Knowledge, Class, and Economics

Knowledge, Class, and Economics: Marxism without Guarantees surveys the "Amherst School" of non-determinist Marxist political economy, 40 years on: its core concepts, intellectual origins, diverse pathways, and enduring tensions. The volume's 30 original essays reflect the range of perspectives and projects that comprise the Amherst School—the interdisciplinary community of scholars that has enriched and extended, while never ceasing to interrogate and recast, the anti-economistic Marxism first formulated in the mid-1970s by Stephen Resnick, Richard Wolff, and their economics Ph.D. students at the University of Massachusetts-Amherst.

The title captures the defining ideas of the Amherst School: an open-system framework that presupposes the complexity and contingency of social-historical events and the parallel "overdetermination" of the relationship between subjects and objects of inquiry, along with a novel conception of class as a process of performing, appropriating, and distributing surplus labor. Readers encounter novel discussions of overdetermination and class in the context of economic theory, postcolonial theory, cultural studies, continental philosophy, economic geography, economic anthropology, psychoanalysis, and literary theory/studies.

Though Resnick and Wolff's writings serve as a focal point for this collection, their works are ultimately decentered—contested, historicized, reformulated. The topics explored will be of interest to proponents and critics of the post-structuralist/postmodern turn in Marxian theory and to students of economics as social theory across the disciplines (economics, geography, postcolonial studies, cultural studies, anthropology, sociology, political theory, philosophy, and literary studies, among others).

Theodore Burczak is Professor of Economics at Denison University and author of *Socialism after Hayek*.

Robert Garnett is Associate Dean and Honors Professor of the Social Sciences in the John V. Roach Honors College at Texas Christian University, USA.

Richard McIntyre is Professor of Economics and Chair of the Economics Department, University of Rhode Island, USA.

Economics as Social Theory
Series edited by Tony Lawson, University of Cambridge

Social Theory is experiencing something of a revival within economics. Critical analyses of the particular nature of the subject matter of social studies and of the types of method, categories, and modes of explanation that can legitimately be endorsed for the scientific study of social objects are re-emerging. Economists are again addressing such issues as the relationship between agency and structure, between economy and the rest of society, and between the enquirer and the object of enquiry. There is a renewed interest in elaborating basic categories such as causation, competition, culture, discrimination, evolution, money, need, order, organization, power probability, process, rationality, technology, time, truth, uncertainty, value, etc.

The objective for this series is to facilitate this revival further. In contemporary economics the label "theory" has been appropriated by a group that confines itself to largely asocial, ahistorical, mathematical "modeling." Economics as Social Theory thus reclaims the "Theory" label, offering a platform for alternative rigorous but broader and more critical conceptions of theorizing.

Other titles in this series include:

What Is Neoclassical Economics?
Debating the Origins, Meaning and Significance
Edited by Jamie Morgan

A Corporate Welfare
James Angresano

Rethinking Economics for Social Justice
The Radical Potential of Human Rights
Radhika Balakrishnan, James Heintz, and Diane Elson

Knowledge, Class, and Economics
Marxism without Guarantees
Edited by Theodore Burczak, Robert Garnett, and Richard McIntyre

Knowledge, Class, and Economics

Marxism without Guarantees

Edited by
**Theodore Burczak, Robert Garnett,
and Richard McIntyre**

LONDON AND NEW YORK

First published 2018
by Routledge
2 Park Square, Milton Park, Abingdon, Oxon OX14 4RN

and by Routledge
711 Third Avenue, New York, NY 10017

Routledge is an imprint of the Taylor & Francis Group, an informa business

© 2018 selection and editorial matter, Theodore Burczak,
Robert Garnett and Richard McIntyre; individual chapters, the
contributors

The right of Theodore Burczak, Robert Garnett, and Richard
McIntyre to be identified as the authors of the editorial material,
and of the authors for their individual chapters, has been asserted
in accordance with sections 77 and 78 of the Copyright, Designs
and Patents Act 1988.

British Library Cataloguing-in-Publication Data
A catalogue record for this book is available from the British Library

Library of Congress Cataloging-in-Publication Data
A catalog record for this book has been requested

ISBN: 978-1-138-63446-6 (hbk)
ISBN: 978-1-138-63448-0 (pbk)
ISBN: 978-1-315-20678-3 (ebk)

Typeset in Palatino
by codeMantra

For Steve and Rick,
our teachers, comrades, and friends

"A superb achievement! This is the definitive collection dedicated to the work of Stephen Resnick and Richard Wolff, the influential scholars who, with their "Amherst School" students, changed Marxian economics forever. It includes piercing yet appreciative evaluations of their bedrock concepts: class, Marxian knowledge, and overdetermination. The authors in this compendium are all the right commentators (former students, colleagues, and famed social theorists), and the editors—Theodore Burczak, Robert Garnett, and Richard McIntyre—have turned in the most insightful, lucid, and useful introductory essay to the work of Resnick and Wolff yet written. A must for undergraduates, graduates, scholars, and activists everywhere, for whom Marxism remains a living tradition."

Jack Amariglio, Professor of Economics, Merrimack College, USA

"Through their teaching as much as their writing, Richard Wolff and the late Stephen Resnick advanced Marxian analysis beyond simple materialism to develop a Marxism that recognizes the importance of multiple forms of identity where social life is interwoven with different types of exploitation and resistance. *Knowledge, Class, and Economics* provides a superb introduction to Resnick and Wolff's thought and offers a set of 30 challenging, fascinating, and stimulating essays that engage with it."

Gerald Friedman, Professor of Economics, University of Massachusetts at Amherst, USA

"History's ironies never end. The interest in Marxism is now more intense than it has been in decades. This collection showcases the scope and depth of the innovativeness of an approach that has breathed new life into Marxism: one 'without guarantees,' one that offers 'hope without guarantees,' a Marxism that calls for continuous reflection, for re-thinking Marxism indeed."

Serap Ayşe Kayatekin, Professor of Economics and Social Science, American College of Thessaloniki, Greece

"This incisive and wide-ranging collection does far more than commemorate the moment of the Amherst School and the possibilities of rethinking Marxism these past thirty years. It shows us what radical thinking looks like today. *Knowledge, Class, and Economics* will soon be required reading across the social sciences and humanities."

Andrew Parker, Professor of French and Comparative Literature, Rutgers University

Contents

Figures and tables

Figures

Tables

Contributors

Masato Aoki is Associate Professor and Chair in the Department of Economics at Simmons College where he teaches in the Honors learning community program and the College of Arts and Sciences. His primary research interests include Marxian economic and social theory and the political economy of education.

Rajesh Bhattacharya is Assistant Professor in the Public Policy and Management Group at Indian Institute of Management, Calcutta. He has a Ph.D. in economics from University of Massachusetts, Amherst. His research interests include the political economy of development (particularly issues of informality and exclusion), Indian economic history, and Marxian theory.

Snehashish Bhattacharya is Assistant Professor of Economics at South Asian University, New Delhi, India.

Theodore Burczak is Professor of Economics at Denison University and author of *Socialism after Hayek* (University of Michigan Press, 2006).

Antonio Callari is the Sigmund M. and Mary B. Hyman Professor of Economics at Franklin and Marshall College.

Lorrayne Carroll is Associate Professor of English, Women and Gender Studies Faculty, University of Southern Maine, Portland. Dr. Carroll teaches and conducts research in early American studies, women and gender studies, and literacy studies. She writes with Joseph Medley on the intersections of economic and cultural formations, specifically on the cultural productions that arise in response to neoliberal economic policies in China and elsewhere.

Anjan Chakrabarti is Professor of Economics, University of Calcutta. His research interests include Marxian theory, development economics, Indian economics, postcolonial economics, and political philosophy. He has authored or edited six books and over 50 academic articles. His latest major work, co-authored with Anup Kumar Dhar and Byasdeb Dasgupta, is *The Transition of the Indian Economy: Globalization, Capitalism* *and Development* (Cambridge University Press, 2015). He was awarded the VKRV Rao Prize in Economics in 2008.

Joseph W. Childers is Professor of English and Dean of the Graduate Division at the University of California, Riverside. He specializes in Marxist, post-Marxist, and historicist theory and criticism, the English novel, and Victorian studies, with a recent focus on working-class and immigrant literature.

Stephen Cullenberg is Professor of Economics at the University of California, Riverside, where he served as Dean of the College of Humanities, Arts, and Social Sciences from 2006 to 2014.

George DeMartino is Professor of Economics in the Josef Korbel School of International Studies at the University of Denver where he is Co-Director of the MA Degree in Global Finance, Trade and Economic Integration. He has written extensively on economics and ethics, and he is the author of *Global Economy, Global Justice: Theoretical Objections and Policy Alternatives to Neoliberalism* (Routledge, 2000) and *The Economist's Oath: On the Need for and Content of Professional Economic Ethics* (Oxford University Press, 2011). He is also co-editor, with Deirdre McCloskey, of the *Oxford Handbook of Professional Economic Ethics* (2016).

Anup Dhar is Associate Professor in the School of Human Studies, Ambedkar University, Delhi, where he is also Director of the Centre for Development Practice. He is currently a member of the editorial board of the *Annual Review of Critical Psychology*. His research interest includes psychoanalysis, philosophy of science, social and political philosophy, and development studies. He is co-author (with Anjan Chakrabarty and Byasdeb Dasgupta) of *The Transition of the Indian Economy: Globalization, Capitalism and Development* (Cambridge University Press, 2015).

Faruk Eray Düzenli is Associate Professor of Economics at St. Mary's College of Maryland and a member of the editorial board of *Rethinking Marxism*. His most recent publications include "Surplus-Producing Labour as a Capability: A Marxian Contribution to Amartya Sen's Revival of Classical Political Economy" in the *Cambridge Journal of Economics* and "Did Marx Fetishize Labor?" in *Rethinking Marxism*.

Kenan Erçel received his Ph.D. in economics from the University of Massachusetts, Amherst; he is now Associate Director at the Fair Labor Association in Washington, D.C., and a member of the editorial board of *Rethinking Marxism*.

Harriet Fraad is a mental health counselor and hypnotherapist in New York City who speaks and writes about the intersection of Marxism and personal life. Some of her latest articles appear in *Imagine Living in a Socialist USA* (Harper, 2014), *Logos* (November 2014), *Truthout* (November

2014), and *The Psychohistory Journal* (Winter 2015). She, Richard Wolff, and Stephen Resnick are primary authors of *Class Struggle on the Home Front* (Palgrave, 2009).

Robert Garnett is Associate Dean and Honors Professor of the Social Sciences in the John V. Roach Honors College at Texas Christian University. His research interests include the meaning and value of pluralism in economics and the moral philosophy of Adam Smith, particularly its connections to Hegel and Marx.

Michael Hillard is Professor of Economics at the University of Southern Maine. He has published widely in the history of capitalism, labor relations, and labor history in journals such as *Labor History, Labor: Studies in the Working Class History of the Americas, Review of Radical Political Economics,* and *Rethinking Marxism.* His current project is *The Fall of the Paper Plantation: A History of Capitalism, Work, and Struggle in Maine's Paper Industry* (forthcoming).

Donald W. Katzner is Professor of Economics and former Chair of the Economics Department at the University of Massachusetts, Amherst. His published research has spanned six general areas: microeconomic and general equilibrium theory, the methodology of building models and analyzing phenomena when measures of appropriate variables are neither available nor reasonably constructible, the analysis of uncertain economic phenomena when it is inappropriate to employ notions of probability (as is often the case when considering economic decision making), the relationship between culture and economic behavior, internal organizational issues within the firm, and the history of the UMass Economics Department during the tumultuous period, 1965–1981.

Vincent Lyon-Callo is Professor of Anthropology at Western Michigan University. He is the author of *Inequality, Poverty, and Neoliberal Governance: Activist Ethnography in the Homeless Sheltering Industry* (University of Toronto Press) and numerous journal articles drawing on his decades of academic research and social service work on homelessness.

Yahya M. Madra received his Ph.D. in economics from the University of Massachusetts, Amherst; he teaches economics at Boğaziçi University, Istanbul, Turkey. He has been a member of the editorial board of *Rethinking Marxism* since 1998. He has published and co-authored articles on various issues in political economy in *Development & Change, Antipode, Journal of Economic Issues, Psychoanalysis, Culture & Society, Subjectivity,* and *European Journal of History of Economic Thought.* Currently he is working on two books: *Late Neoclassical Economics: Restoration of Theoretical Humanism in Contemporary Economic Theory* (Routledge, 2017) and (with Ceren Özselçuk) *Sexuating Class: A Psychoanalytical Critique of Political Economy*.

Richard McIntyre is Professor of Economics and Political Science and Chair of the Economics Department at the University of Rhode Island. He is the author of *Are Worker Rights Human Rights?* (University of Michigan Press) and editor of the Routledge book series *New Political Economy*.

Joseph Medley is Associate Professor of Economics in the Department of Economics, Sociology, and Criminology at the University of Southern Maine. He teaches and conducts research primarily in economic development, focusing on the international economic policies and practices of the IMF, World Bank, and WTO as well as on the history of Chinese economic development. He is currently teaching courses in these areas and on the topic of sustainable, local cooperative development.

Claude Misukiewicz is a historian and managing editor of *History of Political Economy*.

Warren Montag is the Brown Family Professor of Literature at Occidental College. His most recent books include *The Other Adam Smith* (with Mike Hill, Stanford University Press, 2014) and *Althusser and His Contemporaries* (Duke University Press, 2013). Montag is also editor of *Décalages*, a journal on Althusser and his circle, and translator of Etienne Balibar's *Identity and Difference: John Locke and the Invention of Consciousness* (Verso, 2013).

Fred Moseley is Professor of Economics at Mount Holyoke College. His most recent work is *Money and Totality: A Macro-Monetary Interpretation of Marx's Logic in* Capital *and the End of the "Transformation Problem"* (2016, Brill). He is also editor of the recently published English translation of *Marx's Economic Manuscript of 1864–65* (2016, Brill) and was the original organizer of the research group that came to be known as the International Symposium on Marxian Theory, which has published nine collections on Marxian Theory.

Bruce Norton is Associate Professor and economics program coordinator at San Antonio College in San Antonio, Texas.

Erik K. Olsen is Associate Professor of Economics at the University of Missouri Kansas City and research fellow of the Rutgers School of Management and Labor Relations. His research areas include Marxian political economy, microeconomics (with applications to the economics of cooperation and employee ownership), and urban economics. He has published widely in these areas and is currently co-editing the *Handbook of Marxian Economics*.

Elizabeth Ramey is Associate Professor of Economics at Hobart and William Smith Colleges in Geneva, New York.

Jan Rehmann teaches at Union Theological Seminary in New York and at the Free University in Berlin. His research interests include theories of ideology, philosophy of religion, Max Weber, Friedrich Nietzsche, and Ernst Bloch. He is co-editor of the journal *Das Argument* and of the *Historical-Critical Dictionary of Marxism*. His published works include *Max Weber: Modernization as Passive Revolution. A Gramscian Analysis* (Haymarket, 2015), *Theories of Ideology: The Powers of Alienation and Subjection* (Haymarket, 2014), *Pedagogy of the Poor* (2011, with Willie Baptist), "Postmoderner Links-Nietzscheanism – Deleuze and Foucault: Eine Dekonstruktion" (*Argument*, 2004), "Die Kirchen im NS-Staat" (*Argument*, 1986).

Bruce Roberts has published widely in the areas of value theory and the history of economics. He is currently interested in competing conceptions of money and their implications for a value-theoretic understanding of the financial sector.

David F. Ruccio is Professor of Economics at the University of Notre Dame. He was a founding member of the journal *Rethinking Marxism* and served as its editor for 12 years (1997–2009). Ruccio is the author of over 80 journal articles and book chapters. His books include *Development and Globalization: A Marxian Class Analysis* (Routledge), *Economic Representations: Both Academic and Everyday* (Routledge), *Postmodern Moments in Modern Economics* (Princeton University Press), *Postmodernism, Economics, and Knowledge* (Routledge), and *Postmodern Materialism and the Future of Marxist Theory* (Wesleyan University Press).

Ellen Russell is Assistant Professor in Digital Media and Journalism and Society, Culture and Environment programs at Wilfrid Laurier University. Her recent publications include *New Deal Banking Reform and Keynesian Welfare State Capitalism* (2008) and "Why the Rising Tide Doesn't Lift all Boats: Wages and Bargaining Power in Neoliberal Canada" (*Studies in Political Economy*, 2016). She was formerly senior economist at the Canadian Centre for Policy Alternatives and is an occasional columnist on economic affairs for rabble.ca.

Maliha Safri is Assistant Professor of Economics at Drew University. She has published articles in *Signs*, *The Economist's Voice*, *Rethinking Marxism*, and *Performing Diverse Economies* (2016). She has worked for many years in popular economic literacy with worker cooperatives and immigrant communities in New York and New Jersey.

Ian J. Seda-Irizarry is Assistant Professor in the Economics Department at the John Jay College, CUNY, where he teaches courses on Political

Economy and History of Economic Thought. He holds a Ph.D. in economics from the University of Massachusetts, Amherst.

Paul Smith is Professor of Cultural Studies at George Mason University and a long-time member of the Marxist Literary Group. His latest book, *The Renewal of Cultural Studies*, was published by Temple University Press in 2011.

Gayatri Chakravorty Spivak is University Professor and a founding member of the Institute for Comparative Literature and Society at Columbia University. A literary theorist, feminist critic, postcolonial theorist, and professor of comparative literature, she is best known for her essay "Can the Subaltern Speak?" and for her 1976 translation of, and introduction to, Jacques Derrida's *Of Grammatology*.

Andriana Vlachou is Associate Professor at the Athens University of Economics and Business. She has published articles on the political economy of the environment and natural resources in the *Cambridge Journal of Economics, Capitalism, Nature, Socialism, Review of International Political Economy, Review of Radical and Political Economics, Rethinking Marxism, Science & Society*, and other venues. Her edited volumes include *Contemporary Economic Theory: Radical Critiques of Neoliberalism* (Macmillan 1999), *Economic Crisis and Greece* (with N. Theocarakis and M. Milonakis, 2011). She is an editor-at-large of the journal *Capitalism, Nature, Socialism*.

Richard D. Wolff is Professor Emeritus, Economics, University of Massachusetts, Amherst, and currently Visiting Professor of Economics at the New School University, New York. He is co-author (with Stephen Resnick) of *Knowledge and Class: A Marxian Critique of Political Economy* (1987), *Class Theory and History: Capitalism and Communism in the USSR* (2002), *New Departures in Marxian Theory* (2006), and *Contending Economic Theories: Neoclassical, Keynesian and Marxian* (2012). His own recent works include *Democracy at Work: A Cure for Capitalism* (2012) and *Capitalism's Crisis Deepens: Essays on the Global Economic Downturn, 2010–2014* (2015).

Introduction

Marxism without guarantees

Richard McIntyre, Theodore Burczak,
and Robert Garnett

This volume offers a broad, reflective survey of the "Amherst School" of Marxist political economy. The Amherst School developed around the work of Stephen Resnick and Richard Wolff, two economists who came to the University of Massachusetts-Amherst in 1974 as faculty members in a new radical economics program. Beginning with a reading group on *Capital* and other key texts in what they identified as a dissenting, non-determinist tradition within Western Marxism, Resnick and Wolff worked with their Ph.D. students and colleagues from other UMass departments to develop a post-Althusserian critique of economic determinism and a robust class-analytic method of analyzing societies. These ideas were refined and recast in the late 1970s through an initial wave of dissertations, articles, and book chapters in economic history, economic theory, history of economic thought, economic development, and comparative economic systems. The Amherst School expanded further in the 1980s and '90s, shaped by new dialogues within economics and even more by encounters with scholars and perspectives from anthropology, psychoanalysis, evolutionary biology, feminist theory, geography, post-structuralism, postmodernism, postcolonial theory and other fields beyond economics. Through the journal *Rethinking Marxism,* founded in 1988, and a series of large international conferences and smaller semi-annual retreats held on the UMass campus and elsewhere, the Amherst School became a diverse, transdisciplinary space in which to explore the salience of non-determinist Marxian approaches (in particular, the concepts of overdetermination and class) in the context of broad intellectual and social movements of the late 20th and early 21st centuries.

The purpose of this Introduction is to locate the Amherst School with respect to its various antecedents and similar groups in contemporary social theory. In doing so, we identify many concepts and arguments addressed in greater detail by our contributors in the chapters that follow. Marxism at its best is a way of critically analyzing society to support a liberatory vision of a better world. But Marxism also has a lot to account for. The Amherst School seeks to explain the enormous social damage caused by attachments to economic determinism, while at the same time reclaiming from Marx and the dissenting Marxian tradition a powerful, epistemically self-aware, and ethically reflexive class theory to analyze contemporary capitalist and socialist societies.

Marxism without guarantees

What is a Marxism "without guarantees"? Was it not precisely the guarantees that attracted so many adherents to Marxism in the 20th century—the guarantee of being on the side of history, the guarantee of having the true social theory? And does this determinism not give Marxism some credence in popular politics, where the notion that "it's the economy, stupid" is taken as common sense?

Most of the authors of this collection abandon those guarantees. Why do they do this? However well-intentioned its proponents might have been, the course of Marxism's development in the 20th century is probably sufficient to indicate that these would-be guarantees have been tremendously damaging. Yet Marxism is so generally identified as a form of economic determinism that it took a detailed genealogy of a viable dissenting tradition within Marxism by Resnick and Wolff to build a convincing case that there would be something left of the Marxian tradition if it dispensed with that determinism.

What does a non-determinist Marxism look like? The beginning of an answer starts with the new reading of Marx's *Capital* undertaken in the 1970s by Resnick, Wolff, and a contingent of graduate students at the University of Massachusetts-Amherst. They first constituted themselves in the late 1970s as a "journal group" to develop and extend this new reading and eventually founded the journal *Rethinking Marxism,* which began publication in 1988, with Jack Amariglio as its founding editor. In his essay here the second editor, David Ruccio, shows how the Marxian critique of economics and of capitalism developed in the pages of that journal over nearly three decades.

The French Marxist philosopher, Louis Althusser, deeply influenced the journal group. Althusser and his Paris students (Étienne Balibar, Roger Establet, Jacques Rancière, and Pierre Macherey) had famously gone back to the text of *Capital* in the early 1960s to produce the landmark *Reading Capital,* published in French in 1965, although only the essays by Althusser and Balibar were printed in the 1968 French edition, which was translated into English in 1970.

As Rick Wolff notes in the interview that follows this chapter, he and Resnick discovered Althusser through the work of Barry Hindess and Paul Hirst, two UK-based sociologists who had utilized some of Althusser's concepts to produce a non-essentialist analysis of modes of production and social formations. At the time, Hindess and Hirst's approach was exactly what Resnick and Wolff were seeking to counter the determinism of traditional Marxism. They began studying and discussing Althusser's work in the early 1970s and later met with him in Paris, as their own thinking evolved in a similar direction once they began teaching in the newly established radical economics department at the University of Massachusetts-Amherst.[1]

Althusser and his circle sought to criticize the existing Stalinist readings of Marx while staying within a generally Marxian framework. The "traditional" Marxism of the Second International (1889–1916) and official Marxism (after the Bolshevik revolution) were based on a particular reading of Marx and especially Engels. History was seen as having a subject (class struggle) and an end point (communism). Marxism was understood as the science of society, building upon the parallels that Engels drew between the physical and natural sciences. This Marxism provided an integrated world outlook that was seen as a *reflection* of reality consonant with working class life, past and present.

Each form of society was understood to exist in tension between the technological *forces of production* and the legal and organizational *relations of production*. As the forces developed within a fixed set of production relations, these tensions would build and ultimately "burst asunder" in a moment of revolution and transition. Driven by technological change, society would pass through a series of modes of production: ancient, slave, feudal, capitalist, socialist, and finally communist, marking the end of history. The communist revolution would replace the anarchic and uncontrolled process of value creation and distribution under capitalism with a rationally planned, classless society. The task of the revolutionary socialist was not so much to make the revolution but to take advantage of it when it came. History would proceed dialectically but with "iron necessity towards inevitable results" (Marx [1867] 1976, 90). This sketch of Marxian orthodoxy is a bit of a caricature but serves to situate the debates among radicals in Germany and Russia in the years leading up to World War I and gives a sense of the official Marxism that emerged in the Soviet Union in the late 1920s. There were debates between proponents of political and economic determinisms but no debate about determinism itself.

The Great War provoked a crisis in Marxism, first because the workers' movement failed to rise above national differences, as each of the working class parties ended up supporting its government. Then with the establishment and securing of the Bolshevik regime by the end of the 1920s, there was now a successful Marxist-inspired revolution that had firmly consolidated state power, putting it in position to impose its own views on Marxist parties and theoreticians working for the overthrow of capitalism elsewhere.

Even so, the Frankfurt School in Germany and Antonio Gramsci in Italy began to move away from the guarantees given by traditional Marxism in the interwar period. Gramsci saw the Russian revolution as "the revolution against *Capital*" (Gramsci 1917). Capitalism had been expected to meet its great moment of crisis in the regions where it was most developed:

Germany, Western Europe more broadly, and the United States, not in "backward" and mostly non-capitalist Russia (Marx and Engels [1848] 1970, 44). Gramsci also rejected the increasingly loud voice of Moscow in proclaiming the Russian revolution as the model for others, though he held on to the official Marxist belief that the working class must be the agent of socialist revolution because it occupied capitalism's most strategic position.

The Frankfurt School did not retain this belief. Cut off from political practice by the crisis of the workers' movement during and after World War I, Theodor Adorno, Max Horkheimer, and others at the Institute for Social Research returned in the 1930s to methodological questions that the Second International and the Bolsheviks had closed off. They sought answers in psychoanalysis, existential philosophy, non-positivist sociology, and other "bourgeois" disciplines. Here was the beginning of a more open Marxism, albeit one that largely neglected politics and the state.

Marxisms proliferated after World War II. First there was a surge of interest in Marxism outside Europe, in China of course but also in parts of Africa, India, Latin America, and the Middle East. Second, and more directly relevant to the development of the Amherst School, there was an explosion of Marxist theory in France and Italy. The prestige of the Communist-dominated resistance during World War II led to a situation in which the Communists were the main political opposition in both countries. Though the French Communist party was Stalinist, there was an unusually open and vibrant scholarly discussion of Marxism in France, especially in philosophy and history.

The Paris and Amherst readings were similar but differently nuanced, partly because Althusser and his circle read *Capital* as philosophers, while the Resnick-Wolff group approached it as economists. Both Resnick and Wolff had been trained at elite economics graduate departments and were steeped in the Marxian political economy of the *Monthly Review* school. They adopted key concepts from Althusser, such as the epistemological break between the early and mature writings of Marx, contradiction and overdetermination as a new way of understanding causality, and the critique of historicism and humanism. They discerned a dissenting tradition in Marxism that emphasized culture and epistemology rather than just economics by reading back from Althusser through the Frankfurt School, Gramsci, and Lucacs. They found links between this dissenting tradition and the proliferation of non-European Marxisms after World War II that developed orthogonally to the official Marxism of the Soviet Union, shaped by the differently positioned societies of the emerging postcolonial world.

Though they borrowed the notion of overdetermination from Althusser, who in turn had appropriated it from Freud, Resnick and Wolff leaned more heavily on the concept and ultimately recast it in a radically non-determinist way. Overdetermination constituted the key element of Resnick and Wolff's critique of economic determinism. If every social site and level of society (enterprise, family, state, economy, nature, politics, culture, etc.) exists as a bundle of internal relationships and conflicts, and if every site and level affects every other site and level, then our vision of society needs to be decentered. How can we say that any one site determines all others, even in "the last instance"? They replaced the base-superstructure model of traditional Marxism with a model of a decentered totality.

Figure I.1 illustrates what we are calling traditional or official Marxism. The forces and relations of production are affected by culture and politics, but the primary direction of causality runs from base to superstructure. Althusser softened this, saying that the base is determinant only in the last instance.

Resnick and Wolff went further, as illustrated by the series of images in Figure I.2.[2] In a centralized system (A) one aspect of social life is the fundamental cause of everything else, but the other nodes of social life do not interact with each other nor do they significantly influence the fundamental cause. This is similar to the crudest forms of traditional and official Marxism. The distributed model (C) is closer to the Amherst School vision, especially if we presume these dots to be connected to each other in the back of a three-dimensional representation. In other words, there are multiple entry points into social analysis, and every aspect of social life potentially influences every other aspect. Of course it is possible in

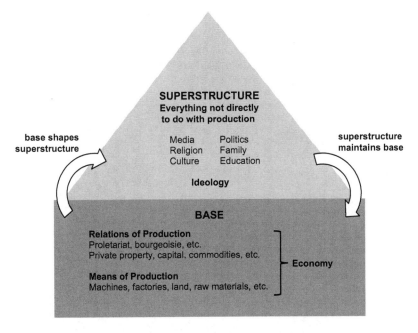

Figure I.1 Traditional Marxist image of society: base and superstructure.

many particular situations to draw a convincing portrait of the economy as determining other parts of society, but this picture is always a creation and not a mere reflection. Image B in Figure I.2 might represent such a conjunctural analysis.

Resnick and Wolff's vision of society (or any nexus of social relations) as a decentered totality opened a space for cultural processes to be analyzed in Marxist terms and for Marxist economic concepts to be understood as cultural forms. Cultural theorists have long made use of dissenting Marxism, especially of the Frankfurt School, but Resnick and Wolff, Jack Amariglio, Antonio Callari, J.K. Gibson-Graham, and David Ruccio created new insights that stimulated discussion between the Amherst School and contemporary cultural theorists, though not without some controversy as shown in the essays below by Montag, Childers, Madra, Rehmann, and Smith.

Overdetermination also has consequences for how we think about theory itself. If we are unable to stand outside of society when we view it, then our starting point must always influence our theories. How we get to that starting point has a lot to do with who we are as people and the great varieties of human culture that each of us always already inhabits. As Resnick and Wolff often said, we care about class processes because … well, it's a long story having to do with our personal history and our beliefs that class has been repressed as an important concept, particularly in the United States, that class processes are important aspects of contemporary social life, and so on. But this means we can only say our theory is *different* from others, not necessarily more *objective*. Consistent with the history of the dissenting Marxian tradition, Resnick and Wolff invoke the works of Gramsci, Althusser, and other Marxists to make this point, as well as non-Marxist sources such as Bruno Latour and Steve Woolgar's

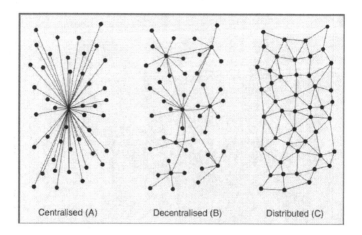

Centralised (A)   Decentralised (B)   Distributed (C)

Figure I.2 Centralized, decentralized, and distributed totalities.

Laboratory Life: The Construction of Scientific Facts (1986) and Richard Rorty's *Philosophy and the Mirror of Nature* (1979). This argument is perhaps the most troubling to their radical economist peers who want to show that mainstream economics is ideological whereas the radical alternative is objectively correct. The Resnick-Wolff approach implies that the first part of that sentence is true, but the second is not. In this, their position is consistent with Althusser's famous no-end-of-ideology thesis. Class becomes the *entry point* for Marxian theory but not an ontological or epistemological essence.

Knowledge, class, and economics

As noted above, the Amherst group differed from the Paris group by reading *Capital* as economists rather than philosophers. One consequence of this difference was that the Amherst group paid closer attention to Marx's theory of value and exploitation. They took the critique of determinism and teleology back to the Marxian economics they had started with and saw that it needed to be transformed. In this, they differed from the post-Marxism of Ernesto Laclau and Chantal Mouffe, whose *Hegemony and Socialist Strategy* (1985) was inspired by Althusser but especially by Gramsci. Laclau and Mouffe dismissed the official Marxist essentialism of class identity and rejected the base-superstructure model. But though Laclau and Mouffe used economic concepts, they had no concept of the economy (Diskin and Sandler 1993). The Amherst group did. Laclau and Mouffe rejected key Marxian economics concepts such as class and labor-power as commodity as essentialist, leading to purely political definitions of capitalism and socialism. As Diskin and Sandler observed:

> The effect of this recomposition is not merely to displace essentialist class concepts from their unique and privileged ontological position (the rightful and necessary comeuppance due every essentialism) but to collapse the theoretical structure of the economic space itself…the appearance of untheorized economic concepts in the second half of *HSS* represents a major consequence of the failure to extend the non-essentialist reconceptualization to the categories of political *economy*.
> (1993, 22–23)

In Laclau and Mouffe, the economy became an undertheorized construct to which culture and politics responded. The Amherst group went farther by *rethinking* rather than merely rejecting Marxian economic concepts. Chief among these was the notion of class.

Beginning in the late 1970s, Resnick and Wolff produced a series of articles that eventually comprised the bulk of their 1987 book, *Knowledge and Class: A Marxian Critique of Political Economy*.[3] These key essays carefully demonstrated that there was much good work in Marx's *oeuvre* and in the

Marxian tradition that did not adopt economic determinism and that a coherent class theory could be constructed by reading Marx's oeuvre as a theory of exploitation rather than (or in addition to) the laws of motion of capitalism. Resnick and Wolff approached *Capital*, in particular, under the influence of Althusser's concept of symptomatic reading. For Althusser, reading a theoretical text was like the Freudian analyst's interpretation of her/his patient's statements. One first had to construct the "problematic": the questions answered but never posed by the text (or posed hundreds of pages before or after the answers). *Capital*, on this reading, constituted a general theory of class society and not, or not only, a theory of laws of motion of an exclusively capitalist mode of production. The particular notion of class that Resnick and Wolff identified in Marx was defined in terms of relationships of exploitation. They read *Capital* as a long essay explicating the ways in which some people lived off the labor of others. Resnick and Wolff showed that over the course of *Capital*'s three volumes, Marx unfolded a compelling theory of the class process, defined in terms of the performance, appropriation, and distribution of surplus labor. Resnick and Wolff elaborated this new reading of Marx's economics in seven other books, and the theory of class they discovered in Marx inspired over seventy doctoral dissertations and many books, articles, and other media by their students and others.[4]

Resnick and Wolff's reading of Marx is innovative in two ways. First they argue strongly for reading all three volumes of *Capital*, placing equal importance on the appropriation and distribution of surplus that Marx discussed in the second and third volumes alongside the more famous analysis of the performance of surplus labor in the first book. They propose a distinction between the fundamental class process of surplus labor extraction (emphasized in Volume 1) and what they call the subsumed class process of distributing that surplus (emphasized in Volumes 2 and 3). They argue that focusing on these class processes, or using them as an entry point into social analysis, is Marxism's *differentia specifica*. Despite the perhaps unfortunate choice of label, the subsumed class process of surplus distribution is not less important than its production, and there are manifold distributions, especially in the form of capital accumulation and luxury consumption by capitalists described in Volume 1, and payments to merchants, bankers, and landlords detailed in Volume 3. Bruce Norton develops this idea most effectively, in this volume and elsewhere, and Norton and others examine different facets of the subsumed class process in the "Capitalism and class analysis" section below. The treatment of these subsumed classes and the move away from the simple two-class model is also relevant for the treatment of crisis, to which we come back briefly at the end.

Second, when using the notion of overdetermination to understand social causality, each site in society is seen to develop differently because of its complex constitution by all other sites. Social development will thus likely be uneven rather than linear, uniform, and progressive, as in traditional Marxism. Marx developed his theory of capitalism by comparing it with slavery, feudalism, and other "pre-capitalist" production modes. The sense in Marx that these modes of production follow one another historically hardened into dogma in official Marxism. As an outcome of the notions of overdetermination and unevenness, Resnick and Wolff and others in the Amherst School discover multiple forms of class processes in *contemporary* society—not just capitalist, but also feudal, "ancient" (petty commodity production), and communal (McIntyre 1995). No society, even the United States, can be understood as simply capitalist so long as other forms of surplus labor are created in households, family-owned and -operated businesses, and worker cooperatives, and so long as much of economic life happens apart from the various fundamental class processes, as in the state and other organizations that function through receipt of distributed surplus labor. Many examples of this are developed in the two books Resnick and Wolff co-edited with J.K. Gibson-Graham, *Class and Its Others* (2000) and *Re-Presenting Class* (2001).

A symptomatic reading of the three volumes of *Capital* also has implications for how we understand the relationship among different parts of Marx's text, as explained in Bruce Roberts's essay. In the traditional reading, Volume 1 is considered foundational for the other volumes. But for the Amherst group, as Marx adds new determinations in Volumes 2 and 3, he literally changes the meaning of the concepts first introduced in Volume 1. For instance "value" means something different in Volumes 1 and 3. Resnick and Wolff sidestep much of the debate over Marxian value theory and the traditional transformation problem by insisting on this reading and the larger point that value-price relationships are not the object of Marx's *Capital* but merely the theoretical means by which Marx renders visible the class dimensions of—the performance, appropriation, and distribution of surplus labor time within—a capitalist economy. Long before the "new solution" to the transformation problem, Wolff, Roberts, and Antonio Callari had shown that the treatment of value-price relationships in Volumes 1 and 3 of *Capital* can be made consistent so long as one allows for the transformation of the concepts of value and value-form at various stages of Marx's analysis (Wolff, Roberts and Callari 1982). In this volume, Bruce Roberts treats value itself as an overdetermined concept. Fred Moseley's related chapter highlights the role of money in Marx's theory of value and surplus value.

In emphasizing the need to read all three volumes of *Capital* with parts of *The Grundrisse* and *Theories of Surplus Value*, Resnick and Wolff draw attention to Marx's general theory of class exploitation and the related importance of surplus labor distribution. The Neo-Marxism that developed out of the Monthly Review school and the Marxian revival of the 1970s focuses mostly on the labor process, the supposed tendency of the profit rate to fall, and one particular distribution of surplus, that to managers for the purpose of accumulating capital. Resnick and Wolff's specification of the subsumed class process of surplus distribution opens a richer analysis of contemporary capitalism. The essays by Olsen, Hillard and McIntyre and by Misukiewicz utilize Resnick and Wolff's treatment of the subsumed class process to analyze the theory of the enterprise, contemporary management ideologies and the concept of planning in the work of the important New Dealer Lewis Lorwin.

The Resnick-Wolff approach bears some similarity to the new reading of *Capital* emerging in Germany. We will take Heinrich (2012) as representative of that reading, as his is the best-known treatment in English. Heinrich does not see Marx as primarily concerned with identifying key contradictions shaping capitalism's future, nor is he looking for specific hypotheses about what is behind the overall path that capitalism traverses, the inner nature of crises, etc. Rather, like Resnick and Wolff, the New German reading sees (1) Marx as devoted to developing a general theoretical framework, and (2) Marx's project as the illumination of capitalism's unfairness and the destructive effects it has on working people.

Heinrich reads Marx primarily as a critic of capitalism, not exploitation more generally. This is in contrast to Resnick and Wolff, who develop out of Marx a general theory of class processes, in which the linchpin category is surplus *labor*, which can be performed in a variety of contexts, and not surplus *value*. This difference has consequences for how one thinks about post-capitalist possibilities. For Heinrich, the transition beyond capitalism must still be an all-or-nothing change, and whereas he seems to see communism as a world without commodity production, Resnick and Wolff see it as a world without exploitative appropriation of surplus labor.

Thus, while the new German reading shares with the Amherst School critiques of economic determinism, historical teleology, and traditional (what Heinrich calls "worldview") Marxism, it retains the ideal of consciously regulated production according to the plans of the associated producers. Somehow, someday, it will be possible for the associated producers to see and to plan the whole. Hence, the new German reading rejects market socialism and does not consider the local and enterprise-centered shifts in class relations that are central for the Amherst School. Heinrich seems to have no real interest in value theory as recast by Wolff, Roberts, and Callari, perhaps because value theory is not as important if one thinks of capitalism as a singular, encompassing system that has to be transcended in total, with no real need to identify exploitation on a local level or to worry about non-class revenues, non-capitalist class processes, and the like. By contrast, Burczak's essay here conceives of a post-capitalist future that eliminates exploitation in production and includes considerable financial regulation, even while retaining private property and market exchange.

Complex class societies and 21st-century socialism

After the fall of the Soviet Union, Stephen Cullenberg (1992) argued that socialism had failed because we asked too much of it. The socialist imaginary in supposedly scientific Marxism was utopian in that any problems in socialist societies were attributed to them being not socialist enough. In other words, when socialism fully arrived it would eradicate poverty, end racism and sexism, stop environmental degradation, entertain your visiting relatives, and so on. In a sense this was the mirror image of neo-liberals who attributed any negatives associated with pro-market reforms to policies that were not sufficiently pro-market.

Cullenberg proposed a "thin" definition of socialism as an alternative to these "thick" descriptions. For him, socialism involved the predominance of collective forms of surplus appropriation, which he took to be the necessary but not sufficient condition for a good society. Ideals shared on the left, such as equality, ending alienation, promoting self-realization, community cohesion, and so on, could not be realized without ending the process by which some lived off the labor of others, i.e., exploitation. But it was significant that Cullenberg described this as necessary but not sufficient, as he saw the possibility of benevolent capitalisms and "hideous" communisms, a point made in more detail in the essay by Safri and Ercel. Russell uses these ideas to recast contemporary anti-capitalism, providing "hope without guarantees."

Cullenberg rethought the concept "socialism" based on Resnick and Wolff's class-analytic framework. Resnick and Wolff used that framework to analyze the most important example of "actually existing socialism," the Soviet Union. From their perspective, the USSR had many successes in terms of economic growth, income and wealth equality, health care, cultural development, etc., and it had many failures in terms of personal freedoms, militarization, famines, etc. But it was generally and widely agreed that the Soviet Union was socialist. Not so according to Resnick and Wolff. For them, the Soviet revolution provoked a shift from private to state capitalism, and the collapse in 1991 swung the pendulum back the other way. They faulted Marxists for being overly concerned with power relationships and property ownership and unconcerned with class. As a consequence, many Marxists tended to think that changing who controlled the means of production (the state in the name of the workers) and who exerted power (the party in the name of the workers and peasants) changed society. Of course it did, but if Marxism's key insight was about exploitative class relations, then these changes were subsidiary. According to Marxian class analysis, the appropriation of surplus labor by non-producers remained the same, even if the identity of the exploiters was altered, as commissars were substituted for capitalists. This leaves a different political legacy than the view that sees the Soviet experience as expressing the "failure of socialism."

The characteristically postmodern propensity to see all types of class processes as possible simultaneously, rather than existing in a sequence of dominant forms, encourages the Amherst School to avoid interpreting the problems of contemporary capitalism as reducible to a primary contradiction between capital and labor.[5] Capitalist and non-capitalist class processes often coexist in a complex modern economy. Satya Gabriel (1989) used this insight to investigate petty commodity production, or as he preferred to call it, the "ancient" class process of self-exploitation. Dropping Marx's assumption that the conditions of existence of non-capitalist modes are the antithesis of the conditions for the capitalist mode, he argued that there was no reason to believe that capitalism would overwhelm and erode the ancient class process. Bhattacharya's essay here picks up this theme and explores the coexistence and reproduction of capitalist and non-capitalist class processes in contemporary India, while Ramey's essay shows the tensions among feudal, ancient, and capitalist class processes in the recent history of American agriculture.

Understanding a complex economy to embody multiple class processes enables creative and contemporary explorations of non-capitalist, non-exploitative alternatives instead of "waiting for the revolution." J.K. Gibson-Graham (1996) wonders why she can practice her feminism in everyday life while her Marxian revolutionary practice has to wait for some apocalyptic moment. Recognition of the multiplicity and diversity of contemporary economic life facilitates new political directions like, for instance, the work of the Community Economies Collective, which engages scholars and activists "to open the economy to ethical debate and provide a space within which to explore different economic practices and pathways" (Community Economies Collective 2016). The essays here by Carroll and Medley, Bhattacharya, Bhattacharya and Seda-Irizarry, Chakrabarti et al., and Spivak develop these and related perspectives on the postcolonial global economy, while DeMartino's contribution explores the ethical implications of overdetermination in *Knowledge and Class* and in the work of the Community Economies collective.

The last section of the book develops a class analysis of everyday life. The essays by Fraad, Lyon-Callo, Ramey, Aoki, and Vlachou examine sex, homelessness, education, and ecology. The Amherst School's attention to everyday life is not unique within Marxism but does mark the first attempt to use Marx's class theory rather than alienation or other concepts of the "early Marx" to analyze daily, lived experiences in capitalism and socialism.[6] Harriet Fraad, in her individual work and also in her collaborations with Wolff and Resnick, is at the forefront in applying class analysis to personal and household arrangements. Surplus labor performance exists in the family and intimate relationships—such relations may be feudal, ancient, communist, and even capitalist—opening up the terrain of the family for class theory. That homelessness, education, and ecology are also class issues is "obvious" but little analyzed. These authors change that.

Once it seems possible to imagine the creation of socialism now rather than in some far-off revolutionary future, it makes sense that writers associated with the Amherst School would look at worker cooperatives as a form of non-exploitation that does not involve overthrowing the old or creating a new "system." Foremost among these is Rick Wolff in his second career as a popularizer of Marxism and master of all media. In the interview with McIntyre, Wolff explains how his position with Resnick shifted over time, from being critics of "economic democracy" in the 1980s to proponents of "democracy at work" in the 21st century. They came to understand that democracy has a very particular and powerful meaning in the American context and that a discourse highlighting democracy can facilitate a discussion about class. That the millions who produce surplus labor have no say over its appropriation and distribution, while the few thousand people who sit on the board of directors do, is an insult to the notion of the United States as a democratic society.

With this entry point, Wolff argues for a "21st century socialism" based on what he calls worker self-directed enterprises. The transition to socialism is now envisioned not as a cataclysmic political event but as something emanating from cooperatively managed enterprises, or as Wolff puts it perhaps too provocatively when he refers to the various spinoffs and garage enterprises in Silicon Valley, as "the achievements of communist enterprises, operated by Republicans in Bermuda shorts in California" (Wolff, in Jhally 2009). This more "microeconomic" approach to creating participatory forms of production at the workplace has great popular appeal but leaves many questions open. How will democratic enterprises relate to the broader community and other social movements? How does the "great relocation" of capital from the old heartlands to the industrializing periphery affect the possibilities for workplace democracy *and* the ability of capitalists to buy off resistance, as they have often done? What about state power? All of these questions are on the table, a sign of a healthy and developing research program and political agenda (Wolff 2012).

We live in what is generally acknowledged to be a time of economic crisis. The difference between the Amherst approach and that of other schools of Marxism is illustrated by the dissimilar ways that crisis is explained. Radical political economists argue over whether a wage squeeze on profits, or disproportionality, or the tendency of the rate of profit to fall is the cause of crisis. Resnick and Wolff bypass this debate with the idea that capitalism *is* crisis and that any particular crisis is most usefully explained by a conjunctural class analysis. In the last decade of their work together, they produced a series of such conjunctural studies on US consumerism, communisms, and the economic crisis of 2008 (Resnick and Wolff 2006, 2010).

Resnick and Wolff saw, before most others did, that this was a serious crisis of *capitalism*, not a banking crisis or a temporary downturn. The kind of capitalism we had from the 1970s to the mid-2000s, fueled by flat wages, debt, and the increasing working day, week, year, and life, simply cannot go on. Wolff develops these ideas further in his filmed lecture, *Capitalism Hits the Fan* (Jhally 2009). The economic and political systems in the United States, Europe, and elsewhere are broken, and the key question is what comes next? A crucial project for Marxists is to demonstrate how transitions to various possible communal forms of surplus labor appropriation and distribution might resolve the crises endemic to private and state capitalisms *better* than merely oscillating between them. Marx's dramatic vision and ethic remain: The problems and contradictions peculiar to communisms are preferable to those of capitalisms (Resnick and Wolff 1995).

But Marx leaves us with neither a well worked out vision of a just post-capitalist society nor a scientific theory sufficient to explicate the "laws of motion" of capitalism. There is no sense pretending that he did. David Ruccio (2015) argues that Marx and Engels should be viewed instead as "critical utopian socialists." In other words, they criticize many of their socialist brethren for developing schemes that are not rooted in the way society actually works, but they also fill their writings with appreciation for the utopian impulse to build a better society and find the seeds of such a society in some unlikely places, like the utopian communities of Robert Owen and the Russian agricultural commune. Some ideas are *dismissible* as utopian because they flow from a purely moral and ethical position, but others are *dismissed* as utopian because they threaten existing social structures that allow the few to live off the surplus labor of the many. The utopian impulse is problematic without the theory of exploitation and a critical edge. But the impulse itself is necessary for any serious project of social change. To build a 21st-century socialism seems to us to require dropping old certainties and embracing a spirit of openness and experimentation.

Notes

1 The history of the UMass-Amherst department is recounted in Katzner (2011). Katzner's essay in the present volume develops the affinity between some strands of non-Marxian economics and Resnick and Wolff's non-determinist Marxism. For a critical treatment of Katzner's account of UMass radical economics, see McIntyre (2015).

2 Thanks to Yahya Madra for pointing us to this diagram. He found it while searching for representations of "rhizome," a concept that Deleuze and Guattari borrowed from botany to indicate their preference for social theories with multiple entry points and hybrid objects as opposed to the "arborist" approach that is more consistent with base superstructure models (the tree and its roots). These particular diagrams were, ironically, developed by Paul Baran of the Rand Corporation (Baran 1964), in the early development of the Internet. This is Paul Baran the engineer, not Paul Baran the influential Marxian economist, though both Paul Barans were born in Eastern Europe, migrated to the United States, and worked at Stanford.

3 Another influential text along similar lines, though published a decade earlier, was Cutler, Hindess, Hirst and Hussain's *Marx's 'Capital' and Capitalism Today* (1977).
4 In addition to *Knowledge and Class*, some of the key texts are Callari, Cullenberg, and Biewener (1995); Callari and Ruccio (1995); Cassano (2009); Cullenberg (1994); Fraad, Resnick and Wolff (1994); Gibson-Graham (1996, 2006); Gibson-Graham, Resnick and Wolff (2000, 2001); Resnick and Wolff (2002, 2006); and Ruccio and Amariglio (2003).
5 These ideas were developed most effectively in the work of Katherine Gibson and Julie Graham (1996, 2006) and their colleagues in the Community Economies network with their notions of deconstructing capitalism and diverse economies.
6 Lefebvre ([1947] 1991) is a good example of the alienation approach.

References

Althusser, L. and E. Balibar. 1970. *Reading Capital*. Trans. B. Brewster. London: New Left Books.

Baran, P. 1964. *On Distributed Communications: I. Introduction to Distributed Communications Networks*. Santa Monica, CA: RAND Corporation. www.rand.org/pubs/research_memoranda/RM3420.html (accessed January 26, 2017).

Callari, A., S. Cullenberg, and C. Biewener, eds. 1995. *Marxism in the Postmodern Age*. New York: Guilford.

Callari, A. and D. Ruccio, eds. 1995. *Postmodern Materialism and the Future of Marxist Theory*. Middletown, CT: Wesleyan University Press.

Cassano, G. ed. 2009. *Class Struggle on the Homefront: Work, Conflict, and Exploitation in the Household*. New York: Palgrave MacMillan.

Community Economies Collective. 2016. "Key Ideas." www.communityeconomies. org/Home (accessed December 19, 2016).

Cullenberg, S. 1992. "Socialism's Burden: Toward a 'Thin' Definition of Socialism." *Rethinking Marxism* 5 (2): 64–83.

———. 1994. *The Falling Rate of Profit: Recasting the Marxian Debate*. London and Boulder, CO: Pluto Press.

Cutler, A., B. Hindess, P. Hirst, and A. Hussain. 1977. *Marx's 'Capital' and Capitalism Today*. 2 vols. London and Boston, MA: Routledge and Kegan Paul.

Diskin, J. and B. Sandler. 1993. "Essentialism and the Economy in the Post-Marxist Imaginary: Reopening the Sutures." *Rethinking Marxism* 6 (3): 28–48.

Fraad, H., S. Resnick, and R. Wolff. 1994. *Bringing It All Back Home: Class, Gender and Power in the Modern Household*. London and Boulder, CO: Pluto Press.

Gabriel, S. 1990. "Ancients: A Marxian Theory of Self-Exploitation." *Rethinking Marxism* 3 (1): 85–106.

Gibson-Graham, J. K. 1996. *The End of Capitalism (as We Knew It): A Feminist Critique of Political Economy*. Cambridge: Basil Blackwell.

———. 2006. *A Postcapitalist Politics*. Minneapolis: University of Minnesota Press.

Gibson-Graham, J. K., S. Resnick, and R. Wolff, eds. 2000. *Class and Its Others*. Minneapolis: University of Minnesota Press.

———, eds. 2001. *Re/presenting Class: Essays in Postmodern Marxism*. Durham, NC: Duke University Press.

Gramsci, A. 1917. "The Revolution against Capital." www.marxists.org/archive/gramsci/1917/12/revolution-against-capital.htm (accessed December 16, 2016).

Heinrich, M. 2012. *An Introduction to the Three Volumes of Karl Marx's Capital*. New York: Monthly Review Press.

Jhally, S. 2009. *Capitalism Hits the Fan*. Northampton, MA: Media Education Foundation.

Katzner, D. 2011. *At the Edge of Camelot: Debating Economics in Turbulent Times*. New York and Oxford: Oxford University Press.

Laclau, E. and C. Mouffe. 1985. *Hegemony and Socialist Strategy: Towards a Radical Democratic Politics*. London and New York: Verso.

Latour, B. and S. Woolgar. 1986. *Laboratory Life: The Construction of Scientific Facts*. Princeton, NJ: Princeton University Press.

Lefebvre, H. [1947] 1991. *Critique of Everyday Life*. London and New York: Verso.

Marx, K. [1867] 1976. *Capital: A Critique of Political Economy*. Vol. 1. London: Penguin.

Marx, K. and F. Engels. [1848] 1970. *The Communist Manifesto*. New York: Pathfinder Press.

McIntyre, R. 1995. "Mode of Production, Social Formation, and Uneven Development, or, Is There Capitalism in America?" In *Postmodern Materialism and the Future of Marxist Theory*, A. Callari and D. Ruccio, eds., 231–253. Middletown, CT: Wesleyan University Press.

———. 2015. "Book Review: *At the Edge of Camelot*, by Donald Katzner." *Rethinking Marxism* 27 (1): 143–149.

Resnick, S. and R. Wolff. 1987. *Knowledge and Class: A Marxian Critique of Political Economy*. Chicago, IL: University of Chicago Press.

———. 1995. "The End of the USSR: A Marxian Class Analysis." In *Marxism in the Postmodern Age*, A. Callari, S. Cullenberg, and C. Biewener, eds., 323–332. New York: Guilford.

———. 2002. *Class Theory and History: Capitalism and Communism in the USSR*. London and New York: Routledge.

———, eds. 2006. *New Departures in Marxian Theory*. London and New York: Routledge.

———. 2010. "The Economic Crisis: A Marxian Interpretation" *Rethinking Marxism* 22 (2): 170–186.

Rorty, R. 1979. *Philosophy and the Mirror of Nature*. Princeton, NJ: Princeton University Press.

Ruccio, D. F. 2015. "Utopia and the Marxian Critique of Political Economy." In *A New Social Question: Capitalism, Socialism and Utopia*, C. Harrsion, ed., 238–261. Newcastle upon Tyne: Cambridge Scholars Publishing.

Ruccio, D. and Amariglio, J. 2003. *Postmodern Moments in Modern Economics*. Princeton, NJ: Princeton University Press.

Wolff, R. 2012. *Democracy at Work: A Cure for Capitalism*. Chicago, IL: Haymarket Books.

Wolff, R., B. Roberts, and A. Callari. 1982. "Marx's (not Ricardo's) 'Transformation Problem': A Radical Reconceptualization." *History of Political Economy* 14 (4): 564–582.

Part I

Knowledge, class, and economics

1 A conversation with Rick Wolff

Richard McIntyre

Conducted over several days in New York City, this extended interview explores Wolff's early years as a product of the *Monthly Review* school of post-World War II U.S. Marxism, the formation and development of his partnership with Steve Resnick, the establishment of and enduring divisions within the radical economics Ph.D. program at UMass-Amherst, the shift in Resnick and Wolff's work after their encounters with Barry Hindess and Paul Hirst's *Pre-capitalist Modes of Production* and the writings of Louis Althusser in the 1970s, and their ongoing collaborative work with current and former Ph.D. students that led to the founding of the journal *Rethinking Marxism* in the late 1980s. The interview also covers tensions between the epistemological and class aspects of Resnick and Wolff's work, Wolff's recent popular advocacy of worker self-directed enterprises, and the relationship between workplace democracy and other social movements.

You initially came out of the Monthly Review *School of Marxism. Can you tell us a little about how this influenced you – and Steve, too, if that's possible?*
For both Steve and me, the *Monthly Review* School of economics was an important influence. I had grown up knowing Harry Magdoff and Paul Sweezy ever since high school. My parents were personal friends of both Magdoff and his wife and Sweezy and his wife. So I moved into being one of their students in almost a family kind of way, because they would socialize together. And in the case of Magdoff, there was an assumption that if anything ever happened to my parents, I would kind of go into that family. It was never put in so many words, but my parents let me know there had been "conversations."

When I graduated from college and decided to go to graduate school rather than to be a lawyer – my father wanted me to be a lawyer but I wanted to learn economics – it was Paul and Harry who said there was only one place I should go, which was Stanford because Paul Baran was a professor there. So I went to Stanford and got in with him. I was his only graduate student. Nobody else wanted to get near this scary Marxist, whereas I was there expressly to do it. Stanford in those days was kind of intimidated by East Coast Ivy League, so it was good for Baran that a student coming from Harvard wanted him. And it was good for me that he wanted me, since I got a lot of attention that I would never have gotten otherwise. He loved cognac, and I learned to enjoy cognac with him. Unfortunately I arrived in September and the following March he had a massive heart attack and died. So at that point I left Stanford, which was an awful place, and went to Yale, which took me because of all the Ivy League stuff and gave me a ton of money.

The program at Yale was wonderful for me. You could earn two degrees, the Masters and the Ph.D., which you could pursue either way: Ph.D. in history and masters in economics or vice versa. I chose the Ph.D. in economics, but I studied history with C. Vann Woodward. I met Staughton Lynd there. He was teaching labor history then, the job that David Montgomery got after him. I learned from all those people, but meanwhile in the economics Ph.D. program there was really nobody to work with except these junior professors: Resnick, who was unapproachable and scary, and his buddy Stephen Hymer. Hymer ended up being on my dissertation committee but not Steve Resnick.

I was intimidated by him. Steve was a hardass at Yale. As a graduate student I remember going to a couple of seminars to hear visiting people. I think it was the first time I heard Paul Krugman. Sometimes somebody famous would come and we would all go. Steve would often be there, and the guy – there were no women – would give his talk, and Steve would sit in a corner and wait, like a lion crouching to get that gazelle. Steve would go after the guy on theoretical grounds, on the econometric stuff. So graduate students backed away from Steve because it was a nightmare to have a teacher do that to you. Not that he would have done that in class. I never had a class with him, but he was tough. Hymer was much softer, which is why he was on my committee rather than Steve. Also Hymer did work on Africa, my dissertation was on Africa, so it made a certain sense.

I didn't become friendly with Steve until we began teaching at City College. We were both living in New Haven and taking the commuter train. We really became friends because we had so many hours together, basically on the train.

In those days the *Monthly Review* had – I don't remember what they called it – these famous lunches at their offices in New York. Any Marxist or radical economist from around the world who had come to New York for whatever reason would have lunch with Harry and Paul. They would have sandwiches brought in, and you would sit around and talk for an hour or two. And because I was very close to them, they would invite me when I was teaching uptown at City College to visit lower Manhattan where their offices were, and I did that very often. I met Theotonio Dos Santos, Joan Robinson, a whole host of people that I wouldn't have met otherwise. I brought Steve with me, and that's how he began to know Paul and Harry.

Steve and I read Sweezy's work and Magdoff's work – all of it closely – talked about it, wrote based on it, assigned it for our students. There was always a lot of respect, admiration, and appreciation for what they were doing and not just for what they had written. They were like mentors, very encouraging. We saw them as people who had kept Marxism alive in the United States in the worst years of the McCarthy period and the Cold War, and they were kind of heroes for having stayed with it. Magdoff was a New York City kid, immigrant parents, City College graduate, scrabbling up the ladder trying to make it. Paul Sweezy was a Brahmin, part of the Rockefeller family, lots of money. He didn't go to City College; he went to Harvard, etc. But they worked together well, as far as we could see. We also met Harry Braverman at those lunches.

So the *Monthly Review* was the inspiration. We admired Magdoff and Sweezy, we respected them, we learned from them. But as we thought more about their work, we began to have disagreements. Mostly not explicit – we didn't bring this up to them. But we talked about them between us.

I'm trying to think about how to characterize this. The first thing that bothered us was that Paul and Harry told us there was no need to study economic theory anymore. The theory issues were settled. Bourgeois theory was neoclassical and Keynes. Marxian theory was them, and the definitive work was Sweezy's *The Theory of Capitalist Development*. We were to learn it, master it and then move on. For them, the important thing for us to do was apply it. For instance, the first article I was commissioned to write for *The Monthly Review* was an article about the rise of multinational banking: how big American banks moved abroad. This article was applied Magdoff/Sweezy, applied *Monthly Review*. They liked it, they published it, that's what I was to do. When they got to know Steve, they appreciated that he had been to the Philippines, that he knew all this stuff about third world countries. They wanted us to apply their approach to problems of development. They wanted us to cash in on our pedigrees. Steve had been to Penn and MIT and I had gone to Harvard and Yale. That's when it became very clear that both of them were victims; they had been pushed out of these jobs. Magdoff had never even gotten in; he was a working class kid....

So they saw you doing what they had not been able to do?
Yeah, a little bit of that. They pushed hard for us to be big shots as Marxists at a fancy university. And I think that, for instance, they were not particularly thrilled with our move to UMass.

Because it was a state university, or in the countryside, or ... ?
They never got that explicit. If I were to guess, it was because it wasn't prestigious enough. Steve had been a young professor at Yale; more of that was what they wanted. My first job offer when I was finishing at Yale was from Johns Hopkins. When I told Sweezy, he urged me to take it. I turned it down, after which James Tobin (at Yale) called me into his office and told me, "You can't do that. No one turns down Johns Hopkins for City College. I can't write a letter for a person who does that." That was a

straight out threat. I never asked him for a letter in any case, because he didn't know me that well.

But what got us upset wasn't that kind of attitude. It was Paul and Harry's notion that the theory was finished that bothered us. By this time we were reading a lot of Marx and were excited by it, as a lot of people were at that time. The idea that the theory was settled when we had so many theoretical questions struck us as very strange. We didn't say much. We were dutiful towards them, they were our masters.

Was there a particular theoretical problem that bothered you?
Yes, there were two, but the really important one was economic determinism. Magdoff and Sweezy were perfectly comfortable with economic determinism. They talked like that, they reasoned like that, and for Steve and me, for whatever complicated reason, this was a problem. We didn't read Marx that way, and we didn't like that kind of argument. I don't think we had a good alternative, but we were very uncomfortable with determinism.

The other theoretical issue we had – really an epistemological question but we didn't know that at the time – was their "history proves" argument. Harry especially (but also Paul) was always telling me, "This is a settled matter, the empirical record shows…." Harry, if you remember his writings, loved to take a proposition that was generally agreed to in the profession and then give you 47 facts that contradicted it. And then he'd make the claim that these 47 facts proved something. I don't think we could have articulated why at that time, but this bothered us.

We began to distance ourselves from them, but there was no trouble between us. We did not air things out with them. That waited until we went to UMass.

Could you say a bit more about your partnership with Steve and why it worked so well and for so long? Initially there was some difference in status. How did you work all that out?
As I said, I got to know Steve at City College. This was my first real job. I had taught both at undergraduate and graduate levels at Yale, but this was still as a graduate student. I got to City College in 1969 and Steve came along, I think, in 1971. He was told at Yale that it was very unlikely that he would get tenure. He made a strategic error. He signed a petition that was circulated by students. I believe the petition was to get the ROTC off campus, which was going around at many colleges and universities at the time. When he signed it, this irritated someone at the higher level. This person spoke to the chair of the economics department who, as a friend, told Steve that signing the petition was viewed as a grievous error. Steve got the idea that he'd better look for another job.

At that time the chair of economics at City College, who had brought me in, was a man by the name of Alfred Conrad who was married to Adrienne Rich, the poet. He had been a professor at the Harvard Business

School and, together with John Meyer, had written a book on the economics of slavery. I remember thinking "Oh my God" when I met him when I visited City College for the first time, because he had an SDS button on the lapel of his jacket. He turned out to be a radical who had taken the job in New York because he wanted to make a radical department there. He thought that was the most exciting thing he could do, and I was the first person hired in that process. Then he went after Hymer, but I think Hymer already had a job at the New School. And then he went after Resnick. (This was before Steve and I were friends.) And he had plans for many more.

Steve was a professor at Yale, remember, when I had been a graduate student. But when he came to City College, we were both professors. He was an associate professor; I was an assistant. There was never any kind of status thing with Steve. I think he found me interesting, and his friendship with Hymer had changed. Hymer had moved to New York and was having horrible psychological and marital problems, and Steve was a much more straight-laced guy, married to his high school sweetheart, etc. So I replaced Hymer in a way as his friend, and the fact that I was a few years younger never made any difference that I ever felt.

By the time we got to UMass we were already good friends, but the move to UMass really solidified it. The first phone calls that Sam Bowles made in putting the department together were to Steve and me, to be the other half of the radical contingent with his buddies, Herb Gintis and Rick Edwards. He wanted us to come up from City College, they would come from Harvard, and we would meet in Amherst and make this thing happen. This is hard to convey, but we very quickly felt "other" in relation to those three. It's hard to explain. Steve had a line that we used for many years. There are two kinds of people in the world: those that will go into the woods to fight with you, and those that will not; those three, uh-uh. It was his assessment that there was something fundamentally unserious about them. This was not a comment on their economics, or their theoretical knowledge, or their qualities as teachers. None of that. This was a comment on their political commitment to anti-capitalism, for lack of a better term. I didn't have this judgment, but I listened to him – smart guy, Steve Resnick. He made this judgment pretty early on. They were our buddies; we had come together. We would cover for each other; we would work as a solid group. And we did for the first five, six, seven years. We supported them and they supported us. But they were different from us. It is hard to explain. Steve and I talked about it often, trying to explain it to ourselves. The words I would use now – I didn't understand it then – they were more interested in the careers; we were more interested in the political project. They had a fundamental distrust of this project being able to go very far. And they felt vindicated in 1990. I remember Sam writing to me once, saying our efforts to change had failed. I remember thinking, "What is he talking about? History has a reverse; does he think it's going to just follow a straight line?" In retrospect they were always more interested in the here and now, not in a broader political project, which I think is what Steve was getting at with who would go into the woods to fight with you. Who do you really trust?

And then Steve and I got more interested in the theoretical stuff. Someone gave me Hindess and Hirst's *Pre-Capitalist Modes of Production*. I don't even know who. I read this book, and I remember calling Steve on the phone and saying, "you've got to get this!" What they had done was written down the theory, the theory of how one class structure is different from another. They really worked it out for you. This is the ancient, this is the capitalist, this is the feudal, and this is the Asiatic (whatever it is). No one had ever done this. And they were answering our theoretical questions.

So you got to Althusser through Hindess and Hirst?
Absolutely. Hindess and Hirst weren't economists, though at first we thought they were. But they were really using Marxist theory to ask the questions we were interested in. This was magnificent, and they kept footnoting and citing Althusser, so of course we picked up on that. We really worked through Althusser. Just to be clear, what Althusser's writings said to us was, "I'm a Marxist, you can be a Marxist, and you don't have to have anything to do with economic determinism." Without knowing it, that's what we wanted, because we didn't like this economic determinism. It made us really nervous, and he was showing us, "You don't need to be an economic determinist. Marx wasn't, I'm not."

What do you think it was for you and Steve that made you so nervous about economic determinism?
Simple mindedness. The criticisms we had read all our lives, in the '50s and '60s when we were growing up. One of the main tools of anti-Marxism was the criticism of its simplemindedness, the childishness, of thinking that people are motivated only by their economic interests. We knew this criticism was right, but we loved Marxism, just not that. When you think about your mother, your father, your siblings, yourself, can you explain what happened in your crazy family by economics alone? Come on. Should it be part of the story? Sure. Economics is what makes the world go round? No. And as we read Marx we could see how people read him as an economic determinist, but we could also see another way, and Althusser said yeah, yeah, yeah. If you take the two together, the preponderance of evidence is that Marx is a critic of economic determinism, not a proponent. Thank you, Althusser. This is before we had any contact with him. We had just read him, like everybody else, thanks to the *New Left Review*.

Let's talk about your relationship with students, which always seemed different to me.
Our teaching was always a part of the rest of our lives, and the rest of our lives always had a great deal in it of building a different society, and

building a movement for that. So for us students were not just sitting in a class to learn some material, or aggrandizing our egos by liking what we were teaching, although I can assure you those students were important to us. But we didn't want just students, we wanted to build a movement, we wanted these students to go out and make this happen on an enormous scale. And that was always important. We wanted them to go into the woods with us! That's what we wanted. I don't know exactly what that meant, but it meant welcoming students into a club, into a society pretty early in the process, where we were all doing something important together. We always talked about this, that what this country needs is lots of people studying Marx, teaching Marx, using Marx, questioning Marx, taking it in new directions, that's fine. But we're building a tradition, that's what we're doing.

So launching the Rethinking Marxism *journal with your Ph.D. students was something you consciously planned?*

Steve and I realized early on how much we needed each other. We even talked about it, and we were not the types to usually talk about these things – which tells you something. But we both understood it, and we said look, this place [UMass] could be impossible if we had to navigate the department alone: its tensions, the politics, the politicking among the students, which got to be difficult sometimes. But there were two of us, two sets of eyes and ears, two people having conversations and bringing back their sense of what's going on. It was invaluable to us, and I think early on we understood that to graduate from UMass – someone like you – and then to go off to another school without someone else to help you: whoa, talk about extra obstacles. That career is going to be very hard. We needed to have an association that could provide support, friendship, a potential colleague you could hire, all of that. We decided early on that there has to be a focus. The journal was a focus. A journal would give us all something we worked on that we could use to communicate our ideas, that we had to write something for or work out a struggle over. Otherwise it would just be either personal friendships or some abstract agreement, which neither of us felt would be sufficient. So the journal, it was natural; you're an academic, make a journal. But that was less important than the group.

And remember we started that journal in the 1980s. Everyone told us we were crazy, that it was a bad time, etc. But we did it anyway because a) the truth of it is, no one knew what was going to happen and b) we had all these other reasons to hold us together as a group. So whether or not it would succeed in some abstract sense, it would succeed if it did that, which it did.

You guys gave students a lot of freedom in writing dissertations, maybe sometimes enough to hang themselves. But for instance you don't require an econometric chapter, which is unusual. Did you worry at all about the fact that people were going out without the pedigree that you have, and with dissertations that might look odd to the profession? Did that ever come up or were you more interested in helping people do what they wanted to do?

No we worried about it. We did push students to have some arithmetic somewhere in their dissertation, to have a model of something that they would at least discuss or do some econometric work on. We did some of that in order to help. But we always did it with humor. It's like writing for the censor. How did Gramsci ever write about Marx without saying "Marx?" How do you do what you want to do without running afoul of the rules? So we reached a decision early and never changed our minds about this. The quality of what came out was much more correlated with the passion the student could bring to it, and therefore if you stifle the passion, constrain students by making them do stuff they don't know, don't like, don't want to do, you will hurt the final outcome. We also believed that you can't do Marxian economics very well if you are spending most of your time mastering neoclassical or Keynesian economics. It's just too much. You can't do it. And if you're a young graduate student, for sure you can't do it. There is just no way out of it. The opportunity cost is that if you are going to do the conventional stuff, you are not going to do the Marxian work very well. And for us, grounding you all in Marxian theory, as really good students of Marx, was more important. Had we discovered that students were losing jobs or being denied jobs because there wasn't more conventional economics in their dissertations, we might have pushed for more. But we never got that feedback. If there were students who had that happen, they didn't tell us.

Was this a point of tension between you and the Harvard group? When I was there in the early '80s, they were pushing people to do fairly standard dissertations with maybe an extra variable for power or race or gender. Or had the parting of the ways already occurred?

They did what they did, we didn't. Sam and Herb flirted with Marxism when it was chic and cool to do that. That was during the first, I'll be generous, the first ten years we were there, and that flirtation had a lot to do with them being caught up, for awhile, in the left economics sub-culture. Sam loved the camaraderie, the solidarity, and Herb did in his peculiar way also.

But by the mid '80s the fad, the fashion of radical political economy was fading, and they did not want to fade with it. Sam and I once had a difficult conversation where he looked at me – he was frustrated, as I was, we weren't communicating well – and said, "I believe in the life cycle of ideas, and all these ideas we had when we came here, they're over." He thought we had to move on. He didn't say this, but he implied that I was stuck in the mud and he was moving forward. He was adapting to a new reality, whereas what I was doing was some kind of fuddy-duddy, antiquarian obsession with the past, something like that. For me Marxism works in fits and cycles, it has had reverses in the past, it will have reverses in the future, but you don't give up on your critical framework because there are a few years in which people who used to be interested lose interest. You have to ask why and you have to think about that, but it's not a justification for giving up on a system of ideas.

I was a Ph.D. student during this period and I think there was a sense in the air that you and Steve were more interested in things that were philosophically rigorous (though you also did the popular economics thing even then) but that Sam especially was interested in popular. So the people who were interested in popular economics would go over here and the people who were interested in philosophical rigor would go over there. Was that your sense?

Yes, except for the caveat that you just mentioned. Not to toot my own horn, but my wife used to say to me in those years, "You are the only member of that department who is an activist doing what they discuss all the time." I built an organization in New Haven. I ran for mayor. I ran for city council. I was the advisor to the AFL-CIO. I was a major strategist for the union groups at Yale. And I spend thousands of hours doing all that stuff.

I always did both academics and politics, and with whatever self-delusion this involved, I told myself that my personality could never stand doing just one or the other.

Was that a source of tension between you and Steve?

Yes. There were times when he resented my activism; it was taking my time and attention away from our intellectual work. On the other hand, he was always supportive of it. It was a tension, even inside of him. He never said to me "You can't do this." Keep in mind the context. How do I say this? I think I'm more of a workaholic than Steve was. But the other way of getting at that, a little dangerous but I'll do it, is that my home life was with a partner who supported, encouraged, and believed in what I was doing, both the activism and the theoretical work.

I'm lucky, I have a wife who believes in the work I do – all of it. I didn't know that when I married her. Luck of the draw. I was 23, what did I know? But whatever it was, I had a person who said, "Write that article. Let's go to the demonstration." Steve had nothing like that.

Let's talk a little more about students. I remember I took the Marx course with Steve. It had this big long reading list. And then for whatever reason I saw the undergraduate Marx syllabus; it was almost the same thing. I wonder how you thought differently about graduate and undergraduate students. Did you think about this consciously?

We thought about it and we talked about it. In the end we didn't think it made much difference. Did we make the graduate course a little more rigorous? Yeah. We made assumptions about what we could do. We would be more likely to write equations on the board about value theory. But that was partly just a difference between Steve and me, which was always there, in every book we wrote together, every article, it was always there. I'll exaggerate a bit here so you get my point. He wanted to write an article that fellow economists would have to acknowledge, however grudgingly, as "pretty good": well argued, proper footnotes, some math if we could get it in there, the right sources that showed we knew what this stuff was. I wanted people to understand what we were saying and worried that if we put too much formal theory in there, they would look at it and go "Argh!" because they don't know what algebra is or how it works, or a differential (d this, d that), and they'd go (Bronx cheer.) We never resolved that. We always compromised.

For example, in our book, *Economics: Marxian vs. Neoclassical,* both the early version and the newer one, *Contending Economic Theories,* all the technical stuff in there is Steve. I mean I reviewed it. I checked for mistakes. I clarified when I thought it looked too murky. But he insisted on that material, whereas I insisted on a metaphor that makes it clear – a story, a way that makes it transparent. It's the same point, but for the economists, they're going to read the equation; they're going to understand it. But they are not going to know what it means. You have to tell them.

And he would compromise. He would understand what I was saying. But he would not write the way I would have written because that would make everyone think we were not serious economists. Look, the man had a point. About the *Contending Economic Theories* book we published with MIT, the last book we wrote together, Steve said, "The students don't buy the book. The teachers buy the book and tell the students to read it. So who do you think the book has to be written for?" And I said, "Yeah, but we want to reach the students. The teachers are a foregone loss anyway." So we would fight, and he would have to acknowledge that I had a point, and I would have to acknowledge that he had a point. The book is a compromise on how to present the material. When we taught together, he would write the equations on the board and I would explain to the students what it meant. Sometimes it worked, and sometimes it didn't. I probably did more verbal explanation because of him, and he probably did more math. I mean, we shaped each other a little bit.

One of our colleagues writing a chapter for this volume told me he is writing it for his graduate students, who hate the epistemology part of Knowledge and Class. *They struggle with the class part but are interested in that, but they hate the epistemology. I've had similar experiences, including some who like the epistemology but hate the class stuff. Did you ever think you were asking people to do too much, by having a different notion of class and asking them to think really hard about the theory of knowledge?*

We worried about it. The first press to which we sent the manuscript for *Knowledge and Class* was Princeton University Press. I don't know why; maybe there was an editor we knew there. Princeton sent it out for review, and then got back in touch with us. They said

This is two books. One book is on philosophy and one book is on economics. We don't like and don't want to publish the first book, but we do like and would like to publish the second book, on economics.

That was a shock to Steve and me because in a peculiar way, as we were walking through Marxian theory, we had begun with what you might call class theory. But through our struggles in class theory, we were drawn into philosophical work, which proved absolutely crucial to us when we came back to class theory to make the contribution we think we were able to make.

So for us, these were closely intertwined. We had a long conversation, more than one, and we decided to say to Princeton, "No, you have to take it all or you are not getting any of it." It was polite, it was friendly, but they said no. Then we sent it to the University of Chicago. We didn't have any relationships there but their editor, who was not an economist, wrote us back and said, "This is great. This is fantastic what you've done. I didn't know there were economists who did this sort of work." We didn't know this at the time, but he was into postmodernism and didn't know there were any economists who had even heard about any of this. And that's why we did it with them. It was very successful; we were one of their top five best sellers in the first year.

I had a good friend, an institutionalist economist, who loved the epistemology. He thought it was great – "exactly what you (Marxist) guys need." But the class stuff, no. It's a lot to ask of people.
It is. Steve and I would marvel at the reactions, and maybe this goes to what you are saying. There would be years in which graduate students would have enormous difficulties with one and not the other. But it had no pattern. There were people like your friend who would celebrate the one and were either unmoved or horrified by the other. But again, it went both ways.

Since I came to New York, I do much more of the class stuff. It's just easier. I do the philosophic stuff less. Someone brought me to the New School, and I did epistemology. I did it for economists to show that prediction is absurd and policy is absurd, you can't do it, etc. I'm pretty good at this, but there was dead silence in the room. Will Milberg, who had invited me, looked around the room and asked, "Doesn't somebody want to question this, challenge this, disagree?" Nothing. For a good number of them, they didn't like this, they didn't want this, but they had never heard it before. This was so off the wall for them. They had the reaction that anybody does when you hear something that is so different and weird. You don't know what to say. You know this is no good, but you don't know how to respond.

We eventually had some conversation. The students said, "You mean I can't say *this* is the way to solve the problem? Then what do I say when the people in leadership ask me for advice or for what policy to try?" Well, you can tell them that on the basis of a whole series of assumptions, policy X might work. But you can't tell them policy X is going to solve their problem. And you have to be honest about the 800 times that people have tried this and it hasn't worked. You've got to do something with that.

They (policy economists) don't have a refutation to these arguments because they have never done this work. So I'm ahead of them. I know their arguments for it, but I also know the other side. And their reaction is "you are taking away from me what I'm doing. I won't let you." Ok, that's fair.

But it's interesting that your popular work now is so extraordinarily successful. …. But that ain't because of me. I wish I could take the credit….

On the other hand, academia just sails on; nothing changes. I assume from what you said earlier, about the difference between you and Steve, that he would have been bothered more than you are to see that the impact of postmodern critique on university economics is virtually zero.
Yes and no. I pushed epistemology on Steve. He read it, but I forced it on him. But then he became more committed to it and adept at it than I was. He was a student who surpassed the teacher. He really was. In his head, there were alternative ways of doing economics, and it had nothing to do with right and wrong. It had to do with who you are, where you came from, how your theoretical work was overdetermined in your life as an individual. And there are these incommensurate alternative knowledge constructions.

Steve and I knew a neoclassical economist at Yale, Richard Cooper. I was his student and Steve was his colleague. He was amazing. You would ask him a question, and he would give you the textbook answer. Everything was convertible into supply and demand, or a production function. He was a wonderful teacher. Wow, you could see it; he was just brilliant at that. And that would come up for Steve and me in later years. One of us would say, "Remember Richard Cooper." The man had mastered that paradigm. Anything that came his way, he could stick it into a neoclassical model. He took pleasure in showing you how to do it.

So, I think Steve, on the one hand, would be upset because our perspective has not prevailed. But he would also take it as a kind of epistemological demonstration that there is no necessity that if a particular underlying reality veers off to the right, these people will not go straight on doing what they have been doing. He would be upset but he would also feel vindicated.

That's interesting. I hadn't thought about that. Your Democracy at Work *writings and talks are eliciting their own dualistic reactions, just as* Knowledge and Class *did. I've seen reviews by self-proclaimed anarchists who say, "This is all fine but he's a Marxist, and you don't need Marxism to do what he's doing." Then at the labor process conference I recently attended in London, the Marxists say, "Well, this is utopianism." How do you react to that?*

I'm familiar with both critiques. I get each from time to time. I would say these people account for 10%, maybe 15%, of my audience. I basically made a strategic decision to just ignore them. This is something that Steve and I talked about a million times. Our most difficult audiences are people who call themselves Marxists.

That has happened to us so much, and for so many years, that it is not even interesting anymore. Marxists, socialists – this is very crude but I'm going to do it anyway – are divided into young and old. I really mean it, chronologically. The older the Marxist or the Socialist, the more likely this utopian critique comes up, and here's how I understand it. For them, for many years, as for us, socialism is public (rather than private) ownership of the means of production, and planning rather than markets. That's it. You can embellish in 27 ways but that's what they want to hear about. They want me to celebrate public vs. private and planning vs. markets. The planning vs. markets is actually less important for them, which is interesting. I try to be gentle, but I lose them when I say 21st century socialism is going in a different direction, that we're not interested in these macro questions, that we're interested in the micro organization of the enterprise. I like planning and I like public ownership, and sure there will have to be coordination among all of these worker self-directed enterprises. But capitalism grew out of feudalism, and eventually the early capitalists figured out how to coordinate themselves. I figure it will happen again that way too with worker self-directed enterprises, where they'll be influenced by the public vs. private and market vs. planning debates. They don't know how to answer me. They live in that old world. They've never been confronted by someone who says, "Socialism, yeah that's what you say. But this is the more important thing for us to be talking about."

So I win, whatever that means. With the anarchists, it depends. If they seem to me to be honest questions, I talk to them about what Marxism has to teach. Anarchism is about control. It's very abstract and very general. It's mostly about citizen-government, and we're not talking about that. We're talking about inside an institution: how does it work, and who's in charge?

This issue of economic democracy was big at UMass when I was a graduate student. But it was mostly other people, not you and Steve. If I remember correctly, you had a critique of economic democracy at that time. Do you still stand by that critique? Have times changed? Is your current analysis somehow different from those of what we might call Progressive economists?

You are absolutely right. Steve and I were consistently arguing over a long period of time against a focus on democracy that had functioned on the left as a substitute for and a distraction from issues of class. For us that was very clear. It was clear in our colleagues, Bowles and Gintis, who in our judgment were obsessed by political issues of democracy, who were really focused on "letting the people decide" and getting everybody to participate, basically taking this from the old SDS idea of participatory democracy. We wanted to say – not that we were against democracy; that would be silly – that an analysis of class is different from an analysis of democracy. Sam and Herb were our counter-points most of the time, since among graduate students those for whom democracy seemed most important tended to end up with them, one way or the other, sooner or later. And it made a certain sense, since neither Sam nor Herb was interested in class. They were really interested in power, and power is closer to this notion of democracy and participation, rather than to exclusion from appropriating and distributing surplus. So we worked very hard to suggest that whatever you think about power, that's a different matter than the production and distribution of the surplus. We want to focus on that class process, because for us that's a separate matter. Class interacts with democracy and power, of course. Overdetermination implies that the class process affects power processes, and vice versa. But we wanted to establish their difference, their uniqueness, and their separate importance for what we were doing.

Let me put it one last way. Sam and Herb – we felt, and we didn't admire this – were tying into an American fetish with democracy. Democracy as a lingo was the issue from day 1. King George III was making a decision without us, and you're not going to tax us without representation. It's an endless mantra in which the good people expand the franchise and the bad people try to restrict. So a few people have too much power, too many people don't have enough, and as leftists we're all about spreading the power. Resnick and I in our meaner moments would say things like

> This is all charming but you are participating in not making a point about one of the things over which we need to discuss democratically: who produces the surplus, who appropriates the surplus and what do they do with it. You leave that out, and yet for us that's what Marx contributed. That's where there is a blind spot.

So even the people who talk a lot about democracy have a peculiar tendency in this country, now and in the 1980s, to see it not in relationship to class but to see it in relationship to a whole other set of topics to the exclusion of class, which brings them back into the consensus in this country that ignores this dimension of production. Power is not the repressed discourse that class is. Sam and Herb are dissatisfied with neoclassical economics because it doesn't include power relationships. In other words – Steve Marglin also does this – the employer is not just trying to find the point where the isoquants cross the price line for efficiency. He's engaged in a power struggle with his employees over something that is going on in production. Sam would get right to that point. We would say,

"Yeah, that something is class." He didn't want that. He was really much more interested in the power relationship. By power I mean who author-izes who to do what, who gives the order, who takes the order, who's calling the shots, who is the price or order taker, all of that. So, Sam would be happy to say he was introducing power into neoclassical economics, since they make no room for it, treating production as an engineering problem. He is saying no, this is a political issue about who is in charge. When we would try to specify what the struggle was over, that's where we would lose Sam.

Do you see your current work as pursuing this connection between democracy and class?

Yes. I would even go further since you are being so polite. This is a con-versation that Steve and I had in his last year or so. The approach Steve and I had taken to debates around democracy, saying, "No, we are doing something else," proved to be a hard sell, harder than we would have liked it to be. So when I started running around the country talking in large meetings, I – like any teacher – wanted my audience to stay with me as I laid out my arguments. It was pretty clear to see when moments came that produced in an audience, who were otherwise with me, a cer-tain consternation, a certain discomfort, a certain "Why are you going in that direction?" So I slowly decided to cash in on the need to talk about democracy, because it seemed to me to be a legitimate way, particularly with an American audience, to get into a whole range of topics. But then I'm always very focused on talking about what that democracy is about. In other words, it's not just that I want people to have more power. I want particular people to have a particular power in a realm from which they have been excluded and about which most of my audience has never thought very much.

You got to a certain moment in the presentation and you lost them?

It's not that I lost them. It's that I got to a certain point and said, "Now, this is *not* about democracy." Look, mostly when democracy is discussed it is just in terms of *who* participates and *who* doesn't. Democracy is very much less focused on *what* the decision is about, the object of the decision as opposed to the subject of the decision, who is making it. So we would attack that and say, "Class is not understood, class is a powerful phenom-enon, class is what we should be talking about, not having more or less participation in decision making *in general*." It is not that people disagreed with me. It is that they didn't understand why I was giving so much im-portance to something they didn't see as significant.

For me to solve that problem, I put the two of them together. I said that we are in favor of democratizing the class process. That allowed me to hold them, because I'm all about democracy, and at the same time I'm all about democracy *here*, over questions of producing, appropriating, and distributing surplus. I found this allowed me to get done the job I wanted at the price of giving a bit more emphasis on the democracy shtick than would have been my preference.

What in your view are the major theoretical issues that need to be explored around the issue of democracy at work?

There are several. Perhaps one of the most important is an area where I can see already trouble coming. By trouble I mean an understandable concern in my audiences that we haven't worked out.

I no longer get much resistance to talking about democratizing the enterprise. People get it when you or I lay out the grotesquely undemocratic way a typical capitalist corporation works, in the traditional way that decisions are made about what to produce, where to produce, how to produce, and what to do with the profits. Who makes those decisions? Who lives with the consequences? The workers have no participation in those decisions. Everyone shuts up, even in my business audiences. By the way, that's another weird thing. I am increasingly invited by business associations, by groups of medical doctors, groups that you think would go right up the wall when they hear this stuff, but they don't. When I lay out that this is a fundamental affront to democracy, I get nothing. You can tell that for many of them this is new, and you can tell I've got them on that point. They're caught in a contradiction that they don't know, at least yet, how to escape.

But that's not the problem. The problem is that the people affected by corporate decisions are not just the mass of workers there. So if you argue, as we do, that they have a democratic right to participate in the decisions whose consequences affect them, then that applies to the larger community as well, the town where the business is located for instance – and not just the town but the region because it transacts across geographic space. I haven't done the work, and neither has anyone else, to render it practical that there be some co-determination between a presumably democratically organized enterprise on the one hand and a democratically organized and operated residential community on the other. How is that going to be done? What are the mechanisms that can give this concreteness so it can be understood, its importance evaluated, and progress made?

I use a number of examples for this. In Germany in the 1920s, after Kaiser Wilhelm had been overthrown, socialists took over. They were namby-pamby socialists, but they were socialists, and they had no idea what to do. One thing they did do was to set up a bi-cameral legislature of a completely new kind, which was kind of a genius move. One house was people elected in the traditional way, by people clumped into traditional regional areas. But workers elected the second house from their workplaces. If your workplace was a certain size, you got a delegate. So this was the labor house, as opposed to the residential house, and all legislation had to be agreed to by these two houses. Not a house and a senate but a labor chamber and a residential chamber.

That's a place to start. I haven't done the work, but there must be books and articles about this, what they did, what worked, where the problems were, where it screwed up. Having spoken last year to roughly 20,000 people in my various talks, there weren't three who knew about this.

So nobody knows the answer, but this is a way of letting people know that this concern for community is not crazy or something that other people have not thought about. If you really believe that people affected by a decision should have a voice in making it, if that's your commitment, then of course you can't stop by having a corporation or enterprise run collectively and democratically by its employees and simply pretend that people who aren't employees have no say and therefore no role in the decision. The truth of this is already recognized in this country because we mandate that certain kinds of business decisions have to be approved by a residential body. You can't build a road over here, you can't pollute the air, etc. Precisely because they understand the interdependence that has to be worked out, political authorities in the United States bring in businesses formally or informally. It is not done in a democratic way, but there is already political recognition of the interdependence.

I remember Julie Graham being involved in a similar argument years ago. Anything else you think needs attention?
Yes, but it is a corollary. Exploitation is defined to mean that there are people in a position to appropriate surplus who did not participate in producing that surplus. If you are going to be strict in your definition, that means people in a subsumed class position inside a corporation, such as the security guards, the secretaries, the clerks, and the managerial functionaries, can't be among the appropriators of the surplus. If they were, you would have an appropriator who is not also a surplus producer. We want to rule that out because this concept of exploitation is what motivates us to be anti-capitalist in the first place. So the way we worked this out, Steve and I, was to say that in a democratic enterprise of the kind we are talking about, the people who appropriate the surplus are indeed limited to those who participate in producing it. Only the people who produce the surplus will appropriate it *and* distribute it.

Bear with me. What then, is the role of the subsumed classes inside the enterprises, the subsumed classes outside the enterprises, and as we just discussed, the residential communities? Answer: their role is to decide *democratically* who gets what share of the surplus that is distributed by the people who produce it. The productive workers produce, appropriate, and distribute it. They do the distribution. But how the distribution is done, the power to determine to whom they distribute shares of the surplus, that is democratically decided by everybody, unproductive and productive workers, people inside and outside the firm: they all do that. This is analogous to what is already happening, but we're going to make it explicit and democratic. It is already the case that to whom the board of directors of a capitalist corporation distributes the surplus is not something that it decides alone. True, the board distributes the surplus. That's how it works. But to whom they give what share is the subject of an influence that's spread very widely in the society. For instance, politicians tell them, "You're going to give us 10% in taxes." The board may not want to do that. This may not have been their choice if they were wholly in charge, but they're not. This is where democratic participation of the unproductive workers and people outside the enterprise comes in. There will have to be real negotiations between the productive workers and these other groups.

Why does the security guard not get to sit at that table?
He gets to sit at the table where the rules for distributing the surplus are decided, but he does not sit at the table where it is decided how surplus is produced or appropriated or what the actual distribution is. His role is limited to participating in deciding to whom and what share that distribution is. And that means that it is the productive workers themselves who decide the size of the surplus, no minor matter. That determines the length of the working day, wage levels, etc. These are significant distinctions.

In a democratic society, it is true that the community as a whole is affected by how many children you and your partner have. Those children will have to be educated in the schools, will have put demands on local pediatric services, and so forth. We do not say that the community has a meeting to tell you when, where, and how to make children. Because we have a notion – and that's what it is, it's a notion – that some things, even though they affect everybody, must remain in the personal domain. You and your partner make you own decisions in the bedroom, when you do it, how you do it, and it may result in a child. The community has a greater interest in leaving the decisions done that way than to have a collective decision about it.

Parallel to this, our community, perhaps influenced by Marx, has the right to say that it will not allow exploitation to occur. We will not let people appropriate surplus that they do not produce. That will be left to the productive workers. But you can't exclude community members from a host of decisions that affect their lives.

You have this relatively worked out. So it sounds more like an education problem than a theoretical problem at this point – or am I missing something?
I would like to believe that but I don't. There may be some big contradictions here we haven't yet encountered. We are at an early stage in puzzling this stuff out, so I am not confident. If you, or someone else, or a student came to me and said, "I smell trouble here. I'm going to work on this," I would be very happy. My guess is that if we got into this, it would be rich. I don't think that we would discover things that would make us discard the whole argument, but we would learn good things along the way.

Have you seen people doing this kind of thing or worrying about these issues in a practical way, say in Mondragon or any of the other larger experiments?

No, not in Mondragon. Where we have gotten this from are people for whom the big issue, for whatever reason, is the interaction between "the community" and "the workplace." Those people have picked up, and rightly so, that everything I say is focused on the enterprise. They feel, "hello, where am I? I'm interested in a democratic community." They like what I say but they don't like that they are left out. They know there is something wrong there, they're the ones who pushed it, and I think they have a point. So that's the way I respond. They feel better when I say that, I don't lose them, but I suspect they know that is a beginning that is way short of where it has to go. But there are other examples. You could talk to Shirley Gedeon or Diane Flaherty or Darko Suvin, people who know something about Yugoslavia and self-managed enterprises. Or early Chinese communes: were they amalgamations of villages and workplace? My guess is that an assiduous piece of work would yield a lot on these fronts.

Let's talk about something you and I have each been thinking and writing about – what you call the Great Relocation. Capital is abandoning some regions, moving to new ones. In part, capitalism has always worked this way, yet there seems to be something new – an exacerbation, faster and more intense than we've seen in the past. We, the editors, are interested to hear how you make theoretical sense of this and what you see as the practical implications for social movements of various kinds.

I don't think I can add much to what I've written, but in any case it's over-determined, which may come as a surprise to you...

Hmmm ... I don't think I've heard that before.

But here are some of the key things, not necessarily in order of importance. The working classes in Britain, Western Europe, North America, and Japan, partly through their own struggles and horrific losses along the way, and partly because the capitalists were able to rip the rest of the world off on a staggering scale, both during and after colonialism and all that, were able to get very high relative wages. Or to make it starker, they were able to get high real wages, while the masses of workers outside those areas suffered a decline of their standards of living as they were drawn into capitalist exploitation, either by providing the food and raw materials for those areas, or as cheap immigrant labor, or in outlying production arrangements.

Over time, these high real wages in the original capitalist countries irked capitalists.

So starting in the 1970s you have a tsunami of capital flowing abroad. The first capitalists who take a risk to set up shop in China, in India, in Brazil – because it's always risky, expensive, and time-consuming to be first – made a commode full of money. Others had to get on board. It was easy to see if you're making shoes in Bristol, England and you see what's coming from Brazil, you gotta go. They're making shoes – OK, not exactly as fancy as yours, but almost the same – and they're charging a third of the price. You're just going to die if you don't figure out a strategy. So, it quickly becomes a flood. And because the natural resources and people in the rest of the world are so numerous, so vast, and we're early in the process of figuring out where they are, there is no end to this racket, no reason to think this is short term.

You read in the newspaper every few months about some company coming back to the U.S. who had left. Sure there will be some, but this return of capital is not going to amount to anything, even though these stories appear regularly. Every couple of months you see a lovely story in the *New York Times* or *Wall Street Journal* about some company opening in Carolina, or Nevada. OK, that's going to happen. But in Bangladesh the monthly minimum wage is under $100. What are you going to do with this?

Is there any way to connect this great relocation of capital to the social movements you are addressing with Democracy at Work? *Are these operating on two different tracks in your mind? Or is there a way to connect them?*
There are plenty of ways to connect the two. But let me tell you something that may seem somewhat tangential. I'm going to be critical now, so correct me because you know more about some of these things than I do. My sense of the struggles of the American Left, by which I mean the unions, the socialist parties, the communist parties, etc., is that they made a horrific strategic mistake from the late 19th century through the 20th century. They fought the class struggle with the capitalist employers around one basic theme: you don't pay us enough. "We want higher wages, better working conditions. But don't worry. We understand. You're the capitalists; we're the workers. We just want a better deal. We want to sell our labor power at a higher price." The reason this was a strategic mistake is that even though the capitalists fought against them, they could meet this demand, and when pushed to the wall, they did. What they could never have done--and here is where the European unions and the European Left are a little better--is to cede their position as surplus appropriators. Had the U.S. Left demanded *that*, their struggles would have been a little harder. But it would have brought the issue to a head, because the capitalists could not have met their demands.

The irony is that now because of the great relocation, the mistake isn't a mistake anymore. In other words, an increasing standard of living is just what American capitalists are not in a position to give you. They can't really because they've put their eggs in a different basket by seeking out low wage labor elsewhere.

The argument then is that global competition won't allow them to pay higher wages in the United States. But why couldn't they take extra profits from having moved abroad and make them available here? That's possible, and it may go that way. If I saw the beginning of that, I might be more inclined to downplay the demand for a higher standard of living. But it seems to me that right now, as I see in my growing audiences, there is a fundamental anxiety among American people that the game is over, that they're done, that they're being pecked to death by ducks, that whether it is social security, or government programs, or police, they are surrounded by changes that are eroding their standard of living. They know it, having begrudgingly come to it, and they are interested in people who explain it. I'm one of those. It is an audience I didn't get before. I have a story to tell about that, and they're interested in it. I tell an entertaining version of it in an educated way, and that makes it a little less scary. In addition, I'm as furious about it as they are, so I have a rapport with my audience. I'm now wondering whether the tide is turning *for* a struggle about what it should not have been about before, namely: wages and living standards. That's the question.

If I saw a recognition on the part of the corporate leadership, or the super-rich who they make rich, that "we're in big trouble, we've got to take a significant portion of our wealth and plow it into these people, we've got to deliver on the rising standard of living promise," then I might change my mind. But I don't see that. There are a few voices. You get Buffetts occasionally, that guy in Oregon who gave all his workers $70,000, but it's isolated. It immediately gets mocked. Those at the top are in an ideological trap; they don't have the mentality to see it that way. Their mentality is, "Grab it all before it disappears." I believe in the power of ideology, so for the moment at least, I'm rethinking my criticism of the conventional demand for higher wages. I still keep my focus on the surplus and economic democracy, but I'm giving more credence to the struggle for the standard of living, because I think it is dwarfing everything else.

That takes me to the social movements. Their leaders are being pressured by the same things that I am. They want this, they want that, but their audiences are shifting the same way mine are, from whatever issues with which they began to a mushier situation. Their original topic is morphing into, "our standard of living is falling apart. Something has to be done about this."

Jesse Jackson writes an article just yesterday about the latest shooting in Ferguson, and he points out that a man who turns out to have been white was killed last week by the police, who the police said was threatening, when they were going after his partner, I guess a woman, in a car they were driving. They suspected the woman of dealing in marijuana, which in California makes her as unique as everybody else, so the police shoot and kill the driver. They were not even after him, a 19-year old white man. The policeman said, "He was coming after me in his car." Three days later, the autopsy reports he was shot in the back. Interestingly Jesse Jackson writes the following, "This story shows we're not facing a race problem, we're facing a class problem." He is not saying this because he suddenly had an epiphany that it's about class. He's always had an understanding, and he knows the Left well enough. I think he is responding to a change in his audience. His audience, which is upset about black lives matter for perfectly understandable reasons, is also noticing, "We are getting shafted like everyone else in the working class, and something has to be done about *that*, not just race."

This is interesting because given how many young black people have been shot by cops, obviously they would be justified in focusing on that particular issue and the incarceration issue, for which the numbers are just awful, I mean off the charts. I think it is doubly significant that someone like him is going in that direction when he really doesn't have to, when he has plenty of justification to stay focused on other issues.

So the $15-an-hour movement, which you might have been mildly critical of 10–15 years ago, now starts to make more sense, given the repositioning of the pieces?
That's right. I mean I would have always supported it, but I would have given the backdrop. We're constantly in this position of demanding more, which is what they can give, and in the end it won't change the basic dimensions of life in that society. For that to happen, we have to change this other thing. And people would give it to me grudgingly, but now I don't even have to say it. They kind of get it.

I got drawn into the living wage movement in Providence, Rhode Island, and I used to say that instead of just asking for a bigger slice of the pie, workers should ask for the pie cutter.
Right, and I would hammer at that – as I try to do with my democracy shtick. If all you ask from Massa is a bigger piece of the pie, you may be lucky enough to get one. But as soon as he thinks he can, he's going to cut you a smaller slice. So why are you leaving the pie cutter in his hands? There's no reason for that.

Part II

Economics without guarantees

2 Strangers in a strange land

A Marxian critique of economics

David F. Ruccio

Do not believe
That, from the sense of all civility,
I thus would play and trifle with your reverence:
Your daughter, if you have not given her leave,
I say again, hath made a gross revolt;
Tying her duty, beauty, wit and fortunes
In an extravagant and wheeling stranger
Of here and everywhere.

Shakespeare, *Othello*

Anyone associated with Marxism, at least in the United States, will have the sensation of living a science fiction novel, like being a stranger in a strange land. This is particularly true in the academy, especially in the discipline of economics, where I have worked for the past 30 years or so.

Economics *is* a very strange land—not unlike the future United States of Robert A. Heinlein's 1961 novel whence I have borrowed the title of my essay (Heinlein [1961] 1987). And those of us who are Marxist economists are often made to feel like Valentine Michael Smith, a human, raised by Martians, who fails to "grok" the strange habits of the humans on planet Earth—although unlike Smith, we will never become celebrities, nor will we be fêted by the elite of our planet Earth, the discipline of economics.

Still, to be honest, we've become somewhat less strange in recent years, with increasing references to Marx and Marxian economics in mainstream media and by mainstream economists.

Here's Nouriel Roubini (2011), a.k.a. Dr. Doom, professor of economics at New York University's Stern School of Business and the chairman of Roubini Global Economics, an economic consultancy firm: "So Karl Marx, it seems, was partly right in arguing that globalization, financial intermediation run amok, and redistribution of income and wealth from labor to capital could lead capitalism to self-destruct."

Roubini continues:

> Firms are cutting jobs because there is not enough final demand. But cutting jobs reduces labor income, increases inequality and reduces

final demand. Recent popular demonstrations, from the Middle East to Israel to the UK, and rising popular anger in China – and soon enough in other advanced economies and emerging markets – are all driven by the same issues and tensions: growing inequality, poverty, unemployment, and hopelessness. Even the world's middle classes are feeling the squeeze of falling incomes and opportunities.

And then, from the other side of the Atlantic, there's George Magnus (2011), Senior Economic Adviser to the UBS Investment Bank:

> Policy makers struggling to understand the barrage of financial panics, protests and other ills afflicting the world would do well to study the works of a long-dead economist: Karl Marx. The sooner they recognize we're facing a once-in-a-lifetime crisis of capitalism, the better equipped they will be to manage a way out of it.

All of which lead to very strange encounters for many of us, such as my being invited on September 22, 2011, to participate in a debate hosted by the BBC program Business Daily about whether or not western capitalism has failed. They explicitly wanted a Marxist perspective on that question. (The best part of that debate actually occurred after they turned off the microphones. One of the participants in the debate—not surprisingly, the representative from the American Enterprise Institute—agreed with my argument that Americans work longer hours than in any other advanced country. However, in his view, that was evidence that Americans are happier than workers in other nations. Americans *like* to work! Well, after the debate was over, the young assistant engineer who had been working the sound board turned to me and asked, "Who is he talking to?!" Of course, I was as incredulous as she was. She then continued, "I'm certainly not happier working 12 hours a day. It's not my choice. And, now that the station has downsized, I not only have to do my own job, but also the jobs of two other people who were let go." I had made an instant friend!)

And then one month later came one of the strangest encounters of my life as a Marxist economist: I received an invitation to speak in Latvia—one of the most anticommunist countries in the world! And the invitation came from Lattelecom, the telecommunications giant and one of the largest companies in Latvia, a country that was in the throes of a neoliberal austerity program, where unemployment had jumped above 20 percent. It was a business conference supported by the prime minister and the CEO of Lattelecom, both of whom were at my talk. And the folks at Lattelecom were the ones who chose the title of my talk: "The New Reading of Marx's *Capital*." I initially thought it was a joke. But, as it turns out, it was real. And they were willing to fly me over to speak about Marx and the current crises of capitalism. So, I did—although, truth be told, to a mostly stone-faced audience (except for the head of the Latvian trade union confederation, who told me he was both surprised and delighted someone had had a chance to speak honestly about Marx and capitalism). And just to make things even more surreal, as I was leaving, the CEO gave me a signed copy of volume 1 of *Capital*, in Latvian!

So—after the crash of 2007–2008, in the midst of what I have come to refer to as the Second Great Depression, and with the rise of the Occupy Wall Street movement—there has in fact been increasing interest in Marx and ideas related to Marx, such as exploitation, socialism, and so on. That has created new openings for many of us. For example, Richard Wolff, a former professor for a number of people whose essays are included in this volume, has a well-known movie (2009) and book (2013) with the title "Capitalism Hits the Fan," who by his own admission can't keep up with the requests for talks and media appearances he receives. Then there's Maliha Safri, who taught a wide range of classes on economics, explicitly nonmainstream economics and noncapitalist alternative economic arrangements, within the Occupy Wall Street movement in Liberty Park. And there are many others—traditional as well as rethinking Marxists, in the United States and abroad—who have received additional recognition for their "strange" ideas in the midst of the ongoing crises of capitalism.

Enrollment in my own class on Marxian economics in recent semesters has been up. And students have been telling me that what they're reading is not at all what they suspected, what they were led to believe by their other professors, and that they do in fact find it refreshing (if somewhat disorienting).

My view, for what it's worth (and perhaps to the consternation of some of my fellow Marxists), is that this new reception of Marx can only be attributed in part to what Marx and contemporary Marxists have to offer. We simply can't take a lot of the credit. This new interest in Marx is, in my view, at least as much a sign of the spectacular failure of mainstream economics, in at least three senses:

- Mainstream economists failed to predict the crash.
- They didn't even consider a crash a remote possibility. The possibility of a crisis starting with (although not necessarily caused by) the housing and banking sectors didn't even exist in their theoretical frameworks.
- Once the crash happened, they simply didn't know what to do. The policy that went along with their models suggested letting the banks and the rest of the economy sort out the multiplying and increasingly deep-seated contradictions and tensions—until, of course, the panic that set in with the failure of Lehman Brothers in September 2008.

The kinds of problems building up for the previous three decades simply didn't figure prominently in their theoretical models and empirical analyses. I'm thinking of problems such as the following: the deregulation of banks and the spectacular growth of the financial sector within the U.S. and world economies; the housing bubble that was supported by prime and subprime bank loans and then sliced and diced into collateralized debt obligations and other derivatives (and backstopped, or so they thought, with credit default swaps); the outsourcing of jobs and the decline of labor unions (which if they paid attention to them at all were seen as freeing up markets); and, finally, the growing disparities in the distribution of income and wealth, reminiscent of the period just before the First Great Depression, when the share of income captured by the top 1 percent approached 24 percent of total income (it was 23.5 percent in 2007), and the share of wealth held by the top 10 percent was almost 85 percent (it was 72 percent in 2007).[1]

Mainstream economists—neoclassical and Keynesian economists, both microeconomists and macroeconomists—either ignored these issues or explained them away as a matter of efficient markets and the essential conditions for economic growth. For example, the financial sector needed no oversight or regulation, because of the idea of efficient markets (which meant that all risk was calculated into prices, and all participants had all the relevant information). Economic inequality was either necessary for growth or, if perceived to be a problem, merely a product of technology and globalization, which could be "solved" by the appropriate worker skills and more education. And, finally, both economic history and the history of economic thought—the history of capitalism and the history of thinking about capitalism—had disappeared as relevant areas of training for mainstream economists. As a result, mainstream economists had no working knowledge of landmark authors in their discipline, not only Marx but Smith (2003), Keynes (1965), and Minsky (1986).

But, after an initial flirtation with Marx, questions about capitalism's failure, and the idea of socialism in the mainstream media, the issue mostly faded from view after the recovery from the crash was declared to have occurred in the summer of 2009.

But the problems themselves continued to grow. We now know the damage inflicted on the majority of people by the worst downturn since the First Great Depression has been enormous and the only real recovery has been at the very top, in the profits of large corporations and the incomes of the top 1 percent. For everyone else, there has been very little improvement.

Let me provide just a few concrete examples: First, U.S. unemployment, which reached a peak of 10 percent in October 2009, remained stubbornly high (at 6 percent or more) for over 6 years (from August 2008 through August 2014). That is just the official (U3) rate. The unofficial rate (U6, which includes discouraged workers and those involuntarily working part-time jobs) was much higher (11 percent or more) for even longer (6 and a half years, from October 2008 through March 2015). Poverty in the United States also grew steadily, reaching 15.1 percent in 2010 (the highest rate since 1993);

since then, it has only dropped to a still-high 14.5 percent (in 2013, the last year for which data are available)—and more than 20 percent of young people (below the age of 18) find themselves in poor households. We also know that more than 30 percent of Americans who find themselves at or below the poverty line work outside the household and that their wages, along with those of most other workers, are still (in real terms) below where they were in June 2009, when the official economic recovery began.[2]

But, as I indicated, there *has* been a recovery—but only in corporate profits (which are at a post-WWII high as a share of national income) and top-1-percent incomes (which, having fallen to 18 percent in 2009, have now returned to above 20 percent as of 2013, the last year for which data are available). Thus, according to Emmanuel Saez (2015), while the incomes of most American families are still far from having recovered from the losses associated with the crash of 2007–2008 (with the result that, during the first three years of the so-called recovery, from 2009 to 2012, only 0.8 percent of total growth went to the bottom 99 percent of households), the incomes at the top have rebounded in spectacular fashion (such that the top 1 percent took home 91 percent of the total growth during that period).

The effects of these fundamentally unequal and ongoing crises are (1) a growing recognition that there has been little or no recovery for the vast majority of the population and (2) people are once again invoking Marx.

Here is Umair Haque (2011) in the *Harvard Business Review*: "Marx's critiques seem, today, more resonant than we might have guessed." And he goes on:

> While Marx's prescriptions were poor, perhaps, if we're prepared to think subtly, it's worthwhile separating his diagnoses from them. Because the truth might just be that the global economy is in historic, generational trouble, plagued by problems the orthodoxy didn't expect, didn't see coming, and doesn't quite know what to do with.

Or Peter Coy (2011) in Bloomberg's *Businessweek*:

> You don't have to sleep in a Che Guevara T-shirt or throw rocks at McDonald's to acknowledge that Marx's thought is worth studying, grappling with, and possibly even applying to our current challenges. Many of the great capitalist thinkers did so, after all.

And more:

> Joseph Schumpeter, the guru of 'creative destruction' who is a hero to many free-marketeers, devoted the first four chapters of his 1942 book, *Capitalism, Socialism and Democracy*, to explorations of Marx the Prophet, Marx the Sociologist, Marx the Economist, and Marx the Teacher. He went on to say Marx was wrong, but he couldn't ignore the man.

However, while references to Marx have certainly increased in recent years, there's no indication these many commentators have actually read Marx (perhaps the *Communist Manifesto*, back in their school days, but not *Capital*) and they certainly haven't read the scholarly work on Marx. Perhaps they were afraid to or didn't know how to, or were just too lazy. But the fact remains, those of us who have actually read *Capital* and have been engaged in a project of rethinking Marxism for the past 25–30 years are still strangers in an increasingly strange land in which the mainstream economic debate continues to oscillate between inflation and unemployment, freeing up or regulating markets, and the necessity—now or in the future—of cutting entitlements and imposing austerity on working and out-of-work people.

Let me turn, then, in the space that remains, to that project of reading and rereading Marx's *Capital*.

* * *

Marx was, of course, a stranger in his own set of strange lands, as he traveled in exile from Germany to France through Belgium and finally to England, where he settled down to write his *magnum opus*.

"A critique of political economy" is the often-overlooked subtitle of *Capital*—and that idea, critique, has taken on increasing significance in my own interpretation of what Marx was up to across the three volumes of *Capital*. It's an idea that Marx (1978) first announces in his 1843 letter to Ruge:

> If the designing of the future and the proclamation of ready-made solutions for all time is not our affair, then we realize all the more clearly what we have to accomplish in the present—I am speaking of a ruthless criticism of everything existing, ruthless in two senses: The criticism must not be afraid of its own conclusions, nor of conflict with the powers that be.
>
> (13)

On this interpretation, *Capital* is a two-fold critique: a critique of mainstream economic theory (the mainstream economic thought of his idea, the classical political economy of Adam Smith, David Ricardo, and the other classical political economists, many decades before the mainstream economic thought of our day, neoclassical and Keynesian economics, had emerged) and a critique of capitalism (the economic and social system celebrated by mainstream economists, then as now).

The idea is that what Marx was doing—and what Marxists after him need to do—is less the application of a particularly Marxian method (whatever it is called or however it is defined) and more the ongoing, ruthless critique of both mainstream economic thought and capitalism.

Let me push that idea a bit further: the starting point of *Capital* consists in the taken-for-granted assumptions of both classical political economy and bourgeois society in order to develop a "ruthless criticism of all that exists, ruthless both in the sense of not being afraid of the results it arrives at and in the sense of being just as little afraid of conflict with the powers that be." It begins by, first, accepting the rules of both mainstream economic thought and capitalism and, then, calling them into question.

I could give many examples, but let me provide just two to illustrate my argument. First, consider the famous opening sentences of volume 1 of *Capital*:

> The wealth of societies in which the capitalist mode of production prevails appears as "an immense accumulation of commodities"; the individual commodity appears as its elementary form. Our investigation therefore begins with the analysis of the commodity.
>
> (1977, 125)

Much to the surprise of many first-time readers, Marx does not begin with history or class but, instead, with the commodity. Why? My view is that it's because the classical political economists then (just like neoclassical and Keynesian economists today) celebrated the great wealth, the "immense accumulation of commodities" (or, in today's language, the national output or Gross Domestic Product) produced by capitalism. That's Smith's *Wealth of Nations* (2003). And, in one sense, Marx agrees: capitalism *does* produce many commodities. So, let's start with the commodity and I'll show you, Marx eventually reveals, that the capitalist production of commodities is also accompanied by the performance of surplus labor and the production of surplus-value, which is the source of capitalist profits. In other words, the immense accumulation of capitalist commodities is based on the exploitation of the direct producers—all on the presumption of the same, very strong assumptions (which Marx summarizes as "Freedom, Equality, Property, and Bentham") as the classicals.

> Freedom, because both buyer and seller of a commodity, let us say of labour-power, are determined by their own free will. They contract as free persons, who are equal before the law. Their contract is the final result in which their joint will finds a common legal expression. Equality, because each enters into relation with the other, as with a simple owner of commodities, and they exchange equivalent for equivalent. Property, because each disposes only of what is his own. And Bentham, because each looks only to his own advantage. The only force bringing them together, and putting them into relation with one another, is the selfishness, the gain and the private interest of each. Each pays heed to himself only, and not one worries about the others. And precisely for that reason, either in accordance with the pre-established harmony of things, or under the auspices of an omniscient providence, they all work together to their mutual advantage, for the common weal, and in the common interest.
>
> (1977, 280)

Why is that significant? Think of all the arguments being made today by mainstream economists—for example, that poor people are not really poor because they have air conditioning and improved cars, or that the goal of economic policy is to promote more economic growth in order to lower unemployment. Both of those arguments follow the classicals, in celebrating the immense accumulation of commodities (whether by individuals or society as a whole), and both of them ignore the existence of exploitation in the production of those commodities, which in turn (as Marx explains in subsequent chapters of *Capital*) produces both poverty and unemployment.

And consider, now, a second example: it is a common sense of bourgeois society that people get what they deserve: just deserts, as it is often put. That's as common sense a proposition as one will find during Marx's time and, even today, in the society in which we live and work. We all get what we deserve, based on individual initiative and the decisions we make every day in markets. At one level, Marx accepts that proposition, or at least uses it as his starting point. Let's assume that people do get what they deserve in commodity exchanges—in exchanges for consumer goods, in the exchanges capitalists are involved in for buying inputs and selling outputs, in exchanging our ability to work for a wage or salary, and so on. Make all those heroic assumptions and, still Marx argues, after the exchanges are completed and we enter the realm of production, capitalists get something they don't deserve: the extra value created by workers. The capitalists, in other words, get something for nothing: they engage in exploitation. And they share that surplus-value with still others: the shareholders in their enterprises, the CEOs who run their enterprises, the banks that finance their purchases and investments, the government that taxes an increasingly smaller share of their profits, even other capitalists with whom they compete in markets. The capitalists (the "industrial capitalists" Marx calls them) appropriate the surplus but don't necessarily get to keep it.

Marx's point is that there's a fundamental injustice at the heart of capitalism, with all kinds of conditions and consequences for the rest of society. That's the essence (to use a much-maligned term) of Marx's critique of both mainstream economics and capitalism. He starts with their (and, today, our) fundamental propositions and ends in a very different place.

In other words, Marx takes these things—mainstream economic thought and capitalism—and makes them different from themselves. He makes them strange. He takes ideas and practices that are a kind of common sense—we're all better off with economic growth, we get access to the necessities of life by freely selling our ability to work for a wage or salary, and so on—and then shows how strange they are, on their own terms.

In other words, reading *Capital* is a bit like Smith's (Mike Smith's, that is) first encounters with Earth-bound humans: everything they take to be normal—like war, clothing, and private property—are, by his Martian standards, simply bizarre. That's what the critique of political economy does and is supposed to do. But in this case, it starts with what others take to be normal—among mainstream economists and among those who think there's no alternative to capitalism—and denaturalizes it, thus making it strange.

That is why, when a student once told me that being in my class on Marxian economic theory was like walking into the "Twilight Zone" (and then stopped himself, embarrassed at the admission and worried that I might be offended), I assured him that I quite liked the idea—that compared to the economics classes taught by many of my mainstream colleagues, sitting in a Marx class *should* feel like an episode of Rod Serling's famous television series.

Having been around as long as I have, I can tell you the disciplines of economics and capitalism are certainly strange lands. So, in many ways, being a stranger and following the method of critique that makes the common sense strange are in fact where I prefer to be.

* * *

I also think it's where other Marxists prefer to be, especially those associated with the journal *Rethinking Marxism*. Over the course of the past few decades, the scholars involved with the journal have paid particular attention to the distinctiveness of the Marxian critique of political economy and, rather than normalizing it, either accepting the protocols of traditional Marxism or making it like the rest of economics, we've taken up the project of extending the concepts and protocols of the Marxian critique, of rethinking it—both uncovering aspects of the Marxian tradition that have been forgotten or overlooked and borrowing from other critical traditions to highlight the differences between Marxism and other approaches to economics. In other words, we've kept alive the project of carrying out a "ruthless criticism of all that exists."

In this sense, we are doubly strangers—strangers (for being Marxists) within the discipline of economics and strangers (for being rethinking Marxists) within the Marxian tradition itself.[3]

However, let me explain immediately, I don't see that double stranger status as being symmetrical or identical. If we follow Georg Simmel (1950) and see the stranger as one who comes today and stays tomorrow—thus distinguishing the stranger both from the "outsider" (who has no specific relation to a group) and from the "wanderer" (who comes today and leaves tomorrow)—then, it is true, some of us have come to both groups (of economists and Marxists) and stayed (because we have doctoral degrees in and make a living teaching economics and have attempted to contribute—through our writing, editing, and other activities—to the rethinking of Marxism). And there's no doubt, as Margaret M. Wood (1934) explained, we have both acted and been perceived, at various times in both cases, as being "in the group but not of it" (45).

But it is also the case that, as *potential* wanderers—who, to continue with Simmel, although we have not moved on, "have not quite overcome the freedom of coming and going"—we have different relations (or, at least, perceived relations) to the two groups. There's no doubt, many of us identify ourselves more as Marxists than as economists. In that sense, we are probably much more willing to come and go from the discipline of economics (even when we are engaged in efforts to stake a claim that what we do as Marxists *is* economics) than from the Marxian tradition (even when what we do and say is often not recognizable as Marxism from the perspective of some traditional Marxists).

Still, like the traders who settle down in the place of their activity, we have stayed within both groups, making our position as strangers stand out even more sharply. We can move about but we are still not "owners of soil."

In one sense, this mobility within both groups reflects and reinforces our status as strangers, as outsiders. Thus, we may speak the language and know the customs but, as so-called native anthropologists (e.g., Takeyuki Tsuda 2015) have discovered, the ability to wander in and out of a group makes it impossible to overcome our identity as strangers.

That's the negative side. But, in another sense, there are real, productive possibilities associated with being a stranger. Simmel suggested that the social relationship of the stranger to the group is associated with, in addition to mobility, objectivity, confidence, freedom from convention, and abstract relations. I want to focus here on one of those characteristics: freedom from convention. It involves, among other things, the ability and willingness to "freely associate," with only minimal attachments to the conventions that bind other enunciations and relations within the group. It is both a free association of ideas—new ways of looking at objects, new ways of making sense of the world—and a free association of persons—since the strangers are free to establish relations among themselves, with different sorts of conventions.

As I see it, those practices of free association (which, of course, echo Marx's reference to "production by freely associated men" [1977, 173]) are the condition and consequence of ruthless criticism—in both economics and Marxism. They form the basis, in other words, of the work of all the strangers who have in their different ways contributed to the project of rethinking Marxism.

* * *

Speaking only for myself, I'm proud to have been part of that project, from the founding editorial board right down to the present, including the 12 years I served as editor. During that time I have witnessed the publication in the pages of *Rethinking Marxism* of an extraordinarily rich and diverse set of contributions to the Marxian critique of political economy. Permit me, because my space is limited, to provide a few illustrative examples from that project.

I want to start with one of the strangest aspects of Marx's critique of political economy, the movement in the first chapter of volume 1 of *Capital* from a very conventional definition of the commodity (conventional, that is, for mainstream economics, then as now) in terms of use-value and exchange-value to the final section on commodity fetishism. I love teaching that chapter, especially at the University of Notre Dame (you can only begin to imagine how uncomfortable I can make a bunch of Catholic students having to talk about fetishism in its various forms and guises). Marx takes this common-sense thing—the commodity—a common sense for both classical political economists and for us, since that's how we acquire many of the things we need for food, clothing, and shelter, and turns it into something bizarre, making it different from itself. It's also both one of the most referred to and misunderstood and misinterpreted sections of *Capital* (especially outside the discipline of economics—what literary or cultural critic would not succumb to the temptation of playing around with that idea?).

Misunderstood because that section is generally interpreted as a kind of false consciousness—that people mistakenly see social relations between things and material relations between persons—that arise during the course of commodity exchange. But, in the pages of *RM*, that reading has been challenged and an alternative interpretation provided, thus making it even stranger. What Jack Amariglio and Antonio Callari (1989) did is suggest, first, that there's nothing mistaken about commodity fetishism— commodity exchange can't exist unless and until people come to believe in and act according to certain notions of freedom, equality, property, and Bentham—and, second, those qualities are the noninevitable product of historical and social processes—politics and culture in addition to economics. In other words, their argument is that the section on commodity fetishism is where Marx raises the issue of economic subjectivity and contests the classicals' insistence on the "natural propensity to truck, barter, and exchange"—and, for that matter, the neoclassical obsession with the given rationality of utility-maximization. Yes, such a commodity fetishism exists (social relations between things and material relations between persons), but there's nothing inevitable, natural, universal, or transhistorical about it. It comes into existence historically, under specific conditions, and needs to be reproduced socially if and when commodity exchange exists. The implication is that commodity fetishism is also contested and is forced to contend with other economic subjectivities, which are also historical and social (and often arise in social contexts alongside and as a challenge to commodity fetishism).

What emerged, partially as a result of Amariglio and Callari's article, was an outpouring of creative work on the problem of subjectivity from a specifically Marxian perspective. In some cases, authors (such as Özselçuk

2006) took a detour through the writings of Freud and Lacan, in order to work through the contradictions of economic subjectivities (which, in the midst of economic dislocation wrought by capitalism and in conjunction with political activity to create a different set of economic arrangements, means that people are sometimes caught between the loss of their existing positions and the desire to create new ones for themselves and others). In other words, Ceren Özselçuk suggests, we need to understand the difference between mourning and melancholy, where the former (mourning) designates a process whereby one works past and through the disabling effects of loss in order to arrive at the possibility of forming new relations and attachments, as against melancholy, which represents a paralyzing attachment to loss. Why is this distinction important? Because with mourning, in contrast to melancholy, a kind of work takes place that involves the production of a new subjectivity, a way of transforming loss and resentment into new possibilities. It creates the possibility—for many people in the world today, whose lives have been devastated *both* by the lost industries they've worked in for much of their lives and by the recent forms of restructuring that have been taking place—of becoming the subjects of new economic identities. It is a process that includes the possibility, key to the Marxian critique of political economy, that they become the collective subjects of their own strange history.

The rethinking of economic subjectivities pertains not only to capitalism; it touches, as well, on noncapitalist subjectivities—such as feudalism (Kayatekin and Charusheela 2004). Against conventional approaches according to which the subjects of feudal exploitation accede passively to "traditional" cultural order, such that agency implicitly becomes identified with the process of "breaking down" tradition and erupting into modernity, it becomes possible to uncover the rich nuances of meaning/cognition in the constitution of feudal subjectivities, nuances that can form the basis for agency within a nonmodernist cultural order. Consider, for example, sharecropping in the U.S. south after the Civil War. One possibility is to see sharecroppers consenting to their feudal exploitation as simply a passive acceptance of fate or an unthinking reflection of a pregiven order. The alternative recognizes the acceptance of hierarchy and subordination generated out of both violent repression and a strong moral perception of the justness through which various members in the hierarchy act out their roles—and which also, importantly, provides the grounds for resistance based, for example, on demands for social dignity.

Readers can probably see where this goes next. The denaturalizing of economic subjectivity that is part and parcel of the Marxian critique of political economy also means that new subjectivities become possible—a process of resubjectivation, if you will. It means, first, moving beyond the idea that capitalism is a total and all-encompassing system (there are moments and elements of noncapitalism all around us) and, second, it means recognizing the emergence of new forms of identity and engagement, local capacities to change the existing order—by recognizing and supporting the pleasures associated with existing forms of noncapitalism and the desire to create still other alternatives to capitalist economic arrangements. It also means recognizing in the famous communist maxim— "from each according to their ability, to each according to their need"—both exposing the scandal of capitalist exploitation and demanding that no one be excluded from sharing in the surplus. These are the new ways of being-in-common (Ruccio 1992) that are implicit, at least on the RM interpretation, in Marx's discussion of commodity fetishism.

Marx continues the critique of political economy beyond commodity fetishism—for example, with the discussion of money (that both expands and destabilizes exchange, thus challenging the idea of Say's Law, that free markets always lead to full employment), the distinction between labor and labor power (thus arriving at the theory of exploitation, as capitalists purchase labor power and end up getting labor, including surplus labor), and then the accumulation of capital, another one of those much-misunderstood and misinterpreted ideas in *Capital*.

The accumulation of capital was central to the growth of the wealth of nations and, of course, is fundamental to the promise of capitalism. Basically, it's the "pact with the devil" that lies at the heart of capitalism: that the capitalists get to appropriate the surplus labor of others in return for reinvesting a large share of those profits, expanding their enterprises, and creating new jobs for workers so that unemployment is kept to a minimum.

Clearly, that hasn't been going so well in the last 6 years (as during many other periods in the history of capitalism), as unemployment has soared and more and more people have been out of work for longer and longer periods of time. That's been the case in the United States just like in Western Europe (where overall unemployment, as of April 2015, still remained at 11.1 percent, and youth unemployment at more than 20 percent). And now, in the midst of the cyclical problems associated with the Second Great Depression, new worries are emerging about both "secular stagnation" (the expectation that, moving forward, growth rates will be lower than was the case in the years before the crash of 2007–2008) and computerized automation (which may, in the next decade or two, eliminate 47 percent of U.S. employment)—further dimming the prospects for anything approaching full employment in the foreseeable future.[4]

Marx takes up this issue of the accumulation of capital in Chapter 24 but many readers don't get it. They assume this is Marx's view when he writes:

Accumulate, accumulate! That is Moses and the prophets! "Industry furnishes the material which saving accumulates." Therefore, save, save, i.e., reconvert the greatest possible portion of surplus-value or surplus product into capital! Accumulation for the sake of accumulation, production for the sake of production: this was the formula in which classical economics expressed the historical mission of the bourgeoisie in the period of its domination. Not for one instant did it deceive itself over the nature of wealth's birth-pangs.

(1977, 742)

Except, as another *RM* writer makes clear (Norton 1988), that's not Marx. That's classical political economy, which "takes the historical function of the capitalist in bitter earnest." In fact, Marx shows, the accumulation of capital—the use of surplus-value for investment in new means of production, raw materials, and additional labor power—is but one of many possible distributions of surplus-value. So, there's no necessity for the accumulation of capital—it is up to the whim and whimsy of individual capitalists, if and when they will accumulate capital—and there are many other uses for that surplus-value, such as distributing those profits to their friends (like CEOs whose incomes are over 200 times the average worker's wage and the bankers on Wall Street who instigated the crash of 2007–2008).

There's no necessity for the accumulation of capital and no necessary laws of motion of capitalism. What this means is that we have to rethink the history of Marxian crisis theory (Norton 2013)—giving up the idea that capitalism's crises represent the unfolding of an inexorable logic, in favor of much more contingent and historically specific explanations (such as the higher levels of economic exploitation we saw emerging in the United States from the mid-1970s onward, leading to housing and financial bubbles that burst and culminated in the crash of 2007–2008). In other words, every capitalist crisis is different, and contemporary contributors to the critique of political economy need to understand both the specific causes of each crisis (such as the present one) and the possibilities for creating alternatives to capitalism both when it is doing well (when the accumulation of capital is working and capitalism is growing) and when (such as now) it clearly is not.

* * *

That's the challenge for us: to continue that project of criticizing political economy, which these days means challenging the terms and implications of contemporary mainstream economics (and, at the same time, rethinking traditional interpretations of the Marxian critique of political economy). We have to criticize the idea that the only alternative theories are neoclassical and Keynesian economics and that we have to stick to capitalist markets—whether celebrated and reinforced with more tax cuts or regulated and stimulated with more government spending. We don't need simply to accept the idea there are no alternatives to an economy in which a tiny minority is allowed to make decisions concerning the surplus that determine the lives and livelihoods of the vast majority of people, both in the United States and abroad.

We need to be familiar with and to study the rules and regulations of that strange land of economics. But we don't have to obey them. Contributing in diverse ways to the critique of economics (such as *RM* authors have been doing, in many more forms and ways than I could possibly cover in this short essay) means that we cannot be anything but strangers in a strange land.

And that's just fine. To borrow the concluding statement about the Man from Mars, it's time "to get to work. He could see a lot of changes he wanted to make."

Acknowledgments

This essay began as a plenary talk for the "Stranger Economies" conference, at the University of Washington, on November 2, 2012. I want to thank S. Charusheela for inviting me to address the conference and to the participants for their comments and questions. I also want to thank the editors of this volume, especially Rob Garnett, for their encouragement to revise the essay for publication and for their suggestions about how to extend the discussion of the stranger. This piece is very much dedicated to Richard D. Wolff and the late Stephen R. Resnick, even though I have included only two direct citations to their work. I have learned a great deal from all of their writings over the years, to say the least; but it is their example as "ruthless critics" that has especially inspired my efforts here and elsewhere.

Notes

1 The data on income are from the World Top Incomes Database (http://topincomes.g-mond.parisschoolofeconomics.eu/, accessed 1 June 2015) and, for wealth, Saez and Zucman (2014).
2 All the data in this paragraph are from official sources: the Bureau of Labor statistics (www.bls.gov/home.htm) and the U.S. Census Bureau (www.census.gov/en.html).
3 And, for some of us, strangers in other senses as well, to the extent that, at least on some issues (e.g., the postmodern critique of modernist epistemologies and methodologies), we have found more encouragement and support from mainstream economists than from traditional Marxists.
4 On the problem of secular stagnation, see Teulings and Baldwin (2014); on the effects of computerization, Frey and Osborne (2013).

References

Amariglio, J. and A. Callari. 1989. "Marxian Value Theory and the Problem of the Subject: The Role of Commodity Fetishism." *Rethinking Marxism* 2 (3): 31–60.
Coy, P. 2011. "Marx to Market." *Bloomberg Business*, 14 September. www.bloomberg.com/bw/magazine/marx-to-market-09142011.html, (accessed 16 September 2011).

Frey, C. B. and M. A. Osborne. 2013. "The Future of Employment: How Suscepti-ble Are Jobs to Computerisation?" 17 September. www.oxfordmartin.ox.ac.uk/downloads/academic/The_Future_of_Employment.pdf, (accessed 2 June 2015).

Haque, U. 2011. "Was Marx Right?" *Harvard Business Review*, 7 September. https://hbr.org/2011/09/was-marx-right, (accessed 10 September 2011).

Heinlein, R. A. [1961] 1987. *Stranger in a Strange Land*. New York: Penguin.

Kayatekin, S. A. and S. Charusheela. 2004. "Recovering Feudal Subjectivities." *Rethinking Marxism* 16 (4): 377–96.

Keynes, J. M. 1965. *The General Theory of Employment, Interest, and Money*. New York: Harcourt, Brace & World.

Magnus, G. 2011. "Give Karl Marx a Chance to Save the World Economy." *Bloomberg Business*, 28 August. www.bloomberg.com/news/articles/2011-08-29/give-marx-a-chance-to-save-the-world-economy-commentary-by-george-magnus, (accessed 19 August 2011).

Marx, K. 1977. *Capital: A Critique of Political Economy*. 3 vols. Trans. B. Fowkes. New York: Vintage.

———. 1978. "For a Ruthless Criticism of Everything Existing" (letter to A. Ruge). In *The Marx-Engels Reader*, R. Tucker, ed., 2nd ed., 12–15. New York: W. W. Norton.

Minsky, H. P. 1986. *Stabilizing an Unstable Economy*. New Haven, CT: Yale University.

Norton, B. 1988. "The Power Axis: Bowles, Gordon, and Weisskopf's Theory of Postwar U.S. Accumulation." *Rethinking Marxism* 1 (3): 6–43.

———. 2013. "Economic Crises." *Rethinking Marxism* 25 (1): 10–22.

Özselçuk, C. 2006. "Mourning, Melancholy, and the Politics of Class Transforma-tion." *Rethinking Marxism* 18 (2): 225–40.

Roubini, N. 2011. "Is Capitalism Doomed?" Project Syndicate, 15 August. www.bloomberg.com/news/articles/2011-08-29/give-marx-a-chance-to-save-the-world-economy-commentary-by-george-magnus, (accessed 16 August 2011).

Ruccio, D. F. 1992. "Failure of Socialism, Future of Socialists?" *Rethinking Marxism* 5 (Summer): 7–22.

Saez, E. 2015. "Striking It Richer: The Evolution of Top Incomes in the United States (Updated with 2013 preliminary estimates)." http://eml.berkeley.edu/~saez/saez-UStopincomes-2013.pdf, (accessed 1 June 2015).

Saez, E. and G. Zucman. 2014. "Wealth Inequality in the United States Since 1913: Evidence from Capitalized Income Tax Data," CEPR Discussion Paper 10227, October.

Simmel, G. 1950. "The Stranger." In *The Sociology of Georg Simmel*, K. Wolff, trans., 402–8. New York: Free Press.

Smith, A. 2003. *The Wealth of Nations,* intro. A. B. Krueger. New York: Bantam Classics.

Teulings, C. and R. Baldwin, eds. 2014. *Secular Stagnation: Facts, Causes and Cures*. www.voxeu.org/sites/default/files/Vox_secular_stagnation.pdf, (accessed 15 August 2014).

Tsuda, T. 2015. "Is Native Anthropology Really Possible?" *Anthropology Today* 31 (3): 14–17.

Wolff, R. D. 2009. *Capitalism Hits the Fan*. Northampton, MA: Media Education Foundation.

———. 2013. *Capitalism Hits the Fan: The Global Economic Meltdown and What to Do About It*. 2nd ed. Northampton, MA: Interlink.

Wood, M. M. 1934. *The Stranger: A Study in Social Relationships*. New York: Columbia.

3 Marxian economics without teleology

The big new life of class

Bruce Norton

Introduction

The Marxian economics Steve Resnick and Richard Wolff encountered as emerging practitioners was diverse in specifics but for the most part consistent in general approach. Influential mid-twentieth-century traditions envisioned capitalism as a system that creates within itself the necessity for its own demise. Accordingly, Marxian economists' task was to identify the basic forces that move the system forward, show how these create developing distress and dysfunction, and link the resulting fundamental dynamics (in conjunction with less predictable economic, cultural, and political forces) to their various manifestations in contemporary economic and social life.

Capitalism's overall dynamics were thought to be ultimately powered by either capitalist firms' inherent nature as accumulation-seeking entities (Paul Baran and Paul Sweezy, and their stagnation-theory predecessor Josef Steindl) or imperatives produced by capitalist competition (various falling-rates-of-profit theorists). Thus these theorists' starting points were one or another abstractly fixed conception of firm behavior. In this sense, as I suggest below, Marxian economics was committed not only to teleological and economic determinist analysis, but also to the related labor necessary to construct an origin. At stake was an originating logic thought to stem from the nature of firms' very existence as units of capital. Only such an origin could insure that, come what may, the capitalist system propels itself toward the telos of inevitably increasing or recurrently deepening distress of a particular kind.

Marxian conceptions of class functioned in these arguments primarily in an instrumental and simplified way. In the late 1960s both major U.S. frameworks needed only a schematic conception of the basic binary—capitalists and productive workers—to develop their respective conceptions of capitalism's inner logic.[1] Marxian economics concerned developmental logics, not class, and what worked to construct developmental logics were simplified behavioral expectations attached to occupants of the basic class positions, capitalists, and productive workers.

Thus, as this paper argues, two of Stephen Resnick and Richard Wolff's distinctive turns—their adoption within Marxian economics of complex causality incompatible with essentialist and teleological reasoning, and the emphatically high valuation they place on Marx's complex class-theoretic approach to capitalist economic life—were closely related with one another. Only once one stopped searching for an originating logic in *Capital* and *Theories of Surplus Value* did a quite different theoretical framework become visible. Class, in our authors' hands, escaped instrumental status and came to center stage. Class processes became a focus of the theory, and began to shape both interpretations and imaginaries—envisioned prospects and possibilities—in ways prior frameworks had not allowed.

Marxian economics in the U.S. in the 1960s and early 1970s

What is Marxian economics about? The field's history is in some ways a short one. The accumulation-theoretic frameworks that shaped its 1960s revival in the U.S. and Western Europe answered the question much as had classical Marxism (as distinct from the analysis in *Capital*) in the years from 1880 to 1914. Marx's primary legacy as they interpreted it turned on the insight that capitalism is a system of interacting firms that unfolds along internally determinate lines to produce transience.[2]

To construct such an argument while retaining a capacity to theorize periods of relative buoyancy as well as periods of evident dysfunction required some accommodation, particularly after World War II. In the United States of the early 1970s creators of the two most influential Marxian economic traditions, falling rate of profit and monopoly capital theory, both solved the problem via a two-step formula for theory elaboration. Both first theorized a set of distress-increasing basic tendencies of the capitalist mode of production or capitalism in its contemporary stage. Each then introduced or admitted the existence of more concrete "external" or historically specific factors thought capable of modifying or offsetting the system's basic tendencies in certain circumstances and for limited periods (wars and epoch-shaping technological innovations like automobiles, as *Monopoly Capital* argued; government interventions or other demand-stimulating developments for falling-rate-of-profit theorist, Paul Mattick, Sr.[3]).

The solution works on the condition that the border between the two types of forces is not permeable. However much the system's basic internal logic can be offset during some periods, it must remain untouched by those historically transient forces, intact and fated to reassume command in due course. Otherwise capitalism's internally produced contradiction cannot be thought to reliably shape the future. The solution works only if one envisions and constructs an origin, a developmental logic internally determined and fixed in abstraction from other aspects of life, shaping without being shaped in turn.

The two traditions' particular visions of the kind of problems contemporary capitalism gestates pointed in utterly different directions. On one side, profit rates tended to fall. Paul Mattick, Sr. (1969 and elsewhere) saw a capitalism wracked by periodic crisis as firms' efforts to compete with one another led to bursts of accumulation followed by profit-strained seize-ups. In the ordinary course of things the resulting crises renew capitalist growth, since by destroying capital values and dampening wages and other costs of production they tend to restore the average rate of profit. But Mattick and others also suggested that the ordinary course of things would not last too long.[4] Capitalist crises were likely to increase in severity. Government demand management in a "mixed economy" could not wish basic capitalist dynamics away. If and when the other actor falling-rate-of-profit theorists invoke—the "subjective" ingredient, a revolutionary-minded and organized working class—materialized, capitalism would face problems not as readily overcome.

On the other side, gross profit income per unit of sales tended to *rise*. Paul Baran and Paul Sweezy saw the "giant firm," which rose to power in the late nineteenth century, as an entity whose appearance required revision of "the basic Marxian laws of capitalism" in this opposite direction (1966, 5, 14–51, 71). The giant firm cuts costs of production but not sales prices; over time in the new system "the surplus tends to rise...." (71). Meanwhile the only two "normal" channels through which surplus income becomes spending, as the book maintained—investment and capitalist consumption (consumption funded by dividend income)—are said to be limited, ordinarily unable to provide adequate outlets for the readily gushing flow of surplus income. As a result, "monopoly capitalism is a self-contradictory system," whose *"normal* state .... is stagnation" (108. Italics in original). Now it is not the working class, presented as bought off by its privileged location within the system, but a coalition of various kinds of dissatisfied and critical groups—racially oppressed, people marginal to the primary workforce, students, anti-imperialists and others—to whom Baran and Sweezy looked for sources of revolutionary resistance and transformation.

In short, the two traditions were antithetical in specifics but homologous in general approach. Both saw Marxian economics as a science that tied the broadest outlines of capitalism's growth and demise to a destructive inner logic of accumulation.[5] On that basis, both frameworks criticized contemporary capitalism's wasteful and irrational workings. Each predicted increasing waste and irrationality of a particular kind as long as the system continued to exist, however much circumstances might temporarily delay the ultimate outcome.

To carry out their critiques both also strictly maintained the border between capitalism's originating inner mechanisms and other aspects of economic and social life. *Monopoly Capital* turned for the purpose to what it presents without further discussion as a tool enabling all "scientific understanding," a model. The book is going to construct a model, as it tells us, and to be useful a model must exclude some factors from analysis. These are the "nonessential" factors. They are rightly kept out so that the model might better "single out and make available for intensive investigation those elements which are decisive" (14). In practice, the decisive forces included inside *Monopoly Capital's* "model" are abstractly set patterns attributed to giant firms' basic nature. The modern corporation is "an engine for maximizing profits and accumulating capital" (47) of a particular sort. In monopoly capitalist conditions its structuring urge to seek and accumulate profit continues to fuel high savings rates even when its purported reinvestment possibilities are systemically diminished (80). Fixed abstractly, the giant firm's compulsions form a pattern, an "'elementary logic' of the system" said to shape every aspect of the whole.

Falling-rate-of-profit theorists' border is less explicitly declared. It emerges as a result, the implication of their unwavering assertion that capitalism's basic structure necessarily nourishes a particular kind of technological change. Capitalists must constantly struggle both to extract surplus value from productive laborers and to cut their costs of production relative to competitors. While lower-cost producers may earn super-profits, higher-cost firms face the prospect of extinction. Falling-rate-of-profit theorists read in Marx the proposition that these competitive pressures fuel growing mechanization of production, and increased mechanization shifts the input mix toward higher values of fixed and circulating constant capital relative to the profit-creating variable capital. Pushed by the struggle to raise their profit rates, firms turn to a strategy that produces an opposite result, as the aggregate rate of profit tends to fall.

Of course these theorists recognize that rates of surplus value (surplus value relative to variable capital) likely also increase. New industries spring up with young technologies, raw materials prices fall, new territories may be exploited, and so on. Reigning conditions of class struggle and various other factors may also sometimes raise aggregate profit rates. In addition, as we have seen, the crises produced by falling profits themselves periodically restore capitalist vitality by pushing costs of production down.

Through it all the border is maintained because whatever else happens falling-rate-of-profit theorists expect the basic profit-dampening dynamic to recur and deepen. Implied by capitalism's constitution, it persists as long as capitalism persists, no matter what other forces come into play in particular sectors or periods. In this approach all that is necessary in order to clearly demarcate capitalism's ultimately shaping internal determination is steadfast commitment to the basic idea: mechanization is an enforced necessity rooted in the very structure of capitalist exploitation and competition, and by raising the organic composition of capital it will, sooner or later, and with varying but eventually greater levels of severity, express itself.

In 1975 (1972 in German) Ernest Mandel pushed the framework further. Criticizing Mattick for the indeterminacy his two-step theorizing introduces (19), Mandel abandoned the border between the capitalist system's unfolding laws and external forces. *Late Capitalism* instead proposed a complex multi-variable analysis that

> will enable us to explain the history of the capitalist mode of production and above all the third phase of this mode of production, which we shall call 'late capitalism', by means of the laws of motion of capital itself, without resort to exogenous factors alien to the core of Marx's analysis of capital.
>
> (42)

For Mandel, long periods of expansion such as the postwar boom are themselves predictable results of capitalism's inner laws. When rate of surplus-value increasing forces (like World War II and the defeat of fascism) interact with transformative technological innovations in motive machine power (such as the "machine production of electronic and nuclear-powered apparatuses since the '40s of the twentieth century"), previously idle surplus-capitals can be committed to investment, and a sustained period of growth results [118]). Resort to "external" growth-stimuli is unnecessary.

But the *"long-term end-results"* (italics in original) revealed through the "laws of development of capitalism discovered by Marx" (Mandel 1975, 43) remain. However richly and complexly Mandel's laws of motion are constructed, the overall system they depict is ultimately doomed, as it remains informed by the originating power common to other falling rate of profit theories. He tells us as much:

> Given the fact of competition, the 'incessant urge for enrichment' which is a feature of capital is really the search for surplus-profit, for profit above the average profit. This search leads to constant attempts to revolutionize technology, to achieve lower production costs than those of competitors, to obtain surplus-profits together with a greater organic composition of capital while at the same time increasing the rate of surplus-value. All the characteristics of capitalism as an economic form are contained in this description, and they are based on its inherent tendency towards ruptures of equilibrium. This same tendency also lies at the root of all the laws of motion of the capitalist mode of production.
>
> (27)

Once again all that is necessary to insure the telos is unwavering commitment to the ultimate power of the origin Marx's capitalist laws of motion are thought to incorporate.[6]

Origins and class theory

How does one construct an origin? Marxian economists' origins turn on abstractly set conceptions of the firm or of the pressures of inter-firm competition. Baran and Sweezy, building on Steindl, construe the capitalist firm's profit reaping and reinvestment behavior as an expression of the firm's accumulating nature, therefore law-like, given, and fixed. Falling-rate-of-profit theorists hypostasize capitalist competition, grounding in the struggle for super-profit a generative pattern of technological development specifiable in advance.

Class concepts are useful in both cases, but for the most part only as supporting players. The class concepts that particularly worked were simple behavior patterns attributed to the two ends of the capitalist/worker binary. Capitalists were profit-seekers and would-be accumulators (whether protected but reinvestment-challenged oligopolists, as one view had it, or constantly endangered competitors, as the other maintained). Mid-twentieth century workers of the higher-income countries were either corrupted and absorbed via their privileged placement within the system (Baran and Sweezy) or configured primarily as exploitation-resisters, actors who left the capitalists few places to turn in their struggle to raise the rate of surplus value other than the ultimate weapon, mechanization.[7]

Once introduced, these class dynamics were treated as understood. These components of life in capitalist economies were known and established. The patterns they traced could be solidified into a model of the "'endogenous' logic of the system" or reified via less formal means. They could not be reexamined, since reevaluating them risked upending the entire argument. In any case, what was ultimately to be investigated was not class. What was to be investigated was how the established behaviors—particularly those attributed to capitalists—interacted with one another and with historically changing forces to shape the self-destructive whole.

Thus, neither the traditions' binary approach to class, nor their attribution of simple, fixed, and already understood patterns of behavior to the two polar sets of actors, was accidental. In 1975 they were carefully cultivated features of specifically "Marxian" economic thought.

Class theory repositioned

In the early to mid-1970s, Stephen Resnick and Richard Wolff began to read *Capital* and *Theories of Surplus Value* differently. The class concepts they encountered were not simple, fixed, bi-polar, or already understood. Indeed the concepts they found were ill-suited for any instrumental role. Painstakingly identified, particularly in *Capital* volumes 2 and 3, where various distributions of surplus value successively come under analysis, Marx's conceptions of capitalist class processes (understood as involving the distribution as well as the production and extraction of surplus value) proliferated. They escaped containment.

If Marx had gone to tremendous lengths to think about class, as Resnick and Wolff suggested, perhaps that thinking is what might be honored in his work and built upon. What might be sought in *Capital* were not after all functional components of an abstract logic. Rather, what one can find are general tools through which capitalism can be understood as turning on the extraction of unpaid labor. Marx's critique of capitalism is then not congealed in a hypothesis. It takes the form of a conceptual framework, a general way to think about economic aspects of life that identifies class exploitation and cares about class justice.

Will this conceptual framework envision transcendent forces? Are the conceptions of class processes provided by Marx to be thought of in the manner of Marxian economists' traditional conception of accumulation? Is class, that is, an aspect of life expressing an internally determinate logic, shaping other dimensions of society without itself being constitutively shaped in return? Our authors said no. They were as firmly committed to a fully relational conception as they were to adding a class-edged focus to that conception's analysis of human existence. No origin preexists the whole, and no abstractly fixed logic propels it forward.

In effect, Resnick and Wolff read Althusser's "Contradiction and Over-determination" and "The Object of Capital" rather than Luxemburg, Grossman, or Steindl, as they re-read *Capital*, and in doing so they saw Marxian economics differently. For them, Marx's class processes face outwards (as an "entry point" or focus), ready to be enriched and changed, as well as to inform. Capitalist firms' surplus appropriation and patterns of surplus distribution are brutally unfair, but how class processes work more precisely depends and changes. Like everything, exploitation and surplus distributions interrelate with other aspects of the whole within which they occur. Class processes are an object for investigation.

As Resnick and Wolff's work soon made very clear (1987), the Marx who produced such a non-essentialist class-theoretic framework had created a heady mix of tools. Once unleashed from service to a system-level telos, concepts of class began to look remarkably applicable at other levels. Indeed, why not think the thought Marxian economic traditions had long rendered impossible to think? If surplus labor is extracted and allocated at the firm level, commodity-producing firms might vary significantly one from another. A firm in which workers find ways to themselves decide how to produce and allocate their own surplus is not a capitalist firm. In this light, local transformational efforts within a commodity-circulating economy are not impossible (or at best insignificant in the face of the overall system's crushing competitive laws of motion). They are very possible. They are underway (see, e.g., the essay by Olsen in this volume).

Economic transformation is then not a project for the future. It is not derivative from political transformation, as traditions that theorize capitalism as an essentially structured totality have generally construed it. In eyes shaped by this variety of Marxian economics, it's a complex and contradictory possibility, but a current one.

As readers of the present volume will know or soon learn, Resnick and Wolff's redirection did indeed nourish an abrupt shift in theoretical and political imaginaries. Class processes can be identified and changed at the level of a firm. Class processes are also at work and in flux within households. In Fraad et al. (1994), the authors and Harriett Fraad distinguished between contemporary types of households on the basis of how surplus labor is performed and appropriated within them (notably feudal, ancient, and communist class structures, with the latter now "developing where few had even thought to look for them, let alone to chart their actual and potential social impacts" [41]). Fifteen years later, the trio relaunched and extended their discussion in a volume that also included new contributions from other authors (Cassano 2009).

An associated school emphasized the open de-centeredness of economies and subjectivities. Communities interact through commodity and non-commodity exchange in ways not derivable from a mode of production's abstractly conceived structure (e.g., Gibson-Graham et al. 2013). If one thinks instead of society "as a decentered, incoherent, and complex totality" one might discern political subjectivities of various unexpected kinds and "multiple point of intervention in class (and non-class) processes at any point in time" (Gibson-Graham 1996, 172).

For their part, Resnick and Wolff used the class process vantage point to rethink the history of the Soviet Union (2002). Efforts to construct socialism, as they found, have sometimes failed to recognize that firm-level class structures wield effects. Top-level political transformation pitched in abstraction from class processes on a local level risks entrapment by the very forces Marx sought to spotlight.

Thus a variety of reenvisioned terrains for analysis and political practice came into view. Theorizing them involved a good deal of fine-grained analysis.[8] To distinguish capitalist from other class and non-class processes, processes occurring in firms, communities, and households require de-conflation. At each site or level non-class and other class processes occur in relation but also distinction to capitalist exploitation. Class is not already known; it is to be investigated, learned about, related to and distinguished from other aspects of life, if efforts for change are to find their way toward building more just and sustainable institutions. Resnick and Wolff both led the way and continually encouraged others' ongoing efforts to work out such issues.

Would there be an associated loss on the more traditional front, Marxian economists' ability to criticize the capitalist system and/or "the economy" as a whole? That was certainly a possibility. The guidelines traditional frameworks offer for such efforts no longer worked. Decade after decade, for example, Paul Sweezy, Harry Magdoff, and others associated with the *Monthly Review* had traced the explosive growth of finance, income inequality, investment stagnation, and other evils characteristic of the U.S. economy's sad fate under the stewardship of the stagnation-generating corporate giants. Bereft of a vision of capitalism's self-produced inner logic of distress, and concerned to distinguish rather than conflate, would the new framework be here defanged?

Again, our authors cleared a path, by the early 2000s taking up the question of "U.S. capitalism" as a whole. Again they began with class. Whatever its material accomplishments, U.S. capitalism "has subjected productive laborers to probably the highest rate of class exploitation (ratio of surplus to necessary labor) in the capitalist world" (2006, 341), and that has had effects on workers' lives. After an initial article in *Historical Materialism* (2003) introducing this hypothesis, Resnick and Wolff took it from there. When several years later financial and economic crisis rocked the world, stripping some of the material accomplishments themselves away, they redoubled their efforts. As we know in recent years Richard Wolff has extraordinarily ably and energetically used public lectures, web presence in texts and videos, books, and a radio program to take the critique to a national and international audience. In his hands (and those of colleagues including David F. Ruccio) Resnick and Wolff's class-focused Marxian economics has translated readily into aggressive aggregate-level criticism—of U.S. capitalism, of European capitalism, of the world economy and of the capitalist system.

These aggregate-level critiques do not presuppose an origin or telos. They do not argue that the capitalist system will inevitably self-destruct;[9] rather, they argue that capitalism is destructive, above all for working people. Thus, the analyses are of a kind with the argument Marx himself chose to highlight (as Part Seven's development of the "general law of accumulation") when he finalized the presentation of *Capital* Volume 1. They are attempts to assess and explain the damage to people and communities capitalism's contemporary functioning has produced. Given higher-income country experience in the decades following 1970, such a critique speaks to a potentially wide public and to develop it no abstractly specified causal nexus or *memento mori* is helpful. Freed from the task of inner logic elaboration, the line of criticism is more direct: the system has not been providing an acceptably stable and reciprocating material basis for many working people's lives, and better and fairer ways to produce and organize a surplus are possible.

It is worth stressing that in this analysis class theory meets contemporary public concerns head-on. The relocation of production to lower-wage nations is in Marxian terms a decision about how to distribute surplus value—a class decision—made under capitalist conditions by a board of directors in interaction with leading shareholders. Worker-directed enterprises, non-capitalist in class structure, distribute surplus differently, seeking at least in good part to maintain and expand domestic jobs and in many cases to sustain community welfare in other ways. Introductory textbooks teach students that every society must answer three big economic questions—what to produce, how to produce, and for whom to produce. To these Richard Wolff adds a fourth, "where to produce." The question is explosive. The firms we have relied on have not made that decision fairly, as he argues, and to change that ongoing state of affairs requires class transformation. Freed from pursuit of an abstract teleological hypothesis, Marxian economics here instead speaks directly to central issues—class issues—of our times.

Conclusion

Departing from the twentieth-century accumulation-theoretic traditions they inherited, Wolff and Resnick produced a new conception of what Marxian economics can entail. They have used it to focus on big issues of historical interpretation, contributing to the critique of contemporary high-income country capitalism from a class-theoretic perspective and rethinking the history of the Soviet Union. They have also used it to redirect critical eyes toward the local and immediate. Situating class processes in local and potentially transformable locations, they've highlighted community, household, and firm-level possibilities. In both ways they have revived and reinvigorated at least one Marx: Marx the theorist of capitalist class exploitation and critic of a destructive but ever-changing capitalism.

If the Marxian class concepts Resnick and Wolff have highlighted can be said to "face out"—ready to be enriched and changed—their future deployment is unpredictable. There are good reasons to think that economic concepts of class are finding increasing use, however. Several decades' experience with neoliberal capitalism's raw edges has surely played a role: predictably a deteriorating economic environment tends to revive interest in class. Resnick and Wolff's persistence and success have created a space of influence, as have the innovative class-focused directions J.K. Gibson-Graham and their many colleagues in the Community Economies group have taken. The many other students and colleagues Resnick and Wolff inspired have also gone on to break new ground.[10]

More generally teleology's grip is on some fronts weakening. Within economics the notion that an abstract logic of accumulation pushes capitalism toward a determinate end-state or end-state-tendency fell out of favor in several Marx-related frameworks in the later 1970s and after. Regulation theory, social structures of accumulation theory, other arguments developing out of the "profit-squeeze" analysis of the crisis of 1965–75 (e.g., Andrew Glyn 2006), and indeed the quasi-traditional Marxian framework produced over the last several decades by Gerard Dumenil and Dominique Levy (2011), all deliberately leave capitalism's future trajectory an open question. If abandoning teleology and focusing upon class were interdependent moves when Resnick and Wolff undertook them, determinism's loosening grip on such frameworks may clear space for new class-theoretic possibilities there as well.[11]

One thing is clear. If such a new space does expand, Marxian econo-mists will no longer need to envision capitalists, productive workers, and unproductive workers—or various groups and kinds of people occupy-ing those class positions—as performers of abstractly pre-ordained roles. Capitalists need not be assumed simply to seek surplus value and then strive to accumulate it as capital; they may turn to a variety of strategies to maintain and further their positions (a point Resnick and Wolff have indefatigably elaborated).[12] And people occupying productive (and un-productive) worker positions might be theorized outside the lines drawn by the yes-or-no question the traditional gaze has posed (whether or not they react to the economic tendencies created by the capitalists by rebel-ling against and overthrowing wage-labor status).[13] A class-focused non-reductive understanding of contemporary problems and transformational potentials might grow. If so, the labors of Stephen Resnick and Richard Wolff will be bearing fruit. No Marxian economists have more emphat-ically insisted on the utter openness of complex determinations. And no one has so compellingly brought Marxian class concepts back to life.

Acknowledgment

The author is indebted to Richard McIntyre, who read the article closely and cleverly multiple times and provided multiple suggestions that greatly improved it.

Notes

1 While Baran and Sweezy saw monopoly capitalism as nourishing growing numbers of unproductive workers, their theory positions these as a *response* to a more fundamental dynamic already set and fixed before consideration of such class positions. Given the capitalists' high profit-earning potential and limited outlets for capitalist consumption or investment spending, the system needs growing legions of sales and other workers to take up the demand slack. Thus these class positions are stressed, but only as symptomatic occupants of a derivative and secondary role.

2 Classical Marxism, however, saw an integral socialism germinating within an integral capitalism, the ultimate product of the contradiction between the cap-italists' private appropriation of surplus value and the increasingly social na-ture of production and its laboring agents, the proletariat (see Diskin 1996 for an illuminating analysis of Engels' *Socialism: Utopian and Scientific*). Thus it ex-tended far more confidently toward the positive than most twentieth century accumulation theorists ventured. What continues more clearly through the twentieth century is the destructive side. Capitalism is seen as undermined by an essential contradiction, whatever its ability to birth a successor.

3 For Baran and Sweezy see especially (1966, Ch. 8). In Mattick's formulation

What was important to Marx was the analysis of capital development on the assumption that there were no interventions in the fetishistic accumu-lation process. Only thus was it possible to detect capitalism's inherent con-tradictions and limitations. Marx's theory does not deny the fact that full

employment can and may be created either by government-induced investments or by an increase in the propensity to consume. It simply does not
discuss such maneuvers. They are, of course, possibilities, provided that
neither policy seriously infringes upon the prevailing social class relations.

(1969, 131)

4 See for example Mattick (1969, 99–100).
5 Such abstractly determinate approaches had a clear prior theoretical and political lineage. The general view of history they aligned with had been constructed and widely popularized by the German Social Democratic Party and
the Second International (1870–1914), not least by Friedrich Engels and Karl
Kautsky. For useful criticism from the point of view of a different reading of
Capital, see Heinrich (2012, e.g. 23–26, 175–78, 196–98). That the system's ultimate demise was economically determined and wired into accumulation's
inherent structure was the fundamental Marxist principle Rosa Luxemburg
(1972) defended so vividly against Eduard Bernstein's criticisms. Nor did the
defeats suffered during and after World War I shake the principle's advocates.
The perspective was sustained and revived in the otherwise quite different
interventions of Henryk Grossman (1929) and Sweezy (1942) both of whom
quoted Rosa Luxemburg's commitment to economic determinacy in support
of their own declared reasoning principles. Grossman in turn greatly influenced Mattick, Sr. As Mattick's Wikipedia entry read on August 1, 2015, after
emigrating from Germany in 1926 at about age 22,

> ... the publication of Henryk Grossman's principal work, *Das Akkumulations
> - und Zusammenbruchsgesetz des Kapitalistischen Systems* (1929), played a
> fundamental role for Mattick, as Grossmann brought Marx's theory of ac-
> cumulation, which had been completely forgotten, back to the centre of
> debate in the workers' movement.

Later Josef Steindl (1952) sketched a conception of a historically determinate
stage-theoretic endogenous accumulation process that influenced Baran and
Sweezy. Roman Rosdolsky's impressive (1977) depiction of the logical structure he saw linking *Grundrisse* and *Capital* also contributed important support
for falling-rate-of-profit theory.
6 A few years later, Mandel's introduction to a prominent new edition of *Capital,*
Volume 1, retraced the position even more vividly, registering a definition of
Marxian economic theory's basic propositions, which students encounter on
first reading Marx even to the current day (Mandel 1977, esp. 12, 81–82).
7 Norton (2001) develops these arguments at greater length.
8 Wolff and Resnick (2012, 133–250) provide an excellent recent introduction to
some of the issues.
9 At least in an abstractly predictable way. I don't mean to underplay the self-
destructive power of capitalism's financial flows with their booms and busts.
And once capitalist firms begin to move production away from their countries
of origin an empirically traceable historically situated process of economy-
destruction may be underway, as Richard Wolff has emphasized.
10 Because I don't feel able to do them justice here, I am deliberately not attempting to sketch the wondrous contributions that Resnick and Wolff's many
friends and students have already made. Some will be evident in other essays
in the present volume. A few are mentioned briefly in my entry on "Accumulation" in Brennan et al. (2017).
11 Such is clearly the case in the work of Dumenil and Levy (2011). Their analysis
of capitalism's uncertain future is open-ended precisely via its central incor-
poration of a more complex, non-binary, and non-pre-specified approach to

class-affiliated political behaviors. Distinguishing broadly among capitalists (defined as owners), workers, and managers, Dumenil and Levy suggest that changing alliances and configurations among actors occupying the three class-position aggregates (periodically shaken up and forced to reform by crises) change the way modern capitalism works from one "phase" to another.

12 For one example see Resnick and Wolff (1987, 164–230). Notably, Dumenil and Levy's capitalist firms are also responsive to a variety of historically changing pressures. In the U.S. neoliberal phase they indeed increase dividend distributions in response to shareholder demands even at the expense of accumulation rates, a conception that displaces reinvestment from the traditionally prioritized position it has held as a claim on surplus value (2011, 62–63 and 143–55). In this respect these authors thus readily abandon the vision of an abstractly fixed accumulation compulsion upon which prior theorists' originating logics were built.

13 Frederic Lordon (2014) maps one provocative route along which cultural theory might develop in a class-focused and non-economic determinist way. His Spinozan affect-theoretic analysis of workers in neoliberal labor markets in effect dethrones the sovereign subject as such an entity might be thought to occupy the productive worker role, much as Wolff and Resnick dislodge the sovereign historical role traditionally played by an unfolding capital accumulation process. Berlant (2011) and Massumi (2015) also open new and bracing paths.

References

Althusser, L. 2005. "Contradiction and Overdetermination." In *For Marx*, B. Brewster, trans., 87–128. New York: Verso.

———. 2009. "The Object of *Capital*." In *Reading Capital*, L. Althusser and E. Balibar, ed., B. Brewster, trans., 77–222. New York: Verso.

Baran, P. and P. Sweezy. 1966. *Monopoly Capital: An Essay on the American Economic and Social Order*. New York: Monthly Review Press.

Berlant, L. 2011. *Cruel Optimism*. Durham, NC: Duke University Press.

Brennan, D., D. Kristjanson-Gural, C. Mulder, and E. Olsen, eds. 2017. *Routledge Handbook of Marxian Economics*. London: Routledge.

Cassano, G., ed. 2009. *Class Struggle on the Home Front: Work, Conflict, and Exploitation in the Household*. New York: Palgrave-Macmillan.

Diskin, J. 1996. "Rethinking Socialism: What's in a Name?" In *Postmodern Materialism and the Future of Marxist Theory*, A. Callari and D. F. Ruccio, eds., 278–99. Hanover, NH: Wesleyan University Press.

Dumenil, G. and D. Levy. 2011. *The Crisis of Neoliberalism*. Cambridge, MA: Harvard University Press.

Fraad, H., S. A. Resnick, and R. D. Wolff. 1994. *Bringing It All Back Home: Class, Gender, and Power in the Modern Household*. London: Pluto Press.

Gibson-Graham, J. K. 1996. *The End of Capitalism (as we knew it): A Feminist Critique of Political Economy*. Cambridge: Blackwell Publishers.

Gibson-Graham, J. K., J. Cameron, and S. Healy. 2013. *Take Back the Economy: An Ethical Guide for Transforming Our Communities*. Minneapolis, MN: University of Minnesota Press.

Glyn, A. 2006. *Capitalism Unleashed: Finance, Globalization, and Welfare*. Oxford: Oxford University Press.

Grossmann, H. 1992 [1929]. *The Law of Accumulation and Breakdown of the Capitalist System: Being also a Theory of Crises.* Trans. J. Banaji. London: Pluto Press.

Heinrich, M. 2012. *An Introduction to the Three Volumes of Karl Marx's Capital.* Trans. A. Locascio. New York: Monthly Review Press.

Lordon, F. 2014. *Willing Slaves of Capital: Spinoza and Marx on Desire.* Trans. G. Ash. Verso: London.

Luxemburg, R. 1972. *The Accumulation of Capital: An Anti-Critique,* ed. K. J. Tarbuck, trans. R. Wichmann. New York: Monthly Review Press.

Mandel, E. 1975. *Late Capitalism.* Trans. J. De Bres. London: Verso.

———. 1977. "Introduction." In *Capital: A Critique of Political Economy, volume 1,* K. Marx, B. Fowkes, trans., 9–90. New York: Vintage Books.

Massumi, B. 2015. *The Power at the End of the Economy.* Durham, NC: Duke University Press.

Mattick, P. 1969. *Marx and Keynes: The Limits of the Mixed Economy.* Boston, MA: Porter Sargent.

Norton, B. 2001. "Reading Marx for Class." In *Re/Presenting Class: Essays in Postmodern Marxism,* J.K. Gibson-Graham, S. A. Resnick, and R. D. Wolff, eds., 23–55. Durham, NC: Duke University Press.

Resnick, S. A. and R. D. Wolff. 1987. *Knowledge and Class: A Marxian Critique of Political Economy.* Chicago, IL: University of Chicago Press.

———. 2002. *Class Theory and History: Capitalism and Communism in the U.S.S.R.* New York: Routledge.

———. 2003. "Exploitation, Consumption, and the Uniqueness of U.S. Capitalism." *Historical Materialism* 11 (4): 209–26.

———, eds. 2006. *New Departures in Marxian Theory.* New York: Routledge.

Rosdolsky, R. 1977. *The Making of Marx's Capital.* Trans. P. Burgess. London: Pluto Press.

Steindl, J. 1952. *Maturity and Stagnation in American Capitalism.* New York: Monthly Review Press.

Sweezy, P. 1942. *The Theory of Capitalist Development.* New York: Monthly Review Press.

Wolff, R. D. and S. A. Resnick. 2012. *Contending Economic Theories: Neoclassical, Keynesian, and Marxian.* Cambridge, MA: MIT Press.

4 Class-analytic Marxism and the recovery of the Marxian theory of enterprise

Erik K. Olsen

Introduction

Stephen Resnick and Richard Wolff's work balances the antagonistic qualities of being both genuinely innovative and profoundly conservative. They ground Marxian theory unequivocally in Marx's writings, especially *Capital* and the associated manuscripts (*Grundrisse* and *Theories of Surplus Value*), to clearly identify and emphasize Marx's unique and distinctive contributions to economic and social theory. At the same time they embrace some of the most provocative ideas of the twentieth century: antiessentialism and antifoundationalism. But those tempted to refer to their work as 'post-Marxism' should take heed: this is not an effort to go beyond Marx but rather an effort to focus attention on what they see as Marx's central contributions while also challenging the dominant social theories opposed to Marxism (Resnick and Wolff 1987, 2005).

Resnick and Wolff's class-analytic approach is often recognized for two important contributions. One is their interpretation of class as a process involving the production, appropriation and distribution of surplus; the other is their commitment to dialectics in the form of overdetermination. These are the "basic entry-point concepts" of their Marxian theory (1987, 281). But they also make a third basic contribution that has not been fully appreciated. This is their emphasis on the productive site as the unit of analysis and, in particular, their carefully articulated Marxian theory of that most basic capitalist institution, the enterprise. The focus on enterprises is also a return to *Capital*, in which a close analysis of the enterprise is the primary method that Marx uses to develop large parts of his critical theory of capitalism. And yet somehow this firm-level analysis is mostly absent from the Marxian tradition. Instead, Marxian economic and social theory is often concerned with questions that are ancillary topics in *Capital*, like prices of production and crisis tendencies or broad social structures and their evolution over historical time. In these approaches the enterprise is not particularly important because it is a subsidiary and subordinate feature of larger societal forces or structures. The action in these other approaches is literally elsewhere, so why concern oneself with the firm?

Marxists during the era of the Second International paid particular attention to the macrostructural relationship between the economic base and the political and ideological superstructure. Despite warnings from both Marx and Engels that the non-economic aspects of society should not be understood simply as passive recipients of determinations emanating from the economy, with some notable exceptions a simple mechanistic interpretation of society is characteristic of Marxism during this period (Olsen 2009). This tendency is even more pronounced in mid-century Marxism. Leading Soviet theorists in the 1940s defined Marxian political economy as "the science of the development of men's social-productive, i.e., economic relations ... in human society in the different stages of its development" (Dunayevskaya 1944, 504) but then reduced these economic relations to simply manifestations of production technology:

> The basic law of historical materialism ... consists in this, that the production relations of men are determined by the character of the productive forces at the disposal of man at a given stage of the development of society.
>
> (505)[1]

These Soviet writers went so far as to propose that Marx's *Capital*, which focuses primarily on capitalism and manifestly contradicts the thesis of technological determinism, is potentially harmful to the study of political economy (Dunayevskaya 1944, 507). Because of this emphasis on the stadial development of social forms driven by the evolution of technology, the enterprise did not have a central role in the study of political economy. It is a peculiar legacy of twentieth-century Marxism that this mid-century Soviet literature, which relies primarily on writings other than Marx's, has come to be seen as "orthodox" Marxism.

Early efforts to provide systematic introductions to Marxist economics in the West (Sweezy 1942; Eaton 1949; Mandel 1968 [1962]) reflect this tendency to emphasize economy-wide phenomena or forces and provide little or no explicit treatment of enterprises at all. This trend in Marxism reached its zenith in the 1950s and then receded. Emblematic of this change was Althusser's "Contradiction and Overdetermination," first published in 1962 (Althusser 1977) and his famous call for a return to Marx's *Capital* (1970a [1965]). Baran and Sweezy gave the enterprise a central place in *Monopoly Capital* (1966) and emphasized the production and use of surplus within it.[2] Braverman's (1974) work on the labor process looks even deeper into relations within the firm. Hindess and Hirst (1975, 1977) develop extensive internal critiques of mode of production and social formation theories, the embodiments of the mid-century holistic approach to Marxism. It is in this *milieu* of declining influence of earlier approaches and growing emphasis on methodological issues and Marx's own work that Resnick and Wolff's class analytic Marxism emerged, and their place in the Marxian tradition is measured alongside these earlier works.

This paper considers Resnick and Wolff's contribution to Marxian theory first by sketching an outline of Marx's treatment of enterprises in *Capital*, then interpreting their theory of enterprise in this light. I also address what is at stake in questions of Marxism and ontology. My central argument is that in *Capital* Marx develops his theory of capitalism primarily through a close analysis of the capitalist enterprise. Fundamentally this is a class theory, and in striving to distill class theory from Marx's voluminous work, Resnick and Wolff return the enterprise to a central place in Marxian theory. This is a distinctively Marxian theory of the enterprise that rejects both the idea that the firm is reducible to the objectives of the individual entrepreneur and that it is simply a reflection or expression of a holistic social logic.

Enterprises in Marx's *Capital*

Marx develops his analysis of capitalism progressively across the three volumes of *Capital*, first focusing primarily on production in industrial capitalist enterprises in volume one, introducing circulation in volume two, and relations between capitals in volume three.[3] The enterprise is the primary frame of reference, and class relations are the central concern throughout the three volumes. Class is a relational process among individuals, and it is these relations and their consequences that are of interest to Marx. Individuals are treated only incidentally, and their place in the theory is made clear from the beginning: "But here individuals are dealt with only in so far as they are the personifications of economic categories, embodiments of particular class-relations and class-interests" (Marx 1967a, 10).

Given the focus on capitalist production, relations between wage workers and industrial capitalist employers occupy the central place in volume one. The concept of surplus value is first developed and then elaborated extensively in this analysis. An initial section introduces commodities, exchange, and money abstractly. Subsequent sections examine the seeming paradox that surplus value emerges from the exchange of equivalents, methods of expanding surplus value absolutely or relatively, the role of the wage relation in the production of surplus value, and the accumulation of capital from surplus value. Each of these topics is dealt with in the context of the industrial capitalist enterprise, and the bulk of volume one consists of a close analysis of this type of enterprise. With the exception of the concluding section of the book, which considers the historical transformations of feudalism in England and clan relations in Scotland, Marx's investigation of capitalist production in volume one is an investigation of the production of surplus value in industrial capitalist enterprises.

Much of volume one focuses on relations between capitalist entrepreneurs and production workers in industrial enterprises, but in the course of this investigation Marx encounters occupations, inside and outside these enterprises, very different from these two. These different occupations can also imply different class positions and involve distinct and conflicting class interests. Marx's best-developed example of class conflict in *Capital* is between employers and production workers, but this leads directly into manifold class differences in the firm. Marx notes that an unavoidable "antagonism of interests" between laborers and their capitalist employers in the labor process necessitates hiring managers and supervisors who do not carry out the actual processes of production but rather oversee it in order to extract labor from the labor power purchased by the entrepreneur (1967a, 330–32).

He first introduces hired managers and "overlookers" very briefly in his analysis of the labor process (1967a, 193) and then returns to them in detail when considering the labor process in large-scale production, referring to them as among the false costs (*"faux frais"*) of production. They are a *false* cost in the sense that they do not directly produce the firm's output, hence are not a true cost of production but rather are necessary to overcome the agency problem inherent in the capitalist wage relation. Marx notes several times in *Capital* that wages of superintendence are deductions from the total profit (surplus value) of the enterprise, and in *Theories of Surplus Value* he ties this directly to the exploitation of production workers with the expression "the exploitation of labor costs labor" (1972, 355). Marx thus introduces a class distinction based around the positions of different groups in relation to the surplus value produced in the enterprise. Some produce it, and others receive it, either directly (entrepreneur) or indirectly through their wages (managers, supervisors).

This class theory relies on the classical distinction between "productive" and "unproductive" labor. For Marx productive labor is that which produces surplus value for a capitalist (1967a, 509). Having established that surplus value is produced only by workers engaged in production, it follows that those who earn wages but are not directly engaged in production are, by definition, "unproductive." Unproductive labor is a cost, which must be paid out of the surplus value realized by the entrepreneur from the sale of output. Marx thus explores not only the *source* of surplus value but also its *use* by analyzing how the surplus created in production provides the resources to support nonproduction activities inside the firm. He later expands this to include class positions outside the firm, such as "ideological" classes (government officials, priests, lawyers, etc.) and workers (such as household servants) whose labor power is not purchased in order to expand the capital of the entrepreneur (446). Marx's frequent use of the term "third persons" (1967a, 522; 1967b, 130, 333–34, 375, 388; 1967c, 343, 355, 381) indicates that this is a class analysis that goes beyond the "two great classes" of the *Communist Manifesto*.

Volume two of *Capital* enlarges Marx's theory of capitalism to include circulation activities, which are first characterized as specific moments (M – C and C′ – M′) in the famous circuit of money capital (M – C – P – C′ – M′). This circuit clearly identifies the important distinction between circulation and production activities. In Marx's taxonomy circulation is nonproduction activity, necessary to secure inputs into production or realize the value of output, not itself a type of production. Expanding his theory in this way requires Marx to consider the class relations between capitalists and workers engaged in circulation activities. Marx is unequivocal that because circulation activities are not production, workers carrying out these activities are, like managers and supervisors, false costs that consume rather than add value for the industrial capitalist (1967b, 149). He characterizes this relation between production and circulation in a way that is strikingly similar to his analysis of the wages of superintendence: "The agents of circulation must be paid by the agents of production" (1967b, 127). This similarity stems from their incomes being drawn from the same source, the surplus labor of workers in production.

Marx further analyzes circulation by considering the role of other commercial activities within the enterprise, such as book keeping or other purely administrative work. In the same way that surplus is the source of income for managers, supervisors and circulation activities, it is also the source of income for various kinds of administrative and accounting activities that are "necessary" for production to take place but are not themselves production. It does not change matters if non-production activities are contracted from other firms specializing in them rather than being done internally to the industrial capitalist enterprise.

> If by a division of labor a function, unproductive in itself though a necessary element of reproduction, is transformed from an incidental occupation of many into the exclusive occupation of a few, into their special business, the nature of this function itself is not changed.
>
> (1967b, 131)

Marx thus extends his class theory of the flow of surplus within enterprises to encompass the flow of surplus between enterprises.

The second part of volume two contains Marx's little-commented-on analysis of the turnover of capital. This involves the capital stock of an individual enterprise, includes numerous examples of what Engels calls "commercial arithmetic" (284) used for calculating the effect of various aspects of turnover on the enterprise, and concludes with a brief consideration of the formation of the aggregate demand for commodities (Chapter 17). The third and final part of volume two then shifts perspective to consider the "process of circulation of ... aggregate social capital" (354) and contains Marx's well-known reproduction schemes. This third section is the only portion that does not use the individual enterprise as the primary frame of reference.[4]

The third volume of *Capital* brings Marx (1967c) back to the analysis of the industrial capitalist enterprise, now in competition with others, and, with some exceptions, the capitalist enterprise remains at the center of his analysis throughout this volume.[5] Parts two and three of volume three deal with controversial topics—the equalization of rates of profit, values and prices of production, and the tendency of the rate of profit to fall—that have occupied a conspicuous and disproportionate place in Marxist economics. But this volume also contains in-depth analyses of the relation of industrial capitalist enterprises with merchant and financial capitalist enterprises and with landlords. Again, Marx returns to the question of the source of income for merchant or financial enterprises, which have their own capital stocks and realize a profit without engaging in production, and landlords who likewise do not produce. Marx's answer to the riddle of how this could occur should, by now, be clear: these non-producing capitalist enterprises derive their income either wholly (merchants) or partially (financial firms) from surplus received from the industrial capitalist enterprise. Landlords likewise receive a share of the surplus created in production in the form of rents.

The conception of capitalism developed in *Capital* emerges from an analysis of a social institution, the enterprise, structured by heterogeneous class relations, with class relations established by reference to the surplus generated in production and characterized by contradictory interests and conflict. The enterprise is very clearly not a simple machine for producing profits, even if that is what the owner might desire. There are also varieties of capitalist firms—industrial, merchant, and finance—each with its own distinctive set of characteristics, and hence the concept of the "capitalist enterprise" is itself diverse. Enterprises exist in relationships with one another intentionally, as in the case of industrial and merchant enterprises, or unintentionally, as in the case of competition between capitalist enterprises.

This is, very briefly, a sketch of the place of the enterprise in *Capital*. But it is also important to reemphasize that the enterprise is central to the analysis Marx develops progressively across these books, and it is remarkable this has had so little impact on most Marxist economic and social theories.

Resnick and Wolff's Marxist theory of enterprise

Marx comments that the ultimate aim of *Capital* is to "lay bare the economic law of motion of modern society" (1967a, 10). Since enterprises are the primary location studied in *Capital*, he must have believed they played an important role in this. Overlooking the forest for the trees, economists have instead tended to search for laws of motion in one or another of the details of *Capital,* and few have looked to the theory of class developed progressively across the three volumes in the context of the analysis of capitalist enterprises.

Resnick and Wolff find Marx's theory of class at work throughout *Capital.* For them this theory is apparent in his consistent attention to the production of surplus and its circulation within and between enterprises. Marxian class theory, as they interpret it, is a process involving the production, appropriation, and distribution of surplus, and the basic elements are well known to anyone familiar with their work: surplus product results from the surplus labor of workers in production; this surplus is appropriated either by the producers themselves (in non-exploitative class relations) or someone else (in exploitative class relations); this surplus is monetized in circulation and then distributed. The production and appropriation moments in this process are characterized by Resnick and Wolff as the "fundamental class process" and the subsequent distribution of surplus as the "subsumed class processes." The fundamental class process may take any of the canonical Marxist forms—communal, slave, feudal, ancient or capitalist—which are identified by referencing a variety of conditions typically associated with these different class relations.

This formulation of Marxian class theory is distinctive. It places the production, appropriation, and distribution of surplus value at the center of Marxian theory and in doing so achieves a synthetic and consistent reading of all three volumes of Marx's *Capital.* From this class-analytic perspective it becomes clear why Marx organizes these books the way he does, focusing first on the production of surplus value in the enterprise, then broadening his analysis to include circulation, and finally introducing multiple enterprises, competition, and the in-depth analysis of trade mark-ups, financial flows, and rents. Their class theory condenses Marx's extensive analyses of the source and use of surplus into a concise theoretical construction. But an underappreciated aspect of Resnick and Wolff's work is that class processes always take place in the context of a specific social site, their term for an institution (Wolff and Resnick 2012, 227–28).[6] They describe a site as composed of individuals in various economic and non-economic relations (1987, 164) and as "… a place in society where various sorts of processes are performed and which define it qua social site" (1987, 231). Sites are inherently heterogeneous and contradictory aspects of a larger heterogeneous and contradictory society, and no single relation or process, or subset of relations or processes, determines their behavior. The relation between site and society is "a relation between overdetermined part and overdetermined whole" (1987, 9).

By situating their class theory in the context of the individual site or institution—enterprise, household, state, etc.—Resnick and Wolff demonstrate fidelity to Marx's enterprise-focused analysis in *Capital,* and with this comes a certain ontological perspective. Sites are elements of a social structure, and by using the site as the primary frame of reference for their analysis, Resnick and Wolff make an important statement about the nature of this structure. The issue here is not microfoundations or fetishizing parts or wholes, but rather interpreting a complex overdetermined whole through one of its aspects. For them, the institution or site is always both a social product and a factor in social development. It is subject to determination by both society and the individuals that populate the site, and, in turn, reciprocally participates in determining both society and these individuals. The site itself always exists in a mutually constitutive relation with other social sites and with phenomena that emerge as effects of composite structures (e.g., prices of production, labor market effects on wages, productivity, profits, and investment).

Sites are also internally heterogeneous, with no limit to their divisibility, irreducible to individuals or their behaviors. But the site provides a frame of reference within which to interpret both the actions of individuals and the influence of social factors. It provides a temporary closure of an aspect of society for the purpose of analysis in what is otherwise a ceaseless dialectic of change. The choice of the appropriate frame or closure is not arbitrary. In *Capital* the enterprise is the basic form capital takes (with the balance sheet of the enterprise being its measure), and it is the location of capitalist production activity, so this is the appropriate frame of reference for an analysis of capitalist class relations. Resnick and Wolff generalize Marx's analysis of capitalist class relations to encompass others (slave, feudal, ancient, etc.) but in doing so retain the site as the frame of reference. Choose a narrower frame of reference and you have an analysis of individuals in isolation; choose a broader frame of reference and you have relations among sites or larger social structures instead of relations among the class positions that populate and structure the enterprise, estate, plantation, household, etc. Sociologists will recognize this as a 'meso' level of analysis, a term that is basically unknown among economists. Meso-level analysis makes monocausal determination implausible by avoiding the two forms of reductionism, atomistic or holistic, that require either pre-social individuals or a transcendental structure that similarly exists outside of society.

Cartesian, Hegelian or overdetermined totality: what is at stake?

For Resnick and Wolff, the point and purpose of Marx's theory of class is to emphasize that capitalism is a system of exploitation or "social theft" wherein the surplus labor performed by workers is appropriated by their capitalist employers (2005). It is a deeply ethical and moral indictment of capitalism intended to make readers aware of this outrage and motivate them to seek a remedy for it through social change. But what is the point and purpose of overdetermination? Why connect class so consistently and intimately with this specific interpretation of dialectics? Dialectics in the form of overdetermination is an explicit and ubiquitous presence in Resnick and Wolff's work, and it is worth considering the implications of this.

Overdetermination obviates the traditional ontological polarity of conceiving of phenomena either as autonomous elements constituting a Cartesian totality or as simple expressions of a Hegelian totality. By Cartesian totality I mean one in which the whole is reducible to individual parts that are internally homogenous and indivisible and whose characteristics are fully formed prior to their assembly into any composite construction (Levins and Lewontin 1985; 1–4, 135–36; Cullenberg 1994; 51–53, 67–70). By Hegelian totality I mean one in which the elements are simply manifestations or expressions of the holistic logic or ideal organizing principle of the whole in which they occur (Althusser 1970a, 17; 1970b, 186–89; Olsen 2009, 179–81).

Lukács gives articulate expression to a Hegelian interpretation of Marxism:

> It is not the primacy of economic motives in historical explanation that constitutes the decisive difference between Marxism and bourgeois thought, but the point of view of totality. The category of totality, the all-pervasive supremacy of the whole over the parts is the essence of the method which Marx took over from Hegel and brilliantly transformed into the foundations of a wholly new science.
>
> (1971, 27)

Lukács qualifies the power of totality over element and argues for a "dialectical conception of totality" leading to a conception of reality as a "social process" (13), but in his later reflections it seems clear that he takes the supremacy of the totality to be primary and subordinates any dialectical complications to this (xx). Holistic ontology implicitly presumes that the logic or purpose of the totality cannot be generated by or found within its constituent elements. Positing the primacy and supremacy of the logic of the totality over the individual elements requires this logic be established beyond the elements, and indeed outside of the totality itself, transcending them both and imposing itself on them from the outside.[7] If this is not the case, and this logic of the totality is instead subject to mutual determination by the elements, it could not be said to exert "all-pervasive supremacy" over them. If the logic or purpose of the whole is generated internally, then changes in the elements will alter this logic or purpose, which violates the notion that determination runs from the whole to the parts. Holistic determination requires sites or institutions be subordinated to an all-encompassing social and historical logic that determines the individual sites without, in turn, being determined by them. In other words, it reduces the relation between the site and society to a form of expression: the site being simply an expression of a force or logic that transcends not only the individual site but the society itself. This is the logic of Hegel's *Philosophy of History* (1956), with its spiritual and transcendental *Idea* whose development transcends the individual societies that express it and has its own teleological logic.

But not only did Marx specifically reject the notion that he proposes a teleological *"marche generale"* imposed by fate on every society inevitably leading to communism (Marx 1942 [1877], 354), the secular equivalent of Hegel's teleological journey of the spirit from initial alienation to the overcoming of this alienation; his analysis of society also lacks the holistic reductionism and transcendental demiurge necessary for this to occur.

By contrast, an overdeterminist ontology describes society as an organic and dialectical unity in which the individual elements shape, and, in turn, are shaped by the others. Part and the whole are always mutually constitutive, and neither part nor whole has ontological priority because neither can be conceptualized without the other. Consider, for example, a capitalist society. The industrial capitalist enterprise can only exist in a social environment that provides the conditions that make it possible, its conditions of existence. Notable among these are workers in the condition of being "free laborers" (Marx 1967a, 169), free in the double sense of being free to sell their labor power as their own commodity, as well as free from ownership of means of production.[8] Likewise, it makes no sense to speak of a capitalist society in the absence of capitalist enterprises. Both the part (enterprise) and the whole (society) have the characteristics they do partially because of characteristics of the other. Part and whole are mutually constitutive. Institutions and society are each consequence and cause, shaped by and in turn shaping one another. Transcendental historical narratives make little sense in an analysis that takes meso-level phenomena seriously because these meta-historical constructions require social sites to simply act out a role assigned to them by the logic of history.

Likewise, the competing ontological perspective that views society as a Cartesian totality ultimately reducible to the behavior of individual agents provides no viable alternative. In these approaches, social phenomena, including society itself, are simply manifestations of the willful behavior of these agents whose likes and dislikes are pre-given. Enterprises, households, and states are epiphenomena of individual choices and actions. For example, neoclassical theories of the enterprise treat it as a singular and unified entity embodying the objective of the entrepreneur. The enterprise, in this theory, responds to price signals in the marketplace in order to realize the single-minded objective of choosing a production plan that maximizes profit.

Marx also assumes the entrepreneur strives to maximize profit, but he emphasizes that the entrepreneur always exists in relationships with groups inside and outside the enterprise whose own interests conflict with this. Furthermore, he ridicules (1967a, 176) the notion that individual choices are free in the classical liberal sense and frequently characterizes market exchanges as superficially voluntary acts that individuals are compelled to engage in by social circumstance. The classical liberal view gives tremendous agency to the individual but ignores the circumstances, culture, ideological conditioning, and a myriad of other social factors that constitute and condition individuals and their choices. The liberal notion of free will presumes a particular atomistic (that is Cartesian) conception of the individual, which Spinoza dismissed long before Marx: "This, then, is that human freedom which all men boast of possessing, and which consists solely in this, that men are conscious of their desire and unaware of the causes by which they are determined" (Spinoza 1995, 284).

Somewhere between the pervasive effects of the Hegelian social totality and the autonomous Cartesian agent lies the process without a subject, the site. Sites are complex, heterogeneous, and contradictory aspects of a larger complex, heterogeneous, and contradictory society, and hence they are neither Cartesian nor Hegelian in nature. The enterprise is then a process without a subject in the same sense that Marx calls individuals "bearers" of social relations. Individuals labor under circumstances and social relations they are both subject to and, through their actions, help to reproduce or overthrow; they are both cause and effect, subject and object. Likewise the site or institution is subject to conditions and agency emanating from inside and outside itself, while producing effects that circumscribe and structure these same conditions and agency.

In Resnick and Wolff's "site," all the elements are mutually constitutive and none has ontological primacy. One or another element may have analytic primacy, that is they may be the focus of our attention for the purpose of analysis, but this does not imply ontological primacy. The site provides a frame that makes the objects (including individuals) within it recognizable as social phenomena without either fetishizing them in isolation or subsuming them completely to the larger social structure.

But Resnick and Wolff also never hesitated to tell their students that there is a political element to their ontological and epistemological choices. As epistemological antifoundationalists, they claim neither greater empirical realism nor logical superiority as the principal reason for embracing overdetermination. Instead, they appeal largely to pragmatic and political motivations. They argue that Marxism competes with other theories for influence in society, and overdetermination is a partisan epistemological position in this struggle, not a scholastic one (1987, 2, 36–37). Its value as an epistemological position is as part of the struggle for social and economic change by advancing Marxist social theory against other theories founded on rationalism or empiricism. Both rationalism and empiricism fail to provide the foundation for the knowledge that is their *raison d'être* (Hindess 1977; 1–22; Rorty 2009, Chapters 3–4), and so the attack on them is also an attack against theoretical discourses premised on them. But this epistemological argument does not address the implications of overdetermination as ontology.

Overdetermination is first an ontological claim—that every object exists in its relationships with all other objects—from which epistemological propositions are then derived. Overdetermination may be a partisan epistemological position, but as ontology it also has important political consequences. Resnick and Wolff's choice, like Althusser's before them, opens up new possibilities for Marxian political practice that are foreclosed by holistic reductionism and its adjunct teleology. Most formulations of dialectics emphasize change. Mutual interaction between elements, and between elements and wholes, implies that change is a general characteristic of phenomena. This conception of society has obvious advantages for those seeking social change, but dialectics involves more than just the notion of change, and endemic change can also be generated by interpretations that embrace holistic reductionism and necessity rather than complexity and contingency. There are political consequences of this. Holistic reductionism, which construes social structures and historical tendencies as all-powerful and omnipotent, is profoundly disempowering. What is the use of political activity if social phenomena are simply manifestations of supra-historical forces acting out in time and space? This whole conception contradicts the idea that class is itself a social product, generated internally to the social structure and its relations, and hence subject to change by social action. This engenders a fatalism that forecloses the possibilities of political practice by putting class relations and their transformation beyond its reach.[9]

J.K. Gibson-Graham's work (1996, 2006) on post-capitalism, for example, would not have been possible in a Marxism that proceeds from a genuinely Hegelian perspective and views social phenomena as simply expressions of a transcendental social essence that imposes itself inescapably through the social structure on its constitutive elements. Their work on post-capitalism begins from a simple set of questions: "My feminism reshapes the terrain of my social existence on a daily basis. Why can't my marxism (sic) have as its object something that I am involved in reconstructing every day? Where is my lived project of socialist construction?" (Gibson-Graham 1993, 10). The answer they find for these questions is that traditionally Marxist discourse produces an understanding of capitalism as something monolithic, hegemonic, and all-encompassing, pervading and determining social and individual life. Conceiving society and economy this way requires socialist activity to be nothing less than striving for the replacement of one unified, singular, capitalist totality with an equally unified, singular socialist one. From this perspective a lived project of socialist construction can occur only after a successful political movement to achieve state power.

In contrast, Resnick and Wolff's emphasis on class relations at sites of production, whether they are households, enterprises, or states, provides a different way of understanding capitalism and allows for a different way of conceiving of socialist class relations. From this perspective, class relations are something occurring between individuals occupying specific class positions in social sites, and this site-level orientation makes it possible to envision and enact socialist or communist practices as part of the lived experience of a workplace, even if this workplace exists among others still characterized by capitalist production relations. Building socialism then involves the transformation of workplace practices, one workplace at a time or many at a time, and either with or without first securing the political power of the state. A site-level orientation also implies that socialism or communism is not something restricted to the actions of states, and rather involves relations in the workplace itself. This suggests a radical re-conception of the objective of socialist or communist construction. The actions of the state may facilitate this transformation of class relations in the workplace, but state power, in itself, does not achieve this.

Conclusion

These two elements we know so well from Resnick and Wolff's work—class and overdetermination—are the beginning of the enduring contributions of class analytic Marxism. But these are not the extent of their contributions. Marxists have sometimes created entire interpretations of Marxism from one or two comments in Marx's work. Seldom has this been done, as Resnick and Wolff do, primarily through a close reading and synthetic interpretation of *Capital* as a whole. Their work is distinctive for its fidelity to Marx's *Capital*, but their orthodoxy is leavened with revolutionary ideas about epistemology and ontology. Resnick and Wolff capture a basic insight of *Capital*, that individuals are indeed the bearers of social relations, which provide the context for their actions, but it is in this bearing that the social relations are observed, and it is in the context of the social site that they are observable. This returns Marxist analyses of capitalism to that most basic institution of capitalism, the enterprise. Since the overwhelming majority of the three volumes of *Capital* proceed through an analysis of the capitalist enterprise, it is remarkable that it has played an almost nonexistent role in Marxian economic and social theory.

The return to a theory of the firm is a return to the focus on exploitation, one of Marx's great insights and indictments of capitalism, and it is integral to a social ontology that escapes from both atomistic and holistic reductionism. These important issues are intimately connected to political practice, and Resnick and Wolff's work enables a badly needed new direction for Marxist political practice. Rick Wolff's current work (Wolff 2012), which endeavors to transform the class relations within enterprises, is one example of this political practice.

The scope of their work has been broad. *Knowledge and Class* presents not only Marxist theories of enterprise and the state, but also a comprehensive interpretation of Marxian dialectics qua overdetermination and a theory of Marxist epistemology that emerges from it. Fraad et al. (1994) expand the analysis to include households and gender relations, and Resnick and Wolff (2002) apply their site-oriented theory of class to understanding the experience of socialism in the Soviet Union. These works demonstrate both the viability and power of Marxist analyses of sites in society. But this work remains unfinished in important ways. They give us a theory of the *communist* class process, something occurring at the site of production, but say little about *communism*, a condition of society. Also, their faith in the revolutionary potential of antifoundationalism and some forms of postmodernism seems unfulfilled. Antifoundationalism has won an unsatisfying victory over foundationalist approaches. It dethroned them, and yet theories that embrace them remain largely unscathed. This suggests that the enduring faith in these theories is itself a complex social product, not subject to being undermined by the recognition that their epistemological presuppositions are untenable.

Acknowledgments

I would like to thank Fred Moseley for his comments on an earlier draft of this paper and Ted Burczak for his careful reading and very thoughtful comments. This work is greatly improved because of their input. Errors, omissions, and other problems remain the responsibility of the author.

Notes

1 See also Economics Institute of the Academy of Sciences USSR (1957), "Introduction."
2 Gillman's (1958) pioneering empirical work also emphasizes the use of surplus value within the enterprise. Given the limited Marxist scholarship in the U.S. in the 1950s and early 1960s, it is remarkable that Baran and Sweezy do not reference Gillman's work, which anticipates some of the central ideas of their book.
3 Marx describes this development explicitly at various points throughout the three volumes (1967a, 11, 564; 1967b, 352–54; 1967c, 25).
4 See Marx (1967b, 352–54) for an overview of the first two volumes of *Capital*.
5 The places in volume three where Marx does not have primarily an enterprise perspective are the second section, dealing with the equalization of rates of profit and the relationship between values and prices, and some portions of his discussion of the credit system. His discussion of "Revenues and Their Sources" at the conclusion contains a discussion of national income accounting, but this is largely to elucidate the ways that the exploitative nature of the capital-labor relation within firms is masked by market transactions and the flows of value between firms.
6 Resnick and Wolff's theories of class and overdetermination were in place before the focus on sites. Their earliest presentation of these concepts addresses the issue of social formations and the transition from feudalism to capitalism in Western Europe (1979). Subsequently they applied their class theory to analyze the income and expenditures of an individual capitalist (1982). Only in *Knowledge and Class* did the site, rather than society or an individual entrepreneur, become the frame of reference for analysis, and it is only in the context of this focus on sites that their thoughts on overdetermination and class are fully realized as a comprehensive theory of Marxism. This site-level orientation remains throughout the rest of their work together and is also distinctive of the work of many of their students after 1987.

7 This is precisely the issue addressed by Althusser with his concept of structural causality. He notes that the purpose of the concept of overdetermination is specifically to address the problem of "the determination of either an element or a structure by a structure" (1970b, 188):

> The structure is not an essence *outside* the economic phenomena which comes and alters their aspect, forms and relations and which is effective on them as an absent cause, *absent because it is outside them*. ... the effects are not outside the structure, are not a pre-existing object, element or space in which the structure arrives to *imprint its mark*: on the contrary, it implies that the structure is immanent in its effects, a cause immanent in its effects in the Spinozist sense of the term, that the *whole existence of the structure consists of its effects*, in short that the structure, which is merely a specific combination of its peculiar elements, is nothing outside its effects.
>
> (Althusser 1970a, 188–89, italics original; see also 1970b, 29)

8 Marx (1967a, 766) uses the example of the Swan River Colony to illustrate the point that capital is a social relation that requires certain social conditions. In this example the unfortunate Mr. Peel is greatly disappointed to discover that while he could import the physical goods needed for a capitalist enterprise along with a prospective labor force, when transplanted from Georgian England to the Australian outback the colonists became independent producers rather than wage workers.

9 This issue is clearly identified by that most astute defender of mid-century stadial Marxism, G. A. Cohen. He argues that political practice cannot itself bring about social revolution, rather it can only be successful in overcoming the fettering of the productive forces by the relations of production in a society pregnant with change (2000, xxviii). He also notes "The political applicability of historical materialism is limited, since it is a theory about *epochal* development, and the time horizon of political action necessarily falls short of the epochal" (342).

References

Althusser, L. 1970a [1965]. "From *Capital* to Marx's Philosophy". In *Reading Capital*, L. Althusser and E. Balibar, eds., 11–70. London: Verso.

———. 1970b [1965]. "The Object of *Capital*". In *Reading Capital*, L. Althusser and E. Balibar, eds., 71–195. London: Verso.

———. 1977. *For Marx*. London: New Left Books.

Baran, P. A., and P. M. Sweezy. 1966. *Monopoly Capital*. New York: Monthly Review Press.

Braverman, H. 1974. *Labor and Monopoly Capital*. New York: Monthly Review Press.

Cohen, G. A. 2000 [1978]. *Karl Marx's Theory of History: A Defense* (expanded edition). Princeton and Oxford: Princeton University Press.

Cullenburg, S. 1994. *The Falling Rate of Profit*. London: Pluto Press.

Dunayevskaya, R., trans. 1944. "Teaching of Economics in the Soviet Union." *American Economic Review* 34 (3): 501–30.

Eaton, J. 1949. *Political Economy*. New York: International Publishers.

Economics Institute of the Academy of Sciences USSR. 1957 [1954]. *Political Economy, A Textbook*. London: Lawrence and Wishart.

Fraad, H., S. A. Resnick and R. D. Wolff. 1994. *Bringing It All Back Home*. London: Pluto Press.

Gibson-Graham, J. K. 1993. "Waiting for the Revolution, or How to Smash Capitalism while Working at Home in Your Spare Time." *Rethinking Marxism* 6 (2): 10–24.

———. 1996. *The End of Capitalism (As We Knew It): A Feminist Critique of Political Economy*. Oxford and Cambridge: Blackwell Publishers.

———. 2006. *A Postcapitalist Politics*. Minneapolis, MN: University of Minnesota Press

Gillman, J. M. 1958. *The Falling Rate of Profit*. New York: Cameron Associates.

Hegel, G. W. F. 1956. *The Philosophy of History*. New York: Dover Publications.

Hindess, B. 1977. *Philosophy and Methodology in the Social Sciences*. Hassocks, UK: The Harvester Press.

Hindess, B. and P. Q. Hirst. 1975. *Pre-Capitalist Modes of Production*. London: Routledge and Kegan Paul.

———. 1977. *Mode of Production and Social Formation*. London and Basingstoke: The Macmillan Press Ltd.

Levins, R. and R. Lewontin. 1985. *The Dialectical Biologist*. Cambridge, MA and London: Harvard University Press.

Lukács, G. 1971. *History and Class Consciousness*. Cambridge, MA: The MIT Press.

Mandel, E. 1968 [1962]. *Marxist Economic Theory*, volumes I and II. New York and London: Monthly Review Press.

Marx, K. 1942. "Letter from Marx to Editor of the *Otecestvenniye Zapisky*" November 1877. In *Selected Correspondence 1846–1895 Karl Marx and Frederick Engels*, Donna Torr, trans., 352–5. New York: International Publishers.

———. *Capital*, volume 1. New York: International Publishers.

———. 1967b. *Capital*, volume 2. New York: International Publishers.

———. 1967c. *Capital*, volume 3. New York: International Publishers.

———. 1972. *Theories of Surplus Value*, part three. London: Lawrence and Wishart.

Olsen, E. K. 2009. "Social Ontology and the Origins of Mode of Production Theory." *Rethinking Marxism* 21 (2): 177–95.

Resnick, S. A. and R. D. Wolff. 1979. "The Theory of Transitional Conjunctures and the Transition from Feudalism to Capitalism in Western Europe." *Review of Radical Political Economics* 11 (3): 3–22.

———. 1982. "Marxist Epistemology: The Critique of Economic Determinism." *Social Text* 6 (Fall): 31–72.

———. 1987. *Knowledge and Class*. Chicago, IL and London: University of Chicago Press.

———. 2002. *Class Theory and History*. New York and London: Routledge.

———. 2005. "The Point and Purpose of Marx's Notion of Class." *Rethinking Marxism* 17 (1): 33–37.

Rorty, R. 2009 [1979]. *Philosophy and the Mirror of Nature*, Thirtieth Anniversary Edition. Princeton, NJ and Oxford: Princeton University Press.

Spinoza, B. 1995. "Letter 58: To the Most Learned and Wise G.H. Schuller, from B.d.S. (1674)." In *Spinoza: The Letters*, S. Shirley, trans., 283–6. Indianapolis, IN and Cambridge, MA: Hackett Publishing Co.

Sweezy, P. M. 1942. *The Theory of Capitalist Development*. New York: Monthly Review Press.

Wolff, R. D. 2012. *Democracy at Work: A Cure for Capitalism*. Chicago, IL: Haymarket Books.

Wolff, R. D. and S. A. Resnick. 2012. *Contending Economic Theories: Neoclassical, Keynesian and Marxian*. Cambridge, MA and London: MIT Press.

5 Uncertainty and overdetermination[1]

Donald W. Katzner

Introduction

Since Immanuel Kant's "Copernican revolution" in the theory of knowledge at the end of the eighteenth-century Enlightenment, philosophical problems of epistemology have substantially ruled the roost. The issues of what is to be said regarding the origin, processes, and validity of knowledge have occupied reflective minds. There is wisdom in the adage that preoccupation with epistemological inquiry has implied the death, or perhaps it should be said the near-death, of metaphysics. The age-old questions of being and becoming have frequently dissolved into those of why observable structures of the 'real' are what they are, in the sense that a believable explanation of their existence can be proposed. To that extent, matters of being, of ontology and the nature of the real, have become the handmaiden of epistemological inquiry. That is, intellectual search has frequently been directed to discovering the descriptive causation of what is, or to the explanation of why what happened did happen or came to be. On a pragmatic level, the search has been for causal explanations.

The logic and theory of overdetermination articulately constructed by Stephen A. Resnick and Richard D. Wolff (1987) have pointed in such directions. At its core, the doctrine of overdetermination directs attention to the understanding of, or at least to throwing light upon, the intricate complexes of determining forces that explain observable states of affairs. Those interconnecting and mutually determining lines of causation call upon categories related to economic, political, cultural, sociological, and ratiocinative complexes of reality. In particular, when thinking about the real, everything—physical, social, mental, etc.—is assumed to interact in a mutually constitutive manner with everything else.[2] Each entity, that is to say, exists only as the result of the combined effects of all other entities. Because of these interdependencies, no single event can be understood by detaching it from the milieu of all events. No phenomenon can be described as the outcome of independently construed (static or dynamic) forces. An economy, for example, cannot be conceived except in relation to all cultural, social, political, psychological, and economic elements of which it is comprised. Furthermore, mental constructs such as concepts, variables, functions, and analyses cannot exist apart from all other concepts, variables, functions, and analyses, nor can an analysis be disentangled from that which it purports to analyze.[3] The only way to conceive and think about physical, social, mental, and analytical elements is discursively, and the knowledge produced from thoughts about those elements exists only as discursive texts.[4] Clearly this approach denies the possibility of analyzing any one piece of reality in isolation from any other piece or collection of pieces.

Moreover, the traditional epistemological dichotomy between observation and thinking becomes blurred.[5] There is no separation between observations of the real world and thoughts about those observations, and it is not possible to explain fully a particular observation as the outcome of a single set of causes or an essence such as the solution of a simultaneous equation system. Unlike rationalism or empiricism, there is no absolute truth, and no single unique procedure generates knowledge. Knowledge, rather, comes from experientially related discourse that recognizes the interrelatedness of observation and thinking, and hence the nonunique (or relative) and nonessentialistic character of truth. On this view, the ability to organize and understand the patterns of happenings in the world rests on deeply penetrating interdependencies. The epistemology of an analysis founded on overdetermination or mutual interaction is referred to as nonessentialistic.

It is in no sense intended as a caricature to suggest that in the overdetermination scheme everything determines everything. Moreover, implicitly in the Resnick-Wolff argument is the idea that differing degrees of perceived relative strengths of determining influences, degrees of more-or-less localized causation, are, at certain times and in specific instances, recognized by the investigator. Indeed, it follows from a careful assessment of overdeterminationism's logical structure that it is because of that phenomenon of recognizability that putatively useful explanatory models of states of affairs can be proposed. As suggested above, the pieces of such models, indeed the models themselves, are mutually interactive with all facets of actuality (including thought processes), and the thing being explained cannot, therefore, be understood as the result of the single cause possibly characterized by the determination of certain parameter values in a convergent time path of an independent differential equations system. Thus variables in the overdetermination approach are defined as being constituted in and through the effects of all other variables of the analysis. They do not exist as detached, isolated, independently specified entities. The same is true of the values that variables may take on. Because variables and their values condition each other's conceptual existence, a change in the value of any variable transforms (among other things) the variable of which it is a value.

Relations among variables are also interactive with each other and are modified when brought together in the conduct of analysis. A relation between two variables is characterized by the unique way in which these variables and the relation itself are affected by all other variables and relations. It is a focal point in a myriad of interlocking effects that continually modulates in the mind of the investigator as the effects are explored. Thus relations, like any other analytical elements, have a kaleidic quality in that they are vulnerable to significant modification or rejection as soon as they are created. Moreover, in parallel to the case of variables discussed above, each relation can exist only in conjunction with the totality of all such relations since each is literally produced by the effects of all others on it. For example, the relation describing the way technology transforms inputs into outputs (what would be called the production function in neoclassical economic analysis) is understood to be the combined result of the interactions of all technological, economic, social, political, and even psychological forces that come together to determine how inputs are transformed into outputs.

However, the primary objective in the present space is not to look directly at the varying possible structures of the overdetermination approach. The inner complexities of the system and its possible application to questions of philosophic and social-scientific interest are well explored by better minds and hands. Here the intention, rather, is to bring to prominence an issue that, on a reasonably comprehensive survey of the relevant literature on overdetermination, does not appear to have been accorded the attention that might properly be given to it. In contemporary, and even in historically more expanded, writings in economics, the matter of uncertainty has been displayed and addressed to varying degrees. By uncertainty is meant simply the question of whether what is claimed to be known can be stated with sureness or certainty or whether degrees of approximation to certainty can be held, and what degrees of confidence can be attached to statements of belief and claims to truth. In the present context the focus is on whether, and in what way and with what analytical results, the concept of uncertainty does, or should, demand a place in overdetermination analysis.

Of course, it cannot be avoided that in the long development of economics as an analytical discipline the very problem of uncertainty has to a large extent been resolved by assuming it away. In the heyday of ascendant neoclassical microeconomics, for example, in the purported explanation of market activity and market systems, it was generally assumed that perfect knowledge, perfectly rapid and frictionless market adjustment mechanisms, and perfect mobility of commodity demands and production factors existed. Similar predispositions of thought informed what was said, from the classical economists onwards, about what became in due course a more fully developed macroeconomics. These constructs were reckoned to provide first approximations to the explanation of real economic conditions. It is to the damage of such intellectual productions that the first approximations only reluctantly gave way to second and what might be thought to be better subsequent approximations.

It would be foolish to imagine that no progress to deeper and deepening explanations occurred. Attempts to flesh out the microeconomic systems by tâtonnement assumptions have been made, various probes to imperfect and monopolistic competition have occurred, and progress has been advanced by analytically marrying to basic analyses the phenomena of real and money capital, influences from the financial sector, and suggestions as to long-run and short-run possible outcomes. The high level of the mathematization of economic argument that in due course invaded theoretical economics has thrown increasing and increasingly valuable light on both immediate and short-run economic systems and on long-run possible outcomes. That has been accompanied by conjectures of possibilities that economic systems may converge to stability or to unstable explosions. Nevertheless, the admission of possible uncertainties into the analytical apparatus of thought has itself proceeded only cautiously and unsurely. It has appeared all too often that the very mathematization involved has been in the interest of epistemological security, or the peace of mind that imagines that elegance of argument implies substantial empirical relevance, rather than appealing directly to the clarification of real-world economic conditions. Against all that, of course, a number of attempts to incorporate uncertainty into the argument have been made, with different postulates as to the meaning of uncertainty and ways of dealing analytically with it. Brief notice shall be taken of some such ways in a moment. The objective in noting them is to place the concept of uncertainty in economic argument against its possible recognition in overdetermination analysis.

It is possible to suggest a rather general concept of the relevance of uncertainty to the respective bodies of analysis, that of overdetermination on the one hand and what may be referred to as the ruling fashion of neoclassical analysis on the other. At this point, recall that the objective and preoccupation of overdetermination is that of gaining an understanding of why what is observable actually exists as the describable state of affairs. In that context, uncertainty, so far as any recognition is given to it, refers simply to the degree of assurance with which statements of determining causes do in fact satisfy claims of what has been described above as nonessentialistic truth. How, in other words, can confidence be held, for example, that a conclusion thought to possess relative truth regarding the explanation of an existing economic state has in fact been reached? Or again, in the course of constructing that explanation, has adequate account been taken of all relevant determining forces and causes, and has the intertwining relation between them been adequately cognized and taken into account? Overdeterminationism, then, in a more expansive form in which recognition is accorded uncertainty, is concerned principally with the question of the manner in which the uncertainty impinges on the confidence that can be held in the adequacy of the explanation.

To the extent that conceptions of uncertainty have been accorded a place in the established neoclassical domain, its principal relevance has been in analytical explanations of choice among future possible outcomes. The upshot of comparisons between the contrasting bodies of analysis now under review is that, from an overdetermination perspective, the investigator may be uncertain of the proprieties of the explanation of *existing* states, whereas the neoclassical approach looks to the *future* and attempts to incorporate uncertainty into a decision-theoretic analysis. It's not that the overdetermination perspective does not allow one to contemplate uncertainty about future outcomes or precludes the analysis of decisions. Rather, in the overdetermination scheme of things, uncertainty arises in a different, more fundamental manner. Further brief comment on such possibilities will be made below.

It would be difficult to overstate the apparent significance of the relation between the two systems of thought in their treatment of uncertainty. Overdetermination analysis calls for the recognition of uncertainty on at least two distinctive levels. First, as has already been suggested, uncertainty conceivably resides in the identification of the most significant elements of the myriad of interconnecting lines of causation. Uncertainty at this level gives rise to the question of whether wisdom has adequately prevailed in the identification of these lines of causation. Second, uncertainty then conceivably exists in the accordance of the relative strengths of what are identified as sources of explanatory influence and of their relative contribution to overall descriptions of real-world states. In such ways, and as implied in the argument to this point, the relevance of uncertainty in an overdetermination analysis is with regard to its contribution to the unsureness of the strength of its claims to nonessentialistic explanation. In that significant respect, the overdetermination system of thought aligns with contemporary styles of postmodern analytics. It raises once again, indirectly perhaps, the conclusion that in the final outcome absolute truth statements are unattainable. Only degrees of truth or significance are recognizable. Or in more direct postmodernist terms, relativity reigns, and truth claims are always contestable. It is for that reason that credibility might be adjudicated in the overdetermination scheme. An approach for evaluating the viability of an overdeterministic explanation in light of the pervasive uncertainty surrounding it will be suggested below.

Since, from the perspective of overdetermination, knowledge arises as discursive texts, uncertainty can be present only in relation to those texts. The texts cannot be uncertain with respect to absolute truth because absolute truth is presumed not to exist. But they are uncertain relative to nonessentialistic truth in that discursive texts are not unique and will generally have different meanings in different discourses[6] and in that texts are capable of change from moment to moment. An individual can never be sure of how long one text will hold sway over other possibilities. Thus uncertainty has epistemological, not ontological, characteristics—there cannot be ontology or absolutely true conditions of real life with overdetermination—only different discursively constructed images, conceptions, or theories of reality. In this framework, one might ascribe to uncertainty a pseudo-ontological-type existence (as a condition of life that might possibly exist), but even in this case, proof of such existence and its meaningful implications reside within a discourse and are not independent of it.[7] Thus uncertainty is only experienced cognitively through discourse. It has no meaningful existence (in the sense of, for example, uncertain future outcomes of actions in neoclassical economics) outside of the discourses that create such meanings.

In addition, from the overdetermination perspective, the understanding of uncertainty as a discursive phenomenon is neither subjectivist nor objectivist; that is, subjectivist in the sense of being based on subjective knowledge such as individual belief or objectivist when the appropriate knowledge foundation is thought to be, in principle, universally observable. Individuals are conscious, at least in part, of the product of the discourses in which they have participated. To say uncertainty is subjective or objective is to locate the knowledge origins of uncertainty in an autonomous individual who is presumed not to exist in the overdetermination context and precludes the understanding that uncertainty emerges from the discourses within which it is theoretically constituted, and from the social conditions in which such discourses arise and change over time.[8]

The point has now been made that uncertainty has a place in the fundamental conceptualization of overdetermination analysis but in a different manner than in neoclassical argument where it has to do principally with future outcomes, decision making, and decision-theoretic analysis. With that in mind, it may be useful to comment briefly on various ways in which theorizing about decision making under conditions of uncertainty has been conducted both within and beyond the neoclassical domain. The reason for doing so is to provide some indication of the manner in which uncertainty might find a more prominent place in the overdetermination argument, particularly in relation to discourses that are concerned with future outcomes and events.

In forward-looking, decision-theoretic analysis, or in arguments directed to issues of economic choice, future possible outcomes have frequently been corralled by applications of the probability calculus. That is, uncertainty has been taken as ontological and essentialistic and has usually been 'measured' in terms of probability—both objective (aleatory) and subjective (epistemological). Objective probability is associated with the likelihood of outcomes of chance mechanisms and the relative frequencies they produce upon repeated trials, while subjective probability arises from degrees of belief held by the decision maker in the likelihood that outcomes are thought to arise.[9] In this manner of understanding decision making, the implications of uncertainty are typically accounted for by employing probability in the essentialistic calculation of expected values and risks. In other words, for analytical purposes future possible outcomes have been reduced to present (possibly discounted) values by taking, respectively, the first and second statistical moments of relevant distribution functions as present-dated magnitudes. Such a procedure has turned future-dated contemplated magnitudes into certainty-equivalents. At the level of choice, then, focus has fallen on that line of action pointing, in terms of certainty equivalents, to decisions that have future consequences. Relevant utility ruminations, some suitably defined decision-theoretic index, or an optimum choice standard may be incorporated as the decision criterion into such an analysis.

Arguments of the kind just suggested are frequently said to be concerned with probabilistically reducible risk, and not with what, in some competing forms of analysis, has been referred to as true or residual uncertainty. The difference in analytical structures turns on the assumption that when one looks to the future and its possible outcomes, one is in a position of complete ignorance. With respect to the future, as Keynes (1937, 214) famously put it, "We simply do not know." That is to say, conditions exist in which it cannot reasonably be said that future possible outcomes can be thought of with respect to likelihood and hence probabilistically defined. The probability calculus and expected values are then of no avail. Indeed, in addition to Keynes, it is well known that Knight (1921, 20 and 233) and Shackle (1972, 19–20) had similar views of uncertainty as it impacts the making of decisions. For them, it is not possible when making decisions to have sufficient knowledge of the future likelihoods to contain uncertainty within the constraints of probability. Shackle's words (1972, 3) echo those of Keynes: "What does not yet exist cannot now be known."

Knight's way of dealing with uncertainty in decision making is with judgment, common sense, or intuition all based on inference from past experience and possibly 'crude' analysis (1921, 211). Keynes (1937, 213–14) argues that for practical decision making it is still necessary to guess at probabilities and reason on the basis of them. Shackle (1969, 422) handles uncertainty in decision making through an analysis that begins with imagination as it leads to what he refers to as potential surprise.[10] In these various ways of coming to grips with uncertainty, the objects of knowledge and sources of explanation are conceived of in an essentialist fashion, and the objective or subjective probability or potential surprise concepts that corral the uncertainty are characterized accordingly.

Essentialist as it may be, Shackle's approach to decision making is clearly different from that of Knight and Keynes. In his view (1969, xi), decision or the choice among available acts that promises or suggests the most desirable outcome is "... more than mere response to circumstances and contains an element which we may call inspiration, which brings essential novelty into the historical sequence of states of affairs. *Decision* (sic) thus becomes the locus of unending creation of history." Addressing uncertainty, Shackle focuses on the imagined possibility of future outcomes rather than on their objective or subjective probabilities. Less knowledge about the possible occurrence of events is required to formulate imagined possibilities than is required to formulate objective or subjective probabilities. In addition, the possibility of attaining a particular imaginative experience could be inhibited or dimmed by a barrier of disbelief. And potential surprise, which may be formulated as degrees of disbelief in, or doubt of possibility (not likelihood) of, is a measure of the strength of that barrier.[11] A precise definition of it may be stated as follows: the potential surprise of an event is the surprise the investigator imagines now that he would experience in the future if the event were actually to come to pass.

In the process of arriving at a decision, each action among which the decision maker is required to choose is associated with a range of possible 'gains' and possible 'losses,' and each gain and loss is accompanied by the potential surprise of its eventuation. One combination of a gain with its potential surprise and a loss with its potential surprise stands out in the decision maker's mind, and that combination serves to characterize and identify the action to which it relates. Based on these characterizations, the decision maker chooses among actions according to a specific choice criterion.[12]

In overdeterminationism, it is possible to relate uncertainty to future outcomes and the analysis of decision making by borrowing from some such thought forms as have now been suggested. Explanations of the making of economic decisions that focus on future outcomes would be created through the development of a discourse that accounts for the myriad influences— economic, social, political, etc.—that interact with decision making in an overdetermined way. What the individual discursively understands about such things as preferences, the current environment and the constraints under which he or she operates, happenings in the past, and conjectures about future possibilities would figure into the analysis. The decision criterion would be overdetermined by a plurality of causes, "overlain with and constituted by contingent and specific social conventions and habits, psychological 'drives' and 'hidden' motivations and desires."[13] Models involving probabilities and expected utilities or potential surprise could be employed subject to the use and limitations set out above. In this way, a kaleidic, discursive vision of the decision-making process could be developed that is subject to change immediately upon its construction.

Moreover, in the context of overdetermination and the uncertainty that permeates it, Shackle's idea of potential surprise provides a language within which to consider the viability of explanation. On the one hand and as indicated earlier, the investigator may see in a particular explanation differing relative strengths of individual forces that might determine an event. These relative strengths could lead him to make judgments as to the relevance of each of the forces at issue. And that judgment, which might involve assessing the imagined consequences of focusing on one force as opposed to another,[14] could be expressed in terms of a nonessentialistic version of potential surprise. That is, the investigator could say now that he would be, in nonunique or relative terms, more or less surprised if, in light of future evidence, knowledge, or other considerations, certain forces turned out to seem more relevant or appropriate than others. On the other hand, since explanation is not unique, the investigator could attach to various competing explanations the relative surprise he feels now he would experience in the future if they were accepted as satisfactory explanations. That satisfactoriness may also take into account the imagined consequences of putting forth the explanation. Thus, in the same way that nonessentialist potential surprise may be used to adjudicate at the point of specifying causal forces and relations, it may be employed to judge the viability of alternative and complete explanatory structures.

Notes

1 The author would like to thank Douglas Vickers for his considerable help.
2 Resnick and Wolff (1987, 2).
3 Georgescu-Roegen's notion of a dialectical concept (1971, 43–45) shares some of the qualities of the idea of an overdetermined concept. For him, a dialectical concept, like an overdetermined one, is a concept whose boundaries cannot be defined clearly and precisely and that overlaps its opposite. However, the extensive interdependences with outside elements of overdetermined notions are not present.
4 Ruccio and Amariglio (2003, 17).
5 Resnick and Wolff (1987, 18–19).
6 Ruccio and Amariglio (2003, 74).
7 Amariglio (1990, 35–36).
8 Ruccio and Amariglio, (2003, 76–77).
9 Hacking (1975, 1).
10 See also Katzner (1998, chs. 2–3).
11 Shackle (1969, 113).
12 A complete description of this decision-making argument may be found in Katzner (1998, ch. 4). See also Vickers (1978, ch. 8), (1987, ch. 12), and (1994, ch. 9).
13 Ruccio and Amariglio (2003, 87).
14 Wolff and Resnick (2012, 368–71).

References

Amariglio, J. 1990. "Economics as Postmodern Discourse." In *Economic as Discourse: An Analysis of the Language of Economics*, W. J. Samuels, ed., 15–64. Boston, MA: Kluwer.

Georgescu-Roegen, N. 1971. *The Entropy Law and the Economic Process*. Cambridge, MA: Harvard University Press.

Hacking, I. 1975. *The Emergence of Probability*. Cambridge: Cambridge University Press.

Katzner, D. W. 1998. *Time, Ignorance, and Uncertainty in Economic Models*. Ann Arbor, MI: University of Michigan Press.

Keynes, J. M. 1937. "The General Theory of Employment." *Quarterly Journal of Economics* 51 (2): 209–23.

Knight, F. H. 1921. *Risk, Uncertainty and Profit.* Boston, MA: Houghton Mifflin.

Resnick, S. A. and R. D. Wolff. 1987. *Knowledge and Class: A Marxian Critique of Political Economy.* Chicago, IL: University of Chicago Press.

Ruccio, D. F. and J. Amariglio. 2003. *Postmodern Moments in Modern Economics.* Princeton, NJ: Princeton University Press.

Shackle, G. L. S. 1969. *Decision Order and Time in Human Affairs.* 2nd ed. Cambridge: Cambridge University Press.

———. 1972. *Epistemics and Economics: A Critique of Economic Doctrines.* Cambridge: Cambridge University Press.

Vickers, D. 1978. *Financial Markets in the Capitalist Process.* Philadelphia, PA: University of Pennsylvania Press.

———. 1987. *Money Capital in the Theory of the Firm: A Preliminary Analysis.* Cambridge: Cambridge University Press.

———. 1994. *Economics and the Antagonism of Time: Time, Uncertainty, and Choice in Economic Theory.* Ann Arbor, MI: University of Michigan Press.

Wolff, R. D. and S. A. Resnick. 2012. *Contending Economic Theories: Neoclassical, Keynesian, and Marxian.* Cambridge, MA: MIT Press.

6 Catallactic Marxism

Marx, Hayek, and the market

Theodore Burczak

When communist *workmen* associate with one another, theory, propaganda, etc., is their first end. But at the same time, as a result of this association, they acquire a new need—the need for society—and what appears as a means becomes an end. You can observe this practical process in its most splendid results whenever you see French socialist workers together. Such things as smoking, drinking, eating, etc., are no longer means of contact or means that bring together. Company, association, and conversation, which again has society as its end, are enough for them; the brotherhood of man is no mere phrase for them, but a fact of life, and the nobility of man shines upon us from their work-hardened bodies.

(Marx [1844] 1978, 99–100)

The life-process of society, which is based on the process of material production, does not strip off its mystical veil until it is treated as production by freely associated men and is consciously regulated by them in accordance with a settled plan.

(Marx [1867] 1978, 327)

Introduction

Friedrich Hayek advocated the idea of catallaxy as a way to think of a society bound together by exchange relationships (Hayek 1976). He argued that we should understand a society in which markets organize the production and distribution of most resources as a catallaxy, rather than as a market economy. The neoclassical concept of economy as "a complex of activities by which a given set of means is allocated in accordance with a unitary plan among the competing ends" may be a sensible description of the economic problem facing an individual person or organization but is misleading and dangerous when applied to society as a whole (ibid., 107). Since the variety of individual trades that occur every day is not motivated by any unitary end but by the diverse ends of individual market participants, Hayek believes we should not use the phrase "market economy" to describe this "complex of activities." The concept of catallaxy reflects the existence of multiple organizations and individuals engaged in exchange to achieve their various ends. Derived from the Greek word for exchange (*katallattein*), catallaxy describes "the order brought about by the mutual adjustment of many individuals in a market" (ibid., 108–109).

For those who think that Marxian theory is ultimately hostile to markets in its understanding of post-capitalist society, the term "catallactic Marxism" remains a difficult juxtaposition, even though there have been many attempts to develop a workable market socialism inspired by Marx's work (e.g., Lange [1936] 1966; Roemer 1996). To be fair, as the second epigraph above demonstrates, Marx at certain moments anticipated a non-catallactic socialist future in which the anarchy and injustice of market competition would be supplanted by cooperative production "in accordance with a settled plan." Marx and his collaborator Friedrich Engels derived this image of a future socialist society at least in part from their philosophy of historical materialism according to which the development of capitalist productive forces (driven by the relentless tendency toward concentration of capital) would erode the need for private property and anarchic market coordination, eventually creating the conditions for social ownership and central planning. As Engels imagined it, capitalist competition breeds large-scale, "socialized" production (meaning large firms, within which the deployment of labor and capital is coordinated by hired managers), eventually culminating in a particular type of socialism.

> The proletariat seizes the public power, and by means of this transforms the socialized means of production, slipping from the hands of the bourgeoisie, into public property. By this act, the proletariat frees the means of production from the character of capital they have thus far borne, and gives their socialized character complete freedom to work itself out. Socialized production upon a predetermined plan henceforth becomes possible.
>
> (Engels [1892] 1978, 717)

Hayek's most famous paper, "The Use of Knowledge in Society" (1945), attacks the tacitly collectivist logic of standard neoclassical models of "market economy" in which all knowledge of production techniques, resource scarcities, and individual preferences is assumed to be "'given' to a single mind" prior to any market exchange. For Hayek, market competition among private owners is essential for individuals to test their separate ideas about how scarce resources should be utilized. The chief advantage of producing for the market is that it poses the threat of loss and offers the benefit of profit, which leads dispersed individuals to discover whether their tacit hunches about and subjective perceptions of economic opportunity are warranted, given others' hunches, perceptions, and preferences. The inherent division and fragmentation of articulate and inarticulate knowledge among separate minds makes top-down central planning impossible, in Hayek's view, especially in a technologically complex society.

Stephen Resnick and Richard Wolff take a major step toward the development of a catallactic Marxism by rejecting the teleology of historical materialism (and essentialist notions of causality in general), including Engels's claim that technological advance and concentration of capital were precursors to social ownership and central planning. Taking their lead from Louis Althusser (1969, with Balibar 1970), Resnick and Wolff find in Marx a radical post-Hegelian notion of overdetermination, a vision of social phenomena in which the perceived lines of causality are complex, indeterminate, and ultimately produced through the interventions of discursively embedded human minds (Resnick and Wolff 1987). Rejecting the determinism and teleology of historical materialism, they argue that the distinctive contribution of Marx was not a discovery of socio-historical laws of motion but a theory of exploitative class processes in which performers of productive labor do not participate in the appropriation of its fruits. Resnick and Wolff put aside the conception of centrally planned socialism that emerges from historical materialism and argue for a non-exploitative future in which production and appropriation are organized communally, i.e., democratically. Their approach to ending exploitation is not hostile in principle to private property and most markets, although the catallactic potential of their "21st century socialism" (Wolff 2014) remains underemphasized and underexplored.[1]

To illustrate the catallactic possibilities of the post-capitalist visions of Resnick and Wolff (and Marx), imagine a world of universal self-employment, a world in which no person hires any other into an employment relation, hence where goods and service are always produced either by independent contractors or by cooperative firms organized on the basis of one person, one vote in the selection of managers who hold ultimate legal[2] decision-making authority regarding productive methods and scale, as well as the appropriation and distribution of the results of the cooperative's efforts. In such a world, the market for wage labor, or labor rentals, would not exist, thereby achieving Marx's goal of "abolishing the wages system" (Marx 1965). Some Marxists argue that this institutional structure would itself suffice to eliminate exploitation (e.g., Ruccio 2011) while others insist that it would not (e.g., Roberts 2011). Regardless of whether one believes that abolishing the wage-for-labor-time market achieves a non-exploitative form of production, this institutional framework is consistent with Wolff's advocacy of workers' self-directed enterprises as a Marxian cure for at least some of the ills of capitalism (Wolff 2012).[3] Others have also reasoned that a world of producers' cooperatives operating within a market system achieves a distinctly Marxian form of market socialism (Burczak 2006; Jossa 2014; Screpanti 2008). The principal question explored in this essay is whether it is *desirable* for socialism to be catallactic, from a Marxist perspective. As one example of critical questions a catallactic Marxism might address, the essay also examines whether there are explicitly Marxian reasons to criticize the allocation of resources among self-employment firms competing for profit via the mechanism of voluntary exchanges of private property.

Socialism after Hayek (Burczak 2006) provides an institutional sketch of and normative justification for a market socialism that integrates a Hayekian theory and advocacy of markets with a Marxian theory and advocacy of non-exploitation. In the name of economic democracy, I propose the abolition of two markets: the market for labor rentals, or wage labor, and the market for common stock, in which ownership of one share of corporate stock gives one vote for the corporate board of directors. The overarching Marxian goal is to end exploitation by placing the legal direction of the firm, the supervision of labor performed inside the firm, and the appropriation of the results of that labor into the hands of the worker-members of the firm. The normative basis of this conception is the anti-capitalist premise that ownership of productive assets should not confer to capital owners the de facto right to direct others' labor time or to appropriate and distribute the firm's output. Working time should always be self-directed, either in self-managed firms of one or in democratic self-employment firms whenever the use of complicated and large-scale capital requires joint production. In addition, following Marx's ([1891] 1978) concern that markets do not necessarily allocate resources to meet social needs in an equitable fashion, *Socialism after Hayek* also contends that a market socialist system requires some sort of non-market welfare provisioning so that access to health care and other basic needs is distributed not according to ability to pay but in a manner consistent with the equalization of capabilities to live free, choice-worthy lives (see also Screpanti 2004). Finally, in order to facilitate entrepreneurship in democratically organized, self-employment firms, the book suggests implementing a wealth tax to fund a universal basic capital account similar to though substantively larger than the capital grant proposed by Thomas Paine in *Agrarian Justice* (Paine [1797] 2000, see also Ackerman and Alstott 1999). These latter provisions would require the state to provide access to social goods and to use the tax and transfer system to facilitate universal self-employment, in addition to imposing a legal framework in which the markets for labor rentals and common stock are no longer allowed. In every other respect, however, this Hayek-Marx vision of market socialism is thoroughly catallactic.

These efforts to advance a different idea of market socialism were inspired by the "catallactic moments" I gleaned from Resnick and Wolff's overdeterminist Marxism. This paper seeks to develop these moments and to consider whether there remain any Marxian reasons *not* to embrace market competition and exchange, assuming that firms are self-directed by their worker-members. I argue that the implicit vision of the good society contained within the overdeterminist Marxian literature bears strong similarities to Hayek's vision of a cosmopolitan, catallactic society. After an initial explanation of this position, the paper explores, first, the extent to which market competition among self-employment firms achieves the abolition of exploitation and, second, whether market competition in the financial sector induces economic pathologies to which Hayekian economics is blind. The Marxian idea of unproductive capital suggests an important set of cases of government regulation of the financial services industry and other forms of unproductive capital that may be warranted, in addition to other essential government roles (namely, state provision of public goods, state regulation of external costs associated with productive activity,[4] and some sort of state-directed redistributive mechanism to facilitate both need satisfaction and entrepreneurship among self-directed enterprises) in a catallactic socialist society.

Catallaxy, equality, and markets

Hayek notes that the term catallaxy connotes not just "to exchange" but also, most notably, "to admit into the community" and "to change from enemy into friend" (1976, 108). With these ideas, Hayek attempts to capture the ways in which market societies promote the development of people who routinely cooperate with strangers. Notable in this connection is the interesting work of Samuel Bowles and Herbert Gintis (2011) showing that people are more oriented toward cooperation and reciprocity than the standard economic model of *homo economicus* would suggest. Moreover, Bowles finds that people in societies where exchange interactions are frequent tend to be more altruistic and more interested in mutuality than in societies where people seldom interact with strangers, as in isolated tribal societies (Bowles 2016, 113–50). For Hayek, the linchpin of a catallactic social/economic order is the acceptance of fair terms of cooperation, which he argues is facilitated by market economies governed by rules that are applied to and enforced on all participants equally.

Jerry Gaus (2015) surveys an extensive social scientific, evolutionary literature contending that humans have developed an egalitarian ethos. Gaus maintains that this egalitarianism expresses itself not it terms of a preference for equal outcomes but as the desire to be free from domination by bullies. We are an egalitarian species in the sense that we want to be treated fairly by others, in a manner that does not threaten our autonomy. We seek a framework of social cooperation such that our interactions with friends and strangers are characterized by mutual respect and consent, not by guile, force, and domination. In a large, diverse society, our egalitarianism results in adherence to "norms of fair transactional treatment" and governance by a set of ends-independent, universally applicable "abstract rules" (ibid., 21). Gaus's argument resonates with Hayek's claim that "it was the very restriction of coercion to the negative rules of just conduct that made possible the integration into a peaceful order of individuals and groups which pursued individual ends" (Hayek 1976, 110). But while Hayek's main point is that catallactic societies produce good results—peace, coordination, and prosperity—Gaus reasons that a market catallaxy coheres with our evolved moral resistance to domination and preference for autonomy.[5]

Contemplating how the egalitarian dimension of the catallaxy concept might apply to the realm of production, the connection between Hayek's catallaxy and overdeterminist Marxism becomes intriguing. Gaus notes that the relationships in the hierarchical firm stand in sharp contrast to the preservation of personal autonomy and avoidance of bullying that he believes are constitutive of exchange relationships. "We evolved to put down the boss, who can now fire us for speaking up" (Gaus 2015, 26). Hence, Gaus concludes, the feature of modern capitalism that is "in tension with the egalitarian ethos" is not market exchange but "the great hierarchical organization that populates market societies: the firm" (ibid., 24). This is precisely where the concerns of Hayekian liberalism overlap with overdeterminist Marxism. The central issue of analysis for overdeterminist Marxism is the performance, appropriation, and distribution of surplus labor. Performing surplus labor does not occur in markets; it occurs in organizations: households, capitalist firms, and non-capitalist institutions. Most people probably spend more time working inside organizations than engaging in the haggling of market exchange (Simon 1991). The question for a catallactically orientated Marxism is whether these productive processes involve exploitation, where producers of surplus labor see this surplus appropriated by those not involved in production, or whether these processes are organized cooperatively, enabling producers to participate in the appropriation of the enterprise output and to "consume their own labor power."

It is hard to reconcile the idea of catallactic friendship with systematic and ongoing exploitation. This is why Marxists speak of class struggle: producers of commodities struggle with the non-producing appropriators of those commodities. Hayek actually recognized the Marxist problematic: "So long as collaboration presupposes common purposes," as it does in capitalist enterprises that must follow accounting conventions of profit and loss, "people with different aims are necessarily enemies who may fight each other for the same means" (Hayek 1976, 110). In the capitalist firm, the disputed means is workers' labor time, particularly in terms of its use. Employers, of course, would like to direct the labor time they have rented in the manner most conducive to enlarging their profits; employees would like to keep their jobs and wages, exercising as little effort as institutionally and psychologically feasible, since they are not the residual claimants—the appropriators—of the results of their working time (Bowles and Gintis 1999). Exploitative institutions are non-egalitarian, unfriendly, and conflictual, hence inherently uncatallactic.

The goal of overdeterminist Marxism is for producers of commodities to serve as the appropriators of those commodities, thereby eliminating exploitation.[6] David Ellerman (1992) calls this "universal self-employment," where workers are always the consumers of their own labor power and where workers in the enterprise participate equally in the appropriation of the firms' product, including any surplus. Resnick and Wolff call workplaces "communist" when productive labor (producers of surplus) also performs the role of appropriator (Resnick and Wolff 2002, 9). Wolff's notion of a workers' self-directed enterprise articulated in his book *Democracy at Work* (Wolff 2012) fleshes out the idea of enterprise communism. Similarly, a communist household is one where its members participate as equals in decisions regarding the production, distribution, and appropriation of household surplus labor. Overdeterminist Marxism seeks to transform fellow workers, and the activity of work itself, from something alien (exploitative, enemy) to something familiar (cooperative, friend); in this regard overdeterminist Marxism is also catallactic. To be sure, friends also struggle, but in communist institutions they struggle as substantive equals.[7]

But what about markets? Can overdeterminist Marxism be *thoroughly* catallactic, in the sense that it might support market exchanges as the principal means by which societies organize the allocation and distribution of resources and products created in self-employment or communist firms and households? Hayek tells us that what he and Adam Smith call a "Great Society," i.e., one organized by markets, "has nothing to do with, and is in fact irreconcilable with 'solidarity' in the true sense of united-ness in the pursuit of known common goals" (Hayek 1976, 111). Perhaps Hayek's polemical declaration of the incompatibility between catallaxy and solidarity will lead some Marxists to reject out of hand the idea of a thoroughgoing catallactic Marxism.

Antonio Callari, for instance, criticizes the idea that a "totalizing Hayekian market imperative could act as a framing for a socialist vision at work in the actual struggles of peoples and communities against the rule of unbridled capital accumulation" (Callari 2009, 371). There is little doubt that the profit motive and market exchange alone cannot effectively coordinate the use of all resources in a manner that Marxist-socialists will find acceptable. As Hayek and other market-friendly economists acknowledge, markets do not effectively and efficiently provide public goods, goods with positive neighborhood effects, and goods that arise out of production processes with diffuse negative externalities (Hayek 2007, 87). Markets might in addition fail to promote an efficient amount of technical change, efficient investment opportunities, and efficient levels of production when there are significant information asymmetries (Bowles and Gintis 1999). We can also obviously challenge the ways in which markets distribute income, wealth, and opportunity in inevitably non-egalitarian and need-blind ways. Yet we must always ask: failure-ridden markets compared to what?

In the 1930s, Maurice Dobb (1937) surveyed the deficiencies of markets and concluded that only scientific central planning could solve the various problems associated with markets. For him, the chief problem with markets was that atomistic competition coordinates resource allocation ex post, after entrepreneurial mistakes have been made. He likened market competition among individual entrepreneurs to a series of trains operating on the same set of tracks. Absent a central timetable coordinating the separate runs over the rails, trains would frequently collide, until experience led the individual train engineers to run at different times. But once this unplanned, spontaneous coordination was achieved, it would be disrupted by the addition or subtraction of new trains or new stops, again setting off a series of wrecks. For Dobb, the obvious solution to the use of the track was a rationally designed timetable. So, too, was central planning the superior method to coordinate the economic activities of the otherwise isolated and dispersed private owners of productive property. Dobb, though, was surely too optimistic about the possibilities of flesh-and-blood government planners to survey the possible range of resource uses and to pick the combination of resources that achieved any sort of social optimum. Nor did Dobb's advocacy of national economic planning face up to the incentive difficulties government planners faced in getting people to perform tasks in a suitable manner when those people did not have any property at stake.

Overdeterminist Marxism recognizes the limits of rational planning (for a good statement about the exaggerated prospects of central planning, see Amariglio and Ruccio 1998). But the space between a full-blown Hayekian, liberal catallaxy and Dobb's version of authoritarian central planning remains to be fleshed out in the development of a catallactic Marxism. As Callari laments, overdeterminist Marxism has not yet articulated a theory of markets.

> [Overdeterminist Marxism] has perhaps been lax in its epistemic responsibility to the knowledge accumulated throughout the long history of Marxian theory; the responsibility, that is, to celebrate and keep on learning from those parts of the work of Marxists, such as critiques of market totalities [i.e., a belief that a self-regulating market system can effectively coordinate the activity of dispersed productive units] and of the purported efficiency of capitalist [profit and loss] accounting, which, though they might have been ensconced in a determinist framework, nonetheless still gave the flower of a radical critique of capitalism.
>
> (Callari 2009, 372)

What follows is an outline of some important issues that a distinctly *Marxian* theory of catallaxy might consider. In particular, we will examine an argument that exploitation can persist, even when producers appropriate the necessary and surplus product, whenever market competition causes a "predistribution of surplus value" that blocks direct producers from the initial receipt of all the value their labor creates. Second, we explore the possibility that profit seeking by unproductive financial capitalists should be checked by government action due to the deleterious consequences it can generate.

Capital intensity and exploitation via the market

One distinctly Marxian line of anti-market critique centers on the extent to which exploitation is truly eliminated by the "abolition of the wages system." The argument that universal self-employment eliminates exploitation depends on interpreting the Marxian idea of exploitation to refer to a process that occurs in production, and only production. Unearthing various passages from Marx, Roberts (2011) puts forth a different idea: exploitation occurs when producers are not able to appropriate the *full monetary value* of their surplus labor because commodities do not always exchange at their labor values. In Marx's famous shorthand description of surplus creation ($M - C - P - C' - M'$), the quantity of money earned via exchange ($M' - M$) might differ from the amount of surplus labor embodied in the produced commodities ($C' - C$). As a result, even if self-employed workers own the commodities they jointly create in a firm, they might not be able to realize in monetary exchange the value of surplus labor time embodied in those commodities. In particular, firms with higher capital intensity might be able to produce at lower unit cost than average, thereby capturing super-profits via the mechanisms of market exchange, at the expense of firms with lower capital intensity. Although Roberts resists this characterization, it is as if the self-employed workers in capital-intensive firms exploit the self-employed workers in firms with low capital intensity. In Roberts's definition of exploitation, however, the members of a self-employment firm operating in a competitive market system are not exploited only if $(M' - M) = (C' - C)$, a result that is unlikely to occur in the typical case.

Is this a Marxian reason to challenge the outcomes of a competitive market process? Perhaps so, if we hold that commodity exchange rates *should* reflect embodied labor values. But for Hayek, understanding how the price system is able to coordinate the activities of diverse and dispersed (self-employment) firms in a market context requires rejecting a "backward-looking" assessment of prices in terms of their consistency with the value of workers' labor time, or of any other production costs. As he puts it,

> [t]he remunerations which the market determines are, is it were, not functionally related with what people *have* done, but only with what they *ought* to do. They are incentives which as a rule guide people to

success, but will produce a viable order only because they often disappoint the expectations they have caused when relevant circumstances have unexpectedly changed.

(Hayek 1976, 116–17)

In other words, market competition coordinates the ideas and activities of dispersed individuals and firms—leading them to economize on the use of scarce resources in a social environment constantly in flux—precisely by rewarding lower-cost producers with higher profits. The question for Marxists is whether a planning process, which dispenses with the profit motive, perhaps replaced with a bureaucratic, scientific, or democratic decision-making authority, only softly constrained (if at all) by cost and benefit accounting, could do a better job of utilizing the ideas and conjectures of diverse, overdetermined human beings about production methods and opportunities. For the most part, as a rule, the answer is probably no.

A clear exception to this conclusion, one that Hayek recognizes, exists when profits are earned by deflecting some production costs onto third parties. Most advocates of markets recognize that passing unpaid costs onto third parties is justification for the intervention of democratic governments to force or incentivize firms, in some way and to some extent, to take these external costs into account. Milton Friedman, for instance, acknowledges that doing so may improve market competition as a coordinating process (1962, 14 and 30).

Does Marxian theory have a parallel argument to insist that democratic governance should regulate democratic self-employment firms operating in a competitive market context to correct the transfers of surplus value/ unpaid labor, via the profit mechanism, from inertial or modestly capital-intensive self-employment firms to innovative or highly capital-intensive self-employment firms? Kristjanson-Gural argues that

> we need to consider the creation of new institutions, informed by value theory, that would seek to reconcile the normative claims of the workers to nonexploitation [by instituting universal self-employment] with the normative claims of workers to get full credit for their labor expended – to avoid or compensate for, in other words, precisely those market transfers that are due to the effects of exchange on the formation of value and exchange-value.
>
> (2011, 358)

Such an institutional structure would clearly not be catallactic, since it would require constant intervention into the market process to correct profit flows to innovative and/or capital-accumulating self-employment firms that do not reflect labor expenditure in that firm. Roberts, who defines capitalist exploitation as the inability of productive laborers to appropriate the full monetary value of their surplus labor and thus maintains that self-employment, by itself, does not eliminate exploitation, takes a more open-ended position, potentially consistent with a catallactic perspective. He asserts that

> to avoid exploitation in a commodity setting [requires] *participatory consent to the process* that establishes that price structure ... from those whose labors create the social surplus or provide conditions for its existence [i.e., consent from all workers and citizens].
>
> (2011, 349–50)

A Marxian reading of the complex set of economic, epistemological, legal, and normative reasoning advanced by Hayek (1960, 1976) could perhaps convince workers to accept the legitimacy of a competitive catallaxy in which innovative self-employment firms earned profits greater than those of the non-innovators, particularly if there were other non-market mechanisms in place to advance basic need provision (e.g., universal access to health care, universal access to education) and ongoing wealth redistribution (e.g., a basic capital grant). Moreover, as Marx and Engels recognized, market competition helps to spur innovation and capital development.

> Modern industry has established the world-market.... This market has given an immense development to commerce, to navigation, to communication by land. This development has, in turn, reacted on the extension of industry....
>
> (Marx and Engels [1848] 1978, 475)

At the end of the day, in a self-employment world, workers as a whole would appropriate all of the surplus value, even though having markets might mean that some workers appropriate more surplus value than average, while other workers get less than average. If, however, there is some mechanism ensuring the satisfaction of basic needs, it is hard to see why it makes sense to sacrifice the efficiency and productivity gains of market competition for a planning process that might be able to keep the performance of surplus labor and receipt of surplus value more closely in line, but only at the expense of significant reductions in social coordination and wealth creation.

Unproductive capitalists and destructive competition

A second line of Marxian resistance to competitive, profit-seeking behavior lies in the observation that some types of profit-seeking behavior, even if pursued by a self-employment firm, are simply resource-transferring rather than resource-creating. Marxian theory, and classical political economics more generally, labels these resource-transferring types of activities as unproductive. In these cases, is there a convincing argument to regulate these sorts of resource-transferring behaviors? As Roberts points out, neoclassical economists criticize and seek to limit what they describe as the self-interested "rent-seeking" behavior of government officials for diverting resources from more productive uses (Roberts 2014, 354–55, n. 12). The Hayek-friendly public choice literature seeks not to eliminate government but instead to provide effective constitutional constraints on government to restrict fraudulent, corrupt, and resource-dissipating activities of public officials. There is an analogous Marxian argument about wasteful capitalist competition, particularly regarding the profit-seeking behavior of unproductive, profit-seeking financial capitalists (Foley 2013). A catallactic Marxism might insist upon careful regulation of at least some types of unproductive, self-employment firms, especially in finance, in ways that Hayekian or neoclassical economists would not accept, since they tend to see nearly all profit-seeking behavior in the private sector as wealth-producing.[8]

To understand this Marxian position, let us consider how overdeterminist Marxism characterizes the distinction between productive and unproductive capital made in classical political economy.[9] Resnick and Wolff (2012, 175) explain:

> Moneylending, landlord, and merchant capital are called "unproductive" capital, because no surplus labor is involved in them. Their self-expansions [of value] do not occur in production. When I lend money to you at interest, I am not employing you or obtaining any commodities from your labor. You must return to me more money than I lent to you. My gain is your loss. In the borrower-lender relationship, no new value is produced, no labor or surplus labor is done, no new commodities are created. The same applies to surplus value obtained through renting out land or merchant transactions.

We will pay special attention to finance, since it has become a particularly important type of unproductive capital due to its growing size and its demonstrated ability after the post-2007 financial crisis to disrupt productive activity. In the U.S., the finance, insurance, and real estate sector surpasses 20% of official GDP, and the rapid loss of jobs in 2008–2009 was instigated by disruptions in the financial sector. Moreover, the primary method through which financial sector profits are earned differs in a crucial respect from profit seeking in the productive sector.

Characterizing finance (and merchanting) as unproductive does not mean that these activities are unnecessary; there must be some kind of institutional mechanism to transfer purchasing power from saving units to borrowing units, for the purposes of funding capital investment and intertemporal consumption smoothing. The issue is that competitive profit seeking from selling and buying financial assets (i.e., money and other paper claims on real resources), or borrowing and lending, is not governed by resource constraints in the same way as is activity in the productive sector (and for that matter, in the unproductive merchanting sector, which depends upon hired labor to truck and market goods and services).

Capitalist productive activities generate profit by hiring, or leveraging, labor. Hiring labor multiplies the hands of the hiring party. If a hard-working, independent producer can make $1 profit per day, it might be possible for that independent to become a capitalist, able to make $1000 profit per day, by hiring 1000 workers, inducing them to work equally as hard and appropriating their output. Productive capitalists leverage labor to increase their profits. A self-employment firm would eliminate the possibility of one employer leveraging many hands to accumulate profit, since all workers would participate equally in the appropriation of profit in such a firm.

Profit seeking in the financial sector operates by hiring, or leveraging, financial capital. A money-lender makes $1 profit per day by assuming a short-term liability at a low interest rate (e.g., by borrowing money from oneself or "depositors") in order to purchase a longer-term asset with a higher interest rate (e.g., by lending money to a productive capitalist or household). In this case, employing more labor in a financial firm does not itself necessarily lead to more lending, since labor does not manu-facture loan capital.[10] Rather, financial institutions generate profit by lev-eraging equity positions through acquiring more financial liabilities—by borrowing more money (through accepting liquid deposits in a bank, for instance)—and using those funds to purchase financial assets (by making bank loans, for instance).

In addition to expanding bank lending, increasing financial leverage can also be employed to drive up the price of what Marx called "fictitious capital," i.e., "ideal sums of money that result via discounting streams of future payments attached to financial assets" (Lapavitsas 2013, 28; see also Marx 1967, 466). Prior to the 2007 financial crisis, for instance, Wall Street investment banks increased their leverage substantially in the process of marketing varieties of mortgage-backed securities at prices that in retro-spect were vastly inflated. From a Marxian perspective, expected future payments expressed in current stock and bond prices are linked to the anticipated flows of surplus value from future exploited labor and other income payments.[11] The key point is that the search for financial profits and competitive pressure to increase financial leverage can lead to a "dis-connect" between the anticipated flows of surplus value and the prices of financial assets, resulting in bubbles, contagion, and a disruption of productive activity.

Leveraging labor in the capitalist enterprise in order to compete for in-dustrial profit does not expose the capitalist system to risk in the same way that leveraging financial capital does. Increased borrowing to acquire more assets leads to a greater possibility of bankruptcy, should some of those acquired assets lose value. In the case of industrial capitalism, if one large firm goes bankrupt, hired labor in that firm loses employment and income, while the value of the firm's capital equipment depreciates. Since one person's spending is another's income, a firm's bankruptcy that reduces the employment, income, and spending of the firm's workers can have a multiplier effect, reducing the income of other producers, although this multiplier effect is generally small. But if a large financial capitalist firm has increased its leverage by funding the purchase of more financial assets through debt, its bankruptcy poses a much larger threat: assets of one highly leveraged financial institution may be the liabilities of another highly leveraged financial institution, and the inability of one to pay its debts to the other may immediately expose the second institution to bankruptcy. And so on. Balance sheets of financial firms are interlocked, thereby endangering a wave of bankruptcies and financial contagion that can be set off by the failure of a large financial firm, à la Lehman Brothers in September 2008. Falling asset prices, rising interest rates, and reluctance to lend can spill over to the real economy, as consumption, investment, and employment follow the reduction in prices of fictitious capital.

Marx expressed this idea as follows. "[D]uring crises and during periods of business depression in general," the ability of industrial capitalists to realize profit declines. Marx goes on:

> The same is true of fictitious capital, interest-bearing paper, in so far as it circulates on the stock exchange as money-capital. Its price falls with rising interest. It falls, furthermore, as a result of the general shortage of credit, which compels its owners to dump it in large quantities on the market in order to secure money. It falls, finally, in the case of stocks, partly as a result of the decrease in revenues for which it constitutes drafts and partly as a result of the spurious character of the enterprises which it often enough represents. This fictitious money-capital is enormously reduced in times of crisis, and with it the ability of its owners to borrow money on it on the market. However, the reduction of the money equivalents of these securities on the stock exchange list has nothing to do with the actual capital which they represent, but very much indeed with the solvency of their owners.
>
> (1967, 493)

The interconnections between financial capital and industrial capital can lead insolvency in the financial sector to insolvency in the industrial sector. Applying a self-employment rule to financial firms, thereby eliminating their ability to leverage labor, will not by itself mitigate the possibility of financial contagion. The logic of increasing profits through leveraging financial capital may not be muted by self-employment and worker appropriation of the gains resulting from that leverage.

This reasoning leads Fred Block (2014) to argue that the financial sector should be "democratized" through various strategies that suppress competitive profit seeking in the financial industry.[12] Most notably, he proposes an expansion of the not-for-profit credit union model for the banking system (which in the context of self-employment firms would imply a codetermined bank management, where depositors shared voting rights with bank workers), the creation of nonprofit, public agencies—pubic banks—involved in lending and security underwriting and policies to encourage decentralized lending institutions. Decentralization is critical so that the people involved in evaluating loan requests have sufficient contextual knowledge of the local economy to assess more accurately whether an individual borrower's plans can reap synergies with other local businesses and their potentially complementary plans. The upshot of his argument is that there is reason to think that concentration in the financial industry and the degree of risk-taking by profit-seeking financial institutions, in terms of both the size and composition of their assets, will not necessarily lead to financial market competition operating in the social interest, even if those institutions are organized according to a self-employment principle.[13] These arguments are particularly salient from a Marxian perspective that sees financial profits as derived from surplus value generated by productive firms.

Conclusion

Chris Sciabarra accuses traditional Marxism of harboring a "synoptic delusion," by which he means a confident belief that we can consciously design economic outcomes according to some principle of distributive justice. Sciabarra believes that Marx recognized "epistemic fragmentation" but thought it was surmountable via the development of productive forces. Some Marxists continue to embrace this vision and maintain that advances in computing power make central planning possible (e.g., Cottrell and Cockshott 2008). Resnick and Wolff, too, are clear that communism does not have to be friendly to market exchange. It can, for instance be consistent with central planning and despotism (Resnick and Wolff 2002, 10). But in view of their foundational commitments to understanding reality as complexly overdetermined and to the inability of discursively embedded human minds to capture a putatively objective reality, overdeterminist Marxists are likely to remain wary of schemes that appeal to technological developments to regulate economic and social life according to a settled plan.[14]

The argument of this paper is that Marxist advocates of a non-exploitative, post-capitalist future can express their core concepts and ideals within a catallactic framework, subject to the exceptions noted above. It may even be desirable to do so if one of the motives to eliminate exploitation is the promotion of human autonomy. Conceivably, the free association of equals might be better facilitated by exchange among self-employment firms—thus wedding Marx and Hayek—than through central planning, although

Marxists (and, in this dimension, their Keynesian allies) are more apt to see the need to regulate the competitive behavior of unproductive financial institutions.

Acknowledgment

Thanks to Antonio Callari, Rob Garnett, Xiao Jiang, Dave Kristjanson-Gural, and Bruce Roberts for comments on earlier drafts.

Notes

1 Resnick and Wolff write: "societies with communist class structures...may display property ownerships that range from the fully collective to the very private. They also may exhibit radically different ways of distributing resources and wealth, from full scale central planning to private markets" (2002, 10).
2 Legal authority only: we must acknowledge that these questions are not necessarily decidable by top management. The knowledge, for instance, of alternative productive techniques often lies further down the institutional hierarchy, for instance with the engineers and other specialized talent that John Kenneth Galbraith famously labeled the "technostructure" (2007).
3 A system of universal self-employment is not identical with Wolff's notion of a worker-directed enterprise, since Wolff indicates that productive workers in a firm would hire unproductive workers into an employment relation, but rather invite them to join a firm membership relation. In Wolff's model, productive workers in a firm would use a "portion of the surplus to hire and provide operating budgets as needed to managers, clerks, security guards, lawyers, and other workers not directly engaged in producing surpluses" (Wolff 2012, 124).
4 Robert Frank (2007) makes a compelling argument that there can be external costs associated with *consumption* activity, specifically the consumption of positional (or status-conveying) goods. He argues that society should consider a highly progressive consumption tax to reduce what he calls wasteful "positional arms races."
5 Interestingly, Gaus acknowledges, "personal autonomy can be endangered by extreme inequalities" (2015, 24). In the U.S., extreme inequalities have been generated in the financial sector, which bear upon the importance of interrogating finance in any discussion of Marx and markets, as discussed below.
6 See note 2. In a self-employment firm, all workers, whether classified as productive or unproductive, collectively appropriate the whole product. Such an arrangement is easier to imagine than one in which the firm's, somehow defined, productive workers appropriate the whole product while hiring the firm's, somehow defined, unproductive workers. The joint notions of division of labor and comparative advantage (i.e., that someone absolutely more productive might have a comparative advantage at an unproductive activity) make the distinction, at least inside a productive organization, difficult to operationalize. The difference between productive and unproductive *capital*, however, plays an important role in the following argument.
7 See Fraad et al. (1989) for a discussion of household communism.
8 Keynesian economists, on the other hand, might be potential allies with Marxists regarding understanding finance to be, at least in part, unproductive *and* sometimes destabilizing. Robert Shiller (2013) has explicitly labeled elements of finance as rent seeking, and Hyman Minsky's (1975) financial instability hypothesis roots financial disorder in profit-seeking behavior.

9 Roberts (2014) provides a detailed and comprehensive discussion of the different ways we might conceive the distinction between productive and unproductive.

10 Polanyi (1944) called money a "fictitious commodity," since it is not produced by labor.

11 Mortgage interest, for instance, is often paid out of wages, which Marx called "secondary exploitation" (Marx 1967, 609).

12 Roemer makes a related argument that financial leverage also tends to concentrate profits in the financial sector into the hands of the wealthy few. Originally, he argued that the solution to this problem was to equalize equity financial positions via a coupon stock market (Roemer 1996). Recently, he has rejected that idea since he doubts that it would be politically robust. As he puts it, "I now believe that as long as there is a culture of greed, there will always be people who will be able to succeed in designing a way around the rules and enriching themselves" (Roemer 2013, 58). Thus, he now supports expanding the existing tax and transfer system.

13 Block explicitly draws upon Karl Polanyi's (1944) argument that finance cannot be part of a well-functioning, self-regulating market system.

14 For an attempt to combine planning and wide-scale participation and personal autonomy see Albert and Hahnel (1992). I believe their attempt ultimately falls short (Burczak 2006, 140–44).

References

Ackerman, B. and A. Alstott. 1999. *The Stakeholder Society.* New Haven and London: Yale University Press.

Albert, M. and R. Hahnel. 1992. "Participatory Planning." *Science and Society* 56 (1): 39–59.

Althusser, L. 1969. *For Marx.* Trans. B. Brewster. New York: Pantheon.

Althusser, L. and E. Balibar. 1970. *Reading "Capital."* Trans. B. Brewster. New York: Pantheon.

Amariglio, J. and D. Ruccio. 1998. "Postmodernism, Marxism, and the Critique of Modern Economic Thought." In *Why Economists Disagree*, D. Prychitko, ed., 237–73. Albany, NY: State University of New York Press.

Block, F. 2014. "Democratizing Finance." *Politics and Society* 42 (1): 3–28.

Bowles, S. 2016. *The Moral Economy: Why Good Incentives Are No Substitute for Good Citizens.* New Haven, CT: Yale University Press.

Bowles, S. and H. Gintis. 1999. *Recasting Egalitarianism.* London and New York: Verso.

——— 2011. *A Cooperative Species.* Princeton, NJ: Princeton University Press.

Burczak, T. 2006. *Socialism after Hayek.* Ann Arbor, MI: University of Michigan Press.

Callari, A. 2009. "A Methodological Reflection on the 'Thick Socialism' of *Socialism after Hayek.*" *Review of Social Economy* 67 (3): 367–73.

Cottrell, A. and P. Cockshott. 2008. "Computers and Economic Democracy." *Revista de Economía Institucional* 10 (19). https://ssrn.com/abstract=1316880 (accessed June 20, 2017).

Dobb, M. 1937. "Economic Law in the Socialist Commonwealth." In *Political Economy and Capitalism.* New York: International Publishers.

Ellerman, D. 1992. *Property and Contract in Economics.* Cambridge, MA: Blackwell.

Engels, F. [1892] 1978. *Socialism: Utopian and Scientific.* In *The Marx-Engels Reader*, 2nd ed., R. Tucker, ed., 683–717. New York and London: W. W. Norton.

Foley, D. 2013. "Rethinking Financial Capitalism and the 'Information' Economy." *Review of Radical Political Economics* 45 (3): 257–68.

Fraad, H., S. Resnick, and R. Wolff. 1989. "For Every Knight in Shining Armor, There's a Castle Waiting to Be Cleaned." *Rethinking Marxism* 2 (4): 9–69.

Frank, R. 2007. *Falling Behind. How Rising Inequality Harms the Middle Class.* Berkeley, CA: University of California Press.

Friedman, M. 1962. *Capitalism and Freedom.* Chicago, IL: University of Chicago Press.

Galbraith, J. K. 2007. *The New Industrial State.* Princeton, NJ: Princeton University Press.

Gaus, J. 2015. "The Egalitarian Species." *Social Philosophy and Policy* 31 (2): 1–27.

Hayek, F. 1945. "The Use of Knowledge in Society." *American Economic Review* 35 (4): 519–30.

—— 1960. *The Constitution of Liberty.* Chicago, IL: University of Chicago Press.

—— 1976. *Law, Legislation, and Liberty, vol. II. The Mirage of Social Justice.* Chicago, IL: University of Chicago Press.

—— 2007. *The Road to Serfdom. Text and Documents: The Definitive Edition*, B. Caldwell, ed. Chicago: University of Chicago Press.

Jossa, B. 2014. *Producer Cooperatives as a New Mode of Production.* London and New York: Routledge.

Kristjanson-Gural, D. 2011. "Value, Cooperatives, and Class Justice." *Rethinking Marxism* 23 (3): 352–63.

Lange, O. [1936] 1966. "On the Economic Theory of Socialism." In *On the Economic Theory of Socialism*, B. Lippincott, ed., 55–141. New York: McGraw Hill.

Lapavisas, C. 2013. *Profiting without Producing: How Finance Exploits Us All.* London and New York: Verso.

Marx, K. 1965. *Value, Price, and Profit.* Peking: Foreign Language Press.

—— 1967. *Capital.* Vol. 3. Ed. F. Engels. New York: International Publishers.

—— [1844] 1978. "Economic and Philosophic Manuscripts of 1844." In *The Marx-Engels Reader*, 2nd ed., R. Tucker, ed., 66–125. New York and London: W. W. Norton.

—— [1867] 1978. *Capital.* Vol. 1. In *The Marx-Engels Reader*, 2nd ed., R. Tucker, ed., 294–438. New York and London: W. W. Norton.

—— [1891] 1978. "Critique of the Gotha Program". In *The Marx-Engels Reader*, 2nd ed., R. Tucker, ed., 525–41. New York and London: W. W. Norton.

Marx, K. and F. Engels. [1848] 1978. *Manifesto of the Communist Party.* In *The Marx-Engels Reader*, 2nd ed., R. Tucker, ed., 469–500. New York and London: W. W. Norton.

Minsky H. 1975. *John Maynard Keynes.* New York: Columbia University Press.

Paine, T. [1797] 2000. "Agrarian Justice." In *The Origins of Left-Libertarianism*, P. Vallentyne and H. Steiner, eds., 81–98. Basingstoke and New York: Palgrave Macmillan.

Polanyi, K. 1944. *The Great Transformation.* New York and Toronto: Farrar & Rinehart, Inc.

Resnick, S. and R. Wolff. 1987. *Knowledge and Class.* Chicago, IL: University of Chicago Press.

—— 2002. *Class Theory and History.* London and New York: Routledge.

Roberts, B. 2011. "Exploitation, Appropriation, and Subsumption." *Rethinking Marxism* 23 (3): 341–51.

——— 2014. "Productive/ Unproductive: Conceptual Topology." *Rethinking Marxism* 26 (3): 336–59.

Roemer, J. 1996. *Equal Shares.* London and New York: Verso.

——— 2013. "Thoughts on the Arrangement of Property Rights in Productive Assets." *Analyse & Kritik* 35: 55–65.

Ruccio, D. 2011. "Cooperatives, Surplus, and the Social." *Rethinking Marxism* 23 (3): 334–40.

Sciabarra, C. 1995. *Marx, Hayek, and Utopia.* Albany, NY: State University of New York Press.

Screpanti, E. 2004. "Freedom and Social Goods." *Rethinking Marxism* 16 (2): 185–206.

——— 2008. *Libertarian Communism.* Basingstoke and New York: Palgrave Macmillan.

Shiller, R. 2013. "The Best, Brightest, and Least Productive?" *Project Syndicate* (September 20). www.project-syndicate.org/commentary/the-rent-seeking-problem-in-contemporary-finance-by-robert-j--shiller (accessed June 12, 2016).

Simon, H. 1991. "Organizations and Markets." *Journal of Economic Perspectives* 5 (2): 25–44.

Wolff, R. 2012. *Democracy at Work: A Cure for Capitalism.* Chicago: Haymarket.

——— 2014. "Socialism and Workers' Self-Directed Enterprises." *Monthly Review* (September 14). http://mrzine.monthlyreview.org/2014/wolff140914.html (accessed June 12, 2016).

Wolff, R. and S. Resnick. 2012. *Contending Economic Theories. Neoclassical, Keynesian, and Marxian.* Cambridge, MA: MIT Press.

Part III
Labor, value, and class

7 Class and overdetermination

Value theory and the core of Resnick and Wolff's Marxism

Bruce Roberts

Introduction

As someone who, over the years, has had the pleasure and privilege to learn from and work with Stephen Resnick and Rick Wolff, I take it as a pleasure and a privilege to reflect on their legacy. I came to UMass, Amherst, as a graduate student in economics in 1975, as a member of the second class admitted in full awareness of the new "radical" program there. I left, ABD ("all-but-dissertation"), to take my first professional job in 1979; my Ph.D. thesis, bearing the signatures of both Wolff and Resnick, was completed and defended in 1981. Those years changed my life.

Those were years of change for Resnick and Wolff, as well. The courses they each taught in fall 1975 reflected their prior work, with no indication of what was to come. A year later, new European influences were prominent, and drafts of papers with a new set of categories and concerns began to circulate. Three years after that, the first published versions of the Resnick and Wolff reading of Marxism began to appear, and in 1987, barely a decade from the first appearance of their new approach, the publication of *Knowledge and Class* solidified the presence of a distinctive new Marxian problematic. A year later, with the appearance of *Rethinking Marxism*, references to the "Amherst School" of Marxism were becoming common.

From the 21st-century perspective, Resnick and Wolff (R&W) are recognized mainly for their focus on class and overdetermination: class as entry point and focus for (mostly qualitative) analyses of social conjunctures, overdetermination as both an epistemological premise (anti-essentialism) and a methodological principle.

The path they took in developing these views is my topic.

There is, I think, a stylized intellectual history in the minds of some observers in which R&W, stimulated by their initial exposure to Althusser and other Europeans, moved from their more traditional American Marxism, gradually opening their perspective to more broadly postmodern trends in philosophy and cultural criticism, leaving their "roots" behind. In this view their journey is a movement away from the traditional concerns of Marxian economics into new territory where older questions and terminology have been superseded by a different epistemological and social agenda, the territory of "postmodern Marxism."

There is undoubtedly some truth in this. *Knowledge and Class* (*K&C*) self-consciously affirms its differences from other Marxian views, and the pivotal place of "overdetermination" in their thinking about both knowledge and class certainly has distinctive consequences. But, I will argue, the stylized notion of a movement from old to new is less accurate than it might appear at first glance. The intellectual journey of R&W never followed a direct path from one position to another, different one; it was a much more circuitous process in which the key steps always involved a return to and rethinking of the core theory in Marx's *Capital*. Instead of a journey from Marx via Althusser to postmodernism, in a real sense they never left Marx at all. Every step they took was motivated and shaped by the same fundamental focus with which they began, a focus on the categories of value and surplus-value and the ways Marx used and developed these categories as the keys to understanding class in capitalism.

In what follows, I develop two themes: (1) R&W's engagement with value categories and the methodology of value analysis is underappreciated as a factor overdetermining both the genesis of and the evolving form taken by their distinctive approach and (2) the choices R&W made concerning value-related issues, in particular the assumptions they imposed, play a consequential role in shaping the class taxonomy that occupies the central place in *K&C*.

Overdetermination

When R&W encountered, criticized, and assimilated Althusser starting in the mid-1970s, they chose to make explicit, extensive use of his concept of overdetermination (earlier borrowed by Althusser, with reservations, from Freud) (Althusser 1977, 101ff and 209). Overdetermination functions, for both Althusser and R&W, as a general premise about the nature and centrality of *relations.* In a late essay, Althusser invokes this core sense of overdetermination in his comment that Marx's theory "presupposes the idea of a causality through relations and not by elements" (1991, 26). On this premise, the terms in a relation are not independent elements that exist prior to or independently of their relationship, instead the terms are literally *constituted by* the relationship of which they are the terms.[1] For R&W, this means that every distinguishable entity we might consider (event, text, social practice or process) is simply a "site" for interactions with all other sites. The notion embraces a complex conception of causality: while mutual and reciprocal causality is certainly a part of the concept, overdetermination additionally implies relations of "constitutivity," the power of each term in a relation to not merely *affect* other terms (i.e., produce changes that then ripple outwards with further consequences) but also to *effect* them, constitute them, participate in determining the *nature* of, not merely the further changes in, every other term with which it is in relation.

In considering the significance of overdetermination as a premise in the works of R&W, there are at least three distinct varieties or dimensions of "relations" that potentially come into play:

(a) relations between theoretical objects and "real" objects taken to be external to discourse;
(b) relations between theoretical objects and other theoretical objects;
(c) relations between concepts within discourse and other concepts within discourse.

Relations (a) above refer to the terrain of epistemology, the basis for knowledge claims (i.e., the "knowledge" content invoked by the title of *K&C*). R&W follow Althusser in viewing Marx as having radically rejected the notion of theory validation via a demonstrable "correspondence" between theoretical objects and real objects; if Marx's thinking emerged as a product of an "epistemological break" from prior conceptions of validity, then the guarantees offered by empiricist and rationalist epistemologies must be set aside. If the act of theorizing is simply an overdetermined moment within a network of relations to all the various non-theoretical practices in its context, then the validity of a theory's claims is something it produces for itself and within itself, alongside the similarly constituted knowledge claims of other theoretical practices.

Relations (b) refer to the nature of the objects constituted by and within theory, the relations of parts and wholes within the "totality" constructed by theory, in particular the social totality (encompassing the "class" content in the title of *K&C*). R&W build from Althusser to a thoroughgoing anti-determinist position, opposing theoretical essentialism or reductionism in every instance (including the last). Their conception of society and economy, of social structure and transition, views the processes expressing class as one site among others, overdetermining but also overdetermined by the other processes that provide its conditions of existence. Class is their theoretical "point of entry," the organizing principle and chosen focus of their Marxian discourse, but not the independent or ultimate determinant of social development.

Given that R&W choose to understand knowledge in terms of the overdetermination of thinking by its relations within the social context, and class as an overdetermined process existing in relation to others within a broader social totality, how should they approach the active *construction* of *conceptions* of these and other (overdetermined) objects? How—by what discursive strategy or method—does Marxist theory go about building a discourse that *adequately poses its objects as overdetermined*?

This is where relations (c) come into play. Only through the deliberate construction of relations between concepts within discourse does theory produce whatever "knowledge effects" it has. "The entities that discourse refers to are constituted in it and by it . . . the connections between the objects [of discourse] can only be conceived as a function of the forms of discourse in which those objects are specified" (Hindess and Hirst 1977, 23, 20). Some terminology (adapted from Althusser's usage) is helpful here. We can distinguish, on the one hand, the connections developed in discourse *between the concepts* that discourse deploys and, on the other, the connections (produced by means of connected concepts) *between the objects* those concepts designate; the former can be referred to as the "diachrony" of the discourse, the latter as its "synchrony."[2] In other words, synchrony refers to characteristics of the constructed *object* of discourse, while diachrony designates the formal development of the discourse, the steps, the protocols governing strategy—in short, the *method*—by which some particular form of synchrony is produced. So, in R&W's understanding of Marxism, overdetermination describes the synchronic nature of the to-be-constructed *object* of discourse, giving a particular form to the relations (a), concerning knowledge, and (b), concerning class, that R&W seek to produce. But what are the implications of overdetermination for the diachrony of their discourse? By what (diachronic) method does R&W's Marxism produce an overdetermined (synchronic) object of discourse? Stating that "everything is overdetermined" is certainly not enough.[3]

Value theory and the method of class analysis

The direct concerns that dominate *K&C* and its predecessor papers are mostly synchronic (how do we understand knowledge? how do we understand social structure and the role of class?), but questions of diachrony, of method, are always present as well. Indeed, the ongoing effort, explicit in both R&W's writing and their teaching, to specify the criteria distinguishing Marxism from alternative theories, and their Marxism from alternative readings, is as much a matter of contrasting methods as of contrasting theory content.

There is an evolving position on method that gradually takes shape in the early R&W papers from the late 1970s. Their first joint publication in the "new" mode ("The Theory of Transitional Conjunctures and the Transition from Feudalism to Capitalism in Western Europe," hereafter *TTC*) appeared in print in 1979 (Resnick and Wolff, 1979a), although earlier drafts were circulating at UMass by late 1976 or 1977. In *TTC*, the relatively brief direct discussions of method invoke the language of Marx's early and somewhat cryptic passage on "The Method of Political Economy" (Marx 1973) in which he asserts that the "obviously ... correct method" involves "rising from the abstract to the concrete" and Althusser's (*For Marx*) elaborations on that passage. R&W write: "Marxian theoretical production begins with a notion of class which it then proceeds to elaborate toward ever more concrete specification and precision" (*TTC*, 7); "discourse ... transforms abstract into concrete concepts of class relations" (*TTC*, 9).

Several of R&W's phrasings in *TTC* show Althusser's influence. When they say that "general" concepts function as the "means for ... specification of alternative particular types of class relations" (*TTC*, 9), there is an unacknowledged, though I think intentional, echo of Althusser's posing of theory in terms of "Generalities I, II, and III": Generalities I, initial abstract concepts, the "raw material" of theoretical practice; Generalities III, the concrete-in-thought, the knowledge "output" of theoretical practice; Generalities II, the "means of production" by which theory "transforms" its raw materials (GI) and produces its outputs (GIII), rising from abstract to concrete (Althusser 1977, 184).

For R&W in *TTC* (as for Althusser in *For Marx*), these early formulations are more accurately seen as descriptions of the evolving form of the *synchronic* object of discourse (as GI becomes GIII), rather than elaborations of the *diachronic* construction of that object (detailing the theoretical work of transformation designated by GII). But there is, nonetheless, the germ of a more specific notion of method. Just as Althusser, having posed the concept of overdetermination in Marxian discourse, draws from it the immediate conclusion that "categories can no longer have a role and meaning fixed once and for all" (1977, 209), R&W similarly draw from overdetermination a "discursive logic" in which "the initial category [is] now changed by the process of theory [as the] object of that analysis" (*TTC*, 9). This notion, that theory acts to transform and *change its concepts* through the process of their application, present but initially vague in *TTC*, was simultaneously emerging in a much more explicit form in another part of the broader R&W research program.

In early summer 1977, Wolff approached two graduate students (Antonio Callari and Bruce Roberts), proposing a collaborative research effort on Marx's theory of value; we would begin with an intensive joint reading of Marx's works of mature theory, and then on that basis produce a collective paper on what made Marx's approach to value analysis unique. While production of that paper was the explicit goal, the research process was intended to support our ongoing dissertation work, with R&W as dissertation supervisors. Six months later, in winter 1977–78, R&W launched a broader collaborative effort by inviting a larger group of graduate students to join in discussions of Marxian ideas more generally, with the long-term goal of founding a new academic journal of Marxian theory. During spring 1978, the "Journal Group" began regular meetings to present and debate our various dissertation projects in light of emerging contemporary literatures (Figure 7.1).

The Wolff-Roberts-Callari (WRC) collaboration on value theory rapidly focused on diachronic issues of method, examining in detail how Marx's GIII are produced from GI, how the GII work of transformation proceeds (not

<u>Fall 1975</u>
- Wolff teaches graduate Marxian Economic Theory ("Marx I") to a large class; syllabus focuses on Marxian value and crisis theory (no references yet to "Althusserian" literature).
- Resnick teaches graduate European Economic History course, focusing on the transition from feudalism to capitalism (no references yet to "Althusserian" literature).

<u>Spring-Summer 1976</u>
- R&W continue to read widely in European Marxism, working from Hindess and Hirst (*Pre-capitalist Modes of Production*) to Althusser and Balibar (*Reading Capital*).
- R&W work on a draft that eventually becomes the "Transition" paper.

<u>Fall 1976</u>
- Wolff teaches graduate "Marx II" course; reading list focuses on Hegel and commentators on Hegel (Kojeve, Hyppolite), Marx's relation to Hegel (Althusser), and Marx's method (Althusser and Hindess/Hirst) R&W generally focused on "the epistemological break" and theoretical anti-essentialism.

<u>Spring 1977</u>
- R&W circulate a draft of the "Transition" paper at UMass
- R&W work on developing the class typology that later appears in their "Concepts of Classes in Marxian Theory" (I) paper.

<u>Summer 1977</u>
- Wolff initiates collaboration with Bruce Roberts and Antonio Callari (WRC) with the goal of producing a paper on Marx's value theory as well as supporting the ongoing dissertation work of Roberts and Callari and WRC undertake intensive group re-reading of Marx's mature texts.

<u>Fall 1977</u>
- R&W work on a draft of "Concepts of Classes."
- WRC begin drafting paper on value in Ricardo and Marx.

<u>Winter 1977–78</u>
- R&W approach selected graduate students, proposing a collaborative effort to launch a new journal of Marxian theory; the "Journal Group" begins regular meetings to discuss Marxian ideas and students' dissertation research.

<u>Spring 1978</u>
- Wolff teaches a small graduate workshop ("Marx III"); announced course goals include developing a Marxist conception of the distinction between Marxist and non-Marxist discourses ("what Marxist Theory thinks theory is"); initial section consists of lecture (with readings including Foucault, Williams, Lecourt, as well as Althusser and Hindess and Hirst) as prelude to detailed study of Marx's *Capital*; final two-thirds of the course is composed of student-led seminar discussion of topics in *Capital*, particularly volumes 2 and 3, as a means to "explore (i.e., develop) the method in Marx."
- Wolff publishes "Marx's Theory of Crisis" in the *Review of Radical Political Economy* (article cites no "Althusserian" sources).
- WRC complete draft of "Marxian and Ricardian Economics: Fundamental Differences"; Callari and Roberts present the paper at the History of Economics Society conference in Toronto, May 1978.

Figure 7.1 Timeline of Resnick and Wolff's intellectual activities, 1975–82.

Fall 1978
- Journal Group meetings continue; members present dissertation prospectuses and R&W papers are discussed.
- R&W circulate draft of "Concepts of Classes" ("Classes I"), then continue work on its sequel/continuation ("Classes II").

Spring 1979
- WRC submit revised version of their paper, now titled "Ricardian and Marxian Economics: A Different View of Value-Price Transformation"
- R&W circulate draft of "Classes II" paper.

Fall 1979
- R&W publish "The Theory of Transitional Conjunctures and the Transition from Feudalism to Capitalism in Western Europe" in the *Review of Radical Political Economy*, along with "Reply to Herb Gintis" (whose critique of R&W was published along with their paper).

1982
- R&W publish "Classes in Marxian Theory" in *RRPE* (a revised version that condensed, combined, and developed the earlier "Classes I" and "Classes II" papers).
- WRC publish their (still further) revised paper, now titled "Marx's (not Ricardo's) 'Transformation Problem': A Radical Reconceptualization," in *History of Political Economy*.

Figure 7.1 (Continued)

surprisingly, the value-theoretic focus was the "transformation problem"!). Over the academic year 1977–78, while R&W were drafting their paper, "The Concepts of Classes in Marxian Theory" (hereafter *Classes I*), WRC produced a draft paper (the first version, which ultimately evolved into two further distinct versions) titled "Marxian and Ricardian Economics: Fundamental Differences" (hereafter *WRC1*). That initial paper sets up several broad distinguishing features of Marx's approach (its distinctive object, method, etc.) in order to then, on that basis, dispute the dominant (neo)-Ricardian interpretation of Marx's volume 3 transformation as a problem of deriving competitive prices and profits from pre-given values and surplus-values, the latter magnitudes treated as independently determined by the physical-technical conditions of production alone (Wolff, Roberts and Callari, 1978a).

The argument in that initial paper concerning method can be sketched as follows. Given his understanding of capitalist class relations as "a complex web of interacting determinations," Marx's theoretical strategy seeks to "weave together the various determinations" in an argument that proceeds through different "levels" of discourse (*WRC1*, 14). Volumes 1 and 3 are different levels, distinguished by the initial absence of "specifically capitalist commodity circulation" (*WRC1*, 15). "Volume 1 is not in any sense a total theory of the capitalist economy. . . . [I]t is merely the completion of one stage of the discursive development of such a theory" (*WRC1*, 49). At this stage, "the definitions of value and value form in Volume 1 were provisional and artificial precisely because they abstracted from the effectivity of capitalist circulation" (*WRC1*, 30). At the next level, though, "it is necessary to rethink, in explicitly capitalist terms, the manner in which social labor is expressed in numerical form" (*WRC1*, 49). "Marx in Volume 3 … is … engaged in a process of reconceptualizing the meaning of the general definition of commodity value, particularizing it, applying that definition" to the new circumstances posed by fully capitalist competition in the circulation of commodities (*WRC1*, 51).

> The concept of a commodity's value is consistently defined and maintained, but this definition is composed of terms ('socially necessary,' 'reproduction') whose meaning … must necessarily evolve with the discursive elaboration of the capitalist basis of commodity production and exchange.
>
> (*WRC1*, 52)

More precisely, concerning this change in meaning:

> The value of commodity output … is constructed in part from the *price of production of the* [consumed] *constant capital goods*," since it is the advance of a quantity of value equal to "*this* magnitude … and not the number of physically embodied labor hours … which takes account of the crucial ['socially necessary'] role played by capitalist exchange as a condition of existence, a precondition, of continued capitalist production.
>
> (*WRC1*, 51)

This initial version of the WRC argument was almost immediately revised to incorporate an improved mathematical exposition, but the basic thesis remained in the second draft ("Ricardian and Marxian Economics: A Different View of Value-Price Transformation," *WRC2*), produced in fall 1978 (Wolff, Roberts, and Callari, 1978b).

Simultaneously, R&W were circulating their *Classes I* paper, which offers a similar characterization of Marx's discursive method. In *Classes I*, R&W explicitly cite Althusser's GI, II, III schema in elaborating their own views more explicitly:

> We distinguish our formulation of Marxian theory … by means of our distinct specification of the [GII] concepts (overdetermination, contradiction, processes, practices, etc.) and our distinct specification of the [GI] concepts as the class process and its conditions of existence. Our [GII] concepts define what we understand as the methodology of dialectical materialism.
>
> (*Classes I*, 15)

In two passages, they then describe the methodology consistent with overdetermination in more specific terms. "[T]he object of [*Capital, I*] is the capitalist class process. The class process is the extraction of surplus labor;

its capitalist form is the extraction of surplus value. ... The formal discourse of *Capital* exemplifies the method of Marxist theory" (*Classes I*, 18).

> In *Capital, I*, ... [Marx's] concept of surplus value presupposes the initial economic concepts of commodity, value, use-value, exchange-value, value-forms, and money presented in the earliest chapters.... . These conceptions are all highly abstract, initial, and provisional; they abstract from the complex and contradictory influences of ... even other economic processes that overdetermine the capitalist class process. As these abstract concepts are elaborated to ever more concretely construct the capitalist class process in its inter-relationship with all the other processes that comprise its conditions of existence, these initial concepts will themselves be changed.
>
> (*Classes I*, 31)

"Initially posed abstract concepts ... are elaborated – transformed conceptually – into more complexly determined concepts" (*Classes I*, 18). Each of these passages (on pp. 18 and 31) describing Marx's methodological development of "more complexly determined concepts" then ends with a footnote directly citing the *WRC2* treatment of the evolving conception of commodity value (notes 12 and 23).

With respect to the understanding of method, these two simultaneous research projects (R&W on class and WRC on value) were clearly benefiting from a "cross-pollination" of ideas. But with respect to content (the object of analysis), there was also significant overlap, more so than may be apparent initially. R&W present their class typology—"fundamental" and "subsumed" classes—as a means to both formalize and extend Marx's value analysis in *Capital*. The concept of subsumed classes appears early on: in *TTC*, it plays a central role in the narrative concerning multi-faceted class struggles in the transition from feudalism to capitalism. Distinct from fundamental classes (initially defined as "performers and extractors of surplus labor"), a subsumed class is "a group which can control exclusively one or another of the conditions of existence of a surplus-extracting class," which then "permits a subsumed class to obtain a transfer of some portion of extracted surplus value from the extracting class" (*TTC*, 8). In *Classes I*, R&W present the category of subsumed class as their "design for encompassing several suggestions scattered throughout Marx's work," in some of his "conjunctural, political analyses" but "more importantly, [in] his complex treatment of merchants, money-lenders and capitalist ... landlords [in] *Capital* 3, Parts IV, V, and VI" (*Classes I*, 27 and note 19).

Resnick and Wolff view their class typology as providing the vocabulary to develop Marx's value theory: in effect, *Capital* 1 poses the *production* of surplus-value (through surplus labor performed within the capitalist fundamental class process) as an initial, relatively abstract conception, and the bulk of *Capital* 3 then rises to a more concrete level by integrating subsumed class processes (providing conditions of existence for surplus-value extraction) as the means of *distribution* and ultimately disposition of that surplus-value. In the published article "Class in Marxian Theory" (*CMT*) that emerged in 1982 from their prior "Classes" papers, R&W make its value-theoretic inspiration quite explicit: they refer to the accounting relations underlying their conjunctural discussions (of taxes, child-rearing, etc.) as "Marxist value equations" (*CMT*, 15) and insist that "Marx's complex class analysis is far more consistently grounded in Marx's value theory than the alternative formulations of the critics" (*CMT*, 2). For R&W, conjunctural class analysis is value theory in application, in action.[4]

The publication of the "Classes in Marxian Theory" (*CMT*) paper in 1982 can be seen as the culmination of the formative period of R&W's theoretical collaboration. That paper, in many ways a direct predecessor to *Knowledge and Class*, no longer contains much of the methodological discussion prominent in previous drafts (the focus is the class categories themselves), but when one reads, in order, the sequence of R&W writings from this period (1977–82), the impact of their value-theoretic concerns in the (uneven) development of their distinctive approach becomes clearer. Their class typology (fundamental and subsumed classes) grew directly from their post-Althusser (re)reading of the value analytics in *Capital 1* and *3*, and their understanding of method—Marx's and their own—took its shape, in part, through cross-pollination with the parallel explicit study of the methodology of value theory in the WRC papers. As argued above, a theory constructed, like theirs, posing class as its object based on the premise of overdetermination faces particular methodological challenges—an overdetermined synchronic object of discourse can be produced only by means of a distinctive diachronic development. That development, in turn, necessarily proceeds in stages. Introducing "new determinations" (capitalist circulation, subsumed class processes) does not simply *add* something to prior conceptualizations; it *reconstitutes*—changes the nature of the overdetermined whole: a differently overdetermined object of discourse must then be produced by means of a differently articulated application of basic concepts. Respecting overdetermination requires this repeated effort of particularization.

In *Knowledge and Class*, R&W give an explicit example, explaining how the concept of "the capitalist" undergoes just this process of change through reapplication. In *Capital 1*, Marx "personifies [exploitation] in its human embodiment, the capitalist," who owns, commands, lends, buys, and sells, as well as exploiting via the capture of surplus labor (*K&C*, 205). But as the discourse progresses, "the capitalist" is transformed: "The meaning of Marx's concept of the capitalist, like that of all other concepts, changes throughout the discourse as Marx introduces ever new concepts in his task of constructing a knowledge of capitalism. The meaning of each of these concepts is overdetermined by the effects of all others upon it. Each changes its meaning as these effects change. The notion of a capitalist in volume 3's construction is far different from that in volume 1 because of the more elaborated knowledge of capitalism Marx presents there..." including "the third volume's subsumed classes, absent from the first volume, [who] secure ... social processes" that "were not the subject of ... analysis in volume 1 ... with its limited focus on the fundamental class process. ... In contrast [to the volume-1 capitalist], the volume-3 capitalist ... is more richly and strictly delimited as one who only exploits labor" while others, including subsumed classes, "perform those social processes required for surplus value's existence" (*K&C*, 205–207).

Value and surplus value in *Knowledge and Class*

I have so far argued that engagement with Marx's value theory was central in the theoretical evolution provoked by R&W's encounter with overdetermination. But since, from Althusser's initial presentation onward, "overdetermination and contradiction" go hand in hand, it goes almost without saying that theoretical development is always uneven, never smooth. R&W's commitments in terms of object and method inevitably provoke choices, with consequences that are not always immediately obvious. The rethinking of value and surplus value in the WRC papers initially cited by R&W poses potential questions.

The more developed version of WRC's paper on value ("Marx's (not Ricardo's) 'Transformation Problem': A Radical Reconceptualization," *WRC3*) was published in 1982, the same year as R&W's "Class in Marxian Theory."[5] There is no explicit treatment of subsumed classes in *WRC3*, but the argument there has potential implications for the value accounting of subsumed class distributions, so a recapitulation of relevant portions of that argument is helpful (Wolff, Roberts, and Callari, 1982).

Consider Marx's familiar representation of the circuit of industrial capital: M – C {Production} C' – M', where value-creation in production is both preceded and followed by exchanges – purchases of inputs and sale of outputs. WRC argue that the task of volume 1 is to show in a provisional way how capitalist income (resulting when M' > M) derives from unpaid labor-time,[6] and this is facilitated by a "carefully chosen device of discourse": Marx's volume 1 assumption ("value-equivalent exchange") that "the particular circulation processes under consideration tend to establish exchange ratios ... determined *solely in production*" (*WRC3*, 569). This means that "each exchange, and therefore the process of circulation encompassing all exchanges, is so specified as to effect no transformation of the quantity of value held by the commodity owner before and after the sale or purchase" (*WRC3*, 570). In terms of value, M = C and C'= M'. Hence, the "social labor-time attached to commodities in production"—"socially necessary" labor—"becomes identical to the ... labor-time physically-technically embodied in the commodity under average conditions of productivity" (*WRC3*, 570). And with circulation thus deliberately pushed "out of the way," not merely value but also surplus value is effectively determined by production conditions: given the reproduction requirements for labor-power, the magnitude of surplus value is governed by technical production conditions (the labor-time technically required to produce the commodities that reproduce labor-power). Thus in volume 1, by assumption, surplus value is independent of exchange and independent of whatever happens to surplus value as it is subsequently distributed.

But in volume 3 Marx drops these assumptions and allows for fully capitalist conditions in both production and circulation—"new determinations" are admitted, in particular a new form for some of the key conditions of existence of capitalist class relations. With fully capitalist competition, equivalence in exchange (at "prices of production") now requires that "commodities with different values ... nevertheless must exchange as equals" (*WRC3*, 573), i.e., in value terms, $M' \neq$ the value of C'. Thus, the exchanges on each side of {Production} entail transfers of value—indeed, in *every capitalist* transaction, equivalent or non-equivalent, value and surplus value are transferred. As argued in prior versions of WRC, "socially necessary" labor in volume 3 is no longer reduced to "physically/technically necessary" labor, with the result that value *and also surplus value* (which is, as Marx repeatedly insists, *unpaid* labor) are no longer determined without reference to exchange conditions.

> Marx's theoretical commitment to overdetermination implies his particular methodological approach ... The fact that surplus value is distributed via commodity circulation necessarily involves the circulation process in the determination of value. Surplus labor in its distinctively capitalist form is *unpaid* labor, labor time for which no equivalent is received; the magnitude of surplus value can therefore only be determined in conjunction with the capitalist structure of payment equivalence in market exchanges.
>
> (*WRC3*, 576)[7]

This argument has potential implications for any change in the level of discourse where "new determinations" are admitted – for example, subsumed class activities as the means of providing conditions of existence for capital. Marx dealt with value-price transformation prior to the subsequent chapters in volume 3 that take up merchants and other subsumed classes, and even though in those chapters (edited and compiled after Marx's death) he only occasionally makes explicit reference to production prices, he regularly invokes the capitalist general rate of profit that presumes them. R&W, however, choose to proceed in their presentations of the subsumed class concept from the premise that, as in volume 1, surplus value is determined prior to and independently of its distribution.

In *CMT* (and subsequently in a more detailed fashion in *K&C*), R&W ground their class analytics in what they see as a basic capitalist accounting identity: the total surplus-value produced is definitionally equal to the total of the subsumed-class distributions made out of that surplus-value (in *CMT*, they express it as S = ∑SC, although it appears that the equals sign should really be an identity sign). In itself, this assumes nothing about the determination of the magnitudes on each side of the equation. But in *K&C*, R&W explain:

> In the case of the specifically capitalist form of the fundamental class process, the subsumed class process refers to the distribution of already appropriated surplus value. As the fundamental class process is the production of surplus value by one class for another, so the subsumed class process is the subsequent distribution of that surplus to other classes.
>
> (118)

The phrasing is telling: by referring to subsumed class distribution as an action "subsequent" to the "already" accomplished appropriation of surplus value, R&W presume the circumstances of volume 1 in which the magnitude of surplus value is determined in production prior to any subsequent dispositions of it. This assumption is made even more explicit a few pages later in *K&C*, when R&W begin their analysis of "the capitalist enterprise engaged in the production of *capitalist commodities*" by stating: "Since our main concern here is the capitalist enterprise, we do not present any further elaboration of these commodities such as would be necessary if we considered their prices of production" (*K&C*, 161).

This is a (diachronic) choice, and it is one with consequences for the nature of the (synchronic) object of discourse. To be clear, the decision to abstract from prices of production and the circumstances that give rise to them (fully capitalist competition in circulation, as described in WRC) means that R&W accept, by default, the basic circulation premise of volume 1: value-equivalent exchange as the norm or "center of gravity." This has three related consequences: (1) values and also surplus values are governed, as in volume 1, by a restricted set of determinants (technical production conditions and the reproduction requirements of labor-powers)—prices simply reflect values and thus have *no independent impact* on value and surplus value magnitudes; (2) surplus value, embodied in C′ and realized in its value-equivalent M′, is given *independent of the subsequent distribution* or disposition of that surplus value; (3) all distributions of surplus value are thus *symmetrical*; all can be understood in the same way as portions distributed out of the "already appropriated" surplus value realized in M′. R&W do not explain why they adopt this diachronic strategy in *K&C*, but several potential reasons can be inferred.

First, it seems that symmetry itself has appeal.[8] In *K&C* (unlike their prior papers), R&W make no distinction between "types" of subsumed classes. All subsumed class revenues are alike as distributions paid out of already appropriated surplus value to secure some condition of existence. The assumption of value-equivalent exchange does not *preclude* an effort to draw distinctions between "types" of subsumed class distribution, but neither does it require or even *encourage* such an effort (whereas the alternative premise of *capitalist* exchange equivalence à la volume 3 does immediately suggest some structural distinctions, as discussed below). So the value-equivalence assumption in *K&C* is fully consistent with the symmetrical treatment of subsumed class distributions toward which R&W seem to have been moving anyway.

Second, R&W seem to regard their treatment as following Marx's own. They document several quotes from Marx, especially those where he critiques the "Trinity Theory," which state or imply that the aggregate magnitude of surplus value (for them, the outcome of the capitalist fundamental class process) is given prior to and independently of the forms and magnitudes of the (subsumed class) incomes that are subsequently distributed from it (*K&C*, 119; 319, n. 139). Indeed, other Marxists with no particular interest in or allegiance to the concept of overdetermination also lay great stress on quotations supporting the independence of aggregate surplus value from its various parts, e.g., Moseley (1993). So there is, arguably, textual support in Marx for treating surplus value as a magnitude independent of its distribution.

Third and most important, R&W clearly regard their assumptions as enabling a simpler and thus more effective pursuit of their principal goal in *K&C*, the class analysis of social sites (enterprise, state, etc.), of the "complex contradictions" and "tensions that characterize each class position" within these sites, and the resulting "possibilities of class and non-class struggles" (*K&C*, 164). R&W seek to understand the "ripple effects" of events, the consequences through time when struggles alter outcomes and thus overdetermine a subsequent cascade of further changes. Presenting a series of open-ended narratives suggesting possible overdetermined trajectories illuminated through the concept of class—what I will describe below as "story-telling" in the best sense—is their driving purpose, and the diachronic steps they take are those they believe will facilitate that purpose.

I don't want to characterize their choice with regard to value and surplus value as "wrong" or as some sort of methodological "mistake." But it's not a choice I would make, for two reasons: First, presuming value-equivalent exchange precludes certain distinctions that are arguably worth making in understanding subsumed classes: it homogenizes some of the richness of the *re*distributive processes in the capitalist marketplace. Second, treating surplus value as independent of its uses is problematic with regard to overdetermination and the discursive strategy that WRC (and also R&W, in previous work) had argued is needed in order to respect overdetermination as a methodological premise.

On the first point: even before considering merchants, bankers, and other subsumed classes in volume 3, Marx introduces a competitive rate of profit and its associated prices, different from values; the WRC papers argue that this implies systematic redistributions of value and surplus value in every exchange, affecting the meaning and magnitude of surplus value understood as *unpaid* labor (labor in excess of the equivalent payment for labor-power). With this as a basis, if discourse proceeds to integrate subsumed classes as part of capital's conditions of existence, it is possible to distinguish three structurally different types of subsumed class activity, which lead to structurally different varieties of surplus value "distribution":

(i)   where subsumed class revenues arise from activities that *directly* alter the price structure (thus altering the redistribution of value and surplus value already present in every capitalist payment, and, in the process, altering the magnitude of *unpaid* labor); examples: independent merchant capital, monopoly pricing power;

(ii) where subsumed class revenues arise from activities not focused on pricing but which nonetheless, by affecting capitalist costs, *indirectly* alter the price structure (with the same redistributive effects); examples: supervisory managers, internal sales staff and other unproductive activities within industrial capitalist firms, rent to landlords;[9]

(iii) where subsumed class revenues are truly *ex post* distributions with no systematic impact on the price structure and therefore no constitutive effect on the magnitude of surplus value; examples: dividend distributions, interest on debt, managerial accumulation activity.

These differences are not apparent when operating on the volume 1 assumption of value-equivalent exchange. Hence R&W are entitled to say: "Thus, persons who occupy the fundamental class position of surplus value appropriator (capitalists) must also occupy the subsumed class position of surplus value distributor" (*K&C*, 131). But not every "distribution" of surplus value requires an active "distributor." In the context of capitalist exchange à la volume 3, distributions made by conscious choice out of realized revenue M′ (type iii) are simply *different* from the (type i) "predistributions" that occur through the price-value deviations that make M′ greater or less than the value of C′ (thus leaving distributable net revenue greater or less than the surplus value originally generated by living labor employed within the firm).

Because their default assumption is value-equivalent exchange, R&W are unable to incorporate some of the broader impact of some subsumed class activities, especially of type (i) above. For example, in R&W's treatment, a competitive capitalist enterprise that has no direct dealings with independent merchant capitals and buys nothing from monopolies would presumably be able to buy and sell commodities at value and thus be uninvolved with and unaffected by any subsumed class distributions made elsewhere to the benefit of merchants or monopolists. The firm would simply make no such distributions out of its independently given quantum of surplus value. But this *ceteris paribus* or "partial equilibrium" approach (treating the enterprise as actually or potentially isolated from and thus independent of activities in its economic and social context) is problematic on value-theoretic grounds. The presence of merchant capitals competing to earn the same general rate of profit as industrial capital alters the *entire* structure of prices (in part by introducing broad-based wholesale vs. retail price differentials), affecting *all capitals*. And if there is a subset of enterprises or industries in which monopoly power permits charging higher-than-competitive prices and reaping higher-than-competitive profits, *all* other capitals necessarily must charge less than otherwise, capture less surplus value, realize lower-than-competitive profits and have *less* revenue for any subsequent distributions (particularly if aggregate surplus value is treated as pre-given, since monopoly profit means that there is simply less surplus value available for the non-monopoly sectors). *No enterprises can be unaffected* when the price structure is impacted by merchant and/or monopoly activities that reconstitute the basis for pricing. On the other hand, enterprise decisions to pay out dividends to shareholders will have many repercussions extending into the future for those associated with these firms, but there are no necessary immediate effects on the basis for exchange equivalence, on the rate of profit, on prices, and so on, i.e., no constitutive effects that change the context for all other firms.

On the second point: treating surplus value as a pre-given magnitude of "already appropriated" surplus labor is hard to reconcile with overdetermination as a premise about the nature of the synchronic whole that is Marx's object. In *WRC3*, quoted above, "Marx's theoretical commitment to overdetermination" *leads* to the dependence of the magnitude of surplus value on "the capitalist structure of payment equivalence," and all of the various WRC drafts make the core argument that a change in the manner in which conditions of existence are secured alters the (synchronic) form of the overdetermined whole, requiring reconsideration of the meaning of basic concepts. As argued above, when independent merchants competing for a share of aggregate surplus value are the means by which industrial capitals are enabled to sell their outputs, exchange "at value" is no longer conceptually consistent. Prices, the structure of payments, must adjust. And if surplus value truly is, at its core, *unpaid* labor, it cannot remain independent and unaffected. How can *"unpaid* labor" be independent of a basic alteration in the price structure governing all *payments*? The introduction of "new determinations" affecting prices and exchange-equivalence should provoke a reexamination, a new particularization, of core categories like value and surplus value. Without such a reexamination, it is hard to see how the diachrony of the discourse fully respects the premise of overdetermination for the synchronic whole under consideration.[10]

It seems that R&W pursue overdetermination in one direction, to the partial exclusion of another. They focus on *ripple* effects (overdetermined consequences through time that can be examined within the existing set of basic concepts) while, at least to some extent, setting aside *constitutive* effects (qualitative change in the social whole that requires reexamination of basic concepts and their articulation). But, I think, overdetermination as a core premise requires both.

It is one thing to say, with Marx—as R&W do—that a "Trinity Theory" treatment of class revenues (wages, profits, rent) as separate and independent sources of value vitiates the insight that current labor creates all new value added. It is quite another to say that relaxing prior assumptions to incorporate major new realms of activity (subsumed class processes) leaves surplus value untouched, independent, frozen in magnitude by a prior, narrower set of determinants. Marx's point (easily consistent with overdetermination) contra the Trinity Theory was precisely that economic phenomena (different class incomes) are *not independent* of each other but are parts of a larger whole. Why, then, should R&W feel obligated to impose an assumption that makes the core category of surplus value independent of the forms of its distribution, pre-given and "already appropriated," a whole that is utterly independent of its changing parts, when overdetermination presumes that *nothing is independent* of its relations to its context (Roberts 1996)?

What R&W do is not "wrong, simply an error." It is a discursive device they adopt to enable their argument to proceed, one that may well not be intended to become a permanent feature of subsequent analyses. It is, however, an unnecessary device, given the WRC work on the diachrony of a discourse that premises overdetermination. Had they wished to do so, I think R&W could have developed the same typology of class and non-class positions even while allowing for constitutive effects on value and surplus value.[11]

Conclusion

Ultimately, class and overdetermination are the core of R&W's Marxism. The former is Marx's chosen object; the latter, the epistemological and methodological principle they read in Marx once they assimilate a broadly Althusserian reading of his theory. Jointly, class and overdetermination provide a shorthand reference to *what* they seek to understand and *how* they then go about building that understanding.

Their class analysis is consistently rooted in Marx's core focus: for Marx, the generation of a material surplus (a *multi*-dimensional surplus: labor, value, product) has both conditions and consequences; in capitalism, those conditions and consequences are the focus of value theory in action. Marxian value theory is the formal accounting language through which one poses and then interrogates the capitalist generation of a surplus as a class phenomenon. When R&W take capitalism as the object of analysis, the very existence of a surplus opens up a series of ongoing and interdependent processes: the production, appropriation, realization, distribution, and deployment of that surplus, with potential struggles emerging at each step and social reproduction always at issue as changes within each process ripple forward and intersect. Each phase provokes questions that lead to the next:

- How and through what sorts of social and technical relationships is the surplus produced?
- How and by whom is that surplus captured as a flow of value?
- To whom and for what purposes is that value distributed (or better, *re*distributed)?
- What struggles are fostered, enhanced, or diminished, and what reproductive consequences may then follow as conditions of existence are transformed?

The architecture of R&W's typology distinguishing fundamental, subsumed, and non-class processes is designed to provide a scaffolding for sophisticated and nuanced treatments of struggle(s), with the presence of the surplus providing the indispensible Marxian context for those struggles. Overdetermination (read in the light of the various Althusserian and postmodern influences that R&W absorbed in pursuing that premise) makes itself felt in *how* their class object is (synchronically) conceived and (diachronically) developed.

I have stressed the importance of the diachrony of successive particularization that incorporates *constitutive* effects and relations among the parts of the social whole; the evolution of R&W's approach in the early years of their collaboration is better understood when that dimension of the methodology of overdetermination is highlighted. But by the time of *K&C*, the *ripple* effects of changes are increasingly the focus of their analysis, and the meaning of overdetermination is consistently demonstrated by presenting alternative "stories" about social possibilities. The distinctive diachronic strategy of *K&C* takes the form of *narrative*, in which the outcome is always open-ended. In *K&C*, the later chapters provide many instances of analysis in the following form: consider "this" particular site of contradiction and/or struggle (the revenues of the enterprise, perhaps, or the tax policy of the state, or the division of labor within the family); suppose "this" action is taken by one of the participants; note the array of possible outcomes, none automatic and each with different further potential consequences; alternatively, though, now suppose "this" different initial action, with its different set of possible consequences, etc. The very *indeterminacy* of the analysis is, for R&W, its virtue. This is why I refer to this aspect of their work as "story-telling."

Story-telling in this sense begins from Marx but goes well beyond any simple mimicry of Marx's texts. For R&W, respect for overdetermination means that class analysis typically takes the form of open-ended narrative, leading to comparison of alternative "stories," rather than pursuit of a determinate "solution" or a predictive "law." I don't mean to suggest that they are math-phobic or in any sense hostile to analytical rigor,[12] merely that they regard mathematics as an aid to *telling better stories*, a way of organizing and "sorting" the conflicting pressures, rather than reducing them to some simpler, determinate form. Hence, as artful and clever master story-tellers, R&W never forget, and never fail to stress, that the overdetermined object of their inquiries (always, in their words, undergoing "ceaseless change" as a result of various "pushes and pulls") is more complex and less comfortably predictable than the outcomes delivered by conventional economic models, Marxian or otherwise.

Over a span of more than three decades, Resnick and Wolff produced a body of work unwaveringly focused on the task they described early on in the 1982 *Classes* paper: producing a "complex class analysis [that] is far more consistently grounded in Marx's value theory than ... alternative formulations." Both the complexity of that analysis and its conscious and consistent grounding are important—and related—parts of their legacy. Readers in general, and especially those of us they influenced as our teachers, are in their debt.

Notes

1 As Althusser paradoxically put it, "The independence of an element is only ever the form of its dependence" (1990, 220).
2 Cf. Althusser's similar posing: "Synchrony represents the organizational structure of the concepts in the thought-totality or *system* (or, as Marx puts it, 'synthesis'), diachrony the movement of succession of the concepts in the ordered discourse of the proof" (Althusser and Balibar 1975, 68). See also Roberts (1981, chap. 1).
3 Logical and (sometimes) mathematical relations between concepts in discourse are constructed as the means to think the overdetermined relations between the theoretical objects those concepts designate. But while concepts designate objects that may be part of an overdetermined synchrony, theoretical concepts do not, *as components of a theory's diachrony*, meaningfully overdetermine each other. Asserting that "concept X and concept Y overdetermine each other" is at best an empty claim and at worst meaningless. For example, if X and Y are "value" and "value-form" or price, theory is obligated to examine the quantitative relation between the two, and *mathematical* overdetermination leads simply to indeterminacy and incoherence (as discussed below, one must instead *show how* the relation changes in the presence of differing overdetermining contextual circumstances).
4 Indeed, R&W's commitment to value theory as an indispensible part of Marxian theory writ large, rather than rejecting value analysis as inherently essentialist, is crucial in distinguishing their work from Cutler et al. (1977) and many others who went down the postmodern road.

5 The published version, "Class in Marxian Theory" (1982), no longer refers to or even cites any of the WRC papers.

6 In several papers, including one in this volume, Fred Moseley has insisted that Marxian value analyses must focus on magnitudes denominated in money, arguing that in Marx's theory, both surplus-value and profit are defined in terms of money and that "the absence of money in the WRC interpretation of Marx's theory means that it cannot be a resolution to the transformation problem" (Moseley, this volume, 9). This critique is simply misguided. As was stressed in *WRC3*, "It is crucial to remember that in any exchange between money and commodities Marx always treats both the money and the commodities as representing magnitudes of social labor time. Thus the magnitudes exchanged are always expressible in units of labor time" (*WRC3*, 572), even though they are also obviously expressible in terms of money. There is nothing of substance at stake here with regard to value accounting, since monetary expressions of value and of exchange-value or production price each represent "a definite social manner of expressing the amount of labour bestowed upon an object" (Marx 1867, 82). Value categories in money differ from their parallel labor-time expressions only by a scalar multiple. It is true that there are more complex circumstances (e.g., an analysis of debt obligations, or one explicitly focused on dynamic changes) where money-denominated magnitudes require direct attention, but the core focus of Marxism as a class analysis always begins with an accounting designed to make visible the flows of necessary and surplus *labor* which may, but do not necessarily, take a monetary form in all analytic or social circumstances. No one other than Moseley will find the discussions in WRC or R&W hard to understand, let alone "contradictory," on this score.

7 See Roberts (1996) for an extended discussion of surplus value as unpaid labor time, interdependent with the structure of payment equivalence established in exchange.

8 Over time, R&W appear to have found it increasingly appealing to posit symmetry in their treatment of subsumed classes. In the early (~1978) *Classes I* paper, R&W distinguished three "types" of subsumed classes ("directors" of processes providing conditions of existence for capital, "unproductive" performers of labor, and landlords and others who monopolize access to conditions of existence); in the 1982 published version (*CMT*), only "Type 1" and "Type 2" remain (landlords/monopolists have been merged into the director group). And in *K&C* (1987), all such distinctions between "types" disappear. The increasing notational complexity in *K&C*, where R&W formally include *non-class* revenues and distributions, may help to explain the appeal of simplifying the typology via the imposition of symmetry.

9 R&W are clearly aware that activities that add to the perceived costs of capitalist enterprises will impact the aggregate rate of profit, and thus also the production prices associated with that rate of profit (1987, 318, n. 136). But their assumption of value-equivalence allows them to bypass explicit elaboration.

10 In their concluding section about "methodological self-consciousness," R&W write: "Our entry-point concepts are defined and deployed in a distinctive way.... The process of deploying our entry-point concepts changes them as well as changing ... the other concepts we encounter. It changes as well the additional concepts we construct as our theorization proceeds. In the course of our book, then, our concepts change. This change is unavoidable because the definition of any concept is nothing other than the varied relations in which it stands to other concepts. ... Each step in the deployment of the concepts of our theory adds determinations to those concepts, enriching and thereby changing their meanings. Our entry-point concepts such as ... surplus ... were

all initially posed and defined so as to permit their further deployment. Their further deployment then develops, enriches, and changes the determinations (relations to other concepts) that give them their … meanings" (*K&C*, 277). With respect to concepts of value and surplus value, I wish they had taken this passage more consciously and explicitly to heart.

11 Personally, though, I am not fully in tune with all the consequences of their complex class and non-class typology in *K&C*. R&W never directly address how their class typology impacts the concept of exploitation. Their first treatment of exploitation defines it as "appropriation of surplus *labor*" by "non-laborers" (*K&C*, 20). But in their developed theory, for example, employees who perform labor in a financial enterprise are not "occupants of [that] enterprise's *class* structure," since they "do not produce surplus *value*," and so, even though they engage in struggles over work conditions and pay, even though they appear to perform surplus labor (labor in excess of the value-equivalent paid for their labor-power), their *"non-class positions"* would seem to preclude them from being subjects of (class) exploitation (*K&C*, 220). This, to me, represents an unappealing and unnecessary conclusion, in comparison to an alternative in which exploitation exists if those who perform labor are not (individual or collective) participants in its appropriation, *whether or not* their surplus *labor* takes the capitalist form of surplus *value* (see Roberts 2011).

12 The WRC papers do indeed present a formal mathematical solution, but as the means to develop the interdependent meanings of categories, not to narrow the spectrum of possible paths or isolate an "equilibrium" outcome or even some (allegedly) necessary tendential result. Similarly, in *K&C*, R&W do produce mathematical formalisms (mostly in footnotes), but even when, for example, they proceed by generating and then analyzing the sign of an expression derived by partial differentiation, the point is to clarify the multiple possible outcomes, not reduce them to one.

References

Althusser, L. 1977. *For Marx*. London: New Left Books.

———— 1990. *Philosophy and the Spontaneous Philosophy of the Scientists*. London: Verso.

———— 1991. "On Marx and Freud." *Rethinking Marxism* 4 (1): 17–30.

Althusser, L. and E. Balibar. 1975. *Reading Capital*. Trans B. Brewster. London: New Left Books.

Cutler, A., B. Hindess, P. Hirst, and A. Hussain. 1977. *Marx's 'Capital' and Capitalism Today*. London: Routledge and Kegan Paul.

Hindess, B. and P. Hirst. 1975. *Pre-capitalist Modes of Production*. London: Routledge and Kegan Paul.

———— 1977. *Mode of Production and Social Formation*. London: Macmillan.

Marx, K. 1973 [1939]. *Grundrisse*. New York: Vintage.

Moseley, F. 1993. *Marx's Method in 'Capital': A Reexamination*. Atlantic Highlands, NJ: Humanities Press.

Resnick, S. and R. Wolff. 1978. "The Concepts of Classes in Marxian Theory." Unpublished manuscript, Department of Economics, University of Massachusetts, Amherst.

———— 1979a. "The Theory of Transitional Conjunctures and the Transition from Feudalism to Capitalism in Western Europe." *Review of Radical Political Economy* 11 (3): 3–22.

—— 1979b. "Reply to Herb Gintis." *Review of Radical Political Economy* 11 (3): 32–36.

—— 1979c. "The Concepts of Classes in Marxian Theory II: Implications for Value Theory." Unpublished manuscript, Department of Economics, University of Massachusetts, Amherst.

—— 1982. "Classes in Marxian Theory." *Review of Radical Political Economics* 13 (4): 1–18.

—— 1987. *Knowledge and Class: A Marxian Critique of Political Economy*. Chicago, IL: University of Chicago Press.

Roberts, B. 1981. "Value Categories and Marxian Method: A Different View of Value-Price Transformation." PhD dissertation, Department of Economics, University of Massachusetts, Amherst.

—— 1996. "The Visible and the Measurable: Althusser and the Marxian Theory of Value." In *Postmodern Marxism and the Future of Marxist Theory: Essays in the Althusserian Tradition*, A. Callari and D. Ruccio, eds., 193–211. Middletown, CT: Wesleyan University Press.

—— 2011. "Exploitation, Appropriation, and Subsumption." *Rethinking Marxism* 23 (3): 341–51.

Wolff, R., B. Roberts, and A. Callari. 1978a. "Marxian and Ricardian Economics: Fundamental Differences." Unpublished manuscript, Department of Economics, University of Massachusetts, Amherst. Presented at the meeting of the History of Economics Society, Toronto, May 1978.

—— 1978b. "Ricardian and Marxian Economics: A Different View of Value-Price Transformation." Unpublished manuscript, Department of Economics, University of Massachusetts, Amherst.

—— 1982. "Marx's (not Ricardo's) 'Transformation Problem': A Radical Reconceptualization." *History of Political Economy* 16 (4): 564–82.

8   Wolff and Resnick's interpretation of Marx's theory of value and surplus-value

Where's the money?

Fred Moseley

Rick Wolff and Steve Resnick have made many valuable contributions to Marxian theory, particularly in their emphasis on class as a process that involves the production and appropriation of surplus-value, the founding and development of the *Rethinking Marxism* journal, supervision of dozens of Ph.D. students at the University of Massachusetts who are now teaching Marxian economics at colleges and universities all over the United States, and the series of international conferences at UMass that brought together Marxian scholars from all over the world. Also important is Wolff's outstanding work as "Marxian media star" and his lectures to popular audiences in which he presents a Marxian analysis of the exploitative nature of capitalism and the causes of the recent (and ongoing) economic crisis.

However, there is one important area in which their contribution is less than satisfactory: their interpretation of Marx's quantitative theory of value, surplus-value, and prices of production. Marx's fundamental theory of value and surplus-value is not discussed much in their work, and when it is discussed, their treatment is generally inconsistent and superficial. The main deficiency, in my view, is that the key role of *money* and *money capital* in Marx's theory is little analyzed in Resnick and Wolff's work.

The first section of this paper is a brief summary of the key role of money and money capital in Marx's theory of value and surplus-value and prices of production. The next section discusses Wolff and Resnick's presentations of Marx's theory of value and surplus-value in their two principal texts: *Knowledge and Class: A Marxian Critique of Political Economy* (Resnick and Wolff 1987) and *Economics: Marxian versus Neoclassical* (Wolff and Resnick 1987). The final section discusses Wolff's joint papers with Bruce Roberts and Antonio Callari on Marx's theory of prices of production and the "transformation problem" (Wolff, Roberts, and Callari 1982, 1984).

The centrality of money in Marx's theory

Marx derives the necessity of money in a capitalist-commodity economy in the very first chapter of *Capital*, in the crucial but often neglected

Section 3. Money is derived as the *necessary form of appearance* of the abstract labor contained in commodities so that the value of each commodity can be compared objectively with the value of all other commodities. Marx concludes Section 3 as follows: "Money as a measure of value is the necessary form of appearance of the measure of value which is immanent in commodities, namely labour-time" (1977, 188).

At the end of Section 3, Marx derives the *price* of commodities as the *quantity of the money commodity*, which is equal in value to (i.e., contains the same quantity of labor-time as) a given quantity of other commodities. From that point on, Marx's theory is about quantities of money or prices that represent, and are thus determined by, quantities of abstract labor. Quantities of money and prices are the variables to be explained (the *explananda*) and quantities of abstract labor are the underlying cause (the *explanans*). Across the three volumes of *Capital*, Marx develops further this abstract concept of price, including most importantly the concept of production prices in volume 3, defined as quantities of the money commodity (more on this point below).

Marx's derivation of the necessity of money from his underlying theory of value is a significant accomplishment in itself and a mark of the superiority of Marx's theory over all other economic theories, including especially neoclassical economics. Marx claims at the beginning of Section 3 that "now we have to perform a task never even attempted by bourgeois economists"–to explain the "mystery of *money*" (1977, 139). One and a half centuries later, bourgeois economists have still made only feeble attempts and have not yet solved the mystery of money. The neoclassical utility theory of value cannot explain the necessity of money, and the neoclassical quantity theory of money does not depend in any way on the utility theory of value.

Chapter 2 of *Capital*, volume 1, is about how commodity owners perceive the need for *money* as a universal equivalent in order to express objectively the value of their commodities to the rest of society. Chapter 3 is a long and substantial chapter (56 pages) whose discussion of the functions of *money* (measure of value, medium of circulation, etc.) is far superior to the prevailing theories of money at the time (Ricardo, Malthus, etc.) and even to today's leading monetary theories.

Part 2 is entitled "The Transformation of *Money* into *Capital*" (emphasis added). As the title of Marx's book suggests, capital is the central concept of Marx's theory, and Marx's concept of capital is defined in terms of *money*—as "*money* that becomes *more money*" (symbolically: $M \rightarrow M + \Delta M$). Chapter 4, "The General Formula for Capital," posits the general formula for capital ($M - C - M + \Delta M$) as the main phenomenon that Marx's theory is intended to explain: how an initial quantity of money becomes more money. Surplus-value is defined as the ΔM that emerges at the end of the circuit of money capital (Marx 1977, 251). The general formula for capital is an abbreviated form of the full circuit of money capital: $M - C - P - C' - M'$.

This circuit of money capital becomes the logical framework for the rest of volume 2 and all of volume 3.

Chapter 5 argues that ΔM cannot be explained as long as the theory is restricted to the sphere of circulation alone (as Marx's theory is restricted in Parts 1 and 2). At the end of Chapter 5, Marx issues his famous challenge to himself and all others: how can we account for ΔM on the basis of equivalent exchange? *Hic Rhodus! Hic Salta!* Chapter 6 argues that ΔM is possible only if capitalists are able to purchase the special commodity labor-power, since labor-power is the only possible source of additional money value (in the "hidden abode of production," away from circulation).

Chapter 7 is the most important in the book and presents Marx's basic theory of ΔM, as determined by surplus labor. Marx's theory of ΔM in Chapter 7 is based on the fundamental labor theory of value assumption that the total price of commodities produced in the economy as a whole (P) is the sum of the constant capital consumed in their production $(C)^1$ plus the new value produced by current labor (N). The new value (N), in turn, is the product of the quantity of current labor (L) and the money value produced per hour $(m)^2$ Algebraically:

$$P = C + N$$
$$= C + mL \tag{1}$$

In Marx's example in Chapter 7, the money value produced per hour is assumed to be 0.5 shillings (determined by the inverse of the labor-time required to produce a shilling of gold). A 6-hour working day produces a money value of 3 shillings, and a working day of 12 hours produces a money value of 6 shillings. From this basic assumption, Marx derives the surplus-value produced (i.e., the ΔM) as the excess of the money new value produced by current labor (N) over the money variable capital advanced to purchase labor-power (V), and this ΔM is proportional to the surplus labor (SL) of workers:

$$M = S = NV$$
$$= m\,(SL) \tag{2}$$

Surplus labor is the excess of hours in the working day over necessary labor (NL), and necessary labor is the number of hours required for workers to produce money new value equal to the money variable capital workers are paid (at the rate of m, the quantity of money-value produced per hour); i.e., $NL = V/m$. In Marx's Chapter 7 example of a typical worker, $V = 3$ shillings and $m = 0.5$ shillings per hour, so $NL = 3$ shillings / 0.5 shilling per hour = 6 hours, and (with a 12 hour working day) $SL = 6$ hours.[3]

Marx triumphantly concludes his exposition of ΔM in Chapter 7 as follows: "27 *shillings* has turned into 30 *shillings*; a surplus-value of 3 *shillings* has been precipitated. The trick has at last worked: *money* has been transformed into *capital*" (301; emphasis added). Money in Marx's theory is not a device for convenient exposition or illustration of labor times; the increase of money capital is the main phenomenon that Marx's theory is intended to explain.[4]

Chapter 8 introduces the key concepts of *constant capital* and *variable capital* that are also clearly defined in terms of money–as the two components into which the initial money-capital that begins the circulation of capital is divided; i.e., $M = C + V$. Constant capital and variable capital are defined as quantities of money capital advanced to purchase means of production and labor-power (the "money laid out" as Marx said many times), not as quantities of labor-time.

Chapter 9 introduces the key concept of the rate of surplus-value, which is defined in terms of a ratio of two quantities of money-capital, the ratio of surplus-value (ΔM) to the money variable capital. In Marx's main example in Chapter 9, surplus-value is equal to £90, and variable capital is equal to £90, so that the rate of surplus-value is 1.0, or 100%.

Parts 4 to 6 of volume 1 are mainly about the various means by which the magnitude of surplus-value (ΔM) can be increased: by increasing the working day, by increasing the intensity of labor, or by reducing necessary labor (by means of technological change and increased productivity of labor). Chapter 17 ("Changes of Magnitude of the *Price* of Labor-power and Surplus-value") is a kind of summary of the theory thus far of how the monetary variables of the price of labor-power and surplus-value (ΔM) depend on the labor-time variables just mentioned.

Part 7 is about the accumulation of capital, which is defined as the conversion of the ΔM appropriated in one circuit into additional money capital (i.e. additional M) in the next circuit. Marx's main example in Chapter 24 is an initial $M = £10,000$ that produces $\Delta M = £2,000$, which is then reinvested as additional M in the next circuit.

Volume 2 is about capital in the sphere of circulation. Part 1 is about different starting points for the circuit of capital. Part 2 is about the turnover time of capital, which is the amount of time between the advance of *money capital* at the beginning of the circuit of capital and the recovery of that money capital plus ΔM at the end of the circuit (turnover time would be inexplicable if the theory were only about labor-times and not about money capital advanced and recovered; labor-times are not advanced and recovered). Part 3 is about the reproduction of the total social capital and all components of capital in the two departments are defined in terms of *money*. Marx's main question in the analysis of the reproduction schemes is how the *money constant capital* that is advanced at the beginning of the circuit is recovered at the end of the circuit out of the price of the product, which was a critique of "Smith's dogma" (according to which constant capital disappears in the aggregate and the total price consists entirely of wages + profit + rent).

Volume 3 is primarily about the distribution of surplus-value or the division of the total ΔM into individual parts, first into equal rates of profit across industries and then the further division of the total ΔM into commercial profit, interest, and rent. All these individual parts of surplus-value are clearly defined in terms of money and would make no sense if defined as labor-times. In particular, prices of production are clearly quantities of money (*prices* after all) and are equal to the sum of the money costs in each industry (which Marx called the cost *price*) plus each industry's share of the total ΔM (determined by its share of the initial M).

Thus we can see that Marx's theory in the three volumes of *Capital* is all about quantities of money capital and how an initial quantity of money capital becomes more money (ΔM) through the exploitation of workers (surplus labor) and how the total ΔM is distributed across industries. *Capital* is the title of Marx's book, and capital is defined in terms of money–as money that becomes more money.

Wolff and Resnick's interpretation of Marx's theory of value and surplus-value

Economics: Marxian versus neoclassical (1987)

This book is a textbook for undergraduate Economics courses, and the main idea is to compare neoclassical economics (Chapter 2) with Marxian economics (Chapter 3). Section D of Chapter 3 briefly presents Marx's basic theory of value and surplus-value (in 8 pages). In subsection D.4, the value of commodities is interpreted entirely in terms of the labor-time required to produce them, and no mention is made of money and price as the necessary form of appearance of value. The labor-value of commodities (W) consists of two main components: embodied labor (EL) (from the means of production) and living labor (LL). Hence (in their notation):

$$W = EL + LL \tag{3}$$

Then in subsection D.5, living labor is divided into two subcomponents in order to explain surplus-value: labor required to produce workers' means of subsistence (LL_p) and the remaining unpaid labor performed (LL_u). Thus, the more detailed equation for the value of commodities is:

$$W = EL + LL_p + LL_u \tag{4}$$

LL_u is also called surplus labor, and surplus-value is defined as surplus labor that is appropriated by capitalists (i.e., surplus-value is defined as a quantity of labor, not ΔM).

The next section of Chapter 3 (Section E) does discuss money but does so in an inconsistent and contradictory way. Subsection E.1 is entitled "What are capitalists?" and the second paragraph begins as follows:

> All capitalists start with a sum of values, usually in the form of money, M.
>
> (Wolff and Resnick 1987, 163)

Here, in contrast to the previous section, "values" seem to be defined in quantities of *money*. However, the causal relation between values as quantities of labor as defined in the previous subsection and values as quantities of money is not explained in this subsection or anywhere else in the book. This key causal relation in Marx's theory should be explained, not glossed over as if identical. The paragraph continues:

> Their goal is to use their money to "make money"–to secure an increment, ΔM, as an addition to their original M. Mathematically this can be stated as $M \rightarrow M + \Delta M$... Marx calls the expenditure on labor power "variable capital" ... Marx call the expenditure on equipment and raw materials "constant capital" ... ΔM is the surplus-value.
>
> (Wolff and Resnick 1987, 163-64)

I agree with these sentences 100%. Capitalist production begins with the advance of money capital (M), and the main goal of capitalists is to "make money" (i.e., ΔM). The initial M is divided into two parts: variable capital expended to purchase labor-power and constant capital expended to purchase means of production (i.e., $M = C + V$); surplus-value is ΔM, a quantity of money. However, two paragraphs later, C, V, and S are *equated with quantities of labor* in the following equations:

$$C = EL$$
$$V = LL_p \qquad\qquad (5)$$
$$S = LL_u$$

Either the definitions of C, V, and S have changed without an explanation from quantities of money in the preceding paragraphs to quantities of labor in these equations, or these equations are illogical. Quantities of money cannot be equated with quantities of labor.

Two paragraphs later, the Marxian concept of capital is defined as "a sum of value–money–which expands itself" (164). Again, I agree completely with this definition of capital as money that expands itself, as M that becomes $M + \Delta M$. However, the theory of surplus-value presented in the previous subsection is entirely in terms of labor and says nothing about ΔM, and the all-important ΔM is not explicitly explained in this subsection or anywhere else in the book.

I recognize that the relation between quantities of labor and quantity of money or prices in Marx's theory is somewhat complicated, especially because of the constant capital component of the price of commodities. However, it is not too difficult to explain that the key assumption in the labor theory of value is that the new value component of the price of commodities (N) is determined by the product of the quantity of current labor required to produce the commodities (L) and the *money value produced per hour of labor* (m): i.e., $N = mL$, as discussed above. From this assumption, it is straightforward to derive the equation for surplus-value ($S = \Delta M$) as the monetary expression of surplus labor ($S = mSL$). I can understand why Wolff and Resnick would want to avoid this complication, but dealing with a little complication is preferable to avoiding the issue, presenting logical inconsistencies, and failing to explain ΔM.

The only other discussion of Marx's theory of value and surplus-value is in Section G ("Capitalist Subsumed Classes"). This section is about the distribution of surplus-value and discusses the division of the total surplus-value into money lenders' interest (S_1), managers' salaries (S_2), merchants' profit (S_3), and the remaining surplus-value (S_r).[5] A positive aspect of Wolff and Resnick's interpretation is that the total amount of surplus-value (S) is assumed to be determined in production and is taken as given as a predetermined amount in the division of the total surplus-value into these individual parts. I agree completely with this interpretation of the logical relation between the production and the distribution of surplus-value (although they do not present a theory of what determines the magnitude of the total surplus-value).

These individual parts of surplus-value are discussed, as they should be, in terms of *money*, not labor, since these payments are made in money to the subsumed classes in the real capitalist economy. The circuit of money lenders' capital is described as: $M \rightarrow M + S_1$ (Wolff and Resnick 1987, 194). The circuit of merchants' capital is described as: $M \rightarrow C \rightarrow M + \Delta M$ (197). Thus implicitly, the total surplus-value–the sum of the individual parts of surplus-value–must also be a quantity of money. However, this contradicts the definition of surplus-value in subsection D.4 as "surplus *labor* appropriated by capitalists" (emphasis added).

In summary, the presentation of Marx's theory of value and surplus-value in Resnick and Wolff's textbook is disappointing. It is very brief, and it does not explain the fundamental causal relation between quantities of labor and quantities of money and prices, and therefore does not explain how ΔM is determined by surplus labor. It is doubly disappointing that this book does not present Marx's theory of money because the book is a comparison of Marx's theory and neoclassical economics, and Marx's theory of money is one of the important areas in which Marx's theory is clearly superior to neoclassical economics (as discussed above).[6]

Knowledge and class *(Resnick and Wolff 1987)*

This book is a scholarly monograph, but unfortunately the presentation of Marx's theory of value and surplus-value is not any better than in the textbook discussed above; if anything, it is worse. As the title suggests, the book is about epistemology and class, and there are only two discussions related to Marx's theory of value and surplus-value. The first is a 10-page section in Chapter 3 ("A Marxian Theory of Classes") entitled "Wages and Profits." Wages are defined as payments for labor, which are in terms of money. Profits are also defined in terms of money, and it is stated that profits do not exist in Volume 1 because its goal is to explain surplus-value, which is defined as surplus *labor* appropriated by capitalists (150). There is no mention of Marx's definition of surplus-value in Volume 1 as ΔM, which was at least briefly discussed in their other book.

This discussion also refers to the "famous section" on the "Valorization Process" in *Capital* (i.e., Section 2 of Chapter 7 of volume 1), but the logic of this important section is not discussed (1987, 150). As mentioned above, the purpose of Chapter 7 is to explain ΔM (i.e., to explain "the transformation of *money* into *capital*"), and ΔM is explained as the product of the quantity of surplus labor and the money value produced per hour. The purpose of this key section is not to explain surplus labor; it is to explain ΔM and its causal connection to surplus labor.

The other discussion of Marx's theory of value and surplus-value in this book is in Chapter 4 ("Class Analysis: A Marxian Theory of the Enterprise"), which presents an analysis of the distribution of surplus-value (i.e., the individual parts of surplus-value) similar to the discussion of this topic in their textbook. The individual parts of surplus-value that are considered are: owners' profit (SC_0), financiers' interest (SC_C), managers' salaries (SC_1), and the remainder of the total surplus-value distributed to state officials, merchants, landlords, etc. (SC_R). Although it is not explicitly stated, the total surplus-value seems to be determined prior to its distribution, as in the textbook, because the "remainder" is calculated in the same way by subtracting all the other individual parts from the total surplus-value. Also as in the textbook, all these individual parts of surplus-value are discussed in terms of *money*, as they should be, since payments to the subsumed classes are made in money. Thus implicitly the total surplus-value is also defined in terms of money, although this is contrary to the definition of surplus-value in Chapter 3 of their book. Again, no theory is presented of the determination of the magnitude of the total surplus-value (ΔM).

The Wolff-Roberts-Callari interpretation of Marx's theory of prices of production

Wolff and Resnick did not individually or jointly write about Marx's theory of prices of production and the "transformation problem." However,

Wolff collaborated with two of his Ph.D. students to write two papers on this subject in the early 1980s. I discuss these papers at length elsewhere (Moseley 2016, 2011). Here I will focus on the absence of money in their interpretation of values and prices of production.[7]

In these papers, Wolff, Roberts, and Callari (hereafter WRC, with apologies) argue that *all* the variables in Marx's theory in all three volumes of *Capital* are defined in units of *labor-time*, including constant capital, variable capital, surplus-value, and even the Volume 3 variables of cost price, price of production, and profit.[8] Money is almost entirely missing from their interpretation, except for a few passing remarks about the money capital advanced to purchase means of production. WRC acknowledge that Marx often expressed or measured labor-times in terms of money, but they argue that this representation is not an essential part of the theory and is only for purposes of convenient exposition or illustration. They maintain that Marx's theory is really about labor-times, even though Marx often chose to illustrate these quantities of labor-time with quantities of money.[9]

Marx explains the all-important phenomenon of surplus-value (ΔM) in terms of labor-time (surplus labor-time), but surplus-value is not *defined* in terms of labor-time. Similarly, constant capital and variable capital are defined as the two components of the initial money capital advanced (the "money laid out") to purchase means of production and labor-power (i.e., $M = C + V$). These definitions are not for convenient exposition, but rather they specify the most important phenomena that Marx intends his theory to illuminate. Capitalism is above all else a *money-making* economy, and Marx's theory explains how this money-making is accomplished through the exploitation of workers (surplus labor). A theory of capitalism whose variables are all labor-times could not explain ΔM and thus would be a very unsatisfactory theory of capitalism.

Why would Marx want to illustrate quantities of labor-time with quantities of money? If his theory really were only about quantities of labor-time, why not illustrate quantities of labor-time directly in terms of labor-hours? Indeed, that is in fact what Marx did in his many examples in *Capital*. But these examples *usually include quantities of money* as well as quantities of labor-time. Marx's labor theory of value is not just about labor-times but is instead about the *causal relation between quantities of labor-time and quantities of money*. In Marx's examples in *Capital*, labor is illustrated in terms of labor-hours, and price (and surplus-value) is illustrated in terms of English money (pounds and shillings); e.g., in the key Chapter 7 of volume 1, discussed above. The Resnick-Wolff interpretation that capital and its components are defined in units of labor-time, so that money plays no essential role in Marx's theory, seems to belie his intentions.[10]

In a three-page Appendix to their most recent textbook, Wolff and Resnick briefly summarize the WRC interpretation of the transformation problem and present it as a "resolution" to the problem (Wolff and

Resnick 2012, 243-46). They discuss the relation between value and price, but they do not explain that "price" in the WRC interpretation is defined as a quantity of *labor-time*, not as a quantity of money. This unstated and unusual definition of "price" as a quantity of labor must be confusing for students who are used to thinking of price as a quantity of money; indeed the notion of price used in the previous chapters of this book on neoclassical economics and Keynesian economics refers to prices as quantities of money. In any case, the absence of money in the WRC interpretation of Marx's theory means that it cannot be a resolution to the transformation problem.

Conclusion

Wolff and Resnick made many outstanding contributions to Marxian theory, but their presentation of Marx's basic theory of value, surplus-value, and prices of production is not one of them. The main weakness in their interpretation is that money and money capital are almost entirely missing. This interpretation overlooks the fact that capitalism is above else a "money-making economy" and that explaining how capitalists succeed in making money is the main question in Marx's theory of capitalism. A more fundamental "rethinking" of the key roles of money, money capital, and ΔM in Marx's theory of capitalism as a "money-making" economy is called for. Capital needs to be defined and analyzed in terms of money (as Marx clearly did) because the purpose of capital is to make *more money*.

With respect to the theory of *class*, a focus on money would provide a better explanation of the specific features of class exploitation in capitalism, because exploitation in capitalism takes place through *the medium of money*–i.e., through the payment of the money wage and then the production of a greater quantity of new monetary value by labor. The payment of the money wage makes it *appear* as if *all labor is paid for*, and for that reason Marx's labor theory of money value is necessary and invaluable in order to dispel this "money illusion" of no exploitation in capitalism.[11]

With respect to comparisons with other theories, Marx's theory of money is superior to other theories, especially neoclassical economics. Neoclassical economics has almost no theory of money and certainly no theory of ΔM. In striking contrast, Marx's theory is all about money and provides a rigorous derivation of the necessity of money as the necessary form of appearance of labor-time, per his initial presentation of the labor theory of value in *Capital* Chapter 1 and a substantial analysis of the main functions of money in Chapter 3. Notably Marx's theory explains the all-important ΔM as the result of the exploitation of labor.

A final reason for expressing Marx's categories in monetary terms rather than in units of labor time is pedagogical. A focus on money in Marx's theory is the foundation of a better pedagogy in teaching Marxian economics from *Capital*. It has been my experience in many years of teaching

Marxian economics that, after a struggle with the difficult Chapter 1, students' interest definitely perks up when we get to Chapter 4 and the "General Formula for Capital": $M - C - M + \Delta M$. They readily agree that ΔM is the main goal of capitalist economies, and they are generally curious to learn more about Marx's explanation of ΔM. Economics majors realize that this all-important question of ΔM was never even posed in their other economic courses, and some start to wonder why.

Notes

1 The first component of the price of commodities is the constant capital consumed in their production because the means of production are purchased by constant capital prior to production, so that the labor required to produce the means of production *has already been objectively and socially represented by the price of the means of production, which is equal to the constant capital advanced to purchase the means of production,* even if these quantities of constant capital are not proportional to the labor required to produce the means of production. The already existing constant capital (a quantity of money) enters directly into the price of the product (another quantity of money), as a given magnitude. See Moseley (2016, 30-31 and 140-42) for further discussion of the constant capital component of the price of commodities produced by capital.

2 Duncan Foley and others have called the variable "*m*" in Marx's labor theory of value the "monetary expression of labor-time," abbreviated as MELT.

3 Marx's theory of surplus-value presented in Chapter 7 is illustrated by the working day of a single yarn spinner, but the same theory applies to each and every worker and thus applies to the total surplus-value produced by the working class as a whole. For further discussion of this macro aspect of Marx's theory of surplus-value, see Moseley (2016, chapters 1-3).

4 For an algebraic summary of Marx's theory of ΔM, see Moseley (2016, ch. 2).

5 Wolff and Resnick do not discuss in this section (or anywhere in the book) the most fundamental aspect of the distribution of surplus-value: the equalization of the rate of profit across industries and the determination of prices of production (i.e., the "transformation problem").

6 In 2012, Wolff and Resnick published a new and expanded edition of their textbook entitled *Contending Economic Theories: Neoclassical, Keynesian, and Marxian.* Chapter 4 is about Marxian economics, and their presentation of Marx's theory of value and surplus-value in this book is almost identical to their earlier textbook–brief and unsatisfactory, especially in its treatment of money.

7 In these earlier works, I have also discussed the following important similarities between the Wolff-Roberts-Callari interpretation of the transformation problem and my own interpretation: (1) constant capital and variable capital are assumed to be the *same* in the determination of both values and prices of production, and thus Marx did *not* "fail to transform the inputs" as is commonly alleged and *there is no transformation problem* in Marx's theory; (2) the value of commodities is analyzed as *products of capital,* rather than as simple commodities; and (3) Marx's two aggregate equalities are always satisfied.

8 WRC do not mention in these papers the individual parts of surplus-value that are discussed by Marx in the rest of Volume 3 (commercial profit, interest, and rent) and which Resnick and Wolff discuss–in monetary terms–in both of their books.

9 Even the concept of "value form" (emphasized by WRC) is defined in terms of *labor-time*–as the "labor-time attached to commodities in the sphere of

circulation," as opposed to labor-time in production. I argue that Marx's concept of "value form" refers to quantities of *money*–as the observable quantities of money that are the necessary "forms of appearance" of unobservable quantities of abstract labor. That is clearly what Marx meant by the title of Section 3 of Chapter 1 of Volume 1 of *Capital*–"The Value-Form"–in which Marx claimed to explain the "mystery of *money*" (Marx 1977, 139; emphasis added).

10 David Kristjanson-Gural (2008) has attempted to incorporate money into WRC's labor-time interpretation of Marx's theory of prices of production, but he does so in a superficial way at the end of the analysis. Only after the rate of profit and prices of production have been determined by the same basic equations as in the WRC interpretation, which defines all the variables in units of labor, does Kristjanson-Gural introduce money, rather than at the very beginning and foundation of the theory. Kristjanson-Gural's extension of the WRC model to include money is discussed in Moseley (2016).

11 Exploitation in feudalism was much more obvious because it took place through direct labor obligations rather than the payment of money wages.

References

Kristjanson-Gural, D. 2008. "Money is Time: The Monetary Expression of Value in Marx's Theory of Value." *Rethinking Marxism* 20 (2): 252–72.

Marx, K. 1977 (1867). *Capital*, Volume 1. New York: Random House.

Moseley, F. 2011. "Recent Interpretations of the 'Transformation Problem,'" *Rethinking Marxism* 23 (2): 186–97.

———. 2016. *Money and Totality: A Macro-Monetary Interpretation of Marx's Logical Method in* Capital *and the End of the 'Transformation Problem.'* Leiden: Brill Publishers.

Resnick, S. and R. Wolff. 1987. *Knowledge and Class: A Marxian Critique of Political Economy.* Chicago, IL: University of Chicago Press.

Wolff, R., B. Roberts, and A. Callari. 1982. "Marx's (not Ricardo's) 'Transformation Problem': A Radical Reconceptualization." *History of Political Economy* 14 (4): 564–82.

———. 1984. "A Marxian Alternative to the Traditional 'Transformation Problem'." *Review of Radical Political Economics* 16 (2–3): 115–13.

Wolff, R. and S. Resnick. 1987. *Economics: Marxian versus Neoclassical.* Baltimore, MD: Johns Hopkins University Press.

———. 2012. *Contending Economic Theories: Neoclassical, Keynesian, and Marxian.* Cambridge, MA: MIT Press.

9 Rethinking labor

Surplus, class, and justice

Faruk Eray Düzenli

Introduction

In this paper, I discuss Stephen A. Resnick and Richard D. Wolff's conceptualization of labor and its theoretical and ethical implications. Discursively privileging one of the definitions Marx advances, Resnick and Wolff construe labor as the performer of surplus. With this articulation, they elaborate their inimitable concept of "class": an economic process—one that is overdetermined by all the other, non-class economic as well as cultural, natural, and political processes—that is defined as the performance, appropriation, and distribution of surplus labor. They then analyze social formations through this particular lens of class, registering exploitative and non-exploitative class processes by tracing the flows of surplus.

Resnick and Wolff's theoretical and political project thus calls for an end to exploitation, now defined as surplus producers' inability to participate in the appropriation and distribution of the surplus. This is indeed a unique contribution to Marxian theory as Resnick and Wolff 's particular definition of class, with its focus on surplus performing labor, differs from other Marxian renditions that construe class and exploitation with reference to (unequal) power relations and/or (unequal) property ownership, which finally allows a reimagining of economic justice from a distinct Marxist class perspective. I conclude this paper by tracing the different ways that Resnick and Wolff's theory of class can be used to conceptualize economic justice.

Marx's labors

Marx advances various articulations of labor throughout his *oeuvre* (Düzenli 2006). For example, he sets himself apart from Hegel and the Young Hegelians with a Feuerbachian humanist framework, which in turn shapes his conception of labor in his early works. As epitomized in the *Economic and Philosophical Manuscripts of 1844*, Marx conceives labor as the productive activity through which human beings come into being—a self-mediated birth through labor; it nevertheless appears, under the regime of private property, as "the activity of alienation, alienation of activity" (Marx 1975). According to the "young" Marx, alienation will be superseded when private property is abolished; only then does labor become the productive activity through which human beings realize their "species-being" by transforming objects furnished by nature to satisfy their ever-developing wealth of needs, thus producing themselves anew in the process.

In *The German Ideology*, Marx, along with Engels, further specifies this particular conception of labor as "self-activity" (Marx and Engels 1975). However, under a division of labor that confines individuals to a limited realm of production, productive-activity, the *differentia specifica* of being human, assumes what Marx and Engels call the "negative form of self-activity." This labor, Marx argues, would be transformed into genuine human activity only with the abolition of the division of labor and private property, which will in turn allow human beings to appropriate the productive forces (the skills and the knowledge the workers acquired, the way the production process is organized, division of labor, among others) as well as the means of production.

With the *Grundrisse*, one can see Marx (1973 [1939]) tentatively yet unequivocally elaborating one of his unique contributions to political economy, the dual nature of labor: labor as creator of useful objects and labor as the producer of values, which in turn attests to labor's potential capacity to produce a surplus, and this is the definition Resnick and Wolff deploy in their class analysis.

Labor as the producer of surplus

Labor as the producer of surplus, as possessing *the potential* to produce more goods and services than what laborers would customarily consume, is the formulation most precisely articulated in *Capital*. Marx (1977) elaborates this particular quality of labor while discussing the relationship between the wage-laborer and the capitalist. Marx assumes that the worker and the capitalist are formally equals in the market, each possessing a property that exclusively belongs to him/her. Each pursues his/her own self-interest, freely exchanging with one another; the former selling a commodity, labor-power, in return for money, and the latter giving up money in return for labor-power. In addition, what they exchange is assumed to be of equal value/worth. Even with these assumptions that characterize the "Eden of innate rights of man," Marx (1977, 254, 280) argues that this equal exchange between the worker and the capitalist has to result in the latter getting more value than what s/he begins with for capital to exist. In order to demonstrate this, Marx focuses on what happens in "the hidden abode of production," where he finds an antagonistic relationship: buyers (sellers) of labor-power attempt to get as much (give as little) labor as possible, thus trying to maximize (minimize) the surplus labor they appropriate (perform).

Marx (1977; cf. Resnick and Wolff 2013) explains surplus-value by distinguishing between two values: the value of labor-power, which is the commodity that the workers sell, and the value that living labor—the use-value of labor-power—produced during the workday. In Marx's accounting scheme, during a portion of the workday laborers produce goods and services the value of which is equal to the wages they receive. He refers to the labor performed during this time as paid or necessary labor. If the workday were to end after the performance of necessary labor, there would be no surplus-value or capital: "if the process is not carried beyond the point where the value paid by the capitalist for the labor-power is replaced by an exact equivalent, it is simply a process of creating value," not surplus-value (Marx 1977, 302). However, since the total value laborers create depends "on the length of time [they are] in action" (Marx 1977, 679), and not the value they receive for their labor-power, and since laborers (are compelled to) continue to work over and beyond the paid portion of the workday, they perform uncompensated, surplus labor, producing surplus-value. If labor "is continued beyond that point, it becomes a process of valorization," a process in which value, by "self-expanding," becomes capital (Marx 1977, 302). Without surplus labor, capital and the capitalist would cease to exist, hence Marx's emphasis on the difference between the use-value of labor-power, or living labor, and its value as a commodity.

For Marx, labor's capacity to produce surplus is not limited to a wage-laborer working for a capitalist; nor does he suggest that surplus only appears in the form of surplus-value. Since not everybody works in any given society, the non-workers' survival depends on the existence of a surplus, whatever the social formation or mode of production is. For example, a tailor who individually produces and appropriates his/her surplus can distribute a portion of it to the state (the church) in the form of income tax (tithe) in order to partially secure the conditions of this ancient, or independent, class process, which then might be redistributed to non-workers in the form of unemployment benefits, food stamps, among other welfare services (charity). In slavery, slaves "do necessary labor, the product of which the slave master allows them to keep to enable them to continue working" (Resnick and Wolff 1987, 149); the remainder, the surplus product immediately belongs to the slave owners. In feudalism, "every serf knows that what he expends in the service of his lord is a specific quantity of his own personal labor-power" (Marx 1977, 170). That is, in addition to performing necessary labor as they produce use-values for their own consumption, serfs also pay rent (a surplus) to the lord either in kind, *corvée* labor, or as money earned from the sale of their surplus product.

Marx also imagines "an association of free [laborers], working with the means of production held in common, and expending their many different forms of labor-power in full awareness as one single social labor force" (Marx 1977, 171). In this communal class process, the laborers collectively produce goods and services; a part of this product would replenish the "means of production" they use and "another part is consumed by the members of the association as means of subsistence," which would correspond to, and be produced by, their necessary labor (Marx 1977, 172). Whatever they produce over and above that would be the surplus product, resulting from their performance of collective surplus labor.[1]

Labor, therefore, in addition to producing surplus-value in a capitalist economy, can and does produce a surplus in non-capitalist—independent (ancient), slavery, feudalism as well as communal—class processes (Resnick and Wolff 1987). Consequently, necessary labor, in its generality, can be defined as labor performed—"time-measured expenditure of human brain and muscles"—in order to produce the goods and services (or their equivalent) considered socially necessary to reproduce the laborers so that they can continue working; labor performed beyond necessary labor is surplus labor (Resnick and Wolff 2006, 93). Thus, in addition to being "the creator of use-values," labor, for Marx (1973, 133), is also a potential to produce surplus, the ability to perform labor over and beyond necessary labor in any class society.[2]

Class: surplus, power, property

To reiterate, Resnick and Wolff use the definition of labor as the producer of surplus to register class processes by tracing the flows of surplus from the site of its production to its various destinations. They begin by differentiating two general types of class processes: the fundamental and subsumed class processes. The fundamental class process focuses on who performs surplus labor and who appropriates and becomes the first, initial possessor of the resulting surplus product. Following Marx, Resnick and Wolff then differentiate various fundamental class processes—independent (ancient), slavery, feudal, capitalist, and communal—in terms of how surplus labor is performed and appropriated. Subsumed class processes concern how the appropriated surplus is in turn distributed to various non-producers. They are equally important for Resnick and Wolff, because the distribution of the surplus to those who provide the conditions of existence of a class process is necessary to prevent the transformation and dissolution of that particular fundamental class process (Resnick and Wolff 1987, 2006).

True to their epistemological and ontological commitments, Resnick and Wolff's intervention in Marxian theory is overdetermined in part by the criticisms of, debates surrounding, and alternatives to, the prevailing, orthodox interpretation(s) of Marxism at the time. In their introduction to *New Departures in Marxian Theory*, Resnick and Wolff (2006, 1) not only briefly summarize their path to Marxism but also suggest how quickly they realized that they had to deal with "the profound problems" of traditional Marxism, particularly, the definition of class. They argue that the prevalent conceptions of class focused on some combination of access to and distribution of property or power (Resnick and Wolff 2006, 2). Resnick and Wolff (2006) attribute the pervasiveness of such articulations partially to a desire to move beyond the "two-class model" that focused on the primary exploited and exploiter classes in a particular mode of production; to account for the complex class structure of modern day capitalism, which could not be accurately articulated by the simple antagonism between the bourgeois and the proletariat; and to support or criticize "actually existing socialisms."

Resnick and Wolff's focus on labor as the producer of surplus is further motivated by the status of the labor theory of value in Marxian theory and in economics more generally. The validity of Marx's labor theory of value was questioned almost immediately after the publication of volume 3 of *Capital* for its inability to explain equilibrium prices solely in terms of labor values. Solutions to this so-called "transformation problem" of labor values into prices followed quickly. If the debate surrounding the presumed impossibility of deriving prices from values did not come to an end with Piero Sraffa's (1960) ultimate verdict on the issue, the final nail on the coffin was delivered by Ian Steedman (1977), or such was the consensus among many non-Marxists and Marxists. As a result, the labor theory of value was seen as an unnecessary and quite unsuccessful detour at best, which rendered it redundant. For others, it was an "embarrassment" for Marxian theory (Bowles and Gintis 1985). Thus, it is not surprising to see attempts to "recover" class as a central, fundamental Marxian category by construing it in reference to power categories and/or property ownership and to conceptualize labor in terms other than its potential to produce surplus.[3]

It was in part a response to this intellectual environment that Resnick and Wolff (2006, 3) returned to Marx and read *Capital* "from a surplus labor perspective," which provided the "organizing focus of Marxian theory." Consequently, they (2006, 2) "took Marx's key insights to be...that all societies organize a portion of their members to produce a surplus output...and that societies differ according to how they arrange the production, appropriation, and distribution of surplus among their members." With this notion of class (and the accompanying conception of labor as the capacity to produce surplus) they analyze the inequalities and injustices in an economy, particularly exploitation.

Exploitation: property, power, surplus

The debates over the validity of the labor theory of value extended to questioning the relevance of exploitation as a concern for Marxian theory; for example, John Roemer (1994) infamously asks "whether Marxists should be interested in exploitation" at all.[4] Many Marxists answered this question in the affirmative and defined exploitation in terms of property, power, and surplus.

For example, Terrell Carver (1987) elaborates a political theory of exploitation based solely on property relations. He argues that neither a labor theory of value nor a theory of coercion (force) is necessary—or relevant—for Marx's theory of exploitation; instead, what is needed is a distinction between work and the ownership of the means of production (Carver 1987, 76, 82). This focus on ownership not only provides Marx with a theory that is applicable to all societies in which unequal property ownership prevails; it also allows one to register exploitation not only in circumstances where there is no surplus, but even where there is loss, "because private ownership of the means of production is still a feature of the economy" (Carver 1987, 70). That is, what matters is not the actual existence, but the *possibility*, of exploitation, which Carver finds to be more relevant and politically promising (1987, 75). Exploitation, he contends, will disappear when no rewards accrue due to individual, private ownership of property, when the means of production are communally owned and democratically controlled (1987, 78).

G. A. Cohen (1988) offers another definition of exploitation as unwarranted ownership of property. After suggesting "the relationship between the labor theory of value and the concept of exploitation is one of mutual irrelevance," Cohen (1988, 209) proposes what he considers to be a much simpler account of the wrongs of capitalism. For him (1988, 228), only the laborer "creates the product, that which has value," but "the capitalist appropriates some of the value of the product," which would mean that the laborer "receives less value than the value of what he creates." Thus, Cohen concludes, the capitalist exploits the laborer. The reason that the capitalist can appropriate "some of the value of what the laborer creates" and that the laborer, not as an individual but as a class, is *forced* to sell his/her labor-power, is the fact that the latter, again collectively, as the proletariat, does not have any meaningful alternatives due to the lack of access to the means of production. Thus *"the private ownership of means of existence which no one has the right to own properly,"* resulting from an unjust initial privatization of "what belongs to us all in common," is why capitalism in general, and exploitation in particular, is morally unjust and indefensible (Cohen 1988, 298, 302; emphasis in the original).

In contrast, others define exploitation by emphasizing the unequal power that exists between the capitalist and the laborer, even though they acknowledge the role of private property as well. For example, Nancy Holmstrom (1977, 360; my emphasis) refers to four features of exploitation: "that it is the production of a surplus, appropriated from the producers, uncompensated for, and *forced*." The forced nature of the performance of unpaid labor, the inevitable involvement of "force, domination, unequal power, and control...both as preconditions and as consequences" of exploitation renders it "evil" (Holmstrom 1977, 364). Similarly, laborers are systematically forced to perform surplus labor (Reiman 1987) as they do not have control over the means of production, or access to them without selling their labor-power, a freedom they are forced have; to put it differently, the "basic cause" of exploitation is the existence of "a minority *controlling* the means of production" (Holmstrom 1977, 360; my emphasis). In addition, laborers are in charge of neither the production of use-values nor the valorization process (the production of surplus-value), which are under capitalist or managerial control; consequently, exploitation becomes "a matter of undemocratic control of production" (Crocker 1972, 201).

According to this power-centered approach, exploitation is necessarily linked with alienation. Laborers not only sell their life activity, which comes under the control of the capitalist (Holmstrom 1977, 365), they are also alienated from their labor, their fellow human beings, and their species-being (cf. Marx 1975a). They are unable to possess the surplus they produce because they are alienated from their product (Crocker 1972, 204; Buchanan 1979, 124; cf. Marx 1975a). Thus, the "theory of alienation supplies content for the concept of exploitation by providing systematic classification of the ways in which human beings are utilized and the forms of harm which this utilization inflicted on them" (Buchanan 1979, 130).

While those who define exploitation in terms of unequal property find Marx's definition of labor as a capacity to produce surplus to be completely irrelevant, power-centered approaches render it secondary to their analyses. For the former, what matters is the fact that someone other than the workers owns the means of production; this creates a distinction between those who labor (those who would sell their labor-power) and those who own (those who would appropriate the product, including the surplus). As a result, the surplus, if it exists, is nothing more than a residual—the difference between what workers produce and what they receive, which leaves no room for surplus producing labor as a category.[5]

According to the power-centered approaches, laborers do indeed produce a surplus due to their lack of access to the means of production, but these are subsumed under, rendered secondary to, unequal power relations. In addition, exploitation is intimately linked with alienation, as the former is now defined first and foremost as workers' inability to control their life activity, as well as the fruits of their labor. In that sense, this approach has a great deal of commonality with the "young" Marx, evoking his articulation of labor in the *Manuscripts*—productive activity through which human beings realize themselves. As such, power-centered analyses do not define exploitation by referring to surplus producing labor, either.

In contrast to property and power approaches to exploitation, Resnick and Wolff (2005) construe it as "social theft." Exploitation is portrayed as a ubiquitous, legalized, yet "criminal" activity in which the products of laborers' creative efforts are appropriated by those who have nothing to do with their production and who return only a portion of those fruits to the workers, keeping the remainder, the surplus, for themselves (at least initially). That is, for Resnick and Wolff, exploitation is the exclusion of direct laborers from appropriation of the surplus they produce, as a result of which they also have no say in how it is distributed. Resnick and Wolff irrevocably base their elaboration of exploitation on unpaid, surplus-labor.

Moreover, Resnick and Wolff (2005, 36) assert that one would "lose the specificity of [the Marxian notion of] exploitation and its social effects" if the focus were on "capitalists' undemocratic power over workers at work ... [and] their accumulation of property." In doing so, one would be "(1) focusing instead on other forms of injustices, or (2) collapsing class and nonclass injustices as if they were identical, or (3) assuming that the eradication of nonclass injustices will necessarily eliminate exploitation as well" (ibid.). For example, the collective ownership of the means of production in socialist economies established in the USSR, China, and other countries would imply an end to class exploitation if class were defined in terms of property relations. Similarly, social democratic gains in American and European states might imply a reduction in exploitation, as workers gain more control/power over economic and political decision-making (Resnick and Wolff 2005, 2006). When one defines exploitation in terms of property ownership or power relationships, "the analytical and hence political distinctness of Marx's economic theory of unpaid labor" is ignored or marginalized so that "actually existing" exploitation in the production process is not confronted but rather rendered invisible (Resnick and Wolff 2005, 36). This may, in turn, strengthen capitalist and other forms of exploitation. Finally, the failure of the so-called socialist countries can be presented as the failure of Marxism (Resnick and Wolff 2005, 2013).

Class justice, class democracy

Again and again, Resnick and Wolff claim that one of Marx's unique contributions to the criticisms of capitalism is "his critique of exploitation inside the production process," the site at which the performance of surplus labor, and the appropriation of its products, occur (2005, 34). In accordance with this definition of exploitation, class justice, or a non-exploitative class process can only be achieved if those who produce the surplus also appropriate and distribute it. Their definition of communism as the appropriation and distribution of surplus labor by productive workers is equivalent to the emergence of "a new kind of class democracy" (Resnick and Wolff 2013, 160): those who *directly* participate in the production of the surplus decide what to do with it after initially claiming it. The basis of this distinct class justice is to be found in "the new ethics that Marx introduced with his idea of class exploitation" (Resnick and Wolff 2005, 34).

Resnick and Wolff's surplus labor approach has inspired numerous contributions to a Marxian theory of class justice and ethics. For example,

Burczak (1998, 2001) calls for the appropriation of the surplus product by all workers inside a firm. Referring to Ellerman's labor theory of property, Burczak considers the workers to be the only responsible agents in the production process. The injustice of exploitation is construed as the treatment of workers as a means toward an end (surplus production) and not an end in themselves, which is an infringement of Kant's categorical imperative. In contrast, Stephen Cullenberg (1998) contends that assigning sole responsibility to some is more in line with the Lockean notion of property rights and can end up excluding others who should be considered as participants in the production of the surplus; consequently, rather than worrying about listing precisely who should be the appropriators, he suggests that those who perform surplus labor should not be excluded from the appropriation of the surplus. From this perspective, one can conclude, despite its claims of equality and all-inclusivity, capitalism entails a "logic of exclusion": not all can—its producers cannot—appropriate the surplus (Özselçuk and Madra 2005).

Bruce Roberts (2011), in contrast, suggests that the fact that workers appropriate their own surplus product does not necessarily mean the end of exploitation because they don't appropriate all surplus-value when faced with "forced value distributions." Workers could have "a *formal but not a real capacity to appropriate* their own surplus labor," and thus continue to be exploited, as surplus-value would inevitably be redistributed in a commodity economy via the price mechanism (Roberts 2011, 346; emphasis in the original).[6] For Roberts (2011, 350; emphasis in the original) the only way to eliminate exploitation "is *participatory consent to the process* that establishes that price structure, from those whose labors create the social surplus or provide conditions for its existence." David Ruccio (2011) disagrees with Roberts, arguing that the inability to dispose over the surplus in its totality does not exploitation make. As long as workers collectively appropriate the surplus product they produce, even though they might "be forced to have the freedom to give up a portion of the surplus," they are participating in a non-exploitative class process, independent of the distributions of the surplus. Ruccio (2003, 88) advances a related argument when he suggests "transnational subcontracting" does not imply "foreign exploitation" as transnational capitalist corporations merely engage in an exchange relationship with local producers, some of which might be non-capitalist.

Adding further nuance to this discussion, David Kristjanson-Gural (2011, 353) argues that, while "the elimination of exploitation at the firm level is necessary to eliminate exploitation," it does not necessarily lead to *class* justice; workers' appropriating their surplus-value does not end the "unfair redistribution of labor time" once value is redistributed through exchange. In contrast to Roberts, he suggests that "the redistribution of value through exchange" and exploitation are qualitatively different forms of class injustice. For example, worker cooperatives could eliminate capitalist exploitation at the firm level yet "face unfair exchange" that results from market competition among the co-ops, thus necessitating the formation of institutions that would address this injustice (ibid.).

Kristjanson-Gural's notion of class justice builds on the arguments of George DeMartino (2003), who discusses how, and by whom, the surplus should be produced, appropriated, and distributed. Evoking the motto Marx (1974) advances in the *Critique of the Gotha Program,* "from each according to his ability, to each according to his needs," DeMartino (2003, 13) suggests that those who can produce the most surplus should do so, and this surplus should be distributed in accordance with "people's distinct needs: those with the greatest needs should receive the greatest shares." Finally, this surplus should be democratically appropriated by all members of a community: in doing so, he situates class justice within the broader context of capabilities equality—"*all* members of society enjoy equal *efficacy*… [and] have equal substantive ability to participate meaningfully in all vital decisions that affect the community"—thus, providing an egalitarian justification for his Marxian conception of class justice (2003, 21; emphases in the original).

Inspired by DeMartino, I construe surplus production, its appropriation, and the claiming of a portion of it as distinct capabilities (Düzenli 2016).[7] I define labor as a surplus producing capability to be "the *ability, freedom and willingness to produce more than what is deemed socially necessary to continue laboring*" and suggest each should contribute to surplus production in accordance with his/her ability, collectively, and willingly, as a result of his/her increased productivity (Düzenli 2016, 1027; emphasis in the original). Each, without exception, should have the capability to appropriate this surplus, and each should have the capability to claim and receive a portion of it, independent of his/her role in its production; thus no one is excluded from any moment of this surplus economy (Düzenli 2016).

Of course, the preceding discussion does not do justice to the wealth of literature on exploitation articulated through the lens of surplus; nor does it provide an extensive summary of the relevant works of the authors cited herein. Nevertheless, perhaps it provides a snapshot of the contributions to a Marxian theory of class justice and ethics inspired by Marx's, and Resnick and Wolff's, surplus labor approach.

Resnick and Wolff's seminal work is all the more important at a time when the Great Recession has led to endless publications that find income inequality or lack of proper regulations to be the fundamental problem(s) of capitalist economies. Resnick and Wolff on the other hand show how capitalism is inherently unstable and prone to crisis; they suggest income inequality is a consequence and not the cause of capitalism's predicament. They remind us that capitalism is an exploitative hence unjust economic system, not to mention an undemocratic one. In a capitalist enterprise, the workers cannot appropriate and decide what to do with surplus-value, let alone have any say in the manner and quantity of surplus-value production. As a result, they have no control over an important aspect of their everyday lives and this is precisely what is wrong with capitalism—and with any class process in which the producers of the surplus do not participate in its appropriation and thus also in its distribution. Resnick and Wolff call for an alternative economic system, one with decentralized, communist enterprises in which workplace democracy prevails, as each worker participates in every decision. The conclusion that workers should take control over their work lives is what makes Resnick and Wolff's project unique, appealing, and pertinent for our times.

Acknowledgments

I would like to thank Ted Burczak and Ruth Toulson for their insightful comments and helpful suggestions.

Notes

1 This surplus product (or likewise the surplus product in any non-capitalist class process) may or may not take the form of surplus-value.
2 What about non-laborers in a non-class society? I think there would be two possibilities. At the very early stages of human existence, with limited technology and know-how, the society could be unable to produce any surplus, barely satisfying the material necessities for survival, thus incapable of supporting the non-laborers. Or, if all labor becomes necessary labor in a communist economy, a possibility Resnick and Wolff (2002, 2006) discuss, surplus labor and surplus product would cease to exist, because the sustenance of non-laborers would be considered part of the necessary labor performed by the society (cf. Marx 1974). I thank Ted Burczak for raising this important question.
3 In contrast, Wolff, Bruce Roberts, and Antonio Callari (1982; Wolff, Callari, and Roberts 1984; Callari, Roberts and Wolff 1998) provide a unique interpretation of and solution to the "transformation problem" in which they reassert the significance of Marx's value theory for his class analysis of capitalism.
4 Even though Roemer (1994, 93) does not see "any logically compelling reason to be interested in exploitation theory," he finds the reasons *behind* Marxists' concern for exploitation—i.e., its basis in differential property ownership—to be compelling. Thus, he (1994, 110) argues that Marxists should "locate the source of exploitation in an unjust distribution of ownership of alienable assets."
5 One can find some common ground between the property approach and the young Marx, given both are highly critical of private property. I would argue, however, these similarities are rather tenuous since for the young Marx, alienation (the *Manuscripts*), or the division of labor (*The German Ideology*) are the more fundamental categories.
6 Roberts provides another example of exploitation that occurs when workers have to make payments to finance capital due to creditors' "effective control over the financial conditions of existence of the enterprise" (Roberts 2011, 346).
7 Amartya Sen (1987) defines capabilities as things a person can do or be and has a reason to value as part of a fulfilling and meaningful life.

References

Bowles, S. and H. Gintis. 1985. "The Labor Theory of Value and the Specificity of Marxian Economics." In *Rethinking Marxism: Struggles in Marxist Theory: Essays for Harry Magdoff & Paul Sweezy*, S. A. Resnick and R. D. Wolff, eds., 31–44. New York: Autonomedia.

Buchanan, A. 1979. "Exploitation, Alienation, and Injustice." *Canadian Journal of Philosophy* 9 (1): 121–39.

Burczak, T. 1998. "Appropriation, Responsibility and Agreement." *Rethinking Marxism* 10 (3): 96–105.

———. 2001. "Ellerman's Labor Theory of Property and the Injustice of Capitalist Exploitation." *Review of Social Economy* 59 (2): 161–83.

Callari, A., B. Roberts, and R. D. Wolff. 1998. "The Transformation Trinity: Value, Value Form, and Price." In *Marxian Economics: A Reappraisal. Essays on Volume 3 of Capital*, R. Bellofiore, ed., 43–56. London: Macmillan.

Carver, T. 1987. "Marx's Political Theory of Exploitation." In *Modern Theories of Exploitation*, A. Reeve, ed., 68–79. London: Sage.

Cohen, G. A. 1988. *History, Labor, Freedom: Themes from Marx*. Oxford: Oxford University Press.

Crocker, L. 1972. "Marx's Theory of Alienation." *Social Theory and Practice* 2 (2): 201–15.

Cullenberg, S. 1998. "Exploitation, Appropriation, and Exclusion: Locating Capitalist Injustice." *Rethinking Marxism* 10 (3): 66–75.

DeMartino, G. 2003. "Realizing Class Justice." *Rethinking Marxism* 15 (1): 1–31.

Düzenli, F. E. 2006. "Re/Presenting Labor: Economic Discourse, Value and Ethics." Ph.D. Dissertation, Department of Economics, University of Notre Dame.

———. 2016. "Surplus-Producing Labour as a Capability: A Marxian Contribution to Amartya Sen's Revival of Classical Political Economy." *Cambridge Journal of Economics* 40 (4): 1019–35.

Holmstrom, N. 1977. "Exploitation." *Canadian Journal of Philosophy* 7 (2): 353–69.

Kristjanson-Gural, D. 2011. "Value, Cooperation, and Class Justice." *Rethinking Marxism* 23 (3): 352–63.

Marx, K. 1973 [1939]. *Grundrisse: Foundations of the Critique of Political Economy*. Trans. M. Nicolaus. London: New Left Review.

———. 1974. "Critique of the Gotha Program." In *The First International and After*, D. Fernbach, trans., 339–59. London: New Left Review.

———. 1975. "The Economic and Philosophical Manuscripts of 1844." In *Early Writings*, R. Livingstone and G. Benton, trans., 279–400. London: New Left Review.

———. 1977. *Capital: A Critique of Political Economy*. Vol. 1. Trans. B. Fowkes. New York: Vintage Books.

Marx, K. and F. Engels. 1975. *Collected Works. Vol: 5*. New York: International Publishers.

Özselçuk, C. and Y. M. Madra. 2005. "Psychoanalysis and Marxism: From Capitalist-All to Communist Non-All." *Psychoanalysis, Culture and Society* 10 (1): 79–97.

Reiman, J. 1987. "Exploitation, Force, and the Moral Assessment of Capitalism: Thoughts on Roemer and Cohen." *Philosophy & Public Affairs* 16 (1): 3–41.

Resnick, S. A. and R. D. Wolff. 1987. *Knowledge and Class: A Marxian Critique of Political Economy*. Chicago: University of Chicago Press.

———. 2002. *Class Theory and History: Capitalism and Communism in the USSR*. London and New York: Routledge.

———. 2005. "The Point and Purpose of Marx's Notion of Class." *Rethinking Marxism* 17 (1): 33–7.

———, eds. 2006. *New Departures in Marxian theory.* London and New York: Routledge.

———. 2013. "Marxism." *Rethinking Marxism* 25 (2): 152–62.

Roberts, B. 2011. "Exploitation, Appropriation, and Subsumption." *Rethinking Marxism* 23 (3): 341–51.

Roemer, J. 1994. *Egalitarian Perspectives: Essays in Philosophical Economics.* Cambridge: Cambridge University Press.

Ruccio, D. F. 2003. "Globalization and Imperialism." *Rethinking Marxism* 15 (1): 75–94.

———. 2011. "Cooperatives, Surplus, and the Social." *Rethinking Marxism* 23 (3): 334–40.

Sen, A. K. 1987. *Tanner Lectures in Human Values: The Standard of Living.* New York and Cambridge, UK: Cambridge University Press.

Sraffa, P. 1960. *Production of Commodities by Means of Commodities: Prelude to a Critique of Economic Theory.* New York and Cambridge, UK: Cambridge University Press.

Steedman, I. 1977. *Marx after Sraffa.* London: New Left Books.

Wolff, R., B. Roberts, and A. Callari. 1982. "Marx's (not Ricardo's) Transformation Problem: A Radical Reconceptualization." *History of Political Economy* 14 (4): 564–82.

Wolff, R., A. Callari, and B. Roberts. 1984. "A Marxian Alternative to the Traditional 'Transformation problem'." *Review of Radical Political Economics* 16 (2): 115–135.

Part IV

Heretical materialism

10 The last instance

Resnick and Wolff at the point of heresy

Warren Montag

There is perhaps no term more associated with Resnick and Wolff's reading of Althusser than "overdetermination" and, at the same time, no term so misconstrued by readers of this reading. Their understanding of Althusser's concept has been described as "everythingism" (Carling 1990) and "indeterminacy" (Silverman 2013) both by those who insist that Resnick and Wolff had either misread the concept as it appeared in Althusser's work, which would then exempt Althusser from the charges levied against their reading of him, and those who, in opposition, argue that the weakness of their formulation is an expression of the fact that "overdetermination" is the weak point of Althusser's *oeuvre* (if not exemplary of its general weakness, imposture, etc.), in which case Resnick and Wolff share in the responsibility imputed to Althusser for the decline of Marxist thought. The particular misreading attributed to them by those readers who regarded Althusser as an important figure in a "renewal" of Marxism or "theory" was their refusal to ground overdetermination as a marker of both the extraordinary complexity and multiplicity of the factors that exercised an effectivity in the configuration of a given historical contradiction in the "determination in the last instance" of this entire configuration by "the economy," as if, in the absence of a determinant last instance, these factors could not cohere into a functioning whole.

Unlike so many of their critics, Resnick and Wolff insisted on deriving the concept of overdetermination from a careful reading of Althusser's actual account of this concept. Their respect for the materiality of writing set them in conflict with the dominant understanding of overdetermination as a theory of the complexity of the historical conjuncture whose existence as system or structure requires the absolute sovereignty of the last instance, "His Majesty, the Economy" (Althusser 1969, 113). They insisted that such an interpretation, which, we should note, substitutes Engels' position in the letter to Bloch, the very position Althusser subjects to criticism in the appendix to "Contradiction and Overdetermination," for Althusser's own position, is constitutively blind to the starkly paradoxical character of "the last instance" exhibited in Althusser's work (Althusser 1969, 111–13). Their recognition of this paradox and its effects gives the work of Resnick and Wolff its power.

The incomprehension and hostility this paradox provoked cannot be explained by the intellectual laziness (one form of which, as Kant remarked, was dogmatism) of the readers of *For Marx*, even if those who turned away in frustration from Althusser did so without really knowing why. Their reactions, in their very diversity, were provoked by Althusser's notion (made visible by Resnick and Wolff's excavation and explanation of that notion) of an overdetermined historical contradiction whose magnitude and complexity gave it the appearance of a miracle, as Lenin put it (Montag 2015) or conferred upon it a kind of sublimity that brought in turn the unrest (*Unrühe*) of perpetual oscillation to a mind simultaneously attracted to and repulsed by the object of its fascination. It is here that Althusser tarried, not with the negative, but with that which resists it: irreducible paradox that no negation can resolve. He not only continued throughout his work to use the formulation "in the last instance," although typically as a kind of incantation to ward off the inescapable fact that no resolution of this paradox was at present possible. In fact, it was Althusser himself who had ruled out the possibility of a "theory of the last instance" at the very moment he introduced the phrase without, however, acknowledging the contradiction or paradox his formula contained: the economy or "the economic" is historically determinant in the last instance, *and* (not "but") "the lonely hour of the last instance will never come" (Althusser 1969, 113).

It is no wonder that readers clung to "the last instance" (whether to adopt or reject it) and systematically overlooked the fact that Althusser had in effect crossed it out, placed it *sous rature*, as if he had employed the phrase precisely in order to be able, by the fact of using it, to cross it out. To gauge the systematic and structural nature of this oversight, it would be difficult to find a more telling case than that of Jacques Derrida. During the course of the long interview conducted by Michael Sprinker concerning his political and philosophical relations with Althusser, Derrida seized upon the "the last instance" after Sprinker used the phrase (Derrida 1993, 207–208). There followed an energetic and lengthy exposition on the fact that the theory of the last instance was evidence of Althusser's inability finally to break with metaphysics in its teleological form. Derrida paused only when Sprinker interrupted him to say that Althusser had actually written that "the lonely hour of the last instance never comes." Derrida stopped and for a moment was confused until, gathering his thoughts, he expressed doubt about the phrase Sprinker had cited; if Althusser really did say such a thing, he, Derrida, had forgotten it. He would have to return to Althusser's text to see for himself. This incident may serve as an allegory of the relation between Resnick and Wolff and the vast majority of Althusser's readers. Their reminder that Althusser's postulation of a determination in the last instance was coupled with his insistence that the last instance never comes remained an unwelcome and disconcerting disruption of the very coherent and absolutely inadequate construction that passed for Althusserianism.

Even reading Althusser's text as closely as possible and in the original French (to follow his protocol of reading), however, does nothing to resolve or overcome the irreducible and stark nature of this paradox. We might move beyond the text to attempt ourselves to overcome it or reconcile its terms in one of two ways: by arguing that the last instance exists but in the form of a deferred presence, a presence or appearance put off, not forever, not even for an indeterminable period of time, that will, because it must, appear at the last or the limit, the *eskhatos*, or by arguing that there is no last instance, no necessary concept of the last instance, not even the concreteness of its ruins, but simply the emptiness of what has never been and will never be (and, it must be added, what Althusser should never have invoked as an explanatory principle). But, as Althusser argued with reference to Freud, there are cases in which we must be able "to understand the *necessity of the paradox* of a body of thought," above all when it is "a thought that never stops saying the same thing, deepening it, but that at the same time says it in forms that are new at every turn and at every turn disconcerting" (Althusser 1996, 94).

To understand the necessity of the paradox that Althusser places before us, we might think of the concept of the "point of heresy" (*point d'hérésie*) introduced by Foucault in *The Order of Things* (1971) but later developed and modified by Etienne Balibar. Foucault, referring to eighteenth-century theories of grammar, speaks of a moment of "*découpage*," that is, of a cut or division that placed before the project of a general grammar the necessity of a choice: "either to pursue its analysis at a lower level than nominal unity, and to bring into prominence, before signification, the insignificant elements of which it is constructed, or to reduce that nominal unity by means of a regressive process, to recognize its existence within more restricted units, and to find its efficacy as representation below the level of whole words, in particles, in syllables, and even in single letters themselves" (Foucault 1971, 99, 181). The division here is constitutive: not only does general grammar from this point on proceed along two divergent paths, but it is now defined by the necessity of a choice, that is, by the impossibility of not choosing (ibid.).

Balibar insists that "there is something in the idea of the point of heresy beyond the classificatory and in some way taxonomic meaning that Foucault gives it in *The Order of Things*" (Balibar 2012). To explain what this might be, he turns to Pascal who examines the concept of heresy not simply in terms of its theological content, but also in formal terms: "what characterizes heresy is that regarding each of the mysteries that are constitutive of the Christian faith and that rest on a unity of contraries, the most fundamental of all being that which concerns Christ himself, simultaneously God and man, the heretic is he who is incapable of upholding the two terms of the contradiction and who chooses (*hairesis*) one of the possibilities so that it may once again become rational and not absurd or incomprehensible" (ibid.). Essential here is the irreducibility of the contraries in their very unity: neither can be reduced to, or even understood, on the basis of the other, nor can there be a third position that would surmount and reconcile the contradiction between them. What was, for Foucault, mere division becomes in Althusser's case active paradox. And while the point of heresy in Althusser's work has nothing to do with the mysteries of faith or a conviction powerful enough to allow the believer to dwell in the darkness of uncertainty, it is nevertheless the case that Althusser was inspired by Pascal's devotion to a Holy Spirit of which nothing remained in the world but the traces of its absence, another paradox, a paradox powerful enough to lead Pascal to the threshold of a kind of materialism.

The point of heresy Althusser sets before us has not been recognized as such, not even as the paradox it is, but has appeared to readers as the index of a problem whose solution was already at hand:

1   the economy is determinant in the last instance, and
2   the last instance will never come.

Expressed in this way, the paradox could appear as a syllogism awaiting only the conclusion that will dispel any doubt: therefore, the economy is not determinant. It was precisely Althusser's refusal to take the next step and draw the inference that seemed unavoidable that divided his readers into two camps, according to whether the economy was or was not determinant (in the last instance). Why would Althusser confront his readers with an incomplete syllogism, which, left as is, is a paradox? Precisely because the lack of a conclusion or solution was not his lack or failure then to be remedied by someone better equipped than he to solve the problem. Rather, the unfinishable syllogism was a "necessary paradox," a paradox determined by the historical conjuncture upon which theory never reflects from the outside because this history is already in it as well as all around it, imposing on theory its uneven and combined development. Caught in an unstable relation of forces between ideas, Althusser's inquiry, quite independently of his efforts, suspended itself. Althusser's paradox thus marks the site of an absence, namely the absence of a theory of causality adequate to Marx's discoveries. Heresy in this sense would be to choose one or the other of the alternatives he has set before us in order to deny the existence of the lack that our impatience refuses to acknowledge.

Although Resnick and Wolff never formulated their intervention in exactly this way, we can say that their intransigent defense of the importance of restoring "the lonely hour of the last instance never comes" to its proper and unsurpassable place as the other term of what we may now call Althusser's point of heresy succeeded in affirming the efficacy of paradox. For the paradox of the last instance was hardly the only one, even in Althusser's early work. Within a year or two of "Contradiction and Overdetermination," Althusser would formulate another closely related, or perhaps the same, paradox in different terms: the paradox of structural causality. In *Reading Capital* he argues that "structure is immanent in its effects, a cause immanent in its effects in the Spinozist sense of the term, that *the whole existence of the structure consists of its effects*, in short that the structure, which is merely a specific combination of its peculiar elements, is nothing outside its effects" (Althusser and Balibar 1970, 188–89).

What does it mean to speak of a cause that exists only in its effects, a cause that cannot exist before or without them, a cause never present except metonymically and therefore finally an absent cause? The fact that we must speak of absent causes and last instances that never arrive reminds us that it is not enough "to shatter all the classical conceptions of causality" for a new conception to emerge. Althusser's paradoxes mark the space constituted by two impossibilities: the impossibility of accepting the old conceptions of determination and causality and the impossibility (neither logical nor eternal, but conjunctural and historical) at this moment of producing a genuinely new conception.

The legacy of Resnick and Wolff is a difficult one, above all because it is difficult to inhabit the paradoxical space that their reading of Althusser has helped to open, that point of heresy whose terms, on the condition that they are held apart, form the gate through which the future may enter.

References

Althusser, L. 1969 [1965]. *For Marx*. Trans. B. Brewster. London: New Left Books.

———. 1996 [1993]. "Dr. Freud's Discovery." In *Writings on Psychoanalysis*, G. Mehlman, trans., 85–104. New York: Columbia University Press.

Althusser, L. and E. Balibar. 1970 [1965]. *Reading Capital*. Trans. B. Brewster. London: New Left Books.

Balibar, E. 2012. "Citoyen Balibar: Entretien avec Etienne Balibar par Nicolas Duvoux & Pascal Sévérac." www.laviedesideés.fr (accessed September 27, 2016).

Carling, A. 1990. "In Defense of Rational Choice Marxism." *New Left Review* 184: 97–109.

Derrida, J. 1993. "Politics and Friendship: An Interview with Jacques Derrida," In *The Althusserian Legacy*, E. A. Kaplan and M. Sprinker, eds., 183–232. London: Verso.

Foucault, M. 1971. *The Order of Things: An Archaeology of the Human Sciences*. New York: Vintage.

Montag, W. 2015. "Althusser's Lenin." *Diacritics* 43 (2): 48–66.

Silverman. M. S. 2013. "'Overdetermined' or 'Indeterminate?' Remarks on *Knowledge and Class*." *Rethinking Marxism* 25 (3): 311–24.

11 Aleatory Marxism

Resnick, Wolff, and the revivification of Althusser

Joseph W. Childers

The work of Steve Resnick and Rick Wolff has been relegated to the margins of the discipline they professed; moreover, they frequently have found themselves at odds, intellectually or strategically, with fellow occupants of these marginal spaces. Perhaps it is appropriate, then, that this essay is itself an outlier in a collection devoted to the assessment of Resnick and Wolff's legacy, as it chronicles their impact from a perspective not founded in economics or even in the social sciences. I make no grand theoretical claims, nor do I engage the finer points of theoretical difference between Resnick and Wolff and those who followed in their footsteps. Instead, I attempt to situate the effect of their work on thinkers who, because they are trained as literary critics and theorists, become disciplinary tourists when traversing Resnick and Wolff's work. Consequently, it may not align with the experience of those who approach Resnick and Wolff from the viewpoint of economics, political economy, sociology, geography, or even art history. Nevertheless, it is arguably through literary studies that "Theory" with a capital "T," especially theory of the poststructuralist sort(s), has established and legitimated itself as central to scholarly discourse in the United States. Furthermore, I want to note the resonance of Resnick and Wolff's work across large disciplinary divides—such as those between the social sciences and the humanities. At least in part, the investment in theory on both sides of that chasm has helped to facilitate the reach and impact of Resnick and Wolff's contributions.

An enormous sector of poststructuralist Theory discourse was (and remains) decidedly Marxian, if not strictly Marxist per se. Even contemporary theoretical articulations ostensibly refusing a Marxist foregrounding of dialectical thinking or of concepts such as value, class, and exploitation are substantially informed by the legacy of Marxist thought and their relation to it. This is especially true in the West. As I point out in the first section below, perhaps the most influential and controversial Marxist thinker of the twentieth century was Louis Althusser. Yet almost as quickly as the work of Althusser began to ascend, it began to be overwhelmed on one side by those who found its repudiation of humanism incompatible with their vision of Marxism and, on the other, by those who regarded his work as too bounded by an epistemology grounded in a rigid notion of structural coherence and unity without totality, a structure only apparent in its effects, thus incommensurate with the emphasis on the aleatory and contingent that became increasingly prominent in Althusser's work (Montag 1998, 72–73).

As I argue below, the work of Resnick and Wolff revolutionized Althusser, offering a liberatory moment that insists upon the aleatory, celebrates it, and indeed finds within it the possibility of an analytic that has broad ramifications for social inquiry in every register. What we are left with is a radicalization of Althusser and Marx that produces an "aleatory Marxism" whose problematic bears as much resemblance to the work of Derrida, Foucault, and other poststructuralist thinkers as it does to the work of Althusser or Marx. Yet unlike Foucault, who never really reconciled himself to his Marxist lineage, or Derrida, who only late in his career fully reconnected with his version of Marx, Resnick and Wolff and their well-known protégés and collaborators, J.K. Gibson-Graham, David Ruccio, and Jack Amariglio, never lost sight of their Marxist heritage.

In lieu of an origin

At a conference at Johns Hopkins University in 1966, a young, iconoclastic French-Algerian philosopher named Jacques Derrida presented the paper, "Structure, Sign, and Play in the Discourse of the Human Sciences." This lecture and its subsequent publication four years later in the conference proceedings, *The Structuralist Controversy: The Languages of Criticism and the Sciences of Man* (Macksey and Donato 1970), effectively opened the floodgates for the "French Wave" of theory, drenching Anglo/American literary critics with the waters of poststructuralist thought. It would be unfair to say that Anglo-American literary theory had been entirely ignorant of the work that had been fomenting in French intellectual circles in the decade or so prior to Derrida's lecture. The works of Levi-Strauss, Sartre, and Merleau-Ponty had found adherents among some younger literary scholars, but most work in literary criticism was heavily influenced either by formalism, especially of the sort practiced by the New Critics such as Cleanth Brooks or Neo-Aristotelians like Wayne Booth, the archetypal criticism of Northrop Frye (which has some similarities to structuralism), Freudian (and to a lesser extent Jungian) psychoanalytic theory, or was indebted to a hodge-podge of varieties of historicism, including Marxist analyses that were very much focused on class but were essentially economistic. Despite their methodological differences, these approaches to literary works and to theorizing how those works generate knowledge share a common presupposition about the *recovery* of meaning, or perhaps better stated, the existence of meaning in a way that informs the operations of the text. That is to say, at a fundamental level, these theories assume a correspondence between meaning and text that insists upon a hermeneutic operation that is primarily exegetic; even if meaning is not entirely recoverable, it is present, represented by the text. Consequently, most Anglo-American literary critics were somewhat ill prepared for the baptism of *différance*, deferral, and decentering that is so much a part of poststructuralist thought and that "Structure, Sign, and Play" invokes in its critique of essentialist, "presentist," epistemologies.

Within a decade of Macksey and Donato's publication of the Hopkins conference proceedings, theory, especially French theory, had established itself as an integral part of the literary criticism industry in the U.S. Journals devoted to theoretical debates (and often particular agendas) such as *Critical Inquiry, New Literary History, Semiotext(e), Diacritics*, and *Representations* arose, displacing in importance organs like *PMLA* and *ELH*, which had been the premier journals of the discipline for more than a generation. *Deconstruction and Criticism* (Bloom, de Man, Derrida, Hartman, and Miller 1979), the "Yale Manifesto," collected in one place seminal essays by Derrida, Paul de Man, Geoffrey Hartman, J. Hillis Miller, and Harold Bloom, essentially legitimizing "theory" as a sub-discipline within literary studies, and linking its pursuit to an interest in contemporary, Continental philosophy. Derrida's *Of Grammatology* (1974) and *Writing and Difference* (1978) became widely available in English and *de rigueur* reading in literature departments across the country. A broad revisioning of Freudian theory was instigated by the translation of a selection of Jacques Lacan's *Ecrits* (1973), as well as his *Four Fundamental Concepts of Psychoanalysis* (1977). Michel Foucault's works also became theoretical must-reads. In 1965 an abridged version of his *Folie et Deraison* was published as *Madness and Civilization* (1965) to lukewarm reviews (Marcus 1975). It received a much different kind of attention when, by the end of the 1970s, *The Birth of the Clinic* ([1963] 1973), *The Order of Things* (*Les mots et les choses*, [1966] 1970), and *The Archaeology of Knowledge* ([1969] 1972), as well as his enormously influential *Discipline and Punish* ([1974] 1977) and *The History of Sexuality, Vol. 1* (1976] 1978), all became available to English readers.

Despite an obvious indebtedness to and influence by Marxian thought—one thinks of Foucault's "Nietzsche, Freud, Marx" (1998) and Derrida's eventual public recognition of his Marxian legacy in *Specters of Marx* (1994)—Foucault's overtly antagonistic stance toward class in analyses of power and Derrida's insistence on the primacy of signifying over the signified were not exactly clarion calls to Marxist critics and theorists. Nor did their Anglo/American fellow travelers uniformly embrace the insights of French poststructuralist Marxists. The most influential works of Louis Althusser, specifically *For Marx* (1969), and *Reading Capital* (with Etienne Balibar 1970), were available in English quite early in the French theory swell, translations appearing in 1969 and 1970 respectively, while the famous "Ideology and Ideological State Apparatuses" (ISA) essay appeared in English in *Lenin, Philosophy and other Essays*, in 1971.

No matter. Distrustful of a metaphysics of deferral and contingency, influential British Marxists like Eric Hobsbawm, E. P. Thompson, and Raymond Williams were careful to distance themselves from the *nouvelle vogue* of poststructuralist theoretical pursuits, and Althusser's work did little to mollify them. Some like Hobsbawm were laconic, stating that Althusser had "practically nothing to offer historians" (MARHO 1983, 37). Thompson was much less restrained, famously writing in his 1973 "Open Letter to Leszek Kolakowski" of his resistance to Continental theory:

> I cannot fly. When you spread your wings and soar into the firmament where Kierkegaard and Husserl, Heidegger, Jaspers, and Sartre and the other great eagles soar, I remain on the ground like one of the last great bustards, awaiting the extinction of my species on the diminishing soil of an eroding idiom, craning my neck into the air, flapping my paltry wings. All around me my younger feathered cousins are managing mutations; they are turning into little eagles, and whirr! with a rush of wind they are off to Paris, to Rome, to California.
>
> (Thompson 1978, 319)

Elsewhere he eschews metaphor and is rather more pointed, "I reject in form all, and in content most, of the work of Althusser" (*ibid.*, 352). Raymond Williams, similarly, in *Marxism and Literature* (1977a) and in "The Paths and Pitfalls of Ideology as Ideology" (1977b) repudiates Althusser's claims, especially in regards to the processes and influences of ideological state apparatuses.

Althusser did have his champions, however, and for a time the possibilities of a new, poststructuralist, linguistically influenced theoretical model made strong inroads among some Marxist academics in literary studies. Under the editorship of Perry Anderson, *The New Left Review* became increasingly critical of the humanist Marxism practiced by the Hobsbawm-Williams-Thompson generation, welcoming essays of the "soaring" variety that Thompson so obstreperously—and entertainingly—despised. A number of young literary theorists, arguably the most well known being Terry Eagleton, used the *NLR* as a venue in which to demonstrate and insist upon the importance of poststructuralist interventions into literary, and Marxist, theory. Even so, Eagleton's efforts are often laced with an ambivalence that is, in many ways, a harbinger of his eventual turning away from Althusser. As early as *Marxism and Literary Criticism* (1976), Eagleton admits that though he finds their work "deeply suggestive" of the relation "they propose between literature and ideology," he also regards the "comments of both Althusser and [Pierre] Macherey [in *Pour Une Théorie de la Production Littéraire*] at crucial points ambiguous and obscure" (19). By the time *Ideology* appears in 1991, Eagleton pronounces Althusser's "model" a "good deal too monistic, passing over the discrepant, contradictory ways in which subjects may be ideologically accosted—partially, wholly, or not at all—by discourses which themselves form no obvious cohesive unity" (1991, 217).

Despite such statements and attempts to reconcile other articulations of poststructuralist theoretical assumptions with Marxist analytics (one thinks of Michael Ryan's *Marxism and Deconstruction* [1982]), the reluctance and distrust that vexed Anglo/American Marxist theories' early interactions with poststructuralism were suspended for a brief time, and Althusser's work was in the ascendancy among those Marxist theorists who recognized that simply dismissing the "linguistic turn" in literary criticism and theory was both nostalgic and unproductive. Hastily presented and often prescriptive and clumsy in its application of Althusserian theory, Eagleton's *Criticism and Ideology* (1976) nonetheless proved exceedingly significant. And even as the more mature Eagleton insists upon the distance between his own theoretical agenda and what he perceives as the shortcomings of Althusser's (especially around theorizations of ideology), the continued, palpable presence of that early influence in his later work remains important to those interested in theories of the aesthetic. Similarly, Fredric Jameson's version of Althusser, specifically in *The Political Unconscious* (1982), informed an entire generation of literary theorists. His admonition to "always historicize" became a kind of watchword for the projects of various literary theoretical models in the 1980s and 90s.

Despite this Althusserian presence, the historicist movements of that era, while often initially reliant on Althusserian conceptions of subjectivity and wary of unexamined uses of the dialectic, increasingly drew either from the carceral Foucault of *The Archaeology of Knowledge* and *Discipline and Punish* or from cultural critics such as Raymond Williams or Stuart Hall. Foucauldian-based "new historicism" as articulated in journals like *Representations*, quickly outpaced the more overtly Marxist inflected "cultural materialism" of critics like Jonathan Dollimore and Alan Sinfield (1985) or Peter Stallybrass and Allon White (1986). And even among that latter group of critics, theoretical allegiances could often be traced to a version of Bhaktinian discourse analysis that bore a greater resemblance to Foucauldian analytics of power and "resistance" than to Althusserian discussions of ideology and overdetermination. In a different, though related, vein in the 1990s and early 2000s, when Gayatri Spivak (1993) began to publish her incursions into Marxian thought around the political implications of rethinking the catachretic signifying process that is "value," she too was concerned to address Foucault and of course Derrida, but not Althusser.

Toward the aleatory

Admittedly the influence of Deleuze and Guattari, Baudrillard, and others began to assert itself at this time, gaining some measure of theoretical turf; nevertheless, it would not be unfair to characterize the theory landscape of literary criticism at that particular historical juncture as primarily divided between acolytes of Derrida and those of Foucault, with those most interested in ideological criticism favoring the Foucauldian. As early as 1978, even a theorist like Edward Said, whose work is overtly indebted to the work of Gramsci (and Althusser), participates in the carving up of theoretical territory, typifying "Derrida's *mise en abime* and Foucault's *mise en discours*" as "the contrast between a criticism claiming that *il n'y a pas d'hors texte* and one discussing textuality as having to do with a plurality of texts, and with history, power, knowledge, and society" (Said 1978, 673). Indeed, the very title of E. Ann Kaplan and Michael Sprinker's volume, *The Althusserian Legacy* (1993), comprising essays collected just prior to and published just after Althusser's death, insinuates that the remains of that particular theoretical agenda are primarily residual. As if to underscore its morbidity, Alex Callinicos' contribution is entitled "What Is Living and What Is Dead in the Philosophy of Althusser" (1993).

The essay in that volume by Stephen Resnick and Richard Wolff, "Althusser's Liberation of Marxian Theory," however, belies the pervasively elegiac mood of *The Althusserian Legacy* and speaks directly to the revivification of Althusser for Marxist theory alluded to in my title. Only three paragraphs in, the authors offer a sort of précis of their relationship to Althusserian thought and to the project that defined their collaboration from its beginning through nearly three decades:

> For us Althusser's work is one of the greatest contributions in the Marxian tradition. His legacy is a profound critique of all determinism enabled by the concepts of overdetermination and contradiction (new "readings" of Marx, as he put it). His critique sweeps away the staunch determinisms that hitherto haunted Marxism: the structuralism and humanism in its social theory, and the rationalism and empiricism in its epistemology. It thus permits a rethinking of Marxism. Marxism may finally be liberated from the conservatism bred by these determinist forms of thought.
>
> (Resnick and Wolff 1993, 59)

Although Resnick and Wolff made similar declarations elsewhere and much earlier, most notably perhaps in their landmark *Knowledge and Class* (1987),[1] the import of their statement in this particular volume is that the collection itself was edited by two *literary* theorists and is the proceedings of a conference organized and hosted by them. The implied audience reaches well beyond the discipline of economics—or that then small subset of heterodox economists and social scientists concerned with the intersection of poststructuralist thought and Marxist theory. Many in that subset would have been regular readers of and contributors to *Rethinking Marxism*, which has been the primary periodical for discussions involving Althusserian-informed post-Marxian theory since the journal was conceived and launched in 1988 by Wolff, Resnick, and a handful of their graduate students at the University of Massachusetts. But *Rethinking Marxism* would have been less familiar to those in the humanities who received their quarterly theory updates from *Critical Inquiry, Representations,* or *Boundary 2.*

Thus the appearance of "Althusser's Liberation of Marxian Theory" is significant because it reaches beyond a discipline, in fact beyond an entire set of disciplines, namely, the social sciences, which to that point had been the most aware of Resnick and Wolff's theoretical insights, though by no means universally—or even pluralistically receptive. Furthermore, their essay resists the overall tone of the collection and presents an Althusserian analytic as a powerful, living approach capable of self-critique, critical flexibility, and enormous radical potential, rather than as a calcified historical artifact worthy of comment but played out in terms of its efficacy. The result is to offer literary theorists an avenue back to a class-based analysis of texts as well as a reason to choose that avenue in the first place. Finally, it is important to note that the very title of Resnick and Wolff's essay enlarges the category in which such theory exists. No longer "Marxist" *per se,* but *Marxian,* that is drawing from, informed by, reliant upon Marxist analytics but not necessarily beholden to a particular version of *Marxism*—a subtlety of language that would have particularly resonated with this enlarged audience of literary theorists and critics.

In that essay Resnick and Wolff outline what is at stake in their argument, and for them it is nothing less than the future of Marxian analysis and theories of the economy and the state. As they point out, "The Althusser that we read has presented us with... powerful new concepts enabling departures in social theory generally and economic analysis in particular" (1993, 59). The implications are startling, and for some, no doubt, discomfiting. For them, Althusser sets in motion a "broad reconceptualization of Marxism" (71). His insights enable a rethinking of both the epistemological and ontological assumptions operating within a Marxian approach. They provide a needed bridge to considering Marxism as a participant in anti-essentialist discourses, and they underscore the slippage of significance in Marxist discourse around terms as seemingly self-evident as "class."[2] The authors are fundamentally arguing that via Althusser we should be thinking Marxism differently and, as a consequence, drawing very different sorts of conclusions about the imbrications of our social practices in the construction not only of the "real" that we inhabit, but also our access to it through perspectives that cannot adequately be considered *en solo* or functioning outside the totality of these practices.

As a prescription for practice, this description may seem vague, even untenable. I want to suggest, however, that Resnick and Wolff have always been less interested in establishing boundaries for theoretical application than they have been in pushing for epistemological shifts. By championing an approach to Marxism and its objects of analysis (i.e., class, exploitation, historical change, subjugation, etc.), which abjures simple—or even complex—correlation as a theoretical/practical standard, they question and refuse the residue of positivism that links so much of Marxist analytics to the very paradigms of thought it putatively opposes. By pointing toward a new way of conceiving of a Marxian analytic, they transfer attention within the discourse to problematics that had heretofore received scant attention or had been largely rejected by "mainstream" Marxist theorists, regardless of their disciplinary training. The implicit consequence of Resnick and Wolff's move in this line of reasoning is to open pathways to a plethora of possible analytical practices that are also always aware of the multiple discourses within which they are operating, by which they are informed, and to which they contribute their own influences in the form of an analytics that is indeed aleatory.

These "problematics" become explicit when Resnick and Wolff emphasize their big "takeaways" from Althusser's work: contradiction and overdetermination. Both are important, but overdetermination perhaps is the more compelling, because the complex theory they glean from Althusser is the entire undoing of the determinism that had hobbled Marxism and its theoretical promise for years. They *teach* both their concept and the implications of overdetermination in this essay, and this leads to an understanding of effects as "processes" rather than entities that are static and traceable even to a "tree" of cause and effect. For critics more comfortable with a Foucauldian (via Nietzsche) model of "genealogy," the similarities are apparent. But by insisting on effects, such as class, as processes that are always forming rather than "formed" and that not only *subject* the individuals included in that process but are also *subjected* to other processes, Resnick and Wolff free their own method from the epistemological and ontological constraints articulated in rationalism and empiricism alike.

Cause-and-effect historicism thus opens up to the broader understanding of subjects, events, and even large-scale processes like class as complex and irreducible to even the most intricate and detailed narratives or matrices of explanation. Like a Derridean notion of meaning that is simultaneously present and absent in a signifier, a complete rendition of a particular moment or even a particular process will always elude us. The very act of attempting to understand and represent such a moment affects its signification.

For Wolff and Resnick, however, this is not the first movement in a symphony of lamentation over the loss of *verstehen* or of praise for radical relativism. Instead, they present it as a radical liberation from prescribed modes of understanding that necessarily bind possibilities of meaning. Rather than bemoan the loss of *singularity* of meaning, no matter how complex, they celebrate the multiplicity of meanings, recognizing that for social analysis to take the next step, that is to intercede in practice, it is imperative to possess as thorough an understanding as possible of the production of meaning. By insisting on the force of overdetermination in social analysis, they resoundingly answer Eagleton's doubts about an Althusserian approach's ability to consider the effects of discrepant, contradictory discourses on subjects.

This is of particular interest to literary theorists who often find themselves drawn to considerations of subjectivity. Without actually offering a new or revised version of subject formation, Resnick and Wolff's project speaks to some of the lacunae in Althusser's "notes towards an investigation" on the topic (Althusser 1971). Eagleton's skepticism, based on what he sees as the "monism" of the Althusserian theory of the subject, is one that has been shared—if not overtly then implicitly—by many literary theorists. Although I would hesitate to make the same assertion about Eagleton's understanding, much of that wider-spread doubt stems from engaging the ISA essay in isolation from the rest of Althusser's writings, especially the work that led him to those investigations. Resnick and Wolff regard *For Marx* and *Reading Capital* as not only formative of but crucial to the analytic they espouse. Their use and explorations of the concepts of overdetermination and contradiction tacitly emphasize the importance of understanding the ISA essay in the context of Althusser's own use and continuing refinement of those concepts, for indeed what they are undertaking here is a *radicalization* that is actually a generalization of certain moments in Althusser whose results may be "excellent" as a poststructuralist reconstruction but may leave many readers less convinced by everything that links these propositions to Althusser himself. In this radicalization Resnick and Wolff refuse the mere repetition of Althusser as recitation in favor of a broader, liberatory engagement. It is arguably in precisely those moments when their work is both the most and the *least* Althusserian, thus dwelling in the contradictory and aleatory.[3]

The liberation of overdetermination

The work done in "Althusser's Liberation of Marxian Theory"—at this writing more than 25 years removed from its composition—helped to draw attention among literary theorists to their larger project, which continues to inform the theoretical investigations of several generations of scholars and theorists. That is not to say that Resnick and Wolff's contributions to Marxist theoretical discourse have been wholly welcomed. Negative reactions to their position have run the gamut from polite and reasoned rejection to *ad hominem* invective. It is not unusual for leftists to level the most withering attack they can imagine by claiming that though their approach may be many things, it is certainly *not* Marxism. "Overdetermination and Marxian Theory: A Socialist View of the Work of Richard Wolff and Stephen Resnick," a commentary on their work (which includes a brief interview with Stephen Resnick) originally appeared in February 2013 on the Socialist Party of Great Britain website and provides a sense of the sort of reception I am describing:

Resnick and Wolff offer a literally infinitely more complex model in which everything is shaped by everything else. They reject historical materialism because they tend to associate classical Marxian theory with the vulgar, mechanical Marxism which emanated as apologetics from the former USSR and other state capitalist regimes. However, by doing so they throw the baby out with the bathwater, rejecting the historical and materialist dimensions of Marxian thought. That said, their practice does not always reflect their ideas as they do often tend to analyse society, culture and politics as reflecting underlying economic and class factors. In fact, when they let their dialectical guard down their work can be insightful and is the reason why some of their work can still usefully be read by socialists.

(The Socialist Party of Great Britain 2013)

A left-handed compliment, at best, this proclamation utterly refuses to acknowledge the value of Resnick and Wolff's theoretical position, apparently willfully misunderstands the philosophical reasons for rejecting historical materialism, and insists upon reverting to precisely the explanatory paradigm that Resnick and Wolff have interrogated and found lacking for the last three decades.

Much more interesting, and far more productive, are the sorts of exchanges that are exemplified by a recent symposium in *Rethinking Marxism* entitled "Revisiting Resnick and Wolff's Reading of Overdetermination." In the essay, "'Overdetermined' or 'Indeterminate'? Remarks on *Knowledge and Class*," Mark S. Silverman (2013) takes issue with what he sees as an imprecision in Resnick and Wolff's use of the term (and thus the concept), "overdetermination." For Silverman, imbricated in this term are at least two distinct meanings: first that "an entity's very being is constituted by the entire network of relations it has with all other entities" and second that "no outcomes can be predicted in advance, regardless of any statement of initial conditions" (311). Silverman argues that this duality of signification leads to a logical confusion, since he contends that the second meaning of the term, synonymous with "indeterminacy" does not logically follow from the first and to suggest otherwise—as he contends Resnick and Wolff do—leads to an epistemological confusion and erroneous conclusions regarding the status of entities' fundamental existence independent of each other.

In the same symposium, Hyun Woong Park's "Overdetermination: Althusser versus Resnick and Wolff" takes issue with Resnick and Wolff's critique of the "essentialist moments" they find in Althusser's theory of overdetermination and the charges of inconsistency they level at the philosopher (2013). For Park, these are not inconsistencies in Althusser's argument nor can they be removed or discounted from the overall structure of Althusser's theory of overdetermination, as Resnick and Wolff suggest. In a generous and respectful though vigorous and detailed response to Silverman and Park, Resnick and Wolff maintain their position that despite Althusser's offering of a way out of economic determinism, he nonetheless falls prey to it in certain instances. Further, they posit that Silverman's claim of "'prediction' is logically impossible." In response to Park, they explain why they "still think that a tension arises in Althusser's work between formulating a notion of overdetermination that in effect rules out any form of causal determination in the last instance and yet affirming economic determination in the last instance" (Resnick and Wolff 2013, 341). As they put it earlier in their reply to Silverman's critique, "We think the concept of overdetermination rejects the possibility of order, certainty, and control in both the epistemological and ontological realms" (346).

In their response, Resnick and Wolff point to a shared reluctance on the part of both Silverman and Park to take the last step, which is to reject the *a priori* ordering that shapes their arguments. Resnick and Wolff pointedly deny the possibility of processes acting outside of and independent of a multiply constituted relationship with all other processes. For them, descriptively, this is a "mess." For Park, somewhat fearfully, it is "chaos." The notions are the same, but the approaches are different. As they point out,

> We read this rejection of independence among processes as the link to Hegel's *Logic*: each and every process only exists (is constituted) by its connection to the other processes. Without that connection, a process has no impact, for it is empty. In this sense, overdetermination is a fully relational concept of causation. To have the economic serving as the ultimate arbitrator of contradictions is the same move as asserting that one aspect of the totality—namely what Park refers to as economic practice—is immune from codetermination: the economic determines (in the last instance) but is itself not determined (in that last instance).
>
> (*ibid.*, 347)

I cite these recent instances of exchange as examples of how the work of Resnick and Wolff continues to foreground the importance of Althusser and to encourage direct engagement with Althusser's work and thought. Luke Ferretter has argued that "though there are few card carrying Althusserian critics today, nevertheless, almost every form of political criticism is indebted, to some extent, to his work" (2006, 143). I would concur and extend his assertion by pointing to the ways that influential theorists from Michel Foucault and Jacques Derrida (who were, at one time, his students) to Judith Butler and Slavoj Žižek can trace a very large part of their own theoretical heritage to Althusser.

Yet I also contend that we cannot discount the efforts of Resnick and Wolff in keeping the Althusserian "moment" alive. The impact of their work across disciplinary boundaries has been truly remarkable. This is especially notable in the scholarship of many of those they directly influenced, who have made a point of interrogating the interstices between disciplinary practices as sites where key cultural criticism and theoretical work can, indeed must, take place. For example, *Whither Marxism: Global Crises in International Perspective* (Magnus and Cullenberg 1995) set the stage for a rethinking of the place of Marxism in the post-Soviet world as well as provided a forum for Derrida's introduction of large portions of *Spectres* (1995). *Postmodern Materialism and the Future of Marxist Theory: Essays in the Althusserian Tradition* (Callari and Ruccio 1996) with essays by Negri, Balibar, Montag, and Elliott, to name only a few, helped to recast the connection between poststructuralist and Marxist thought while *Postmodernism, Economics, and Knowledge* (Amariglio, Cullenberg, and Ruccio 2001) continued that discussion through essays designed to pose the poststructuralist Marxist problematic to the disciplines of economics and political economy. More recently, *Economic Representations: Academic and Everyday* (Ruccio 2008) effectively highlights the ubiquity and constitutive force of the economic as representational trope, and *Sublime Economy: On the Intersection of Art and Economics* (Amariglio, Childers, and Cullenberg 2009) takes up issues of value and representation that dwell at the juncture of two seemingly disparate, but nonetheless mutually constitutive, discourses.

Beyond these collections, which demonstrate the breadth of Resnick and Wolff's influence across a panoply of disciplines in the humanities and social sciences, concentrated studies such as J.K. Gibson-Graham's *The End of Capitalism (As We Knew It)* (1996) and Ruccio and Amariglio's *Postmodern Moments in Modern Economics* have made extraordinary contributions that have productively disrupted the ways we think, talk, and write about strategies for instigating social change. Gibson-Graham's concept of "capitalocentrism," for instance, underscores the dominant practice of representing economic activity of any kind in its relationship to capitalism (opposed to it, engendered by it, subsumed by it, etc.). By focusing on the discursive power of this practice, Gibson-Graham can provide alternative representations of economic activity that are not continually re-instantiating the exploitative functions of capitalism. Ruccio and Amariglio's volume takes up a related discursive task, identifying in modern economic thought those *aporia* that in fact undo or "deconstruct" the very "foundations" upon which modern economics claims its authority. Like Gibson-Graham, Ruccio and Amariglio are arguing for an epistemological shift that would unbind our way of thinking about how we value everything from labor to knowledge. And, very much in the vein of Resnick and Wolff, they embrace the contingent and the aleatory, for it is there that revision and liberation actually take place.

Such contributions are powerful, and as I have suggested from the outset directly attributable to their commitment to *radicalizing* Althusser, pursuing and insisting upon the aleatory implications of his insights, and thus freeing his thought from precisely the epistemological limits that Resnick and Wolff stress in their response to Silverman and Park. Rather than accede to the fetish for order and *science* that vexes the early Althusser and that they openly criticize, Resnick and Wolff embrace the "mess," recognizing the liberatory potential for analysis that begins with the presupposition of complex, perpetual process and interaction within the political, cultural, and economic realms of social existence. Given that economics as a discipline and Marxism as ideology and analytic are steeped in traditional humanistic ontologies and epistemologies that insist on essentialist concepts of meaning and its production, this has been no small feat. To reach across disciplinary lines so effectively that their contributions have been much noted (and highly engaged) by theorists and practitioners in the humanities as well as the social sciences speaks to the intellectual weight and merit of their analysis.

Some, especially on the Left, have labeled their efforts "Amherst Marxism," a term often applied derisively by their critics (see Clarke 2004; The Socialist Party of Great Britain 2013). It is an appellation, however, that should be celebrated by those generations of scholars and theorists who have reaped such tremendous benefits from their insights, for it situates a moment in the advancement of Marxian thought that has, in the spirit of Althusser, remained provocative and a basis for praxis as well as theory. In many ways, what Resnick and Wolff have provided is a place to begin the difficult but rewarding theoretical work of thinking differently, of beginning, like Gibson-Graham, Amariglio, Ruccio, and others, to participate in and help drive that epistemological shift. Their radicalization of Althusser has made this possible, has opened the door to new ways of thinking not only about Althusser and Marx but of materialism itself. The least that we have learned in this journey is that discursive practices are not merely descriptive, but constitutive, and as our discourse—our thought—comes to terms with the aleatory, we expand the possibilities for a liberated existence.

Notes

1 See Cullenberg and Wolff (1986) for another example. For others, one could peruse any volume of *Rethinking Marxism* from the past 29 years to find many excellent instances of vigorous and theoretically robust theoretical work informed by a critical engagement with the work of Althusser.

2 Resnick and Wolff, together with J.K. Gibson-Graham speak directly to the importance of the need for a "multidirectional foray" into "relatively unexplored territory: Marxian class-theory." As they point out in the introduction to *Re/presenting Class: Essays in Postmodern Marxism,* "The *theory of the capitalist totality* has been developed at the expense of the *theory of class* (Gibson-Graham, Resnick, and Wolff 2001: 1; see also Norton 2001).

3 I am indebted to Rob Garnett for this insight, which arises from his reading of a September 1964 letter from Derrida to Althusser regarding, "Marxism and Humanism," which became the last chapter of *For Marx*:

I found the text that you sent to me *excellent*. I feel as close as one possibly could to that 'theoretical anti-humanism' that you set out ... I was less convinced by everything that links these propositions to Marx himself. There is probably a great deal of ignorance in my mistrust and in the feeling that other – non-Marxist – premises could lie behind the same antihumanism. What you set out on pp. 116 et seq. shows clearly the way Marx broke away from a certain humanism, a certain conjunction of empiricism and idealism, etc. But the radicalization often appears to me, in its most powerful and alluring moments, very Althusserian. You'll tell me that the 'repetition' of Marx must not be a 'recitation,' and that deepening and radicalizing him is being faithful to him. True. But in that case don't we end up with the same result if we start out with Hegel or Feuerbach?

(Peeters 2013, 148, original emphasis)

References

Althusser, L. 1969. *For Marx*. Trans. B. Brewster. New York: Pantheon.

———— 1971. *Lenin and Philosophy and other Essays*. Trans. B. Brewster. London: New Left Books.

Althusser, L. and E. Balibar. 1970. *Reading Capital*. Trans. B. Brewster. London: Verso.

Amariglio, J., S. Cullenberg, and D. Ruccio, eds. 2001. *Postmodernism, Economics and Knowledge*. New York: Routledge.

Amariglio, J., J. Childers, and S. Cullenberg, eds. 2009. *Sublime Economy: On the Intersection of Art and Economics*. New York: Routledge.

Bloom, H., P. de Man, J. Derrida, G. Hartman, and J. H. Miller, 1979. *Deconstruction and Criticism*. New York: Seabury Press.

Callari, A. and D. Ruccio, eds. 1996. *Postmodern Materialism and the Future of Marxist Theory: Essays in the Althusserian Tradition*. Hanover, NH and London: Wesleyan University Press.

Callinicos, A. 1993. "What Is Living and What Is Dead in the Philosophy of Althusser." In *The Althusserian Legacy*, E. Kaplan and M. Sprinker, eds. 39–50. New York: Verso.

Clarke, S. 2004. "Resnick and Wolff's *Class Theory and History*." In *Research in the History of Economic Thought and Methodology, volume 22, part 1*, W. J. Samuels, ed., 355–63. Bingley, UK: Emerald Group Publishing Ltd.

Cullenberg, S. and R. Wolff. 1986. "Marxism and Post-Marxism." *Social Text* 15: 126–35.

Derrida, J. 1974. *Of Grammatology*. Trans. G. Spivak. Baltimore: Johns Hopkins University Press.

———— 1978. *Writing and Difference*. Trans. A. Bass. Chicago: University of Chicago Press.

———— 1994. *Specters of Marx: The State of the Debt, the Work of Mourning, and the New International*. Trans. P. Kamuf. New York: Routledge.

Dollimore, J. and A. Sinfield. 1985. *Political Shakespeare: New Essays in Cultural Materialism*. Ithaca: Cornell University Press.

Eagleton, T. 1976a. *Criticism and Ideology: A Study in Marxist Literary Theory*. London: Verso.

———— 1976b. *Marxism and Literary Criticism*. Berkeley: University of California, Press.

———— 1991. *Ideology*. New York: Verso.

Ferretter, L. 2006. *Louis Althusser*. New York: Routledge.

Foucault, M. 1965. *Madness and Civilization: A History of Insanity in the Age of Reason.* Trans. R. Howard. New York: Vintage.

——— [1966] 1970. *The Order of Things.* New York: Pantheon.

——— [1969] 1972. *The Archaeology of Knowledge.* Trans. A. M. Sheridan Smith. New York: Pantheon.

——— [1963] 1973. *The Birth of the Clinic: An Archaeology of Medical Perception.* Trans. A. M. Sheridan Smith. New York: Pantheon.

——— [1974] 1977. *Discipline and Punish: The Birth of the Prison.* Trans. A. Sheridan. New York: Vintage.

——— [1976] 1978. *The History of Sexuality, Vol. 1.* Trans. R. Hurley. New York: Pantheon.

——— 1998. "Nietzsche, Freud, Marx." In *Aesthetics, Method, and Epistemology,* Vol. 2, J. Faubion, ed., 269–78. New York: The New Press.

Gibson-Graham, J. K. 1996. *The End of Capitalism (As We Knew It): A Feminist Critique of Political Economy.* Oxford, UK and Cambridge, MA: Blackwell.

Gibson-Graham, J. K., S. Resnick, and R. Wolff, eds. 2001. *Re/Presenting Class: Essays in Postmodern Marxism.* Durham, NC: Duke University Press.

Jameson, F. 1982. *The Political Unconscious: Narrative as a Socially Symbolic Act.* Ithaca, NY: Cornell University Press.

Kaplan, E. and Sprinker, M., eds. 1993. *The Althusserian Legacy.* New York: Verso.

Lacan, J. 1973. *Four Fundamental Concepts of Psychoanalysis,* J-A. Miller, ed., A. Sheridan, trans. New York: Norton.

——— 1977. *Ecrits: A Selection.* Trans. A. Sheridan. New York: Norton.

Macksey, R. and E. Donato. 1970. *The Structuralist Controversy: The Languages of Criticism and the Sciences of Man.* Baltimore: Johns Hopkins University Press.

Magnus, B. and S. Cullenberg, eds. 1995. *Whither Marxism: Global Crises in International Perspective.* New York: Routledge.

Marcus, S. 1975. *Representations: Essays on Literature and Society.* New York: Columbia University Press.

MARHO, The Radical Historians Organization. 1983. *Visions of History.* New York: Pantheon.

Montag, W. 1998. "Althusser's Nominalism: Structure and Singularity (1962–66)." *Rethinking Marxism* 10 (3): 64–73.

Norton, B. 2001. "Reading for Class." In *Re/Presenting Class: Essays in Postmodern Marxism,* J. K. Gibson-Graham, S. Resnick, and R. Wolff, eds., 23–-55. Durham, NC: Duke University Press.

Park, H. W. 2013. "Overdetermination: Althusser versus Resnick and Wolff." *Rethinking Marxism* 25 (3): 325–40.

Peeters, B. 2013. *Derrida.* Cambridge, UK: Polity Press.

Resnick, S. and R. Wolff. 1987. *Knowledge and Class: A Marxian Critique of Political Economy.* Chicago: University of Chicago Press.

——— 1993. "Althusser's Liberation of Marxian Theory." In *The Althusserian Legacy,* E. Kaplan and M Sprinker, eds., 59–72. New York: Verso.

——— 2013. "On Overdetermination and Althusser: Our Response to Silverman and Park." *Rethinking Marxism* 25 (3): 341–9.

Ruccio, D., ed. 2008. *Economic Representations: Academic and Everyday.* New York: Routledge.

Ryan, M. 1982. *Marxism and Deconstruction: A Critical Articulation.* Baltimore: Johns Hopkins University Press.

Said, E. 1978. "The Problem of Textuality: Two Exemplary Positions." *Critical Inquiry* 4 (4): 673–714.

Silverman. M. S. 2013. "'Overdetermined' or 'Indeterminate?' Remarks on *Knowledge and Class.*" *Rethinking Marxism.* 25 (3): 311–24.

The Socialist Party of Great Britain. 2013. "Overdetermination and Marxian Theory: A Socialist View of the Work of Richard Wolff and Stephen Resnick." www.worldsocialism.org (accessed February 2015).

Spivak, G. C. 1993. *Outside in the Teaching Machine.* New York: Routledge.

Stallybrass, P. and A. White. 1986. *The Politics and Poetics of Transgression.* Ithaca: Cornell University Press.

Thompson, E. 1978. *The Poverty of Theory and other Essays.* London: Merlin Press.

Williams, R. 1977a. *Marxism and Literature.* Oxford: Oxford University Press.

——— 1977b. "The Paths and Pitfalls of Ideology as Ideology." In *Times Higher Education Supplement,* 10 June.

12 Process

Tracing connections and consequences

Yahya M. Madra

An uncanny Marxism

Steve Resnick and Rick Wolff's rethinking of Marxian political economy has led to a theoretical formation that has proved to be uncannily resistant to domestication by the mainstream of the Marxian tradition. This is despite the fact that it is constructed upon a close reading of the three volumes of *Capital* (Marx 1976, 1978, 1981) together with the *Theories of Surplus Value* (Marx 1963, 1969, 1973). With their self-conscious insistence on the epistemological impossibility of accounting for the whole of the overdetermined field, they have created a powerful *estrangement* (*alienation* or *distancing*) *effect* on the standard Marxist reader. Bertolt Brecht used this concept (*Verfremdungseffekt*) to describe a theatrical technique he applied to dislodge the audience from the comfort of losing itself in the narrative (Jameson 1998). By copiously reminding the reader that their story is a partial and partisan one, Resnick and Wolff refused to entertain the historicist and determinist fantasies that have long captured the imaginations of Marxists. Their somewhat outsider status in relation to the Marxian tradition may be, in large part, emanating from this powerful estrangement effect that results from their epistemological self-awareness.

But there is more here than their rhetoric of partiality and partisanship. Their reading of Marx stands out because a most uncompromising and radical concept structures their thoroughgoing rethinking: the concept of *process*. In fact, this cornerstone concept, together with the concept of *overdetermination*, is itself partly responsible for anchoring their rhetoric of partiality and partisanship to an anti-essentialist epistemology and a non-reductionist ontology.

The concept of *process* is both an effect and a cause, simultaneously constituted by and constitutive of a complex overdetermination. It is an *effect* of Resnick and Wolff's own reading of the concept of overdetermination that they propose as a critique of the modernist theories of causality, whether humanist or structuralist. Yet, it is also a *cause*, to the extent that the concept of overdetermination attains its "estranging" quality as a result of their invention of the notion of process.

These two concepts, process and overdetermination, can only be properly understood in relation to each other. This is how Resnick and Wolff define them:

> To generalize Marxian theory, each process in society is understood as the site of the interaction of the influences exerted by all the others. In other words, the existence and particular features of any one social process are constituted by all the other processes comprising a society. Each social process is the effect produced by the interaction of (i.e., is overdetermined by) all the others. Each process is overdetermined as well as a participant in the overdetermination of every other process in the society.
>
> (1987, 24)

According to Resnick and Wolff, each "process" is a "site" (which is also a category that has a very specific meaning in their work) continually pushed and pulled in contradictory directions by all the other processes. Every process is at one and the same time constituted and constituting; no process has any existence or meaning without the others.

According to Jack Amariglio, as a concept of causality, overdetermination also entails a critique of identity:

> [O]verdetermination does not permit us to view the constituent elements of a process of determination as essential, non-contradictory, positive components or variables that retain their initial character upon interaction with one another. Overdetermination stresses the changing and contradictory nature of the articulated processes and demonstrates that the very effectivity of these processes transforms each of them as they form a new and distinct product: a social event or conjuncture. These new products, as sets of social processes, serve as the further conditions of existence or raw materials for other events or conjunctures.
>
> (Amariglio 1984, 19)

These notions of process and overdetermination imply a radical flattening of social ontology: agency is everywhere and nowhere; no process can be ontologically (causally) more privileged than the others.[1] Consequently, the subject-structure dualism is also torn down, as subject is conceived as a process in a perpetual state of becoming, constituted by and, in turn (albeit in no privileged manner), constitutive of all the other processes.

But where does this concept, process, come from? What are its constituents? What are Resnick and Wolff's intellectual sources in developing their ascetic understanding of process and overdetermination? What are the intellectual currents from which their novel conceptualizations arise? While their own references, in particular those that they develop in *Knowledge and Class*, are the obvious places to look, it is also useful to place their formulations into a larger theoretical anti-humanist, post-structuralist context. In that regard, even though the concept of process is a critique of the static notions of structure and monadic notions of identity fairly widespread in economics, it is in fact, in part, a product of structuralism, a philosophical orientation whose development, starting with Ferdinand de Saussure and Sigmund Freud, spans the entire twentieth century.

In tracing the philosophical and epistemological connections and theoretical and methodological implications of the concept of process, two important lineages will be delineated: one developing in relation to structuralism (heterogeneously emerging in a wide range of disciplines, such as linguistics, psychoanalysis, anthropology, and mathematics) and the other in response to the Marxian struggle with the Hegelian dialectic. On the structuralism side, Deleuze's symptomatology of structuralism (2002 [1967]) will be used to elaborate the notion of process. On the side of dialectics, Resnick and Wolff's appropriation of Lenin, Lukacs, and Mao will be linked to the "Final Althusser." The dual rejection of Cartesian monadism and Hegelian holism led Resnick and Wolff to an ontological notion of *subjectivity as a process*. Yet, missing in this notion is the retroactive logic (Lacan 2006 [1970], Fink 1997) of the overdetermined theory of subjectivity immanent in the concept of entry point that they elaborate in their discussions of anti-essentialist epistemology. The overdetermined subject has to recover by way of ideology critique and analysis the overdetermined (unconscious) theoretical "choices" always already made in the past. There is an ethics embodied in this recovery that involves assuming a retroactive responsibility for one's entry point. Yet the unidirectional nature of their ontological notion of *subjectivity as a process* does not incorporate this ethical insight or account for its epistemological implications. Finally, the constitutive role that the concept of process played in the formalist turn in class analysis will be discussed.

Structuralism: from the symbolic to the topological

The structuralist provenance of the concept of process compels us to explore its homology with the linguistic category of *sign*. Indeed, Resnick and Wolff themselves invoke Saussure and his structuralist linguistics as an influence, early on in *Knowledge and Class*, in the context of their discussion of epistemology:

> Saussure has exercised considerable influence upon us as well, both directly and through its role particularly in shaping the work of Althusser … In our conceptualization of theory we develop certain of Saussure's notions, particularly those concerned with language's synchronic structure and the "arbitrariness" of its constituent signs, although in ways different from his own development of them.
>
> (Resnick and Wolff 1987, 17)

However, Resnick and Wolff's reading of Saussure spills over the episte-mological register and forms the nucleus of their relational understanding of *overdetermination* as a critique of ontologies of identity:

> [L]anguage is a system of differences in which all elements are defined solely by their relations with one another.... What distinguishes it is what constitutes it. Difference creates the characteristic (or the feature) in the same way that it creates *value* and the unit itself.
>
> (cf. Resnick and Wolff 1987, 17; emphasis added)[2]

Admittedly, overdetermination is interpreted differentially in diverse theoretical contexts, but there is an agreement as to its sources in the turn of twentieth century linguistics (posthumously published in 1916, *A Course in General Linguistics* was based on Saussure's Geneva lectures, 1907–1911) and psychoanalysis (in particular, Freud's *The Interpretation of Dreams* from 1899). Jacques Lacan gave Freud's discussion of the logics of *condensation* and *displacement* a linguistic meaning by drawing not only on the difference between paradigmatic (relations of substitution, similarity, and difference) and syntagmatic (relations of words in a sentence unfolding contiguously) axes of language but also on Roman Jakobson's discussion of the metaphoric and metonymic (corresponding) axes of aphasia (Lacan 2006 [1970]). Lacan's oft-cited phrase, "unconscious is structured like a language," is a summary of the symbolic meaning of the concept of overdetermination. Returning to Freud's suggestion that the golden road to the unconscious is found by tracing the condensations and displacements of repressed meanings in dream formations, slips of tongue, jokes and other cultural formations, Lacan argued that the unconscious is structured through overdetermined relations of condensation and displacement and constituted within the symbolic order.[3]

In this vein, recall that Ernesto Laclau and Chantal Mouffe, in their much-cited treatment of overdetermination, famously argued that the concept "is constituted in the field of the symbolic, and has no meaning whatsoever outside it" (1985, 97). Their emphasis on the symbolic character of overdetermination is quite understandable, especially given that their understanding of structure is defined in a minimalist fashion as a field of difference constituted around the metonymic and metaphoric axes of displacement and condensation, respectively.

Yet neither the concept of structure nor the concept of overdetermination as a causal category needs to be limited to the symbolic domain. In this regard, Gilles Deleuze's 1967 essay "How Do We Recognize Structuralism?" is insightful.[4] Through a carefully woven discussion of the writings of Jakobson, Levi-Strauss, Lacan, Foucault, Althusser, Barthes, and the *Tel Quel* circle, Deleuze (2002 [1967]) introduces seven criteria to discern what defines structuralism as a philosophical orientation that cuts across disciplines. Let us try to read Resnick and Wolff's framework through his symptomatology.[5]

Deleuze's first criterion to identify structuralism is the presence of a constitutive reference to the symbolic order. Deleuze defines the symbolic as the "third" register that places a wedge between the real and the imaginary registers (2002 [1967], 171). Here, the symbolic order figures as the fundamental condition of human sociality, as the condition that introduces the dimension of metaphor that separates speaking beings from other animals. In structuralist anthropology this third register is constituted through taboo (the prohibition of incest), in psychoanalysis through the paternal law and in structuralist linguistics through the language itself. Yet, Deleuze extends the domain of applicability of the idea of structure beyond this focus on the symbolic to the topological.

According to his second, *topological,* criterion "the elements of a structure have neither extrinsic designation, nor intrinsic signification" (2002 [1967], 173) but are defined in a "necessarily and uniquely 'positional'" manner (*ibid.,* 174). Deleuze points out that the positional sense that the elements of a structure have is neither "a matter of a location in a real spatial expense, nor of sites in imaginary extensions, but rather of places and sites in a properly structural space, that is topological space" (*ibid.,* 174). Deleuze explains this topological sense by way of an example from the physical world—an unexpected choice given that the structures are supposed to make sense only at the level of the symbolic, which has its bearings in the differential structure of language.

> Or take genetic biology: the genes are part of a structure to the extent that they are inseparable from "loci," sites capable of changing their relation within the chromosome. In short, places in a purely structural space are primary in relation to the always somewhat imaginary roles and events which necessarily appear when they are occupied.
>
> (*ibid.,* 174)

This topological and relational account of structure is similar to the more "developed" conceptualization of overdetermination where "each process is the effect produced by the interaction of all the others" (Resnick and Wolff 1987, 24). To begin with, viewed from Deleuze's perspective, Resnick and Wolff's concepts of decentered structure and overdetermination and, in particular, their "analytical separation" of processes into four types (cultural, economic, political, and natural) gain a particular significance that may not be conceivable from a strictly symbolic understanding of structure and overdetermination. The *cultural* processes that refer to the production and dissemination of *meanings,* the *economic* processes that refer to the production and distribution of means of production and consumption of *values,* and the *political* processes of design and regulation of *power and authority* are all easily accommodated within the symbolic understanding of overdetermination. Yet the fourth category of *natural* processes that refers to the movements of *matter and energy* is more difficult to accommodate within a strictly symbolic understanding of structure and causality. In fact, their conceptualization of the natural as yet another process within the system of overdetermined causality may quite plausibly be deemed theoretically illegitimate—unless one extends the concept of structure, as Deleuze does, to include the topological dimension. The topological criterion is in fact strongly present in Resnick and Wolff's framework, as their own definition of overdetermination includes a constitutive reference to the category of "site," where each process is conceived as the *site* of the contradictory "interaction of the influences exerted by all the others" (1987, 24).

Deleuze's third criterion differentiates between "a system of *differential* relations according to which the symbolic elements determine themselves reciprocally, and a system of *singularities* corresponding to these relations and tracing the space of the structure" (2002 [1967], 177). This co-presence of the systems of differentiality and singularity enables us to appreciate the importance of what may appear to some critics to be a "flattening of ontology."[6] Granted, there is a formal (and perhaps estranging) quality to the concept of process *qua* site. Morphologically each process, as the locus of the constitutive effectivity of the relational system of processes, is identical to the others, and as such no process shall be causally more privileged than another. This is what critics may mean when they argue that Resnick and Wolff's ontology is flat; it is indeed an implication of the system of differential relations. But, it has to be considered together with a reading of each and every process, to the extent that it is a product of the conjunctural coming together of the contradictory push and pull of its conditions of existence, as a *singularity*. The "flat ontology" diagnosis papers over the possibility of treating each process simultaneously as a part of a system of differential relations (without causally privileging any one) and as incarnating an irreducible singularity that defies any isomorphic homogeneity. This irreducible singularity is also a corollary of the concept of an overdetermined conjuncture as a contradictory unity of heterogeneous forces, since the analysis of conjuncture requires differentiation of structure in time and space.

The fourth criterion introduces this dimension of time and space by positing a difference between the *virtual* structures, which may be "totally and completely differential" but undifferentiated, and the *actual* structures "embodied in a particular actual form (past or present)" where actualization of the structure entails differentiation in space and time (Deleuze 2002 [1967], 179). Even though each process is formally a *virtual* site ("totally and completely differential"), it can only get *actualized* through the constitutive effectivity of a historically determined and specific set of processes, attaining a topological quality in the relational system of overdetermination through its differentiation in space and time. This movement from virtual to actual is an ontological account of how each site, as an overdetermined process, ever changing, is always already marked by the singularity of its historicity.

The fifth *seriality* condition states that to become animated every structure must be multi-serial (at least two) in such a manner that they relate to each other in a displaced and dislocated manner (Deleuze 2002 [1967], 181–83). The "process" ontology of overdetermination multiplies different categories of processes, related in a serial manner (economic, cultural, political, and natural processes; class and non-class processes; fundamental and subsumed class processes; the process of surplus distribution to a proliferating set of recipients; and so on) since each process is constituted by (or animated by) a series of other processes. In other words, the movement from *virtual* to *actual* happens through the constitutive (and contradictory) relations among (always) a multiplicity of series.

The sixth condition is the *"Empty Square"* condition, which states that every structure must be organized around "a wholly paradoxical object or element" (Deleuze 2002 [1967], 183)—not unlike the empty space in sliding puzzles that constantly displaces itself so that the game functions (*ibid.*, 185). Resnick and Wolff's concept of entry point, to the extent that it is simultaneously an *essence* that interrupts the virtual differentiality and an *emptiness* that is waiting to be actualized through differentiation, is precisely the name that they give to the paradoxical element, "Empty Square," that causes the structure to unfold diachronically.

And finally the seventh criterion, *from subject to practice*, where a *nomadic* subject, who is "less subject than subjected," who is broken up, distributed, dissipated, and shifted from place to place, works on the contradictions of and the moments of dislocation in the structure by "following and safeguarding the displacements, on its power to cause relations to vary and to redistribute singularities, always casting another throw of the dice" (Deleuze 2002 [1967], 191). We will return to these final three criteria below when we discuss the double-sided conceptualization of the subject's simultaneous inevitable dispersion into its constitutive processes and deliberate collation around the entry point and the formalist turn enacted by the notion of class as an adjective. But before doing so, we will first trace the other lineage of materialist dialectics.

Contradiction and overdetermination: a materialist dialectics

The second lineage of Resnick and Wolff's concept of process is that of the Marxian tradition in its struggle with Hegelian dialectics. Their approach to Vladimir Lenin's and György Lukács' readings of Hegel's maxim, the truth is the whole, and Mao's discussion of the complex nature of contradiction (with its emphasis on "contradiction" and "ceaseless change") is important. This lineage, for Resnick and Wolff, culminates in Althusser's "Contradiction and Overdetermination" and the notion of the overdetermined conjuncture as a transformation (or better yet explosion) of Hegel's orderly, teleological, and essentialist concept of contradiction. I will further trace the connections of this thread to the "Final Althusser" of aleatory materialism (Althusser 2006; see also the introduction to Callari and Ruccio 1996).

Despite their Althusserianism, Resnick and Wolff have not shied away from affirming Hegel's dialectical method, and they have done so persistently over the span of their career. In the first chapter of *Knowledge and Class*, they find in Hegel an *avant la lettre* response to Saussurean "infinite regress of meaning production" (1987, 28). They invoke Hegel in the context of developing their notion of "entry point" as "a starting point to make sense of ... ceaseless mutual effectivity of terms." The image they paint provides an account of what they mean by the concept of process as an overdetermined site.

> To borrow an image from Hegel, the specification of any idea is without meaning; it is completely empty until we begin to construct its complex determinations, its linkages to other ideas, its conceptual conditions of existence. Only these give it life and character. Thus each discursive idea of a theory can only take on its meaning in relationship to all the other ideas of the discourse. Each term is thus understood to exist as the locus of effects emanating from the other terms of the theory. Its meaning is literally constructed by them.
>
> (Resnick and Wolff 1987, 28)

Even though this is a depiction of the process of theorizing, it should also be read in a truly Hegelian fashion as an adequate account of how "[o]ur process of approaching constituted objective reality repeats the virtual process of Becoming of this reality itself" (Zizek 2004, 56). Rather than reading this short circuit between the epistemological and the ontological as a rational isomorphism of thought, we can read it through Deleuze's symptomatology as an opening into the topological, in excess of the symbolic notion of overdetermination.

Each process is a vanishing point, an emptiness, without all the other processes that provide conditions of existence that give it life and character. Returning to the Hegel connection a decade later, Wolff (1996) gives a dialectical account of how their concept of entry point provides them with an operational methodology to interrupt what they called in 1987, "the infinite regress of meaning production"—another name for the underlying virtual differentiality, the "ceaseless mutual effectivity of terms." Through a reading Hegel's *Logic*, Wolff offers a "Hegelian rethinking and extension" to Althusser's concept of overdetermination:

> Overdetermination can thus be reformulated as containing, initially, its own negation, namely, an essentialism. To begin an overdeterminist

explanation immediately involves its own negation in the form of an essentialist argument... It is a momentary affirmation of a priority within the web of interacting aspects of any totality.... To set out to construct overdeterminist analysis entails, then, immediately and unavoidably, its own annulment by an initial essentialist moment.... Yet this essentialist moment, insofar as it figures within an overdeterminist explanation, is a *determinate* negation of that perspective and thus dependent on it. Moreover, the essentialist moment will, in turn, be negated or annulled by overdetermination in a rather classic Hegelian rhythm.

(1996, 156)

An inescapable essentialism initially squeezes overdetermination into an entry point. However, this contraction is immediately negated by the very logic of overdetermination. As its conditions of existence, its presuppositions, are gradually discerned, the contingency of its origins are also progressively exposed, and its status as an essence is negated. The dialectical method is first and foremost a procedure to reveal the tendential emptiness of a process through enumerating its conditions of existence. Needless to say, one cannot say the whole. But, rather than seeing this as an epistemological inadequacy, a failure to account for the reality, this can be seen, first, as an inevitable consequence of the "virtual process of Becoming" at the ontological and topological level, and second, as an outcome of the ontological impossibility of occupying an Archimedean position from which to survey the social, leading to the inescapability of always already occupying a partial and partisan position.[7] These two levels, however, are intricately linked. Partiality (and as a result, inevitable partisanship) is an outcome of the very situatedness of anyone attempting to theorize the *whole*; always existing in ceaseless change, in the "virtual process of Becoming," it is ontologically (topologically) and not just epistemologically (symbolically) impossible to say it *all*.

This reading may appear controversial, especially given the fact that Resnick and Wolff have always taken pains to distinguish the matters of epistemology from those of ontology, arguing that a discourse with an essentialist epistemology can entertain non-reductionist ontology and vice versa. For instance, the critical realist project combines a non-reductionist, relational ontology with a realist epistemology (Ruccio 2009). But this does not change the fact that their own discourse implicitly posits an intimate link between the two registers. The short circuit between epistemology and ontology that the dialectical method reveals is an outcome of the immersion of the knowing subject within the overdetermined being. To put it differently, the argument is not that their dialectical method is mimicking ontology (a rationalist isomorphism of thought). Rather, it is that it is impossible for Resnick and Wolff to even begin thinking about epistemology without referring back to ontology. Their treatment of process through the dialectical method is precisely the point in their discourse where epistemology meets ontology.

Their reading of Lenin and Lukács also depicts the complex relationship between epistemology and ontology through an affirmation of Hegel's maxim, "the truth is the whole," as their point of departure. For Lenin, as it is for Hegel, the whole as truth includes "all the processes of nature and society, including thought." When Lenin writes "every notion occurs in a certain *relation*" or "in the eternal change, movement of notions," Resnick and Wolff find an incipient understanding of process and overdetermination (Resnick and Wolff 1987, 65).

Lukács, like Lenin, takes the Hegelian maxim "the truth is the whole" as his point of departure with *the* proviso that the whole is an "ensemble of relations," in which "[e]very substantial change … manifests itself as a change in relation to the whole and through this as a change in the form of objectivity itself" (Resnick and Wolff 1987, 70). The totality, Lukács writes, "is the concrete unity of interacting contradictions," a structured articulation of totalities with differential levels of complexities and a historical reality that "is changing, disintegrating, confined to a determinate, concrete historical period" (cf. Resnick and Wolff 1987, 71).

Mao accentuates contradiction as an irreducible aspect of each process, an idea that was already present in Lenin's and Lukács' reading of Hegel's dialectical account of identity and opposition, being and becoming. The import of Mao for Althusser (1969) and Resnick and Wolff is in his accents on the multiplicity of contradictions and the diversity of concepts of contradiction. The notion of contradiction is precisely what makes it impossible to think of the conditions of existence in a functionalist manner: Each process is always becoming as a contradictory outcome of the push and pull of its conditions of existence.

Undoubtedly, Althusser's posthumously published writings on the "philosophy of encounter" resonate with the radical sense of contingency and contradiction that permeates Resnick and Wolff's concept of overdetermined totality as a contradictory "ensemble of relations." In fact, Althusser's discussions of overdetermination as a concept of conjuncture, with its multiplication of the categories of contradiction (Althusser 1969), and the concept of history as a "process without a subject or goals" (Althusser 1976) gain a new radical meaning in light of Althusser's philosophy of encounter where history is conceived as a "site of an infinity of encounters between heterogeneous forces the outcome of which could never be predicted" (Montag 2013, 16; see also Callari and Ruccio 1996).

Neither monads nor spirits

With its topological density, virtual differentiality, and irreducible singularity, the concept of *process* occupies a central place and serves a critical role in Resnick and Wolff's project of rethinking Marxism. The centrality of process has three important consequences for the construction of their theoretical framework: it is a springboard for their critique of ontology, it provides the basis for their theory of the subject, and it leads the way toward their formalist turn in class analysis. The remainder of this section and the subsequent two sections will address these consequences in that order.

As a critique of ontology, the concept of process is intimately linked to their understanding of overdetermination as a critique of humanist as well as structuralist theories of causality, and it enabled them to foreground *change and becoming* against *fixity and identity*. Their emphasis on relationality, the ensemble of relations, and becoming remains a significant advance on much of the modernist social theorizing of causality.

This dual break from Cartesian and Hegelian notions of totality and causality was already present in Althusser's articulation of the notion of structural causality (Althusser and Balibar 1970, Cullenberg 1994). Looking back from the perspective of the "Final Althusser" of aleatory materialism, we are able to appreciate how the concept of structural causality, far from being a context for a last-instance determinism, is indeed *the* concept to capture the contradiction-generating overdetermination of each process by the "ensemble of relations" among all the processes. The emphasis here is on "relations" among processes rather than "processes" themselves, as structural causality exists only in its effects, in the way processes relate to one another. Althusser summarizes this point when he writes, "the idea of causality [is] through relations and not by elements" (1991, 26; see also Roberts 1996, 199–201). The emphasis is also on "contradiction" rather than "reconciliation," as the concept of overdetermination implies the proliferation of contradictions rather than a reduction to a "fundamental" one. This is, indeed, in striking contrast with both Cartesian atomism where the cause springs forth from the parts (e.g., rational actors, monads) that are themselves undetermined and Hegelian holism where the whole (e.g., History, Spirit, Mind) gives shape and direction, a destination, a telos for the ensemble of parts to arrive at. Hence Althusser's (1976) most famous and efficient theoretical anti-humanist formula, "process without a subject and a goal," is central for Resnick and Wolff's double rejection of both Anglo-Saxon (predominant among neoclassical economists) and Continental (predominant among classical Marxist economists) varieties of determinism.

Retro-active path to the subject

The second consequence pertains to the rejection of the subject-object dualism that characterizes modernist thought. The concept of process provides them with the theoretical armature they need for their rejection of humanist and structuralist theories of subjectivity. The Althusserian notion of "process without a subject or a goal" is primarily directed against the Hegelian notions of Spirit as the Subject of History and the harmonious reconciliation of State and Civil Society, on the one hand, and the Cartesian world populated by monadic individuals (e.g., *homo economicus, homo psychologicus*) who, through their interactions, eventually arrive at an equilibrium state (e.g., *economic order*), on the other hand (see also Althusser 1996). In this vein, Wolff and Resnick conceptualize *subjectivity as a process*:

> Overdetermination implies that each of us is a singular being precisely because of the different array of determinations combining to constitute each ... [N]o one can be conceived to be a decision-making island, an isolated entity. Rather, we are all interconnected.... [I]ndividuals are ... composed of multiple, ceaselessly shifting, and potentially conflictual "subjectivities." ... [W]e all are a complex bundle of potentially conflicting and conflicted subjectivities interacting and vying with one another and overdetermining our social behavior.
>
> (2012, 280–81)

As a critique of theories of causality, overdetermination renders the assignment of a privileged agency to the individual theoretically illegitimate. Nevertheless, Resnick and Wolff's theorization of *subjectivity as a process* fails to account for that something that exceeds the ceaseless push and pull of the network of contradictory determinations, a singular something that renders the incalculable subject ethico-politically culpable, if not causally privileged. For Freudo-Lacanian psychoanalysis, accounting for this ethico-political excess of the subject is essential for social transformation, for constituting an ethical-social link that can cultivate a minimal distance to social fantasies. The key point here is to conceive of choice not in terms of rational choice but as an unconscious act that has happened in the past. The ethico-political act of the subject is to retroactively recover and assume the responsibility of this unconscious choice (Zizek 1989).

Despite its far-reaching, radical implications for ontology, there is something temporally unidirectional in the manner in which Resnick and Wolff conceptualize each process (including the subject) as always in a state of ceaseless change, always *becoming*. This is despite the fact that the concept of overdetermination, within its linguistic and psychoanalytical lineages, implies a non-linear (retroactive) concept of temporality: the meaning of a signifier (*process*) is not only determined relationally by all the other signifiers (*processes*) in a synchronic manner, but also diachronically in a retroactive manner by the addition of each new signifier to the chain of signification (see also Roberts 1981, 1996).

In clinical practice, the notion of retroactivity is central for producing an anti-essentialist, theoretically anti-humanist understanding of trauma. Contrary to the common idea, trauma is not an ontological priority but an initially mere senseless cut/rupture/interruption (symbolic castration enacted in the process of the infant's accession to language) that gains its constitutive status for the subject only retroactively through its subsequent significations and narrativizations, leading to the formation of a fundamental fantasy (Fink 1997). The aim of the analytical process is to recover the contingency of the significations and narratives about the self and the others and hopefully gain a minimal distance to the subject's own fundamental fantasy structured around the original cut. For psychoanalysis, overdetermination, functioning through condensations and displacements, describes this logic of retroactive constitution of the subject around his or her constitutive trauma. While the figurations, narratives, and memories are singular and make up the contradictory formation that we call *subjectivity*, the subject itself is an effect of the signifying process, the traumatic cut introduced by the representation of the subject with a signifier to other signifiers.[8] It is this category of the subject as an effect of the accession to language, to the symbolic order that can *neither* be fully accounted for by the notion of *subjectivity as a process* nor be reduced to an ideological construct.

Somewhat unexpectedly, we can discern in Resnick and Wolff's discourse the elements of a theory of the subject that make use of this notion of retroactivity and that are in excess of the ceaseless push and pull of overdetermination (see also Madra 2015). In particular, in their treatment of the process of *theorizing* (defined as the production of thought-concrete for making sense out of concrete-real) in *Contending Economic Theories*, they note that "everyone engages in economic theorizing" (Wolff and Resnick 2012, 6) and that all people, whether they are conscious of it or not, "necessarily use some economic theory throughout their life" (*ibid.*, 7). This is almost a working assumption for them, and to foreground it as such may help us to shed a new light on their unwavering resolve to compare and contrast different and contending economic theories with respect to their entry points and logics. In efforts to analyze discourses, their aim has been to help readers (be it a lay-person or a student of economics) recover a choice that they have already (consciously or unconsciously) assumed in subscribing to one or another dominant theory that has historically been in mainstream circulation. They do this by revealing the very contingency of the entry point (the necessity and inevitability of an arbitrary cut), the historical overdetermination of the emergence and development of a discourse, and the impossibility of entertaining a non-partisan position (the non-existence of a meta-position). The logic of retroactivity informs their theoretical practice. Their aim in writing *Contending Economic Theories* (2012) is to encourage their readers to own up to a theoretical choice that is always already made: to create the conditions under which the reader can assume responsibility for his/her fundamental fantasy, recover the spontaneous or unproblematized theoretical choices and discern the contingent foundations of the more elaborate theories built around them. Yet, they want more; they also want to convince the reader to disassociate from the dominant economic ideologies and embrace a new entry point, a new theory (re-identification). The arbitrary and essentially meaningless initial cut of the entry point is precisely that which is in excess of the push and pull of overdetermination, that cannot be reduced to it. Yes, the content of the cut, constituted retroactively, is overdetermined, but the inevitable cut itself is irreducible to the push and pull of overdetermination. Unfortunately this implied theory of subject (premised upon the non-linear temporality of the retroactive logic of theoretical practice) does not spill over to the content of their theoretical practice of class analysis, and its implications remain limited to the fields of epistemology (the recovering of the contingency of entry point) and methodology (the rhythm of the dialectical method).[9]

Class as an adjective: the formalist turn

A third consequence of turning the concept of process into an ontological axiom pertains to Resnick and Wolff's formalization of class analytics as the study of diverse forms of production, appropriation, and distribution of surplus labor: it enables Marxists to rip class analysis from the historicity of its origins and to formalize it in order to carry it toward ever-new contexts in an irreducibly heterogeneous concrete-real.

Thinking of class as a process, "not as a noun, but as an adjective," as Resnick and Wolff put it, is a major breakthrough. To the extent that process is a site of the contradictory push and pull of its conditions of existence, it is, in essence, an emptiness, a vanishing point that is always becoming. Consequently, the objective is not to define fixed class identities and measure the distance of the consciousness of concrete subjects from those identities (as in the debates on class consciousness) but rather to explore how class and non-class processes combine into contradictory formations that are always in transition. In contrast to the classical Marxian tradition, where class antagonism is defined as a conflict between classes (noun) *qua* identities or positions, for the anti-essentialist Marxism, class antagonism *as such* (qua constitutive negativity), first and foremost, pertains to the impossibility of achieving a harmoniously reconciled class formation, since each class process is a site of the contradictory push and pull of its conditions of existence, including those that pertain to subjectivity and class consciousness. Conflicts among class positions, compared to this fundamental impossibility of constituting a harmonious class relation, are secondary. Specific class formations are historically contingent institutional configurations to organize the class process; they are attempts to distribute subjects to class positions and shape the parameters within which conflicts are waged. In this sense, they function like defense formations; conflicts among class positions within class formations are institutional attempts at domesticating a more fundamental impossibility by containing the effects of overdetermination and contradiction within manageable bounds (Özselçuk and Madra 2005).

If the emptiness ("site") part of the definition of the concept of process enables us to identify the precise theoretical location of the constitutive negativity in the class process, the conditions of existence part of the definition enables us to rethink "difference" in class analysis. When considering the consequences of the concept of process, we can cite a number of important constitutive debates in the Marxian tradition. Resnick and Wolff and the Amherst tradition have engaged in many of them: the problem of transition from feudalism to capitalism (Resnick and Wolff 1979, Kayatekin and Charusheela 2004); the question of forms of the commune (e.g., Amariglio 2010); the ideas of socialism and communism (e.g., Ruccio and Amariglio 2003); the debate on the articulation of modes of production in the context of development (e.g., Chakrabarti and Cullenberg 2003); the question of social formation (e.g., Olson 2009); and post-capitalist economic politics (Gibson-Graham 2006).[10]

What is significant here is a tendency to push the envelope beyond the "big five" class formations (i.e., ancient, slave, feudal, capitalist, communist) and to think of class difference materializing across a range of criteria depending on the historically specific cultural, political, economic and natural conditions of existence. In this manner, the methodological flexibility of the concept of class process as an empty site constituted by the contradictory determinations of its ever-multiplying series of conditions of existence is not betrayed, since there might be an infinite number of class formations. Yet, we have to be careful not to entertain an idealist or empiricist notion of the infinite here, as there are an infinite number of class formations only in the virtual sense of the word. The centrality of the negativity qua impossibility of instituting fully reconciled class formations is the cause of a virtual differential infinity, even if in actuality all we have is historically specific and finite differentiations—yet, even if these differentiations are finite and circumscribed by their historicity, they surely are inexhaustible by the big five.

Conclusion

The concept of process is uncanny because Resnick and Wolff always insisted on reminding us, at the risk of undermining their own discourse, of their partiality and partisanship and because the concept has controversial implications for Marxian theories of causality and subjectivity and the methodology of class analysis. In terms of causality, it is a radical break with both atomistic and holistic forms of determinism and as such is not accepted by Analytical Marxists (an important rival research program in the 1980s) or by Classical Marxists (from which Resnick and Wolff broke). In terms of subjectivity, to the extent that they remained in fidelity to Althusser's formula "process without a subject and a goal," the concept implies a thoroughgoing critique of theoretical humanism and its essentialist notion of human subjectivity, as well as centered notions of structure where the latter is treated as an anthropomorphized Subject with intentionality and pre-determined directionality (historical telos). Since these theories of causality and subjectivity are so prevalent in various currents of Marxism, Resnick and Wolff's concept of process ends up being indigestible for those currents. And finally, the shift from class as a noun to class as an adjective creates an additional break from the traditional Marxist politics structured around the privileged figure of the proletariat and offers a new politics of class transformation at the level of class formation rather than simply that of class identity (Gibson-Graham 2006). This new politics of class, combined with theoretical shifts listed above, has created a novel form of Marxism—albeit one that is (still) not easily recognizable by large sectors of the Marxian tradition.

Acknowledgments

The author would like to thank the editors of the volume, Ted Burczak, Rob Garnett and Ric McIntyre, and Ceren Özselçuk for their labor of reading and thoughtful comments. The usual disclaimer applies.

Notes

1 To my knowledge, the idea that overdetermined ontology is flat was first articulated in written form, pejoratively, by Herbert Gintis (1979) in his response to Resnick and Wolff's article (1979) on the debate on transition from feudalism to capitalism.

2 In these paraphrased fragments from Saussure, we already see the traces of a more foundational homology between (linguistic) *sign* and (economic) *value*. See also Saussure (1959 [1916], 79). The determination of the meaning of a sign (i.e., the stabilization of the relation between a signifier and its signified) can be thought as homologous to the determination of the value of a commodity (i.e., the stabilization of its relative price). The (economic) value of a commodity is determined in its relation to, or through its differential relation (according to a set of socially determined criteria) to, all the other commodities. In a similar manner, the linguistic value (meaning) of a sign is also determined relationally and differentially. See Amariglio and David F. Ruccio's (1999) discussion of the misuses of the category "economy" in literary theory and the post-structuralist tradition in general.

3 During the last decade of his life, Lacan's discourse on the relation between the structure and the subject, while not abandoning the imaginary and the symbolic registers, placed the accent increasingly on the affective investments, entanglements, and cathexes of the subject, using topological models, e.g., a Moebius strip (Fink 1997).

4 For the relevance of Deleuze for the Althusserian School, see Stolze (1990). For a more focused treatment of this particular text and the exchange among Deleuze, Althusser, and Macherey regarding an earlier draft, see Stolze (1998). For a convincing Deleuzean reading of Resnick and Wolff's framework, see Rebello (2006).

5 The term, from another text by Deleuze written in the same year as the "structuralism" essay, refers to the efforts of a clinician in making a

diagnosis by collating a number of symptoms under a single name (1991 [1967], 15–16). His own effort to identify structuralism through a number of symptoms is an instance of symptomatology as practiced in the field of critical philosophy.

6 If all processes have the same morphological structure, what happens to the specificity of the cultural, the political, the economic or the natural? See Miklitsch (1995) for a careful critique of Resnick and Wolff's treatment of the cultural in their work.

7 For Wolff, this constitutes a response to George DeMartino's (1992) critique of their methodological practice. According to DeMartino, the impulse to enumerate an endless list of determinants falls into a kind of realism of overdetermination, which he calls the "overdetermination fidelity complex."

8 According to Lacan's famous formula, "[a] signifier represents the subject to other signifiers" (Lacan 2006 [1970]). Althusser, in his memoir *Future Lasts Forever*, gives an excellent example of this when he writes about the traumatic nature of his name, Louis—the name of his maternal grandfather and mother's lover and a homonym of "him" in French (1995, 38–39).

9 In his discussion of the logic of *Capital*, Bruce Roberts (1981) argues that the concept of overdetermination pertains to the diachronic unfolding of concepts within Marx's discourse where new concepts reconfigure the earlier concepts, modifying their meaning (*referents*). In particular, Roberts used this idea to trace how the referents of the signifiers value and value-form get progressively modified from volume 1 to volume 3 of *Capital*. To turn the homology around, the concepts within a discourse could themselves be conceived as processes that are determined retroactively by the introduction of new concepts into the theory.

10 See also the contributions by Jonathan Diskin and Richard McIntyre in Callari and Ruccio (1996).

References

Althusser, L. 1969. *For Marx*. Trans. B. Brewster. London: New Left Books.

—— 1976. *Essays in Self-criticism*. Trans. G. Lock. London: New Left Books.

—— 1991. "On Marx and Freud." *Rethinking Marxism* 4 (1): 17–30.

—— 1995. *The Future Lasts Forever: A memoir*. New York: The New Press.

—— 1996. *Writings on Psychoanalysis: Freud and Lacan*. O. Corpet and F. Matheron, eds., J. Mehlman, trans. New York: Columbia University Press.

—— 2006. *Philosophy of the Encounter: Later Writings, 1978–1987*. O. Corpet and F. Matheron, eds., G. M. Goshgarian, trans. London and New York: Verso.

Althusser, L. and É. Balibar. 1970. *Reading Capital*. Trans. B. Brewster. London: New Left Books.

Amariglio, J. 1984. "Economic History and the Theory of Primitive Socio-economic Development." Ph.D. Dissertation, Department of Economics, University of Massachusetts, Amherst.

—— 2010. "Subjectivity, Class, and Marx's 'Forms of the Commune'." *Rethinking Marxism* 22 (3): 329–44.

Amariglio, J. and D. F. Ruccio. 1999. "Literary/Cultural Economies, Economic Discourse and the question of Marxism." In *New Economic Criticism: Studies at the Intersection of Literature and Economics*, M Woodmansee and M. Osteen, eds., 324–39. London and New York: Routledge.

Callari, A. and D. F. Ruccio, eds. 1996. *Postmodern Materialism and the Future of Marxist Theory. Essays in the Althusserian Tradition*. Hanover and London: Wesleyan University Press.

Chakrabarti, A. and S. Cullenberg. 2003. *Transition and Development in India*. London and New York: Routledge.

Cullenberg, S. 1994. *The Falling Rate of Profit: Recasting the Marxian Debate*. London and New York: Pluto Press.

de Saussure, F. 1959 [1916]. *A Course in General Linguistics*. New York: Philosophical Library.

Deleuze, G. 1991 [1967]. "Coldness and Cruelty." In *Masochism*, J. McNeil, trans., 9–138. New York: Zone Books.

——— 2002 [1967]. "How Do We Recognize Structuralism?" In *Desert Islands and Other Texts 1953–1974*, D. Lapoujade, ed., M. Taomina, trans., 170–92. Los Angeles and New York: Semiotext(e).

DeMartino, G. 1992. "Modern Macroeconomic Theories of Cycles and Crisis: A Methodological Critique." Ph.D. Dissertation, Department of Economics, University of Massachusetts, Amherst.

Freud, S. 1953–74 [1899]. Vols. 4 and 5 of *The Standard Edition of the Complete Psychological Works*. 24 vols. Edited and translated by J. Strachey. London: Hogarth.

Fink, B. 1997. *A Clinical Introduction to Lacanian Psychoanalysis: Theory and Technique*. Cambridge and London: Harvard University Press.

Gibson-Graham, J. K. 2006. *A Postcapitalist Politics*. Minneapolis: University of Minnesota Press.

Gintis, H. 1979. "On the Theory of Transitional Conjunctures." *Review of Radical Political Economics* 11 (3): 23–31.

Jameson, F. 1998. *Brecht and Method*. London and New York: Verso.

Kayatekin, S. and S. Charusheela. 2004. "Recovering Feudal Subjectivities." *Rethinking Marxism* 16 (4): 377–96.

Lacan, J. 2006 [1970]. "The Instance of the Letter in the Unconscious or Reason Since Freud." In *Écrits*, B. Fink, trans., 412–41. New York: W.W. Norton.

Laclau, E. and C. Mouffe. 1985. *Hegemony and Socialist Strategy: Towards a Radical Democratic Politics*. Trans. W. Moore and P. Cammack. London and New York: Verso.

Madra, Y. M. 2015. "'Everyone Engages in Economic Theorizing': Reading *Contending Economic Theories* for a Theory of Subjectivity." *Rethinking Marxism* 27 (2): 288–92.

Marx, K. 1963. *Theories of Surplus Value, Part 1*. Moscow: Progress Publishers.

——— 1969. *Theories of Surplus Value, Part 2*. Moscow: Progress Publishers.

——— 1973. *Theories of Surplus Value, Part 3*. Moscow: Progress Publishers.

——— 1976 [1867]. *Capital Volume 1*. Harmondsworth: Penguin/New Left Books.

——— 1978 [1884]. *Capital Volume 2*. Harmondsworth: Penguin/New Left Books.

——— 1981 [1894]. *Capital Volume 3*. Harmondsworth: Penguin/New Left Books.

Miklitsch, R. 1995. "The Rhetoric of Post-Marxism: Discourse and Institutionality in Laclau and Mouffe, Resnick and Wolff." *Social Text* 14 (4): 167–96.

Montag, W. 2013. *Althusser and His Contemporaries: Philosophy's Perpetual War*. Durham: Duke University Press.

Olson, E. 2009. "Social Ontology and the Origins of Mode of Production Controversy." *Rethinking Marxism* 21 (2): 177–95.

Özselçuk, C. and Y. M. Madra. 2005. "Psychoanalysis and Marxism: From Capitalist-all to Communist Non-all." *Psychoanalysis, Culture and Society* 10 (1): 79–97.

Rebello, J. T. 2006. "The Economy of Joyful Passions: A Political Economic Ethics of the Virtual." *Rethinking Marxism* 18 (2): 259–72.

Resnick, S. A. and R. D. Wolff. 1979. "The Theory of Transitional Conjunctures and the Transition from Feudalism to Capitalism in Western Europe." *Review of Radical Political Economics* 11 (3): 3–22.

—— 1987. *Knowledge and Class: A Marxian Critique of Political Economy.* Chicago: University of Chicago Press.

Roberts, B. 1981. "Value Categories and Marxian Method: A Different View of Price-Value Transformation." Ph.D. Dissertation, Department of Economics, University of Massachusetts, Amherst.

—— 1996. "The Visible and the Measurable: Althusser and the Marxian Theory of Value." In *Postmodern Materialism and the Future of Marxist Theory. Essays in the Althusserian Tradition*, A. Callari and D. F. Ruccio, eds., 193–211. Hanover and London: Wesleyan University Press.

Ruccio, D. F. 2009. "(Un)real Criticism." In *Ontology and Economics: Tony Lawson and His Critics*, E. Fullbrook, ed., 263–74. London and New York: Routledge.

Ruccio, D. F. and J. Amariglio 2003. *Postmodern Moments in Modern Economics.* Princeton and Oxford: Princeton University Press.

Stolze, T. 1990. "A Marxist Encounter with the Philosophy of Gilles Deleuze." *Rethinking Marxism* 3 (3–4): 287–96.

—— 1998. "Deleuze and Althusser: Flirting with Structuralism." *Rethinking Marxism* 10 (3): 51–63.

Wolff, R. D. 1996. "Althusser and Hegel: Making Marxist Explanations Antiessentialist and Dialectical." In *Postmodern Materialism and the Future of Marxist Theory. Essays in the Althusserian Tradition*, A. Callari and D. F. Ruccio, eds., 150–64. Hanover and London: Wesleyan University Press.

Wolff, R. D. and S. A. Resnick. 2012. *Contending Economic Theories: Neoclassical, Keynesian, and Marxian.* Cambridge: MIT Press.

Zizek, S. 1989. *Sublime Object of Ideology.* London and New York: Verso.

—— 2004. *Organs without Bodies: Deleuze and Consequences.* London and New York: Routledge.

Part V

Appraising the postmodern turn

13 Marxism's double task

Deconstructing and reconstructing postmodernism

Jan Rehmann

Introduction

The conference panel on which Rick Wolff and I started this discussion was titled "Marxism and Postmodernism: Enemies or Allies?"[1] The title was meant to highlight the polarized, polemical terms in which the postmodernism/Marxism relationship is often cast in the intellectual field. When Rick and I organized this panel, however, it was clear that we each intended to overcome this dichotomy and to open up a differentiated debate on both the contradictions and possible encounters. Though I focus on the contradictions between the two formations, I refuse to accept the either-or question posed by the conference panel title. Critiquing an intellectual formation, learning from it and building theoretical-political alliances are not mutually exclusive and depend on the concrete research project and debate. I have no objection to using valuable aspects of postmodernist theories, but I do maintain that such usage should not be made without awareness of the overall shift from critical Marxism to postmodernism. It is my contention that Rick Wolff's self-description as a "postmodern Marxist" underestimates and glosses over the theoretical and political "costs" this shift entails.

Postmodernist and poststructuralist theories have been widely praised for overcoming Marxism's tendencies of economism, determinism, class-reductionism, totalitarianism, you name it. Finally, social theory and social movements abandoned their fixation on class rule and state domination and turned to the microphysics of power in everyday life. Finally they gave up what Lyotard described as the typically modernist meta-narrative, which not only applied to the metaphysical novels of traditional philosophy, but was also against the "emancipation of the rational and working subject" (Lyotard [1979] 1984, xxiii), which was, of course, a marker for Marxism and socialism. Finally they left behind the boring labor of *ideology-critique* and focused on the minute fabric of discourses and micro-powers. This has become the main meta-narrative of postmodernism, a meta-narrative that claims to do away with "modernity" altogether, not only with its predominant ideologies but also with its most powerful socialist and anti-imperialist critiques. Since this success story of postmodernism is still predominant in large parts of academia, in particular in the humanities, I will focus in this presentation on a theoretical critique of some basic tenets of postmodernism. I am aware that I bend the stick in one direction. I know of course that there are many different and contradictory theories that can be subsumed under this label, and I am of course not denying that Marxist theory can learn from these competing approaches. But my main point is that behind the conspicuous success story of postmodernism there is a *serious theoretical loss*.

In what follows I would like to raise the following objections:

1   It was not postmodernism that taught Marxism how to overcome its economistic, deterministic, and class-reductionist tendencies. It was rather Marxist critical theories, in particular theories of ideology and hegemony, that formulated a thorough and substantial critique of these tendencies;

2   Most of the postmodernist and poststructuralist theories marked a *serious step back* from the analytical level of these theories of ideology and hegemony; in their majority, they delegitimized a Marxist critique of capitalism, successfully sidelined the influence of critical theories in academia and social movements, and thus functioned as an integral part of neoliberal ideologies; and

3   Marxist theories can and must certainly learn from postmodernist approaches, but they need to be both *deconstructive* and *reconstructive*, in order to reinterpret the fruitful insights in a renewed *critical social theory*.

Marxist self-criticism

Let me begin with the inner-Marxist critique of economism and determinism, which started quite some time before Althusser took up and refurbished Freud's concept of "overdetermination." Some valuable insights that Althusser considered to be "humanistic" and thus still "ideological" and "pre-Marxist" are to be found in the early Marx. In his *Theses on Feuerbach*, Marx distanced his "new materialism" from "all previous materialism" by the characteristics that it conceived of reality no more as an object but as a "sensuous human activity, practice, [...] subjectively" (Marx [1845] 1976, 3). When, in the *German Ideology*, Marx and Engels gave an early account of their historical-materialist method, they described this subjective practice in an integral and non-deterministic way and differentiated it into five aspects: in order to survive, humans need to produce their means of subsistence; they develop new needs; they propagate their kind and create relations between men and women, parents and children; they engage in a twofold "production of life," of one's own in labor and of fresh life in procreation; they develop language and consciousness as a "social product" (Marx and Engels [1845] 1976, 41–44).

Unlike some other passages that insist on the "determination" of people's consciousness by their social being (Marx [1859] 1987, 263, for example), this account is not interested in hierarchizing these aspects; they are not conceived of as "different stages" with one having historical or ontological priority over the others, but rather as "moments that have existed simultaneously since the dawn of history" (Marx and Engels [1845] 1976, 43). When Marx and Engels distance themselves from idealistic philosophies of consciousness, they don't do this here from the objectivist position of an underlying dichotomy between (primary) being and (secondary) consciousness, but rather because these philosophies severed consciousness from the integral context of social praxis.

Many debates on determinism, overdetermination, and co-determination are too much fixated on the relationship between already fixed instances of society (economy, politics, culture, etc.) and forget that these instances are in fact institutionalized and ossified forms of social practices. A praxeological approach would need to distinguish for example between concrete activities of people, which are never completely determined but surrounded by a certain space of possibilities, and the respective *fields* of activities, in which these activities take place. Determination is a quality not of the singular action, but of the structured field, because it contains "switches" that determine what is considered to be successful or unsuccessful activity and thus give regular feedback to the acting subjects. Diverging actions thus coalesce around converging experiences, which are then repeated again and again, become fixed habits and are then handed down as such. "Laws" are only "resulting laws," in which the interactions typical for a field of activities are condensed. In this sense one could say that determination is a result of indetermination (cf. Haug 2013, 220–21).

Antonio Gramsci in his *Prison Notebooks* fought a constant battle against any kind of mechanical determinism that undermined Marxism's potentials as a *philosophy of praxis*. The notion that we have been defeated for the moment, but the "tide of history is working for us in the long term," can certainly be helpful in providing some perseverance in the struggle, but it is also a kind of religious opium of the subaltern classes, a "substitute for the Predestination or Providence of confessional religions," and as such it can become a cause of passivity and "idiotic self-sufficiency" (Gramsci 1971, 336–37). Gramsci thus applied Marx's famous critique of religion to Marxism itself. There is no guarantee in history whatsoever, everything depends on our capacity of analysis and organizing and alliance building. This also applies to the experience of economic crises.

Over and over again, Gramsci warned his comrades who believed and hoped that the crisis would necessarily lead to a collapse of the capitalist system. No, he argued, the expectation that the economic crisis opens the breach in the enemy's defenses, so that one's own troops can rush in "in

a flash" and obtain a definite strategic victory, is an economistic and deterministic prejudice that belongs to the paradigm of an outdated model
of revolution as a "war of maneuver" (Gramsci 1971, 233). This model succeeded the last time in 1917 in Russia and then failed in the developed
capitalist countries of the West because of the very complex structure of
their civil society (*ibid.*, 236). Under the conditions of a "war of position,"
an economic crisis cannot by itself produce fundamental historical events,
but only "create a terrain more favorable to the dissemination of alternative ideas" (*ibid.*, 184, 235). The ruling classes are usually able to adapt to
the situation and to regain the control that was slipping from its grasp.
No automatism here either. There is never a direct equation between what
is going on in the "economy" and on political and ideological levels. The
working class can be fragmented into competing factions and thereby absorbed into the bourgeois hegemony of the ruling power bloc or it can
develop its own hegemony from below, or a combination of both—it all
depends on its capacity to act and to alter the power relations in "civil
society" and "political society."

Taking up Gramsci's reflections on an "interregnum," where the ruling class "has lost consensus," is no more "leading," but only "ruling,"
whereas the masses are skeptical toward all general formulas (Gramsci
1975, 311–12), one could argue that today's neoliberal capitalism has become increasingly incapable of actively mobilizing its subjects and thus
relies more and more on a "passive consensus," which can in turn be maintained as long as credible and appealing democratic-socialist alternatives
are either not yet worked out or effectively barred from a wider public. It
is possible to observe and predict the general tendency that capitalism's
authoritarian and disciplinary-panoptic inclinations grow in significance.
It cannot however be determined beforehand for how long and to what
extent the elites and their ideologues will succeed in shifting the blame to
trade unions, Mexican immigrants, Muslims, and other enemy-images, or
at what point the fundamental contradiction between capitalism and democracy becomes visible and opens the way to new anti-capitalist movements and alliances.

This critique of economism and determinism was then continued in
the so-called "ideology-theoretical turn" of the 1970s and 1980s, initiated by Louis Althusser and developed further e.g., by Stuart Hall and
the research group *Projekt Ideologietheorie* in Berlin, in which I had the
chance to participate. This "ideology-theoretical turn" marked a major
paradigm shift against the former prevailing notion of ideology as a
form of *false consciousness* that was to be derived from the "economy."
The response was basically: you must not reduce the concept of ideology to a phenomenon of consciousness. If you want to understand why
and how subjects "voluntarily" submit to alienated and restrictive conditions of life, you need to take the proper "materiality" of the ideological seriously, that is, you need to investigate its material reality as an

arrangement of apparatuses, certain types of intellectuals, of rituals, and forms of praxis. Gramsci had described this arrangement as "hegemonic apparatuses." Althusser tried to reconceptualize this materiality with his theory of "ideological state apparatuses" (ISA) and of ideological "interpellations" that grasp the subjects' attention and format their subjectivity. This ideological subjection not only impacts consciousness, but also anchors itself unconsciously in bodily dispositions and attitudes of "habitus" (Bourdieu).[2]

A second achievement of Marxist ideology theories, mostly *after* Althusser (and partly against him), was the insight that ideological subjugation works not only in a one-way top-down manner. Rick Wolff pointed out that the plurality of the "modes of production combined in social formations" were transmitted to the ISA and thus led to a panoply of contradicting interpellations to which the individual subjects are subjected (Wolff 2004, 765–66). This implies of course a stronger agency of the subject: subjected to contradicting interpellations, s/he needs to balance and prioritize them, which might imply rejecting some in order to be able to respond to others. Stuart Hall has shown that the *coding* of an ideological message and its *decoding* by the interpellated subject are not necessarily the same. The subjects might, for example, accept the predominant ideology full-heartedly, or they might hear the interpellation and decide that it's not applicable to the given situation ("negotiated code"), or they might interpret the message in a *"globally* contrary way"—Hall calls this an "oppositional code" (Hall 1993, 517). Often the same ideological symbols and values are interpreted and claimed in an opposite way. The *Projekt Ideologietheorie* conceptualized this as "antagonistic reclamation"—ideological values are interpellated by antagonistic forces (cf. Haug 1987, 71–72, 94; Rehmann 2014, 254–61). Different classes, genders, and generations interpret very differently what *God's Will* is, what *justice* means, what *morality* proclaims, etc. Under certain circumstances, subaltern classes can claim these ideological values as well, turn them around and reappropriate them. But they can also by the same token be *reabsorbed* into the mainstream. The ideological is a field that is traversed by manifold social antagonisms and struggles.

Taking out social contradictions

Getting to my second point, I would like to argue that it is in particular these two achievements of Marxist ideology theories, the *antagonistic reclamation* of ideological instances and values and the *materiality* of the ideological, that got all but lost in the transition to postmodernism. For illustrating the first loss, I take as an example the way Michel Foucault dissolved *ideology* into *knowledge* and *discourse*, which he then later transformed into the concept of *power*. In his *Archeology of Knowledge* he argued that the ideological functioning of science can be observed where it is "localized" in knowledge and finds its place in a "discursive regularity," where it "exists as a discursive practice" (Foucault [1969] 1972, 185). This transfer of the concept of ideology to the concepts of knowledge and discursive practice led to an overgeneralization that took out the critical sting. Foucault has bid farewell to the question of ideology before he even raised it. To raise the question of ideology would mean to search in both "science" and "knowledge" for specific forms and modes of functioning that organize a 'voluntary' submission to the respective relations of domination (and for those that resist such a submission).

According to Foucault, discourses are not to be searched for "theoretical contradictions, lacunae, defects," but are rather to be described on the level of their "positivity" (Foucault [1969] 1972, 186). As Dominique Lecourt observed, Foucault distanced himself from an early version of Althusser's ideology theory (Lecourt 1975, 199–200), in particular from his concept of a "symptomatic reading," by which he tried to identify the "lacunae [...] and blanks" in a text, to unveil the inner link between what is seen and what is unseen, and to lay open the textual ruptures that indicate the interference of a second text in latency with an opposite logic (Althusser and Balibar [1965] 2009, 28–29). By replacing this Althusserian project of a sophisticated textual ideology-critique with his "happy positivism" (Foucault [1969] 1972, 125), Foucault abandoned the analytical task of relating the respective formations of knowledge to the underlying social perspectives, and of differentiating between the inherent ideological or subversive and anti-ideological dimensions.

What got lost is the theoretical understanding that the social production of knowledge takes place in antagonistically structured fields, where, as Althusser remarked, "the class conflicts of the practical ideologies combine with the theoretical ideologies, the existing sciences and philosophy" (Althusser [1974] 1976, 147–48). According to Michel Pêcheux, Foucault did not understand that discursive formations are to be analyzed on two levels, namely, on the one hand from a "regional" standpoint, which identifies its internal relationships, and on the other hand from a class perspective, which is able to explain why ideologies invoke the same higher values but "under contradictory modalities that are connected to the class antagonism" (Pêcheux 1990, 258).

This blind spot persisted when Foucault from 1971 onwards transferred his concepts of discourse and knowledge into his concept of *power*. As I tried to show in a study on postmodernist Neo-Nietzscheanism (Rehmann 2004, 112–20), Foucault took his concept of power directly from the late Nietzsche and identified it with the "will to truth" as such. However one decides to distinguish between the different periods of Foucault's works, the connection of power, knowledge, and truth is the main axis from the early 1970s to the late studies on Greek Antiquity, Stoicism, and early Christianity in the 1980s. He located the enigmatic force of power on a deep level "underneath the old theme of the sense, the signified, the signifier" and conceived of it explicitly as an alternative to the Marxist concepts of "exploitation," "appropriation," and the analysis of state apparatuses (cf. Foucault 2001, 1180–81; Foucault [1975] 1995, 26).

This methodological decision overlooks however that for Marx relations of production and appropriation of unpaid surplus-labor were not just economic "facts," but constituted a highly condensed and institutionalized "power network" (cf. Poulantzas 1978, 36). Marx's *Critique of Political Economy* shows how fetishism and exploitation function as hidden power mechanisms of modern capitalist domination by which the cooperative powers of the producers are alienated and handed over to the capitalist class. It is one thing to argue that there are manifold manifestations of power beyond and relatively independent from class-relations; it is quite another to define power as a reality of its own, outside and underneath the social relations of production and domination. In the context of this anti-Marxist detachment of "power" from exploitation, I find Resnick/Wolff's strict separation between "class," defined as surplus-appropriation, and "power," as a non-class category, not helpful (cf. Resnick and Wolff 2006, 119ff, 125ff; Resnick and Wolff 2013, 158f; Wolff 2013, 29f). Since the capacity to make decisions about what to produce, how to produce, and how to distribute the surplus are dependent on the power relations of the society in question, the different definitions of class can be translated into each other.

Similar to his concept of discourse, Foucault's concept of power dissimilates the contradictions between a power of domination from above and a collective agency from below (in the Spinozian sense of *potentia agendi*, capacity to act). It is not used as an analytical tool to decipher social relations and respective capacities to act but designates a vague quality somehow attached to knowledge and truth claims, no matter by and for whom, of what kind, and to what ends. The qualitative questions of *whose power, what power,* and *the power to do what* are excluded from the analysis. Nicos Poulantzas rightly pointed out that Foucault's alleged microphysics of power was in reality an essentialist construct of a "Master-Power" as the prime founder of all struggle-resistance. Behind the rhetoric of a multiple micro-power lies the idea of a "phagocytic essence" that invades and penetrates both the mechanisms of domination and of resistance, glossing over all social contradictions and struggles (Poulantzas 1978, 149 and 151). This disguised essentialism is a serious step back from the level of analytical differentiation of Marxist ideology theories. Whereas these theories tried to grasp how the "organic intellectuals" of opposite classes or hegemonic blocs struggle about the interpretation and application of ideological values, poststructuralist methods have shown hardly any interest in distinguishing opposite or different social perspectives within discourse formations and power configurations.

The de-materialization of human practices

Connected to this backdrop is the second theoretical loss. What got lost is the *"materiality"* of the ideological, its reality of hegemonic apparatuses, of different types of intellectuals, and of ideological practices and rituals. This was exactly what set apart Marxist *ideology-theories* from a mere critique of false consciousness in the first place. Postmodernist and poststructuralist theories have emerged to a large extent from a radicalization of the "linguistic turn" and have therefore focused in fact almost entirely on language and texts. Dominique Lecourt has already criticized Foucault's *Archeology of Knowledge* for remaining in an "archeological circle" and thus being unable to conceive of the interlocking of discourse formations and their material-institutional base and of ideological subject production, the social mode of production, and social struggles (1975, 205ff). When Foucault in his *History of Sexuality* derived the modern dispositive of sexuality from the discursive obligations of religious *confession* ([1976] 1990, 19ff, 58ff), he created indeed a new paradigm that helped overcome a narrow understanding of what he described as a Freudo-Marxist "repression hypothesis."

But confession was in reality not just a discursive meeting point of sex and "will to truth," but an integral part of a powerful ideological state apparatus. Furthermore, confession could develop such an effective power to detect and thus construct the stirrings of desire, because it operated in the context of systematic repression: mandatory confession was introduced by the same Lateran Council in 1215 that systematized the inquisition against heretics; whoever did not show up once a year was excluded from the church and could not get a church burial. It was framed and percolated by repression, functioned in conjunction with and as an ideological complement to it. Gramsci's notion of "hegemony protected by the armor of coercion" or Althusser's modified idea that the ISAs reproduce the relations of production under the "shield" of the repressive state-apparatuses (cf. Gramsci 1971, 263; Althusser [1971] 2001, 101) provide a much more adequate and comprehensive framework of analysis.

The shift toward a one-sided linguistic interpretation can be illustrated with the example of the biased reception of Wittgenstein's concept of *language games* by postmodernist approaches. In his *Philosophical Investigations* of 1945, Wittgenstein defined "language games" as "the whole, consisting of language and the actions into which it is woven" (Wittgenstein 1958, §7). The concept was intended to highlight that speaking is part of an encompassing activity, of a "form of life" (Wittgenstein 1958, §23). The meaning of words is the "kind of use they have" (*ibid.*, §10), exemplified by the practical communication between builder A and his assistant B, during which the former employs the words "blocks," "pillars," "slabs," and "beams" as elements of operational calls to have his assistant deliver these labor-items (*ibid.*, §2). One could of course ask why Wittgenstein used the ambiguous term "language game" instead of describing "the whole" of language and actions in terms of a Marxian or Gramscian *philosophy of praxis* (cf. the arranged dialogue among Wittgenstein, Gramsci, and Brecht, in Haug 2006, 69–91). Lyotard's *La condition postmoderne* shows in an exemplary way how this ambiguity of the term can give occasion to a fundamental displacement of meaning: according to his reading, subjects dissolve in a dissemination of language games, and the social bond that connects them is "linguistic" ([1979] 1984, 40). The outcome is the exact opposite of what Wittgenstein tried to demonstrate: whereas Wittgenstein conceived of language as embedded in socially structured praxis forms, Lyotard severs language from its material and practical conditions.

My argument is of course not that discourses have no importance for social analysis; to the contrary! Speeches, texts, and images are an important part of ideological subjection and struggles, discourse formations determine what is thinkable and imaginable in a certain time period, and it is no coincidence that one of the first discourse theories was developed within a Marxist framework by Michel Pêcheux, who tried to combine Althusser's ideology theory with a linguistic analysis of speeches and texts (cf. Pêcheux 1975). But whereas Marxist ideology-theories investigate the production of speeches and texts in connection with the respective ideological apparatuses and fields, postmodernist theories tend to isolate them from the practical and institutional contexts in which they are embedded. The result is a disembodied linguistic idealism.[3] The undeniable fact that language is found everywhere as a component of social practices and relations is pushed to the point that language seems to be *all* there is.

The consequence of this one-sidedness is that postmodernism's valuable deconstructive project of a de-*natural*ization of fixed meanings and identities regularly morphs into an overall de-*material*ization. By this I mean both a de-*material*ization of human practices and relations, which reduces the social to the symbolic, and a de-*material*ization of the body and thus a disembodiment of human subjects, who appear as effects of discourses and of chains of signifiers. Such a transition from de-naturalization to de-materialization occurs, for example, when Judith Butler, in order to challenge the presumption of one's sex as a "simple fact or static condition of one's body," explains the "materiality" of the body as an "effect of power," while power is in turn conceived of as a reiteration of "norms" (Butler 1993, 2; cf. Butler 1990, 12 and 189). This has provoked numerous criticisms from "materialist feminists," which is all the more interesting as some of them (e.g., Susan Bordo) started out from Foucault as well, but then came to the conclusion that the body must be at the center of feminist theory. Carol Bigwood claims that the poststructuralist body has no terrestrial weight (1998, 103); Rosemary Hennessy argues that Butler reduces materiality to the symbolic and thus drops social relations and in particular the fundamental relationship of capitalist exploitation out of her analysis (2000, 60f, 120f); Karen Barad states that

Butler cannot overcome the gap between the discursive and the material, because she considers matter to be the result of the agency of language and culture and does not recognize matter's own dynamism (2007, 64ff, 132ff, 194, 208).

The tendency to de-materialization was one of the hooks by which the mainstream currents of postmodernism could be co-opted into various neoliberal ideologies of an "immaterial," "weightless" mode of production and life. Hennessy describes postmodernist concepts of the subject in terms of an "eerie immateriality" coupled with an obsessive fetishized visibility of sexual identity, both of which correspond to accelerated commodification, deregulated labor markets, habitual mobility, and an increased fluidization of everyday life (2000, 106ff, 111, 115). As Luc Boltanski and Eve Chiapello have demonstrated, neoliberalism internalized not only the typical 1968 demands for "authenticity," but also what were seemingly their opposite, the demands for radical deconstruction of the exigency of authenticity; the various deconstructive schools especially facilitated the construction of a new adaptability (2005, 441ff, 451ff, 461, 498).

Toward a renewed ideology-theory

This leads me to my third and concluding point. Considering the significant theoretical shortcomings and the political ambiguities of postmodernism, I have serious doubts whether an overall fusion of Marxism and postmodernism as expressed in Rick Wolff's self-description as a "postmodernist Marxist" is sustainable. It glosses over fundamental contradictions and tensions and restricts the ideology-critical potentials of Marxism. I would like to propose instead that Marxist theory has a double task, a *deconstructive* and a *reconstructive* one. It should continue to critique whenever postmodernist theories de-materialize and disembody social life or repress the antagonisms and contradictions that run through the social fabric of capitalism. It needs to identify where the postmodernist celebrations of social fragmentations and simulacra intersect with (or are propelled by) the illusions of fictitious capital and tightly connected to the ideological imaginary of High-Tech-Capitalism.

A Marxist theory of ideology goes of course beyond the denouncing or pulling apart of a competing theoretical formation. It aims deeper and tries to grasp the inner connections between a specific stage of capitalism and the predominant subjectivities that emerge from it. In this vein, Frederic Jameson described postmodernism as a "superstructure" in the transition from Fordism to post-Fordism that produced a new "structure of feeling" (1991, xiv); for David Harvey, it marks a new round of "time-space-compressions" in the organization of capitalism, generated by the pressure of capital-accumulation (1990, 306f, 327ff). Since it is also a "mine-field of conflicting notions" (*ibid.*, viii and 292), we need to look for its inner contradictions, just as Marx analyzed the culture of modernity dialectically as a conflicting field of progressive potentials and destructive forces. Postmodern theories are usually not able or willing to self-critically scrutinize their anchorage in and inner connection with High-Tech-Capitalism—for this they would need a Marxist ideology-theory as a reliable ally.

At the same time, Marxist theory ought to pick up and reinterpret all the productive insights of postmodernism. There are for example interesting intersections between Derrida's concept of *deconstruction* and Marx's concept of a *dialectic* that regards "every historically developed form as being in a fluid state, in motion, and therefore grasps its transient aspect as well" ([1867] 1976, 103). Foucault's analysis in *Discipline and Punishment* of specific spatial arrangements (he called them *dispositifs*) by which disciplinary techniques are ingrained in subjects can fruitfully be reinterpreted in the framework of a Marxist theory of ideology (cf. Foucault [1975] 1995, 202–203). In this sense, the *Projekt Ideologietheorie* has used Foucault's concept of spatial dispositives for its studies on German fascism. It demonstrated that fascism's spatial and architectural arrangements, its ideological rituals and practices, had a stronger impact on people's imagination than mere systems of ideas: Orthodoxy is trumped by Orthopraxy (*PIT* [1980] 2007, 77 and 104–105). Judith Butler questioned Althusser's overly monotheistic top-down model of interpellation and argued that the interpellating "law" is not only obeyed or refused, but might also be ruptured, turned into hyperbole, submitted to parody. Such a "constitutive failure of the performative" in turn opens up the possibility that ideological interpellations can be "resignified" and turned against their violating aims (Butler 1993, 124).

Reinterpreting these and many other valuable insights and pointing out the theoretical limits of most postmodernist approaches are not mutually exclusive. Postmodernists' almost exclusive fixation on discourses and sign-systems (even when they deal with the body) prevent them from reconnecting their analyses with the macrostructures and hegemonic relations of society. Foucault's promise of an "ascending" analysis starting out from the microstructures of power and moving up to the macrostructures of class and state domination could not be kept, because he had no theoretical account of how power is being accumulated and assembled. Here, Bourdieu's emphasis on the modes of "conversion" between different kinds of power, or, in his terminology, among economic, cultural, social, and symbolic "capital," can help fill this gap. After having learned our postmodern lessons in the domains of epistemology and methodology, we need to take up the project of an ideology-critique that operates with a theory of the ideological as a "conceptual hinterland" (Haug 1993, 21). For this, we need to release the fruitful methods and findings of poststructuralist approaches from their narrow framework and re-embed them in a renewed critical social theory.

Notes

1 Panel at *Rethinking Marxism* conference, September 19–22, 2013, chaired by Serap Kayatekin, with presentations by Jan Rehmann and Richard Wolff.
2 On Bourdieu's relevance for a materialist theory of ideology, cf. Rehmann (2014, 221 ff).
3 McNally uses this term in his critique of Derrida's disembodied notion of language, which in his opinion reproduces what Marx analyzed as "fetishism," namely, the alienating rule of abstract value over use value, of abstract average labor over concrete labor (McNally 2001, 56ff, 66ff).

References

Althusser, L. [1974] 1976. *Essays in Self-Criticism*. Trans. Grahame Lock. London: New Left Books.

———— [1971] 2001. "Ideology and Ideological State Apparatuses. Notes towards an Investigation." In *Lenin and Philosophy and other Essays*, B. Brewster, trans., 85–126. New York: Monthly Review Press.

Althusser, L. and E. Balibar. [1965] 2009. *Reading Capital*. London: Verso.

Barad, K. 2007. *Meeting the Universe Halfway. Quantum Physics and the Entanglement of Matter and Meaning*. Durham, London: Duke University Press.

Bigwood, C. 1998. "Renaturalizing the Body (with the Help of Merleau-Ponty)." In *Body and Flesh. A Philosophical Reader*, D. Welton, ed. 99–114. Oxford: Blackwell Publishers.

Boltanski, L. and E. Chiapello. 2005. *The New Spirit of Capitalism*, transl. by Gregory Elliot. London, New York: Verso.

Butler, J. 1990. *Gender Trouble: Feminism and the Subversion of Identity*. New York: Routledge.

———— 1993. *Bodies that Matter*. New York: Routledge.

Foucault, M. [1969] 1972. *The Archeology of Knowledge*. Trans. A. M. Sheridan Smith. New York: Pantheon Books.

———— [1976] 1990. *The History of Sexuality. Volume I: An Introduction*. Trans. R. Hurley. New York: Vintage Books.

———— [1975] 1995. *Discipline and Punish. The Birth of the Prison*. Trans. A. Sheridan. New York: Vintage Books.

———— 2001. *Dits et écrits I, 1954–1975*. Paris: Quarto Gallimard.

Gramsci, A. 1971. *Selections from the Prison Notebooks of Antonio Gramsci*, ed. Trans. Q. Hoare and G. N. Smith. New York: International Publishers.

———— 1975. *Quaderni del carcere*, Four volumes, critical edition of the Gramsci Institute, V. Gerratana, ed. Torino: Einaudi.

Hall, S. 1993. "Encoding, Decoding." In *The Cultural Studies Reader*, S. During, ed., 507–17. London, New York: Routledge.

Harvey, D. 1990. *The Condition of Postmodernity*. Cambridge, MA and Oxford: Blackwell.

Haug, W. F. 1987. *Commodity Aesthetics, Ideology & Culture*. New York and Bagnolet: International General.

———— 1993. *Elemente einer Theorie des Ideologischen*. Hamburg: Argument-Verlag.

———— 2006. *Philosophieren mit Brecht und Gramsci*. Hamburg: Argument-Verlag.

———— 2013. *Das Kapital Lesen aber Wie? Materialien zur Philosophie und Epistemologie der marxschen Kapitalismuskritik*. Hamburg: Argument-Verlag.

Hennessy, R. 2000. *Profit and Pleasure. Sexual Identities in Late Capitalism.* New York, London: Routledge.

Jameson, F. 1991. *Postmodernism, or, The Cultural Logic of Late Capitalism.* Durham: Verso.

Lecourt, D. 1975. *Marxism and Epistemology: Bachelard, Canguilhem, and Foucault.* Trans. B. Brewster. London: New Left Books.

Lyotard, J. -F. [1979] 1984. *The Postmodern Condition: A Report on Knowledge.* Minneapolis: University of Minnesota Press.

Marx, K. [1845] 1976. "Theses on Feuerbach." In *Marx Engels Collected Works* (MECW), Vol. 5, 3–5. London: Lawrence & Wishart.

———— [1859] 1987. "A Contribution to the Critique of Political Economy." In *Marx Engels Collected Works* (MECW), Vol. 29. London: Lawrence & Wishart.

———— [1867] 1976. *Capital. A Critique of Political Economy,* Volume I. Trans. B. Fowkes. London: Penguin Books.

Marx, K. and F. Engels. [1845] 1976. *The German Ideology.* In *Marx Engels Collected Works* (MECW), Vol. 5. London: Lawrence & Wishart.

McNally, D. 2001. *Bodies of Meaning. Studies on Language, Labour, and Liberation.* New York: State University of New York Press.

Pêcheux, M. 1975. *Les vérités de la palice.* Paris: Maspero.

———— 1990. *L'inquiétude du Discours. Textes de Michel Pêcheux,* selected and presented by D. Maldidier. Paris: Éditions des Cendres.

Poulantzas, N. 1978. *State, Power, Socialism.* Trans. P. Camiller. London and New York: Verso.

Projekt Ideologietheorie (PIT). [1980] 2007. *Faschismus und Ideologie,* new edition by K. Weber. Hamburg: Argument-Verlag.

Rehmann, J. 2004. *Postmoderner Links-Nietzscheanismus. Deleuze & Foucault. Eine Dekonstruktion.* Hamburg: Argument-Verlag.

———— 2014. *Theories of Ideology. The Powers of Alienation and Subjection.* Chicago: Haymarket Books.

Resnick, S. and R. Wolff. 2006. *New Departures in Marxian Theory.* London, New York: Routledge.

———— 2013. "Marxism." *Rethinking Marxism* 25 (2): 152–62.

Wittgenstein, L. 1958. *Philosophical Investigations,* Third Edition. Trans. G. E. M. Anscombe. New York: Macmillan.

Wolff, R. D. 2004."Ideologische Staatsapparate/repressiver Staatsapparat." In *Historisch-Kritisches Wörterbuch des Marxismus* (HKWM), Vol. 6.1, W. F. Haug and P. Jehle, eds., 761–72. Hamburg: Argument-Verlag.

———— 2013. "Religion and Class." In *Religion, Theology, and Class: Fresh Engagements after Long Silence,* J. Rieger, ed., 27–42. New York: Palgrave Macmillan.

14 Overdetermination
The ethical moment

George DeMartino

Introduction

A paradox emerges in Steven Resnick and Richard Wolff's foundational text, *Knowledge and Class* (1987). I refer to the striking underdevelopment of the ethical moment in the articulation of their entry point concepts of class and overdetermination. By "ethical moment" I mean the normative basis and entailments of their commitment to these concepts. Resnick and Wolff comment briefly on the Marxian ethical imperative to embrace class as an analytical category in support of a class-transformative political project, but these remarks appear principally in their textbook, *Economics: Neoclassical vs. Marxian* (Wolff and Resnick 1987), not in *Knowledge and Class*. But the normative grounding of their commitment to overdetermination as an epistemological, ontological, and methodological premise—the subject of this essay—is neglected altogether.

And yet, and as Resnick and Wolff are acutely aware, theoretical choices such as the selection of entry point concepts are terribly consequential; hence ethically laden. It bears emphasis: in Resnick and Wolff's antiessentialist approach to economic and social theory, concepts and explanatory logics are understood to be chosen for their effects—for their theoretical and political productivity. They are not dictated by the nature of the world. Why, then, do they leave the ethical moment underspecified, particularly with regard to overdetermination?

The paradox explored

Throughout *Knowledge and Class* and in much of their other work, Resnick and Wolff treat the concept of class, the practice of class analysis, and the project of class transformation with unparalleled care. In particular, they refuse to embrace the definitions of class that appear throughout the social sciences—such as those that reduce class to relations of power, property, or status (Resnick and Wolff 1987, ch. 3). They advance an alternative conception of class, the precedent for which they find in Marx, defined in terms of the social processes by which societies organize the performance, appropriation, and distribution of surplus labor. Resnick and Wolff develop this concept in extraordinary detail—not least by elaborating upon the relatively abstract account of surplus production and appropriation that appears in volume 1 of *Capital* with insights Marx develops in volumes 2 and 3 and in other writings. This integrative theoretical work is wonderfully productive. It yields an account of class processes that is non-reductionist and more nuanced than so many other Marxian (and non-Marxian) treatments.

That said, Wolff and Resnick's treatment of the ethical dimensions of class processes—and of their commitment to the concept of class—is largely intuitive. As befits a textbook approach intended to introduce students to Marxian insights, the discussion is appealing in its simplicity. In their words, "the class division of society into exploiters versus exploited...is unjust and has an undesirable influence upon every aspect of that broader society" (Wolff and Resnick 1987, 9). Elsewhere in the same text they argue that "Marxian theory conveys its own ethical messages. One of the most significant messages concerns the class process itself. Those laborers who produce goods and service should own them and decide what to do with them..." Productive workers, those who generate surplus, "should control and distribute that surplus as their own" (1987, 125). The analysis continues as follows:

> If and when this does *not* occur in a society, Marxian theory claims that a kind of social theft takes place: some individuals "steal" the surplus labor (or its fruits) from those who have produced it. The term "social theft" seems warranted because the thieves (the receivers of surplus) *take* what others (the performers of surplus labor) have produced; they give nothing in return.
>
> Just as we become angry when personal theft strikes our families, so, too, Marxism exhorts us to become angry at this social theft of the labor of one group by another.
>
> (1987, 125, emphasis in original)

Finally, neoclassical theory, which validates "individualism and free markets," serves "to hide and perpetuate class injustice" (1987, 9).[1]

Though underdeveloped, the normative moment in Resnick and Wolff's attachment to class resonated among their students, many of whom were left-leaning activists attracted to the economics program at the University of Massachusetts because of their commitment to Marxian theory and to class emancipation. Some attempted to specify more precisely a normative indictment of exploitation. One example is a debate that appeared in the pages of *Rethinking Marxism*, involving Ted Burczak (1998, 2001), Steve Cullenberg (1992, 1998), George DeMartino (2003), and others about the nature of exploitation, which examined *inter alia* questions pertaining to why exploitation is morally indictable. A central question in the debate concerned what arrangements would have to hold in order for the appropriation of workers' labor to be just. Despite various disagreements, all of the contributors to that debate and most other Marxian scholars who probe class relations take it as given that exploitative class processes are normatively suspect.

If the normative moment in Resnick and Wolff's attention to class and exploitation is underdeveloped, the normative moment in their commitment to overdetermination is absent altogether. We find in *Knowledge and Class* an unwavering commitment to overdetermination in the authors' conceptions of ontology, epistemology, and methodology—in the nature of the world, the nature of knowing, and the social science practices Resnick and Wolff embrace. Yet Resnick and Wolff do little to motivate or justify their commitment to overdetermination. Like class, overdetermination is treated as an entry point that distinguishes the Marxian framework from others. But it remains ethically unmoored. Why is this?

It's a matter of ontology

The simplest answer would be that overdetermination is a non-negotiable, pre-theoretical ontological datum that *just is*. Following Althusser (1977), one might argue that the mature Marx discovered a new "continent" of social reality, a world structured by relations of complex contradiction and overdetermination. The embrace of overdetermination implies the rejection of a social ontology marked by causal reductionism, stable identities, independent and dependent variables, or any sort of telos in which society evolves from one pre-scripted stage to the next. In this view, overdetermination imposes itself *objectively* on the world about us. And if that just happens to be the way the world *is*—if the world bears the imprint of overdetermination all the way down—then good theory must reproduce, capture, or otherwise reflect it in social analysis. In this view, the normative moment is excised altogether.

In my own earliest engagement with Resnick and Wolff, my dissertation work (1992), I concluded that this was in fact Resnick and Wolff's own perspective. I claimed that in practice they had come to treat overdetermination as an objective ontological category and that they then sought to advance a form of social theory that was faithful to it. In so doing (I argued), they had fallen into the very same essentialist epistemological error they criticized in others—that of believing that social theory must reflect the truth of the social world it sought to map. This error, I argued, undermined Resnick and Wolff's ability to elaborate compelling social analysis since it prevented them from offering explanatory accounts of events in the world. In a world marked ontologically by overdetermination, after all, there could be no cause and effect, no relations of necessity, no stable generative structures, and so forth. All was to be recognized, essentially, as contingent: the identities and properties of all objects (and agents) were fundamentally unstable and perpetually in process of becoming. One way to capture this is to say that in the Resnick-Wolff framework, a monism of contingency had come to replace the monism of necessity that marked orthodox, structural Marxism or the necessity/contingency dualism around which much western Marxian scholarship was constituted throughout the 20th century (see DeMartino 1993).

I now think my critique was at least partially mistaken. Resnick and Wolff do not explicitly take the view that the world is marked by an over-determinist ontology that good theory must capture. Like all other concepts, overdetermination appears in this work not as a non-negotiable ontological given, as an objective statement about the way the world *is*, but instead as a terribly consequential theoretical *choice* that theorists can make as they try to create knowledge of the world. For Resnick and Wolff, all choices in social theory matter, concretely and politically. Ontological, epistemological, and methodological concepts don't just describe the objects and practices in the world; they participate in shaping that world. As Resnick and Wolff took pains to demonstrate, theories transform lived realities in vital ways. They emancipate as well as oppress; they shape the actors who populate the worlds that the theories themselves animate. Theories give and take away life; they create and take away rights, freedoms and opportunities, identities and capacities, and much else besides. Not least, theories open up and close off imagined alternatives; distinguish the normal and acceptable from the abnormal and deviant, the human from the non-human, the legitimate from the illegitimate, and the worthy from the unworthy. The meanings that theories impart are then inscribed in and reinforce social practices, identities, norms, and institutions. Theoretical critique must then be understood as political engagement that can have powerful, concrete effects.

But if, as the overdeterminationist framework itself claims, the embrace of overdetermination is a consequential *choice*—one that ramifies in all these ways (and more)—then it would seem, necessarily, to entail ethical substance. Indeed, how could there *not* be ethical considerations in the theoretically and politically charged decision to operate within a theoretical framework that features the radical contingency associated with overdetermination, when one recognizes all that is at stake in the choice?

Resnick and Wolff signal their attachment to the view that decisions regarding social theory, including its ontological and epistemological precepts, are ethically laden in this way:

> [Marx] ridiculed the idea of "dispassionate analysis," which he suspected was the disguise of analysts who preferred to excuse rather than expose social injustices. Every analyst, Marx believed, makes a particular commitment to social values and to a particular kind of future society.
>
> (Wolff and Resnick 1987, 128)

This passage occurs in Resnick and Wolff's discussion of their commitment to the analytical category of class. It perforce applies equally to the choice of ontological and explanatory logics (e.g., overdetermination/anti-essentialism vs. determinism/essentialism). Resnick and Wolff can't have it any other way without violating their own deepest theoretical commitments.

And yet, to repeat the point, reading within the lines of *Knowledge and Class*, we find little attention to the normative case for overdetermination. One of the notable features of Resnick and Wolff's foundational work is that their commitment to overdetermination emerges here as *direct* rather than *ethically mediated*. The commitment to overdetermination appears with surprising immediacy, as if no motivation or rationale (ethical or otherwise) were required. As noted above, this silence stands in contrast to the admittedly underdeveloped ethical grounding the authors offer as context for their commitment to class analysis and class emancipation.

Resnick and Wolff's asymmetric treatment of class and overdetermination reflects tendencies in the predominant traditions in social and political philosophy, on one hand, and epistemology and ontology, on the other. Much contemporary political philosophy attends to the ethical question explicitly when theorizing analytical categories (e.g., inequality or justice) and appropriate forms of political, economic, and social organization. We can think in this context of the work of John Rawls (1971), Robert Nozick (1974), Michael Walzer (1983), Martha Nussbaum (1992), Amartya Sen (1992), and various contributions to the Marxian tradition (e.g., Lukes 1987; Geras 1985, 1992; see also Marx 1977). Ethical positions are advanced, and claims about social arrangements are then inferred to some degree or other from these ethical positions. For instance, Sen (1992) and Nussbaum (1992) defend their claims for equality of capabilities on the basis of their vision of freedom as human flourishing. In contrast, literature on epistemology and ontology, and explorations in the philosophy of science more broadly, tend not to grapple as deeply or explicitly with ethical questions. In these fields, logical (and empirical) rather than ethical arguments tend to predominate.[2] One epistemology or ontology is typically advocated over another on the basis of what its advocates see as the objective argument. I think we find the same asymmetry in Resnick and Wolff. They present at least an attenuated ethical defense of their commitment to class analysis, but they do not offer a comparable ethical defense of their epistemological and ontological claims. In Resnick and Wolff we *begin* with a commitment to overdetermination—it is not derived from or linked to any ethical position. There is, in short, a side-stepping around the ethical question as concerns overdetermination—one that parallels the side-stepping that broadly appears in epistemological and ontological inquiries.

I hope I have by now demonstrated the existence of the paradox I asserted at the outset: *though the Resnick-Wolff commitment to overdetermination must be and is deeply normative, they do not probe the ethical basis of this commitment.*

If this claim is correct, then we might ask the question, on what grounds is the side-stepping around the ethical moment of the commitment to overdetermination justifiable? We have already ruled out one possible defense—that the world *just is* structured by the relation of overdetermination. If that answer is unavailable, then is there an alternative, suitable defense, within the overdeterminationist framework itself, of the ethically unmediated commitment of Resnick and Wolff to overdetermination? In what follows I explore and reject the best candidates and then argue that the ethical entailments of overdetermination are in fact among its most powerful attributes.

It's all preferences and interests

One possible resolution of the paradox is that the choice of overdetermination in epistemology and social theory is simply a matter of preference, aesthetics, or interests, about which nothing more can be said. One's preferences, aesthetic judgments, interests: these are the outcome of the radical contingency that overdetermination entails. Some of us are overdetermined in such a way that we find overdetermination appealing, and some of us are not. Nothing more can be said apart from the unfurling of each theorist's peculiar autobiography. Asking whether the presumption of overdetermination in epistemology or ontology is right or wrong would be like asking, in the destabilizing rhetoric that Wolff employed so effectively in his pedagogy, *what color is Tuesday?* It is a nonsensical question; a category error. Or worse: invoking normative grounding can be and often is a strategic ploy of the man on a mission. When we claim of a certain epistemology or ontology that it is ethically right or wrong, we are actually engaging in what Wolff so often calls a *"hustle."* We are attributing to our contingent tastes an exalted status they do not deserve so as to amplify our influence and exert power over others. Ethical claims are suspect in this account because they attempt to disguise preferences and the interests to which they are attached, to make them appear as something they are not. *So the ethical question is not just wrong-headed or nonsensical, it is dangerous.* Better, then, to disengage from ethical debate, other than to ridicule others' ethical naiveté or duplicity. How then could one possibly claim that overdetermination is in one way or another sanctified by ethics? Resistance against the power plays of others requires that we expose ethical claims for what they so often are: efforts at rhetorical misdirection, sleights of hand that seek unwarranted influence for its purveyors.[3]

My guess is that virtually all students of Resnick and Wolff have had conversations with their mentors in which Resnick or Wolff advanced one form or another of the "ethics as tastes" or "ethics as a hustle" argument. The more we students pressed our professors on the normative foundations of their theoretical commitments, in feeble attempts to rescue them from what we viewed as their radical moral relativism, the more Resnick and Wolff distanced themselves from normative assessment altogether. To the question, *"What is your moral anchor?"* would come the reply *"Why do you need a moral anchor?"*

Thinking back on these exchanges, with the benefit of twenty-five years' distance, it seems to me now that Resnick and Wolff were more concerned to disrupt their students' comfortable moral intuitions than to make a theoretically rigorous argument. The pedagogical point was not to impugn or destroy our ethical commitments; it was to wean their audiences (perhaps including their own former selves) from the habit of thinking that their commitment to the study and development of Marxian theory required an extra-discursive scientific or ethical warrant. The point was that our ethical stances, too, are best theorized as products of overdetermination—they, too, are implicated in complex contradiction. The associated point was that there is no escaping overdetermination—there is no place to stand beyond one's own overdetermined position and perspective to evaluate social processes, theories, and practices.

In this regard Resnick and Wolff were making a point rendered with greater circumspection by other scholars. Martha Nussbaum's rejection of "metaphysical realism" comes to mind. Nussbaum rejects the idea that in crafting normative propositions we have access to some immutable truth about the nature of the world or of humanity. But importantly, and unlike Resnick and Wolff, Nussbaum (1992) nonetheless defends a rational basis for generating reasoned normative judgment, one that follows Aristotle rather than Plato in generating insights about the world. So does the cultural relativist Michael Walzer, who recognizes that even the most radical social critic has to live within and draw upon the existing cultural system he inhabits, replete with the social meanings that history makes available to him. "Where else," he asks, "can he live?" (1993, 168) But for Walzer, too, the critic's contingent historical positioning does not diminish the force of his imminent social critique (cf. Nussbaum and Sen 1989). For these scholars, the fact that there is no unimpeachable foundation for ethical judgment—that "[t]here is no authoritative centre, no Jerusalem from which meanings go forth" (Walzer 1993, 170)—complicates ethical reasoning, to be sure. But it does not reduce all ethics talk to a hustle or a power play designed to assert influence by illicit means.

Dethroning ethics

The argument that ethics ought not to be reduced to metaphysical claims yields an alternative but related explanation for neglecting the ethical moment in one's theoretical commitments. The alternative recognizes that ethical judgments are indeed sensible, legitimate, and even inevitable in a framework that takes overdetermination seriously. But it claims that ethics must be de-sanctified: ethics talk must lose its privileged status as the paramount guide to individual belief and behavior and also its privileged status as the paramount criterion for assessing social institutions and practices. This is an important intervention. When one considers the ethics tradition in political philosophy, one finds a set of foundational claims about how we should live that are taken to trump other kinds of claims. When "mere" preferences conflict with "deep" ethical principles, the ethical principles are taken to govern. One person's preference to instrumentalize another, as through enslavement, comes up against not just the preference of the other not to be enslaved, but also the far weightier Kantian categorical imperative that precludes that kind of objectification regardless of the preferences of the actors (and even the willingness of an agent to be enslaved). In that controversy, it is argued, the categorical imperative must win out. It is not surprising, then, that in the long history of ethical engagement, ethical positions have tended to be associated with essentialist visions. They are predicated variously on the word of a deity, a governing ontology, a universal human nature, and so forth. The power of ethical claims to trump other kinds of claims derives from their purportedly deep origins in the substrate that sustains and even defines human existence—Nussbaum's metaphysical realism; Resnick and Wolff's "anchor." But for their essentialist footing, ethical edicts would have less authority over us.

This argument implies that within an overdeterminationist framework, and for the sake of theoretical consistency, ethical claims must be cut down to size. In the words of Resnick and Wolff:

> Marxian theory admits no final, absolute standards for truth, justification, and so forth. Such absolute concepts belong to epistemological standpoints different from and opposed to that of Marxian theory.
>
> (1987, 29)

In this account, then, ethical propositions are to be understood as one kind of contingent claim about how we should live. Once we understand that, once we reject the essentialisms that underlie ethical thought, we may come to find that there is little point in attending to ethics at all. One might say that an overdeterminist who carefully and painstakingly examines the ethical defenses of his preferred epistemology or ontology just doesn't get it. He would be like an atheist who seeks cover for his claims about the way humans should behave in the word of God. *You can do it, but what's the point?*

Nussbaum rescues us from this implication. Rejection of metaphysical realism, she argues, presents an obstacle to reasoned judgment only for those who presumed its presence. For the rest, she asks, why do they "conclude that the absence of a transcendent basis for judgment—a basis that, according to them, was never there anyway—should make us despair of doing as we have done all along, distinguishing persuasion from manipulation?" (1992, 213). She continues as follows:

> In fact, the collapse into extreme relativism or subjectivism seems to me to betray a deep attachment to metaphysical realism itself. For it is only to one who has pinned everything to that hope that its collapse will seem to entail the collapse of all evaluation—just as it is only to a deeply believing religious person, as Nietzsche saw, that the news of the death of God brings the threat of nihilism. What we see here, I think, is a reaction of *shame*—a turning away of the eyes from our poor humanity, which looks so mean and bare—by contrast to a dream of another sort. What do we have here, these critics seem to say? Only our poor old human conversation, our human bodies that interpret things so imperfectly?
>
> (Nussbaum 1992, 213)

Nussbaum provides a basis for refusing this shame. Not having presumed the need for an unimpeachable normative anchor, some sort of invariant meta-standard to guide and validate our judgments, the anti-essentialist should not be troubled in the least by its absence. For the anti-essentialist, the dismissal of metaphysical claims ought not to obstruct the search for reasoned normative judgments. Instead, recognition that there is no anchor should reorient the search for ethical precepts in an altogether healthy direction, away from Platonic "rim of the heavens" defenses of normative values that presume to know more than mere mortals can in fact know (Nussbaum and Sen 1989, 309; see also Nussbaum 1994, 18).

To sum up: we have before us three justifications for the relative neglect of the ethical moment in overdetermination in the work of Resnick and Wolff. The first claims that overdetermination is an objective ontological fact, recognition of which entails simply accounting for what is. The second sees ethics as an overdetermined matter of taste and interest and ethics talk as an illicit attempt to persuade and to exert influence over others. The third grants the legitimacy of ethics talk but dethrones ethical claims from their privileged position that derives from deep essentialisms, which render ethics largely uninteresting, distracting from the real business of Marxian scholarship, or otherwise off-point.

Though there is some evidence of all three perspectives in the work of Resnick and Wolff, they certainly do not commit to any one of them, and with good reason. None succeeds in sustaining the neglect of ethics in an overdeterminist framework. Something else is involved here. My sense is that Resnick and Wolff's avoidance of ethics reflects a concern that if they were to give the ethical moment any serious play in their epistemological or ontological accounts, any weight at all, they might then put at risk their commitment to overdetermination. Ethical arguments can spin off in all sorts of directions, after all—taking on a life of their own and leading us down paths we may not be happy to travel.[4] Had they sought to derive or defend their theoretical stances by reference to a precarious chain of ethical reasoning, they might have placed their (or their students') commitments to overdetermination in some jeopardy. I read in Resnick and Wolff an unwillingness to do that—a refusal to have their commitment to overdetermination put at risk by subjecting it to ethical engagement. The direct, unmediated attachment to overdetermination that I touched on earlier is an attempt to resolve this problem by placing this attachment out of harm's way, thus insulating it from ethical critique. To say it another way, since Resnick and Wolff in fact explicitly claim no ethical warrant for their attachment to overdetermination, they could consistently maintain the view that ethical critique of that commitment is off-point, irrelevant, and/or uninteresting.[5]

The ethical entailments of radical contingency: J.K. Gibson-Graham and the community economies collective

There are no doubt other possible explanations for Resnick and Wolff's relative neglect of the ethical question—for their largely having side-stepped the ethical moment in the direct path they chart to overdetermination. The explanations given above amount to little more than informed speculations. I want to suggest that irrespective of the reason, it is a mistake to repress the ethical moment in overdetermination, not just for the sake of theoretical consistency, since treating overdetermination as an ethically unmediated analytical category makes little sense within an overdeterminationist framework, but also because the ethical entailments of overdetermination are among its most theoretically and practically important, powerful, and exciting features. To see this, I need to pose a second question: *Just what ethical entailments are reflected in a commitment to overdetermination in ontology, epistemology, and social theory?*

One compelling answer has emerged in the work of the Community Economies Collective (CEC) and the Community Economies Research Network (CERN) and in the work that launched that project—the work of Katherine Gibson, Julie Graham, and their collaborators (Gibson-Graham 1996, 2006, 2011).[6] From their first essays in the 1990s, to their recent work with Gerda Roelvink and others on the Anthropocene, to their new book with Jenny Cameron and Stephen Healy (Gibson-Graham, Cameron, and Healy 2013), the ethical moment in Gibson-Graham has become increasingly explicit, careful, sharply put, and compelling. Elsewhere (DeMartino 2013) I explore the ethical nature of this body of theoretical work and political practice in depth. Here I can just summarize a few of the key ethical features of the CEC project.

Against ontology

Gibson-Graham demote ontology from its disciplinary role in shaping what is and what is not possible in the world. For them, the embrace of radical contingency that overdetermination entails is entirely presumptive. Indeed, no claim is made here about the way the world really is. Overdetermination is adopted without ontological defense or apology because of its extraordinary usefulness in opening up the political, economic, and social terrain for perpetual, *unscripted* social experimentation, inventiveness, and joyful discovery. For instance, the openings implied by overdetermination allow Gibson-Graham to presume, look for, and find all sorts of non-capitalist economic practices and institutions—right here, right now, in the belly of the supposed capitalist beast (the advanced, "developed" economies) as much as in the supposedly less-developed global south. The commitment to overdetermination allows for exploratory expeditions, which are not burdened by any sort of disciplinary ontological categories or forces, in search of non-capitalist forms. In this context, ontology is theorized as the produced result of discursive and material practices rather than their grounding. "What would it mean," they ask, "to view thinking and writing as productive ontological interventions?" (2008, 614) What can and can't be brought into existence, survive, grow, or be replicable or scalable—these are not dictated by a sutured social totality driven by the unified logic of capital accumulation, human nature, or any other ontological structures, but emerge instead in part from knowing practices (cf. Laclau and Mouffe 1985). As they put it:

> When ontology becomes the effect rather than the ground of knowledge, we lose the comfort and safety of a subordinate relation to 'reality' and can no longer seek to capture accurately what already exists; interdependence and creativity are thrust upon us as we become implicated in the very existence of the worlds that we research.
>
> (Gibson-Graham 2008, 620)

The choice to presume overdetermination finds expression in the CEC's commitment to a form of class (and other forms of) emancipation that entails construction rather than resistance. If capitalism is not ontologically secured, then meaningful political interventions might require, in the first instance at least, little more than mapping the diversity of economic forms all about us so as to acknowledge their viability and (perhaps) desirability as alternatives to capitalist economic practices and institutions (DeMartino 2003). *Seeing differently* in the ways that overdetermination enables us to do is therefore a radical act of decentering that need not entail confronting, resisting, or overturning capitalism. In the hands of CEC scholars, overdetermination gives rise to a political imagination that permits class and other forms of emancipation. This is overdetermination's most vital role in radical scholarship and activism—to enable the recognition, formation, and sustenance of more ethical social practices.

Overdetermination entails a multifaceted emancipation. It suggests the immediate possibilities that exist for becoming other than we are; for living differently than we do; for forming relationships other than those in which we are entwined. Overdetermination signals perpetual aperture that extends not just to the institutions and practices we construct, but also to our identities and subjectivities. And the opportunities for becoming that it signals apply not just to the subjects of the economy, but to radical researchers themselves as they seek to chronicle and otherwise contribute to projects of social transformation.

Transforming the academic researcher

Recognition of the ethical moment in the commitment to overdetermination encourages new understandings of the efficacy of radical scholars and the obligations they face as researchers and advocates of the communities they purport to serve. There is much to be said on this score. Here, I touch on just two aspects that are central to the work of Gibson-Graham and the broader CEC project.

Over the years Gibson-Graham have come to emphasize a peculiar ethical mandate for academic researchers: to banish the skeptical voice from analytical work. This is the authoritative voice that adjudicates initiatives by reference to theory that purports to be adequate—adequate in the sense of being able to distinguish viable projects of emancipation from the unviable, revolutionary projects from reformist, palliative endeavors, and productive, generative initiatives from dead-ends. They challenge themselves to reinvent themselves, moving away from arbiters of social processes—*what can this puny worker coop possibly achieve?*—to "conditions of possibility" of the diverse economy they hope to instigate and support. Contrary to received academic methods, they reject the role of detached observers who presume that they can discern the limitations of the political and economic projects unfolding around them by reference to a restrictive ontology. To do this they employ Nietzche's notion of "self-artistry" and Foucault's concept of "self-cultivation." They address these concepts to their own thinking:

> The co-implicated processes of changing ourselves/changing our thinking/ changing the world are what we identify as an ethical practice. If politics involves taking transformative decisions in an undecidable terrain ... ethics is the continual exercising of a choice to be/ act/or think in certain ways.
>
> (Gibson-Graham 2008, 618)

For CEC researchers, "hybrid research collectives" have emerged as a model for the kind of praxis that overdetermination enables—praxis, that is, that yields new identities and practices. Rather than maintain the academically sanctioned arms-length separation of knowing subjects from the objects of their deliberations, the hybrid research collectives place researchers and community members in intimate contact as they experiment together—remaking themselves while inventing new economic identities, practices, and institutions (Gibson-Graham and Roelvink 2009). The collective challenges the epistemic status of researchers as the authority on matters pertaining to its practice while recognizing and benefiting from their particular skill sets, networks, institutional affiliations, and other assets that can help to legitimate and sustain the collective's experiments in new forms of economy.

Ignorance-based praxis

A second (related) ethical entailment of overdetermination concerns the emancipatory implications of its epistemology. In the work of Gibson-Graham and the work of the CEC, unrelenting epistemic inadequacy—the inescapable ignorance that overdetermination implies—is turned against those theories that purport to know too much. With Eve Sedgwick, Gibson-Graham disparage the scholar's attachment to "strong theory" that features "an embracing reach and a reductive field of meaning" (Gibson-Graham 2008, 618; Sedgwick 2003). Strong theory discounts and marginalizes possibilities for transformation that don't measure up when assessed against the dictates of some essentialist theory or another. Strong theory appeals to academic vanity by emphasizing epistemic capacities rather than epistemic limitations. It authorizes the privilege and status of the expert and the legitimacy of her influence in public affairs and governance. Rejecting the pretensions and constraining influence of strong theory, Sedgwick and Gibson-Graham advocate "weak theory":

> The practice of weak theorizing involves refusing to extend explanation too widely or deeply, *refusing to know too much*. Weak theory could not know that social experiments are doomed to fail or destined to reinforce dominance; it could not tell us that the world economy will never be transformed by the disorganized proliferation of local projects.
>
> (Gibson-Graham 2008, 619, emphasis added)

The cited passage demonstrates how, in Gibson-Graham's hands, *the epistemic inadequacy that is associated with overdetermination is transformed from debility to capacity*. It authorizes observation without judgment. Theory that is cognizant of its limits is not willing to discount new ideas and practices on grounds that they can't succeed. A wonderfully radical and destabilizing praxis emerges here: theory that expects novel, unscripted, and peculiar initiatives—without judgment about their significance, depth, or logic and without demands that they be "self-sustaining," "scalable" or otherwise "adequate"—enables these initiatives to emerge, achieve recognition, and even flourish. This kind of ignorance-based praxis also generates capaciousness—providing lots of room for many people, institutions, and ideas. The emancipatory point is that we don't ever know already what we can't be, become, or do. An embrace of unrelenting ignorance permits the flourishing of all sorts of heretical discourses that might excite imaginations and inspire heretical practices. The empowering ignorance that overdetermination entails permits and perhaps even privileges the proliferation of small-scale initiatives, *too small to fail*, that are understood as localized experiments in living rather than the enactments of the blueprints that other kinds of theory (including orthodox Marxism) purport to offer. Finally, for present purposes, recognition of our inability, ever, to manage the world we hope to affect—also an entailment of overdetermination—weans us from what feminist theologian Sharon Welch (2000) calls "an ethic of control," where we position ourselves as social engineers, and replaces it with what Welch calls an "ethic of risk," one that foregrounds the uncertainties that always attend political practice and require of us extraordinary care as we learn how not to harm as we pursue our emancipatory projects (see also Berry 2005 and Jackson 2005).

Conclusion

There is much more to be said about all of this. For my part, the central lesson is that stripping ethical claims of their essentialist or metaphysical foundations, as Resnick and Wolff (and Nussbaum, Walzer, and many others) urge us to do, hardly implies the illegitimacy or inutility of ethical inquiry. To the contrary: the commitment to radical contingency and ignorance that overdetermination entails *does not separate us from ethical reasoning—it follows from it.* To choose overdetermination is to stake out an ethical position in defense of perpetual aperture, creativity, innovation, productive ignorance, and audaciousness and risk taking that is combined with abiding care and humility. Overdetermination is a deeply consequential choice, an inescapably ethical act. We employ it most effectively when we make the ethical connection explicit, open it up to critique, refine it, and see what we learn. Yes, there are risks here. But if the work of the CEC is any indication, those risks are well worth taking.

Acknowledgments

I am indebted to Stephen Resnick, Richard Wolff, and many other scholars in the Association for Economic and Social Analysis (AESA) for innumerable discussions over the years of the concept of overdetermination and in particular of its ontological, epistemological, and ethical status. Special thanks are due to Rob Garnett, who read and offered suggestions on several drafts of this paper and who over the years has helped me clarify my own thinking on the issues examined here.

Notes

1 In a more theoretical text they argue that "communist instead of exploitative class structures comprise a worthy goal in themselves. This is a moral, ethical, and even aesthetic judgment" (Resnick and Wolff 2002, 12). Even here, however, Resnick and Wolff do not continue the thread of the argument to tease out just what moral, ethical, and aesthetic standards inspire and support this judgment.

2 I mean only to convey an asymmetry in the center of gravity in these various domains, without denying the many important exceptions to the rule. Notable exceptions include the epistemological critiques offered by pragmatists, such as Rorty (1979), and feminist contributions to philosophy of science, which illuminate the gendered theoretical commitments that infuse the nominally objective perspectives that inform the predominant positions (Harding 1986; Hartsock 1998). See also Elgin (1989) and Goodman (1989), both of whom emphasize the normative choices that epistemological stances entail.

3 Haskell (1996) attributes a similar but more cynical stance to Stanley Fish, who identifies freedom of speech as "a political prize" rather than "an independent value"—but one that masquerades behind an apparently apolitical principle of inalienable right. In Haskell's view, Fish's treatment is "Machiavellian": his advice

> transforms free speech from a matter of obligation that may constrain us to act against our own wishes into a rhetorical ruse that liberates us to take advantage of suckers, including all who believe in such ephemeral things as independent value.
>
> (78)

See also Fish (1994, ch. 8). I thank Rob Garnett for directing me to Haskell's work.

4 As one example, Nozick's "side-constraint" approach to rights leads him to endorse voluntary slavery—a conclusion he would not likely have taken to be the most attractive feature of his libertarianism (1974, 331).

5 Why then are Resnick and Wolff willing to supply a normative defense for their attachment to the concept of class? Two reasons seem plausible. First, Marx himself and the broader Marxian tradition had already supplied the basis for an ethical critique of class oppression (for a recent contribution to the literature see Martin 2008). Second, the idea of exploitation as social theft is readily available and intuitively accessible. Drawing on it is rhetorically useful for animating the Marxian approach to political economy. The same cannot be said of the concept of overdetermination, which, upon first approach, is intuitively convoluted and even opaque.

6 For the work of CEC and CERN scholars see: www.communityeconomies.org/Home

References

Althusser, L. 1977. *For Marx.* Trans. B. Brewster. London: New Left Books.

Berry, W. 2005. *The Way of Ignorance.* Berkeley, CA: Counterpoint Books.

Burczak, T. 1998. "Appropriation, Responsibility, and Agreement." *Rethinking Marxism* 10 (2): 96–105.

———— 2001. "Ellerman's Labor Theory of Property and the Injustice of Capitalist Exploitation." *Review of Social Economy* 59 (2): 161–83.

Cullenberg, S. 1992. "Socialism's Burden: Toward a 'Thin' Definition of Socialism." *Rethinking Marxism* 5 (2): 64–83.

—— 1998. "Exploitation, Appropriation, and Exclusion." *Rethinking Marxism* 10 (2): 66–75.

DeMartino, G. F. 1992. "Modern Macroeconomic Theories of Cycles and Crisis: A Methodological Critique." PhD dissertation, Department of Economics, University of Massachusetts, Amherst.

—— 1993. "The Necessity/Contingency Dualism in Marxian Crisis Theory: The Case of Long Wave Theory." *Review of Radical Political Economics* 25 (3): 68–74.

—— 2003. "Realizing Class Justice." *Rethinking Marxism* 15 (1): 1–31.

—— 2013. "Ethical Engagement in a World beyond Control." *Rethinking Marxism* 25 (4): 483–500.

Elgin, C. Z. 1989. "The Relativity of Fact and the Objectivity of Value." In *Relativism: Interpretation and Confrontation*, M. Krausz, ed., 86–98. Notre Dame, IN: University of Notre Dame Press.

Fish. S. 1994. *There's No Such Thing as Free Speech and It's a Good Thing, Too*. New York City: Oxford University Press.

Geras, N. 1985. "The Controversy about Marx and Justice." *New Left Review* 150 (March/April): 47–85.

—— 1992. "Bringing Marx to Justice: An Addendum and Rejoinder." *New Left Review* 195 (September/October): 37–69.

Gibson-Graham, J. K. 1996. *The End of Capitalism (as we knew it): A Feminist Critique of Political Economy*. Cambridge, MA: Blackwell.

—— 2006. *A Postcapitalist Politics*. Minneapolis, MN: University of Minnesota Press.

—— 2008. "Diverse Economies: Performative Practices for 'Other Worlds.' " *Progress in Human Geography* 32 (5): 613–32.

—— 2011. "A Feminist Project of Belonging for the Anthropocene." *Gender, Place and Culture* 18 (1): 1–21.

Gibson-Graham, J. K., and G. Roelvink. 2009. "An Economic Ethics for the Anthropocene." *Antipode* 41 (S1): 320–46.

Gibson-Graham, J.K., J. Cameron and S. Healy. 2013. *Take Back the Economy: An Ethical Guide for Transforming Our Communities*. Minneapolis, MN: University of Minnesota Press.

Goodman, N. 1989. "Just the Facts, Ma'am!" In *Relativism: Interpretation and Confrontation*, M. Krausz, ed., 80–85. Notre Dame, IN: University of Notre Dame Press.

Harding, S. 1986. *The Science Question in Feminism*. Ithaca, NY: Cornell University Press.

Hartsock, N. 1998. *The Feminist Standpoint Revisited and Other Essays*. Boulder, CO: Westview Press.

Haskell, T. L. 1996. "Justifying the Rights of Academic Freedom in the Era of 'Power/Knowledge.' " In *The Future of Academic Freedom*, L. Menand, ed., 43–90. Chicago, IL: University of Chicago Press.

Jackson, W. 2005. "Toward an Ignorance-based Worldview." *The Land Report* 81 (Spring): 14–16.

Laclau, E., and C. Mouffe. 1985. *Hegemony and Socialist Strategy*. London: Verso.

Lukes, S. 1987. *Marxism and Morality*. Oxford: Oxford University Press.

Martin, B. 2008. *Ethical Marxism: The Categorical Imperative of Liberation*. Peru, IL: Open Court Publishing.

Marx, K. 1977. *Capital, Volume 1*. New York: Vintage Books.

Nozick, R. 1974. *Anarchy, State, and Utopia*, New York: Basic Books.

Nussbaum, M. 1992. "Human Functioning and Social Justice: In Defense of Aristotelian Essentialism" *Political Theory* 20 (2): 202–46.

———— 1994. *The Therapy of Desire*. Princeton, NJ: Princeton University Press.

Nussbaum, M. and A. Sen. 1989. "Internal Criticism and Indian Rationalist Traditions." In *Relativism: Interpretation and Confrontation*, M. Krausz, ed., 299–325. Notre Dame, IN: University of Notre Dame Press.

Rawls, J. 1971. *A Theory of Justice*. Cambridge, MA: Harvard University Press.

Resnick, S. A. and R. D. Wolff. 1987. *Knowledge and Class*. Chicago, IL: University of Chicago Press.

———— 2002. *Class Theory and History: Capitalism and Communism in the U.S.S.R.* New York: Routledge.

Rorty, R. 1979. *Philosophy and the Mirror of Nature*. Princeton, NJ: Princeton University Press.

Sedgwick, E. 2003: *Touching Feeling: Affect, Pedagogy, Performativity*. Durham, NC: Duke University Press.

Sen, A. 1992. *Inequality Reexamined*. Cambridge, MA: Harvard University Press.

Walzer, M. 1983. *Spheres of Justice*. New York: Basic Books.

———— 1993. "Objectivity and Social Meaning." In *The Quality of Life*, M. Nussbaum and A. Sen, eds., 165–77. Oxford: Clarendon Press.

Welch, S. D. 2000. *A Feminist Theory of Risk*. Minneapolis, MN: Fortress Press.

Wolff, R. and S. Resnick. 1987. *Economics: Marxian Versus Neoclassical*. Baltimore, MD: Johns Hopkins University Press.

15 The cost of anti-essentialism

Paul Smith

Rewind

I always have to remind myself that my view of the work of Steve Resnick and Rick Wolff will probably never quite transcend a certain disciplinary distance. I am no economist, and despite the many intellectual points of reference I might share with them, that is a major issue. By the same token, it's clear to me that one part of their influence over the last 20 or 30 years is in the very fact that they have persuaded scholars like me—in the humanities and qualitative social sciences, let's say—that we need to get more real about the economic side of the political economy we profess! This was true, for me at least, way back in the early 1990s when I first came across their work. *Knowledge and Class* (Resnick and Wolff 1987) had appeared several years before, and the AESA and *Rethinking Marxism* were gathering steam. Resnick and Wolff were widely seen as leading thinkers in an epic transdisciplinary shift that was taking place in the humanities and social sciences, and in Marxism itself, broadly under the aegis and influence of the so-called continental theory that was finding its way into every corner of American intellectual life, even the retrograde discipline of economics. In that maelstrom Resnick and Wolff provided a unique and valuable perspective since they were both part of the new wave and were also economists.

I hope I can be indulged a moment to rewind and talk about a little bit of the history of that time that isn't recorded anywhere else. For most of the 1990s I was President of the Marxist Literary Group (MLG) that had been founded by Fredric Jameson in the 1970s and held (and still does hold) an annual "summer camp" event, the Institute on Culture and Society. At some point in the early '90s I invited Wolff and his colleagues to come to Carnegie Mellon, Pittsburgh, where we held the Institute, to join us in the development of new interdisciplinary thinking about Marxism. They were gracious enough to do so on several occasions. I can no longer recall everyone who came or everything that happened over the course of several summers. But I do recall with great pleasure that Wolff himself came, as did other friends such as Jack Amariglio, Steve Cullenberg, Antonio Callari, Julie Graham, and Katherine Gibson.

For Marxists in the MLG, many of whom were employed in humanities departments but working mostly in isolation, this was a moment when we were trying hard to reconcile our Marxism with many of the new trends in theory in the humanities and social sciences, including the beginnings of cultural studies in America and under pressure to integrate questions and perspectives of gender, race, ethnicity, and other axes of difference. We also were trying to keep up with developments in Marxism itself (Althusser in particular was still in need of some digestion) even as we began to encounter the challenge of post-Marxism, represented most obviously in the work of Ernesto Laclau and Chantal Mouffe (1985), who also accepted my invitation to the Institute on several occasions and who generated perhaps even more unease and controversy than the AESA people. I think it's fair to summarize by saying that the MLG contingent had quite a few members who thought that Resnick and Wolff's new anti-essentialism, associated with post-Marxism and accompanied by lots of other theory and the rise of identity politics, was really just one more wrinkle in the chronic production of bourgeois theory and that it was destined to inflict further damage on Marxist theory and politics.

Given the differing positions, some lively interchanges were to be expected. I can no longer recall the details of those many discussions and debates, though I do know that they were not always calm and sedate, and sometimes not even very friendly! Several huge shouting matches between the sadly departed Mike Sprinker and the long-suffering Antonio Callari over the role of value in Marx's discourse became legendary. And I do remember with amusement when a kind of hushed bemusement settled over pretty much the whole MLG audience when it was invited by Julie Graham to consider to what extent the United States really is a capitalist society. On a less contentious level, I recall a lengthy exposition by Wolff himself on the concept of overdetermination that was universally agreed to be masterful. I personally learned a lot from my short but difficult conversation with Wolff about Mao (whose relation to Resnick and Wolff's thought is, I suspect, more crucial than it might at first appear).

It would be wrong to suggest that somehow in the last quarter century all the dividing lines that appeared in those meetings in Pittsburgh have disappeared and still more wrong to say that the theoretical or political problems that were raised in those discussions have all been solved. What can be said, however, is that this was a time of extraordinary intellectual energy for Marxist thinking in the United States and that Wolff and his colleagues had a lot to do with it because of their willingness to challenge the stodginess and obstinacy of what we eventually agreed to call "orthodox" Marxism (Kellner 1995). In many ways, their work allowed what might best be described as a loosening up of Marxist theoretical discourse, allowing entrance to some of the fundamental contributions of continental theory in its structuralist and post-structuralist forms, while remaining firmly committed to the struggle for "a society freed of self-perpetuating inequalities of power, wealth, and social standing which constrict and distort the potentialities of human life" (Resnick and Wolff 1987, 279). (I shall return to this formulation of a left project at the end of this essay.) In other words, the possibility was still open that the theoretical turn could be put to the service of social change and even revolution.

Apart from the present essay, I think that the only recorded mark of the several encounters between the MLG/ICS and Wolff and his colleagues is a 1994 interview I conducted with Wolff, which was published in the MLG journal, *Mediations* (Smith 1994).[1] In retrospect it can be admitted that there was more than a little skepticism behind some of my questions. Like others in my group at that time, I was not sure how Resnick and Wolff's particular spin on Marx's distinction between productive and unproductive labor was earned and worried that the notion of subsumed class processes would put a barrier between the processes of capitalist exploitation and all other social formations. It was not easy then, nor is it now, for a lot of Marxists to accept definitions of class processes that seem to unmoor them so completely from the specific process of capitalist exploitation itself. It was to that nexus of problems that I referred when I asked Wolff about the theoretical and political cost of promoting "a view of class processes not only in non-essentialist ways but also in non-determinist ways" (1994, 8). As a kind of extension of that question, I asked him about the tendency in their work to separate the formation of class power from that of state power (1994, 10–11). The bottom line here, and still a question of some concern, is an anxiety that Resnick and Wolff tend to divide off the economic from the political in a familiar move of bourgeois thought, and it should be admitted that a lot of the anxiety had been generated by encounters (mine and others') with the work of Laclau and Mouffe (1985), which is marked by many similar conceptual moves.

Wolff answers me very patiently in that interview and without betraying too much surprise at my ignorance! He reiterates his trenchant anti-essentialist positions in regard to the question about class processes, refusing to allow that "class processes [can be] the ultimate cause, goal, determinant, telos, etc. of all the non-class processes" (1994, 8). And with the question about the separation of politics and economics, he makes the interesting (but I think ultimately unconvincing distinction): "We separate precisely in order to understand how these two sets of aspects (processes) of social life participate in overdetermining one other. That is, no wall divides the realms" (11). Finally, perhaps his most telling and therefore useful (and I would venture, correct) answer to my questions at the time comes in his remarks about Laclau and Mouffe's work. While allowing a "complex relationship" between the two bodies of work, and while sharing a version of commitment to overdetermination as a principle, Wolff criticizes Laclau and Mouffe for, as it were, going too far: "Where traditional Marxism celebrated the essential and socially determined role of economics . . . they go to the other end and celebrate the virtual evaporation of economics from critical social analysis" (13).

Play

Wolff's answers to my interview questions back in 1994 rely utterly on and indeed repeat the theoretical arguments mapped out by him and Resnick in *Knowledge and Class* and elsewhere. That book had an interesting reception at the time, both within political economy and in broader interdisciplinary contexts and amongst Marxists. I asked a research assistant to gather together a few contemporaneous reviews, and she came up with a good selection that, although I'm sure I didn't read any of them at the time, did seem and sound familiar, exemplary even.[2] Many of them say similar things, to the extent that the responses can be rather easily categorized. One category of critiques comes from the positivist left who have already given up on the concept of surplus value and its extraction, and so would always already have no time for *Knowledge and Class* since Resnick and Wolff's argument about the totality depends upon that fundamental class process.

Another category is more philosophical, or rather gives more priority to the epistemological arguments of *Knowledge and Class*. Resnick and Wolff come in for a lot of criticism on the grounds that the logic of their work leads to a hopeless relativism and to non-explanatory theory. These are the kinds of criticisms that Resnick and Wolff foresee (and maybe even embrace) when they summarize some of the charges that follow "from our use of overdetermination. These include nihilism, in which no meaning or purpose attaches to life; radical relativism, in which statements are merely different from one another; 'everythingism,' in which no one can say anything definite about something without saying something about everything, which is an impossible task; and so on" (2013, 348).

As Resnick and Wolff suggest, many such criticisms are direct responses to the logic of overdetermination and, concomitantly, their reading of Althusser. I want to say right here that there's no doubt in my mind that Marxism can no longer operate without the concept of overdetermination and that it is unavoidably part of Resnick and Wolff's legacy that they have made that the case. At the same time, frankly, there is something a little too blithe about Resnick and Wolff's attitude to such criticism. After all, the manner in which they insist that the principle of overdetermination *necessarily* and *inevitably* demands such an uncompromisingly anti-essentialist theoretical position as theirs is itself, logically, a kind of essentialism! The more they posit the utterly indeterminate character of the overdetermined totality, the more their famous "starting point" (Resnick and Wolff 1987, 25) of class processes as a way of grasping that totality will always appear logically arbitrary, always a tendentious choice rather than an epistemological necessity. Some of their reviewers and critics have, of course, pointed this out before. As Jon Gubbay says:

> [C]hoosing class as the entry point smuggles an essence back into the theory... Arguably, class might have been chosen as the entry point for theorizing on the basis that it is a crucial causal factor in tensions and developments of capitalist society – but their anti-essentialist stance rules this out, even as a tentative hypothesis.
>
> (Gubbay 1989, 145)

Resnick and Wolff's absolute commitment to the logic of overdetermination and a non-essentialist theory can't but remind us of a similar commitment to groundlessness in Laclau and Mouffe's post-Marxist work. I noted earlier Wolff's distancing of his and Resnick's position from Laclau and Mouffe on the grounds that the latter elide economics altogether; I tend also to agree with some of the distinctions pointed out by Diskin and Sandler (1993), who claim that the path opened by the concept of overdetermination goes potentially in many different directions (as the concept itself might always already predict!). They characterize Laclau and Mouffe's path as purely political, one that in its effort to understand social articulation stubbornly turns politics into the only game in town. Diskin and Sandler make what seems to me a compelling case for a path that would from the outset "[t]ake seriously the constitutive power of exploitation" (1993, 186).

So even if there are major differences, especially in the final commitments of the work, it is hard not to notice what Resnick and Wolff share with Laclau and Mouffe. That is, each of these pairs of authors is anything but hesitant in carving out a spectacularly extremist position in regard to the perceived essentialism of the Marxist tradition. Indeed, both explicitly find fault with Althusser for not going far enough with anti-essentialist logic. Laclau and Mouffe, for example, bemoan Althusser's stepping back from "[his] original formulation" of overdetermination, which had promised "a break with orthodox essentialism not through logical disaggregation of its categories ... but through the critique of every type of fixity, through an affirmation of the incomplete, open and political character of every identity" (1985, 104). They complain that his stepping back from the logic of this concept is a result of his ultimately wanting to have his cake and eat it too, wanting the logic of overdetermination to be in the end determined by the famous "last instance."

This is not so different from the view of Resnick and Wolff. In their 2013 response to a *Rethinking Marxism* article by Hyun Woong Park (2013), which had attempted to save Althusser from the "having his cake and eating it too" critique, Resnick and Wolff accuse Althusser of precisely *not* having "escaped the tension in his work between, on the one hand, affirming an economic determinist anchor and the certainty that follows from its use and, on the other hand, rejecting that same anchor and certainty" (Resnick and Wolff 2013, 347). In the same response, Resnick and Wolff again fully embrace what they call the "mess" of a social world produced by overdetermination and co-determination and charge critics such as Park with foolishly seeking "anchors" (Park's word) in response to the dangers of chaos. Such critics are simply not courageous enough; they cannot "take that last step of letting go of determinism." Even Althusser is not brave enough.[3]

There is often something that sounds, as I've said before, a little blithe in Resnick and Wolff's rejection of the kinds of criticism they receive. And, frankly, their exhortation to the rest of us to just have the guts to give up on the quest for certainty and come join them in the "mess" conceived by anti-essentialism often comes across as a kind of macho intellectual challenge. And as with Laclau and Mouffe, the absolutism of the claim can sometimes seem to lead to mere scholasticism. But rather than respond to it on that level, and without trying to trip up Resnick and Wolff on their own logic, I want to pose the issue a little differently and ask: What is or has been the *cost* to Marxist theory of this intransigent anti-essentialism, this embrace of non-stop overdetermination? The answers I adumbrate here are at best provisional, but I do want to claim that the purism of Resnick and Wolff's anti-essentialism is hardly *necessary,* and when it is carried through with all their determination (excuse the pun) it can in fact be very costly to Marxism. In particular, I want to focus on the elision (underutilization might be a better term) of two classic Marxian concepts—agency and history—and their relationship.

Agency

"There is no entity, no group of persons, that can be properly designated as a class," Resnick and Wolff assert, and to think any other way would be to adopt "an essentialist mode of analysis" (Resnick and Wolff 1987, 161). In this short essay, I can't examine closely the whole tapestry of reasoning Resnick and Wolff use to back up these bald assertions, though I do believe that an important part of Resnick and Wolff's legacy and the challenge it offers resides within the lines of that reasoning. Their opening gambit of rethinking Marx's distinction between productive and unproductive labor is an important theoretical move that makes possible their own related distinction between fundamental and subsumed class processes (1987, 124 ff.). Here already the anti-essentialist principle has made any definitions of class or collectivity very "messy." Furthermore, even within the overdetermined and co-determined mess of class processes, they see individual subjects who can be in multiple class positions *and* in multiple non-class positions all at once, bound up in a plethora of overdetermined and co-determined social relationships, including those of other class positions, and inevitably demonstrating contradictory motives and actions. From these theoretical propositions they advance what I take to be one of their most important positions:

> [T]he interests or struggles of persons are determined, or rather overdetermined, by all the processes of social life, not merely by the class processes they immediately participate in. The concepts of class struggles and class interests must refer, in a non-essentialist Marxian theory, to the objects of those struggles and interests.
>
> (1987, 163)

Again, without going too deeply into these assertions or the reasoning beneath them, it seems to me clear that what is rendered extremely problematical in this account is any sense of individual or collective agency. I should emphasize that the problem here is *not* that Resnick and Wolff eradicate the proletariat as the privileged historical agent of change. (We Marxists all know enough by now to be thinking that a little differently!). Equally, the problem is not that I would want to argue for the need for prediction in regard to social activism (as Silverman [2013] does). Rather, it is more that Resnick and Wolff's logic cannot lead to anything but the most random or voluntaristic kind of action on the part of human subjects.

As Gubbay remarked, when pointing similarly to Resnick and Wolff's concept of class processes, *Knowledge and Class* "greatly impoverishes the possibilities of agitational discourse" (1989, 145). One critic suggested that the political implications of *Knowledge and Class* can be only some kind of a "defanged . . . self-mutilated Marxism" (Dugger 1988, 689). I would put it less extremely but still suggest that the book's argument, or its logic, runs the risk of eliding any and all mechanisms for collective agency. When all class processes are so endlessly overdetermined, there can be neither empirical nor theoretical basis for class antagonism or struggle—only topical, opportunistic, random, or voluntarist processes.[4]

History

Agency is of course a crucial political term for Marxism, and it is generally theorized in that tradition in relation to historical process. History and agency produce each other—that is what it means that we are humans living in a polis. I think it might not necessarily replicate some *prima facie* essentialist aspect of Marxism if I were to suggest that one of the strengths of the Marxist tradition has been the way it is has tried to understand long-term changes in the mode of production and between modes of production. Marxism posits that such changes expose a historical logic—and it has been Marxism's job to grasp and explain that logic—as capitalism emerges and develops across time. This is one of the principal methodological drivers of Marxism, from which political concepts such as agency derive. However, once we conceive of the social totality as an overdetermined/co-determined "mess," the question of historicity is immediately muddied.

The sections of *Knowledge and Class* that take up particular institutional forms within the overdetermined totality as case studies deal, as we know, with entrepreneurial and state institutions. But even with the best will in the world, it becomes hard to see these analyses as anything but ahistorical and ultimately theoreticist. The details of the institutional processes have no historical detail or actual material reference at all. Even a short section devoted to a "concrete example" is entirely suppositional (Resnick and Wolff 1987, 213). Resnick and Wolff insulate all their cases from any historical context and gather them into some strange synchronic image. Such a synchronic image serves to elide historical change and also pretends that whatever explanatory power it has can be abstracted and generalized across different times and places. What is missing, then, is historicity. A synchronic snapshot of all the overdetermination in the world is no doubt going to look like Brownian motion—a mess. But a Marxist sense of historicity cannot be satisfied by a synchronic analysis and will always want to ask how this moment's mess differs from the previous moment's mess and try to learn from such questioning something about the logic of historical movement.

One of Resnick and Wolff's major influences, Louis Althusser, was especially sensitive to questions of time, history, and historicity. His *Reading Capital* contains several chapters whose central concern is to establish a specifically Marxist (and definitely non-Hegelian) notion of history, while at the same time defending Marxism from the charge of historicism (Althusser and Balibar 1970). Obviously, to Althusser's way of thinking most theories of history are empiricist and thus ideological, and he is particularly scathing about any appeal to history that assumes "a model of a continuous and homogeneous time" or assumes that contemporaneity can be grasped (1997, 110 and 115). I mention this here because it seems to me important to see that Althusser's moment of theorizing historicity is in fact the very moment at which he steps back from the commitment to absolute overdetermination that Resnick and Wolff would want him to make. In other words, the historical nature of any conjuncture allows us to see it as something other than arbitrary relativism. And here, of course, the spirit of Althusser's thinking is informed by and in tune with Marx's own insistence on the *narrative* of capitalism, a dialectical narrative in which the very structures and mechanisms of capitalism demand that it keep on going, keep on repeating its processes, such that it expands from being a predominant social process to becoming the dominant one.

What I am getting at here is perhaps akin to an operation Fredric Jameson recently conducted in his book, *Representing Capital*, where he draws out the historicity in Marx's thinking by pointing to

> the identity and difference between the stages of capitalism, each one remaining true to the latter's essence and structure (the profit motive, accumulation, expansion, exploitation of wage labor), at the same time that it marks a mutation in culture and everyday life in human relationships.
>
> (2011, 9)

Jameson would no doubt be summarily dismissed by Resnick and Wolff at the mere sight of that word "essence," just as they abandon Althusser at the point of his infamous "determination in the last instance." But as he explores the logic of *Capital*, Volume 1, Jameson makes clear that what is fundamentally at stake is the nature of the Marxist dialectic itself. It is in this movement of identity and difference that the generative power of dialectical thinking resides, leading him to conclude that

> The dialectic is then a mode of thinking able to combine the singular and the general in a unique way, or better still, to shift gears from the one to the other and back again, to *identify* them in such a way that they remain different.
>
> (Jameson 2011, 134)

The point, then, is that having the anti-essentialist guts to conceive of the social only as an overdetermined chaos may come at a substantial, cost inasmuch as Marxist notions of agency, history, and even the dialectic itself are elided.

Fast forward

So I want now to fast forward to the present, or to the very recent past, to our own supposedly "post-recessionary" moment, where we find that, although *Knowledge and Class* was published almost 30 years ago, Resnick and Wolff are still to be heard rehearsing the theory that first hatched in that book. I already quoted above from their response to a symposium on their understanding of overdetermination. This piece must be one of the last things that Stephen Resnick wrote before his death in early 2013, and yet it retains all the energy and clarity of *Knowledge and Class*. In fact, what is most remarkable about this 2013 iteration is that it might even constitute a kind of doubling down on the earlier arguments since it embraces with even more enthusiastic confidence this notion of the chaos of the social:

> That being exists in contradiction – pushed here and there – is equivalent to arguing that its motion is indeterminate. That is what we mean and always meant by a process pushed in different directions by its contradictory nature. Sometimes we try to capture this indeterminacy by using the descriptive word 'mess'.
>
> (Resnick and Wolff 2013, 342–43)

Not too far removed from that 2013 symposium, Rick Wolff was making the lecture rounds, addressing the 2008 crisis by way of a talk that later became a widely circulated video (2009) and eventually a book, *Capitalism Hits the Fan* (2010). He also published a couple of other books that were similarly directed to a non-specialist reader, *Democracy at Work: A Cure for Capitalism* (2012) and *Occupy the Economy: Challenging Capitalism* (2012). Around this time, I was teaching a small graduate seminar in the Cultural Studies Ph.D. program at George Mason University—a wide-ranging but theoretically intensive class looking at various political-economic responses to the recent crisis and its attendant shifts in the global economy.

One of our texts in the seminar was the video of *Capitalism Hits the Fan*. The students in the class knew their Marx, had read a lot of Althusser, and had probably read a few things in *Rethinking Marxism* even if they didn't know Wolff's (or Resnick's) work in itself. I can't pretend that they much liked what Wolff says in the video, and in some ways they were quite taken aback by it. They spontaneously launched a critique of the kind of history that Wolff tells about the long-term origins of today's financial capitalism. Wolff's is a very conventional linear and crudely periodized narrative, driven largely by the use of a single concept (the long-term rise of wages between 1820 and 1970). He then turns his attention to the 1970s, a period also explained by way of wages, only this time by way of their stagnation. Finally, he deals with the financial bubble and the crisis itself.

Apart from the very underdetermined nature of the narrative that Wolff offers, the students were struck by the way he deals with "the working class." First of all, he uses the term as if there were no problem locating its referent. Second, he appears at many points in the narrative to be blaming the working class for the predicament that in fact capitalism makes for them. At one point the working class is depicted as reactionary and greedy spendthrifts, at another as all too eager to go along with financial capital's lending binges. In general, Wolff talks about the working class as if the problems facing it were of its own making and even avoidable, rather than being determined by the labor regime that sets the value of and the conditions for labor as a commodity at any given moment. These features of the video are somewhat troubling, but perhaps not as much as Wolff's effort to outline a plan for getting the U.S. economy beyond the crisis. It turns out that the model he has in mind is the Silicon Valley start-up, which he lauds for its workplace democracy and its entrepreneurial labor. The future, as he puts it, is a bunch of Republicans in Bermuda shorts in California.[5]

To me, and I think to many on the Left, very little is appealing in that model. Be that as it may, the most remarkable aspect of this video to me is that it appears to be completely unrelated to the theoretical work that I was discussing before. Or at least, none of that work appears in the video. Now, nobody—probably least of all Wolff himself—would claim that public manifestos of this sort are somehow obliged to be theoretically purist or even theoretically tuned in. Yet I think it's legitimate to wonder about the relationship between this kind of analysis and Wolff's urgent and trenchant convictions around overdetermination and anti-essentialism. I am not at all sure I want to answer the question, because it would seem on the face of it that either (a) there is no real connection, rendering the theoretical work moot or (b) this anodyne and problematical political agenda is where the theoretical work has led.

Pause

I don't know whether Steve Resnick would have endorsed his friend's recent political tracts. But in any case, I think the kind of politics that Resnick and Wolff's work at its best can foster and promote is better expressed in their phrase I quoted earlier, that they are looking to usher in "a society freed of self-perpetuating inequalities of power, wealth, and social standing which constrict and distort the potentialities of human life" (Resnick and Wolff 1987, 279). There is no choice but to have solidarity with those goals, obviously. But there are different ways of getting there and different theories and knowledges that underpin those various ways. So, as I think about the long legacy of *Knowledge and Class* and the theoretical work it has challenged, provoked, and produced, I keep coming back to a problem that can perhaps be isolated in one word from Resnick and Wolff's statement: self-perpetuating. Resnick and Wolff's absolutist anti-essentialism and their view of the social as a totally unanchored play of determinations can leave us with a sense of a world that simply exists and reproduces itself, a world of uncontrollable Brownian motion that defies individual or collective human understanding and intervention.

Of course, the criticisms I've been rehearsing of Resnick and Wolff (and of Wolff alone in the last part of this essay) are meant to be friendly. So I want to finish, in a spirit of solidarity rather than critique, by quoting something Wolff wrote about Althusser, but I'll replace the name Althusser by the names Resnick and Wolff:

> Precisely because of the social goals, theoretical achievements, and political importance of [Resnick and Wolff]'s work, they need to be critically engaged, extended and transformed as a central task of the renewal of Marxism. Like all before [them], [Resnick and Wolff] leave ambiguous legacies, incomplete arguments, and all sorts of

contradictions – all raw materials indispensible to the next period of Marxist theoretical and political activity, now more than ever.

(Wolff 1998, 92)

Yes indeed, and still "now more than ever," as we are propelled fast forward by a capitalism whose chronic crises just keep coming thick and fast, and where more and more people around the globe appear to be willing to hear what Marxism might have to say to them.

Notes

1 For the record, and for the sake of convenience, I've posted a rudimentary scanned copy of that interview on my website: http://mason.gmu.edu/~psmith5/WolffInterview.pdf.
2 My thanks to Esma Celebioglu for this labor.
3 "We likewise fault Althusser for hesitating at that last step" (Resnick and Wolff 2013, 347).
4 My frequent references to Laclau and Mouffe are a product of the fact that in the 1980s and early 1990s their work threw up many of the same questions as that of Resnick and Wolff, specifically because of their anti-essentialist agenda and the kind of political agenda that it might predicate. I have criticized Laclau and Mouffe's politics on the basis of their reticence on the question of agency. My argument is that what I call their "secret agent" cannot give rise to a politics that would challenge the power and the scale of the state in contemporary society (Smith 1991).
5 If only Wolff had read Richard Barbrook's and Andy Cameron's famous essay, "The California Ideology": www.comune.torino.it/gioart/big/bigguest/riflessioni/californian_engl.pdf.

References

Althusser, L. and É. Balibar. 1970. *Reading Capital*. Trans. B. Brewster. London: New Left Books.

Diskin, J. and B. Sandler. 1993. "Essentialism and the Economy in the Post-Marxist Imaginary: Reopening the Sutures." *Rethinking Marxism* 6 (3): 28–48.

Dugger, W. 1988. "Review of *Knowledge and Class*." *History of Political Economy* 20 (4): 688–90.

Gubbay, J. 1989. "Dialectics and Class Analysis." *Contemporary Sociology* 18 (1): 144–7.

Jameson, F. 2011. *Representing* Capital: *A Reading of Volume One*. London: Verso.

Kellner, D. 1995. "The End of Orthodox Marxism." In *Marxism in the Postmodern Age*, Callari et al., eds., 33–41. New York: Guilford Press.

Laclau, E. and C. Mouffe. 1985. *Hegemony and Socialist Strategy*. London: Verso.

Park, H. W. 2013. "Overdetermination: Althusser versus Resnick and Wolff." *Rethinking Marxism* 25 (3): 325–40.

Resnick, S. and R. Wolff. 1987. *Knowledge and Class: A Marxian Critique of Political Economy*. Chicago, IL: University of Chicago Press.

——— 2013. "On Overdetermination and Althusser: Our Response to Silverman and Park." *Rethinking Marxism* 25 (3): 341–9.

Silverman, M. 2013. "'Overdetermined' or 'Indeterminate'? Remarks on *Knowledge and Class*." *Rethinking Marxism* 25 (3): 311–24.

Smith, P. 1991. "Laclau's and Mouffe's Secret Agent." In *Community at Loose Ends*, Miami Theory Collective, 99–110. Minneapolis, MN: University of Minnesota Press.

———— 1994. "Interview with Richard D. Wolff." *Mediations* 18 (1): 5–17.

Wolff, R. 1998. "A Note on Althusser's Importance for Marxism Today." *Rethinking Marxism* 10 (3): 90–92.

———— 2009. *Capitalism Hits the Fan*. Northampton, MA: Media Education Foundation.

———— 2010. *Capitalism Hits the Fan*. Northampton, MA: Olive Branch Press.

16 Marxism and postmodernism

Our goal is to learn from one another

Richard D. Wolff

In following Jan Rehmann's comments, I have two luxuries: (1) to likewise bend the stick although in the opposite direction and (2) to structure my comments as responses to certain of his. Both sets of comments below are moments in an on-going discussion that is far from concluded. After all, the encounter of central elements of Marxism and of postmodernism is also far from finished.

In a peculiar agreement that should have worried more of those who agreed, most Marxists and most postmodernists have pushed the notion that they are enemies. Indeed, overheated rhetorics on both sides were often provocations or responses to provocations from one to the other. Many seemed concerned to guard the purity of one side from contamination by the other. Too bad: the result was fewer gains from the interaction than both sides badly needed.

Rehmann is right that Marxism's critical theorists, especially in and inspired by the Frankfurt School, had opened lines of inquiry well before postmodernism resumed, developed, and extended them. Yet this fact supports seeing postmodernism and Marxism as working on allied themes and goals at least as much as it warrants denigrating the unique contributions of the latter. In my view, postmodernism was chiefly a significant break with a largely bourgeois modernism and only secondarily a critique of the modernism that Marxism had too often and too uncritically absorbed into itself. The critical theorists grasped this point but earlier and in less developed and less profound ways because the huge wave of postmodernism had then not yet crested among bourgeois thinkers. That wave took all the earlier anticipations of postmodernism, grasped them as such, and wove them together into a much more powerful critique that then caught up what critical theorists had said inside Marxism and took it much, much further.

Frankly, I am neither much surprised by nor much interested in the ways postmodernists opposed to Marxism or socialism have used postmodernism against them. I am concerned when Marxists fail to learn the crucial practical and theoretical lessons postmodernism can teach. It would be tragic for Marxism's development to miss the practical and theoretical gains available to Marxists who carefully and critically integrate postmodernist insights as they develop the Marxian tradition.

The damage done, practically as well as theoretically, by economism inside the Marxian and broader socialist traditions is difficult to overstate. Critiques of and dissents from economism have not been strong enough to dislodge that modernist concept from the minds of many Marxists and socialists. Not a few critiques hesitated to make the clean break fearing that to do so meant a departure from their basic political and ideological commitments. Others shifted to alternative determinisms (of power, consciousness, etc.). Most did not reach far enough down into the most basic ontological assumptions about how different aspects of society relate to one another. Neither did they engage what an epistemological rejection of all determinism in the relation of thought to society could and should contribute to a critique of economism. Althusser's importance lies just there in pushing Marxism to reach down into those depths. That is why his brilliant development and application of Freud's "overdetermination" concept—to society and to thought in relation to society—is such a transformative moment in the engagement of Marxism with a postmodernism it can interrogate for its own advance.

Or at least that advance was made possible by Althusser's work when that was not lost in tediously repeated exercises of mutual rejection by postmodernists and Marxists. They usually missed utterly what was possible with and what was at stake in deploying "overdetermination" systematically in both social theory and epistemology. To prevent that loss for Marxism was a major goal for Steve Resnick and me when we published *Knowledge and Class* in 1987. The ongoing enmity between Marxism and postmodernism has persistently limited success in many people's efforts to achieve that goal.

To be blunt, what overdetermination enabled conceptually was the rejection of epistemological as well as ontological determinism. In epistemology, that means simply that no theory captures some singular truth valid across all theories; no such truth exists. Alternative theories construct and include their own notions of truth. Truths are as plural and multiple as the theories that construct and then appeal to them; they are internal to those theories. The contradictions and contests among alternative theories have unfortunately often led their respective champions to resort to endless, lame efforts each to raise their theory's particular truths (relative or internal to their theory) to the exalted level instead of the one absolute truth valid across all theories. The epistemological absolutism of classical religions lived and lives on in the absolute truth fetish of later, secular theories that claimed otherwise to have made great strides beyond religions.

For Marxism, epistemological overdetermination means that Marxian theories do not capture any absolute truth. They do not relate to non-Marxian theories in the manner of true to false (or scientific to ideological when such terms substitute for true and false). Marxian theories represent ways of thinking about the world—ways of appropriating the world for thinking beings in the world—that differ from alternative, non-Marxian theories. Since ways of thinking participate in overdetermining ways of acting in the world, how one thinks helps shape how one acts. And that helps shape how the world is and becomes. So how people think, which particular theories or mixes of theories they use, matters to the life experiences of everyone in the world we "share," (but of course we have theoretically differentiated ways of thinking about—different concepts of—what "share" means).

That is why each of us feels close to some theories and distant from others, agrees with some and not others, or applauds the actions associated with some theories and not those associated with others. Theory matters and so becomes another of the world's objects of debate and struggle. Nothing is gained and much risked and lost by conceiving of that struggle in terms of absolute truth and falsity. That is a lesson of history drawn by those whose theories of history (Marxian and non-Marxian) include the embrace of epistemological overdetermination.

Within a Marxian ontology or social theory, overdeterminism means that any and all aspects of past or present societies are understood to be the products of all the other aspects. If, only for convenience, we group social aspects under four subheadings—natural, economic, political, and cultural—overdetermination means that any one existing event, movement, person, desire, individual attribute, etc. is the product of all the others have existed or do exist. Economic events are overdetermined by natural, political, and cultural events. Any one cultural movement is the combined effect of all other cultural and also economic, political, and natural aspects of societies preceding or coexisting with that cultural movement. A political passion results from the combined effects of all the other political, cultural, natural, and economic processes predating and coexisting with that passion.

Marxists who engage critically with postmodernism and consequently integrate the concept of overdetermination into their Marxian theories do not shy away from key implications. If any and every historical event or movement or person is overdetermined by an infinity of other social aspects, processes, or events, then it follows that a full explanation for or account of that event, movement, or person is not possible. To do that is simply too big a task for humans, singly or together, to accomplish; it is like leaping unassisted over tall buildings or stopping time. It follows further that all explanations of events, movements, persons, etc. are inherently partial, incomplete, unfinished, and thus forever open. That includes all Marxian explanations. Everything overdetermines all the forever-open theories: all social changes (including developments inside each theory) affect all theories whose changes then react back upon society in an endless, open dialectic. Here lies yet another way to reject absolutist claims of a truth that transcends a particular theory. Indeed, apropos historical periods when many theories agree on some explanation of events, movements, persons, etc., a commitment to overdetermination precludes inferring some absolute truth from such agreement. Rather, the question would be what particular conditions of time and space overdetermined such agreement.

In sum, Marxian theories that engage postmodernism can draw and have drawn invaluable lessons, such as the concept of overdetermination, to support and advance the rejection of economism. A broadened, enriched, and extended Marxian tradition resulted. One major cause of so many remaining unaware of how the Marxian tradition has grown and evolved over the last 30 to 40 years through its complex engagement with postmodernism is the unproductive repetition of assertions that they are inherently enemies.

Let me turn next to Rehmann's notion that "the different definitions of class can be translated into each other." Here our disagreement raises the matter of overdetermination in another way. For thousands of years, at least since ancient Greece, populations have been conceptually divided— actually "classified"—into subgroups called "classes." The noun derived from the verb. Social theorists found it useful to break up populations into subgroups much as biologists and chemists break up their objects of analysis into plants and animals, atoms and molecules, and so on. Two key subgroups emerged over the centuries as key classes for social theory and political action. The first subgroups were differentiated according to wealth: the property they owned and/or the income they received. Thus we can read writings about the rich versus the poor classes, the middle class, etc. The second set of key subgroupings focused not on wealth but rather on power: the ruling class versus the ruled, those with much authority over others versus those with none and those in the middle, etc. These were the quite different property and power definitions of class. Theorists for many, many centuries have used one or the other or combinations to analyze, govern, and rebel against social systems. Yet they are irreducibly different concepts, different definitions of class. Depending on which one or combination is deployed, the theorist reaches different conclusions about the problems of and solutions for the societies examined through such theories.

Marx used these very old property and power concepts of class in his own social criticism, but he also added another, new and different definition. In this he displayed a revolutionary's impatience with the efforts of those who had gone before him. Those revolutionaries' understandings of class in terms of unequal social distributions of wealth and power yielded revolutions that had never yet succeeded in ending those inequalities or even coming close. Marx inferred that their heroic revolutionary projects had missed some aspect of society that needed change if equalized wealth and power were ever to be achieved in a durable way. And Marx set himself the task of finding what that missed aspect of society might be and what to do about it.

What Marx found and wrote extensively about was an aspect of society largely overlooked by the centuries of theorists who had worked with concepts/definitions of class in terms of wealth ownership and/or power wielded. That aspect was every society's particular organization of the production and distribution of a surplus. The latter referred to the difference between its total output of basic goods and services and the portions of that output (a) given back to the producers for their consumption and (b) used to replace the used-up inputs to production. What remains from total output after removing (a) plus (b) Marx called the "surplus." It is variously distributed to all sorts of people in each society. Some of those people do not participate in producing basic goods and services and thus consume without producing; they live off the surplus. Others both produce and also get distributed shares of the surplus. How each society particularly organizes its surplus—who produces the surplus, who distributes the surplus, who receives such distributions of the surplus, how and why distributed portions of the surplus are allocated among recipients—differentiates one society from another, shapes how each society functions and changes over time. To analyze a society through the lens of its organization of the surplus is what Marx meant by his new class analysis. Classes are defined in relation to the production, appropriation, and distribution of surpluses. That is Marx's analytical focus on capitalism across the three volumes of *Capital*.

Marx's class-*qua*-surplus definition yielded a different analysis of capitalism from those of his forebears including those who made great use of the older wealth and power definitions. For Marx, every society's organization of the surplus participated in overdetermining that society's distribution of wealth, income, power, and so on. And, as he showed, wealth and power distributions likewise participated in the overdetermination of a society's organization of its surplus. Marx's work demonstrated the interdependence of class-*qua*-surplus with class-*qua*-wealth and class-*qua*-power.

The motivation driving Marx's theoretical innovation was to inform revolutionaries that their projects to overcome unequal social distributions of wealth and power—with which he agreed—required attention to and the transformation of societies' organizations of the surplus. Marx's political message: to overcome the inequalities and needless sufferings of slavery, feudalism, and capitalism (where tiny minorities of their populations owned most of the wealth and exercised most of the power over others) required reorganizing the production and distribution of the surplus. Wealth and power distributions were indeed participants in overdetermining the social organization of the surplus. But the reverse was equally true. Only by changing the organization of the surplus—from exploitative (a minority of mostly non-producers appropriates the surplus produced by the producers) to non-exploitative (the producers themselves collectively and uniquely appropriate their own surplus)—would enduring equalizations of wealth and democratizations of power become possible. In short, the centuries of demands for the latter required the transformation of slavery, feudalism, and capitalism finally into communism as alternative organizations of the surplus, alternative class structures (using Marx's definition of class in surplus terms). Most of the above is lost if, as Rehmann suggests, "the different definitions of class can be translated into one another."

That some postmodernists took the insight that thought and/or language mediates everything we know and say about the world and exalted it to the notion that thought and language are the ultimate causes of the world is true but no longer a very compelling critique. It is the postmodern analog to Marxists who read Marx's examination of how the capitalist economy influenced politics and culture and exalted it into the economic determination of politics and culture. Matters of focus and emphasis have a long history of morphing into assertions of last-instance determinism by the less discerning.

Such exaltations deserve criticism to recover the insight at their roots without the overgrowth of excessive, insupportable claims. Here Rehmann and I agree. But the risk has often been that the criticisms overreach the other way to lose the original insight. Everything is mediated by language, and that reality needs to be taken into account analytically. Everything is shaped by economics and that likewise needs to be taken into account analytically. Marxism has largely done (and too often overdone) the latter; it has rarely done the former.

Marxism and Marxists were often stung by postmodernism's dismissal of all absolutist truth claims. Because so much of the Marxist tradition had been deeply caught up in and by the predominant modernism of the 19th and most of the 20th centuries, the postmodernist critique provoked modernist Marxism's defensive response. Only a few Marxists were open, like Althusser, to interrogating whether and how postmodernism's critiques might assist in modernist Marxism's self-criticism. They felt the urgency of that self-criticism if Marxism was to escape the dead ends confronting its modernist forms especially as their political expressions (Communist Parties and then Communist Party governments) imploded after the Second World War. Marxism has made considerable progress on that escape and on constructing the alternative vision and goals that drive its contributions to 21st-century history.

Part VI
Postcolonial Marx

17 Global Marx?

Gayatri Chakravorty Spivak

Since 1978, my teaching of Marx, and my awareness that the text was written in German, was short on secondary scholarship but interactive, attempting to move with a diversified and changing world. Brilliant projects like David Harvey's distance learning summary of Marx's writing (2016) became complicit with the technological will to power through knowledge. What is it to "know" what Marx wrote? "Knowing" Marx's writings preserves the old conviction that the idea of knowledge is knowledge about knowledge, halting Thesis 11 before its end: the supplementary task is to try to change the world. "Knowing" work must be supplemented by the double-bind of one-on-one teaching possibly producing collectivities: Thesis 3 (Marx 1947 [1888], 121–23). The supplement is dangerous, because it suggests that what is offered as a totality is incomplete and introduces the incalculable, since all must forever look beyond, to an undisclosable future of use—"poetry from the future" (Marx 1974 [1852], 149). My own work is so openly supplemental that I need fear no ancestor-worship. It is in that spirit that I have asked the question of global Marxism.

Attempting to move with a diverse and changing world and acknowledging Marx's own acknowledgment of the limit of his thinking in the differences among the many drafts for and the actual reply to Vera Zasulich in 1881 (Marx 1989 [1924], 346–71), I attempt to situate Marx's urbanist teleology, as others have before me (Baer 2006; Spivak 2012).

My argument circles around Antonio Gramsci's well-known remark, in *Prison Notebook 10*, in reference to Marx (1975 [1859]):

> The proposition contained in the Preface to *A Contribution to the Critique of Political Economy* to the effect that men [sic] acquire consciousness of structural conflicts on the level of ideologies should be considered as an affirmation of gnoseological [*gnoseologico*] and not simply psychological and moral value. From this, it follows that the theoretical-practical principle of hegemony has also gnoseological significance. . . . The realization of a hegemonic apparatus, in so far as it creates a new ideological terrain, determines a reform of consciousness and of methods of knowledge. . . . When one succeeds in

introducing a new morality in conformity with a new conception of the world, one finishes by introducing the conception as well; in other words, one determines a reform of the whole of philosophy.

(2000, 19)

Our general idea about Marxism is usually a violent change in governance, dependent upon regime change, the will and wisdom of a leader, supported by a responsible government. What we have seen over the last hundred years is that the success of the system depends a great deal on the power of the people—either in education or resistance—in conjunction with the capacity of the head of state to protect his or her national economy over against the incursions of the global economy in the interest of redistribution.

This model could not be fully followed by the great revolutions of the twentieth century because the diversified populations of the Russian empire and China, the two mammoths of Eurasia, were not equally resistant or educated, largely rural rather than urban, too dependent upon charismatic leaders, as were the Balkans, and their idea of gender empowerment was too mechanical.

Today, the charismatic leader supported or challenged by a resistant or motivated population model is threatened by the impersonal anti-humanist selective absolutism of global capitalism. The supposedly well-educated peoples of the European socialist or social-democratic sector are remodeling the resources of the welfare state either in reaction to what is elegantly called the "visible minorities," moving into those "developed" spaces by the vicious inequalities and violence/corruption attendant upon the abstract march of capital harnessed to unregulated greed, or against the miniature globality of the European "Union," a collection of debtor and creditor states. The postcolonial nations are neo-patrimonial, using the structures of democracy to preserve the status quo. Economic growth has no connection to social inclusion.

Marx knew the nature of capital, even if he did not know our worldly modernity. He said that capital, if it could, would want to move *mit Gedank-enschnelle*, at the speed of thought (1973 [1939], 548 and 631). With the silicon chip, capital can move at an even greater speed. The neuro-ethicists can so far only describe how the brain behaves in the modes of right and wrong. They have not been able to upgrade the computer in the head, although silicon technologists affirm that the newest model robots can be programmed for empathy.

I attended many sessions at the May 2016 World Economic Forum on Africa in Kigali, Rwanda. "Africa's Fourth Industrial Revolution" was run in a brisk British way. Jon Ledgard, Director of "Afrotech and Future Africa" at the Ecole Polytechnique Fédérale de Lausanne and founder of RedLine droneports and cargo drone network, spoke of the fact that roads and railways will not be constructed in Africa in the foreseeable future and that the skies were under-used. (A previous session was devoted to liberalizing air travel.) Therefore, said Mr. Ledgard, transportation should take place via drone ports, which would house robots. Apparently, one was already under contract for such a thing, or perhaps I misunderstood and it was already open, in Rwanda.

The entire discourse at the Forum reminds one of Marx's remark in "The Trinity Formula," that those who promote the unlimited social productivity of capital alone can fortunately forget the theft of "surplus value" (1981 [1894], 953). Steve Resnick and Rick Wolff (1987) have taught us how to go back and back and back along the chain of these promises and once again arrive at the fact of the theft of surplus value that allows capitalism to flourish.

"Who will build the drones?" Another participant, Neil Gershenfeld from MIT, answered "fab-labs": working the digital to assure that you can yourself build anything you want to, changing 2D to 3D. In answer to a question from a young African about joblessness in Africa today, Gershenfeld told us that we should change the idea of how to get things, that getting a job and making money in order to get things was not the only way. You could make what you wanted.

"Launching a new fab lab requires assembling enough of the hardware and software inventory to be able to share people and projects with other fab labs," says part of the online promo. Apply here Resnick and Wolff's lesson of working back to the theft of surplus value.

You will remember the astonishment of folks like James Steuart and Adam Smith at facing the sudden invention of a way of working that is not to make things for yourself or for a person who wanted you to make a thing for him or her but rather to make objects in great quantities for selling and making money, over and over again. James Steuart gave the name "industry" to this way of working, unlike anything known before (Steuart 1966 [1767], 468). There are pages, particularly the first pages of the *Wealth of Nations*, full of exclamation points (Smith 1976 [1776])—the great surprise, having to change the idea of making. Now here, within that last framework, is being offered, at the tip of technology, ways of going back to the other way, except through a denial that that historical framework was still at work and would displace itself with this new bit of digital idealism. There is no room for discussing this here, especially since I myself am unprepared to do so. But I place this here as an extreme form of the promise of globalization with which distance learning is complicit. Just change the idea of the interaction of learning—its transference—and you can know what Marx really thought, while you are in a position to make your computer in a fab lab.

What escapes the program (we have spoken of robots) is the contingent as such. The pursuit of the contingent is the edge of the technological will to power through knowledge. However, the power to be surprised by the contingent is now becoming less and less available because of the global

disincentive for imaginative training. It is within this lack that I will locate the persistent necessity for something that can, somewhat unrecog-
nizably, be called "global Marx." Is it the most accurate name for what I
will describe? That question is contained in the question mark in my title:
"Global Marx?"

Before I join the pursuit of the contingent, I want to go back to Antonio
Gramsci's comment on the Preface to *A Contribution to the Critique of Political Economy*: "Marx's proposition . . . should be considered as an affirmation of gnoseological value."

> "Gnoseological": in the logic of gnosis, knowing; a word-fragment that
> is still in colloquial English use: diagnosis, prognosis, words related
> to healing or the impossibility of healing – the double bind of healing.

Quintin Hoare and Geoffrey Nowell-Smith translate Gramsci's *gnoseologico* as "epistemological" (Gramsci 1971). "Actually between 'gnoseologico'
and 'epistemological' there is no difference," Italian political philosopher
Michele Spanò writes. Yet they are two different words. Therefore, their
so-called identity is a heterotautology. In this difference-as-identity of a
smooth translation I will place the globalizability of Marx today.

> "Gnoseological": learn to talk the talk well; "epistemological:" learn to
> re-imagine myself as knower and the object of knowing as knowable
> in order to try to walk the walk.

I have said above that "gnoseological" in diagnosis and prognosis carries the double bind of healing as the impossibility of healing, not only
in individual but also social "abnormalities." For those unfamiliar with
"double bind," let us call it living within equally insistent contradictory
instructions. Gramsci recognizes that Marx wishes to introduce the
worker into the double-bind of the contamination of manual labor by intellectual labor—not only the knowledge of the technology of capital, but
its gnoseology—so that any worker could become a "dirigent." This is the
task of the new intellectual in the party as well as in civil society. Leadership training for all.

Marx's "Preface" was written in 1859. The body of *A Contribution* was
written between 1861 and 1863. This was as much a preparation for *Capital*
volume 1 (1990 [1867]) as were the multilingual notebooks known as the
Grundrisse, first published in 1939. As we know from Marx's letter to Engels of 1862, amidst all of this, he discovered the secret of surplus value,
which he describes in *Capital* 1 as the *"Sprengpunkt"* or "pivot of his critique," and everything changed (1990 [1867], 132; translation modified). He
discovered the secret of reproductive heteronormativity, that every excess
in the human and upper primate emerges out of the differences between
needing and making. Marx described it in human terms: the worker

advances the capitalist his labor and the capitalist repays less than he gets out of it since the worker needs less than s/he makes. He also describes it in rational terms: labor power is the only commodity which, when consumed, produces value.

The "Preface" to *The Contribution to A Critique of Political Economy* belongs to a period before Marx's preoccupation with the unique logic of surplus value. Here the emphasis is indeed on gnoseology, to *know* that ideology is a more conflictual text than the scientifically precise economic base and to tease out that relationship. However, this text already lays down the possibility of backtracking from gnoseology—knowing and laying down the right stuff, David Harvey—to epistemology—constructing civil society as the object of knowledge, because it does not preclude the inclusion of the writer's own ideological production and because it makes us move toward being folded together "within the framework of the old society," emphasizing the complicity with the prevailing relations of production (Marx 1975 [1859], 426). For the Preface is nothing if not an account of epistemological performance: how a student of philosophy with a minor in jurisprudence puts himself in school to become the writer of the text it would introduce. Our last step as teachers and students of Marx is to open this apparently end-stopped narrative into the persistence of the run-on—a continuing commitment to the historic and generational.

Why, in a text about global Marxism, am I mentioning the World Economic Forum at all? It is to forge a practice that acknowledges complicity, not always with our consent, in every detail of the corporatist operation of the globe today. I cannot know what a cosmopolitical revolution would look like. But I do know that its principal agent can no longer be imagined as the internationally conscientized collective agent helping actively in a change in state-structure. In spite of Resnick and Wolff's already-mentioned demonstration of the continuing importance of the theft of surplus value upon which stands industrial capitalism, we have to admit that industrial capitalism is no longer produced by the definitive working class of the nineteenth and early twentieth centuries. Facing global capitalism, the struggle for "another world" is staged in the discontinuous confrontation of the misnamed international civil society and the subalternized citizen, within which labor, with international solidarity undone by nationalism and the factory floor "pulverized" by electronic resources, has its own discontinuous place.[1] The WEF is also gnoseological, by way of the techniques of knowledge management. I want to conclude with the critique of knowledge management by way of opening Marx to globality, with a question mark. This is why I have here marked a complicity—a folded togetherness—of nineteenth century confidence in scientific socialism and twenty-first century confidence in the social productivity of globalized capital with the twentieth century disaster area of communo-capital complicity, as carefully studied in Resnick and Wolff's Marxist analysis of the former Soviet Union (2002).

The World Economic Forum is basically engaged in "improving the state of the world" through Development, i.e., insertion into the circuit of capital with no critical subject-formation (Spivak 2017 forthcoming). The persistent epistemological transformation of the gnoseological—the all-knowing Research wing of Research and Development—is neglected by it, as it is neglected by cutting-edge work on techniques of interviewing (Lederman 2016). The goal is to enhance corporate social responsibility by folding it into the field of values such as "human dignity" and "common good." Assigning such values to one and all reflects the absolute failure of the epistemological effort toward grasping the heterogeneity of the developer and the developee—not to mention between the research methods of R & D on the one hand and, on the other, Policy. Any serious consideration of a just world has to consider the relationship between Policy and socialization, a very far epistemological cry from "the general will of the global." This is where a global Marx must allow its tight focus upon the proletarian to waver into the classed, gendered, raced (non)citizen.

* * *

The first part, then, is about where we go, and how we intervene, in order to have any bit of impact in the global policy field: Research and Development, international civil society, World Economic Forum. What can become of Marx's vision in this sorry collection of underdevelopment-sustaining mechanisms supporting capitalist ambition and greed? The Trades Union Advisory Committee of the nation-state-oriented Organization for Economic Co-operation and Development (currently focused on industrial nation-states)—a haven upon that hapless terrain—must still talk about establishing friendly relations with business and collective bargaining, job security rather than revolution.

This second part, by contrast, is about an academic debate. This is one of two broad academic debates regarding Marx:

1   Can Marx be followed today?
2   Should Marx be considered a humanist or materialist?

My position on Balibar's *Philosophy of Marxism* is just a taste of the first debate (Balibar 2014). Etienne Balibar is the felicitous heir of Marx within the Marxist tradition in its proper place of origin and development—a French philosopher deeply trained in German classical philosophy. I am fortunate enough to be able to call him my friend. At his suggestion, I have consulted his brilliant book, *The Philosophy of Marx* (2014).

I write as a woman with no institutional training in philosophy, with thirty years of work in a backward district of West Bengal, where the general social oppression of the landless illiterate outcasts and aboriginals was certainly ameliorated by the Communist-Party-Marxist, the party in power that also engaged in goon politics in certain rural sectors and lost the elections after thirty-four years. My involvement with western Marxism is through the soft margins of the U.S. Left, a rather different story. I owe a great deal to Resnick and Wolff for achieving that entry.[2] Before I put together my response to Balibar's challenge in his magisterial and wise slim book, I should perhaps put this section in contact with the previous one and repeat that my discussion of the Global Future Council on Ethics and Values at the World Economic Forum is an indication of the politically incorrect effort required to rectify (*pace* Balibar) persistently the digital idealism of Antonio Negri and Michael Hardt's massive volumes that posit a "multitude" automatically produced, advanced now into a consideration of social media as agent of change.[3] The World Economic Forum shares this view.

My ignorant alliance with my learned friend is by way of his conviction that one must "argue" with Marx. I also do agree with him that "Marxism is an improbable philosophy today" (Balibar 2014, 118), and so make peculiar contacts. Even if improbable, Marxism is not more impossible than anything else.

Rather than follow Marx to the letter, I harness my Marxist engagements to the tendency to go as far as possible:

> De Man goes on to say that the shift from history to reading typical of his generation "could, in principle, lead to a rhetoric of reading reaching beyond the canonical principles of literary history which still serve, in this book, as the starting point of their own displacement." "Reaching beyond" can mean displaced to another place. How far beyond? As far as I pull, in these times? Altogether elsewhere? At least into an understanding, as the best universities counsel students to cut their dissertations to market demands, that an aesthetic education inevitably has a meta-vocational function?
>
> (Spivak 2012)

Comparably, as our best philosophers call Marxism improbable, pulling Marx into the global economic, the belly of the beast, to suggest that repeatedly rectified ingredients for a doctrine, recognized as such, may be what we need to make Marxism work in a globalized situation where the first wave of Marxist experiments are coming undone?

Like Balibar, I do not think Marx "postmodern." In the spirit of Thesis 3, I think the changeful task is "persistent," adding to the thought of Marx, Gramsci, Balibar, and all my brothers, the dimension of generational turnover, a gendered concern of a teacher of other people's children. Interpretation is originary, each a halfway house with the "walk the walk"—the point is to change the world—imperative included and leading beyond—by way of the dangerous supplement.

Balibar perceives the ambiguities, contradictions, and amphibologies in Marx. He makes the important suggestion that "no theorist, when he has effectively found something new, can *re-cast* his own thinking. . . . Others will do that" (Balibar 2014, 112; other perceptions on 21, 27, 33, 92, 102 and *passim*). For me, this double bind is the very defining character of life, action, thought—the condition of impossibility as the only available condition of possibility, a persistent rewriting of improbability.

Before I learned the lesson of the double bind in the late seventies, I taught and wrote in another way, what in Balibar becomes dismissive:

> Revolution and science (revolution in science, science of revolution): ... [this] alternative was never resolved by Marx. This also means that he never accepted sacrificing the one to the other, which is a mark of his intransigence.
>
> (Balibar 2014, 115)

I taught it as "the heterogeneous dialectic of knowing and doing" (1987, 50),[4] an asymmetry that opens to action.

Marx thought Hegel calculated everything for the mind. Therefore, for the heterogeneous dialectic of knowing and doing, we go not to *The Science of Logic* (Hegel 2010 [1812]), as Lenin had suggested (Lenin 1960 [1914]) but to "The Beautiful Soul" in *The Phenomenology of the Spirit* (Hegel 1977 [1807]) that Lacan describes as metonymic of psychoanalysis (Lacan 2006 [1948], 242).[5]

Marx was haunted by Hegel, not by a question of his being a Hegelian or not. Ever since finishing his doctorate, he was interested in finding out the economic reality of life under capitalism. Taken by the brilliance of Hegel's method, he attempted to work out the phenomenology of capital (not onto-phenomenology). The lesson we learn is that capitalism is for capital's sake and therefore unreal. Hence, the socialist use of capital cannot be just for capital's sake alone.[6]

As soon as he understood that capitalism is based on the theft of surplus value, Marx also understood that the play of capital and labor was in terms of contentless value, and that the contents that appear along the line of play as moments of real-ization, were always traces or forms of appearance—*Erscheinungsformen*. There are some who think of land in this land-grabbing phenomenology of primitive accumulation as completely real. Marx quotes Ovid in heavy mockery: "and now in addition the ground, inorganic nature as such, *rudis indigestaque moles* 'a rough unordered mass' in its full sylvan primordiality. Value is labor. So surplus-value cannot be earth" (Marx 1981 [1894], 954; translation modified).

Yet, in "The 18th Brumaire of Louis Bonaparte" Marx distinguishes the revolution of the nineteenth century as content rather than phrase: "Previously the phrase went beyond the content; [in the social revolution of the nineteenth century] the content goes beyond the phrase" (Marx 1974

[1852], 149). This is close to a passage in "Beautiful Soul," where Hegel is writing about "the moral intuition of the world [*Weltanschauung*]": "[T]he antinomy. . .that there is a moral consciousness, and that there is none, or that the validation of duty [for Marx socially just action] lies beyond consciousness, and conversely, takes place *in* it" (Hegel 1977 [1807]).

This was seen by Hegel to be "a contradiction. . . by content." And when this thinking "in which the non-moral consciousness counts for moral, and its accidental knowing and willing is taken as fully potent, felicity granted to it by way of grace [perhaps a reference to Kant's metaleptic invocation of 'effect of grace' in the Appendix to the *Critique of Pure Reason*]"—it is seen as a contradiction "by form" (Hegel 1977 [1807], 383; translation modified).[7]

Marx, for whom phenomenological definition has become part of mental furniture, is here choosing the double bind of the antinomy of ideology: we can/we cannot—for the social revolution of the nineteenth century as "content"—over the "formal" reconciliation of the antinomy in the mere "phrase" of the revolutions of the past: we can do good. This is also an indication that socialism is not just the use of abstract average labor power to build a just society, for the abstract by definition has no content. There would be content in the nineteenth century revolution—the poetry of the future—not just abstract planning, a point to which we return below.

Everybody knows that *Geist* is hard to translate. It is clear, however, that it is not consciousness—*das Bewusstsein*—and not reason—*die Vernunft*. Like capital, *Geist* by itself cannot "do." Hegel charts the course of its estrangements in Part C.BB of *Phenomenology*. However, when it is contaminated by *Gewissen*—psychologistically (and unfortunately) only translatable into English as "conscience"—it can only stage the "doing." Marx finds in this predicament of self-consciousness, instantiated in this constellation, the fact of human beings making their own history but not able to choose their roles. *Geist* shot through with *Gewissen* can hold *Wissen* and *Wollen*—knowing and willing—but not actually know and will. This counter-intuitive way of a spatializing structure is hard for Marx's English translators to grasp. But let us continue: *Bewusstsein* or consciousness cannot really think good and bad, although programmed to think it can and must. On the other hand, it must have the conviction, and it must talk about this conviction collectively, and thus it can bring about abstract collective consciousness. Of course Marx, not a Hegelian, did not act this out in such detail, but all the generalizing convictions – all the writing, the talks, the meetings—use this in action, even as they emphasize the separation of individual subjectivity—in the vanguard or the masses—from its ideological production. Since Marx is not obliged to show that he is a correct or incorrect Hegelian, this rough ironic parallel between *Gewissen* (conscience) and ideology cannot easily be discarded.

Hegel uses the words *Tat, Tätigkeit, Tun, handeln, Handlung*—German words for doing or action—to show whether duty was being done. Of course, the word *Arbeit* (work/labor) is never used. This is where Marx staged the phantasmagoria of the action of labor power, and in his work, unlike in Hegel, the dialectic becomes heterogeneous, in contrast to Hegel, for whom the separation between knowing and doing is kept brilliantly and counter-intuitively intact.

From time to time Hegel warns that the staging of the phenomenology of *Geist* into human psychological types short-circuits the account of the march of philosophy. But the text often seems to ask for this transgression. Marx, as Fanon later more vividly, steps into this transgression and attempts to move the system away from "the mind alone."

Balibar charts Marx's lifetime move from an evolutionist history toward its undoing—by way of the experience and study of failed revolutions (1848, 1871), the tendency of left movements to move away from Marx's methods, and, finally, the out-of-system (or anti-systemic) potentialities of the agricultural communes in Russia. The consequence of this chain of displacements is described this way by Balibar: "I am tempted, rather, to believe that Marx never, in fact, had the time to construct a doctrine because *the process of rectification went faster*" (2014, 117). I see this as Marx's great gift, autodidact as he was, acquiring knowledge as new needs opened up, not only to be constrained to but creatively to be able to learn from his mistakes—again a chain into which we can, transindividually and responsibly, insert ourselves (Balibar 2014, 30). A persistent set of epistemological performative instructions kept overtaking the stern requirements of a gnoseology. Given the *Aufhebung* into globalization, this persistence is our difficult guide.

The thinking of globality requires thinking the contemporary. "In globalization every site is contemporary," I have written elsewhere, "and yet also unique. We therefore call it a double bind" (2010, 510). Balibar is able to grasp this intuition of globality in Marx: "communal form was '*contemporary*' (a term to which Marx insistently returned) with the most developed forms of capitalist production, the technique of which it would be able to borrow from the surrounding '*milieu*'" (Balibar 2014, 108). Expanding our field of activity beyond the "pulverized" factory floor is part of such borrowing.

For Christine Buci-Glucksmann, this particular thought of globality is still in the future. However, her reading of Gramsci reading Marx "beyond the letter" and her rendering of gnoseology as epistemology ("they are the same thing," says Michele Spanò) through Gramsci's idea of the "critic-practical act," are deeply resonant with my own (Buci-Glucksmann 1980, 348 and 351).

In *The 18ᵗʰ Brumaire of Louis Bonaparte* (1974 [1852]), Marx suggests that the real long-term result of the French Revolution was, paradoxically, to strengthen the power of the executive. Some of us have felt the long-term result of the great revolutions in China and Russia was to bring about a globalizable world. Following in the same great narrative mode, it can be said that, just as the Industrial Revolution made capitalist colonialism necessary, so does the technological revolution make global governance necessary. And just as monopoly capitalist colonialism did not represent mercantile capitalist colonialism, so does this haphazard global governance not resemble a magnified world state, on the model of nation-state governance. The world's charter is written by finance capital. World trade is financialized. The anthropocene flourishes through greed. Climate is changed drastically.[8] Victims of inequality suffer natural and social disasters more drastically than those not. Class apartheid in education produces rape-culture and bribe-culture above. Stoppage of imaginative training produces rape-culture and bribe-culture below. Democracy is exported on the spear-point of trade blackmail and war. In spite of the abstractions of finance, the bull market is driven by affect: investor confidence. And the subprime crisis is driven by family values.

Behavioral economics, attempting to thicken rational choice, is no match for this ethical catastrophe. If international socialism died of an ethics-shaped hole, global capitalism, although it is not as embarrassed to talk the ethical talk, will continue to live with the same terminal disease— an ethics-shaped hole. Into this void steps the World Economic Forum, wanting to turn capitalism toward social justice with inadequate imaginative resources but an acknowledgment of complicity in the narrow sense ("we alone have done this"). Its strongest tradition of amelioration is sustainable underdevelopment, a phrase I have already used.

The World Economic Forum is a large, non-profit, private-sector organization, admonishing civil society, examining the decimation of the constitutional state, and considering redress to corporate, military, and extra-state violence, the consequences of inequality, and climate change, to name a few. It attempts to re-think technology by making it sit down with Amnesty International and Africa. It moves from local and national to regional, perhaps to access the global. Access to global, in spite of digital idealists, is not a certainty here. It is not prepared to be taught what it cannot know—how not to control top-down.

The distance in kind between the top (WEF and Columbia University), bottom (the largest sectors of the electorate—"citizens!"—in Africa and Asia), and hapless middle (undocumented immigrants) makes the task of the teacher complex. The international civil society—confusing equality with sameness and thus denying history or teaching income-production and thus serving capital, is useless. Here one invokes the complicity—folded-togetherness—of fund-raising radicals and the corporate world. Of Research and Development, I have written above. It is upon this rough terrain that Gramsci's "new intellectual" must push the question mark in "global Marx?" into a possibility, supplement the question mark as copula—gnoseology into epistemology over and over again, working by the surreptitious light of the hidden declarative: "This is happening." (We remind ourselves that the supplement fills a need but also shows the incompleteness of what it supplements. Here the intellectual's tendency is to remain, as a "beautiful soul," in the question mark forever.)

Before I had participated in Abu Dhabi, and in response to the Occupiers of Wall Street as well as W.E.B Du Bois, Gandhi, and others on the General Strike, I wrote in *Rethinking Marxism*:

> Like Rosa Luxemburg, we can perhaps claim that the citizens' strike is no longer a step back toward the bourgeois revolution. Our example is not just Occupy Wall Street, a citizen's strike which started in 2007 as no more than a first move, but also the Eurozone, the "broad Left" in Greece, shoring up after financial disaster as a result of the capitalist policies of the creditor state/debtor state policies of the European Union. If, at the inauguration of the International Working Men's Association [at a meeting of the Chartists where Marx introduced the word International into the Workingmen's Association], Marx had felt that workers should keep abreast of international politics and diplomacy, enough to intervene at this moment of capitalism's negation, the citizen, the agent of the general strike redefined, must keep abreast of the laws regulating capital.
>
> (2014b, 10–11)

Now, the citizen and the corporatist acknowledge complicity in seemingly turning capital to social, the baseline of socialism. (Gender is still caught in family values—read sanctioned rape and reproduction—in most of the world. That is future work.) Let us stop for a moment on the "seemingly," the semblance of an unmediated interest in social justice. As I have urged before, the corporatist actually works to preserve the interest of capital. The epistemological undertaking is therefore for the 99%, the citizens.

The 99%'s rearrangeable desire, then, should be in the embrace of the teacher's agential slot for the electorate—often from within a liberation theology (more future work here to gender theology into the intuition of the transcendental, "belief" to imagination). There is a deep interest in inequality and the "slaves" involved in the commodities we enjoy, on all impressionistic sides, opening to Marx's insight of the fetish-character of the commodity, with a rough and ready idea of the social relations of production and no understanding of surplus value.[9] However, the point now is to see the subaltern as subject ungeneralizable by the Forum, their numbers replenished as capital marches on, not just proletarian as universal subject.

As Marx counseled a homeopathy of reification—appropriate the quantification of labor to turn capital into the service of the social—so does my wary move toward the nature of corporate benevolence acknowledge a homeopathy: the undoing of the distinction between public and private about which we at U.S. universities worry endlessly. As Crystal Barto-lovich comments:

> Subjected to tutelage of breakfast cereal icons and branded peer pres-sure throughout their lives, students are rarely going to be transformed into revolutionaries in fifteen weeks, no matter how "radical" their English or sociology professors may be [Bartolovich does not mention that their radicalism does not shun the complicity of corporate fund-raising for project support]. Nevertheless, coming out of a generally conservative climate into the liberal university, bright students can develop their "critical-thinking" skills in ways useful to business and government so long as they don't think too critically for too long – something that corporate elites do not appear to be concerned will happen. They know their professors are small fish in a very big pond.
> (2013, 44)

Ours is an invitation to get out of this acceptance of powerlessness as normal, to stop us-and-them-ing, to acknowledge complicity and act the conjuncture.

* * *

In closing, I will emphasize that the agent of production of the social today is the citizen rather than the wage worker as such. The subaltern voter and the subalternized citizen need to be welcomed into the Marxist struggle of moving capital into the social incessantly. The fact that the subaltern can vote and be "developed" (not just robbed of indigenous knowledge and DNA) has made a huge conjunctural change that is usually ignored. The internationally divided, often adversely gendered, hopelessly exploited proletariat is of course also a member of this lowest stream of citizen-ship. To produce in this large, ungeneralizable global subaltern group a rearrangement of the petty bourgeois "desire to get rich" (Marx 1964 [1932], 286) to a socialist desire to build a just world is the (im)possible task. "Socialism is about justice, not development," I can hear Teodor Shanin declaim.[10] In 1844, the Hegelian statement that conviction spoken and dis-cussed (in *Sprache* and *Rede*) creates a general consciousness was noted as ignoring class divisions and conflicts by the young Marx. As Marx kept "rectifying," the result of this possible general consciousness is presumed to undo the proper names of modes of production. This intuition remains in the very late Marx: "if both wages and surplus-value are stripped of their specifically capitalist character—then nothing of them remains, but simply those foundations of the forms that are common to all social modes of production." We will come back to this passage.

The epistemological cut between the early humanist and the later ma-terialist Marx (Althusser 1969 [1965]) is too tight. The materialist Marx discovers the importance of the use of the abstract average as the "social" of socialism. Describing the centrifugality or *Zwieschlächtigkeit* of the commodity, his own specific discovery, will allow the worker/citizen to restrain her/himself to contain the march of capital. Simply having the abstract tool (gnoseology) is not enough. While "normality" works by greed, or at least self-interest, even if enlightened, the socialized worker/citizen must want this self-restraint in the interest of social collectivity. Here Marx's unexamined humanism, sustained throughout the abstract materialist work (canny enough to know practically that the workers have petty bourgeois ideologies) sustains his conviction that once fully aware of this by way of the ownership of the means of production, its agents, the workers, will exercise the freedom to subsume self under collectivity for a bigger project. It goes without saying that Human Rights intervention, although necessary in the short run, generally working toward restoration of often-unknown rights by shaming states through public interest litigation does not enter the epistemological task required by Marx's hope and plan, as Gramsci understood.

Let me add the aporia between liberty (autonomy, self-interest) and equality (alterity, unconditional hospitality), bringing forward some points I have made above. The democratic structure, body count, one equals one, is arithmetical and impoverished. It does not produce a democratic society. The democratic structure presupposes a democratic society—a performative contradiction. This is why most post-colonial nations are neo-patrimonial: using the structures of democracy to preserve structures of patronage, bribe-culture, sustained by rape-culture; and preserving class-apartheid in education, so that votes as body count can be counted on indefinitely. This performative contradiction, therefore, invites us to make mind-sets change, an epistemological performance—a call to teachers.

We interrogate the absurdity of arithmetic equality, one person one vote, given the race-class-gendered unevenness of subject-production. Indeed, even if we achieved the impossibility of an absolutely egalitarian race-class-gender situation, 1=1 would remain an underived disability count of the "normal" human body, "able" always approximate and depreciating (like capital) within this inflexible arithmetic as the "majority" moves from birth to unevenly spaced death, other "majorities" shoving the sociograph at the same time. This does not disqualify democratic principles, but rather points at the difficulty of any claim to an affective collective solidarity in the name of political agency within the constraints of democratic principles. It is an insoluble problem. The solution is not to ignore it; however, you want to understand the declarative. To remind the world of such inconveniences is the task of the humanities.

The irreducible conditionality of the human animal sits uneasily and irresolvably within the abstractions of democratic rationalist unconditionality. The two cross unevenly as life-expectancy is marked by class, gender, and race. It certainly cannot be solved by informal markets or voting blocs. The paragraphs above suggest that the arithmetic structure of democracy requires for democratic functioning not only an informed electorate, but also a basic imaginative flexibility, allowing for an epistemological performance where the least "disabled" subject knows that the world is not intended primarily for it, and that its way of knowing is contingent. The relationship between Marx*ism* as we know it and this post-anthropocentric epistemological perception—rather different from the easily declared post-humansim of the sustainable underdevelopers of environmentalism—is too massive to be launched here. I will content myself with another word on the formation of democratic judgment.

One-on-one and collective; a more careful alternative to consciousness-raising of various sorts: vanguardism to promote class-consciousness; organizing for collective bargaining and job security; legal awareness seminars; citizenship training; identitarian voting-bloc pre-party formation; gender-babble encompassing all. One-on-one pedagogy for collectivity, millennially tested within race-class-gender parameters, is the equivalent of what classroom teaching could be today: the careful work of learning and rearranging desires to contain the march of capitalism and to respect the rights of others who do not resemble me. Yet the politically correct formulas that circulate within our crowd are extended only to our self-consolidating other, not further. I give you an example from my limited but deep and intimate study: the six rural elementary schools that I have been teaching and training at for decades now.

The social groups there, including my teachers and co-workers, are fully aware of millennial caste-oppression, but know nothing about colonialism, which departed seventy years ago. They have never seen white people. The schoolbooks are not written for them, so the gender and multicultural (religion) banalities have to be taught straight. Gender and religious common ground must be dealt with outside of the classroom, and Europe cannot be ignored.

I try to make the groups friendly with the wretched map of the world on the back cover of the old geography book. There is no map of the world in the new government textbooks. I point at the northwestern corner of the huge Eurasian continent and tell them that that is Europe and that though it is so small, it won. I discuss with them how it won and even use such mid-Victorian examples as James Watt watching the lid dance on the pot of boiling water: the emergence of the rationality of capital—the beginning of industrial capitalism—accessible apparently to a high school student. I can then begin to introduce into the style of pedagogy the lesson of using capital for socialism. For, although until five years ago, the party in power was Communist-Party-Marxist, the secret of the theft of surplus value was not taught in school or in the party office.[11] There is no factory floor, and yet they vote.

I remind myself not to be an "improver" (hard for a teacher) and discuss with my increasingly more aware co-workers (male and female teachers and supervisors) from these social groups the fact that I am not drawing profits from the work for and with them. Although they are not well acquainted with the world map, know nothing about colonialism, and have not seen any factories of any significant size, they do understand what profit or *munafa* is. They are subaltern, they have no special psychological essence, they are not "the East," "the Non-West," or to use the awful phrase, "the global South"; they are examples of a general argument that notices that they vote in a postcolonial nation that they do not know as such.

The argument from Eurocentrism now belongs to another class that must also deal with a limiting concept of "Europe" in global capitalism, that Europe is a part of a much larger world now. Europe's moment was historically important but not all-consumingly determining. Not everyone has to have a correct interpretation of the English and French revolutions. It is enough to think of the relationship between the Chartists and the Reform Bills, even Labour and New Labour; of the 18th Brumaire, even Aimé Césaire and Frantz Fanon versus Valéry Giscard d'Estaing. The sun rises at different times upon the globe today. When the stock exchange closes in London, it must wait for Tokyo and then Mumbai, and in-between opens the turbulent and unstable speculative "marriage of socialism and capitalism," where the "turnover rates are ten times higher," altogether different from the sober decision for a mixed economy taken in the New Economic Program in 1921. The beginning of the end: without the epistemological support imagined by Du Bois, Gramsci, and Fanon, this leads to a wild eruption of the uniformization/universalization of capital rearing to break through, like the steam in the steam engines that we traveled by in my childhood and adolescence: Shanghai and Shenzen (Spivak 2014a).[12]

These are examples where our politically correct formulas might not work. Yet even here, one can teach epistemological performance through a rearrangement of the desire for an impossible self-enrichment, which only gels into petty bourgeois ideology in the most cunning fashion. Marx-via-Gramsci-limited by Zasulich must be extended here, and it must be remembered that the subaltern is by definition not generalizable. My example will not travel to details of socio-cultural life in other parts of India, as it will not in the large and diversified sectors of the subaltern in Africa, in Latin America. This is the one-on-one. The collectivity is the entry into citizenship, which will destroy subalternity. The citizen as such is generalizable, as is the proletarian as such. That is the displaced global Marx. For the diversified ungeneralizable unverifiable singular aesthetic, we do not look to Marx.

And yet.

Many committed readers of Marx feel that *Capital* volume 3 is both continuous with and transgressive from volumes 1 and 2. One of the most famous "transgressive" passages is the invocation of "the realm of freedom." In closing, we will read it together to suggest that Marx's robust unexamined humanism, developed from the early task of correcting Hegel ("[t]he only labour Hegel knows and recognizes is *abstract mental [geistig]* labour"), so far felt as the *Zwieschlächtigkeit* or centrifugality in the word "social"—the abstract average and yet the place of human development— here gives us an empty space—"the realm of freedom" (Marx 1981 [1894], 958–59)—which we can occupy to introduce the incalculable, the supplement always considered dangerous by mechanical Marxists—imaginative training for the ungeneralizable singular aesthetic—persistent preparation for the ethical reflex—the absence of which in general education brought the first set of revolutions to heel (Marx 1964 [1932], 386).[13]

The passage invites careful reading.

In *Capital* I, Marx proposes counter-intuitively that exchangeability is already present in nature ("[i]n considering the labour process, we began by treating it in the abstract, independently of its historical forms, as a process between man and nature" (Marx 1990 [1867], 643). This presupposition, never relinquished, supplies the basis for the broader proposition, that labor is a human fact – the argument that can be broadened to the proposition that we can make more than we need in *every* act of life and thought. Marx, interested only in the economic sphere, compliments capital:

> It is one of the civilizing aspects of capital that it extorts this surplus labour in a manner and in conditions that are more advantageous to the development of laborpowers, to social relations and to the creation of elements for a renewal on a higher plane than under the earlier forms of slavery, serfdom, etc.
>
> (1981 [1894], 958; translation modified)

It is important that he is not speaking of capital*ism* here. In this passage, Marx is looking forward to the socialist use of capital. I am thinking especially of phrases such as *"gesellschaftliche Verhältnisse,"* where the adjective could almost be "socialist" and the noun is the more philosophical *Verhältniss*—suggesting a philosophically correct structural position rather than the more colloquial *Beziehung* (relationship)—and of *höhere Neubildung*, which is almost *Aufhebung* or sublation. This is what capital does. The problem, once again, is that the capital*ist* use simply "disappears." This is where our globally diversified effort can teach and practice Marxism by persistently *de*-humanizing greed as the *primum mobile*—the dangerous supplement, one-on-one yet collective.

In the next movement of this rich paragraph, Marx once again generalizes, bringing all modes of production together, bringing *Gemeinschaft* and *Gesellschaft* together. Here is the loss of the proper names of modes of production as a subjunctive goal, a blow to gnoseology. Marx brings up once again that exchangeability begins in nature. Before capital, nature ruled the human like a blind power. In socialized capital, "associated producers govern" this originary exchangeability, "human exchange of material [*Stoffwechsel*, usually 'metabolism,' translates literally into 'exchange of material'] with nature in a rational way" (translation modified). The entire world, all modes of production together, is the realm of necessity that supports human development for its own sake. This is the site of the epistemological struggle, where the question mark becomes the copula that opens the supplement that displaces itself and continues questioning, again and again. If in the globalized practice of marxism (small m), the agent for turning capital to socialist uses must be the citizen, for Marx s/ he remains the worker. Therefore, our passage ends with the effort to provide more time for the realm of freedom that will no doubt be released if the realm of necessity is socialized.

No doubt. Marx's description of such a prepared realm of necessity is without reference to the epistemological—one-on-one yet collective— struggle required to produce a general will for social justice.

Here is the passage. First Marx takes the small peasant (the least likely candidate) as proof of the illusion that capitalism is the norm. Then he shows us how easy it is to disprove this illusion by painting that effortless picture of a socialist state.

> Because a form of production that does not correspond to the capitalist mode of production [the self-employed small peasant] can be subsumed under its forms of revenue (and up to a certain point this is not incorrect), the illusion that capitalist [structural] relationships are the natural [structural] relationships of any mode of production is further reinforced. If however one reduces wages to their general basis, i.e. that portion of the product of his labour which goes into the worker's own individual consumption; if one frees this share from its capitalist limit and expands it to the scale of consumption that is allowed on the one hand by the existing social productivity (i.e., the social productive power of his own labour as effectively social) and on the other hand required for the full development of individuality; if one further reduces surplus labour and surplus product, to the degree needed under the given conditions of production, on the one hand to form an insurance and reserve fund, on the other hand for the constant expansion of reproduction in the degree determined by social need; if, finally, if one includes in both (1) the necessary labour and (2) the surplus labour . . . that those capable of work must always perform for those members of society not yet capable, or no longer capable of working – i.e. if one strips both wages and surplus-value of their specifically capitalist character – then nothing of these forms remains, but simply those foundations of the forms that are common [*gemeinschaftlich*] to all social [*gesellschaftlich*] modes of production.
>
> (1981 [1894])

Today, efforts at imagining social justice are seldom more than top-down efforts at preserving the movement of global capital: Development as "insertion into the circuit of capital without subject-formation." To imagine the Gramscian lesson in this globalized conjuncture, the "leftist" polarization of subject-formation and the collective abstraction of capital/social must be persistently undone by the new intellectual in a class-, gender-, and race-sensitive way. The move to socialize capital cannot be assured by "a shorter working day." The forming of the subject for the ethical reflex housed in the responsible outlines of a general will for socialization in the fullest sense, on the broad relief map of the globe, sometimes undone by centuries of extrinsic and intrinsic violence, inhabited by many first languages, obliged to recognize, if necessary in the idiom of the subaltern, that, as I have insisted above, the contingent, beyond programming, rises in the difference between need and capacity to make and cannot be caught by knowledge management. Today's methodology of choice can be fearlessly confronted only if it becomes the deep background of a classroom teaching to rearrange desires, teaching also the risks of walking the walk that would then begin to be desired.

The invaluable work toward a will to justice is destroyed by a confidence in so-called toolkits and templates. The desire for such speedy solutions must be rearranged with the training of the imagination, to understand that to change gnoseology to epistemology today we must first understand that the toolkit closes off the contingent. If the toolkit is telling the top how to help the bottom, the bottom is thought as needing no more than material aid for income production and the reduction of poverty. Movements that are advertised as "from below" need to have their leadership/vanguard structure carefully read. This remote, infinitely complicated struggle cannot be assigned to knowledge management.

The new intellectual must teach how to make toolkits—even on the subaltern level—as halfway houses to be undone by the contingent rather than offer toolkits as a solution to the problem of action. Some of us have been criticizing the UN, for example, on the use of platforms of action to diffuse and manage violence against women. Some of us have been criticizing the mere statisticalization of such things as development and progress. All of this has to be integrated into a persistent critique of knowledge management so that meetings to achieve solutions do not work as if for children, with leaders who divide collectivities into groups, with instructions to produce lists of items that are collected as the groups are put back together. This is not the way that the imagination will be trained for epistemological performance so that unconditional ethics can be introduced to move capital into social justice. This is the work that we must continue to do persistently in order to make "Marxism" global.

I want to close with a word on gender. Within scientific socialism, the empowerment of gender was stiffly rational. One can find proof of this in the writings of Alexandra Kollontai (1980) and latter-day writers such as the Chinese feminist Dai Jinhua (2002). Today gender empowerment through micro-credits and financial independence—taking employability as the bottom line of human dignity—follows the same sort of autonormative agenda. Here gendering as the type case of reproductivity must be acknowledged. Just as in the epistemological project of *Capital* 1, the worker was invited to rethink himself epistemologically as an agent of production rather than victim of capitalism, so also, and on a broader base, women must understand that men take more and give less and that women are not themselves the victims of phallocentrism but the agents of production. The need for legitimate passage of property must not be the excuse for keeping them in confinement. Integrating this to capitalism takes us from Engels through Thomas Picketty (2014) into listening to the gendered subaltern subject. If you think this is bio-politics, try to imagine more flexibly.

And an envoi: globality is my brief, and I have tried to attend to it, with a question marking the need for a persistent and effortful move from gnoseology to epistemology, from knowledge management to intellectual labor, from rational choice to imagination, moving poison to medicine, capital to social, rearranging desires as the generations pass. I have referred to a contemporary vanguard, the Global Futures Council of the World Economic Forum. The subtext: work must be supplemented by the production of the subaltern intellectual: focused, local, intense work, attempting to produce in the largest sectors of the global electorate an understanding of the importance of the right to intellectual labor—a labor that is almost impossible to teach in the face of millennial cognitive damage, in the face of the imperative to obedience. At the World Economic Forum, Klaus Schwab, the Founder and Executive Chairman, spoke of moving from and between the local and national into the regional, in preparation for the global. The subaltern are people who have not been welcomed into all the nationalisms of the previous centuries and yet, in some sectors, have become multinational now as labor export, often undocumented. There one does not practice or teach leadership, but learns to follow how to teach. But that is another talk, another walk, another theater. For now, think that limit as center, not margin, as we part company.

Notes

1 Word used in unpublished 2001 conversation with the editor of *Asia Labor Monitor*.
2 Resnick and Wolff were the first and perhaps the only economists to see any value in my work, as reflected in my class-notes-based essay "Scattered Speculations on the Question of Value" (Spivak 1985).
3 Most expansively developed in Hardt and Negri (2004).
4 In a bolder formulation, Jean-Luc Nancy declares: "'To speak of freedom' is accordingly to suspend philosophy's work. And this is in fact the very possibility of a 'philosophizing' " (1993, 3).

5 Lenin writes: "It is impossible completely to understand Marx's *Capital*, and especially its first chapter, without having thoroughly studied and understood the *whole* of Hegel's *Logic*. Consequently, half a century later, none of the Marxists understood Marx!" (1960 [1914], 180).

6 I cite here Amina Mohamed, currently running for the position of Chairperson of the African Union Commission, and Alicia Bárcena, the Executive Secretary of the U.N.'s Economic Commission for Latin America and the Caribbean, neither noticeably Marxist, yet both pushing for sustainable development driving the market rather than vice versa, as is the case now.

7 Already in 1844, Marx alluded to this section of the *Phenomenology*: "[t]he 'unhappy consciousness,' the 'honest consciousness' the struggle of the 'noble and base consciousness,' etc. etc., these separate sections contain the *critical* elements" (Marx 1964 [1932], 385). Our (Marx's) task is to supplement intellectual with manual labor.

8 Dipesh Chakrabarty's brilliant work (2016) points the way to acknowledging the subject/agent bind into planetarity. However, given his theoretical base, he is obliged to ignore the challenges of the heterogeneity of knowing and doing.

9 A moving example of this interest is "Are My Hands Clean?" (Reagon 1985, performed by Sweet Honey in the Rock, 1988, Flying Fish Records).

10 Unpublished conversation with the author.

11 Theft of surplus value is not mentioned in Mao's groundbreaking essay on the peasant revolution in Hunan province (Zedong 1971 [1927]). Early Bolsheviks often made the point that the Russian revolution was better than the German because it involved both workers and peasants. For Gramsci's "subalterns" too, there was no factory floor.

12 My description of Shanghai and Shenzen is taken from Wong (2006).

13 Even here, Marx notices the usefulness of the method: "Hegel adopts the standpoint of modern national economy" (translation modified). Marx himself proceeds from "national" to "political" economy in subsequent writings.

References

Althusser, L. 1969 [1965], *For Marx*. Trans. Ben Brewster. London: New Left Books.

Baer, B. C. 2006. "Ghost-Work: Figures of the Peasant and the Autochthon in Literature and Politics, 1880s–1940s." PhD dissertation, Department of English and Comparative Literature, Columbia University.

Balibar, E. 2014. *The Philosophy of Marxism*. Trans. C. Turner. London: Verso.

Bartolovich, C. 2013. "Small Fish, Big Pond." *Academe* 99 (6): 44.

Buci-Glucksmann, C. 1980. *Gramsci and the State*. Trans. D. Fernbach. London: Lawrence and Wishart.

Chakrabarty, D. 2016. "Humanities in the Anthropocene: The Crisis of an Enduring Kantian Fable." *New Literary History* 47 (2–3): 83–98.

Gramsci, A. 2000. *The Gramsci Reader: Selected Writings*. Ed. D. Forgacs. New York: New York University Press.

Hardt, M. and A. Negri. 2004. *Multitudes*. London: Penguin.

Harvey, D. 2016. "Reading Marx's *Capital* with David Harvey." http://davidharvey.org/reading-capital/, (accessed 7 January 2017).

Hegel, G. W. F. 1977 [1807]. *Phenomenology of Spirit*. Trans. A. V. Miller. New York: Oxford University Press.

——— 2010 [1812]. *The Science of Logic*. Trans. G. D. Giovanni. Cambridge: Cambridge University Press.

Jinhua, D. 2002. *Cinema and Desire: Feminist Marxism and Cultural Politics in the Work of Dai Jinhua.* Eds. J. Wang and T. E. Barlow. London: Verso.

Kollontai, A. 1980. *Selected Writings.* Trans. A. Holt. New York: Norton.

Lacan, J. 2006. "The Function and Field of Speech and Language in Psychoanalysis." In *Écrits*, B. Fink, trans. New York: Norton.

Lederman, R. 2016. "Fieldwork Double-Bound in Human Research-Ethics Reviews: Disciplinary Competence, or Regulatory Compliance and the Muting of Disciplinary Values." In *The Ethics Rupture: Exploring Alternatives to Formal Research-Ethics Review*, W. C. van den Hoonaard and A. Hamilton, eds., 43–72. Toronto, ON: University of Toronto Press.

Lenin, V. I. 1960 [1914]. "Conspectus of Hegel's Book *The Science of Logic*." In *Collected Works*, Vol. 38, 85–241. Moscow: Progress Publishers.

Marx, K. 1947 [1888]. "Theses on Feuerbach." In *The German Ideology*, C. J. Arthur, trans., 121–3. New York: International Publishers.

—— 1964 [1932]. *Economic and Philosophic Manuscripts of 1844.* Ed. D. J. Struik, trans. M. Miligan. New York: International Publishers.

—— 1974 [1852]. "The Eighteenth Brumaire of Louis Bonaparte." In *Surveys from Exile*, B. Fowkes, trans. Harmondsworth: Penguin.

—— 1975 [1859]. "'Preface' to *A Contribution to the Critique of Political Economy*". In *Early Writings*, R. Livingstone and G. Benton, eds., 424–8. Harmondsworth: Penguin.

—— 1973 [1939]. *Grundrisse.* Trans. M. Nicolaus. New York: Penguin.

—— 1981 [1894]. *Capital: A Critique of Political Economy*, vol. 3. Trans. D. Fernbach. New York: Vintage.

—— 1989 [1924]. "Letter to Vera Zasulich." In *Marx/Engels Collected Works*, vol. 24, 346–371. London: Lawrence and Wishart.

—— 1990 [1867]. *Capital: A Critique of Political Economy*, vol. 1. Trans. B. Fowkes. London: Penguin.

Nancy, J.-L. 1993. *The Experience of Freedom.* Trans. B. McDonald. Stanford, CA: Stanford University Press.

Piketty, T. 2014. *Capital in the 21st Century.* Trans. A. Goldhammer. Cambridge, MA: Harvard University Press.

Reagon, B. J. 1985. "Are My Hands Clean?" Washington, DC: Songtalk Publishing.

Resnick, S. and R. Wolff, 1987. *Knowledge and Class: A Marxian Critique of Political Economy.* Chicago, IL: University of Chicago Press.

—— 2002. *Class Theory and History: Capitalism and Communism in the USSR.* New York: Routledge.

Smith, A. 1976 [1776]. *An Inquiry into the Nature and Causes of the Wealth of Nations.* Chicago, IL: University of Chicago Press.

Spivak, G. C. 1985. "Scattered Speculations on the Question of Value." *Diacritics* 15 (4): 73–93.

—— 1987. "Speculations on Reading Marx: After Reading Derrida." In *Poststructuralism and the Question of History*, D. Attridge et al., eds., 30–62. Cambridge, MA: Cambridge University Press.

—— 2012. *An Aesthetic Education in the Era of Globalization.* Cambridge, MA: Harvard University Press.

—— 2014a. "Postcolonial Theory and the Specter of Capital." *Cambridge Review of International Affairs* 27 (1): 184–98.

—— 2014b. "General Strike." *Rethinking Marxism* 26 (1): 9–14.

———— 2017 (forthcoming) "Development." In *Political Concepts: A Critical Lexicon*, J. M. Bernstein, A. Ophir, and A. L. Stoler, eds. New York: Fordham University Press.

Steuart, J. 1966 [1767]. *An Inquiry into the Principles of Political Economy*. Ed. A. S. Skinner. London: Oliver and Boyd.

Wong, S. M. L. 2006. "China's Stock Market: A Marriage of Capitalism and Socialism." *Cato Journal* 26 (3): 389–424.

Zedong, M. 1971 [1927]. "Report on the Investigation of the Peasant Movement in Hunan (March 1927)." In *Selected Readings of Mao Zedong*. Beijing: Foreign Language Press.

18 Primitive accumulation and historical inevitability

A postcolonial critique

Anjan Chakrabarti, Stephen Cullenberg, and Anup Dhar

> Who is the ethical subject of humanism? The misadventures of international communism might teach us something about the violent consequences of imposing the most fragile part of Marx, the predictive Eurocentric scenario, upon large parts of the globe not historically centered in Europe.
>
> Gayatri Chakravorty Spivak (2012, 27)

Is there a hidden aspect of historical inevitability, a teleology, inscribed in Marx's *Capital*? One could argue that there is, and that would certainly qualify as one reading of *Capital*. In this paper, however, we invoke the writings of 'late' Marx to produce a different reading—of *Capital*, the book, and 'capital', the concept—a reading that in turn challenges the idea of 'historical inevitability.' The idea of historical inevitability—with regard either to either the *birth* of capitalism (marked by the concept of 'primitive accumulation' for example)—or the *demise* of capitalism (marked by concepts such as the 'falling rate of profit' or the 'auto-crisis' of capitalism) has haunted much of classical Marxism, a kind of Marxism deeply problematized by Stephen Resnick and Richard Wolff. In the encounter with the question of historical inevitability, our focus is on the concept of primitive accumulation[1] and its two differing renditions in Marx: first in *Capital* and then in 'The Russian Road/Question'—in other words, first in 'scientific' Marx (Althusser 1969) and then in 'late' Marx. We show how late Marx revised the concept of primitive accumulation and challenged the idea of historical inevitability. Building on Resnick and Wolff's incisive interpretation of Marx's *Capital* and our understanding of *late* Marx (Dhar 2003, 47–66; Chakrabarti and Dhar 2009, chs. 6 and 7) we offer a different interpretation of Marx's writings on primitive accumulation and a distinct theorization of primitive accumulation, both of which can be used to explore the phenomenon of capitalist development in its many complexities, especially in the global South.

The political import of the vexed question of historical inevitability cannot be underestimated in the context of the BRICS nations (Brazil, Russia,

India, China and South Africa) where this logic is often presented as a legitimate and powerful weapon, even within the mainstream Left, in the ongoing attempt to socially engineer the transition of these (putatively backward) economies to capitalism. The question of transition in such countries often gets resolved through the perspective of *historical inevitability* of a march of economy and society to capitalism. History triumphs over politics in this case.

The context of transition (to capitalism) in England and the West helped to engender Marx's 'critique of political economy' and 'theories of surplus value.' That of course does not make his theory false; his theorization of surplus labor and the defamiliarization of capitalism from its Political Economy moorings remain meaningful even to this day and in contexts beyond the regions mentioned above. No matter where capitalism thrives and notwithstanding its variegated forms, it remains by definition an exploitative organization of surplus (value) in the context of the commodity form of the material forces of production, labor power, and use values. Moreover, in his effort to theorize capitalism, Marx ended up giving us a clue to conceptualizing the 'economy' as diverse, in which capitalism is one social form among many that co-exist. If we reconceptualize capitalism in the manner Marx suggests in *Capital* and the *Grundrisse*—in terms of the organization of surplus labor in a dialectical space of mutual interaction with other processes including non-capitalist ones—we end up with a decentered, disaggregated understanding of the economy in which capitalism is a part and not the whole. This decentered notion of economy stands in sharp contrast to the predominant view in mainstream discourses (Left, neoclassical and otherwise) in which economy is synonymous with capitalism, a phenomenon Gibson-Graham (1996) call capitalocentrism. We contend that this reinterpretation of Marx was one of the central contributions of Resnick and Wolff (1987, 2002, 2006) who, by formalizing Marx's resistance to capitalocentrism and the Political Economy that formalizes it, helped to ensure that Marx would remain a specter to haunt the tragic consensus of our times.

It is true that there has been a resurrection in recent times *for* (Werner Bonefield 2001, Paul Zarembka 2001, Massimo De Angelis 2001, Jason Read 2002 to name a few) and *against* (Michael Hardt and Antonio Negri 2000) the concept of primitive accumulation; others such as David Harvey have favored replacing it with "accumulation by dispossession" (2004). In a detailed encounter with these positions elsewhere (Chakrabarti and Dhar 2009), we have shown that, notwithstanding their diverse and contending positions and their attempts to situate the concept of primitive accumulation in a non-teleological perspective, the concept remains trapped in either or both capitalocentrism and orientalism and as such continues to be under-theorized. While Resnick and Wolff's class-focused Marxian theory helped to develop a new evaluative space of economy and capitalism that challenges capitalocentrism, an adequate theorization of primitive accumulation requires that the theoretical frame be revised even further by revisiting and recasting the question of transition through an encounter with the orientalist dimension. Otherwise Marxism, no matter how much one deconstructs the economy and capitalism to circumvent capitalocentrism, will remain Eurocentric and orientalist (Dhar 2003; Chakrabarti, Dhar and Cullenberg 2012, ch. 1).

We contend that the clue to rethinking primitive accumulation was offered by a different Marx, which is also perhaps 'an Other Marx,' the Marx who revisits the question of the birth of capitalism, this time in the context of a different circumstance, history and space. This displacement of the given rendition of primitive accumulation is based on late Marx's encounter with the non-Western world in general and the Russian Mir in particular (Marx 1970, 1975, 1983, 1989). Our description of this particular encounter and engagement rests principally on Marx's correspondence with Vera Zasulich (Marx 1970). This was Marx's encounter with the Russian agrarian economy that was not capitalist. This was also Marx's (late) encounter with the question of the possible transition from a predominantly agrarian non-capitalist economy to an industrial capitalist economy in a largely non-European world. In other words, it was also about the birth of industrial capitalism through primitive accumulation. This experience made Marx revisit the question of *historical inevitability.* Late Marx thus comes to face economies and forms of life that were different (the Russian rural commune for example) and that could not be devalued or necessarily mutate along capitalist lines. Taking off from late Marx, we have retheorized and renamed this space as the world of the third, where world of the third is distinct from what has come to be known as third world, where world of the third is that which marks *differance*[2] with respect to (global) capitalism and the third world is that which is its 'lacking other' (Chakrabarti, Dhar and Cullenberg 2012). This turn to late Marx renders unfamiliar the *given* rendition of primitive accumulation.

Why revisit this engagement of Marx (a German refugee in England, coming from Western Europe) with Zasulich (a Russian, coming from Eastern Europe as also from a landmass that spills largely into Asia or perhaps Russia is that largely Asian landmass that spills into Europe)? It is because late Marx encounters primitive accumulation in a non-Western setting, having encountered it once before in the context of England and British rule in India. Departing from his view of primitive accumulation in the context of England, he asks again how primitive accumulation will take shape in a non-Western setting in general and how it would take shape in Russia in particular. Equally importantly for us, he grapples with the question of whether primitive accumulation is inevitable. Marx asks: Can we not bypass the process of primitive accumulation?

This encounter of Marx with the non-Western world can be taken as a precursor to a retheorization of primitive accumulation in the context of capitalist development. It also marks for us a *turning away* from the original

Marx, from a westernized Marx to what could be called an *ab*-original Marx, a Marx that is at the same time ab-original (i.e. other than the White Western Original) and also attuned to questions emanating from what could be called with qualifications the 'aboriginal world.'

The other genealogy of capitalism

Capitalism in the West, including England, progressed through the conduit of globalization under colonial conditions. That allowed on the one hand for capitalism to grow organically from within; on the other, this organic development was mediated through the restructuring of colonized spaces that in turn began the process of implanting a regulated capitalism from outside. In short, there are at least two genealogies of capitalism, one whose organization was driven from within and the other a consequence of a drive from outside. Consequently, the societal configurations it produced and the opposition that capitalism faced in the West and those in the colonial countries could not have been the same. The juxtaposition or perhaps collapse of these two historically distinct entry points in the study of capitalism is a mistake. It is a mistake because the juxtaposition or collapse means a non-appreciation of 'coloniality' in the theorization of economy and capitalism. The significance of 'coloniality' and then 'development' in the theorization of capitalism is not merely spatial/territorial but can be traced to aspects of Orientalism, where the invocation of a 'lacking/devalued other' (in this case third world) in relation to the West marked the quintessential western/modernist rationale. The overdetermination of capitalocentrism and orientalism produced the dualism of modern capitalism (as normal) and the other as traditional/pre-capitalism—hence abnormal, hence in need of assimilation/ annihilation.

The point however is not whether the (post)colonial experience is acknowledged in the 'evaluative space' (as is now quite common); the issue is the evaluative space *itself*. To have that Other canvass in the evaluative space is what we see as the *post-colonial imperative* in the process of (re) theorizing the idea of capitalism and its underlying political economy. The problem is compounded by the weight of what could be called the western-ness (or Eurocentrism) of extant Marxism. Much of Marxism has remained unaware of this problem (one can call it *sanctioned ignorance*), been at times dismissive (*untheorized arrogance* as in the case of debates on the Asiatic mode of production) or anxious and afraid of facing it. The overwhelming body of western Marxist work—and we say western with some trepidation—shares with the liberals some anxiety on the question of the (post)colonial. Finally, one must contend with the changing nature of capitalism at present; when capitalism is taking a global form from within, contemporary global capitalism displaces and changes the cartography of these economies in ways that are distinct from the phase indicative of the rise of western capitalism in which capitalism acquired its global form through colonialism. The transition of the post-colonial countries is indicative of an overdetermined and contradictory space marked by the pastness of capitalism (that took shape first through colonialism and then development) as also the futureness of global capitalism seen as procreating from within rather than from outside. The challenge is to theorize the idea of capitalism in the context of this transitional cusp and in a manner that unpacks its deep-seated fissures and conflicts. To do this, one must confront the question of the (post-colonial) Other as a theoretical impasse. Our work is a contingent, provisional attempt to attend to this impasse through the invocation of the concept 'world of the third' (Chakrabarti, Dhar and Cullenberg 2012, 2016; Callari 2016).

In short, if one is to reconceptualize primitive accumulation—primitive accumulation in existing form as not just an inalienable moment in the birth of capitalism but as underlying an orientalist representation and description of the Other—then there is a need to examine capitalist development in a critical mold, which also involves producing a different conception of economy such that it can be rescued from its totalizing moorings in capitalism. Resnick and Wolff do precisely this. In the southern context, a context marked by both capitalocentrism and orientalism, we try to problematize the equally totalizing idea and figure of 'third world,' through the invocation of what we have called a counter-concept: world of the third.

In the present context of capitalist development, such an intervention shifts the terms of reference from third world-ism *to* world of the third, and in so doing questions the concept and process of development itself— development understood in terms of the transition of the pre-capitalist third world in the image of the modern capitalist West. It thus imparts a spin to what has hitherto been considered necessary or historically inevitable; in the process it questions what was deemed as developmental in the milieu of third worldism; it also puts to question the somewhat naturalized nature of the violence of primitive accumulation, violence that looks justified if one looks at it from the perspective of the *lacking other* of third world, violence that looks totally unjustified if seen from the perspective of the world of the third or the worldview of the third. The violence of primitive accumulation was hitherto deemed necessary and inevitable, and an integral part of historical progress in a third worldist milieu. From the context and perspective of world of the third, that violence is deemed unjust, and through that a critique of violence embodied in capitalist development emerges. In the process, one moves from a *description* of the bloody birth of capitalism or *prescription* for the inevitable annihilation of the lacking other of third world, to a critique of primitive accumulation itself.

A brief theoretical summary of the concept of capitalist development is necessary to organize our subsequent intervention on primitive accumulation.

The epistemology of capitalist development

One of the values of Resnick and Wolff's reinterpretation of Marxism is its class-focused approach, whereby the economy is constituted by the combined effects of overdetermined and contradictory class processes (i.e., varieties of capitalist and non-capitalist class processes) appearing in conjunction with non-class processes and giving rise to numerous socioeconomic forms. Because it is decentered and disaggregated, the economy cannot be reduced to capitalism, which in turn paves the way for the following question: How can a decentered and disaggregated economy be transmuted into a 'dual economy'? Does this transmutation involve the reduction of the whole of the economy—a rather complex, contradictory and overdetermined whole—to a *part* called capitalism? Indeed, the epistemological imperative of economic dualism makes a particular class process—the capitalist class process—the pre-given privileged center of the economy. Such capitalocentrism reduces the otherwise decentered and disaggregated economy into two homogenous wholes—capitalism and the disposable remainder, 'non-capitalism' (Gibson-Graham 1996).

This dual economy model opens for analysts, policy makers and practitioners a perspective to relocate the otherwise decentered and disaggregated economy through the prism of capitalism; a dualist economic structure is thus constitutionally ingrained within a monist worldview. Notably, countries in the 'South' have the additional legacy of orientalism, which is often not given due importance in the rendition of the economy. Orientalism structured the way the 'South'-ern (economies) came to be seen through the cultural-political experience of colonialism. Referring to Homi Bhabha's definition of colonial discourse, Escobar noted that

> although some of the terms of this definition might be more applicable to the colonial context strictly speaking, the development discourse is governed by the same principles; it has created an extremely efficient apparatus for producing knowledge about, and the exercise of power over, the Third World.
>
> (2012, 9)

Weaving its way into development in the post-colonial phase, orientalism turned the dualistic frame into one that not only differentiated between capitalism and non-capitalism (the hallmark of capitalocentrism), but where non-capitalism is rendered devalued/backward/traditional. Consequently, the term 'non' is replaced by 'pre,' where 'pre' is that which is stuck in archaic time-space; non-capitalism is reduced to *pre*-capitalism. Thus the dualism of capitalist class process and pre-capitalist class process becomes at times the dualism of modern/tradition, city/rural and industry/agriculture, or formal/informal. The category 'third world' emerges as placeholder and shorthand for the 'second in all of the above.' This foregrounding of a pre-capitalist third world/other in turn forecloses the language-logic-ethos-experience of the world of the third/ Other (Chakrabarti, Dhar and Cullenberg 2012; Chakrabarti 2014).What however is the world of the third? The world of the third is constituted by a multitude of class and non-class processes that includes a variety of non-capitalist class processes materializing in its overdetermination with other economic as also cultural, political and natural processes.[3] World of the third societies conceptually-territorially *differ* from and *defer* capitalism. As we shall explore now, it *is* the world of the third, and *not* the third world that is the target of primitive accumulation. Rather, third world is the category that legitimizes primitive accumulation.

Primitive accumulation in *capital*

Building on the case of England as his site of analysis, Marx defined primitive accumulation as:

> [T]he historical process of divorcing the producer from the means of production. It appears as primitive because it forms the *pre-history* of capital and of the mode of production corresponding to capital.
>
> (1990, 875)

This process thus involves two transformations. First, it transforms the extant social means of production and subsistence into the service of creating capital and, second, it transforms the immediate producers (i.e., peasants, attached principally to land-agriculture as also the artisans, attached to their tools and their produce) into (free) wage-laborers (Marx 1990, 873–74). The end result of the two is the creation of a potential labor market where labor power can be (freely) exchanged, thereby acquiring the status of a commodity. For a worker to be 'free' under capitalism means that she must not own or possess independent access to means of production and subsistence, and she must be detached from the shared environment that previously sustained her forms of life. Primitive accumulation forwards a theory of how a condition of existence for the origin and expansion of capitalist production—labor power—is created as a commodity:

> The capitalist system pre-supposes the *complete separation* between the workers and the ownership of the conditions for the realization of their labor. As soon as capitalist production stands on its own legs, it not only maintains this separation, but reproduces it on a *continually extending* scale.
>
> (Marx 1990, 874)

How could such a massive change in conditions of human existence be achieved, and who would take the lead to enact it? Here, Marx referred to multiple sources, including colonial plunder, which can be held responsible for producing the desired effect of 'separation.' Following an interpretation of Marx by Read (2002), separation by itself does not lead to the creation of wage labor. It is followed by moments of "bloody legislation" designed to impose strict control over the disenfranchised peasants and artisans and the normalization exercise a la Foucault operating through ideological apparatuses a la Althusser that "obliterates the memory of the past modes of production as well as any traces of the violent foundation of the new mode of production" (45). The historic process of primitive accumulation even in its classical form is long and would see many dynamic variations in forms of wage labor before it settles down to one conducive to the workings of a modern capitalist enterprise in a generalized commodity production system. We are aware of warnings that the labor market in post-colonial countries such as India does not represent the classical market for labor power that was supposed to be the target of primitive accumulation, but this might appear to be a hasty conclusion if one takes a longer and a more expansive view of history. Moreover, one needs to consider that in countries such as India peasants may have more options concerning their access to, or ownership of, means of production including land, which, due to different historical circumstances, was not available in settings such as nineteenth-century England or twentieth-century Soviet Union. Therefore, it is not correct to say that primitive accumulation and hence the history of labor will unfold in the same way, as Marx warned, in all countries.

The above three moments of force (involving aspects of violent separation, disciplining and normalization) are telescoped in the process of primitive accumulation and unfold through an ensemble of repressive and ideological apparatuses. This was Marx's response to the classical political economists and their modern incarnation in neo-classical economics, which represents the birth and evolution of capitalism as simply a matter of thrift and entrepreneurship and in which the element of force is purportedly absent or accidental (Perelman 2000, 2001). In contrast to the latter's a-historical reading of capitalism, Marx's analysis is a reminder of the *social and historical constitution* of capitalism in the past and the present. In this history, the dissolution of the feudal mode of production, the violent origin of the capitalist mode of production and the history of colonialism, on their own and in relation to one another, defined the make-up of capitalism as also its specificity across time and space.

While accepting the contribution of Marx, there are by now many dissenting voices to this rather teleological rendition of primitive accumulation. However, the issue we are pursuing here is not merely one of historical proof (of primitive accumulation) but of its theorization in the context of transition in late industrializing countries, including those with a colonial legacy. To that end, we now examine late Marx's attitude toward the 'Russian question' to map out the *turn* Marx gave to his initial rendition of primitive accumulation.

Primitive accumulation in late Marx

Confronted with what is known as the 'Russian question' Marx revised his position on the question of historical inevitability.[4] To begin with, Marx clearly expressed his displeasure with any translation of the genesis of capitalism in Western Europe into a general historico-philosophical theory of either development or transition, imposed by fate on all people.

> I expressly limited the "historical inevitability" of this process to the countries of Western Europe. Why so?... [W]e are dealing here with the *transformation of one form of private property into another form of private property*. The land tilled by the Russian peasants never having been their *private property*, how is this to be applied in their case?
>
> [D]oes this mean that the development of the "land commune" must necessarily follow the same lines under all circumstances? Certainly not. Its constitutive form allows the following alternative: either the element of private property implied in it gains the upper hand over the collective element, or vice versa. Everything depends upon the historical background in which it finds itself...Both these solutions are possible *a priori*, but both obviously require entirely different historical environments.
>
> (1970, 152 and 156)

One needs to ask: Does this go against the grain of the argument that seeks to place primitive accumulation as a necessary sub-moment of history, as an event that in facilitating a move from the feudal to the capitalist mode of production will take society one stage closer in the direction of communism? It is necessary to confront this position since primitive accumulation was used by Marxists to legitimize an array of policies pointing to a social engineering of hitherto and erstwhile 'socialist' nations; we are pointing to instances of 'socialist' primitive accumulation in the former Soviet Union and the current one in China to facilitate capitalism in the name of 'socialism with Chinese characteristics.'

To this logic of inevitability encompassing even the Radical terrain, Marx would say this about the Russian situation:

> At the same time as the commune is being bled and tortured and its land made barren and poor, the literary lackeys of the "new pillars of society" refer ironically to the wounds which have been inflicted on the commune as symptoms of its spontaneous decrepitude. They claim that it is dying a natural death and the kindest thing would be to put an end to its agony. Here we are no longer dealing with a problem to be solved, but quite simply with an enemy who must be defeated. In order to save the Russian commune there must be a Russian revolution. And the Russian government and the "new pillars of

society" are doing their best to prepare the masses for such a catastrophe. If the revolution takes place at the right time, if it concentrates all its forces to ensure the free development of the village commune, the latter will soon emerge as the regenerative force in Russian society and as something superior to those countries which are still enslaved by the capitalist regime.

(1970, 161)

Through his particular rendition of primitive accumulation in the Russian context—primitive accumulation as violence, as unjust—Marx can be understood as deconstructing the idea of the inescapable historicity and the scientific inevitability tied to the origin and evolution of capitalism and industrial society. He is also unveiling in the process the 'masked political character' of capitalism and primitive accumulation as also the 'not-so-hidden hostility' of the modern West to what we have called the world of the third.

This we believe is a landmark revision that late Marx is announcing. Three aspects of the revision can be highlighted. First, when faced with the question of whether the 'event' of primitive accumulation should be accommodated or not in Russia's transition path, Marx seems to be veering toward a clear 'no.' He thus turns what was previously the simple historic fact of primitive accumulation into a critical political concept. This turn in Marx is part and parcel of an unambiguously critical position vis a vis capitalism. Given that primitive accumulation announces the birth of capitalism, it is to be opposed. The Marxist description of primitive accumulation must not be a defense of it. This shift in Marx takes final shape when in the Preface to the Russian edition of the Communist Manifesto, he writes: "...present Russian communal land ownership can serve as a point of departure for a communist development."

Second, Marx's analysis provided the decisive shift in understanding primitive accumulation as a multifaceted and continual process rather than a once-and-for-all big bang program. In the case of England, as we explained, Marx emphasized the expropriation of land, as a *condition* of primitive accumulation. However, following his Russian studies, he wondered whether expropriating land from the peasantry was a necessary condition for primitive accumulation. Is expropriating land from the peasantry the same as expropriating the tillers of the land?

In order to expropriate the tillers of the land it is not necessary to drive them from their land as was the case in England and elsewhere; nor is it necessary to abolish communal property by an usake. Just go and deprive the peasants of the product of their labor beyond a certain point and you will not be able to chain them to their fields even with the help of your police and army.

(Marx 1970, 159)

This marks a significant departure from a property-centric reading of primitive accumulation toward emphasizing the importance of the multi-faceted conditions shaping *forms of (rural) life*. Rather than simply land or forcible eviction, Marx was referring to policy-induced alterations such that the world of the third societies, as referred to in an earlier quote, grow anemic and meet their end. Primitive accumulation also concerns how the conditions of existence governing world of the third societies can be changed in multiple ways (through unfavorable modification in terms of trade, debt, knowledge, technology, capital-labor ratio, access to water, forests, etc.) in order to bring about a major *dislocation* (see Chakrabarti and Dhar 2009 for the distinction between displacement and dislocation) in forms of life such that they finally get dismantled; in the present and future, they disappear, as if, of their 'own free will' dying a 'natural death' even if the cause may be the wounds inflicted in some past. In the end, there is no recognition of the wound that is inflicted and only the decrepit body remains visible, a very familiar story even in today's transition economies.

Some immediate consequences of this revision follows. One, primitive accumulation is better understood as an ever-changing menu of altered conditions of existence that leads to a gradual and at times quick dismantling of world of the third forms of life. This also reveals that there is no *one* trajectory of primitive accumulation. Rather, depending upon the conditions of existence being altered in such societies, primitive accumulation would take different paths and forms. Next, one needs to revise the idea of the 'complete' at the moment of *separation* (which Marx initially seems to suggest in his case study of England). Thus, there is no need for emphasizing complete separation from the means of production such as land. Separation itself needs to be rethought, which in this case would appear to be 'separation' from any conditions of existence (such as from the ability to draw water for agriculture or from cash to make payments as in done through demonetisation policy in India) that in turn would ensure that the world of the third subjects including peasants and artisans are unable to reproduce their extant forms of life or what they seek. The fact that world of the third subjects, even if they may have ownership of resources including land, are unable to reproduce their livelihood should be a sufficient condition for securing their formation and existence as wage labor. Therefore, the purported direct connection between creation of wage labor and loss of ownership of property needs to be revisited.

Third, Marx's Russian turn marks a move away from the capitalocentric-orientalist approach to development. The Russian transition discussion posed the difficult issue of whether Russia should take the path of capitalist development as it had unfolded in England. Marx's answer is unambiguous. One need not be enslaved to capitalism in thinking of paths of development. Rather, the *path* itself must be open to thinking. To *think*, the path then opens the field for alternative constructions and deviations from the current one. It opens the very question of transition as a theoretical concept.

Having many paths to development requires at least a theorization of economy that is decentered and dis-aggregated, actually and potentially. Did Marx give us any clue regarding the need to reconceptualize the economy as decentered and disaggregated? Referring to land communes in Russia, which he saw as the point of reference and departure for alternative constructions of economy and society, Marx observes:

> .... a commune in which the arable land has become private property, whereas forests, pasture and waste land, etc., have remained communal property.

And, one page later:

> [A]lthough arable land remains communal property, it is redivided periodically among members of the land commune in such a way that each person cultivates by himself the fields assigned to him and appropriates the fruits of his own labor, whereas in the archaic communities production was communal and only the products were distributed.
>
> (1970, 154–55)

In land communes, then, Marx is clearly pointing to the presence of independent class enterprises and, for 'archaic' communities, communist class enterprises. In fact, given the form of 'community economies' that prevailed in Russia then and to which Marx was referring, many other kinds of class enterprises could very well have been present, including those with communitic class process. Communitic class process refers to two possible scenarios where (i) even as direct producers may collectively (C) produce surplus, only one of these producers (A) would appropriate the surplus and the rest would be excluded, and (ii) even as direct producers perform surplus labor individually (A), the appropriation is done collectively (C) such that nobody is excluded from participation in it. The former constitutes CA communitic class process and the latter AC communitic class process (Chaudhury and Chakrabarti 2000). An example of a CA communitic class process is a family based agricultural farm in which all members labor but where only one member, say, the male head of the family who also is a direct producer alongside others appropriates the surplus individually by excluding the rest (this is in contrast to slave, feudal and capitalist class forms in which the appropriators are not direct producers of surplus); an example of AC communitic class process is an agricultural arrangement where farmers farm individually in their respective lands but decide to come together to appropriate the surplus collectively (this is in contrast to the communist class form where a collective performs and appropriates surplus). In *Letters from* Russia, Rabindranath

Tagore reflected on his experience in the Soviet Union where he had observed class-organizational forms-farms of AC communitic kinds, kinds that were representative of the related dyad: *'collective appropriation'-'individual production.'* Tagore saw such class-organizations as solutions to the contradictions inherent in the couple 'forced collectivization/free individualism.' In addition, other exploitative class organizations such as slave, feudal and even small-scale capitalist enterprises may prevail on their own or in tandem with other class enterprises in such spaces.

Having moved away from the nineteenth century discourse of historical inevitability, we interpret Marx as pointing to independent and communist class enterprises (and other arrangements) with reference to land organizations and a theorizing of primitive accumulation as a process of dismantling existing or possible forms of non-capitalist existences. What this calls for is the need to consider the presence of different class arrangements within world of the third societies so that both the form of primitive accumulation and resistance to it can be precisely located and analyzed. This demands a movement from (1) the categorization of the economy as a homogenous body to that which is decentered and disaggregated and (2) the decrepit, devalued stature of 'other' forms of life that later came to be defined as third world to the differing-deferring Other, world of the third.

The first of these items entails a different conception of the economy that cannot be captured in terms of the 'mode of production' approach in the classical Marxian mold. To this end, Gibson-Graham (2008) urge us to relocate the *place* of the economy away from its capitalocentric moorings. Resnick and Wolff's class-focused approach, paving the way for a decentered and disaggregated economy, becomes decisive. This is crucial because the concept third world reduces the heterogeneity of the world of the third into stereotypical imagery—the 'victim third' (poor, marginalized, excluded, ignorant, etc.), the 'evil third' (hysterical, irrational, archaic, etc.) and 'the redundant other' (projects of Gandhianism, post-capitalism, post-development, communism, etc.). Once incarcerated within third worldism, primitive accumulation cannot but be necessary. It is only when we have relocated the 'third world other' into the 'world of the third Other' that new possibilities in contrast and opposition to capitalist development emerge. Movement away from capitalocentrism is thus necessary but not sufficient in the context of transitional economies. One must also confront, in conjunction with it, orientalism.

We however do not consider world of the third societies as desirable per se. There is no question of valorizing world of the third societies. In the process of constructing this conceptual-territorial space, no claim is made regarding its site of existence (rural or urban), its economic status (it could be rich or poor, exploitative or non-exploitative), its cultural ethos (it could be fundamentalist in some axis or more than liberal in others), its political institutions (it could be closed or open ended with regard to rules of authority and control) and its relation with nature (it could be friendly or non-friendly toward its surrounding environment). Importantly, then, there is no *a priori* value judgment (good, bad, useful) attached to the world of the third. The idea of the world of the third offers us a concept of the *outside*; an outside to the circuits of global capital, both spatially and perspective-wise.

The class-focused understanding of world of the third renders communist class enterprises and AC type communitic class enterprises, large and small scale, viable possibilities. Moreover, taking Marx's broad canvas into consideration, the struggle for the collective organization and action in agrarian societies must be conjoined with the struggle for the collective in industrial societies such that "the return of modern societies to a superior form of the 'archaic' type of collective ownership and collective production" (Marx 1970, 157) is achieved. Marx thus reversed what by the classical historical inevitability thesis is termed 'progressive' into the 'regressive,' and the 'regressive' into the progressive.' His clue also carries the important lesson that the choice for transition economies need not be between modern capitalism and third world, but one could also think of the path of a struggle against capitalism combined with a reconstruction of world of the third toward a post-capitalist society. The central issue is not 'historical inevitability' but a position based on justice arguments and options to access and shape moral subject-positions geared toward unalienated life (Bilgrami 2014).

Recasting the theory of primitive accumulation

Against the backdrop of our interpretation of Marx's encounter with the 'The Russian question,' one could ask: What would a theoretical framework look like that (1) questions capitalocentrism and orientalism, (2) generates a decentered and heterogeneous understanding of the 'what are not capitalist' spaces (disaggregating these into numerous modes of performance, appropriation, distribution and receipt of surplus, and from within such disaggregated spaces communist and communitic forms—existing and imagined—can take shape), (3) embodies different historical paths of primitive accumulation and hence of capitalism in a manner that unpacks the 'regressive' substance in the so-called 'progressive' logic advanced by the protagonists of development discourse, and (4) permits a political standpoint based on the justice considerations of non-exploitation, fair distribution and development justice?

In our examination conducted over the years, working through all of these features, we have tried to advance a Marxian framework that deploys *class* as processes of surplus labor to produce an evaluative space containing an assortment of economic arrangements—capitalist and 'what are not capitalist.' It is to also open the discursive terrain to the idea of the *world of the third*—world of the third as the *outside* to the circuits of global capital—as against third world, where third world is what the 'new pillars of society' assume as and attest to be in a process of natural decay due to its self-imposed decrepitude and where 'the kindest thing would be to put an end to the agony of the terminally ill.' We have hence been trying to reinterpret the position of (late) Marx, to relocate the place of primitive accumulation and in the process rethink its relation with (global) capitalism and the world of the third. Let us present a brief summary of what may emerge.

We make two observations regarding our conceptualization of primitive accumulation. First, and this is especially common in the context of the southern countries, there is nothing that prevents a subject from holding polymorphous class and non-class positions. Any theory must incorporate (and not erase as is often the case) such polymorphisms. For example, a wage laborer (say, working in the city) could also be the (absentee) owner-appropriator of an agricultural farm. Interestingly, he occupies multiple positions: that of an appropriator of surplus value in the agricultural farm, distributor of surplus value in the same farm and performer of surplus labor in an industrial enterprise. As explained earlier, there is nothing necessarily antithetical between a property-owning individual (even with attachment to land) and a wage laborer; driving the person's livelihood below the subsistence basket of goods and services is enough to reduce him to a wage laborer. As intricate interlinkages between agriculture and rural non-farm employment or agriculture and industry develop, the multiplication of such varied interlinked positions occupied by a segment of rural individuals should not surprise us. Primitive accumulation that emphasizes the exclusivity of pure wage labor (as against property ownership), as in the classical rendition, would run into trouble in capturing and explaining the complexity of such phenomena. In contrast, our frame is able to consistently integrate multiple subject positions and their shifting interlinkages.

Second, it is becoming evident that the old thesis promising a breakdown of agriculture resulting from the logic of growth through industrialization has undergone some modifications, at least in countries such as India. The promised transformation from agrarian society toward a full-fledged industrialized capitalist economy has taken quite an unpredictable turn as far as the promised accommodation of 'surplus' rural labor force into the modern capitalist economy is concerned. A remarkable turn in the discourse of development has been to clear the growing modern capitalist sector from any responsibility in integrating the migrating population from agriculture into its ambit, which previously remained one of the central theses of not only the (Lewisian) dual economy imagination, but also the promise of primitive accumulation wherever it appears. Whether due to the rapid rise in population, the labor-substituting technological changes, simply the inability of industrial capitalist economy to grow quickly enough, the perverse nature of the ongoing breakdown in agriculture or a combination of all these factors, the point remains that the accommodation of workers from agriculture toward large-scale industrial production has not materialized.

Instead, another so-called third world 'traditional' sector, dubbed as the informal sector, has grown in volume and importance in the last 50 years absorbing, by default, a large reservoir of people coming from agriculture who are unable to find work in the capitalist industrial economy; the informal sector can be seen as a safety net that can potentially absorb 'leftover' populations from agriculture. The informal sector can be split into two where one part—through outsourcing, subcontracting, offshoring and body shopping—has emerged as economic supplement to (global) capitalist enterprises while another part remains *outside* the circuits-camp of (global) capital (Chakrabarti, Dhar and Cullenberg 2012). The second part of the informal sector making up the world of the third exists in urban as well as rural areas. This testifies to the further point that primitive accumulation does not simply work with respect to the world of the third agriculture, but also the world of the third informal sector where the latter's conditions of existence are expropriated or reset to facilitate the control and march of (global) capital (Chakrabarti, Chaudhury and Cullenberg 2009).

Given these clarifications, we have made an effort to rethink the transition of economies such as India through the mutually intersecting, reinforcing and compensating axes of neoliberal forms of globalization, global capitalism and inclusive development (Chakrabarti, Dhar and Dasgupta 2015). As part of this transition, the economy that is otherwise decentered and disaggregated is relocated into the mutually constitutive dyad of on the one hand the circuits-camp of global capital and on the other the world of the third. The otherwise diverse economy is represented, through the combination of capitalocentrism and orientalism, as a dual framework in which the world of the third is displaced as lacking/devalued qua third world or its metonymic substitutes such as 'social capital' or hapless community a la World Bank. The relocation of the lived world of the third as third world is decisive for global capital to dredge its way through into the privileged center in the logic of development. Seen from above, development qua progress is now represented as the march and expansion of circuits-camp of global capital, which, as it unfolds, cannot avoid a confrontation with world of the third societies that are now threatened with 'separation' from their erstwhile cluster of concepts, events, mental state and identities that underpin their forms of life. Evidently, since the logic of capitalist development is founded on securing, facilitating and expanding the circuits-camp of global capital, the process of primitive accumulation that works continuously on what we call the world of the third appears in multifaceted forms. That is, the expansion of the net of global capitalism disturbs-dislocates-displaces the world of the third in diverse ways and, as explained earlier, through various strategies and means. Broadly, the forms could be divided into two: the non-classical and the classical form (Chakrabarti and Dhar 2009, chs. 7–8).

The *non-classical* form pertains to changing one or two conditions of existence of world of the third societies (such as changing the ground levels of water through the sudden setting up of the production unit of a global industrial capitalist enterprise in a rural area) such that the world of the third has no alternative but to first be dislocated and then disintegrated. The *classical form* takes the form of wholesale displacement of world of the third societies and life forms; it has been much discussed. Either way, primitive accumulation is impacting world of the third economies such as India massively and in the process reshaping the circuits-camp of global capital and the world of the third at a frantic pace. However, the more mundane non-classical forms of primitive accumulation (that imply not direct land acquisition but other avenues of dislocation of world of the third societies by changing their conditions of existence) unfolding rapidly are not really accounted for by the policy makers; their discursive unaccountability renders them absent from the policy making paradigm of the state. In India's transition, for example, the high growth rate regime achieved through the expansion of circuits-camp of global capital and the growing resistance of world of the third subjects to what they see as injustice has initiated a rethinking of the rationale and models of land acquisition as also of the subsequent legal changes for land acquisition. In so far as the Indian state is considered, it is one form of primitive accumulation—direct land acquisition—that has particularly caught attention (not least because of fierce resistance movements). However, primitive accumulation through the non-classical route could and does unfold intermittently and unevenly in dispersed time and space, producing varied processes that turns world of the third societies into anemic and decrepit (hence disposable) existences of third worldliness.

Amidst high economic growth, India's long run agrarian crisis and rural disintegration symbolized by recurrent events of distress migration, indebtedness, land loss, farmers suicide, environment degradation, etc., stand as an example of this process of transition built on producing the decrepit imagery of the third world and facilitating its torturous process of decay and decline. The informal sector that keeps growing as the ghostly-ghastly shadow of the circuits-camp of global capital presents an analogous picture of a struggling economy; it awaits the historically inevitable end of formalization as projected and actively sought by International Labour Organization and the present Indian state, the latest being the latter's attempt to hollow out the vast unofficial informal economic space (where almost all the transactions take place through cash) by sucking out liquidity through the demonetization policy. Whether it is over an entire region or taking place intermittently across a region, primitive accumulation thus symbolizes an assortment of dislocations that are an integral component of development logic and that in turn enable an expansion of the circuits-camp of global capital. It also never allows the world of the third to settle into what Marx called "normal development"—development experienced, understood, imagined, conceptualized, practiced and modeled by the world of the third itself or on its own terms. It was a point emphasized by Marx, especially after the turn to the Russian Road, but one that was not greatly valued by his followers.

Acknowledgment

We are thankful to Richard McIntyre for his comments and observations.

Notes

1 In the German original of *Capital*, Volume 1, Marx used the term *Ursprüngliche Akkumulation*, which could be translated as *original accumulation* or primeval accumulation – a form of accumulation that is present at the origin of the capitalist class process. However, *Ursprüngliche Akkumulation* was translated as "so-called primitive accumulation" and "the secret of primitive accumulation" in the English editions of the German original produced by Progress Publishers, a translation that relegated this form of accumulation to the past or pre-history of capitalism. While we agree on the importance of using the term 'original accumulation,' we use the term primitive accumulation here to avoid confusion and to ensure continuity in the long-standing debates we address.
2 Following Derrida (1982), *differance* is the mutually constitutive state of *difference, differing* and *deferring*.
3 Strictly speaking, it can also include capitalist class processes of certain types, such as the simple reproduction type (Chakrabarti, Dhar and Cullenberg 2016).
4 Marx (1970, 75, 83, 89); Bailey and Llobera (1981); Shanin (1983); Dhar (2003, 47–66); and Chakrabarti and Dhar (2009, ch. 7).

References

Althusser, L. 1969. *For Marx*. Trans. B. Brewster. London: New Left Books.

Bailey, A. M. and J. P. Llobera. 1981. *The Asiatic Mode of Production: Science and Politics*. Georgetown: Routledge/Chapman and Hall.

Bilgrami, A. 2014. *Secularism, Identity and Enchantment*. Cambridge: Harvard University Press.

Bonefield, W. 2001. "The Permanence of Primitive Accumulation: Commodity Fetishism and Social Constitution." *The Commoners*: September.

Callari, A. 2016. "Marxism from the Outside: A Take on World of the Third and Global Capitalism." *Rethinking Marxism* 28 (2): 263–70.

Chakrabarti, A. 2014. "A Post-Colonial Critique of Economic Dualism and Its Politics." *Journal of Contemporary Thought* 40 (Winter): 158–65.

Chakrabarti, A. and A. Dhar. 2009. *Rethinking Dislocation and Development: From Third World to World of the Third*. Routledge: London and New York.

Chakrabarti, A., A. Chaudhury, and S. Cullenberg. 2009. "Global Order and the New Economic Policy in India: The (Post)colonial Formation of the Small-Scale Sector." *Cambridge Journal of Economics* 33 (6): 1169–86.

Chakrabarti, A., A. Dhar, and S. Cullenberg. 2012. *Global Capitalism and World of the Third*. World View Press: New Delhi.

—— 2016. "(Un)doing Marxism from the Outside." *Rethinking Marxism* 28 (2): 276–94.

Chakrabarti, A. Dhar, and B. Dasgupta. 2015. *The Indian Economy in Transition: Globalization, Capitalism and Development.* Delhi: Cambridge University Press.

Chaudhury, A. and A. Chakrabarti. 2000."The Market Economy and Marxist Economists: Through the Lens of a Housewife." *Rethinking Marxism* 12 (2): 81–103.

DeAngelis, M. 2001. "Marx and Primitive Accumulation: The Conscious Character of Capital's 'Enclosures.'" *The Commoners*: September.

Derrida, J. 1982. *Margins of Philosophy.* Chicago: University of Chicago Press.

Dhar, A. 2003. "Other Marx: Marx's Other." In *Other Voice*, Kolkata, 47–66.

Escobar, A. 2012 [1995]. *Encountering Development: The Making and Unmaking of the Third World.* Princeton: Princeton University Press.

Gibson-Graham, J. K. 1996. *The End of Capitalism (as we knew it): A Feminist Critique of Political Economy.* New York and London: Blackwell.

——— 2008. "Place-Based Globalism: A New Imaginary of Revolution." *Rethinking Marxism* 20 (4): 659–64.

Hardt, M. and A. Negri. 2000. *Empire.* Cambridge: Harvard University Press.

Harvey, D. 2004. "The New Imperialism: On Spatio-Temporal Fixes and Accumulation by Dispossession." *Socialist Register* 40: 63–87.

Marx, K. 1970. "First Draft of the Reply to V. I. Zasulich's Letter." In *Karl Marx and Friedrich Engels, Selected Works,* Volume three. Moscow: Progress Publishers.

——— 1975. "Letter to Otechestvenniye Zapiski." In *Marx-Engels Selected Correspondence*, S. Ryazanskaya, ed. Moscow: Progress Publishers.

——— 1983. "Marx-Zasulich Correspondence: Letters and Drafts." In *Late Road and the Russian Road: Marx and the Peripheries of Capitalism,* T. Shanin, ed. New York: Monthly Review Press.

——— 1989. *In Pre-Capitalist Economic Formations.* Trans. J. Cohen. New York: International Publishers.

——— 1990. *Capital.* Vol. 1. Trans. B. Fowkes. London: Penguin Books.

Perelman, M. 2000. *The Invention of Capitalism.Classical Political Economy and the Secret History of Primitive Accumulation.* Durham: Duke University Press.

——— 2001. "The Secret History of Primitive Accumulation and Classical Political Economy." *The Commoners*: September.

Read, J. 2002. "Primitive Accumulation: The Aleatory Formation of Capitalism." *Rethinking Marxism* 14 (2): 24–49.

Resnick, S. and Wolff, R. 1987. *Knowledge and Class.* Chicago: University of Chicago Press.

——— 2002. *Class Theory and History: Capitalism and Communism in the USSR.* New York: Routledge.

———, eds. 2006. *New Departures in Marxian Theory.* London and New York: Routledge.

Shanin, T., ed. 1983. *Late Marx and the Russian Road; Marx and the Peripheries of Capitalism.* London, Melbourne and Henley: Routledge and Kegan.

Spivak, G. 2012. "More on Power/Knowledge." *The Spivak Reader.* D. Landry and G. Maclean, eds. New York: Routledge.

Zarembeka, P. 2002. "Primitive Accumulation in Marxism: Historical or Transhistorical Separation from Means of Production." *The Commoners*: March.

19 Draining the "blood energy"

Destruction of independent production and creation of migrant workers in post-reform China

Joseph Medley and Lorrayne Carroll

Introduction

Stephen Resnick told fantastic stories. Early in his career, he was particularly adept at fashioning arguments that questioned neoclassical economic discourse in order to advance his ideas about developing economies (Hymer and Resnick 1969). As he altered his perspective, he began explicitly to criticize, then to supersede, the limits those forms of discourse imposed (Resnick 1975). Later, in collaboration with Richard Wolff and many of their students at the University of Massachusetts, he developed a powerful new rhetorical approach to building economic theories, emphasizing class processes and transitions as key concepts for interrogating and understanding the narratives that underwrite economic history and development; these processes shift, coalesce, disperse, and reassemble dependent on multiple factors, including factors well outside neoclassical economic purview (Resnick and Wolff 1979). Working from this theoretical vantage point, Resnick's later work with Wolff challenged neoclassical economic histories of development by offering a complex, nonessentialist reading of how economies move from feudal to capitalist processes.

Satyananda Gabriel, Wolff and Resnick's student and a scholar of Chinese economic transition, notes that "[t]ransition/development is constituted by the logic of the interaction of countless social and environmental processes producing a trajectory of change that is always partially seen and understood in social analysis" (2006, 7). Our reading of Chinese economic development both recognizes the shifting, *"partially* seen" nature of these processes and seeks to make them clearer. To do so, our study calls on Resnick's early, careful attention to the rhetorics of economic theory and, in particular, on his challenges to—and transformations of—the impoverished heuristics that drive neoclassical economic development discourse. We therefore ground our analysis in Resnick's correctives to some of these dominant tropes, particularly the master trope of "markets."

We emphasize the misleading neoclassical characterization of "markets" as exclusively capitalist, private-property-based phenomena. Conversely, following Resnick, we examine the transitions and coincident, class-*differentiated* market formations that appeared in post-1978 China. Our narrative challenges the reductive view that capitalist transition in China began immediately post 1978 with the introduction of markets; rather, with a detailed analysis of class processes dependent on Resnick's, Wolff's and Gabriel's work, our story reveals that the transition to capitalist processes occurred more than a decade later, after early-1990s policies began to support technologically advanced, foreign-funded export industries in order to improve the productive forces in China. Most importantly, these policy changes severely undermined the conditions that supported ancient production in the earlier reform period and thereby drove millions of rural agricultural, manufacturing, and commercial producers out of business and into wage labor markets far from home.

This study is indebted to the elaborations of Resnick and Wolff's work found in Gabriel's critical reading of the Chinese economy, specifically, to Gabriel's study of China's ongoing transition to a mix of state and private capitalisms. Gabriel's redeployment of Resnick and Wolff's theory of transitional conjunctures (whose initial focus was on Western Europe) to rethink Chinese development offers a compelling study of transitions among feudal, ancient, and capitalist production as they operate within the Chinese economy.

As Gabriel's arguments make clear, theory is a cultural production,[1] a point latent in Resnick's early studies published in mainstream economic journals and made explicit in his later books and articles with Wolff. To emphasize the cultural dimensions of Resnick's economic analysis, we put his theories and our findings in conversation with selected works of contemporary Chinese fiction. Drawing on the tropes, characters, and stories created by Chinese authors who lived through and animated these transitions with their fictions complements and enriches the economic and social analysis in our project.

In addition to the cultural representations of this period, we examine recent texts written by Chinese economist and former Chief Economist of the World Bank, Justin Yifu Lin.[2] While we use Lin's data to provide evidence of the changes in the Chinese social and economic formation, our reading challenges Lin's analysis of the data and his characterizations of these transformations and their meanings (Lin 1992).[3] By rethinking the data from the theoretical perspectives that Resnick, Wolff, and Gabriel developed, we argue that Lin's findings effectively institute neoclassical economic analysis and prescriptions as the rubric of Chinese Communist Party policy. Thus the complex and mutating positions of Chinese economic policy from 1978 to the present day are usefully captured in Gabriel's observation that "Zhou Enlai's *Four Modernizations* and Jiang Zemin's 'Well-off Society' all point in the same direction: the path toward telos is delineated by technological sign posts not class analysis" (Gabriel 2006, 155). Furthermore, as Gabriel argues, "Socialism with Chinese characteristics is a way of defining socialism as whatever type of social formation arises out of CPC rule" (*ibid.*); that is, socialism is whatever the central government declares it to be insofar as the productive forces are advanced. According to Gabriel, the "modernists" were able, after Mao's death, "to generate widespread acceptance of the notion that adopting new technologies *by whatever means necessary* constitutes successful socialism" (*ibid.*, 154). Our argument makes clear that adopting economic formations and disciplines predicated on capitalist processes of production also fits snugly under the rubric, and Lin's work exemplifies this fit.

Lin's narrowly *neo*-neoclassical development discourse, set forth in *New Structural Economics* (Lin 2012), contrasts sharply with Resnick's rich, humane, rigorous theory and practice. In our investigation, the contrast between the two approaches reveals the weaknesses in Lin's perspective and in his reading of the Chinese economic data. This chapter, then, can be viewed as a conversation, itself an homage to Resnick's garrulous gathering of ideas, data, students, colleagues, scholars, workers, and activists. In this conversation, we follow one of Resnick's early models in our attempt to make evident the *fabulous* dimensions of economic development discourse: the possibilities and foreclosures, the "partially seen" and the hegemonic assertions of self-evidence, as they play out in the lives of Chinese rural workers.

Z goods/Z processes

Resnick recognized early in his career that neoclassical economic theory constricts the range of analysis in which the consequences of the theory play out. In particular, he made clear that neoclassical theory doesn't examine the heterogeneity of the labor process; that is, the theory treats labor as a homogenous factor inserted into a technologically determined production process. Significantly, the language in which development theory has been—and in many cases, continues to be—expressed reflects this perspective. Resnick and Hymer's 1969 article on agrarian reform presents an intriguing, if partial, remedy for the oversight. Resnick and Hymer postulate the qualitatively distinct production processes of "Z goods" as a missing element, unaccounted for within mainstream models of agrarian sector production. By including in their discussion this heretofore ignored aspect of labor processes in the agricultural sector— labor performed *alongside and distinct from agriculture*—they complicate the reductive binary that "postulate[s] an agrarian sector allocating its labor between two major activities, agriculture and leisure or non-work" (Resnick and Hymer, 493). Notably, they provide examples of Z goods but do not define or delimit their specific characteristics or the mode of their production. Rather, they seek to extend readings of the full range and diversified work of agricultural producers by creating a space and a category for examining multiple forms of production relations in rural areas as part of a revised neo-classical development theory. Explicitly, this formulation posits an expanded approach to development theory that problematizes the capitalist/traditional binary of neoclassical economics and emphasizes both the positive and the negative consequences of transition.

In theorizing Z processes as an analytic category, Resnick and Hymer stretch the boundaries of neoclassical economic analysis *and* continue to work within its logic. Z goods represent a way to account for production that remains invisible or "partially seen" within neoclassical metrics because the analytic provides a means with which to measure formally excluded or mischaracterized production. Therefore, in making Z goods legible and—critically—*measurable*, Resnick and Hymer's theorizing abides within neoclassical frameworks and methodologies even as their work extends their functionality by opening up the question of whether capitalist transitions are "good" for the populations drawn into them.

Acknowledging their model's fit within neoclassical theory, however, we note too that Resnick and Hymer stretch the restrictive discourses of development theory, forcing the theory to a greater tolerance for ambiguity and for as-yet untheorized but significant effects. By recognizing and beginning to theorize these effects of Z goods production, Resnick and Hymer offer it as an irruption within neoclassical development theory, one that opens possibilities for rethinking the ways we see (or don't see) labor processes, how we represent what counts as agrarian production, and how we come to understand the effects of the transformation of these activities.

Resnick emphasized Z goods production processes as a key factor in understanding transformation in developing economies in his 1970 *Journal of Economic History* paper on the history of export expansion in Burma, Thailand, and the Philippines. Here, he expands and clarifies the definition of Z processes for his model "to explore the historic behavior of the transitions from agrarian to commercial societies" (51). Resnick's model focuses on two types of labor activity in an agrarian economy: the effort devoted to the production and cultivation of crops and the time spent on a multitude of home or artisan handicraft and service activities, such as the spinning and weaving of cloth, the processing and milling of rice, the manufacture of assorted implements, the provision of transportation and housing, and so forth (*ibid.*, 51).

This expanded definition of Z processes provides a critical tool for our study of the several economic transformations in the Chinese countryside in the period of "reform." Attending to home/artisan production and service activities, small manufacturing, and transportation through the lens of Z processes, we find openings for, and later restrictions on, the access to conditions for self-reproduction for Chinese rural populations starting in 1978. Moreover, for a fuller understanding of these conditions, we rely on Gabriel's emphasis on *ancient* class processes as nonexploitative, wherein "the individual ancient producer is also the ancient appropriator and distributor" of surplus (Gabriel 2006, 12). As we argue, the consequences of the transformation in Z processes of production, through multiple, sometimes overlapping class processes and within broader economic reform policies, play out in people's lives and in the landscapes, rural and urban, in contemporary China.

Resnick and Hymer's conceptualization of Z processes makes possible an incipient multi-class model of manufacturing and trade that complicates the neoclassical analytic binaries pre-modern/modern, irrational/rational, traditional/capitalist. Theorizing the category of Z processes thereby enables the conceptualization of a space in which noncapitalist processes of manufacturing and trade could complement noncapitalist agricultural processes in order to provide practitioners with potentially expanding means of production *and* consumption. This approach thereby allows us to posit expanded reproduction of noncapitalist class relations, markets, and rural sector investment and consumption levels over time. Attending to Z goods production processes thus advances an inquiry into the real possibility for greater than subsistence standards of living resulting from "peasant" control and allocation of their self-produced surplus and the possibility to improve such a standard. Moreover, examining Z goods production throughout the period of reform in China reveals the ways in which this self-produced surplus can be—and was—reduced, disrupted, eroded, or smashed, as we have found in the experiences of rural Chinese peasants/producers.

In addition, an important claim in our overall argument is that Resnick's *JEH* article introduced into the neoclassical model elements necessary to conceive the formal rudiments of *imperialist* disruption and structural dislocation of "traditional" peasant economies—whether feudal or ancient—in poor/underdeveloped countries. These interventions produced poverty in the disrupted local communities alongside an extension of capitalist markets. Resnick showed, by theorizing a barely disguised imperialist "trade effect" that imported goods displaced local handicrafts production. As well, an imperialist "land transfer effect" dispossessed small agricultural producers. Integrating local production into international capitalist markets undermined peasant self-reproduction and could substantially reduce their incomes and force them into capitalist production and trade networks.[4] He also raised the possibility that, while these transformations of peasant economic activities could lead to the systematic displacement of peasant producers from self-reproductive activities, they could also substantially erode their real incomes from agriculture and handicrafts manufactures to below subsistence levels and thus "free them" to seek subsistence by selling their labor power in capitalist labor markets. That is, Resnick showed how the spread of "imported" capitalist economic relations in poor/underdeveloped countries might lead to impoverishment of the mass of the population and their forced "freedom" to become wage laborers.

Resnick's Z goods model, therefore, imaginatively introduces imperialist effects into neoclassical models of development and then associates these effects with primitive accumulation in developing nations. Their agricultural resources and peoples are compelled by privation to enter into a global network of capitalist relations of production. We extend Resnick's theorizations to reconceptualize the effects of Chinese Communist Party (CCP) economic reforms. In the process, we stress that CCP policies directed toward improving the nation's productive forces, which initially increased and stabilized rural living standards, eventually undermined how those incomes were produced. Peasants were often unable to maintain incomes and cover rising costs so that many were pushed to migrate long distances to seek wage-labor in export-oriented, foreign-funded firms.

Policies and disruptions in the Chinese rural economy up to 1978

While Chinese peasant workers' production and self-appropriation of agricultural surplus grew after the 1950s post-revolution land reform, under the Great Leap Forward (GLF), their labor was resorbed into the state's communal production, appropriation, and redistribution system. During the mid-1950s, it was difficult for the state to transfer peasant-produced surpluses at a sufficient rate and in sufficient volume to support rapid industrialization in urban areas. Consequently, the Chinese state considered implementation of alternative modes of surplus production and appropriation in the countryside.

Working from Resnick and Wolff's theory of class processes as both overdetermined and grounded in a focus on control of surplus, Gabriel characterizes the period from the late 1950s until just before the 1978 reform era as "feudal," while he rejects a modernist Marxist theorizing that constructs "an essentialist model of feudalism" (2006, 15). Rather, his analysis illuminates the multiple, interdependent factors that organized the social and economic formations in Chinese society during this period. In so doing, he elaborates on and applies Resnick and Wolff's model of class processes to mid-twentieth-century Chinese conditions (*ibid.*, 27 and 119–20). Significantly, the pre-reform state feudal formation, notwithstanding its social welfare functions, depended upon increased work by rural peasants yet afforded peasants continuously diminishing incomes (Peng 1998, 1).[5]

Moreover, the social-political arrangements of the collective era reorganized the life and work of agricultural producers, who had experienced a degree of independence and prosperity due to the land reforms immediately post-revolution. According to Gabriel, during the 1950s, these workers had labored within "the ancient class process (productive self-employment)" (2006, 119), so the move to more concentrated collectivization and commune-based social and economic regimes effectively diminished their opportunities for independent production as well as for self-appropriation and allocation of surplus product. This class transformation meant that peasants were unable to guarantee minimal levels of family consumption through self-provision.

Despite some extended periods of increased output, economic data on consumption levels in rural areas indicate that malnourishment and even starvation accompanied substantially increased corvée labor. The benefits from additional output were transferred to state-managed industrial firms to support more rapid industrial accumulation in urban areas. The rural sector agricultural surplus funded urban industrialization rather than adding capacity to store grain, to build up grain reserves, or to move food from areas of high production to areas of low production. Peasant net incomes, communally and individually, were reduced to bare minimums to enable the transfer of agricultural surplus to support urban industrial expansion.

Consonant with Resnick's emphasis on the human costs of economic development as well as with Gabriel's insistence that social transformation is economic, political, and *cultural*, we note that analysis of this data is most revelatory when read in dialogue with cultural representations of agrarian workers' lived experiences. That is, the cultural work that accompanied or reflected upon the agrarian labor represents a key element in these class processes. For example, contemporary fiction by Mo Yan, Chinese novelist and Nobel Laureate, interweaves the economic and social changes of this period and uncovers the disruptions and privations that peasants suffered in order to feed urban industrialization. In the Preface to one of his early short story collections, Mo Yan writes of his childhood in Shandong during the early 1960s: "We were like a pack of starving dogs, haunting the streets and lanes sniffing the air for something to put inside our bellies" ([2000] 2001, ix).[6] The image of "starving dogs" powerfully depicts the hunger that afflicted peasants in the countryside but doesn't make explicit reference to its causes. However, his 1996 historical fiction, *Big Breasts and Wide Hips*, that examines twentieth-century Chinese history through figures of female embodiment, does suggest that these privations could be traced to the exploitative structures conditioning state feudalism.

Beginning in 1900, the novel moves through seven chapters, each detailing an era of violence and dislocation, from the Boxer Rebellion to the reform era. The accumulating effects that economic, social, physical, and emotional trauma visited on the countryside in the shift from independent production to state feudal processes proliferate in the lives of the collectivized workers, represented by Mo Yan, again, as humans reduced to animals:

> In the spring of 1960, when the countryside was littered with the corpses of famine victims, members of the Flood Dragon River Farm rightist unit were transformed into a herd of ruminants, scouring the earth for vegetation to quell their hunger. Everyone was limited to an ounce and a half of grain daily, minus the amount skimmed off the top by the storekeeper, the manager of the dining hall, and other important individuals.
>
> ([1996] 2004, 430)

The overall effect of the disruptions and concomitant reconfigurations of peasant identities was to severely depress output in both rural and urban areas. For the central state policy makers, the recognition that depressed rural output led to political instabilities, as well as starvation, interrupted the transition to centralized state feudalism. Within this context, Mao re-empowered Zhou Enlai as chief economic planner, to develop and implement policies, including changes in modes of production, that would "stabilize" production and restore rural people's livelihoods (Kueh 1995, 14).

From 1961 to 1962, Zhou and his supporters changed labor allocation and compensation from the commune level all the way down to the production teams (Kueh 1995, 20–1). Pre-figuring the 1979 Household Responsibility System, family-level production units were "supplemented by the expansion of private plots (*ziliu di*), rural trade fairs (*ziyou shichang*), and sideline activities on private account (*zifu yingkui*)" (*ibid.*, 21). Thus, ancient production was established as the predominant mode of agricultural organization and surplus appropriation. Additionally, "reduced state extractions (due to accelerated increase in grain imports to serve urban needs), coupled with the receipt of the majority of the state chemical fertilizer supply" (*ibid.*, 21), increased the net income of family farms. These policies secured conditions under which peasants' labor would allow them, under all but the most adverse circumstances, to self-provide both means of consumption and the means to expand future production. Despite narratives to the contrary, the Great Proletarian Cultural Revolution (GPCR) did not obliterate these gains because

> [e]ven at the height of the commune system, Chinese peasants still possessed what is known as 'private plots'—the land that was owned by the collectives but worked by the peasants themselves. The land was not tradable but the revenue rights were private. The production on private plots was not taxed and returns accrued to the peasants with the assignment rights to the land.
>
> (Huang 2003, 33)

Despite a severe North China drought in 1972, crop output continued to increase at about 3% per annum during the 1970s, supplemented by the effects of the "five industries" investment program. In particular, investments in increased electrification, improved water resources—storage and delivery systems—increased manufacture of agricultural equipment, and local, rural production of chemical fertilizers supported the consistent increases in agricultural output. From 1970 to 1978, the index of capital investment in agriculture doubled, while chemical fertilizer use tripled (Lin 1992, 40, Table 4). These factors much more than compensated for the shift of labor from rural agriculture to rural industry in those years. In addition, during this period, Chinese rural research scientists were developing some of the first hybrid wet rice seeds. Substantial increase in output from these hybrid seeds was only realized when this new technology was implemented later, coincidently, during the peak reform years.

Feudal to ancient: agricultural reform, 1978–1984

Resnick, Wolff, and Gabriel remind us to think complexly in terms of class relations, not simply non-capitalist/capitalist but along a number of dimensions. We note, for example, that the Zhou-Deng axis of policies was manifest in both the early 1950s and, in the countryside, from 1962 to '78. Consistent with their reading of Marx's *Critique of the Gotha Program*, the Zhou-Deng model of *socialist* organization of production shifted decision-making and surplus control to the household level in order to closely link direct producers' input of effort to their reward (Deng 1980). Increasing the use of capital equipment, other inputs (especially chemical fertilizers), and improving agricultural infrastructure (roads, irrigation systems, expanding agricultural research on seeds and electric generation) across provinces further enhanced the forces of production. In our reading, then, CCP state policies supported the extension of ancient production in *both* periods, as a means to increase investment, output, and incomes of hundreds of millions of direct producers in China's rural areas.

Through these "modernist Marxist" policies, leading up to the 1978 reforms, Chinese rural workers participated in a hybrid formation of ancient production at the level of direct agricultural production that was complemented by state feudal relations of production in large-scale agriculture, rural industries, and infrastructure investment at the commune level. Therefore, while most analyses (see Lin 1987, 1992, 2012; Huang 2008) emphasize discontinuity between pre-reform and post-reform periods, our reading finds certain continuities only made visible through the lens of a class analysis shaped by Resnick, Wolff, and Gabriel's work.

In particular, our analysis of the economic effects of the reform era contrasts sharply with mainstream Chinese interpretations, especially those of Chinese economist Justin Yifu Lin. Lin's work exemplifies the mainstream state interpretation of reform and its consequences because it reproduces the neoclassical "flattening" of economic analysis critiqued by Resnick, Wolff, and Gabriel. Lin's reading of Chinese economic reforms is undergirded by the powerful neoclassical assumption that non-capitalist formations can never produce the efficiencies of capitalist economic organization. Lin provides a simple narrative of pre-reform "planned economy" and post-reform "market economy," in which the "planned" economy is deemed unproductive while the "market" engenders efficiency and higher incomes. "The main fault in the economic system," he argued, "was low economic efficiency arising from structural imbalance and incentive problems" (Lin, Cai, and Li 1996, 212).[7] Thus, the central claim of Lin's neoclassical and contemporary state-sponsored Chinese analyses of the rural reforms of 1978 is that the reforms were market-oriented and *therefore* highly successful. This claim begs a basic analytical question: what were the distinct class features of these reforms and the markets that they established? Moreover, do these conventional analyses overlook or intentionally elide the previously outlined successes of pre-reform rural agricultural policies, those that sought to provide "socialist" incentives by directly linking incomes to effort?

In critiquing Lin then, we focus on the very continuities his analysis ignores. Neoclassical analysts, and Lin in particular, effectively claim that the bulk of agricultural output and income increases can be attributed to an instantiation of capitalist property relations and labor processes in 1978. We see this shift, however, as a transition from feudal to ancient class processes, that is, to the absence of exploitation in those processes of independent production that permit ancient producers to obtain the full net value of their production. Lin's analysis elides the critical changes in access to individual production and, instead, seeks to claim these improvements under the banner of capitalist market incentives, property relations, and labor power markets.

It's important to note here the complex rhetorical maneuver Lin uses to occlude the productivity achieved through these ancient class processes and to attribute that productivity instead to what he claims are the newly instituted—and, by his estimation, highly efficient—capitalist relations. Writing in 1987, he is retroactively reading capitalist relations back into early reform rural economic conditions in order to justify future institutional transformations that will establish capitalist class processes. This deft substitution appears in his argument for "intelligent government" and advances the integration of China into imperialist networks:

> [F]or the development of an economy, it is necessary, at the risk of over-generalization, to have a system that encourages individuals to actively seek for and innovate *new profitable income streams* and the system also allows individuals who invest their time, effort, and money on these activities to reap the profits for themselves. Institutional arrangements with such a character—or more explicitly a system of

clearly defined and well-enforced property rights in goods, factors of production, and ideals—are inherently public goods. They cannot be established by the induced institutional innovation process. Without the whole-hearted support of government, such institutional arrangements will not exist in a society.

(Lin 1987, 39–40 original emphasis)

Key to our understanding of Lin's purpose here is his insistence on reducing all relations to capitalist relations. In contradistinction, Resnick and Hymer make possible our reading, which seeks to tease out—and make legible—the complexities in class relations and the consequences for the ancient producers.

In addition to Lin's rhetorical and theoretical legerdemain, his claims about market efficiencies and "improved" capitalist property relations are belied by the facts presented in his own data. As the Household Responsibility System was implemented during 1979 to 1981, the percentage of participating households rose from 1 to 45% (Lin 1992, 38, Table 3) while the crop output index (*ibid.*, 40, Table 4) rose from 107 to 109. In other words, the movement from almost no participation to close to half participation in two years of reform only produced about 2% increase in crop output. Further, in 1983, after the participation rate increased to 98% (*ibid.*, 38, Table 3), the index of crop output rose to 129, presumably exhausting the effects of the transition to "capitalism." However, the next year a tiny 1% increase in household participation in the new system purportedly caused another 10% jump in agricultural output (the index of crop output rose from 129 to 142 (*ibid.*, 40, Table 4).

Clearly, an immediate connection between the implementation of market reforms and increase in the rate of output growth is not tenable when big increases in participation are matched by small increases in output and tiny increases by large jumps in output. Instead, these statistics point to the joint impacts of class transformation—moving from state feudalism to ancient production and several other factors: the low cost provision of output-boosting inputs (agricultural equipment, new hybrid seeds, and the complementary increase in irrigation and chemical fertilizers); substantially increased (planned) prices for requisitioned and above-quota crops; local market sales; and—let's be frank—excellent weather in the key year of comparison, the anomalously productive 1984.

Weather has an inescapable and widely variable impact on agricultural output. Abysmal weather in the years 1959 through 1961 deeply depressed the output figures for those years and provided an unusually low baseline for the subsequent ten years of strong (5% per annum) agricultural growth in the "commune" period. On the other hand, the burst of agricultural output between 1978 and 1984 was exaggerated by the excellent weather conditions in 1984. Were we to remap the reform period as 1979

(1% household responsibility participation; agricultural output index = 107) to 1983 (98% household responsibility participation; agricultural output index = 129), the compounded growth rate of crop output would be less than 5% a year—about the same as during the commune-dominated period 1963 to 1970. The fact that periods characterized by purportedly contradictory policy regimes (from Lin's perspective, planned versus market) had such similar and high growth rates suggests the possibility that Lin's reading is not the whole story.

First, the post-1978 policies can be read, alternatively, as formalizations and extensions of the class transitions brought about by Zhou's post-1961 reforms. For example, Zhou's early reforms, like the 1979 Household Responsibility System, explicitly focused decision-making, surplus appropriation and rewards at the household level while allowing commodity production in agriculture. Some producers—especially grain producers—sold some of their crops at state-set prices while they could sell other, additional crops, of a composition they chose, at local and regional markets. The individual productive unit, the household, bore the direct costs of production and possessed the right to dispose of the output and retain the net revenues. These revenues were subject to other deductions, such as local taxes as well as healthcare and educational costs for individual household members. Thus, we see that the post-1978 reform policies, from this perspective, constituted an *extension* of the class transition from state feudalism to ancient production.

What is startling, however, in this comparison is that *planned* prices were changed in 1978 as part of the reforms. The long-depressed procurement prices for agricultural outputs, e.g., for grain and cotton, which provided a major subsidy to urban industrial investment and accumulation, were dramatically increased over 20% by weighted average, and the above-quota prices (i.e., the amounts paid for above-quota levels of output) were increased 40%. These increases, combined with allowing farmers to continue to market their sideline crops, boosted the incomes of the nation's over 800 million peasants by 30%. Additionally, *planned* input prices were sharply reduced, as shown by the abrupt rise, by 40%, in the ratio between overall agricultural output prices to input prices (Lin 1992, 37).

Households responded to the state-planned boost in their potential net revenues not only by increasing their efforts per hour worked but also by allocating more, now relatively inexpensive, resources to agricultural production. For example, from 1978 to 1984, capital equipment use rose by about 65%, chemical fertilizer use rose about 70%, and direct labor inputs rose by 15% (Lin 1992, 40). Crop output, measured in weighted physical output, rose 40% over the 1978–84 period. Consequently, agricultural incomes nearly doubled. Therefore, much of the dramatic surge in farm incomes, which consolidated rural support for these early reform policy changes, was "paid for" by a change from one state policy to another: the intentional *elimination* of agricultural output price suppression and the associated rural subsidy to urban industrial growth and the *institution* of planned complementary changes in both input and output prices that yielded substantial income increases to ancient production in agriculture.

Feudal to ancient: industrial reform, 1978–1984

During the pre-reform 1970–78 period, rural manufacturing enterprises and output increased rapidly. Toward the end of the GPCR, as factional fighting intensified in the cities, state-owned enterprises (SOEs) that formerly sold their output to rural areas were shut down for political reasons. Their "place" within the structure of production and distribution was assumed by newly developed rural commune enterprises. Consequently, rural enterprises' "output value was increased from 9.25 billion yuan in 1970 to 27.2 billion in 1976, with an average annual growth rate of 25.7%. ... By 1978, their output value reached 49.3 billion yuan in 1970 constant prices" (Lin and Yao n.d., 4). In conjunction with this "rural industrialization" at the commune level, many associated supply opportunities were seized by micro household firms that then employed surplus agricultural labor.

When these changes were formalized by explicit rural industrial and commercial reforms in 1984, households were permitted to independently manage small industries, construction, transportation, and commercial enterprises, often employing only a few family members. These household enterprises were considered self-employment businesses, while larger concerns were designated by a different category: "Self-employment businesses are single proprietorships, and in China they are formally known as individual businesses (*geti hu*) or individual economy entities (*geti jingji*) in the Chinese statistical reporting system" (Huang 2008, 58). Households set up five million new firms. By 1985, the number of such small family firms more than doubled to 12 million, most of which were organized by small groups of farm families (Lin and Yao n.d., 6).

In Resnick's terms, these are the firms whose labor processes constitute China's Z sector. Moreover, following Gabriel and Resnick, they function as ancient producers. As these rural industrial enterprises grew during the 1984–85 period, they employed millions of rural residents, and "[b]etween 1984 and 1988, growth averaged 27 percent" (Huang 2008, 119). The blossoming of these millions of firms was fed by increases in agricultural incomes: per capita consumption in rural areas increased 6% a year prior to 1984 (Lin and Yao n.d., 6).

Post-1978 reform in agriculture was complemented by policies that extended ancient processes to rural industry, construction, transport, and commerce. Higher farm incomes allowed households to increase agricultural investment, including irrigation infrastructure, capital equipment, and fertilizers. Along with farm incomes, these Z processes rapidly became important sources of income and thus of rural peasant self-support: "By 1988, a typical rural household had 545 yuan in net per capita income. Of this, 118 yuan came from wage earnings and 58 yuan came from nonfarm business earnings" (Huang 2008, 119). Lin and Yao's data capture the economic transformations in the countryside during this period:

> In 1978, only 9.5% of the rural labor force was engaged in industrial activities, and only 7.6% of rural income was contributed by the non-farm sectors; by 1996, 29.8% of the rural labor force was working in local industry, and non-farm income accounted for 34.2% of rural total income.
>
> (Lin and Yao n.d., 1)

Trade in rural markets facilitated exchange between rural agricultural producers and local manufacturers. Rural producers brought their agricultural goods into local towns and county seats and then brought locally produced consumer goods back. Commerce and construction grew. The number of rural enterprises grew from 1.5 million in 1978 (mostly former commune enterprises in the "five industries") to over 23 million in 1996, while the number of employees grew from 28 million to more than 135 million.

By 1994, household businesses numbered 22.5 million and employed almost 54 million persons (Huang 2008, 79). These ancient firms built houses and produced simple furnishings and basic consumer goods. They also equipped small farms with improved means of production, provided transport of agricultural goods to, and *marketed* their products at, regional towns. In so doing, these small, ancient firms participated in a web of related activities, mutually supplying basic items to much of the Chinese rural populace. Consequently, millions of ancient firms provided and augmented employment and incomes for tens of millions of producers. The firms enabled a substantial portion of the self-provisioning of these rural communities, as well as providing the source, along with agriculture, of sufficiently higher incomes to raise the majority of Chinese peasants above the poverty level. The conditions that permitted peasant self-provisioning, that is, the reproduction of the conditions of existence for ancient production, were secured by state planning policies. Growing peasant incomes provided ready markets for their outputs, whether means of production or consumption.

However, these class transformations and the income gains they produced were short-lived. In the early 1990s, the Chinese Communist Party (CCP) fundamentally shifted its economic policies. The CCP decided to speed up and intensify the development of China's productive forces by shifting massive amounts of resources to support foreign-funded, export-led industrialization. Deng explained this policy shift in a series of speeches while visiting Special Economic Zones (SEZs). Huang Ping, a Research Professor and Deputy Director at the Chinese Academy of Social Sciences, writes:

> In 1992 Deng Xiaoping made what may be considered his final but most important move in his lifetime—an inspecting tour around southern China. He delivered a series of speeches that significantly pushed forward the process of marketization of economy in China. We may consider Deng's tour as the most important landmark since the reform began in 1979. After these speeches, the whole nation was seen to move in full swing toward a marketization.
>
> (Huang 2003, n.p.)

The dominant wing of the CCP believed that China's productive forces would stagnate (as in the Soviet Union) if they were unable to integrate and master the technologies developed by capitalist firms. Deng's speeches were translated into policy by Jiang Zemin, General Secretary of the CCP and President-in-waiting:

> In June 1992, Comrade Jiang Zemin explicitly put forward the concept of "socialist market economic system" for the first time on the basis of Comrade Deng Xiaoping's southern talk…it is a market economy making full use of both means of regulation and market; it is a market economy actively involved in economic globalization.
>
> (*People's Daily Online* 2012)

Related to this shift toward capitalism, investment in infrastructure to support the SEZs—seaports, airports, rail service, roads, communications, power generation, and distribution—increased. On the other hand, policies that had secured conditions of existence for a rural ancient farming, rural industry, rural transportation, and commerce were reversed. Significantly, the CCP took steps to eliminate financial mechanisms that recycled ancient surpluses to ancient accumulation of means of production and growth.

Instead, the state began to draw upon ancient surpluses to expand investments to support coastal city and SEZ industrialization while undermining the capacity of ancient farms, communes, and industries to succeed financially. Huang Yasheng notes that "In the 1980s, rural China experimented with substantial financial liberalization, the main elements of which were (1) adoption of an accommodating and supportive credit policy towards the private sector by state banks, (2) the proliferation of informal financial instruments, and (3) tacit permission for informal financial instruments…" to support the small family farm/firm sector (Huang 2008, 139). He argues

A consistent theme running through the bank policy documents of the ABC [Agricultural Bank of China] in the 1980s is that the ABC and the RCCs [rural credit cooperatives] should provide loans to rural residents to engage in non-farm activities.

(ibid., 146)

These institutions, under the direction of the ancient producers themselves, gathered the surpluses produced by ancient farmers and craftspeople to make them available to invest in existing farms/firms and for funding the development of new ones. As Huang points out, "the three original features of the RCCs... [are that] they would be organizationally reliant on RCC members, managerially democratic, and operationally flexible" (2008, 146). These financial institutions became important elements in support of the expanded reproduction of ancient class processes. Lending to households increased by 50% over the period 1982–88 (2008, 68) and, in particular, "[i]n 1985, RCCs accounted for 76.8 percent of all agricultural loans and 47.8 percent of all loans extended to TVEs" (2008, 146). In addition to the RCCs, rural cooperative foundations [RCFs] were set up in the 1980s to serve as the means for small independent producers jointly to control collective productive assets. The RCC-RCF formation served as a mechanism that allowed small producers jointly to possess means of production that might then function as collateral for small operating loans. Thus, during the 1980s, the RCFs operated as informal savings and loans for their members, in which membership shares could serve as collateral for small business loans. They therefore became a crucial source of funds to support the development of ancient business income and employment growth.

However, in the early 1990s "...the Chinese state began to systematically stamp out those providers of capital [in rural areas] outside the state banking system" (Huang 2008, 139). For example, "[in] 1993, the RCFs that took and lent deposits were absorbed into the RCCs; in 1996, the rest of the RCFs were absorbed into the RCCs. From that point on ...the average rural household bank loans in real terms never exceeded their 1987 level" *(ibid.,* 141 and 146). The RCCs' capacity to serve their members was finally explicitly curtailed when they were redefined as "local government financial institutions" *(ibid.,* 156) and removed from the control of the ancient producers.

Ancient surpluses were rerouted into the state banking system, and local producers were financially crippled along with the institutions that had nurtured them, so "[b]y the late 1990s...the RCCs experienced massive operating problems and they contracted dramatically in number. In 1985, there were more than 400,000 RCCs in the country. ... By 2003, only 91,393 RCC branches remained" (Huang 2008, 156). The rapidly deteriorating financial position of the ancient farms and firms is starkly evidenced by the parallel fate of these institutions: "The shareholder equity of the

RCCs was reported to be 63.2 billion yuan in 1995.... 15.1 billion in 1998, and - 8.5 billion by 2003" (*ibid.*, 156). These changes cut off the supply of finance to independent producers in rural areas and allowed the reallocation of those funds to export-focused, foreign-funded private firms.

Small, rural ancient firms were unable to get the necessary funds to advance technologically to produce consumer goods competitive with those of the export firms, even in local, rural markets. As we saw above, "[t]he sharpest reversal occurred in rural finance. Many very useful financial experiments were terminated and credit constraints on small-scale, low-tech, and labor-intensive rural entrepreneurship were tightened" (Huang 2008, 111). Without access to low-cost finance to support investment and technological improvement, the competitive position of ancient producers was eroded relative to the now favored export-oriented capitalist firms.

Thus, even though business income grew in real terms in the early 1990s, that growth was at a fraction of the rate prevailing in the 1980s. In particular, there was a significant shift from ancient business income to wage income. For example, "[i]n the 1990s, rural households largely maintained the same growth rate in wage income as they did in the 1980s" (Huang 2008, 122). Local paid employment per household unit rose from an average of 87 days during the 1986–88 period to 143 days in the 1992–99 period, while migrant labor days rose from 49 days to 75. Between these periods, the average income per day from local employment (in constant 1978 yuan) fell from 9 to 6 yuan while it rose from about 4 yuan to 7 yuan for *migrant* labor (*ibid.*). Huang concludes, "Because the local employment markets were overcrowded, rural residents sought jobs elsewhere.... They made this 'constrained choice' despite the demonstrably lower and decreasing returns from paid employment" (*ibid.*, 124). Not only were ancient producers pushed toward wage labor, but also they were forced to migrate great distances for a small absolute increase in their income necessary for subsistence.

The reforms of 1978 eliminated communal healthcare and educational obligations. The new rural township and village governments were not provided the resources by central authorities that would allow them to assume these responsibilities. In 1980–84, the resulting combined cost burden was about 8% of total rural household consumption expenditures. By 1990–94, the combined burden averaged about 16%, despite the growth in rural household incomes. From 1998 to 2002, the burden rose to an average of 22% (Huang 2008, 247). Consequently, increasing pressure was placed on rural households to pay much more for these services, even as their agricultural incomes stagnated because crop prices fell due to increased competition from larger and more mechanized operations closer to big-city markets. Rural households also suffered from constricting opportunities to self-provide through independent manufacturing, transport, and commerce. Conditions of existence for ancient firms eroded as they lost this planned competition with export firms in local markets and as ancient farms were threatened by yielding below-subsistence net incomes for families. These financial and distribution reforms destroyed the conditions of self-reproduction for millions, then tens of millions, then hundreds of millions of ancient producers. The Z goods processes were smashed and these ancient producers suffered from a form of primitive accumulation driven by the turn toward the global capitalist economy by the CCP.

Ancient to capitalist: blood energy

In order to raise the level of productive forces to integrate into the global economy, the CCP had to manage the transition from state feudalism and ancient production to state and private capitalisms. The Chinese state's creation and support of SEZs produced new modes of exploitation in nascent urban areas. Many of the firms that initially benefited from these pro-capitalist policies were among the larger TVEs located near major cities, along the east coast and readily accessible to Hong Kong, Taiwan, and Singapore, the gateways to the US-dominated global economy. Their particular geographic circumstances set up a bifurcated process of capitalist transition. Over the next decade, many of the TVEs that were situated close to export centers were privatized by government permission and transformed into explicitly capitalist firms.

The SEZ policies, however, concomitantly reversed a two-decade-long trend of supporting the expansion of ancient production in agriculture, manufacturing, transportation, and commerce to reduce poverty in rural areas. As state-appropriated surplus was redistributed to support expansion of the SEZs, constituted by urbanized, technologically advanced, foreign-funded export industries, many of the dispossessed and increasingly re-impoverished rural ancient producers migrated to these new zones of modernizing capitalism to seek wage labor in order to survive the destruction of ancient farms and firms.

In 1969 Resnick and Hymer argued that the substitution of agricultural and small firm production of Z goods by large-scale industrial goods can produce destructive results: "[M]arket systems, even when they improve overall allocation and division of labor, may well hurt the interests of some factors of production" (1969, 505). Moreover, Resnick's early critique of exploitation and emerging imperialist processes, which he continued to develop throughout his career, appears in his and Hymer's cautionary final paragraph:

> If adequate redistribution mechanisms do not exist, the gains from trade will be spread unevenly, and certain parties, instead of sharing in the increased wealth, may even be immiserized. More important, increased specialization disrupts the social structure and causes great

stress and strain. New divisions of labor and the interdependence they imply require new political and social relations among members of society.

(1969, 506)

As we have seen, millions of Chinese ancient producers were "immiserized" by the transformations in state policies, from those that supported rural independent production to those that privileged large-scale private property and capitalist markets. What Resnick feared, Justin Yifu Lin embraces as the work of a necessary collaboration between "intelligent government" and "market forces." The contrast between Resnick's careful, humane theorizations and Lin's neo-neoclassical parroting of Chicago-style "incentivization" manifests in the life of Xu Sanguan, protagonist of Yu Hua's 1995 novel, *Chronicle of a Blood Merchant* (Yu 2003). The novel's portrayal of Chinese peasant life from the post-Revolutionary era to the mid-1980s provides a "chronicle" of how blood selling exploded from an infrequent practice used "to pad out a lean year or to live a little better in a fat one" to a crucial component of peasant incomes (Pomfret 2001). Yu Hua employs traditional metaphors of "blood" and "blood energy" to trace the ever-diminishing opportunities for self-provisioning, family support, and, ultimately, sheer survival afforded to Xu Sanguan and his fellow villagers as the mid-80s reforms take hold. Losing work at a factory, one of the TVEs decommissioned by the move toward urban SEZ manufacture, Xu Sanguan faces the related loss of medical and educational supports for his family. He approaches corrupt "Blood Chief Li" more and more frequently, imploring Li to allow him to sell his blood at shorter—and illegal—intervals. That is, as the new economic policies dispossess workers from stable employment and social supports, Xu Sanguan becomes increasingly desperate. Blood Chief Li can't allow Xu Sanguan to give any more blood, but Li offers him a solution:

> You really have no shame, do you? Thickest skin I ever saw. So out of respect for your thick skin, I'm going to give you a little suggestion. Even if *I* won't let you sell any blood, you can always go somewhere else. Try another hospital. *They* won't know that you've just sold blood somewhere else. They'll be happy to take your blood. Get it?" Blood Chief Li saw Xu Sanguan nodding his head. "That way, you can sell as much blood as you want. And you can sell your life away along with it for all I care.

(Yu 2003, 210)

Li's advice, although set in the novel's 1980s milieu, necessarily echoes the early '90s rise of blood markets in China, when both Chinese and foreign companies "began buying blood" for plasma products.[8] Xu Sanguan thus takes his body to market: "He was on his way to Shanghai," passing through

17 towns, but only six were county seats. "He would go ashore in all six of these towns to sell blood. He would sell his blood all the way to Shanghai" (Yu 2003, 211). Xu Sanguan's journey downriver to Shanghai, selling his blood, concretizes the distinction he makes earlier between factory labor in the TVE and blood selling: "I've only just learned what it means to sell the kind of energy that comes from the blood. What I earn in the factory is just sweat money, but what I earned today is blood money" (*ibid.*, 16).

The difference between ancient production that characterized Z manufacture in the Chinese countryside and the dislocations and dis-possessions attendant on capitalist relations in the later reform era are clear: blood is the final possible Z good for rural workers. It is, in fact, the last product of the ancient producer, whose blood energy, and, in Xu Sanguan's case, actual blood represents the new class relations, ones predicted by Marx's famous metaphor of capitalist as vampire. We end the story of Z goods, economic reform in rural China, and this transfor-mation in class processes with a final admonition from Resnick, and a call to further "conversations" that challenge the consensus of contem-porary economists, such as Justin Yifu Lin and global capitalist apolo-gists: "A development program that ignores the historical lessons of the great transformations of the past is likely to continue its present course of a fractured and fragmented political and economic life" (Hymer and Resnick 1969, 506), drained and exhausted, exploited by those forces that crave the last drop of blood.

Notes

1 "[E]xplaining the dynamics of Chinese social transformation requires an un-derstanding not only of economic and political processes, but also cultural processes (of which theory is a sub element" (Gabriel 2006, 2).
2 Justin Yifu Lin was born in Taiwan in 1952. Lin embodies the transmission of Taiwan's model of capitalist development, interpreted through the lens of the Chicago economics program, to the PRC. See the admiring profile of Lin by Evan Osnos (2010).
3 Lin draws his data from "e-level panel data from 1970 to 1987 for 28 of the 29 provinces in mainland China [there is no data from Tibet]" (1992, 35).
4 Resnick argues, "As the agrarian economy became linked to world markets, the effective demand generated for its products caused a dramatic reallocation of work effort and a shift in indigenous demand from the production and con-sumption of Z goods to the expansion of agricultural crops for export and the consumption of imported manufactures" (1970, 52).
5 "Even though two decades of collective farming had accomplished impressive advances in terms of yields per *mu* of farmland, peasants' real income stag-nated and payment per workday declined" (Peng 1998, 1).
6 Mo Yan notes the changes in literary topics that accompanied economic and political transformations of this period, including the "rise of so-called scar literature, personal accounts of the horrors of the Cultural Revolution" ([2000] 2001, xv).

7 Earlier in this same article, the authors assert that "to attain a sustained, smooth growth, it is imperative for China to complete the transition from the planned economy to a market economy" (1996, 202).

8 The literature on the resulting explosion of AIDS cases in China, due to pooled blood in the plasma-collection process and to tainted blood transfusions, is massive. Pomfret (2001) reports that "the blood market got a massive boost in 1993" in a state push "to export blood products to earn foreign exchange." Therefore, the novel's fictional events presage the actual events of the novel's historical moment: Yu Hua refers specifically to the AIDS villages and blood markets as key inspirations for *Chronicle*. See Michael Standaert's interview with Yu Hua (Standaert 2003).

References

Deng, X. 1980. "Answers to the Italian Journalist Oriana Fallaci." *People's Daily Online*. http://en.people.cn/dengxp/vol2/text/b1470.html (accessed January 17, 2017).

Gabriel, S. 2006. *Chinese Capitalism and the Modernist Vision*. London and New York: Routledge.

Huang, P. 2003. "China: Rural Labor Under the Uneven Development of Recent Years." www.usc.cuhk.edu.hk/PaperCollection/Details.aspx?id=2487 (accessed April 19, 2015).

Huang, Y. 2008.*Capitalism with Chinese Characteristics: Entrepreneurship and the State*. New York: Cambridge University Press.

Hymer, S. and S. Resnick. 1969. "A Model of an Agrarian Economy with Non-agricultural Activities." *American Economic Review* 59 (4, Pt. 1): 493–506.

Kueh, Y. Y. 1995. *Agricultural Instability in China, 1931–1990: Weather, Technology, and Institutions (Studies on Contemporary China)*. Gloucestershire, UK: Clarendon Press.

Lin, J. Y. 1987. "An Economic Theory of Institutional Change: Induced and Imposed Change." Yale Economic Growth Center, Paper #537.

—— 1992. "Rural Reforms and Agricultural Growth in China." *American Economic Review* 82 (1): 34–51.

—— 2012. *New Structural Economics: A Framework for Rethinking Development and Policy*. Washington, D.C.: World Bank Publications.

Lin, J. Y. and Yao, Y. n.d. "Chinese Rural Industrialization in the Context of the East Asian Miracle." China Center for Economic Research, Beijing University. http://services.iriskf.org/data/articles/Document118102006240.3176996.pdf (accessed April 19, 2016).

Lin, J. Yifu, F. C., and Zhou L. 1996. "The Lessons of China's Transition to a Market Economy." *Cato Journal* 16 (2): 201–31.

Mo Yan. 2004. *Big Breasts and Wide Hips*. Trans. H. Goldblatt. New York: Arcade Publishing.

—— 2001. "Preface." In *Shifu, You'll Do Anything for a Laugh*. Trans. H. Goldblatt. New York: Arcade Publishing.

Osnos, E. 2010. "Boom Doctor." *The New Yorker* 86 (11 October): 31 www.newyorker.com/magazine/2010/10/11/boom-doctor (accessed January 17, 2017).

Peng, Y. 1998. "Agriculture, Rural Industries and Peasant Income in China," *Development and Society* 27 (1): 1–31.

People's Daily Online. 2012. "China's Socialist Market Economic Reform and its Strong Theoretical Consciousness and Confidence." http://en.people.cn/100668/102793/7980397.html (accessed January 17, 2017).

Pomfret, J. 2001. "The High Cost of Selling Blood: As AIDS Crisis Looms in China, Official Response is Lax." *Washington Post*, 11 January: A01 www.washingtonpost.com/archive/politics/2001/01/11/the-high-cost-of-selling-blood/d0dbe9ab-11d3-4179-908f-0c43d3cf94a9/ (accessed June 6, 2016).

Resnick, S. 1970. "The Decline of Rural Industry under Export Expansion: A Comparison among Burma, Philippines and Thailand, 1870–1938." *Journal of Economic History* 30 (1): 51–73.

——— 1975. "State of Development Economics" *American Economic Review* 65 (2): 317–22.

Resnick, S. and R. Wolff. 1979. "The Theory of Transitional Conjunctures and the Transition from Feudalism to Capitalism in Western Europe." *Review of Radical Political Economics* 11 (3): 3–22.

Standaert, M. 2003. "Interview with Yu Hua." http://u.osu.edu/mclc/online-series/yuhua/ (accessed June 6, 2016).

Yu, Hua. 2003. *Chronicle of a Blood Merchant*. Trans. A. F. Jones. New York: Anchor Books.

20 Problematizing the global economy

Financialization and the "feudalization" of capital

Rajesh Bhattacharya and Ian J. Seda-Irizarry

Introduction

Financialization is perhaps the most controversial aspect of the series of transformations that have altered the face of capitalism in the last four decades. Broadly speaking, financialization refers to the dominance of financial capital over other forms of capital, evident in "the increasing role of financial motives, financial markets, financial actors and financial institutions in the operation of the domestic and international economies" (Epstein 2005, 3). The most significant aspect of financialization, emphasized by heterodox economists, is the purported "separation" of finance from material production. In empirical accounts, this separation refers to a set of associated phenomena, e.g., the subjugation of manufacturing to financial interests (Orhangazi 2011), the rise to power of financial over productive capitalists (Dumenil and Levy 2011), the trade-off between short-term profit maximization and long-term growth (Stockhammer 2004), and so on. At a more theoretical level, separation has been understood in terms of the privileging of financial profits over real production of value as the dominant mode of valorization of capital (Arrighi 1994, Krippner 2005, Foster and Magdoff 2008) or as the 'autonomization' of capital from its material bases (Teixeira and Rotta 2012, Rotta and Teixeira 2016, Paulani 2014).[1]

Despite its rich historical-empirical content and theoretical insights, the literature on financialization, in general, suffers from a tendency to study it in isolation from other transformations of the global economy and to focus on richer capitalist economies only. More specifically, while connecting financialization to neoliberalism, the literature has not explored it in connection with other strands of critical literature on neoliberalism—notably, the literature on primitive accumulation as a strategy for enhancing corporate profitability (Harvey 2003, Perelman 2000 and 2002, Sanyal 2007, Basu 2007, Bhattacharya 2010) and the literature on the "global value-chains" (Bair 2005, Gereffi and Korzeniewicz 1994, Gereffi et. al 2005) that captures the new economic geography of global production. The connection among these transformations can be understood using the Marxian category of (ground) rent. Very few works have explored the link between financialized capital and the organization of production in global value chains (Milberg 2008, Milberg and Winkler 2009, Palpaceur 2008, Newman 2009). Teixeira and Rotta (2012) have investigated the connection among "new enclosures" of knowledge-products, ground rent, and financialization. Serfati (2008) has tried to connect financialization, global value-chains, and the significance of rents in corporate strategies. The absence of these theoretical connections sustains the separation thesis in the existing literature on financialization. Once we recognize these connections, the separation thesis as currently articulated must give way to a new theoretical problematic, one we refer to as the *feudalization* of capital. Feudalization of capital points to the set of processes that forge an inseparable yet distanced connection between capital and labor that relies on primitive accumulation and extraction of rent. For this connection to become visible, we must eschew the richer capitalist economies as the unit of analysis and look at the global organization of production.

We believe that Marx's contributions concerning financial capital are extremely relevant to the current debate on the separation of finance and production. Specifically, his understanding of financial or interest-bearing capital as the most *fetishistic* form of capital is central to our endeavor.[2] The purported separation of finance from production then becomes one of misunderstanding the distance between value-producing labor and the profits realized in finance as the apparent autonomy/dislocation/separation of the latter from the former. In other words, fetishization of financial capital renders invisible living labor as the source of surplus value.

In this essay, we seek to develop a theoretical critique of the separation thesis by following the leads provided by those who have made the connection among financialization, global value chains, and the importance of rent in corporate strategies. However, we also point to the shortcomings of these attempts to reconceptualize global capitalism. We argue that the literature of financialization continues to be blind to the presence of non-capitalist production spaces in the global economy that are subjected to control by mercantile and financial capital, with revenues flowing from such control largely appropriated by firms headquartered in the richer capitalist economies, and to the salience of primitive accumulation for rent-earning capital.

Our critique builds on the contributions of Stephen A. Resnick and Richard D. Wolff (1987), particularly those enabling complex and disaggregated analyses of the economy (Bhattacharya and Seda-Irizarry 2015, 674–76). More specifically, we find their distinction between different forms of *capital* and *capitalism* particularly illuminating. One of the insights following from their Marxian framework is that an economy is labeled capitalist because the capitalist class structure is *prevalent* in the social formation of which it is a part, but not because it is the only class structure present in the social formation. The social formation can and often does include non-capitalist class structures, and sometimes the latter constitutes a significant or even the major part of the economy.[3] Further, the capitalist class structure consists of a set of specific articulations between productive (industrial) and unproductive (merchant, financial) forms of capital in any social context. A class structure is called capitalist because class exploitation in production is capitalist in character, not because productive capital is dominant over unproductive capital. Hence, a capitalist class structure can exist in which unproductive capitalists have greater power over productive capitalists. Similarly, unproductive capital can be and has always been deeply connected to non-capitalist class structures whenever they are present in the social formation. Moreover, unproductive capital can be associated with expansion of both capitalist and non-capitalist class structures at the same time, or they might facilitate the expansion of one at the cost of the other. Thus, financialization has to be located in a more complex picture of the economy, particularly when we are taking the global economy as the unit of analysis. However, while Resnick and Wolff's works allow us to problematize the economy by making a distinction between class structures and the social formation containing them and by disaggregating the connections between different forms of capital and non-capitalist class structures, we argue that the salience of primitive accumulation and rent as a source of revenue for capitalists has been largely ignored in their work.

The following section presents the separation thesis as a theoretical problem in the literature on financialization and briefly reviews the literature connecting financialization with global value chains and the significance of rent in corporate strategies. The third section builds on the contributions of Resnick and Wolff to argue that if we acknowledge the complex relations between different forms of capital and non-capital—which may together constitute a capitalist social formation—then the separation thesis cannot be sustained as a Marxian proposition. Instead, a different transformation of the global economy becomes discernible, which is elaborated in the fourth section on "financialization and non-capital." It argues that any account of capitalism that does not recognize non-capitalist class structures obscures the continuous and central role of primitive accumulation to the valorization of capital. Capital may subject its non-capitalist "outside" to primitive accumulation to secure its conditions of existence, without necessarily dissolving the latter (Bhattacharya 2010). This opens up a theoretical connection among primitive accumulation, rent, and financialization. The last section concludes.

Financialization and the separation thesis

The point of departure of the separation thesis is the observed slowdown in physical capital accumulation in the richer Western economies relative to the post-WWII Golden Age. Since the same period also witnessed rising financial profits, it has been argued that financial accumulation has happened at the cost of physical capital accumulation. These empirical observations have given birth to a literature on the purported trade-off between financial and productive investment. This trade-off has been linked to the rise of shareholder value as the dominant principle of corporate governance (Lazonick and O'Sullivan 2000), a class-offensive against the workers in advanced countries (Harvey 2010), the deregulation of the financial sector since the 1970s (Crotty 2009 and 2011), the global dispersion of production of goods and services (Milberg 2008, Milberg and Winkler 2009), and structural changes within the United States as the center of global capitalism (Bakir 2015, Kotz 2015). This trade-off approach to the separation thesis has been criticized on two grounds; a) it takes advanced countries—individually or as a group—as the unit of analysis, and b) it takes the post-WWII Golden Age rate of physical accumulation as the comparator. As McNally (2011) points out, if capital is not territorially fixed, then the world-economy is the appropriate unit of analysis of accumulation of capital, not the nation-state. In particular, the focus on advanced countries hides the dramatic increase in the rates of physical capital accumulation in developing countries, most notably East Asian countries and two of the largest economies of the world, India and China. Outsourcing and offshoring of production to developing countries—linking financialization to global value-chains—could explain the dramatic rise in physical capital accumulation in developing economies and concurrent slowdown in the developed countries, thus ruling out a trade-off at the global level. Second, McNally (2011) also points out that the post-WWII Golden Age capitalism should not be taken as the period of comparison, since it was an exceptional period, driven by the post-war reconstruction of Western Europe and Japan and exceptionally low competition in world markets.

A second approach to the separation thesis emphasizes the connection between financialization and structural transformations in capitalism. Arrighi (1994) argues that financialization occurs when a certain mode of accumulation of productive capital exhausts itself so that capital seeks to transform itself from productive to its unproductive forms and prefers financial or mercantile profits over direct production and accumulation of surplus value. Financialization, according to Arrighi, represents the end to long cycles of capitalist expansion. Thus, current financialization is a symptom of the exhaustion of the "American" century of productive accumulation that began around 1870s and started showing signs of exhaustion in the 1970s. Also within the structuralist tradition, Kotz (2011 and 2015) uses the *social structure of accumulation* (SSA) framework to analyze financialization as a 'mode of accumulation,' and Boyer (2000) uses the *regulation* framework to understand financialization as a 'regime of accumulation' succeeding the post-WWII Golden Age phase. In both of these frameworks, there is the notion of exhaustion of a 'mode' or 'regime' of accumulation, which ushers in the subsequent one, and financialization is traced to the 'exhaustion' of the previous 'mode' or 'regime.' In this respect, their works have a certain affinity with Arrighi's, even though the latter uses the *longe durée* approach of the French *Annales* school of historiography.

In all of these formulations, financialization represents a phase (cycle, regime) during which production is subjugated to finance, the productive to the unproductive, and the 'real' to the 'fictitious.' Implicit in these formulations is the belief that finance becomes *independent* of material production—i.e., it separates itself from the processes of value-creation—and even expands at the cost of the latter. Hence, all accounts of financialization, historical or contemporary, link this separation to capitalist crises. The theoretical puzzle implicit in framing the separation thesis was pointedly presented in Pollin's review of Arrighi (1994): "[In the M-M′ circuit] where do the profits come from if not from the production and exchange of commodities?" (1996, 115).

Pollin locates three possible sources of financial profits: (1) a general trade-off between capitalists that are making money and other capitalists that are losing money, hence a redistribution of surplus value within the capitalist class itself (e.g., financial firms or financial wings of firms gaining at the expense of non-financial firms or non-financial wings of firms); (2) a redistribution of income in favor of financial capitalists through the extension of credit to the working class (who make interest payments to financial firms) or indirectly when industrial capitalists increase their profits without increasing surplus value—by lowering tax burdens or decreasing real wages—and then redistribute some of these additional profits to financial firms in the form of interest payments;[4] or (3) enhanced financial profits can also accrue when financial firms enable industrial capitalists to shift their funds into more profitable areas of material production and are then able to capture a share of the resulting expansion of surplus value (Pollin 1996).

The literature on financialization provides arguments and empirical evidence showing how all three of the above sources have been important for the expansion of financial profits. For example, Stockhammer (2004), Crotty (2005), and Orhangazi (2008) have examined the performance of non-financial vis-à-vis financial corporations in the neoliberal era, emphasizing the negative impact of financialization on real investment. Lapavitsas (2009) has highlighted how expansion of the sphere of circulation and the stagnation in production has led to a process of 'financial expropriation' where profits are extracted from wages. Finally, Harvey (2003) and Guttman (2008) have focused on asset stripping, mergers, and acquisitions as strategies to increase profitability.

At the same time, the literature on financialization has ignored two parallel transformations in global capitalism: the ascendance of intangible capital (knowledge-capital) as a driver of financial profits and the geographical dispersion of production embedded in global value chains. Though there has been a substantial literature on both these transformations, few scholars have connected them to financialization and even fewer have done so from a Marxian perspective.

One thought-provoking contribution in this regard is by Teixeira and Rotta (2012) who draw novel connections among financialization, rent, and knowledge-commodities. They point to the salience of knowledge-commodities in contemporary capitalism, e.g., "privatized knowledge and commodified information, such as computer software, chemical formulae, cultural and musical production, engineering secrets, and patented knowledge" (454). Using Marx's definition of value as that "determined not by the labor-time originally taken by their production, but rather by the labor-time that their reproduction takes" (1993, 522), they assert that knowledge-commodities are valueless because labor is employed in their production but not in their reproduction (except for the material content of the storage and transportation devices that constitute an insignificant component of its market price). The price of such "valueless" commodities is therefore the result of monopoly property rights—just like land, which has no value but yields ground-rent to its owner. For Teixeira and Rotta, therefore, the return to capital in production of knowledge-commodities is not surplus value from direct production but "rent" earned from monopolizing the knowledge-product and leasing or selling it to producers who make rental payments to use these knowledge-commodities in production. The owners of the knowledge-commodities get a cut of the surplus value generated in production by others using the knowledge-commodities. Teixeira and Rotta argue that "new enclosures" pertaining to privatization and commoditization of potentially freely reproducible knowledge-commodities points to the salience of rent and rent-bearing capital in contemporary corporate strategies of maximizing profit.

Teixeira and Rotta understand financialization as one aspect of the transformation of capitalism, in the sphere of finance. Its counterpart in the sphere of production is "valueless" commodities. Both of these transformations—financialization and valueless commodities—are said to be manifestations of a single process, the "autonomization of social forms" in capitalism from their "material bases." Fundamental to understanding the *logic* of autonomization is the recognition that capital "has the tendency to expel its own content" (Teixeira and Rotta 2012, 451). Specifically, the contradiction of capital is that, even though living labor is the source of new value, and hence surplus value, capital "both depends on and expels productive labor" (*ibid.*). Thus, for example, the objective of production of knowledge-commodities is not the direct exploitation of laborers through appropriation of their surplus labor time. In fact, strictly speaking, the laborers producing patented knowledge-commodities are not "exploited" in the Marxian sense, since they are not producing value or surplus value but are producing monopolizable "valueless" commodities that are nonetheless essential conditions for the production of value and surplus value elsewhere. In this conception, rent-bearing capital distances itself from production and productive laborers.

As far as social forms in capitalism are concerned, autonomization consists in the *retreat* from the M – C – P – C' – M' (productive capitalist) circuit and its associated M – C – M' (mercantile capitalist) circuit to the pure M – M' (financial capitalist) circuit. The dominant social forms of capital in contemporary capitalism are financial or "fictitious" capital and rent-bearing capital, which are forms farthest removed from real value-producing activities, which we will explore in detail in the next section. But Teixeira and Rotta's work, in pointing to valueless commodities and knowledge-rents as the increasingly dominant elements in securing financial profits, is also susceptible to Pollin's question: Where do interest and rent come from, if not from real production in which capital is exploiting labor? To find an answer to this vexed question, we suggest that we look beyond the heartland of financialization—namely, the richer capitalist economies—and beyond the capitalist economy itself. The literature on global value chains offers important clues in this respect.

In the era of financialization, a new economic geography of production has emerged in which firms in the developed and developing countries occupy specific locations in the global value chain of production, with most of the value captured as returns to intangible capital (i.e., rents) by large firms in developed countries that specialize in the higher-end operations of the value-chain such as design, logistics, branding, and the like (Guttmann 2008).[5] One of the earlier works that connected financialization to the emergent economic geography of production was Saskia Sassen's writing on "global cities" in which she argued that the vertical disintegration of production and its global dispersal is accompanied by a corresponding centralization of command and control functions in "global cities" like New York, London, and Tokyo where financial markets have been instrumental in intensifying such centralization (Sassen 2000, 81–82). This pattern of globalization is different from the colonial pattern of trade, where underdeveloped countries specialized in primary products and developed countries specialized in industrial products. We return to this point in the section on "financialization and non-capital."

The imperatives of finance in such global organization of production are clearly noted by Milberg and Winkler (2009):

> We find that the expansion of global production networks has served a dual purpose in the evolving corporate strategy. Cost reductions from the globalisation of production have supported the financialisation of the non-financial corporate sector, both by raising profits and by reducing the need for domestic reinvestment of those profits, freeing earnings for the purchase of financial assets and raising shareholder returns.
>
> (2009, 2)

In our view, a clear understanding of the connections among financial-ization, global value-chains, and appropriation of surplus value in the form of rent implies that the separation thesis cannot be sustained. At most, the separation of production from finance is a regional empirical phenomenon confined to select western economies. When we consider the role of global value chains, as we do in the next two sections, what emerges is a more disaggregated picture of global production of surplus in both capitalist and non-capitalist production spaces and new forms of the appropriation of that surplus in the form of rent. In the process, the "outside" of capital and the process of primitive accumulation become theoretically visible—but only by moving beyond the capitalocentric limits of the existing literature.

Forms of capital and capitalism: a critique of the separation problem

Any account of financialization in contemporary capitalism must explain the relations among different forms of capital, the relation between different forms of capital and non-capitalist production, and hence what capitalism means in the face of such heterogeneity. Traditionally, Marxists understood capital as "self-expansion of value," i.e., something that exists only in order to grow. The simplest form that captures this self-expansion is the circuit of money-capital, $M - M'$ In this circuit, value can expand in different ways. It can expand because the money-capitalist has advanced unproductive loans to any economic agent and gets a cut (as interest) of the diverse incomes generated in production. It can expand because the money-capitalist has lent money as capital to the undertaker of production and gets a cut from the surplus value (as interest) generated in production. The cut can be from either capitalist or *non-capitalist* surplus value, depending on the class structure in which the borrower participates. Money-capital can also expand when it is invested in monopoly rights over conditions of production (e.g., land or knowledge) and it earns rent. Interest-bearing capital and rent-bearing capital are different instances of the same circuit of capital at work.

In the circuit of mercantile capital, $M - C - M'$, capital valorizes itself by enabling the circulation of produced commodities. Mercantile profit is a cut of the surplus value generated in the production of commodities. The source of mercantile profit can be either capitalist or non-capitalist surplus value depending on whether mercantile capital is invested in the circulation of capitalist or non-capitalist commodities. Finally, the connection between capital and production is most intimate in the case of the circuit of productive capital, i.e., $M - C - P - C' - M$. Here, capital can only valorize itself by being involved in the actual process of production, through direct appropriation of produced surplus value.

In a social formation, the multiple connections between the different circuits of capital and the different (class) forms of production yield a complex economic totality. A class structure is defined in terms of the social relations entailed in the processes of production, appropriation, and distribution of surplus labor performed by direct producers (Resnick and Wolff 1987). By a capitalist class structure, we mean the specific configuration of class relations that sustain the circuit of productive capital. In Resnick and Wolff's view, the concept of "social formation" then refers to a social totality exhibiting multiple and ever-changing class structures (*ibid.*, 118). Social formations are often named after the class structure "prevalent" in the social formation at that particular time, where "prevalence" is often but not necessarily understood in terms of the class structure's dominance in the share of the total surplus in society. Capitalism refers to a social formation in which the capitalist fundamental class process is "prevalent." Unlike capital and capitalist class structures, which are theoretical categories, capitalism is a historical category that refers to the context of a particular social formation.[6]

Sustained valorization of capital in any social conjuncture is ultimately based on the value created in production. To pose a fundamental disconnect between valorization of capital and value-creating activities, i.e., to pose something like "valorization without value," is therefore to subscribe to a non-Marxian position. There is nothing in the conceptualization of a capitalist class structure that rules out the possibility that the landlord or the money-capitalist may end up possessing more surplus value than the productive capitalist. The logic of self-expansion of value might require that capital be fluid among its forms so as to bypass any obstacles to its expansion. For individual firms, this need for fluidity might require transformations in the production and appropriation of surplus, like the geographical dispersion of production to take advantage of lower unit costs (due to lower wages for territorially less mobile workers), or it might imply a diversification of activities to secure already-produced surplus (e.g., productive capitalist firms developing financial branches). These and other possibilities can combine in ways in which rent-bearing and interest-bearing capitals are more prominent than productive capital. However, it does not mean that capital has separated itself from value-creating activities. The capitalist class-structure, i.e., the productive circuit of capital, can be prevalent and yet the productive capitalist's share of total surplus value can be less than those of financial and rent-bearing capital. In fact, faster accumulation of financial or rent-bearing capital can enable faster rates of accumulation of productive capital through expanding the supply of loans and purchase of equities. Consider the example of the iPhone:

> The largest share of the value created by the iPhone accrues to providers of distribution and retail services in the United States and to Apple, mainly to its innovations in design, marketing and supply-chain management. For each iPhone 4 sold, at a retail price of USD 600, Apple earns around USD 270, while Korean firms supplying core

components earn USD 80, and Chinese enterprises that undertake the assembly earn USD 6.5, a mere 1% of the total value.

(OECD 2013, 23)

The fact that Apple earns large rents from "valueless" knowledge-commodities such as design or branding does not subtract from the significance of "value-creating activities" in Korean and Chinese capitalist factories. In this case, one class-position—the "landlord class-position" of Apple by virtue of its monopoly rights over iPhone's design—has greater ability to capture surplus value than the productive capitalists in China and Korea. However, this doesn't prevent high rates of accumulation of productive capital in China or Korea, nor does Apple valorize its capital without an underlying production of commodities.

In advancing the autonomization thesis, Teixeira and Rotta (2012) have inadvertently fallen into a trap that theoretically privileges the social forms of capital prominent in western economies (symbolized by Apple, Nike, Reebok, or Monsanto). Capitalism—understood at the global level—is about the prevalence of the capitalist class process in the production of surplus value, not the dominance of this or that form of capital. In the same vein, as we argue in the next section, the "prevalence" of the capitalist class structure does not rule out the presence (or even numerical significance, for example, in employment) of non-capitalist class structures in the social formation. Coffee is often grown by small peasant families in various countries of Latin America, Africa, and elsewhere, and the fact that big capitalist firms, who may themselves be highly active in the financial sphere, control that trade, does not mean that the entire coffee chain exhibits a capitalist class structure.

A more disaggregated analysis of the global economy can open up the debate on financialization to newer theoretical possibilities. When considering capital as a process (i.e., self-expansion of value) at the micro-level, the strategic choices of a firm are a response to the entire context. It is possible for the self-expansion of value to involve a retreat from direct production (i.e., a retreat from class-exploitation of workers) in certain social contexts (richer capitalist economies, for example) and an expansion in other social contexts (developing economies, for example), as an outcome of the pursuit of surplus value. This geography of exploitation is determined by the degree of resistance to class-exploitation, the level of productivity of workers, the policies of the respective governments, and so on, in different jurisdictions. Therefore, in certain regions, financial capital may appear socially prevalent while in others industrial capital may be socially prevalent. If we focus on the class process in production, then we realize that the mobility of capital across jurisdictions, which has expanded in the neoliberal era under free trade policies across the world, coupled with the immobility of workers under stricter immigration policies, creates the conditions of precisely such an economic geography of exploitation. Correspondingly, the prevalent form of capital will also vary across global regions, making it imperative to analyze capitalism at a global level in order to sustain a Marxian account.

Financialization and non-capital: a critique of capitalocentrism

The account of capitalism in the debate on financialization gets further problematized if we bring in non-capitalist class-structures linked to productive, mercantile, interest-bearing or rent-bearing forms of capital. Unfortunately, even those who make a connection between financialization and global value-chains fail to recognize the articulation of non-capitalist class structures in developing countries into circuits of capital dominated by capitalist firms, often headquartered in the developed countries. Failure to recognize non-capitalist production sites obscures the flows of value between non-capitalist and capitalist class structures within and across nations and the significance of primitive accumulation. For example, Teixeira and Rotta (2012) draw the analogy between knowledge-commodities and land but do not bring out the full implications of the centrality of primitive accumulation ("new enclosures") to the production of valueless commodities and the appropriation of knowledge-rent. This is because to posit primitive accumulation as a process constitutive of capitalism requires the acknowledgment of an inescapable (non-capitalist) "outside" of capital (Bhattacharya 2010).

In the literature on global value chains involving coffee and other agricultural products, athletic footwear, sporting goods, and the like, we often find that sometimes a major part of the production is done by peasants, family enterprises, and petty producers at the lowest level of the global value chain. Much of this production goes on within non-capitalist class structures, often using just family labor in home-based production. These direct producers are often located in developing countries and get an insignificant share of the value. The bulk of the value is retained by retailers and parent firms who provide the design specification and the brand name. In Marxian terms, non-capitalist surplus value is extracted by mercantile capitalist firms or captured as rents by firms who provide a crucial element that cannot be imitated, whether knowledge-commodities like patented designs such as Nike or Reebok, brand image, or consumption ambience (Starbucks). But the source of these mercantile profits and rents is the non-capitalist surplus value produced in the developing countries. The reduction of all economic sites and class processes to capitalist ones hides an important source of surplus value for merchants and rent-bearing capital: non-capitalist value.[7]

Thus looking only at capitalist production sites and their rate of accumulation of physical capital does not exhaust the potential sources of value for financial profits. Financial profits can expand on the basis of *non*-capitalist surplus value. While the example of Apple products in the previous section mainly illustrates the presence of *capitalist* firms in China or South Korea in its global value chain, textiles, coffee, footwear, and sportswear are well-known examples of *non-capitalist* units (characterized by feminized work in many cases) in the global value-chain led by highly financialized capitalist firms.

The financialization of the dominant firm is reflected in the rising significance of "intangible capital"[8] or "knowledge-capital" in the firm's strategies. In the past, global competition was driven by accumulation of physical capital; today it is driven by the accumulation of knowledge/intellectual/intangible capital. As Belloc and Pagano (2012, 448) argue, "[i]f a good like knowledge is moved from the public to the private sphere, the legal positions on intellectual property influence the comparative advantages of nations and cause patterns of asymmetric development." As production gets globally dispersed, what matters is not the dominance of material production and physical capital, but rather the prevalence of immaterial production (Hardt and Negri 2001) and knowledge-capital (Burton-Jones 1999). Immaterial production based on knowledge-capital dominates the global value-chains. In the past, firms specializing in industrial products ruled over those that produced primary products; today, firms specializing in immaterial production dominate firms specializing in material production in the global value chains.

The elements constituting these new forms of capital clearly belong to the domain of culture, knowledge, and communications; investment in intellectual capital now outstrips that in physical capital in several advanced countries. According to an OECD report (2013), in Sweden, the United Kingdom, and the United States, investment in knowledge-based capital matches or exceeds investment in physical capital. The report emphasizes that the importance of knowledge-capital will increase in the future as countries compete over the upper segments of the value chains given that the "allocation of value depends on the ability of participants to supply sophisticated, *hard-to-imitate* products or services" (OECD 2013, 23, emphasis added).

As Milberg argues, "many 'manufacturing' firms do not manufacture at all, providing only brand design, marketing, supply chain logistics and financial management services" (2008, 425). The reason behind this strategy is that as productive capacities develop in other countries, only the most *hard-to-imitate* parts of the production process become the means of extracting greater value. Investment in intangible assets creates instruments that secure monopoly rights over conditions of production (because it is hard or illegal to imitate), forcing producing firms to yield a greater share of their value to the providers of such conditions of production.

Once we recognize the importance of rent in the contemporary era of financialization, we must also recognize the processes of primitive accumulation that transform the conditions of non-capitalist production across the world. The introduction of genetically modified seeds, the extension of intellectual property rights to living organisms like plants, and "theft" of traditional knowledge all contribute to the production of what Teixeira and Rotta call "valueless" knowledge-commodities that yield rents to the firms with state-protected property rights in these commodities. Scholars have often referred to these novel forms of primitive accumulation as "new enclosures" or "second enclosures" (May 2000, Boyle 2003, Evans 2005). The introduction of knowledge-commodities through these "new enclosures" can lead to the extraction of heavy rents from both capitalist and non-capitalist producers. Primitive accumulation, therefore, does not necessarily lead to the dissolution of non-capitalist class structures; instead, it might alter the conditions of existence of non-capitalist production such that the producers must pay rent for access to crucial conditions of production, e.g., Monsanto selling patented seeds to peasants. This aspect of financialization, in our understanding, contributes to the "feudalization" of an economy we have so long been accustomed to refer to as capitalism.

Conclusion

In this essay we have argued that the separation problem is at the heart of a substantial part of the contemporary discourse on financialization. Within the literature on financialization, we have singled out those contributions that have connected financialization to global value and commodity chains, the production of knowledge-capital, and to the significance of rent in driving various financial strategies of firms. While recognizing the significance of these contributions, we have found them to be trapped within capitalocentric discourses where the experience of the richer countries remains the focus. Using the insights from Resnick and Wolff, we have offered a more disaggregated view of capital, capitalism, and the world economy.

In our view, any discussion of the global economy must recognize the empirical possibility of two related but distinct phenomena: (1) the simultaneous existence and uneven development of capitalist and non-capitalist class structures and (2) the complex articulation of different forms of productive and unproductive capital with each other and with non-capitalist economy. In doing so, one must recognize the significance of traditional forms of primitive accumulation as well as instances of new enclosures in securing rent for dominant financialized firms. Investment in knowledge-capital appears as an increasingly dominant instrument for extraction of rent from both capitalist and non-capitalist producers within a transformed economic geography. For us, such a Marxian analysis renders the separation problem an untenable proposition. What we refer to as the feudalization of capital is the set of processes that contribute to an accumulation of (unproductive) capital through control over conditions of production rather than direct exploitation of workers—a strange distancing of capital from labor that is more reminiscent of what we have come to call the pre-capitalist era. It has been our purpose in this essay to introduce certain theoretical problems in the ongoing debate on financialization in the hope of eliciting more responses in this direction.

Acknowledgment

We are thankful to Ted Burczak for detailed comments on draft versions of the chapter.

Notes

1 The separation thesis seems to pose a fundamental challenge to Marx's theoretical contributions given the latter's emphasis on the *connections* among labor, value, and the various forms of surplus value (industrial profit, commercial profit, rent, interest, dividends, and so on). The cited works of the "autonomization school" are a Marxian response to this challenge.
2 "In interest-bearing capital, the capital relationship reaches its most superficial and fetishized form" (Marx [1883] 1993, 515).
3 Sanyal (2007) gives an account of capital's hegemony over postcolonial social formations where capitalist accumulation may in fact be accompanied by an expansion, rather than the dissolution, of the non-capitalist space.
4 Financial profits can arise from either current or anticipated future value flows. When credit is extended to the working class to finance investment in durable assets (houses) or when credit is extended to firms for investment in capital goods, financial profits are premised on the future value flows (Lapavitsas 2009). When such claims to future values are commoditized as financial assets, speculation in the face of radical uncertainty invariably affects exchange-values, leading to "spurious" future values. Part of financial profits in such cases is purely mercantile profit from selling "commodities" that are nothing but claims on future value, whether real or spurious. Such profits can therefore be a redistribution of real or spurious surplus values.
5 For the case of coffee, see Newman (2009).
6 See Resnick and Wolff (1987, 118–21 and 141–43) for a detailed discussion of the distinction among capital, capitalist class structure, social formation, and the prevalence of a class structure in social formation.
7 This point is argued forcefully by Ruccio, Resnick, and Wolff (1991, 35).
8 In the business literature, intellectual/intangible capital often refers to a set of assets: human capital, structural capital, or relational capital. While human capital is a familiar term, the other two refer to very specific firm-level assets and capabilities. Structural capital refers to organizational structure, culture, and procedures as well as patents, trademarks, and copyrights and other intellectual properties of the organization enhanced through R &D (Martín-de-Castro et. al 2006). Relational capital includes customer relationships, supplier relationships, trademarks, trade names, licenses, and franchises (Bontis 1998, Joia 2000).

References

Arrighi, G. 1994. *The Long Twentieth Century: Money, Power, and the Origins of our Time*. London: Verso.
Bair, J. 2005. "Global Capitalism and Commodity Chains: Looking Back, Going Forward." *Competition & Change* 9 (2):153–80.

Bakir, E. 2015. "Capital Accumulation, Profitability, and Crisis: Neoliberalism in the United States." *Review of Radical Political Economics* 47 (3): 389–411.

Basu, P. K. 2007. "Political Economy of Land Grab." *Economic and Political Weekly* 42 (14): 1281–7.

Belloc, F. and U. Pagano. 2012. "Knowledge Enclosures, Forced Specializations and Investment Crisis." *European Journal of Comparative Economics* 9 (3): 445–83.

Bhattacharya, R. 2010. "Capitalism in Post-Colonial India: Primitive Accumulation Under *Dirigiste* and *Laissez Faire* Regimes." Ph.D. dissertation. Department of Economics, University of Massachusetts, Amherst.

Bhattacharya, R. and I. Seda-Irizarry. 2015. "Re-centering Class in Critical Theory: A Tribute to Stephen A. Resnick (1938–2013)." *Review of Radical Political Economics* 27 (4): 669–78.

Bontis, N. 1998. "Intellectual Capital: An Exploratory Study that Develops Measures and Models." *Management Decision* 36 (2): 63–76.

Boyer, R. 2000. "Is a Finance-led Growth Regime a Viable Alternative to Fordism? A Preliminary Analysis." *Economy and Society* 29 (1): 111–45.

Boyle, J. 2003. "The Second Enclosure Movement and the Construction of the Public Domain." *Law and Contemporary Problems* 66 (1/2): 33–74.

Burton-Jones, A. 1999. *Knowledge Capitalism: Business, Work and Learning in the New Economy.* Oxford: Oxford University Press

Crotty, J. 2005. "The Neoliberal Paradox: The Impact of Destructive Product Market Competition and 'Modern' Financial Markets on Nonfinancial Corporation Performance in the Neoliberal Era." In *Financialization and the World Economy,* G. Epstein, ed. 77–110. Northampton, MA: Edward Elgar

——— 2009. "Structural Causes of the Global Financial Crisis. A Critical Assessment of the New Financial Architecture." *Cambridge Journal of Economics* 33 (40): 563–80.

——— 2011. "The Realism of Assumptions Does Matter: Why Keynes-Minsky Theory Must Replace Efficient Market Theory as the Guide to Financial Regulation Policy." In *Handbook of Political Economy of Financial Crises,* G. Epstein and M. Wolfson, eds., 133–58. New York: Oxford University Press.

Dumenil, G. and D. Levy. 2011. *The Crisis of Neoliberalism.* Cambridge: Harvard University Press.

Epstein, G., ed. 2005. *Financialization and the World Economy.* Aldershot: Edward Elgar.

Evans, P. 2005. "The New Commons vs. The Second Enclosure Movement: Comments on an Emerging Agenda for Development Research." *Studies in Comparative International Development* 40 (2): 85–94.

Foster, J. B. and F. Magdoff. 2008. "Financial Implosion and Stagnation." *Monthly Review* 60 (7): 1–29.

Gereffi, G. and M. Korzeniewicz, eds. 1994. *Commodity Chains and Global Capitalism.* Westport, CT: Praeger.

Gereffi, G., J. Humphrey, and T. Sturgeon. 2005. "The Governance of Global Value Chains." *Review of International Political Economy* 12 (1): 78–104.

Guttmann, R. 2008. "A Primer on Finance-Led Capitalism and Its Crisis. Introduction." *Revue de la régulation. Capitalisme, institutions, pouvoirs* 3 (4): 1.

Hardt, M. and A. Negri. 2001. *Empire.* Cambridge: Harvard University Press.

Harvey, D. 2003. *The New Imperialism.* New York: Oxford University Press.

—— 2010. *The Enigma of Capital and the Crises of Capitalism*. New York: Oxford University Press.

Joia, L. 2000. "Measuring Intangible Corporate Assets: Linking Business Strategy with Intellectual Capital." *Journal of Intellectual Capital* 1 (1): 68–84.

Kotz, D. 2011. "Financialization and Neoliberalism." In *Relations of Global Power: Neoliberal Order and Disorder*, G. Teeple and S. McBride, eds., 1–18. Toronto: University of Toronto Press.

—— 2015. *The Rise and Fall of Neoliberal Capitalism*. Cambridge: Harvard University Press.

Krippner, G. 2005. "The Financialization of the American Economy." *Socio-Economic Review* 3 (2): 173–208.

Lapavitsas, C. 2009. "Financialisation, or the Search for Profits in the Sphere of Circulation." School of Oriental and African Studies, Discussion Papers 10.

Lazonick W. and M. O'Sullivan. 2000. "Maximizing Shareholder Value: A New Ideology for Corporate Governance." *Economy and Society* 29 (1): 13–35.

Martín-de-Castro, G., J. E. Navas-López, P. López-Sáez and E. Alama-Salazar. 2006. "Organizational Capital as Competitive Advantage of the Firm." *Journal of Intellectual Capital* 7 (3): 324-37.

Marx, K. 1993 [1883]. *Capital: Volume 3*. London: Penguin.

May, C. 2000. *The Global Political Economy of Intellectual Property Rights: The New Enclosures?* New York: Routledge.

McNally, D. 2011. *Global Slump: The Economics and Politics of Crisis and Resistance*. Oakland, CA: PM Press.

Milberg W. 2008. "Shifting Sources and Uses of Profits: Sustaining U.S. Financialization with Global Value Chains." *Economy and Society* 37 (3): 420–51.

Milberg, W. and D. Winkler. 2009. "Financialisation and the Dynamics of Offshoring in the USA." *Cambridge Journal of Economics* 34 (2): 275–93.

Newman, S. 2009. "Financialization and Changes in the Social Relations along Commodity Chains: The Case of Coffee." *Review of Radical Political Economics* 41 (4): 539–59.

Organization for Economic Co-Operation and Development (OECD). 2013. *New Sources of Growth: Knowledge-Based Capital. Key Analyses and Policy Conclusions – Synthesis Report*. <www.oecd.org/sti/inno/knowledge-based-capital-synthesis.pdf> (accessed June 10, 2015).

Orhangazi, O. 2008. "Financialisation and Capital Accumulation in the Non-financial Corporate Sector: A Theoretical and Empirical Investigation of the U.S. Economy: 1973-2003." *Cambridge Journal of Economics* 32 (6): 863–86.

—— 2011. "'Financial' versus 'Real': An Overview of the Contradictory Role of Finance." *Research in Political Economy* 27: 121–48.

Palpaceur, F. 2008. "Bringing the Social Context Back in." *Economy and Society* 37 (3): 393–419.

Paulani, L. 2014. "Money in Contemporary Capitalism and the Autonomization of Capitalist Forms in Marx's Theory." *Cambridge Journal of Economics* 38 (4): 779–95.

Perelman, M. 2000. *The Invention of Capitalism: Classical Political Economy and the Secret History of Primitive Accumulation*. Durham: Duke University Press.

—— 2002. *Steal This Idea: Intellectual Property Rights and the Corporate Confiscation of Creativity*. New York: Palgrave Macmillan.

Pollin, R. 1996. "Contemporary Economic Stagnation in World Historical Perspective." *New Left Review* I/219: 109–18.

Resnick S. and R. Wolff. 1987. *Knowledge and Class: A Marxian Critique of Political Economy*. Chicago: University of Chicago Press.

Rotta, T. and R. Teixeira. 2016. "The Autonomization of Abstract Wealth: New Insights on the Labor Theory of Value." *Cambridge Journal of Economics* 40 (4): 1185–201.

Ruccio, D., S. Resnick, and R. Wolff. 1991. "Class Beyond the Nation-State." *Capital & Class* 15 (1): 25–41.

Sanyal, K. 2007. *Rethinking Capitalist Development: Primitive Accumulation, Governmentality and Post-colonial Capitalism*. New Delhi: Routledge.

Sassen, S. 2000. "The Global City: Strategic Site/New Frontier." *American Studies* 41 (2/3): 79–95.

Serfati, C. 2008. "Financial Dimensions of Transnational Corporations, Global Value Chain and Technological Innovation." *Journal of Innovation Economics* 2 (2): 35–61.

Stockhammer, E. 2004. "Financialisation and the slowdown of accumulation." *Cambridge Journal of Economics* 28 (5): 719–41.

Teixeira, R. and T. Rotta. 2012. "Valueless Knowledge-Commodities and Financialization: Productive and Financial Dimensions of Capital Autonomization." *Review of Radical Political Economics* 44 (4): 448–67.

21 Reproduction of noncapital

A Marxian perspective on the informal economy in India

Snehashish Bhattacharya

Introduction

The informal economy is viewed through contradictory lenses in development discourse. On one hand, it is seen as a pre-capitalist remnant acting as a drag on capitalist development or simply as the failure of capitalist development. On the other hand, it is seen as a seedbed of an emerging capitalism in which micro-entrepreneurs participate in commodity production to earn profit and expand their businesses, often working innovatively under severe constraints. In this essay, I present an alternative perspective on the informal economy in the context of recent growth experiences in India. Over the last decade and half, India's impressive GDP growth rates have given rise to a widespread celebration of the Indian economy as a success story of global capitalism. Yet the vast majority of the Indian working population continues to labor in the informal economy, in production processes that would be classified as noncapitalist (namely, household production with no strict separation between capital and wage labor). This poses a deeper question about the very concept of the informal economy, namely: Can it be understood as a homogenous economic space in which all enterprises are similar in terms of their production processes and that stands as the binary opposite of the capitalist formal sector?

To probe more deeply into the production and labor processes of informal enterprises, I draw upon the class analysis and overdeterminist Marxist framework developed by Stephen Resnick and Richard Wolff (1987 and 2006). I begin by discussing the theoretical conundrum posed by the stubborn existence of the informal economy amid sustained economic growth in the capitalist sector and the problems associated with the received dualism between formal and informal economies. I then analyze the case of India and explore the various class processes in the Indian informal economy. In particular, I explore the differential abilities of capitalist and noncapitalist informal enterprises to produce and distribute surplus and to achieve expanded reproduction. By way of conclusion, I consider the implications of this analysis for understanding the nature of postcolonial capitalist development.

Informality, dualism, and capitalist development

Traditional development discourse—in which economic development is synonymous with development of capitalism—assumes that noncapitalist structures will break down and dissolve as capitalist production relations expand and penetrate all parts of the economy. Since Lewis (1954), the so-called "less developed" or "labor surplus" economies have been characterized as backward due to a pervasive lack of capitalist development. In such classic "dual economies," the formal industrial production structures, comprising the capitalist sector, are limited to a small part of the entire economy, employ only a small fraction of the total labor force, and are surrounded by vast peripheries of pre-capitalist structures, mostly in agriculture. The development challenge in such societies, then, becomes the problem of transition to a full-fledged capitalist structure, like the way "advanced" economies are organized. The latent idea is that, with such a transition, the entire working population will be transformed into capitalist wage labor. A rapid industrialization process is supposed to be the instrument of this transition by drawing out surplus labor from the pre-capitalist peripheries.

Such a transition is possible only through a process of primitive accumulation, where the capitalist expansion in the formal industrial sector leads to a dissociation of the direct producers in the pre-capitalist peripheries from their means of labor, leading to their dispossession and turning them into capitalist wage laborers (Marx [1867] 1977). However, when the informal sector was "discovered" in the 1970s, it was already seen that in such "less developed" economies, this "double freedom" of labor—freedom from the ownership of their means of subsistence and the freedom to choose their own masters—is not actualized. The dispossessed direct producers are not transformed into wage laborers but rather are pushed in the burgeoning informal sector in both rural and urban regions. Over the following decades, the informal sector, though supposed to be a temporary or a transient phenomenon that would wither away as the industrialization process gathered momentum, showed a remarkable tenacity.

From traditional Marxist perspectives, the reason for the persistence of the formal/informal dualism is assumed to be either (1) the failure of capital to wash away the pre-capitalist remnants due to the comprador nature of domestic capital under the influence of imperialism and its resultant failure to bring about a full-fledged capitalist transformation or (2) the functional value of pre-capitalist economic spaces, continuing to exist because they fulfill the needs of capital and are thus fully subsumed to the logic of capital. For example, the informal sector produces cheap intermediate goods for the capitalist industries as well as cheap wage goods for the industrial workers, thereby aiding the process of capitalist surplus extraction in the formal sector. Such approaches visualize the entire economic space in terms of the logic of capital and its reproduction. In other critical approaches, the logic of reproduction of the informal sector is seen to be distinct from that of the formal capitalist enterprises. They are not oriented toward production of surplus, and hence remain outside the margins of the capitalist economy. In this framework, the informal sector is a unitary noncapitalist sector in which all household enterprises are motivated only by their own subsistence.

In short, there are two contradictory radical theories of the informal economy. The first provides a functionalist analysis, where the reproduction of the informal sector is understood in terms of the logic of capital. This represents a classic instance of capitalocentrism (Gibson-Graham and Ruccio 2001), where the informal sector is devoid of its own logic of existence and can only be explained in light of capital. In the second approach, the persistence of noncapital is seen to be a result of the dualism in the economy, where the entire informal sector is seen as outside the domain of capital, and all the differences and the dynamics within the informal sector are reduced to a singular logic of subsistence.

In much of the mainstream narrative, by contrast, the informal sector, formerly seen as a drag on the possibilities for capitalist growth, is now celebrated as a site of budding micro-entrepreneurship and the mechanism for inclusive development, providing livelihood to the vast majority of the working population who need not throng the gates of capital asking for employment. In this narrative, it is possible to have a depoliticized process of transition, where the direct producers reconnected with their means of production can reproduce themselves by participating in the market process, thereby exonerating capital from its responsibility to generate employment for the masses.

Both mainstream and radical discourses obscure the various class processes—i.e., the processes of performance, appropriation, and distribution of surplus labor—within the informal economy and the internal dynamics of the noncapitalist informal enterprises. In this essay, I question these standard representations of the informal economy by showing that the informal economy is a site of heterogeneous class processes. Through an analysis of the appropriative (or "fundamental") and distributive (or "subsumed") class processes of the informal manufacturing enterprises (Resnick and Wolff 1987), I show that there is a dualism even within the informal sector and that it is possible, conceptually and empirically, to distinguish capitalist and noncapitalist spaces within this sector. These two spaces have differential abilities to produce as well as to retain surplus, thereby giving rise to different possibilities for accumulation, expanded reproduction, and growth. As a concrete illustration, the next section looks through a class lens at production processes in the informal manufacturing enterprises in India.

Informal enterprises and class processes

Even after a relative success of the industrialization policy in post-independence India in modernizing the economy, the onset of pro-market reforms since 1991, and the high rate of economic growth over the past couple of decades (particularly between 2001 and 2011), it might be surprising to find that only about 15 percent of the entire work force in India—roughly 73 million out of a total labor force of about 460 million workers in 2010—is employed within the formal segments of the economy. The rest, about 85 percent of the work force, eke out their livelihood in the informal economy. Even within manufacturing, which is often considered to be the most dynamic segment of the economy driving the process of economic transformation, about 70 percent of the workforce is engaged in its informal segment (NSSO 2013).

For statistical purposes, the informal sector in India is defined as all unincorporated private enterprises owned by individuals or households engaged in the sale and production of goods and services, operated on a proprietary and partnership basis, with less than ten total workers. Thus, the firms are inextricably aligned with the households, often without having any separate existence.

A close look at the informal economy, however, reveals that it is not uniform or homogenous in terms of the production processes—the labor process and the way in which value is produced and distributed within a firm. The understanding of the entire informal economy as having an essential predetermined logic of its own (either same as or antithetical to the pre-given logic of the formal economy) erases the heterogeneous class processes that shape the dynamics of the enterprises in this economy. An overdeterminist class-focused understanding, in contrast, opens up the possibility for seeing this economic space in terms of a complex, diverse, and interconnected set of social (economic, political, and cultural) relations that are shaped, perhaps partially but nevertheless importantly, by the class processes.

The informal enterprises are classified in two types, namely, own account manufacturing enterprises (OAMEs henceforth) and establishments. In the OAMEs, production is organized using family labor without employing any wage labor, whereas the establishments predominantly exhibit a capitalist class process in which the owners of the enterprises employ some wage labor. The OAMEs constitute about 84 percent of all informal manufacturing enterprises, while the establishments constitute the remaining 16 percent—thus, the production processes in a vast majority of informal enterprises are noncapitalist, marked by an absence of any capital-wage labor relation.

However, an important aspect of *all* informal enterprises, including the establishments, is that in almost all firms, the owner participates in the labor process along with one or more family members, giving rise to different types of class processes within the enterprise. In the establishments, the predominant capitalist class process may often seem to be accompanied by a self-exploitative (ancient) class process (in the instances when the owners themselves participate in the production process of the firm and perform surplus labor) and even by a feudal class process, where the owner of the enterprise appropriates the surplus labor of other non-employed members of the household working in the enterprise.[1] As Marx points out: "Of course he [the capitalist] can, like the man who is working for him, participate directly in the process of production, but then *he is only a hybrid, a man between capitalist and worker,* a 'small master'" (Marx [1867] 1977, 423, emphasis added).

Similarly, in the OAMEs, a self-exploitative (ancient) class process, where the owner appropriates his or own surplus labor, often goes hand in hand with a feudal class process, where s/he appropriates the surplus labor performed by other household members, or with a communal class process where the household workers collectively appropriate the total surplus labor performed within the household enterprise.[2] However, in the absence of any capital-wage labor relations, these OAMEs are marked by an absence of the capitalist class process. Nevertheless, in terms of class processes, the identity of the firm in the informal sector is fractured and does not display any singular class process.

In order to get a notion of surplus in the "capitalist" enterprises, one must estimate the value of labor power of hired workers and the necessary labor of family workers, including the owner. The noncapitalist enterprises participate in the market process, and while the total net returns from the sale of their produced commodities become the net earning of the enterprise, an estimate of their surplus can be determined only after calculating the consumption fund necessary for the reproduction of the customary standard of living of the household workers (just as this must be done to arrive at a notion of the value of labor power of a wage worker).

While these ancient and feudal workers do not receive a wage, the value of their necessary labor can be inferred from the commodity basket that they purchase to maintain their customary standard of living. For example, while discussing necessary labor and the value of labor power, Marx argues:

> If, instead of working for the capitalist, he [the worker] worked independently on his own account, he would, other things being equal, still be *obliged to work for the same number of hours in order to produce the value of his labor-power,* and thereby to gain the means of subsistence necessary for his own preservation or continued reproduction.
>
> ([1867] 1977, 324, emphasis added)

The retained earnings of the enterprise comprise total revenues minus payment for the means of nonwage labor, wages of hired labor, and other payments made to secure the conditions of the existence of the enterprise. A *part* of these retained earnings is the *net* surplus of the enterprise that can either be used for accumulation purposes for expanded reproduction of the enterprise or for consumption purposes of the household to raise their standard of living. In the latter case, the household would receive a distributive class income as the owner of the enterprise.

The total surplus value produced in each enterprise is distributed as distributive class payments to secure the economic, political, and cultural conditions of existence of the enterprise. Such payments would include payment of rent for hired assets and land, interest payments for loans, and bribes and other payments to administration, police, and political parties to secure the rights to transact and conduct business, particularly when the informal enterprises work in the shadowy area of legality.

The existence of such multiple class processes within an enterprise may give rise to specific contradictions and tensions. To reproduce the conditions of existence for the capitalist class process, the kind of necessary distributions from the total surplus might be different—or even contradictory—from the distributions that might be needed to reproduce the conditions for the ancient or feudal class processes. For example, if the owner of an enterprise, who is often the head of the household, decides to distribute a larger proportion of the surplus to augment the household's total consumption, this would siphon away a part of the net surplus that could be used as an accumulation fund to undertake expanded reproduction of the enterprise. In this case, the noncapitalist structure of the household obstructs expansion of the enterprise. On the other hand, if an enterprise is unable to produce enough surplus to satisfy its conditions of existence, the household members working in the enterprise have the "flexibility" to reduce their consumption basket, pushing their standard of living below the customary standard, to allow for the survival of the enterprise. Similarly, the success of a capitalist class process in an informal enterprise might lead to employment of a larger number of workers, thereby, over time, replacing the household workers and changing the nature of the enterprise in the capitalist direction.

Thus it can be seen that it is impossible at two different levels to posit the informal sector as a homogenous space. The sector is comprised of two different segments—the enterprises that exhibit a predominantly capitalist class process (establishments) and those that are marked by the absence of a capitalist class process (OAMEs). Further, even within each kind of enterprise, one can see the existence of multiple class processes that might often be in contradiction with one another. This breaks the notion of informal economy as centered, uniform, and homogenous, as is often posited in the existing development literature. In the next section, I investigate the different possibilities of reproduction for the capitalist and noncapitalist enterprises within the informal economy.

Surplus in non/capitalist enterprises

It is possible to interpret the data on the informal manufacturing enterprises in India—produced by the successive rounds of detailed surveys of such enterprises carried out every five years by the National Sample Survey Organization (NSSO)—in the class terms outlined above.[3] A look at the three most recent rounds of such surveys, carried out in 2000–2001, 2005–2006, and 2010–11, covering the entire decade of fast economic growth in India, gives a sense of how class processes shape the reproduction of the heterogeneous informal economy.[4]

The Gross Value Added (henceforth, GVA) derived in Table 21.1 below gives a sense of the total value produced in an enterprise, net the constant capital or the means of labor. GVA is equivalent to the total wage fund or the consumption fund of the workers and the total surplus produced in the enterprise. As there is a large degree of heterogeneity among the informal firms and, consequently, a high level of dispersion in GVAs, I use the median values of the economic variables to get a sense of the characteristics of the typical OAME and establishment.

As Table 21.1 shows, there is a huge difference in GVA between the OAMEs and the establishments, and this difference has only increased over the decade. For example, in 2000–2001, the GVA of an average OAME (INR 21697) was about 16 percent that of an average establishment (INR 135609).[5] In 2005–2006, the ratio of the former to the latter fell to about 12 percent, and in 2010–11 it was about 13 percent. Over the decade, the GVAs of an average OAME increased by 15 percent, while that of an average establishment increased by about 39 percent. Similarly, in per-worker terms, the GVA per worker of an average OAME (INR 15233) in 2000–2001 was about 37 percent that of an average establishment (INR 41236).[6] This ratio fell to about 31 percent in 2005–2006 and to about 34 percent in 2010–11.

From their GVA, the enterprises need to distribute payments to various claimants who provide the conditions of existence for the internal class

Table 21.1 Gross Value Added (GVA) in OAMEs and establishments (median values in Indian rupees at constant 2011 prices).

	OAME				Establishment			
Year	GVA	GVA per worker	Net GVA	Net GVA per worker	GVA	GVA per worker	Net GVA	Net GVA per worker
2000–2001	21,697	15,233	21,255	14,945	135,609	41,236	73,727	56,258
2005–2006	15,629	12,584	15,246	12,310	134,225	41,026	71,088	53,489
2010–2011	24,960	20,100	24,660	19,710	187,800	58,920	100,800	85,740

Source: Calculated from the 56th, 62nd, and 67th Rounds of NSSO surveys of unorganized manufacturing sector in India.

processes. For the establishments, after paying off the claimants outside the enterprise, as well as the wages for the hired workers, whatever is retained constitutes the net GVA or the net income for the household. For OAMEs, on the other hand, this net GVA or net income is simply the difference between the total GVA and the outside payments. The ratios of the net incomes of the OAMEs to that of the establishments in 2000–2001, 2005–2006, and 2010–11 were 29 percent, 22 percent, and 25 percent, respectively. The stark difference between the OAMEs and the establishments is thus further reflected by the differences in their net GVAs over the decade.

The ratios of net income per household worker of the OAMEs and the establishments for these years were 27 percent, 23 percent, and 23 percent, respectively. The bleakness of the conditions of the household workers in the OAMEs, and the huge gap between the conditions of the OAMEs and the establishments, become all the more striking when it is seen that, on an average, the earnings of the hired worker in the establishments (viz., INR 26568, INR 28268, and INR 36000) have been almost twice that of the net income of the household workers of the OAMEs in all three time periods.

In order to get a sense of the surplus produced by enterprises, it is crucial to know the value of labor power of the unpaid household workers in the enterprises (which is roughly equivalent to the wage fund or consumption fund in the case of the hired workers). By identifying the wages per worker for similar types of enterprises—in terms of industry groups, rural and urban sector, and GVA per worker—that employ labor, it is possible to find an analogous consumption fund for the household workers in OAMEs.[7] For establishments, this idea of consumption fund for the household workers can be derived in terms of the average wage paid to the hired workers in the same establishment. Thus, an estimate of the total surplus of an enterprise for both OAMEs and establishments would be given by the difference between the total GVA and the total wage/consumption fund of all workers (both household and hired) in the enterprise. After making distributive class payments from this surplus to secure the economic, political, and cultural conditions of existence of the enterprise, the amount left with the enterprise, i.e., the net surplus, can be used for accumulation and expanded reproduction of the enterprise, or for augmenting the consumption fund of the household.

Table 21.2 Surplus and net surplus in OAMEs and establishments (median values in Indian rupees at constant 2011 prices).

Year	OAMEs		Establishments	
	Surplus	*Net surplus*	*Surplus*	*Net surplus*
2000–2001	7,749	7,395	41,535	34,317
2010–2011	8,424	8,028	63,840	53,400

Source: Calculated from the 56th and 67th Rounds of NSSO surveys of unorganized manufacturing sector in India.

In order to focus on the changing ability of capitalist and noncapitalist enterprises for growth and expanded reproduction over the decade of high growth in India, the surplus and net surplus of the OAMEs and establishments for 2000–2001 and 2010–11 are given in the above table (Table 21.2). The surplus produced and appropriated in a median OAME in 2000–2001 and 2010–11 was about 19 percent that in the median establishment in 2000–2001, and only about 13 percent at the end of the decade in 2010–11. Similarly, the net surplus for a typical OAME in 2000–2001 was about 22 percent that of a typical establishment, while in 2010–11 it was about 15 percent that of the median establishment. To put it into perspective, the typical OAME had about INR 616 (or USD 14) net surplus per month in 2000–2001 and INR 669 (or USD 15) per month in 2010–11. In other words, the OAMEs had next to nothing left as net surplus that could be used for their growth. Further, as is apparent from the above figures, the distributive class payments of these enterprises from their total surplus is also negligible, showing that the enterprises either cannot or do not pay much to secure the conditions of their existence. Thus, over the decade of high growth, the divergence between economic conditions of the noncapitalist OAMEs and the capitalist establishments, in terms of both the surplus and the net surplus, has only increased.

This unambiguously brings out the duality within the informal sector. While both the capitalist and noncapitalist enterprises encompass a variety of class processes, there is a stark difference between the two kinds of enterprises in terms of their ability to secure the conditions of existence and for expanded reproduction. The average noncapitalist enterprise (OAME) produces some surplus and is just about able to undertake a process akin to simple reproduction. However, the low volumes of surplus and net surplus in such enterprises lead to their precarity. In contrast, the informal capitalist enterprises are able to produce and retain a significant amount of surplus, which can be a source for accumulation and expanded reproduction. Given that the prospective consumption funds for household workers in the OAMEs are much lower than the median wages of hired workers in the establishments, it is evident that the OAMEs can produce even the minimal amount of surplus necessary for their existence only by pushing the standard of living of household workers below the average standards for wage workers in the capitalist enterprises. This also implies that any net surplus that the noncapitalist enterprise might be able to retain after paying off various outside claimants is likely to be used for augmenting the consumption fund of the household in an attempt to attain a better standard of living, rather than for accumulation and expanded reproduction. Thus, the class processes in the various kinds of informal enterprises shape, to a large extent, the structure of dualism *within* the informal sector and the disparate possibilities for securing the conditions for existence and growth of the capitalist and noncapitalist spaces in the informal economy.

Class, dualism, and the politics of postcolonial development

Nonessentialist class analysis provides an understanding of the differential abilities of the capitalist and noncapitalist spaces to reproduce themselves successfully and to gain prevalence in the economic formation. The lack of ability of the noncapitalist enterprises to produce and retain a significant amount of surplus limits any possibility of their expansion and makes their sustained reproduction uncertain. It is possible for these enterprises to produce even this surplus partly because the median noncapitalist enterprise incurs very low operating expenses—by using household labor, by avoiding explicit costs of production through encroachments and illegal sharing of privately supplied services (e.g., electricity), and by sharing common assets (e.g., land in slums) (S. Bhattacharya 2010; R. Bhattacharya 2014). The lack of such costs, along with the unity of the direct producers with their means of labor, enables the enterprises to retain a net income, part of which is used to meet the subsistence needs of the household workers. Even the low amount of surplus necessary for satisfying the conditions of existence of the enterprises can be produced only by maintaining a standard of living of the household workers below that of an average wageworker in the capitalist enterprises. In the event enough surplus is not produced to cover the payments necessary for the enterprise to survive, a lowering of the real income of the household workers (below a socially determined subsistence level) becomes a real possibility.

The vast terrain of noncapital engraved in the heart of postcolonial capitalism in India signifies a basic dualism within the economy. To grasp the implication of this dualism, it is necessary to understand the reasons for the coexistence of the capitalist and noncapitalist economic spaces and the contradiction between them. In the 1960s and '70s, a critique of the functionalist and reductionist theory of the noncapitalist economy, as I briefly outlined earlier, was developed in the context of Latin America (see, for example, Nun 2000, Quijano 1974). Kalyan Sanyal (2007) pushes this argument further in his original critique of the accumulation process under postcolonial capitalism.[8] In this understanding, the noncapitalist space is constituted by a "marginal mass" —or, in other words, a *surplus population*—a mass of working people who are not directly needed for the self-expansion of capital. This surplus population is not functional to, or subsumed under, the dynamics of capital in every instance, and thus the existence of the noncapitalist enterprises cannot be reduced simply to the needs or the vicissitudes of capital. Sanyal argues that the incompleteness of the process of primitive accumulation under postcolonial capitalism produces the surplus population: the exclusionary process of capitalist growth leads to the expropriation of the masses from their means of livelihood without simultaneously transforming them into wage labor for capital. Unable to enter the domain of capital as wage labor—even the capitalist enterprises within the informal economy—because of its vast size and lack of employment opportunities, this surplus population survives precariously in the noncapitalist informal economy. The noncapitalist enterprises thus serve as a 'reservoir' or 'sink' for the surplus population. Given that these enterprises represent a mode of basic survival for the households that do not have access to other ways of earning a livelihood, they are likely to persist even when they are performing precariously.[9] Thus, in postcolonial economies like India, the development of capitalism through primitive accumulation and exclusionary growth processes simultaneously creates the scope for continued existence of a noncapitalist economy, however unstable and fragile.

It is often argued in the development discourse (for example, Chen 2014) that the dire condition of the (noncapitalist) household enterprises can be addressed by moving toward a more inclusive paradigm of capitalist development, where the enterprises are given some access to funds, credits, training, and market openings. However, this argument misses the complexity of the process of postcolonial capitalist development. While such interventions might strengthen the household enterprises in some cases, other outcomes are also possible. For instance, it might lead to a differentiation between the noncapitalist enterprises, giving rise to a capitalist dynamic in some of them. This might entail a process of primitive accumulation, leading to further dispossession of some of the noncapitalist producers from their means of labor and thereby undermining the economic conditions of subsistence of the surplus population.

There is, however, another possibility where the noncapitalist space flourishes and is able to provide an economic shelter to the surplus population by thwarting the predatory thrusts of capital. This would be feasible, for instance, if the household enterprises could pool their resources and collectively organize themselves as workers' cooperatives. Such cooperatives, through political mobilization, might be able to compel the state to provide them with various economic resources (which might require a transfer of resources from the capitalist space), as well as to set up a barrier to entry for capital to this noncapitalist space. The formation of such workers' cooperatives, with their nonexploitative class structures, is also more likely to prevent the capitalist dynamics that lead to the dispossession of the noncapitalist producers and thereby to subvert the exclusionary process of capitalist development. This underlines the contradictory and the political nature of the process of development. There is no certainty regarding the final outcome of this process—it is open-ended, conjunctural, and without guarantees.

Acknowledgments

I would like to thank Ted Burczak for his detailed comments and suggestions. I would also like to thank Surbhi Kesar for excellent research support and for several discussions. I am indebted to Lopamudra Banerjee for many discussions and for her comments and insights.

Notes

1 In a majority of establishments, the number of wage laborers employed is usually greater than that of family members employed.
2 For analyses of different kinds of noncapitalist class processes within the enterprise or the household, see Gibson-Graham et al. (2001) and Resnick and Wolff (2006). See also Gabriel (1990) for a nonessentialist Marxian theory of self-exploitation.
3 While not all enterprises surveyed by the NSSO conform to the official definition of the informal sector given above, for all calculations in this essay only the enterprises that conform to that definition have been considered. Further, while NSSO provides data on 24 industry groups in informal manufacturing, in the rest of the essay, the following 8 industry groups, which make up more than 95 percent of informal enterprises, have been considered: food products and beverages; tobacco products; textiles; apparel; wood and wood products; nonmetallic mineral products; fabricated metal products, except machines; and furniture.
4 For other versions of nonessentialist class analyses of Indian informal or small-scale sector, see Chakrabarti et al. (2009) and Chakrabarti and Thakur (2010).
5 All prices are in real terms, deflated at 2010-11 prices. The exchange rate of Indian rupees (INR) in terms of US dollars (USD) in the 2010–11 financial year was INR 100 = USD 2.22 (or, 1 US dollar was worth about 45 Indian rupees).
6 Here "worker" designates a full-time worker. Where the enterprises employ part-time workers, I follow the usual convention of considering two part-time workers as one full-time worker.
7 The closest approximation of an OAME is an establishment in the same industry group where production is carried out mostly by household workers along with a single hired worker, with similar levels of GVA per worker (and with similar location—rural or urban). Note that the median wage of hired workers in such *similar* establishments—which operate at a much smaller scale than an *average* establishment—is usually lower than that of the hired workers in the informal capitalist enterprises.
8 For critical engagements with Sanyal's (2007) work on postcolonial capitalism and the role of the informal economy, see Chatterjee (2008 and 2016), Sanyal and Bhattacharya (2009), Bhattacharya (2010), Bhattacharya et al. (2013), Chakrabarti (2013), and Gidwani and Wainwright (2014), among others. Also see Sanyal (1993) for an articulation of a social formation as a capital-noncapital complex.
9 As I argued above, such household enterprises might try to survive even by pushing the standard of living of the household workers below the socially determined levels. For capitalist enterprises not so much driven by the logic of subsistence, it would not make much economic sense to persist under such circumstances.

References

Bhattacharya, R. 2014. "The Informal Sector and the Role of Urban Commons." *Yojana* 58 (October): 46-48.

Bhattacharya, S. 2010. "Non/Capital, Class and Development: The Case of Informal Manufacturing in India." Ph.D. dissertation, Department of Economics, University of Notre Dame.

Bhattacharya, R., S. Bhattacharya, and K. Sanyal. 2013. "Dualism in the Informal Economy: Exploring the Indian Informal Manufacturing Sector." In *Development and Sustainability: India in a Global Perspective*, S. Banerjee and A. Chakrabarti, eds., 339–62. New Delhi: Springer.

Chakrabarti, S. 2013. "Interrogating Inclusive Growth: Formal-Informal Duality, Complementarity, and Conflict." *Cambridge Journal of Economics* 37 (6): 1349–79.

Chakrabarti, A. and A. Thakur. 2010. "The Making and Unmaking of the (In)Formal Sector." *Critical Sociology* 36 (3): 415–35

Chakrabarti, A., A. Chaudhury, and S. Cullenberg. 2009. "Global Order and the New Economic Policy in India: The (Post)Colonial Formation of the Small-Scale Sector." *Cambridge Journal of Economics* 33 (6): 1169–86.

Chatterjee, P. 2008. "Democracy and Economic Transformation in India." *Economic and Political Weekly* 43 (16): 53–62.

—— 2016. "Rethinking Postcolonial Capitalist Development: A Conversation between Kalyan Sanyal and Partha Chatterjee." *Comparative Studies of South Asia, Africa and the Middle East* 36 (1): 102–11.

Chen, M. 2014. "Informal Employment and Development: Patterns of Inclusion and Exclusion." *European Journal of Development Research* 26 (4): 397–418.

Gabriel, S. 1990. "Ancients: A Marxian Theory of Self-Exploitation." *Rethinking Marxism* 3 (1): 85–106.

Gibson-Graham, J. K. and D. Ruccio. 2001. "'After' Development: Re-imagining Economy and Class." In *Re/Presenting Class: Essays in Postmodern Marxism*, J. K. Gibson-Graham, S. A. Resnick, and R. D. Wolff, eds., 158–81. Durham and London: Duke University Press.

Gibson-Graham, J. K., S. A. Resnick, and R. D. Wolff. 2001. *Re/Presenting Class: Essays in Postmodern Marxism*. Durham and London: Duke University Press.

Gidwani, V. and J. Wainwright. 2014. "On Capital, Not-Capital, and Development: After Kalyan Sanyal." *Economic and Political Weekly* 49 (30): 40–47.

Lewis, W. A. 1954. "Economic Development with Unlimited Supplies of Labour." *The Manchester School* 22 (2): 139–91.

Marx, K. [1867] 1977. *Capital: A Critique of Political Economy*, Volume 1. New York: Vintage Books.

National Sample Survey Organisation. 2013. *Employment and Unemployment Survey, NSSO 66th Round, July 2009 – June 2010*. New Delhi: Ministry of Statistics and Program Implementation.

Nun, J. 2000. "The End of Work and the "Marginal Mass" Thesis." *Latin American Perspectives* 27 (1): 6–32.

Quijano, A. 1974. "The Marginal Pole of the Economy and the Marginalized Labour Force." *Economy and Society* 3 (4): 393–428.

Resnick, S. A., and R. D. Wolff. 1987. *Knowledge and Class: A Marxian Critique of Political Economy*. Chicago and London: University of Chicago Press.

——, eds. 2006. *New Departures in Marxian Theory*. Oxon and New York: Routledge.

Ruccio, D. 2010. *Development and Globalization: A Marxian Class Analysis*. London and New York: Routledge.

Sanyal, K. 1993. "Capital, Primitive Accumulation, and the Third World: From Annihilation to Appropriation." *Rethinking Marxism* 6 (3): 117–30.

—— 2007. *Rethinking Capitalist Development: Primitive Accumulation, Governmentality and Post-Colonial Capitalism*. New Delhi: Routledge.

Sanyal, K. and R. Bhattacharya. 2009. "Beyond the Factory: Globalisation, Informalisation of Production and the New Locations of Labour." *Economic and Political Weekly* 44 (22): 35–44.

Part VII

Capitalism and class analysis

22 Management ideologies and the class structure of capitalist enterprises

Shareholderism vs. stakeholderism at Scott Paper Company

Michael Hillard and Richard McIntyre

Management ideologies and the class structure of capitalist enterprises

The relationship of owner, manager, and banker is a longstanding problem in social theory, dating at least to Marx. Marx recognized an important shift in the capitalism of his time when in *Capital* volume 3 he noted that the formation of joint stock companies meant the "[t]ransformation of the actually functioning capitalist into a mere manager, administrator of other people's capital, and of the owner of capital into a mere owner, a mere money-capitalist" and that this transformation led to "a whole system of swindling and cheating by means of corporation promotion, stock issuance, and stock speculation. It is private production without the control of private property" (Marx 1981, 570). Classical Marxian theory (1870–1914) emphasized the increasing role and influence of financial capitalists, and this has continued in contemporary neo-Marxist work on "financialization."

Keynes (1936), Berle and Means (1932), and Tawney (1926) dealt with the relationship between owner and manager differently during the interwar period. They argued that the classical defense of property rights did not extend to passive owners, so that non-managing owners should be seen more like rentiers. Thus, they would be subject to Keynes's argument in favor of the euthanasia of the rentier. After World War II theorists of managerial capitalism such as Chandler (1977), Marris (1964), and Galbraith (1967) argued, perhaps optimistically, that once management was liberated from the dictates of ownership the firm need no longer maximize profits and thus, in theory anyway, could distribute enterprise surplus in a number of ways, some of which were more socially beneficial than others. Indeed, many enterprises in the post-WWII period did distribute surplus to workers and communities in a kind of patriarchal stakeholder capitalism. We will analyze such firms below.

In the 1980s there was a strong reaction against managerial capitalism and an emphasis on shareholder value. The idea that management's *primary* purpose was to increase the wealth of the owners became the centerpiece of speeches by corporate executives and management theorists alike. In the United States at least, this became a new orthodoxy. We call this new orthodoxy "shareholderism." This is contrasted with the ideology of stakeholderism (sometimes called "jointness") in which all claimants to the surplus are imagined to have a "seat at the table." This latter was an updated version of managerial control that sought enhanced worker participation with the goal of increasing productivity.[1] We use our case study to show how a third ideology of enterprise communism can emerge from the struggle between shareholderism and stakeholderism, an ideology focused more on who appropriates the surplus than how it is distributed.

We follow Wolff and Resnick in seeing various management ideologies as attempts to prioritize one or another distribution of surplus (Wolff and Resnick 2013, 223–27). We use the following equation to illustrate this point:

SV = rent + interest + management salaries + accumulation + merchant payments + taxes + dividends + advertising + community payments + excess wages

This indicates that surplus value, the difference between the firm's revenues and expenses on productive labor, depreciation, and raw materials, is fully exhausted by these "subsumed class" payments: payments to landlords, bankers, managers (for both salaries and capital accumulation), merchants, the state, advertising, community activities (charities, youth sports teams, etc.), and wages over and above what is necessary given the value of labor power in the firm's area.

Shareholderism is an ideology that says that enterprise management should maximize dividends (and share values) by minimizing these other payments and possibly by increasing surplus value through speed up, moving the enterprise to places with a lower value of labor power, or other strategies. Part of this ideology involves defining the firm not as a going concern but as a potentially decomposable bundle of assets.

This is directly opposed to the vision of the enterprise in stakeholder theory, where the firm is understood to be a "going concern," an institution whose common purpose continues regardless of the lives of its individual members and whose working rules are largely established by custom and appeals to fairness, ultimately enforced by the state. While this particular view is due to John R. Commons, something similar was at work in the writings of all the managerial theorists, including Veblen, Berle and Means, Galbraith, Marris, and their contemporary descendants like Osterman. Here the distribution of the surplus should be whatever maintains the enterprise as a going concern.

Following Resnick and Wolff (and others),[2] we understand these theories to be constitutive of and not merely reflective of changes in the economy. Much of the institutional and radical literature sees a new institutional regime or epoch of capitalism emerging in the last several decades. The general frame is the contrast of a managerial era of the enterprise to a subsequent financialized era. What they share is the notion that in any historical period there is a "ruler" of the enterprise, "top managers" after World War II, and financiers since the 1980s. In these simple stories, these rulers control the strategies of the firm associated with distributing the surplus. The institutional structures associated with these enterprise regimes define an epoch of capitalism.

Labor and employment relations scholars, grounded in institutional thought, have used "financialization" to mean a shift away from a previous period of managerial capitalism, with largely negative effects on workers' well being, although the size of these negative effects is understand to vary between coordinated (Germanic) and liberal (Anglo) forms of capitalism (Jacoby 2008, Applebaum and Batt 2014). A consequence, sometimes implied but sometimes clearly stated, is that there has been a change in who controls the corporation, in particular a shift away from management and toward control by stock owners and financiers. This manifests in the increased attention to shareholder value, prioritization of financial over industrial activities, and the rising influence of financial/legal departments vs. engineering and labor relations/human resources departments. Some radical political economists share this institutionalist position, though they tend to focus more on the rise in financial relative to industrial activities and the implications of this shift for macroeconomic performance, social inequality, and financial crises (Stockhammer 2009). Once again, though, there is a sometimes implied and sometimes stated shift in corporate (and societal) control from industrial capitalists to financiers, industrial to banking capital, etc.

We have learned from and have some sympathy with each of these positions. Indeed our case study illustrates some of the negative social effects of prioritizing stock owners over other stakeholders. But we think the evidence for a change in the form of capitalism is weak and prefer not to see this as a new epoch or as signaling the dominance of one group of capitalists over another. We have criticized this epochal way of understanding capitalism elsewhere (McIntyre and Hillard 2013). Historical scholarship has demonstrated that the social cooperation implied by the "limited capital labor accord" of the post-World War II era was inaccurate and misleading. It created an image of a desirable golden age of capitalism that never existed and implied that this nirvana could be reconstituted through cross-class cooperation. We believe that essentializing financiers in the current era similarly misses the complex and contradictory setting for the appropriation and distribution of surplus in our own time. It draws attention away from the appropriation and distribution of surplus value in favor of a focus on power differentials between fractions of the capitalist class.

We note that similar patterns of firm dependence on profits from financial activities were widely described in the era before the Great Depression. In fact Marx noted the periodic tendency of capitalists to forget that production is a necessary moment in the circuit of capital in *Capital* volume 2, when he wrote:

> The process of production appears merely as an unavoidable intermediate link, as a necessary evil for the sake of money-making. All nations with a capitalist mode of production are therefore seized periodically by a feverish attempt to make money without the intervention of the process of production.
>
> (1978, 137)[3]

Nor do we find that the victory of financial over "real" economic forces is an adequate description of contemporary capitalism. As Greta Krippner argues in her important study of financialization, "the distinction between forces operating 'inside' and 'outside' non-financial corporations is becoming increasingly arbitrary. Non-financial corporations are beginning to resemble financial corporations..." (2005, 202). Krippner dismisses the idea that "financialization" signifies the victory of one group of capitalists over another, instead pointing to the classical Marxist literature on finance capital as more correct, i.e., financialization means the *union* of finance and industrial capital. She tells a macro story of the unity between financial and industrial capital but does not investigate how this works at the level of the enterprise or industry. That is partly what we are undertaking here.

We do not want simply to revive Marxian notions of finance capital, however. Classical Marxism shares with contemporary radical political economy a conservative epistemological assumption that the world exists independently from our conception of it. In other words, the role of theory is to capture a political economy that exists independent of that theory. We see the relationship between owners and managers as complex and contingent, and it is constituted in part by the very narratives that are produced to try to understand that relationship. So our focus is on the rhetoric of shareholderism, a rhetoric that insists that maximizing shareholder value is the only way to be competitive and, in so doing, creates a world in which managers in fact focus on shareholder value.

Stakeholderism and shareholderism at Scott Paper

Scott Paper Company is infamous as an archetype of financial engineering and shareholderism, based on the events that unfolded under "Chainsaw Al" Dunlap's dramatic and very short reign in the mid-1990s (Beer and Nohria 2000, Greenhouse 2008,). Students of stakeholderism, especially those interested in high-profile efforts to change industrial labor processes, frequently called "high performance work organizations," also know Scott for its elaborate, partially successful "Jointness" program—a six-year endeavor that commenced in 1988 (Getman and Marshall 1993, Hillard 2005). It thus makes an interesting case study, in which cross-cutting narratives reflecting both perspectives were at play, out of which developed a third oppositional narrative initiated by workers.

Between 1985 and 1995 shareholderism and stakeholderism co-existed at Scott, which by the early 1990s began to exemplify a critical point made by Harvard Business School professors Michael Beer and Nitkin Nohria about the difficulties U.S. manufacturing corporations were then facing:

> An examination of many other organizations will show a mixture of these strategies, often in uneasy co-existence. We argue that both theories have validity. That is, each of them does promote objectives that management explicitly or implicitly intends to achieve. But each also has costs, often unintended. The problem managers face is resolving the tension between theory E [shareholderism] and theory O [stakeholderism] in a way that obtains the benefits of each and minimizes the negative consequences of each. *Too often, these theories are mixed without the resolution of the inherent tension between them. This leads, we argue, to maximization of the costs and minimization of potential benefits of each theory.*
>
> (2000, 3–4)

As a weak corporate performer in a high-revenue, low profit-margin manufacturing industry, Scott (and the paper industry in general) was an obvious target for takeover threats emanating from Wall Street. Scott's leadership recognized its growing vulnerability and developed an elaborate set of "Theory O" strategies to rebuild its competitiveness through improved relations and practices with various stakeholders, but especially by reforming labor-management relations. CEO Phil Lippencott and his top executives saw the company's contentious labor relations as a central problem; its "Jointness" initiative was among the nation's most aggressive campaigns to reorganize labor processes and create a changed culture conducive to productivity, quality, and ultimately profitability improvements. Scott's leaders were also negatively inspired by the scorched-earth tactics of rival International Paper (IP), which provoked a strike in 1987 with the intention of deposing unions and firing workers in a number of plants. Scott thus initiated a six-year experiment: treat its workers (at least in its narrative) as sovereign partners in the company's fortunes, give their union representatives and the workers themselves a greater "voice" in the labor process, and thus demonstrate the validity of stakeholderism. The project came to an abrupt end when Dunlap took control of the company in late 1994.

At the same time, however, Scott was under intense heat from Wall Street analysts. Scott's profits remained low, and the benefits of the stakeholder approach it was pursuing were taking years to materialize. Moreover, paper is a cyclical industry; any progress in producing better and less costly paper was overwhelmed by depressed sales and margins when a recession hit in 1990 and 1991. The slow economic recovery in 1992 and 1993 continued to retard financial performance.

Fairly early on in Scott's Jointness plan, senior Scott executives leading the effort were challenged when Scott's financial department questioned the entire strategy. One of these pro-Jointness executives (we'll call him Mr. Smith) was shocked by what he saw as the advent of a wrong-headed logic that would undermine the new stakeholder approach before it had a chance to succeed.

> I could see it coming, that's one of the reasons I got out when I did... They used to have a President's meeting, which was all the top people of Scott... (in 1989) the focus of that meeting all of a sudden shifted, from being 'we're no longer interested in being just a good company, we want to be an outstanding company,' or something like that. And so the whole focus at that meeting was, how are we going to raise our margins up, or returns up, from an ROI of 8-to-10, up into 14, or something like that, so we could be pre-eminent—that was the term they used: 'we want to be a pre-eminent company.'
>
> ... I went to some of the finance people that I knew in Treasury and Corporate Planning [who were staff to the Finance Vice President], and said: 'These numbers don't add up, they don't make any sense at all.' And they said: 'Well, that's what they told the guy who was going to make the speech. We told them that those numbers weren't reasonable and weren't accurate, and were impractical.' And he [the VP of Finance] said: 'I'm just trying to make a point; those guys aren't smart enough to understand that anyway.'[4]
>
> And that was the sort of attitude at that point, in my mind, was that, all of a sudden, all we had to do was to put pressure on people, and people would, we'd cut cost, that we could become a preeminent company. And they had lost the whole concept of the philosophy of what it takes to build, I think, a long-term term preeminence into an organization.

Within a short period of time, under additional pressure from the 1990-91 recession, CEO Lippencott's allegiance began to transition to the shareholderist perspective, though he also allowed the Jointness programs to continue at Scott's 16 local mills, many of which were beginning to show results.

We look at how these conflicting corporate narratives played out in one of these local Scott mills: S.D. Warren, of Westbrook, Maine. The

Westbrook mill had a rich and complicated labor relations culture. It was the last major paper mill in Maine to unionize, thanks to a complicated founders' culture of paternalism that long thwarted unionization, but it also produced a highly rebellious set of union locals that emerged around the time that Scott Paper bought S.D. Warren Company in 1967.[5] Jointness was received differently across Scott's many mills, depending on local culture and the deftness, or lack thereof, of mill managers. The Westbrook mill's workers and unions were at the recalcitrant end of the spectrum.

Between 1988 and 1990, international union leaders, corporate HR executives, and consultants made appearances at Westbrook to proselytize the strategy and then initiate trust-building exercises and training. The initiative was met with a cool reception from union leaders and went forward without the masterly touch of longtime mill manager Howard Reiche. Reiche was trained in the pre-union, "S.D. Warren" era, oversaw the transition to unionized labor relations, and, crucially, had maintained the community stakeholder tradition forged during the S.D. Warren era that lasted until the Scott takeover. Seeing an uncertain future but a likely end to his latitude to maintain a managerial ethos, Reiche retired in 1988. In the coming six years, Westbrook had three different mill managers come from "away." These managers were seen as the archetypal outsiders who poorly understood the mill's operations, failed to develop a rapport with the workers and their union leaders, and acted as mouthpieces for "corporate."

Scott put the Westbrook unit up for sale in early 1991, while keeping the plant in production. The Scott corporate office stated that it was "refocusing its product strategy" and, most importantly, directly introduced the language and agenda of shareholderism. The mill's local workers and long-time local managers embodied years and decades of a coherent daily practice in the complex art of making high-end publication paper, united by a shared identity as part of the all-encompassing "Mother Warren" that reveled in memories of the company's paternalistic 19th-century founders. Scott's corporate leadership viewed "Mother Warren" as a mere bundle of decomposable assets to be assessed and, if necessary, sold off. The message of change was not subtle: the mill's most recent outside manager suspended major production for a day and gathered nearly all of the mill's 2,000 workers and managers at a nearby sports Expo center, announcing to a stunned crowd: "all assets are under review." Initially, this simply meant that Westbrook was for sale. Over the next two years it became clear that this strategy extended to examining each operation within the capital-intensive mill separately; individual "assets" could be sold off one by one if merited.[6] "Although several potential buyers toured the 1,800-worker mill, company officials indicate no one has wanted to buy the mill as a whole. But, according to [UPIU Local 1069 President Bill] Carver, Scott is now entertaining offers to sell off individual operations."[7]

The largest "asset up for review" was the mill's finishing department. Coated publication papers needed to be cut and packaged before delivery. Female employees dominated the department, and it was the locus of an antiquated "bonus" piece-rate system that was the primary tool for wringing efficiency from an older operation. Scott was developing a larger "sheeting" facility in Allentown, PA, at the time, but it also offered Westbrook's workers the chance to use a Jointness project to cut costs sufficiently to restore its profitability and keep the operation at Westbrook. Consultants involved in the process identified a $90 per ton savings target that would raise ROI from 3% to a desired 15–20% range and make the survival of this "asset" worthwhile to the company's shareholders. Even though Westbrook workers and managers collaborated and exceeded the proposed savings target, Scott decided to close the operation and move it to Allentown. The willingness of the mill's unions and workers to demonstrate their ability to improve the profitability of "assets" was of little interest to central corporate managers, despite their pronouncements.

Scott set out to refocus the mill's product line, narrowing it to the new specialty products (Ultracast, "release" peel and stick products) and away from its traditional niche in high-end coated publication papers. In turn, it began to ship publication grades to other mills within the S.D. Warren division. This was taken badly by Westbrook's workers, who saw this as a poorly conceived gambit, and ultimately backfired on Scott while accelerating Westbrook's decline. Making high-end publication papers required a good deal of craft knowledge not present at other mills that produced "commodity grade" (i.e., cheaper standardized products like toilet paper), and Warren paper grades produced at other mills were of poorer quality, ruining Warren's brand. This development coincided with the company's refusal of the unions' offer to buy the mill. Union leaders claimed that, unable to sell the mill to a corporate buyer, Scott was now pilfering Westbrook's valuable products on its way to an uncalled-for debasement, if not destruction, of the company.

A third approach: enterprise communism

Westbrook workers developed a third narrative articulated by leaders of the mill's largest union local, Local 1069-UPIU. Westbrook's workers and managers conceived their mill as a flagship operation with many advantages over other mills in the S.D. Warren division and in their market. This meant they saw the firm as a viable enterprise with a future. The workers responded to Scott's intention to sell the mill by making their own offer to buy it. The thinking and actions of Local 1069 were fueled by Maine paper workers' existing anti-corporate culture, with paper union locals in Maine adopting a language of opposition to corporate greed.[8] This thinking was critical of Wall Street's growing impact—disruption—of the state's paper industry.[9] Finally, worker consciousness at S.D. Warren was powerfully shaped by a sharpening shared memory of the "Mother Warren" era. Central to this vision was an interpretation of the mill's decline as being caused by changes in corporate governance of their workplace, in particular the loss of a stakeholderist ethos shaped by local ownership. Together, we argue, these factors constituted the emergence of what we are calling "enterprise consciousness."

After the attempt to buy the mill failed, S.D. Warren and the rest of Scott's mills then experienced the traumatic Dunlap reign. At Westbrook as elsewhere, Dunlap made immediate cuts, moved to undermine or suspend collaborative workplace projects, and then pursued sale of the firm in parts. The S.D. Warren Division was sold to South African Pulp and Paper Products, Limited (SAPPI) the next year. SAPPI's purchase was heavily financed with junk bonds, and when the firm's hopes for continued strong sales and profit margins in coated publication papers faded in the late 1990s, it began a radical retrenchment of its U.S. operations, including a large layoff at Westbrook in 1999.

In the end, Warren's workers (and many managers) were not persuaded by either the shareholder or stakeholder narrative. A third narrative arose out of a local culture and especially memory of Warren's distinct paternalism that preceded the Scott era. Memories celebrated a kind of "class justice": stories about how the generations of Warrens and later other "family" owners' voluntarily "gave back" company profits to its workers in generous community public works. They recalled having the highest wages in Maine and an economic security vastly at odds with the market realities faced by other workers in the state, as workers' descendants were almost automatically given preferential hiring treatment. This narrative shaped the workers' plan to buy and run the mill; the workers were the only one of the mill's original stakeholders still present. Moreover, the outsider initiatives of Scott's central corporate leadership were seen as irrelevant to the local skill and craft knowledge essential to making the world's best publication papers. Thus, worker ownership and self-management offered a way to stay competitive and to restore the class justice of which Scott, a "distant, out-of-state" corporation (a common local formulation), had deprived the Westbrook mill.

What differs here from similar stories of deindustrialization, such as the celebrated struggles of Youngstown steel workers (Lynd 1982 and 1987, Russo and Linkon 2002), is the context: Workers were reacting to shareholderism and what appeared to be a fork in the road. Behind them was a form of welfare capitalism in which the firm's owners distributed the surplus in part for the benefit of the community and the workers. One path forward was shareholderism, which the workers could clearly see meant destroying the valuable enterprise on which their lives depended. The other path was nurturing the mill's vitality via worker ownership or a change in who *appropriated* the enterprise's surplus. By the late 1980s, paper workers statewide had come to view paper executives as purveyors of a new greed that sought to destroy Maine's paper unions and the very mills themselves, through the new emphasis on "assets." In Gramscian terms, at this particular juncture these workers made at least part of the journey from "common sense" to "good sense."[10]

Proponents of shareholderism such as economist Michael Jensen saw a strict discipline and especially a willingness to break up old manufacturing companies as a way to make capitalism work better for consumers and shareholders (workers not so much). Advocates of stakeholderism sought a high road alternative to union busting and layoffs as a way of helping stressed U.S. manufacturing operations survive and with luck prosper. Missing from the world of corporate leadership, or even labor relations' experts at the time, were alternatives that put workers at the center of reform. Warren's workers used memory of the past to conceive such an alternative that also served as a critique of shareholderism and stakeholderism, at least in the versions proffered by Scott corporate leadership between 1988 and 1994.

If the "economic imaginary" defines the range of ways people conceive of possible forms of economic life, then we argue that these workers developed, or at least began to develop, a radical imaginary (Gibson-Graham 2003 and 2006). For them, "enterprise consciousness" meant seeing the enterprise as a vital, valued, and efficacious institution that supported their willingness to take new directions in opposition to shareholderism. S.D. Warren workers used their understanding of the past, influenced by reaction to union busting by incompetent management and radical critiques of corporate work reorganizations, to indict the capitalist practices they confronted. For Warren's workers, the arrival of the language and practice of shareholderism crystallized both their oppositional consciousness and their bid to become the mill's owners.

We see this as relevant to a current movement to engender "cooperative economies" and even "enterprise communism"—worker-owned enterprises modeled on Mondragon (Alperovitz 2011, Wolff 2012, Gibson-Graham 2003 and 2006). This movement looks at the United States economy as diverse and open to change from within rather than wholly colonized by corporate capitalism.[11] As popularized by Wolff, Alperovitz, and Gibson-Graham, ethically guided cooperative enterprises—that can occupy empty spaces of the predominantly capitalist landscape—offer one avenue for progressive change that can be realized at the local level, while also creating ethical economic communities supportive of broader social movements.[12] Building a "cooperative enterprise consciousness" is a counter-hegemonic project, most likely to be potent when it emerges organically from already-existing, supportive working-class narratives. While Westbrook's workers do mine the understandings and memories of patriarchal welfare capitalism, they also create a forward-looking alternative.

Acknowledgment

We thank Ted Burczak for his expert and patient editorial work.

Notes

1 As large corporations were buffeted by new demands for large and fast performance of stock prices, stakeholderism—focused as it was on building long term organizational capacity—stood at odds with new shareholder driven practices that "re-engineered" enterprises, pushed them to shrink to a "core competency," and shed other major operations. Stakeholderism was a rearguard strategy, and its centerpiece was "transforming" work practices to promote quality, and it inherently involved trust-building measures. Notably, the older managerial capitalism sought limited input from workers, typically through collective bargaining, but it now sought to have workers internalize an ethic of restructuring that meant giving up traditional union protections for an uncertain combination of higher productivity and higher pay. In Maine, the site of our case study, shareholderism persisted, withstood some attacks, and lost others. See Hillard (2005), Osterman (1999), Beer and Nohria (2000).

2 For instance, Mackenzie (2006).

3 This is the viewpoint of finance. Marx also noted the bourgeois tendency to see commerce as the center of the economic process without the intervening problem of production: "It is typical of the bourgeois horizon...where business deals fill the whole of people's minds, to see the foundation of the mode of production in the whole of commerce corresponding to it, rather than the other way round" (ibid., 196). This is the viewpoint of merchant capital, so clearly described by Lichtenstein (2012) and the example of Wal-Mart, which portrays itself as a marketplace of always-low prices, with production hidden or written out of the script entirely. The relation between the financial and merchant narratives could be fruitfully explored but not in the space we have here.

4 We are struck by this statement, if true, because of the rhetorical strategy implied—asserting the intellectual superiority of shareholderism over stakeholderism.

5 The Warren Company was founded in 1854 and was a single mill company until the 1950s, when it embarked on an expansion that added mills in Michigan and Alabama.

6 "S.D. Warren publicly said in October 1991 that it needed to review all of its operations in Westbrook to find ways to cut costs and be more profitable." "S.D. Warren Accused of 'Destructive' Actions," *Portland Press Herald*, November 3, 1992. Tom Lestage, a union leader and later President of the mill's largest union local, described this event in two interviews. He elaborated on the advent of a decomposability mindset: "We were told [initially] the intent was to sell the facility in total as one unit, and then about a year went by when they didn't have a lot of bidders, or interest shown for the sale of the entire facility, they [Scott's corporate leaders] opened up their minds to piecemeal [sale of mill "assets"]. *Thomas Lestage Interviews*, Westbrook, Maine, August 4, 2000 and May 11, 2013.

7 "Workers Study Paper Mill Buyout," *Portland Press Herald*, December 12, 1991.

8 Local 1069 played a leading role in a statewide support movement in a dramatic strike at Jay, Maine, at the state's International Paper Company mill. "IP" successfully crushed Jay's workers, but not before the event unleashed a statewide, even regional, movement across many paper mill towns as workers and their families joined a battle with the moniker "Stop Corporate Greed." See Getman (1998) and Hillard (2005).

9 In 1989, Georgia Pacific (GP) effected a hostile takeover of Great-Northern Nekoosa, which owned Maine's largest, two-mill paper complex. Under pressure of heavy interest payments and slow sales the following two years, GP essentially suspended investment and major repairs during the two years it owned the Maine mills before it sold out to Boater Inc. in December 1991. "Wall Street Gem no Millinocket hero," *Bangor Daily News*, December 30, 1997.

10 Gramsci distinguishes common sense, the diffuse, popular, and generally conservative conventional wisdom of any period, and good sense, by which he means something more critical and coherent built out of that common sense. See the section on "The Philosophy of Praxis" and especially "Critical Notes on an Attempt at Popular Sociology" in Gramsci (1971).

11 See especially Gibson-Graham (2006, xix–xxxiii and 1–5).

12 In an interesting twist, some in this movement offer up the idea that only workers in an enterprise can claim a moral status as, in Jensen and Meckling's (1976) language, "residual claimants." See Burczak (2006).

References

Alperovitz, G. 2011. *America beyond Capitalism: Reclaiming Our Wealth, Our Liberty, and Our Democracy.* Cambridge, MA: Democracy Collaborative Press/Dollars and Sense.

Applebaum, E. and R. Batt. 2014. *Private Equity at Work: When Wall Street Manages Main Street.* New York: Russell Sage.

Beer, M. and N. Nohria. 2000. "Resolving the Tension between Theories E and O of Change." In *Breaking the Code of Change*, M. Beer and N. Nohria, eds., 1-33. Boston: Harvard Business School Press.

Berle, A. and G. Means. 1932. *The Modern Corporation and Private Property.* New York: Transactions Publishers.

Burczak, T. 2006. *Socialism after Hayek.* Ann Arbor: University of Michigan Press.

Chandler, A. 1977. *The Visible Hand: The Managerial Revolution in American Business.* Cambridge: Harvard University Press.

Galbraith, J. K. 1967. *The New Industrial State.* Princeton: Princeton University Press.

Getman, J. 1998. *The Betrayal of Local 14: Paperworkers, Politics, and Permanent Replacements.* Ithaca, NY: ILR Press.

Getman, J. and R. Marshall. 1993. "Industrial Relations in Transition: The Paper Industry Example." *Yale Law Review* 102 (8): 1804–95.

Gibson-Graham, J. K. 2003. "Enabling Ethical Economies: Cooperativism and Class." *Critical Sociology* 29 (2): 123–61.

———. 2006. *A Postcapitalist Politics.* Minneapolis: University of Minnesota Press.

Gramsci, A. 1971. *Selections from the Prison Notebooks.* Ed. Q. Hoare and G. N. Smith. New York: International Publishers.

Greenhouse, S. 2008. *The Big Squeeze: Tough Times for the American Worker.* Norwell MA: Anchor Press.

Hillard, M. 2005. "The Failure of Labor-Management Cooperation at Two Maine Paper Mills: A Case Study." In *Advances in Industrial & Labor Relations*, volume 14, D. Lewin and B. Kaufman eds., 121–171. Bingley, UK: Emerald Group Publishing Limited.

Jacoby, S. 2008. "Finance and Labor: Perspectives on Risk, Inequality and Democracy." *Comparative Labor Law and Policy Journal* 30 (1): 17–66.

Jensen, M. and W. Meckling, 1976. "Theory of the Firm: Managerial Behavior, Agency Costs, and Ownership Structure." *Journal of Financial Economics* 3 (4): 305–60.

Keynes, J. M. 1936. *The General Theory of Employment, Interest, and Money.* London: Palgrave McMillian.

Krippner, G. 2005. "The Financialization of the American Economy." *Socio-Economic Review.* 3(2): 173-208

Lichtenstein, N. 2012. "The Return of Merchant Capitalism." *International Labour and Working Class History* 81: 8–27.

Lynd, S. 1982. *The Fight against Shutdowns: Youngstown's Steel Mill Closings.* San Pedro: Singlejack Books.

———. 1987. "The Genesis of the Idea of a Community Right to Industrial Property in Youngstown and Pittsburgh, 1977–1987." *Journal of American History* 4 (3): 926–58.

Mackenzie, D. 2006. *An Engine Not A Camera: How Financial Models Shape Markets.* Cambridge: MIT Press.

Marris, R. 1964. *The Economic Theory of Managerial Capitalism.* New York: Basic Books.

Marx, K. 1978. *Capital,* volume 2. London: Penguin.

———. 1981. *Capital,* volume 3. London: Penguin.

McIntyre, R. and M. Hillard. 2013. "Capitalist Class Agency and the New Deal Order: Against the Notion of a Limited Capital Labor Accord." *Review of Radical Political Economics* 45 (2): 129–48.

Osterman, P. 1999. *Securing Prosperity – The American Labor Market: How it Has Changed and What to Do about It.* Princeton: Princeton University Press.

Resnick, S. and R. Wolff. 1987. *Knowledge and Class: A Marxian Critique of Political Economy.* Chicago: Chicago University Press.

Russo, J. and S. Linkon. 2002. *Steeltown U.S.A.: Work and Memory in Youngstown.* Lawrence: University of Kansas Press.

Stockhammer, E. 2009. "The Finance Dominated Growth Regime, Distribution, and the Present Crisis." Working Paper, Department of Economics, Vienna University of Economics and Business, http://epub.wu.ac.at/136/1/document.pdf (accessed Jan.28, 2017).

Tawney, R. H. 1988 (1926). *Religion and the Rise of Capitalism.* Livingston: Transaction Publishers.

Wolff, R. 2012. *Democracy at Work: A Cure for Capitalism.* Chicago: Haymarket Books.

Wolff, R. and S. Resnick. 2013. *Contending Economic Theories: Neoclassical, Keynesian, and Marxian.* Cambridge: MIT Press.

23 Lewis L. Lorwin's "Five-Year Plan for the World"

A subsumed class response to the crises of the 1930s

Claude Misukiewicz

It was at Amsterdam last August that for the first time a group of Russian economists sat in with a congress of their fellows from Western Europe and America. They told of their five-year plan and a nation at work in the midst of world-wide depression and unemployment. And it was an American economist who, by sheer mastery of his subject and the lucidity of his analysis, became the spokesman for the westerners in their half articulate belief that through economic planning the stresses of modern industrialism may be reconciled with self-government and freedom. To the engineers and economists, business and labor leaders and government officials of a score of nations he gave a philosophic basis for social progressive planning.

—*The Survey* (Lorwin 1931b)

Introduction

The encounter between Lewis L. Lorwin of the Brookings Institution and Valerian V. Obolensky-Ossinsky of the Soviet Union's State Planning Commission was the climax of the World Social Economic Planning Congress, which met in Amsterdam, August 23–29, 1931. The Congress occurred during a period of intense intellectual ferment that Lorwin would later describe as "the Great Turn of 1930–32," a moment when the idols of business leadership and laissez-faire policies were shattered, clearing the way for a "rapid and spectacular conversion to a new faith in the powers and rationality of governmental and collective action" (Lorwin 1941, 426). Then, a chorus of voices from business, academia, labor unions, and churches all called for "economic planning" (Beard 1932b), which became a promise of FDR's 1932 presidential campaign (Roosevelt 1933), although there was little agreement about the meaning of the phrase. Historians have tended to neglect this sea change in public opinion, focusing instead on the Roosevelt administrations that followed. This essay shifts our attention backward, to begin recovering a rich, nearly forgotten intellectual heritage that helps us understand the policy debates of the New Deal.

It also examines these debates from a fresh perspective, Marxian class analysis, to argue that Lorwin's address to the Congress was an intervention in *class struggle*. This is an absurd claim if the term is understood as the violent contest between two great classes described in *The Communist Manifesto*. That narrow definition has pushed class analysis into the margins of historiography by making "class struggle" something exceptional, rather than part of daily life. This essay, however, employs a different understanding of class, one identified by Stephen A. Resnick and Richard D. Wolff as Marx's "unique surplus labor notion of class" (2002, 8).

Resnick and Wolff ask us to exchange traditional notions of class, as categories of people defined in terms of property and power, for Marx's innovative view of class as a set of processes: the fundamental class process, in which surplus labor—that labor beyond what is necessary for the laborer to reproduce herself—is produced and appropriated; and the subsumed class process, in which shares of that surplus are distributed to those who provide necessary conditions of existence—economic, political, and cultural—for the continuation of the fundamental class process (Resnick and Wolff 2006, Wolff and Resnick 2012). Specifically, the capitalist fundamental class process (CFCP) occurs at the site of commodity production. There, a laborer performs, for part of the day, *necessary* labor in exchange for a wage. This exchange is not a class process. The CFCP occurs when the laborer performs additional unpaid labor; this is the *surplus*, which is appropriated by her employer.

If *exploitation* occurs when surplus labor is appropriated by someone other than the direct producer, then slaves, serfs, and proletarians are exploited when their surplus labor is appropriated by slave masters, feudal lords, and capitalists, respectively. In contrast, exploitation does not occur in the communist class process, in which laborers collectively appropriate their surplus labor, or the ancient class process, in which individuals appropriate their own surplus labor. Because the Soviet model was one pole of the planning debates, we should note that Resnick and Wolff argue that the predominant class structure of Soviet industry was not communist, but rather a form of state capitalism in which state agents assumed the role of capitalist boards of directors to appropriate and distribute the surplus labor of Soviet workers (2002, 85–103).

In *Capital*, Marx describes how several subsumed class positions provide *economic* conditions of existence for the CFCP and receive their share of surplus in a specific form. Merchants are one example; they help realize the surplus value embodied in goods and receive their portion through wholesale discounts. Resnick and Wolff extend this analysis to include those who provide capitalism's political and cultural conditions. These include agencies of the state, which build infrastructure, enforce contracts, educate children, and police communities. Industrial capitalists make subsumed class payments to the state through tax payments. In addition, some conditions of the CFCP are secured through the work of foundations funded through the direct contributions of capitalists. These institutions produce knowledge that supports the management of capitalist enterprises, enables the state to superintend the capitalist system, and provides cultural justification for the CFCP. Examples include the Russell Sage Foundation and the Brookings Institution, then the employers of the Congress's organizer, Mary Van Kleeck, and Lorwin, respectively.

Marxian class analysis shows that individuals may participate in multiple class and non-class processes, rather than belonging to a single group. Thus, the category "capitalists" includes those who appropriate surplus labor as well those who receive a distribution of it, and while all "workers" sell their labor power, only some perform surplus labor. While the participants in capitalist class processes are enmeshed in antagonisms over the production and distribution of the surplus, they are simultaneously dependent upon the robust functioning of the fundamental class process for their livelihoods.

Resnick and Wolff's reformulation of class transforms their understanding of class struggle. "Struggle," Resnick and Wolff explain, occurs when "the overdetermined contradictions embedded in social processes have fused to motivate intense collective efforts to change the process in question" (2006, 115). "Class struggle," specifically, is distinguished by its *object*—a change in fundamental and/or subsumed class processes—rather than by the individuals and groups involved (Resnick and Wolff 2006, 115).

The Marxian tradition has long been divided on economic determinism. Resnick and Wolff went beyond the critique of determinism toward a rigorous rejection of every kind of *essentialism*, the presumption that "any apparent complexity...can be analyzed to reveal a simplicity lying at its core" (1986, 2–3). Resnick and Wolff read in Marx a radical alternative to essentialism, which they described in terms of overdetermination and contradiction. Overdetermination presumes that all aspects of existence—natural, economic, political, and cultural—are mutually constitutive, that is, simultaneously cause and effect. Every process, therefore, is inherently contradictory because of its multiple, contradictory constituents, and therefore always subject to change. Because causal factors are innumerable, no theory can be more than partial and there can be no objective standard of truth by which to evaluate contending theories. Resnick and Wolff embrace a "nonabsolutist epistemology," to conclude: "Theories are differently true; truths are irreducibly plural" (2013, 376). A Marxian history of economic thought, therefore, understands economic theories, practices, and policies as mutually constitutive, the effects of a multitude of contradictory processes as well as the causes of others.

The road to Amsterdam

To understand the Congress, we need to know something about its antecedents and its participants. While Lorwin's proposals seem heretical by today's standards, this was less the case in 1931. Lorwin was part of an institutionalist movement that was prominent within the economic mainstream and which seemed poised to overtake neoclassical theory (Rutherford 2011, 7). The movement included philosopher John Dewey, historian Charles A. Beard, and economists Thorstein Veblen, Wesley C. Mitchell, John R. Commons, and Walton Hamilton. Both Columbia University, where Lorwin earned his doctorate, and the Brookings Institution, where he would work for a decade, were institutionalist strongholds. This school of thought focused on the origins and development of *institutions*, a broad concept that embraced the laws, customs, habits, and traditions that structure economic life (Atkins et al. 1933). The form of these institutions is subject to constant change through diverse processes. For institutionalists such as Walton Hamilton, the mutability of institutions suggested that their development could be socially directed: "Competition, property, the price structure, the wage system, and like institutions refuse to retain a definite content....To insist upon treating such things genetically or as in process is nothing more than to insist that they are subject to conscious control" (1919, 310). While the question of economic planning is now often reduced to a choice between market mechanisms and state intervention (Ruccio 2011, 17–21), the institutionalists contemplated legal, cultural, and political transformations outside the conventional boundaries of economics. Institutionalists were critical of capitalism, without advancing an alternative, and of neoclassical theory, though their criticism was muted by their pluralism. Thus, at the end of the decade, Lorwin would describe the theoretical innovations of the 1930s as "the process of reconciling some of the ideas of the neo-classical economists with what had long been regarded as the heresies of J. A. Hobson, Henry Gesell [*sic*], Thorstein Veblen and Karl Marx" (1941, 100).[1]

The experience of planning during the World War helped prepare the way for proposals like Lorwin's. Then, the US government intervened in the economy to an unprecedented degree, pressing numerous economists and social scientists into the service of wartime planning. The massive increase in war production with little consumer hardship convinced many that the economy had untapped capacities that could be realized through planning (Barber 1985, 2).

The Congress

The five-day Congress was comprised of 18 consecutive formal presentations and 80 commentaries offered by 60 discussants (Van Kleeck 1932a, 5). The meticulous care with which the Congress was organized and its proceedings published attests to the gravity of the project, as does the prominence and diversity of those attending. The Congress attracted participants from more than two dozen countries, with the preponderance from Western Europe:

Rudolf Wissell, the former German secretary of labor; Fritz Napthali, the head of the German trade union research association; Friedrich Pollock, a leading member of the Frankfurt Institute for Social Research; French journalist and politician Bertrand de Jouvenel; Dutch social democrat F. M. Wibaut, the eminence grise behind Amsterdam's exemplary municipal housing development project; Albert Thomas, the director of the Geneva International Labor Bureau...and leading industrialists from many countries.

(Horn 1996, 74)

In addition to Van Kleeck and Lorwin, more than 40 Americans attended including a US Congressman, the president of the International Brotherhood of Electrical Workers, and executives from American Telephone and Telegraph, Chemical Bank and Trust, Metropolitan Life Insurance, Miami Copper, and Western Electric. Members of the National Bureau of Economic Research attended as did numerous academics. Frances Perkins, an ally of FDR who would become a leading figure in the New Deal, also attended (Fleddérus 1932b). Major presentations were made by Harlow S. Person, director of the Frederick Taylor Society (Person 1932), and Edward A. Filene, president of the retail giant, Wm. Filene's Sons' Company (*New York Times*, 1931b), as well as by Lorwin and Van Kleeck.

A five-year plan for the world

Lorwin had taught at universities and been a foreign correspondent and investigative journalist before joining the Brookings Institution in 1925. There, he was encouraged to write *Labor and Internationalism* (1929), a comprehensive historic survey of European labor movements and their strategies to unite workers across borders (Lorwin and Shaughnessy 1962, 108). Lorwin traveled widely while researching the book and met many government and labor officials and other researchers, including those at the International Labour Organization, which he would join in 1935, and the Frankfurt Institute for Social Research, the seedbed of critical theory that Lorwin would help migrate to New York City (Wheatland 2004). During these trips Lorwin learned about various economic planning efforts and was impressed by the national economic councils of France and Germany.

In 1931, a series of events impelled Lorwin to the forefront of debates about planning. He was encouraged to write about the councils by the editor of the *Electrical Workers' Journal*. That article led to another in the *New Republic*, which garnered national attention and was discussed in many newspapers (Lorwin and Shauggnessy 1961). As Lorwin described, the French council drew together 47 delegates representing consumers, labor, and capital, to conduct research and advise the prime minister. The German economic council, mandated by the Weimar Constitution, was a kind of economic parliament, with 326 members representing a multitude of economic positions and occupations and working through 11 standing committees. For the United States, Lorwin envisioned "a federal economic council which would aid the American people to visualize their economic life as one vast enterprise and to guide it safely between the Scylla of inflation and the Charybdis of depression" (1931a, 295). It would comprise 100 delegates drawn from organizations representing "trade associations, national labor unions, farmers associations," and other diverse economic interests (Lorwin 1931a, 296). Lorwin believed a privileged position should be accorded to some professions: "special representation should also be given to science, management and research, considered as a single group, on the basis that these hold a peculiar place in society, tending to take an objective view and to reconcile conflicting interests" (1931a, 297). The council would collect data, study specific issues, and offer recommendations to Congress and government agencies (Lorwin 1931a, 296).

Lorwin's articles joined an avalanche of proposals. By April 1932, the Commerce Department was tracking two dozen proposals for economic planning including those of the American Federation of Labor; historian, Charles A. Beard; the Chamber of Commerce; Stuart Chase, economist and advisor to Franklin Delano Roosevelt; Senator Robert LaFollette, chairman of the Senate Committee on Manufactures; George Soule, editor of the *New Republic*; and Gerard Swope, president of General Electric (US Dept. of Commerce 1932, 118). In the wake of Lorwin's article, LaFollette enlisted him as a consultant to his committee, and Lorwin was invited to the Congress in Amsterdam (Lorwin and Shauggnessy 1961).

At the Congress, Lorwin began his address with a moral challenge, declaring that the audience confronted "the greatest paradox of all times— the paradox of misery and privation in a world of immense economic resources and productive power....We must meet this paradox or declare ourselves mentally and morally bankrupt"(1932a, 257). Lorwin viewed the Depression as part of a profound, global transformation: "we are experiencing a world-wide process of social change from the unlimited economic individualism and political liberalism of the XIX century to new and not yet full perceived economic and political forms of the XX century" (1932a, 258). Lorwin argued that these circumstances demanded nothing less than a conversion of faith:

> The laissez-faire of the nineteenth century was based upon a metaphysics of the providential guidance of natural law. The planning of the twentieth rests its case on a philosophical faith in the power of man to promote orderly economic and social change through scientific research and constructive imagination.
>
> (1932b, xl)

For Lorwin, the Depression was partially rooted in the failure of competitive capitalism—market structures had changed irrevocably. Now, competitive markets governed only a portion of the economy, and industry was fragmented into four categories: (1) "decentralized industries in which competition still holds," (2) "industries where a few large corporations practically fix prices—though with an eye to possible competition," (3) "industries where monopolistic prices prevail," and (4) the "areas of industrial life where price is regulated by public authority" (Lorwin 1932b, vxi–vxii). Consequently, markets now functioned in ways that were pernicious rather than beneficial. For example, competition still motivated producers to increase their productivity and capacity—with the potential to produce greater quantities at lower prices—but these social benefits were seldom realized. Instead, "the tendency is to try to restrict production in order to maintain profitable price levels" (Lorwin 1932b, xxv). Such strategies had a devastating effect on employment. Meanwhile, producers in relatively competitive markets, including farmers, tended to overproduce as demand fell, driving themselves into bankruptcy. Though Lorwin was critical of monopolies, he also associated them with efficient management, technical innovation, and increased productivity. They could not, therefore, be dismantled without a devastating loss of output. Lorwin's analysis was built upon a technological determinism: It was technological development that dictated the concentration of capital into fewer, larger corporations. As a result, the economy had greater productive capacity but was also subject to increasingly frequent and severe crises. Lorwin believed this vulnerability made planning inevitable.

Lorwin cited another negative consequence of competition: It exerted downward pressure on wages that exacerbated a tendency toward underconsumption. "It is because of its subservience to maximum profits that business is unable to extend mass purchasing power to the degree necessary for the solution of present-day difficulties….either through increasing wages and salaries or through lowering prices or…both" (1932, xxvi). Low wages spelled underconsumption but also made possible "excessive saving," which arises when "a large proportion of the national income finds its way into the hands of small groups in the form of rents, profits, and high salaries" (Lorwin 1932, xxvii). Lorwin suggested three measures to redistribute these funds: a guaranteed annual wage, a universal reduction of working hours, and the introduction of the various forms of social insurance already common in Europe (1932, xxviii).

Drawing on the example of wartime planning, Lorwin envisioned a network of government and voluntary agencies working in coordination with a central government authority. Rather than reacting to the exigencies of war, however, this new apparatus would guide long-run economic change to achieve socially defined goals. For example, if output had heretofore been limited by lack of effective demand because consumers lacked sufficient income, planning would transform the equation of supply and demand to "an equation between maximum capacity and maximum real need achieved through direct conscious control" (Lorwin 1932, xvi). This spelled new responsibilities for both government and business, holding them accountable for:

> meeting the real needs of the people and of utilizing all available productive capacity to do so at minimum possible prices allowing for reasonable profits... .Where any price or series of prices appeared excessive or incapable of meeting the needs of the consumers, they would create a prima facie case for the agency to intervene. Thus producers could be allowed to make their own prices subject to investigation and inquiry by the planning agency, and all business would have to reckon with the idea of a fair and reasonable profit. ....Under this scheme there is an approximation to the ideas of *social price,* and a varying range of return in relation to social service.
>
> (Lorwin 1932b, xvi, emphasis added)

"Social price," Lorwin explains, would be determined "on the basis of costs plus whatever surplus may be necessary to carry out the larger social purposes" (Lorwin 1932b, xvii). Lorwin's breezy tone seemingly reduces the determination of social price to an accounting problem, but the concept raises difficult questions. How much profit is "fair and reasonable"? By what calculus can "social service" be quantified and rewarded? Marx claimed that commodity fetishism obscures the complex social relations embodied within a commodity's price. To disaggregate a price into its components, as Lorwin suggested, is to risk exposing the conflictual, arbitrary nature of those relations. Lorwin discussed social price in his preliminary paper only, perhaps his fear of conflict caused him to drop the subject permanently.

If there was broad consensus about planning's necessity, there was little about its meaning (Balisciano 1998). One of Lorwin's unique contributions to these debates was his typology that identified four main types of economic planning. One was an "absolute-socialist type," totally centralized and completely egalitarian. This served as a rhetorical foil against its opposite, absolute laissez-faire; Lorwin dismissed both as relics of the previous century. By always stipulating the presence of markets, Lorwin may have hoped to sidestep the argument, advanced by Ludwig von Mises and others, that their absence made the calculation of prices impossible.

Lorwin also described planning of the "voluntary-business type," championed by business leaders, which exhorted businessmen to extend their sense of responsibility beyond their particular enterprise to encompass stewardship of the economy as a whole (Lorwin 1932b, xxiv). While advocates of this position called upon government to assume a larger role in regulating the economy, they insisted that it remain "subordinate to business in the main functions of guidance and leadership" (Lorwin 1932b, xxiv-xxv). Lorwin rejected voluntary-business type planning as insufficiently democratic and, because it left all major decisions in the hands of business leaders, likely to be counter-productive.

Lorwin termed Soviet planning "the partial state socialist type," because only some industries were planned. Lorwin criticized not Soviet planning, *per se*, but rather its association with political dictatorship and the collective ownership of the means of production. As an alternative, Lorwin stated that one may,

> assert the possibility of unified direction without either a dictatorship and without abolishing completely and all at once the rights and institutions of private property.... Such planful control would undoubtedly have to limit the powers of individuals and corporations, and subject the making of profits to social ends, but such control would not eliminate individual and group initiative on a private basis.
>
> (1932a, 263)

Lorwin termed this alternative, "social-progressive planning." In response to the Soviet claim that planning required collective ownership, Lorwin argued for a focus on coordination alone (1932a, 261). For comparison, consider that Charles A. Beard proposed the dispersal of *both* ownership and control of industry through the government purchase of corporate stocks and their redistribution to directors, managers, and employees (Beard 1932, 117–40).

Lorwin explained that "the social-progressive type" of planning "proceeds from the conviction that economic leadership is not, and should not be, a monopoly of the business man. Our understanding and guidance of economic life will be greater and better," Lorwin claimed, "if management and labor, and technical and scientific workers are brought together for the purpose of supplying both planning and the executive powers for carrying out plans" (1932b, xxix).

This raises the question of why business would accept increased responsibility and diminished autonomy. As Lorwin explained:

> In all democratic countries, economic planning involves the balancing of opposing group and class interests. But I believe that such balancing would become possible after a while, given the large and dynamic plans which would hold the promise of activity and economic advance....For one must face the situation and realize that the alternatives are becoming more and more either the willingness to accept the dictates of a rational concept of national and social welfare, or social revolution.
>
> (1932, xxix)

Lorwin's social-progressive planning appealed to contradictory emotions, appropriating some of the excitement that Soviet planning inspired while exploiting the anxieties it provoked. Lorwin understood that business acceptance of planning depended on a carrot, the promise of secure, if somewhat limited, profits, and a stick, the threat of popular rebellion.

The culmination of Lorwin's address was a "Five-Year Plan for the World," probably the only proposal of its time that attempted to address both the Depression and worsening international tensions through international economic planning. This portion of Lorwin's address was reported in the *New York Times,* the Associated Press, and many newspapers around the world (*New York Times* 1931a, Lorwin and Shaughnessy 1961, 193–94). For Lorwin, economic recovery required the resumption of international trade, which depended upon the initiative of the industrialized, creditor nations. His position contrasts sharply with those of Charles A. Beard and George H. Soule, who believed that creating a domestic market adequate to purchase the national output should be the first priority (Beard 1935, Soule 1932). This was based on their recognition that US imperialism had been fueled by the quest for foreign markets for domestic overproduction. Their so-called isolationism was, in part, motivated by international solidarity.

While Lorwin's case for national economic planning proceeded from a critical diagnosis of the economic crisis, his proposal for international planning glossed over the origins of the international crisis. Instead, Lorwin expressed moral imperatives:

> The growing economic unity of the world calls for a new sense of world solidarity based upon equal opportunity for all nations, and makes every attempt to perpetuate the division of the nations of the world into victors and vanquished, exploiters and exploited, a crime against human welfare.
>
> (Lorwin, 1932b)

Lorwin's long-range goals included restoring and maintaining the living standards of the advanced countries and "a leveling up of standards and an increase of mass purchasing power in the less developed but potentially promising countries of the world" (1932b, 268–69). To achieve these goals Lorwin proposed four measures for at least a five-year period: (1) a moratorium on war debts and reparations; (2) a series of international loans from the "chief lending countries" to promote productivity and increase "world purchasing power"; (3) a series of "international agreements for the division and control of the world market by producers of raw commodities and some manufactured goods"; and (4) establishment of a World Planning Board, possibly under the auspices of the League of Nations" (1932b, 268–99).

"The working class becomes the ruling class"

Valeryan Obolensky-Ossinky joined the revolutionary movement while he was a student, fought in the failed revolution of 1905, and held a variety of high-level positions in the new Soviet state, the Communist Party, and the Communist International (Comintern). Ossinsky repeatedly criticized the concentration of power at the highest levels of the party. In 1918, as one of the Left Communists, he warned that the party's control over production and its embrace of capitalist management methods would have dire consequences: "Socialism and socialist organization will be set up by the proletariat itself, or it will not be set up at all: something else will be set up—state capitalism" (1975). Lenin, however, rebuked and suppressed the Left Communists, effectively prohibiting further debate on the nature of Soviet class relations. At the Congress, Ossinsky could not play the role of the critical Marxist; he was limited instead to the role of the diplomat, arguing his country's official positions before a hostile world.

The first of three Soviet presenters, Ossinsky offered a detailed history of Soviet economic policy and celebrated its unique achievements in the face of great adversity. As he told the Congress, planned socialist reconstruction was the reason why,

> a backward country, which suffered enormous losses in the world war and which later experienced equally ruinous intervention and civil war, was able ten years after a mass famine, not only to restore everything that was ruined but to advance forward at a pace absolutely unparalleled in history. It...is making uninterrupted progress at the height of a world crisis. These achievements have been accompanied by the reduction of the working day to seven hours and by the radical improvement of the working conditions of workers in town and country.
>
> (Ossinsky 1932, 308)

But first, Ossinsky took aim at Lorwin and other planners, deriding them as "champions of capitalism" bent on redeeming the system (1932, 291). Ossinsky argued that the profound cultural transformations Lorwin imagined were wholly unrealistic. It would be impossible for the capitalists to disregard their habits, experience, and training and begin working cooperatively, either voluntarily or under compulsion. Even if implemented, he asserted that Lorwin's proposal would intensify, rather than calm, class conflict because it would produce constant friction among the groups represented on the planning boards, require an expanding bureaucracy of management, cause indecision and inertia among business leaders, and give way to constant insubordination, abuses, and corruption, and "such a hampering and disruption of the economic processes that the situation would be equivalent to the worst of crises" (Ossinsky 1932, 297). But this would not happen, Ossinsky concluded, because "it is altogether impossible to imagine that the employers who actually wield power and force will allow themselves to be brushed aside" (1932, 297). Planning would succeed only in lifting antitrust restrictions and therefore "only strengthen the position of the big monopolist corporations" (Ossinsky 1932, 295).

Further, Ossinsky warned that Lorwin's plan was feeble in the face of the economic forces determining world history, inexorably making the world less stable and more violent. Competition among capitalists accelerates the vertical and horizontal concentration of industry, which only heightens competition and forces it across borders: "The struggle for markets, for spheres of influence for the investment of capital, and for cheap raw materials is transferred to the world arena. Monopolist groups in control of state power...contend with each other for the partition of the world and for the control of as many dependent colonial territories as possible" (1932, 293–94).

Ossinsky went on to explain how the World War and the Treaty of Versailles had "created a whole new system of oppressing and oppressed states and nations" and set in motion "the preparations of the imperialist groups for a new war" (1932, 294). In retrospect, Ossinsky's words sound horribly prophetic: "the imperialist groups who possess all the economic resources, all the instruments of violence of the modern state, as well as the powerful ideological weapons of science, the schools, the church, the press, etc., are prepared to go to any length, including even the mass extermination of human beings...to maintain and extend their rule of oppression" (1932, 293–94).

Soviet planning was succeeding, Ossinsky argued, because it was founded on society's common ownership of the means of production: "The socialization of the means of production naturally signifies the abolition of classes and all class distinctions" (1932, 298). With this change in ownership, "power passes into the hands of the working class, that is, the working class becomes the ruling class until classes and class distinctions are abolished" (Ossinsky 1932, 301).

The poles of the debate

Although Lorwin and Ossinsky's analyses appeared to be polar opposites, they are in many ways parallel. Both appealed to anti-capitalist and utopian longings. From the perspective of Marxian theory, Lorwin deployed the promise of planning as an ideological justification for private capitalism, just as Ossinsky used the promise of communism to justify state capitalism. Both Lorwin and Ossinsky excluded the question of worker self-management, though the concept of workers' control was known to them. Property was of central importance for both planners. For Ossinsky, the collective ownership of property was the *sine qua non* of socialist economic planning. Lorwin, instead, embraced the sanctity of private property, believing this would forestall a major objection to planning.

We can also discern parallel national exceptionalisms, American and Soviet, in their presentations. Both minimized the prevalence of class conflict within their states, assuming their governments to be motivated by loftier moral concerns. And each expressed confidence in the legitimacy and efficacy of his state—Lorwin assumed his nation to be a popular democracy while ignoring the degree to which it was a class dictatorship, and Ossinsky assumed that the Soviet Union was ruled by its working class rather than the Party.

The world view of each planner was built upon similarly essentialist foundations. While Lorwin's determinism was technological, Ossinsky's was economic. Ossinsky assumed that: (1) capitalist societies are divided by profound, irreconcilable class antagonisms; (2) monopoly capitalists are politically dominant and able to dictate policy, even within liberal democracies; and (3) these class conflicts within states inevitably translate to inter-imperialist competition, including war. In Ossinsky's narrative, these conflicts and tensions are mutually reinforcing, building inexorably toward cataclysm. In contrast, Lorwin presumed that the same societies were (1) united by the interdependence of classes; (2) able to achieve democratic consensus because of their common interests, and (3) capable of taking collective action to avert economic crisis and war. If Lorwin and Ossinsky's one-sided perspectives had been integrated, they would have gone far toward describing the complex and contradictory nature of these societies.

The Soviets could be faulted for underestimating the resilience and adaptability of capitalism and the imperialist powers. These failings, however, are overshadowed by the fact that the Soviets were the only speakers at the Congress to sound the alarm about the coming global conflagration. If Lorwin's proposal failed to prevent war, it nonetheless prefigured elements of the postwar economic order, imagining institutions similar to the United Nations, the World Bank, and the International Monetary Fund. Contrary to Lorwin's rhetoric of solidarity, however, these institutions would dominate less-developed nations and undermine national economic and political experiments. In some respects, Lorwin's naïveté about international relations was consistent with his approach to class relations: He assumed a harmony of interests among nations, underestimated their potential sources of conflict, and disregarded the inequalities of power among them. Betting always on the good intentions of the powerful, he left their power and economic incentives intact, while he discounted the agency of the powerless.

While a full assessment of Ossinsky's claim that capitalist planning would "only strengthen the position of the big monopolist corporations" (Ossinsky 1932, 295) is beyond the scope of this article, it would prove remarkably similar to Lorwin's own evaluation of events a few years later. Lorwin's proposals were credited with helping to inspire the National Industrial Recovery Act (NRA) of 1933. Although the NRA fell far short of what Lorwin had proposed, it made some provision for the representation of diverse economic groups (NPA 1995, 3–4). But as Lorwin would soon admit, the results were disappointing: "The NRA has not given representation to consumer interests, to managerial interests, or to technical interests; it has given but very scant representation to labor interests; it has given undue preponderance to the business interests" (1935, 118).

Class as groups or class as process?

In 1934, Lorwin offered an explicit view of class relations and, we may infer, the role of planners. He explained that western societies had reached an impasse because the two great classes had failed to lead in the common interest: While capitalists "showed a sad incapacity to establish leadership based on social needs and moral values," labor "proved unable either to assume the hegemony of the state or to impose by force the program of socialism which they had preached for more than half a century" (1934). In the midst of crisis, however, a new social force emerged, which Lorwin called "middle-class insurgents" (1934, 16–22). Their legitimacy rested on their potential to act as "the reconcilers of conflicting interests and groups....As against the class struggle of the Marxians, as against the competitive conflicts of capitalism, the spokesmen of the middle classes offer to build up a new social system based upon an organic solidarity in which group inequalities and group interests are happily merged in a higher national purpose" (1934, 17).

Lorwin's tripartite model follows a common essentialist pattern: Regardless of their heterogeneity, the members of the large aggregates—capitalists, labor, and the middle class—are assumed to share characteristics that determine their outlook and behavior. Such models typically valorize one group as the universal class, capable of leading the others because its particular interests coincide with those of society in general. This class-as-aggregate approach, however, seems at odds with the specifics of this historical moment: the Congress included representatives of each "class"; the epochal shift in economic beliefs that Lorwin called "the Great Turn" cut across "class" lines; and the policies proposed at the Congress, such as higher wages, could not be easily categorized in terms of the "class" interests they served. Furthermore, even in 1934, Lorwin recognized that these "middle-class insurgents," rather than defending "solidarity," were contributing to fascism in Italy and Germany.

In contrast to Lorwin's approach, Resnick and Wolff's reformulation of Marxian theory understands class struggle as contention over class processes rather than conflict among groups. One implication is that Lorwin's intervention can be read as a *subsumed class rebellion*. *Subsumed class*, not because of the individuals or groups involved, but because it attempted to reinvent the capitalist class processes by creating new methods, new institutions, new ideas, and even new professions that would help secure the conditions necessary to perpetuate the CFCP. Lorwin's proposal promised to revive the CFCP by mediating conflicts among capitalists, as well as between capital and labor, by recalibrating the distribution of the surplus.

From the viewpoint of Marxian class analysis, Lorwin's rebellion seldom exceeded the boundaries of the CSCP, because it neither challenged the predominance of the CFCP nor proposed an alternative, such as the communist fundamental class process.[2] Lorwin's intervention was no less a *rebellion*, however, because it challenged economic orthodoxy, criticized business conduct, and sought to bring production and distribution under a degree of collective, democratic control. While his proposal promised to *revive* the CFCP, by coordinating production and redistributing income, it also threatened to *undermine* the CFCP, by circumscribing the prerogatives of capitalists and subjecting formerly private decisions to public scrutiny.

Conclusion

By directing our attention toward class processes, Resnick and Wolff have shown us how to discern the lineaments of class conflict within debates about economic policies and doctrines, even those that exclude the concept. Their contributions offer historians the means to enlarge the scope of Marxian theory within historiography and show us ways to expand its influence in contemporary debates. Today, as in Lorwin's day, there are critiques of capitalism and proposals for change that can be understood as subsumed class rebellions. Now, as then, most economic debate centers on how to reform the capitalist class processes in ways that promote desired combinations of fairness, opportunity, prosperity, or other goals. Whether or not the proposed reforms can achieve their stated purpose, they are likely to justify and reinforce capitalist class processes, just as they did in Lorwin's time. But today's subsumed class rebels may choose to break from this pattern and go beyond renovating the capitalist class processes. By choosing instead to produce the knowledge, culture, and institutions that provide the conditions of existence for the communist fundamental class process, today's subsumed class rebels may create new ways to transform society and themselves.

Acknowledgment

This paper would have been impossible without the support of Christine Skwiot and Ian Fletcher. It benefited from the comments of Richard McIntyre and Jane Rago, although the usual caveats apply.

Notes

1 Lorwin was probably referring to Henry George. "Henry Gesell" may be a conflation of George with his admirer, Silvio Gesell.
2 Lorwin's address to the Congress was nonetheless cited as evidence of his "disloyalty," leading decades later to his dismissal from the US Department of Commerce (Storrs 2012).

References

Atkins, W. E., D. W. McConnell, C. D. Edwards, C. Raushenbush, A. A. Friedrich, and L. S. Reed. 1933. *Economic Behavior: An Institutional Approach.* Boston: Houghton Mifflin.

Balisciano, M. L. 1998. "Hope for America: American Notions of Economic Planning between Pluralism and Neoclassicism, 1930–1950." *History of Political Economy* 30 (supplement): 153–78.

Barber, W. J. 1985. *From New Era to New Deal: Herbert Hoover, the Economists, and American Economic Policy, 1921-1933.* Cambridge: Cambridge University Press.

Beard, C. A. 1932a. "A 'Five-Year Plan' for America." In *America Faces the Future,* 117–40. Boston: Houghton Mifflin.

———— 1932b. *America Faces the Future.* Boston: Houghton Mifflin.

———— 1935. *The Open Door at Home: A Trial Philosophy of National Interest.* New York: Macmillan.

Fleddérus, M. L., ed. 1932a. *World Social Economic Planning: The Necessity for Planned Adjustment of Productive Capacity and Standards of Living; Material Contributed to World Social Economic Congress, Amsterdam, August 1931.* The Hague: International Industrial Relations Institute.

————, ed. 1932b. *World Social Economic Planning: The Necessity for Planned Adjustment of Productive Capacity and Standards of Living; Addendum to Material Contributed to World Social Economic Congress, Amsterdam, August 1931.* The Hague: International Industrial Relations Institute.

Hamilton, W. H. 1919. "The Institutional Approach to Economic Theory." *The American Economic Review* 9 (1): 309–18.

Horn, G. 1996. *European Socialists Respond to Fascism: Ideology, Activism and Contingency in the 1930s.* New York: Oxford University Press.

Lorwin, L. L. 1929. *Labor and Internationalism.* New York: MacMillan.

———— 1931a. "A Federal Economic Council: Concrete Suggestions for a Program of Economic Planning." *The New Republic* (April 29): 294–7.

———— 1931b. "A Five-Year Plan for the World: Shall We Seek Temporary Painkillers or Lasting Cures?" *The Survey* 67 (5): 231–5.

———— 1932a. "The Problem of Economic Planning." In *World Social Economic Planning,* M. L. Fleddérus, ed., 257–69. The Hague: International Industrial Relations Institute.

———— 1932b. "The Problem of Economic Planning." In *World Social Economic Planning: Addendum,* M. L. Fleddérus, ed., xvi–xl. The Hague: International Industrial Relations Institute.

_____, 1934. "Some Aspects of the Planning State." *The American Political Science Review.* 28(1): 16-22

———— 1935. "Socialism, Fascism and Democracy." *Annals of the American Academy of Political and Social Science* 180 (July): 114–8.

———— 1941. *The Economic Consequences of the Second World War.* New York: Random House.

Lorwin, L. L. and D. F. Shauggnessy. 1961. "The Reminiscences of Lewis L. Lorwin." Columbia Center for Oral History Archives, Rare Book and Manuscript Library. New York: Columbia University.

National Planning Association. 1995. *The National Planning Association at Work: Six Decades of Providing Solutions to America's Challenges,* 3–4. Washington, DC: National Planning Association.

New York Times. 1931a. "Urges 5-Year Plan to Restore World: Dr. Lewis L. Lorwin Tells Group at Amsterdam that First Step Is Moratorium." August 26: 10.

New York Times. 1931b. "High Wages Urged on Social Congress." August 27: 8.

Obolensky-Ossinsky, V. V. 1932. "The Nature and Forms of Social Economic Planning." In *World Social Economic Planning*, M. L. Fleddérus ed., 291–340. The Hague: International Industrial Relations Institute.

Osinsky, N. [1918] 1975. "On the Building of Socialism." *Kommunist* no. 2 (April). Quoted in Brinton, M., *The Bolsheviks and Workers' Control*. Montreal: Black Rose Books.

Person, H. S. 1932. "Scientific Management as a Philosophy and Technique of Progressive Industrial Stabilization." In *World Social Economic Planning*, M. L. Fleddérus, ed., 153–204. Geneva: International Industrial Relations Institute.

Resnick, S.A. and R. Wolff. 1986. "Power, Property and Class." *Socialist Review* 16(2): 97-124.

Resnick, S. A. and R. D. Wolff. 2002. *Class Theory and History: Capitalism and Communism in the U.S.S.R.* New York: Routledge.

—— 2006. *New Departures in Marxian Theory*. New York: Routledge.

Roosevelt, F. D. 1933. *Looking Forward*. New York: John Day.

Ruccio, D. 2011. *Development and Globalization: A Marxian Class Analysis*. London: Routledge.

Rutherford, M. 2011. *The Institutionalist Movement in American Economics, 1918–1947*. Cambridge: Cambridge University Press.

Soule, G. H. 1932. *A Planned Society*. New York: Macmillan.

Storrs, L. R. Y. 2012. *The Second Red Scare and the Unmaking of the New Deal Left*. Princeton: Princeton University Press.

U.S. Department of Commerce. 1932. "Sponsors of Plans Presented to Date on Economic Planning for America." *Congressional Digest* 11 (4): 118.

Van Kleeck, M. 1932a. "Analysis and Review of the Congress." In *World Social Economic Planning: The Necessity for Planned Adjustment of Productive Capacity and Standards of Living; Material Contributed to World Social Economic Congress, Amsterdam, August 1931*, M. L. Fleddérus, ed., 14–34. The Hague: International Industrial Relations Institute.

Wheatland, T. 2004. "The Frankfurt School's Invitation from Columbia University: How the Horkheimer Circle Settled on Morningside Heights." *German Politics and Society* 22 (3): 1–32.

Wolff, R. D. and S. A. Resnick. 2012. *Contending Economic Theories: Neoclassical, Keynesian, and Marxian*. Cambridge: MIT Press.

Part VIII

Communism without guarantees

24 Bad communisms

Maliha Safri and Kenan Erçel

Resnick and Wolff's many communisms

The recent appearance of Alain Badiou's *Communist Hypothesis* (2010) and two high-profile edited collections, *The Idea of Communism* Volume 1 (Douzinas and Žižek 2010) and Volume 2 (Žižek 2013), signifies a return to theories and histories of communism. We see Stephen Resnick and Richard Wolff's work as hovering over this new excitement, at home with and presciently anticipating the contemporary struggle to rethink the concepts and possibilities of communism. We are bold enough to claim that Resnick and Wolff's theoretical contribution is the missing piece these works—and all of us—sorely need: a theorization of communism without guarantees.[1]

At heart, Resnick and Wolff's theorization of communism is "thin," refusing to assume that communism provides a solution to all forms of alienation, poverty, discrimination, inequality, and other social ills (Cullenberg 1992). Instead, Resnick and Wolff (1987) define communism as a class process: a collective of producers that appropriates and distributes the fruits of its own surplus labor. Communism stands in stark opposition to capitalism, slavery, and feudalism. In all of the latter, a small subset occupies the position of appropriator and distributor of surplus, excluding and exploiting the direct producers.

In *Class Theory and History* (2002), Resnick and Wolff wrote a chapter, "The Many Forms of Communism," in which they lay out many overdetermined possibilities for communism. First, they examine how communism could coexist with a variety of property structures. While traditional Marxism automatically equates capitalism with private property, Resnick and Wolff carefully posit that communism could be organized by private property arrangements (amongst other property regimes). Workers engaged in a labor market and in collective appropriation and distribution of surplus in a privately owned firm would be one such possibility. As a concrete example, workers engaged in contemporary self-directed enterprises (or worker collectives) may own their means of production and also engage in market exchange. Their collective appropriation of surplus means that the fundamental class process is a communist one, even if it is fully engaged in labor and commodity markets.

Resnick and Wolff examine the spectrum of power relations that is possible within communism, ranging from one extreme to the other. On the one hand, they offer the possibility of a despotic communism, in which political power is vested in the hands of a few, perhaps even only one—in contrast to a fully social democratic communist polity in which everyone equally shares political power, irrespective of class position.[2] George Demartino (2003) develops this idea in his work on the different dimensions of "class justice," in which distributive justice necessitates addressing the rights and needs of those who are not directly productive workers but who nonetheless have a social stake in the surplus. Madra and Özselçuk (2010, 2015) sharpen the stakeholder approach by focusing on Marx's well-known description of communism as "from each according to his ability, to each according to his need." They argue that in contrast to the masculine logic of capitalism (where only the board of directors is legally empowered to appropriate and distribute the surplus), this communist axiom unfixes who is the rightful appropriator/distributor of surplus.[3]

Resnick and Wolff suggest that inequality could arise and worsen over time, despite widespread prevalence of communism. Communism could be characterized by "stability and instability, concentration and competition, alienation and solidarity" (Resnick and Wolff 2002, 61). Antagonism is ever-present. Instead of a Marxist politics that promises harmony and a non-conflictual social totality, theirs is one in which division and antagonism are not only possible but ineradicable.

In Resnick and Wolff's own words: "communisms are as variable as capitalisms" (2002, 70). The definition of communism is not fixed to one idea, one incarnation, or one set of ideal possibilities. It also means that communism is not a description of a utopian state (echoing Marx and Engels's description of a non-utopian understanding of communism in the *German Ideology*).[4] Marx and Marxists such as Resnick and Wolff make the case for communism not because it will solve all social antagonisms but because it is the only class process in which exploitation would cease to characterize fundamental class relations. Communism would be considered just or ethical because it is the only non-exploitative way to organize the economy.

Yet even if communism is non-exploitative, that doesn't mean it is always "good." Communism can be bad: nondemocratic, unstable, rife with corruption and contradiction. Resnick and Wolff insist we avoid the presumption "that communist class structures would necessarily survive" (2002, 54). This is perhaps the most salient difference between Resnick and Wolff's Marxism and the more hopeful post-capitalist politics of Gibson-Graham (1996, 2006). Resnick and Wolff's emphasis is on contradiction, on the light *and the dark* within communism.[5]

In this essay, we focus on the dark side of communism. We take our cue from the mischievous glee we remember Stephen Resnick taking when teaching "bad" communisms in the classroom—which, it must be noted, he never characterized as such. He did this, of course, not because he approached the matter from an anti-Marxist position (e.g., *The Black Book of Communism*), but because an intellectual investigation must go everywhere, confront everything, and present a "ruthless criticism." In other words, we are not analyzing these forms of communism from the perspective of those for whom "bad communism" is a redundancy—as communism is inherently bad, evil, etc.—but from the perspective of those who advocate for it but think it would be a disservice to communism to not recognize its presence in places where one would rather not find it. The particular examples of "bad" communism discussed below correspond to different and increasingly larger scales: from a certain profession (sexual labor), to a large sector within the economy (agriculture), to a social formation in its entirety (Asiatic Despotism).[6] We draw on the work of Resnick and Wolff on this theme and also from their students, Jack Amariglio and Marjolein van der Veen, who investigated the topics of Asiatic Despotism and sexual labor respectively in their Ph.D. dissertations under Resnick and Wolff's mentorship and in subsequently published work.

Communist forms of sexual labor

Sexual labor is a highly charged and divisive issue among feminists. While radical feminists typically consider sexual labor to be demeaning and exploitative by its very nature, sex radicals and prostitutes' rights advocates regard it "as work, as an occupation susceptible like others to exploitation."[7] The agenda of the former camp is mainly geared toward eradication of this category of labor through, if need be, drastic measures like criminalization of sex work, while the latter camp calls for traditional forms of labor advocacy like unionization. In her class-analytical approach to the issue, van der Veen (2001) attempts to reconcile the two camps, and in so doing, performs a Hegelian *Aufhebung* and preserves the insights of both perspectives while transcending them.

Van der Veen argues that like other goods and services, sexual labor is performed in various class settings. It might take the form of slavery as, for example, is the case with the victims of human trafficking, which certainly warrants an abolitionist agenda. However, sexual labor might also take the form of capitalist wage labor whereby the sex worker sells her labor-power to the employer owning, for example, an escort agency, a striptease club, or a brothel. A class-analytical point of view agrees with the sex radicals that the distinction between slavery and capitalist forms of sexual labor is fundamental and cannot be dismissed on the grounds of the sexual nature of work. Nonetheless, van der Veen's approach differs from the sex radicals in that the sex radicals' non-Marxist conception of exploitation focuses on unfair compensation or unsafe working conditions and informs a struggle against the employer for their improvement or against the state to decriminalize sexual labor. In contrast, the class-qua-surplus perspective problematizes the very existence of an employer who appropriates surplus from the direct producers—in this case, the sex workers (van der Veen 2000, 2001).

An interesting and maybe scandalous implication of the class-qua-surplus perspective, however, is that, under certain circumstances, sexual labor might assume communistic forms. Van der Veen writes about the formation of organizations, such as COYOTE (Call off your Tired Old Ethics), PONY (the Prostitute Organization of New York), the Red Thread in Amsterdam, and the Prostitutes Collective of Victoria in Australia (van der Veen 2000, 134 and 136). It is worth noting that most of the examples above are not so much sites of communist production as they are support or advocacy groups organized as collectives. An admittedly rare example of the former is Lusty Ladies in San Francisco, a collective that organized as a union in 1997 and later evolved into a worker cooperative (Looking Glass Collective) in which all workers (peep-show performers and support staff, such as bouncers and janitors) were members. Faced with rising rents and falling revenues as Internet porn rapidly assumed prominence, the collective was forced to close in 2013 (Mulder 2015).

As the experience of Lusty Ladies demonstrates, communist forms of sexual labor may succumb to various pressures and dissolve. Or to resist those pressures, workers may need to increase their work hours, thus expanding their absolute surplus labor, or pay themselves less. The performance of sexual labor in a communist class setting does not guarantee total control over the fruits of one's labor, either. For example, in a society where sexual labor is criminalized, a collective of prostitutes might feel pressured to allocate a portion of their surplus to the law enforcement agents in the form of bribes. Sex workers who are organized as a communist collective might still have to endure harsh working conditions, the daily threat of sexual and other physical forms of violence, and the ever-present risk of a sexually transmitted disease. Such challenges notwithstanding, a class-analytical approach shifts the terrain of the debate *from* whether the sexual labor is inherently exploitative *to* whether the sexual labor is performed in an exploitative class process. In other words, whether a sex worker is exploited is not inferred directly from the nature of the service commodity exchanged, but derives from the ways in which the surplus labor embodied in this service commodity is produced, appropriated, and distributed.

Collectivized farms in Soviet Russia

While the USSR was widely acclaimed as the preeminent example of existing socialism, Resnick and Wolff took a certain kind of perverse delight in showing that for the most part, the Soviet experiment did not foster communist class processes. Resnick and Wolff (2002) argued that the Soviet experiment was largely built upon the foundation of "state capitalism," because the state occupied the crucial role of appropriating and distributing surplus generated by workers, in much the same way that the corporate board of directors usurps surplus of its employees in private capitalism. In the absence of a class-qua-surplus analysis, the Bolsheviks "neither destroyed ancient, feudal, and capitalist structures, nor could they recognize their failure to do so" (*ibid.*, 153).

There was one exception in this trajectory, and that came in the 1930s with the creation of large collective farms, the *kolkhozes*. This policy largely emerged because Soviet industrial workers could not obtain the rising quantity of food and raw materials they required. When the state tried to requisition and seize agricultural output from the peasant majority (or "ancient" farmers, as they are called in Resnick and Wolff's work) and remaining small capitalist *kulak* farmers, severe conflicts erupted. Switching to money rents and state-imposed unfavorable terms of trade for agriculture did not solve the problem, and all three strategies led to failure, as peasants could not survive with what little was left to them. The solution to this conflict between industry and agriculture was to herd most peasants into private collective farms, creating "the first and only large-scale establishment of communism in Soviet history" (Resnick and Wolff 2002, 178). The hope was that collective farms would be easier to control than the mass of small peasants and kulaks who were considered anti-socialist; indeed, the collectivization took place under the name of "finishing the anti-capitalist revolution" in Soviet Russia. Those who resisted the process were killed or imprisoned *en masse*.

Resnick and Wolff argue that despite the centrality of the state in the process of forced collectivization, the collective was nonetheless the first body to appropriate and distribute surplus labor. No individual farmer could touch or lay claim to the product that belonged to the collective. The revenues from sales were deposited into a "kolkhoz savings account" from which distributions were made by the collective. However, in order to meet the growing needs of an ever-privileged industrial sector, the state required surplus distributions from these collective farms, without going so far as to become a direct appropriator. Collectives were subject to a mandatory output quota to be sold to the state at under-valued prices (in addition to having to pay taxes and rents for the tractors leased from the state). They were also pressured to distribute surplus to collective farm needs. Starting in 1932, the remainder could be legally sold in local private markets at higher prices. This revenue was not sufficient, though, to assure the survival of the families in the collective farm, contributing to famine in 1932–33.

As a result, early in the 1930s, the state assigned individual plots to peasants and allowed the peasants to sell this produce in local private markets to ease the burden of the low prices that the state set for requisitioned agricultural commodities. Resnick and Wolff draw upon accounts and journals of farm chairmen to show that these individual plots actually saved the majority of households from starvation, providing for most of their vegetable, potato, and milk consumption. This set in motion a never-ending contradiction for farmers, between their identities and class positions as individual peasant farmers, which sustained their lives in important ways, and their positions within the collective farm. Most of the output from collective farms was sold to the state at the below-market prices it imposed, while all output from individual plots of land could be sold in uncontrolled local private markets at higher prices. Thus, state pricing continually undermined communist class structures in collective farms, despite other policies that aided and improved productivity on collective farms.[8]

In the post-WWII period, state policies increasingly transformed private collective farms (*kolkhozes*) into state farms (*sovkhozes*). The latter grew from a small minority in the 1930s to comprise almost 45% of the total number of state and collective farms by 1990, according to the 1990 Statistical yearbook of the USSR. Resnick and Wolff argue that the *sovkhoz* was a "state capitalist" structure since the state designated its own agents to serve as surplus-appropriating boards of directors and adopted a wage-remuneration system, proletariatizing collective farm workers. Yet, since individual plots of land still remained, workers in state farms and the remaining private collective farms could divert much of their energy and labor toward their individual family plots. Perhaps due to the blindness to class-qua-surplus, the state diminished and eventually killed the most widespread experiment with communism in Soviet history, an experiment that itself killed millions and starved many more.

Despotic forms of the commune

Taking up Marx's distinction in the *Grundrisse* (1993 [1939]) between Asiatic and Germanic forms of the commune, Amariglio (2010) offers new insights into both. We find his work salient because it introduces all of the thorny issues of subjectivity in relation to communism. In many "ideal/ized" understandings of communism, there is an implied subjectivity, often conjoined with an "ideal" political process: the collective gathers as a group of producers, all of whom have a collective subjectivity in which they recognize each other as equals and comrades. This ideal form of subjectivity and collective process can be linked to a "good," democratic, Germanic commune of small peasants, a topic Marx explores in the *Grundrisse*. Amariglio draws on this work to show that in the Germanic form, peasant families were first and foremost members of a clan, and membership in that clan allowed families to lay claim to the means of production and surplus.[9] The family was merely a "molecule of the self-representation and existence of the commune" (Amariglio 2010, 334). Challenging the idea that those separate molecules (or individual peasants) formed the basic character of the commune, Marx argued that communal property should be distinguished from private possession.

In contrast to this form of the commune, there is the despotic commune, perhaps a "not-so-good" way communism can come into this world. In the *Grundrisse*, Marx refers to examples of this despotic commune as an Asiatic form and as the original form of the commune when humans settled into agricultural cultivation.[10] The cohesion of the commune is "represented by a 'comprehensive unity' that often takes the form of a despot, who, Marx claims, is seen by the members of the commune either as the 'father of many communities' or as an intermediary for an 'imagined clan-being, the god'" (Amariglio 2010, 334). Since the despot represents the commune, Marx's discussion implies that when the despot determines the distribution of surplus to various ends—for example, toward the construction of aqueduct and irrigation projects or community feasts—that distribution is undertaken by the commune itself.

Amariglio tackles the dismissal of despotic communism as a false form, one in which the despot disguises his individual appropriation under the cover of standing in for the collective. Even if some forms such as the Germanic are democratic and others such as the Asiatic are not, "they are communism, in economic terms, nonetheless" (2010, 332). This argument hinges on accepting as real the ways in which the clan/commune ideologically configures the despot as standing in for the commune itself. Amariglio writes about the Asiatic form:

> [T]he *Grundrisse* is eye-opening for Marx's insistence on taking seriously the notion that there is no meaningful difference between the "real" and the "imaginary" when it comes to the actions of the clan/commune on its own behalf. ... No distinction is drawn between the real, empirical direct producers and the commune, an imagined unity with a form of representation in a person/body that may not "actually" perform necessary and surplus labor.
>
> (Amariglio 2010, 334–5)

There is no difference between the subjective or ideological realm (what the commune believes of the despot) and the objective realm (the material moments of appropriation and distribution). Or rather, they are fused together, which means that the commune undertakes appropriation of surplus in and through the figure of the despot.

Related to this discussion is one about how the individual is constituted and experiences his/her own subjectivity. Amariglio urges us to see how individuality is constituted differently and variously understood within alternative historical junctures. He references the many types of individual that Marx surveys: the isolated individual, private individual, real individual, social individual, and natural individual, among others. The different ways in which individuals are constituted must map onto the varieties of communism as well. Amariglio argues, "Some kinds of individuality give rise to the idea that direct producers are independent and separate elements in the collective, whilst others beckon towards a more 'social' form of individuals" (2010, 336).

In the Asiatic commune, perhaps the ideological relation between the despot (who represents the "higher unity" of the commune) and the individual commune members might also be connected to the issue of the existence or non-existence of hierarchy and equality within the commune. If, for instance, there is disagreement over any matter, then the despot, representing the commune, has greater weight, importance, and decision-making power than any other individual. Nonetheless, this despotic and, arguably, non-egalitarian and hierarchical commune remains a form of communism. It shows that the process of appropriation as well as the subjectivity in communist projects can take many forms, some that involve participatory and democratic processes, and others that do not.

Why bad communism?

It is intriguing that as ardent proponents of communism, Resnick and Wolff unabashedly own up to "bad" forms of communism discussed above. It would have been much easier for them to "thicken" the definition of communism with qualifications that would preempt such dreary labor practices from being labeled communist or to forge a chain of equivalence between sex labor-patriarchy-capitalism-slavery and define exploitation to be inclusive of all forms of sexual labor. It would have been much easier to broaden their "state capitalist" conception of the urban, industrial Soviet Russian economy so as to include the collective farms and, in so doing, not only disown the unfathomable devastation that resulted from that epic failure of a social engineering, but also put the blame of all the suffering on capitalism. And, too, it would have been much easier to portray communism as inherently democratic and antithetical to Asiatic Despotism.

While we do not purport to provide an exhaustive explanation of the motivations behind Resnick and Wolff's non-disavowal of "bad" forms of communism, we think that part of the explanation has to do with the ability of bad communisms to throw into sharp relief the *differentia specifica* of the moment of appropriation. An analogy with modern capitalism might be helpful in illustrating this point. In Volume 3 of *Capital*, Marx describes the joint-stock corporation, the pinnacle of modern capitalist enterprise. Özselçuk and Madra (2005) draw on that work to show how the traditional capitalist-cum-entrepreneur dissolves into various functions performed by other entities with the emergence of the joint-stock corporation. With the growth of financial capital, the capitalist can borrow the requisite capital instead of providing it. Other functions (managing, accounting, marketing, direct labor) can also be delegated to other entities (managers, accountants, marketing department, employees). The board of directors at the helm of the corporation does not have to perform any of these functions. In fact, in contemporary business, "corporate boards of directors rarely own significant proportions of the firm's outstanding stock" (Resnick and Wolff 2002, 79). Once the justification evaporates for a "return to the entrepreneur" based on his role in production or capital ownership, "[p]rofit thus appears as simply the appropriation of other people's surplus labor" (Marx 1991 [1894], cited in Özselçuk and Madra 2005, 87). The moment of appropriation is distilled into its purest form, revealing that the capitalist really is the exception to the exchange of equivalents, receiving something for nothing.

Concentrating on bad communisms similarly helps crystallize the moment of collective appropriation by the direct producers. In the same way the capitalist on the board of directors is stripped from all the productive functions that have traditionally justified claims on the surplus, to be left with nothing but the role of appropriator, the collective of producers in bad communism is similarly devoid of most positive characteristics typically attributed to communism by its proponents and reduced solely to the role of collective appropriators of their own surplus. For example, in the case of sexual labor, a collective of prostitutes can engage in a communist class process while being subject to violence or working grueling hours. From Resnick and Wolff's point of view, this analysis shows not only the impossibility of equating communism with safe, decent working conditions, but also that the former is possible without the latter.

The above-mentioned class analysis of Soviet collective farms is of particular interest to us, not only because it was undertaken directly by Resnick and Wolff but also because it is quite telling that in their many decades of co-authorship, the concrete historical example of communism they investigated most deeply was forced Soviet collectivization. They take great pains to pore over diaries of collective chairmen to describe how appropriation is undertaken by the collective, despite the foundational violence that had created the collective farms and the continuing pressures from the state that severely limited the collective's discretionary distribution of surplus value. Interestingly and tellingly, far from being treated as an aberration, "bad" communism is the primary historical case of communism that emerges in Resnick and Wolff's work. We think they pay this example special attention because it exposes the distilled moment of appropriation, much as Marx's volume 3 analysis of the corporation does for modern capitalism.

Bad communisms allow us insight into appropriation that "enchanting"[11] communisms obscure; they expose what cases of good communism might render murky: the singularity of the moment of appropriation. Ultimately, the exclusion or inclusion of producers in that moment of appropriation is the key to distinguishing between exploitative and non-exploitative class processes. This is both a blessing and a curse: a blessing because it relieves communism of the burden of being the panacea of all social antagonisms, and a curse for the very same reason. Communism is now compatible with many of the social ills it is supposed to cure or, at least, mitigate. One can see communism in sex labor, *kolkhozes*, and Asiatic Despotism.[12] Thus, the liberating effect of the thin definition of communism comes at a high cost. Communism can no longer claim the moral high ground in every case and might concede it to capitalism, depending on the circumstances. For instance, the employees in a worker collective might fare worse than counterparts in a "high-road" capitalist firm[13] in terms of compensation, working conditions, personal fulfillment, and so on.

Here we see the scandalous nature of Resnick and Wolff's contribution to Marxian theory. Their commitment to communism is not grounded in its positive entailments and, arguably (and maybe paradoxically), it is a stronger commitment for that. Their unwavering resistance to thicken the definition of communism by augmenting it with desirable attributes might seem self-destructive to the uninitiated. Yet, the robustness of their class analytical framework is evident from the vast array of insightful contributions published in this volume, the *Rethinking Marxism* journal, and elsewhere.

Notes

1 In "Marxism without Guarantees," Stuart Hall (1986) argued that even without economic determinism, or a determinist attitude toward ideology, Marxism contributes something useful to social thought and action. In making this argument, Hall does for Marxist theories of ideology what we think Resnick and Wolff do for Marxist theories of communism.
2 We return below to Jack Amarglio's work on despotic forms of communism (Amariglio 2010).
3 When they posit communism as "an ethico-political shift that gives up the enjoyment of achieving an ideal "form of the commune" that can ultimately "fix" the production and division of surplus," Madra and Özselçuk (2010) help us see that what Resnick and Wolff present as an "exclusive class democracy," in which only productive workers appropriate and distribute the surplus, is ultimately a kind of impossible fantasy in which the rightful appropriators are identified, enumerated, and defined once and for all. Once the closed set of "rightful appropriators" is opened beyond producers to any stakeholder, then that set will always be provisional to the prevalent politics. In time, a new claimant may come along (for instance, environmental considerations have appeared where they may not have 100 years ago) that re-opens the contestation over surplus appropriation.
4 Marx and Engels write scathingly on this point in the *German Ideology*:

> These "socialists" or "true socialists," as they call themselves, regard foreign communist literature not as the expression and the product of a real movement but as purely theoretical writings which have been evolved by a process of "pure thought." It never occurs to them that, even when these writings do preach a system, they spring from the practical needs,

the conditions of life in their entirety of a particular class in a particular country...Communism is for us not a *state of affairs* which is to be established, an *ideal* to which reality [will] have to adjust itself. We call communism the *real* movement which abolishes the present state of things. The conditions of this movement result from the premises now in existence.

(1998 [1848], 481 and 57)

5 Gibson-Graham also deploy the concept of contradiction and develop a nuanced understanding of post-capitalist politics. Yet in their examples of post-capitalist politics, they rarely connect non-exploitative class processes to oppressive ones. They (Gibson-Graham 2001) seek a "politics of enchantment" and, to that end, identify possibilities that would draw people's desire toward post-capitalism, not dull it.

6 While differences in scale certainly have a bearing on the class analysis, the significance of this dimension is only alluded to, but not explored, in this article.

7 Jo Bindman, from Anti-Slavery International, continues: "Then sex workers can be included and protected under the existing instruments which aim to protect all workers from exploitation" (Kempadoo and Doezema 1998, 8).

8 The state provided conditions of existence for collective farms, such as modern tractors, new laws mandating general meetings and assemblies, and technical aid.

9 Amariglio also deals with the added complication that patriarchy meant that only male family heads were admitted into the democratic assembly of the Germanic commune. Marx ambiguously "toggles between family and male head of household as the prevailing subject of production/appropriation" (Amariglio 2010, 333). Therefore, the Germanic commune is far from the full ideal of a completely egalitarian version of a commune, but it is the one Marx presents as the "second type" in the *Grundrisse*, in contrast to the first Asiatic type.

10 Like Amariglio (2010), we leave aside the extensive debates on the orientalism of Marx's treatment of Asiatic despotism. We think that despite the name, the analysis of despotic communes could equally apply to western societies, contemporary as well as historical ones.

11 We recall the work of Gibson-Graham (2001) on "class enchantment" here. In their insightful treatment of the film "The Full Monty," they describe the different kinds of transformation experienced by the former steel workers as they form a communist collective of strip-tease workers. Two workers come to terms with their queer sexuality and fall in love, another comes to terms with his crippling body-image issues and rejuvenates his marriage, and another repairs his relation with his son. Collective members "swerved" and became new subjects, liberated in multiple ways, and the total effects were greater than the instantiation of a pure communist class structure.

12 We should note that Amariglio's analysis of the Asiatic despot as a stand-in for the commune is not commensurate with the other two examples discussed above. The introduction of subjectivation at the societal level renders the sub-levels of analysis irrelevant; it overrides them. How the members of the commune relate to the despot colors the entire social formation and its class character.

13 For example, the "B-corporation" is a form of business that includes positive impact on its employees, the society and the environment among its legally defined goals alongside profit. Such Benefit Corporations are accountable to their shareholders on not only financial performance, but social and environmental impact as well.

References

Amariglio, J. 2010. "Subjectivity, Class, and Marx's 'Forms of the Commune'." *Rethinking Marxism* 22 (3): 329–44.

Badiou, A. 2010. *The Communist Hypothesis*. London and Brooklyn: Verso.

Cullenberg, S. 1992. "Socialism's Burden: Toward a 'Thin' Definition of Socialism." *Rethinking Marxism* 5 (2): 64–83.

DeMartino, G. 2003. "Realizing Class Justice." *Rethinking Marxism* 15 (1): 1–31.

Douzinas C. and S. Žižek, eds. 2010. *The Idea of Communism – Volume 1*. London and Brooklyn: Verso.

Gibson-Graham, J-K. 1996. *The End of Capitalism (As We Knew It): A Feminist Critique of Political Economy*. Cambridge, MA: Blackwell Publishers.

——— 2001. "Class Enchantment." *Theory & Event* 5 (3): <http://muse.jhu.edu/journals/tae/> (accessed December 28, 2016).

——— 2006. *A Postcapitalist Politics*. Minneapolis: University of Minnesota Press.

Hall, S. 1986. "Marxism without Guarantees." *Journal of Communication Inquiry* 10 (2): 28–44.

Kempadoo, K. and J. Doezema. 1998. *Global Sex Workers: Rights, Resistance, and Redefinition*. Psychology Press.

Madra, Y. M. and C. Özselçuk. 2010. "*Jouissance* and Antagonism in the Forms of the Commune: A Critique of Biopolitical Subjectivity." *Rethinking Marxism* 22 (3): 481–97.

——— 2015. "Creating Spaces for Communism: Postcapitalist Desire in Hong Kong, the Philippines, and Western Massachusetts." In *Making Other Worlds Possible: Performing Diverse Economies*. G. Roelvink, K. St. Martin and J. K. Gibson-Graham, eds., 127–52. Minneapolis: University of Minnesota Press.

Marx, K. 1991 [1894]. *Capital*, Vol. 3. Trans. D. Fernbach. Harmondsworth, UK: Penguin.

——— 1993 [1939]. *Grundrisse*. New York: Penguin.

Marx, K. and F. Engels. 1998 [1848]. *The German Ideology*. Amherst, NY: Prometheus Books.

Mulder, C. P. 2015. *Transcending Capitalism through Cooperative Practices*. New York: Palgrave Macmillan.

Özselçuk, C. and Y. M. Madra. 2005. "Psychoanalysis and Marxism: From Capitalist-All to Communist Non-All." *Psychoanalysis, Culture & Society* 10 (1): 79–97.

Resnick, S. A. and R. D. Wolff. 1987. *Knowledge and Class: A Marxian Critique of Political Economy*. Chicago: University of Chicago Press.

——— 2002. *Class Theory and History: Capitalism and Communism in the USSR*. London: Routledge.

van der Veen, M. 2000. "Beyond Slavery and Capitalism: Producing Class Difference in the Sex Industry." In *Class and Its Others*, J.-K. Gibson Graham et al., eds., 121–42. Minneapolis: University of Minnesota Press.

——— 2001. "Rethinking Commodification and Prostitution: An Effort at Peacemaking in the Battles over Prostitution." *Rethinking Marxism* 13 (2): 30–51.

Žižek, S., ed. 2013. *The Idea of Communism – Volume 2*. London and Brooklyn: Verso.

25 Hope without guarantees

Overdeterminist anti-capitalism amidst neoliberal precarity

Ellen Russell

Introduction

Stephen Resnick and Richard Wolff invite us to reject exploitation, which they define as the appropriation and distribution of surplus labor by those who have not performed it. Yet they do not seek to persuade us to share their agenda for class transformation by invoking any assurances that the absence of exploitation necessarily entails the presence of the many potential attributes of a putatively (and variously defined) "good society." Theirs is a "thin" conception of class transformation (Cullenberg 1992), devoid of guarantees that the elimination of exploitation will necessarily advance other radical agendas. Collective production, appropriation, and distribution of surplus labor might (or might not) coexist with inequitable power, property, and income distributions, harmful environmental practices, undemocratic and other abhorrent political practices, various oppressions and other objectionable characteristics. As is argued elsewhere in this volume, there is the logical possibility of "bad" communisms as well as "good" communisms.

Resnick and Wolff's epistemological commitment to overdetermination precludes the possibility of asserting guarantees concerning the future convergence of various radical goals and the elimination of exploitation. As a promissory assertion concerning a future outcome, a guarantee is predicated on a theory of causation that makes such assertions about future outcomes intelligible. Guarantees concerning attributes of communist futures are conceivable in a determinist epistemological environment, where the correct analysis correctly executed produces foreseeable (or at least probabilistically foreseeable) results. Such guarantees are not available to the overdeterminist. From this epistemological perspective, the elimination of exploitation would overdetermine (and be overdetermined by) all other social, political, economic, and natural considerations. Thus the synergies (and antimonies) between class transformation and other radical agendas are not knowable, *a priori*. Certainly intellectuals and activists informed by overdetermination aspire to muster all available capacities to advance their many desired objectives, but this undertaking is devoid of assurances about the outcomes of these efforts.

Not only must Resnick and Wolff refrain from framing their case for the elimination of exploitation in promissory terms, they must argue on behalf of exploitation as their "entry point" without recourse to guarantees. They are acutely aware that hegemonic discourses routinely deny the existence of exploitation, let alone accord exploitative class processes any analytical or normative significance. Resnick and Wolff must argue on behalf of the existence, importance, and implications of exploitation while refraining from the discursive strategies familiar in a cultural environment permeated with determinist analytic and rhetorical conventions. As overdeterminists, they cannot assert that exploitation is the/a "correct" entry point of analysis, since their rejection of empiricist and rationalist epistemology denies them the possibility of asserting such truth-claims.[1] Since the proposition that only labor creates value cannot be proven (or disproven), the existence of exploitation cannot be established as "truth" (or dispensed with as "false"). Resnick and Wolff's anti-essentialism denies them any grounds from which to insist on opposition to exploitation as the necessary priority for radical social transformation. For those accustomed to determinist epistemology and the assertion of truth-claims as the *lingua franca* of discursive persuasion, it is a shocking proposition to embrace an anti-essentialist political and intellectual project that eschews what has been a prevalent means of justifying one's ontological commitments.

Thus Resnick and Wolff can offer no guarantees that their political and intellectual project is starting in the "right " place or that it will end in the "right" place (indeed they would contest the essentialist and teleological implications of these notions of starting, ending, and "right"). The rejection of such promises puts their overdeterminist Marxism at odds with prominent aspects of two of the intellectual legacies that deeply influenced their thought. As economists trained in the discipline as it is practiced in leading American economics departments, they were immersed in the celebration of certainty (or at least probabilistic certainty) via systematized models motivated by predictive intent and framed around essentialist entry points and teleological conceptions of equilibrium. As Marxist economists embarking on their academic careers in the 1960s and 1970s, they were also surrounded by appropriations of Marx informed by similar determinisms. For example, the base/superstructure approach influential within economistic Marxisms employs conceptions of cause and effect that share the essentialisms and teleologies of neoclassical economics.

While Resnick and Wolff's critique of determinism—of the left and the right—implies that their overdeterminist Marxism is inhospitable to promissory appeals, the pursuit of radical social change nonetheless has an anticipatory dimension. Whether we want something, or want to be rid of something we don't like, the pursuit of social change entails some regard to possible and desired outcomes. In *Cruel Optimism*, Lauren Berlant describes such attachments (including political attachments) as "optimistic, if we describe optimism as the force that moves you out of yourself and into the world in order to bring closer the satisfying something that you cannot generate on your own" (2011b, 1–2). These objects of desire—such as political projects—are, for Berlant, "a cluster of promises we want someone or something to make to us and make possible for us" (*ibid.*, 23). Yet Berlant cautions us that such optimistic attachments may be "cruel," in the sense that our attachment to these objects of desire may constitute an obstacle to our flourishing (*ibid.*, 1). When our optimistic attachment to such promises compromises our capacities to pursue that which we desire, we are afflicted with a "cruel optimism."

This chapter entertains the possibility that promises asserted on behalf of communist futures constitute a "cruel optimism." Depicting possibilities in promissory terms may compromise our sober assessment of how we might pursue potentials that are not necessities. Because promises imply a deterministic invocation about future knowability, they collude with a denial of the pervasive uncertainty and contradictory dynamics animating any overdetermined context. In seeking certainties, we turn our backs on the possibilities that might be fostered via astute engagement with indeterminacy. It would be a "cruel optimism" to derive our inspiration for communist futures from assertions about necessity that impair our ability to analyze and act in the perilous and shifting terrain in which we seek to promote our desired objectives. As Stuart Hall has eloquently cautioned in his famous entreaty for a "Marxism without Guarantees,"

> [G]iv[ing] ourselves all kinds of those necessary guarantees that we may think that we need to have, in order to convince ourselves that we are really on top of the historical process. But to carry that guarantee in our back pockets will prevent us from actually being able to come to terms with the real world.
>
> (1983, 39)

Hall invites us to consider "cruel" attributes of the guarantee that may sabotage the radical social change it ostensibly seeks to promote. By way of accepting Hall's invitation, this chapter explores the possibility that the rejection of the guarantee implied by an anti-determinist Marxism might support an optimism that engages fruitfully with the complexities of anticipation and hope that animate radical aspirations.

We may be persuaded that elimination of exploitation creates auspicious conditions for the pursuit of many other desirable (however defined) potentialities, but the extent to which the elimination of exploitation may foster diverse radical objectives is contingent upon the uniquely overdetermined circumstances in which non-exploitative class processes evolve.

Fortunately, vigilant attention to the ceaseless, profound, and mutually constitutive interaction between class processes and their others is a distinguishing characteristic of overdeterminist Marxism. Shorn of guarantees, overdeterminists can only remain alert to opportunity amidst uncertainty. We can hope that non-exploitative class processes might overdetermine conditions in a manner supportive of other transformative radical demands, and use our capacities to discern and analyze contradictory and shifting dynamics in order to seize opportunities to advance these possibilities.

To invite consideration of opportunities that are not necessities, including the ways in which we make meaning of and take action to engage with uncertain possibilities, this discussion focuses on Resnick and Wolff's conception of culture: "the diverse ways that human beings produce meanings for their existences" (Resnick and Wolff 1987, 20–21). Theirs is an explicitly process-focused concept of culture—a complex totality of practices situated in a specifically overdetermined context. Thus cultural processes inform and are informed by economic processes (including exploitative class processes), political processes (the design and regulation of authority), and natural processes (including biological and physical factors). Since culture exists in a relationship of mutual constitutivity with the totality of all other processes, culture both shapes and is shaped by political, natural, and economic processes (such as exploitation).

Focusing on cultural overdeterminants that might promote the embrace of potentiality and the tentativeness of debate rather than essentialist or teleological promise, this chapter begins with a discussion of the role of promises in the debilitating condition known to Walter Benjamin (1999) and subsequent theorists as "left melancholia." It then examines the interaction of contemporary neoliberal economic and cultural factors that might support the rejection of attachment to promises and the embrace of process-oriented conceptions of collective economic futures. Via the concept of "precarity," it considers the resignification of the notion of the promise. In lieu of the promises of previous determinist radical discourses, it explores the opportunities for encouraging radical imaginaries devoid of promises, invested in possibility without guarantee. If circumstances promote this attachment of hope to collective possibilities, this cultural milieu offers a hospitable terrain in which to pursue Resnick and Wolff's overdeterminist anti-capitalist project.

Cruel guarantees and invigorated possibilities

Hope supports us to imagine and act in pursuit of a society that we view as "better" (in whatever ways) than the status quo. While hopes reflect the desire and the possibility that we might successfully achieve our aspirations, guarantees depict aspirations as certainties. Happy are the determinists who are redeemed when their predictions prove correct(ish), but more familiar are the disappointments as unforeseen developments thwart the presumed journey from cause to effect. Determinist Marxisms have often sought to encourage political struggle by offering guarantees buttressed by their necessitarian interpretations of crisis tendencies, historical imperatives, programmatic requirements, or other such essentialist or teleological inevitabilities. Just as often, such promises have been disappointed. Despite their repeated disappointment, why do such guarantees have such a persuasive appeal?

The promise that one's political project will ultimately prevail conveys an enticing comfort by reassuring us that the dangers of our struggle will be rewarded. But by shielding us from the anxieties provoked by the unvarnished encounter with the unknown, the comfort offered by the guarantee is also debilitating. By colluding with our unconscious resistance to confronting the perils of the unknown, the guarantee perpetuates a fantasy of knowability that impairs our ultimate political efficacy. Just as our psychic struggles with the loss of our fantasies of omnipotence lay the ground for a mature reconciliation of both the fragilities and capacities of selfhood, in the political realm our renunciation of the illusory comforts of the omniscient guarantee enhances our capacities to tolerate (and even seek out) the risk, indeterminacy, and changefulness that invigorates collective anti-capitalist struggles. A political culture invested in promissory pronouncements concerning the outcomes of political struggle offers a cruel optimism in that it undermines the resilience that might be cultivated via the confrontation with unknowability.

In her "Resisting Left Melancholy," Wendy Brown paints a vivid portrait of the debilitating consequences afflicting a left that does not come to terms with such losses. Many of the "losses of the left" considered by Brown address the fantasy of knowability: the loss of a unified analysis, the loss of an inexorable and scientific forward movement of history, and the loss of theoretical and empirical coherence (1999, 22). She links these losses to an unavowed loss of the promissory dimension of left political commitment:

> But in the hollow core of all these losses, perhaps in the place of our political unconscious, there is also an unavowed loss- the promise that left analysis and left commitment would supply its adherents a clear and certain path toward the good, the right, and the true.
>
> (1999, 22)

Following Walter Benjamin's earlier examination of "left melancholia," Brown invokes Freud's distinction of melancholia and mourning to explore the emotional and psychic implications of our relationship to loss.[2] While mourning is a process in which grieving an avowed loss has the possibility of resolving in a manner that makes the formation of new attachments possible, melancholia depicts an unconscious and pathological relationship to loss in which the relentless hold of the lost attachment thwarts the possibility of new attachments. Left melancholy speaks to this stultifying attachment that fossilizes political desire, as the melancholic remains incapacitated by the unavowed loss of that which does not exist and is unable to embrace what might be.

The left melancholic prefers to cling to such illusory promises (however often they are disappointed) rather that confront the loss of these perceived certainties in order to embrace tentative possibilities. For Brown the left melancholic is rendered a "revolutionary hack who is, finally, attached more to a particular political analysis or ideal—even to the failure of that ideal—than to seizing possibilities for radical change in the present" (1999, 20). Clinging to such illusions costs the left dearly. Brown claims that a melancholic left "literally renders itself a conservative force in history-one that not only misreads the present but installs traditionalism in the very heart of its praxis, in the place where commitment to risk and upheaval belongs" (*ibid.*, 25).

Brown points us toward a recognition of the "cruel optimism" of anchoring our hopes in certainties. To the extent that the left leaves unexamined these pernicious dimensions of the guarantee, we diminish our attentiveness to the opportunities inherent in the indeterminacy of each overdetermined context of our struggles. Our political efficacy is further compromised if the left's dependence on guarantees is complicit with a wider cultural veneration of safety, security, and conformity.

There are additional troubling dimensions of the reliance on promises to shield ourselves from the anxieties provoked by the encounter with the unknown. Viewed from an overdeterminist perspective, promises made to motivate commitment to political action appear as naïve, disingenuous, infantilizing, or worse.[3] Possibly such promises are the crass manipulation of the vulnerabilities of the promisee by a promisor eager to cultivate a grandiose stature as an external authority vested with the omniscient capacity to make credible truth-claims. Those of us experiencing doubt regarding the plausibility of such promises must either concede that our political betters are able to access knowledge unavailable to us or find ourselves unable to sustain our connection to a leftist culture in which hope is predicated on guarantees that we cannot view as credible. In either case, the vitality of the leftist political movements is compromised. Those unable to sustain the illusion that others know what is unknowable may see no option but to become politically disengaged. Those who repress their own awareness of unknowability to preserve their faith in deterministic promises are susceptible to the most troubling forms of political authoritarianism.

How might the overdeterminist Marxism promoted by Resnick and Wolff enable us to embrace hope while avoiding the "cruel" attributes of the guarantee? In contemplating ways to reconsider and rearticulate hopes and fears in the service of possibility, I have found it instructive to revisit

Resnick and Wolff's distinction between objects and processes in their rethinking of Marxism. They conceive of class as a process (that of performing, appropriating, and distributing surplus labor) rather than an object category demarking certain groups of people (however that category might be defined—say a specified relation to the means of production). One of the important attributes of this process-oriented class analytic is its versatile and inquisitive investigation of the endless ways a given class process is overdetermined by (and overdetermines) the "others" of class (the confluence of evolving historical, regional, legal, gendered, raced, and many other processes). Guarantees concerning the characteristics of future communisms are inimical to their process-oriented analytics since the attributes and implications of communist class processes in any particular overdetermined context cannot be foreseen (other than via a minimal definitional assertion that communism will be characterized by the collective performance, appropriation, and distribution of surplus labor).

We might mourn the loss of any perceived guarantees concerning the attributes of a society without exploitation. But mourning these illusory promises invites the possibility of reorienting hopes toward different communist possibilities. We might encourage our "optimistic attachment" to process rather than outcome, specifically the collective processes entailed in the collective performance, appropriation, and distribution of surplus labor.

For the present discussion, we will highlight only a few aspects of non-exploitative class processes that potentially inspire optimistic attachment to communist class processes. While capitalist economic processes systematically deprive us of the ability to appropriate and allocate the surplus value that we collectively create, communist class processes require us to determine collectively the various possible uses of surplus value. Communist class processes offer the possibility that we might chose to distribute our surplus value to support various radical agendas. At the very least, capitalists would be deprived of the ability to allocate surplus value to subvert these radical agendas. But workers' collective control over their surplus value potentially facilitates many more ambitious aspirations, as long as we mobilize to take advantage of the opportunities that a communist class process affords.

While no promises can be offered concerning the possible consequences of the elimination of exploitation and the collective deliberation concerning the allocation of surplus value, we do know that a shift from capitalist to communist class processes will overdetermine all other societal processes. As we engage collectively to analyze and deliberate over priorities, to address disagreements and to make the many decisions entailed in producing, appropriating, and distributing surplus value in our workplaces, these collectivist economic processes would in turn influence further political and cultural transformations. Both because our political, cultural, and natural landscapes will be overdetermined by these communist class processes, and because we will have at our disposal the surplus value with which to fund our collectively determined priorities, we may credibly hope that non-exploitative class processes offer advantageous conditions from which to pursue radical agendas regarding democratic political institutions, the opposition to oppressions, a rethinking of our collective relationship to the environment, and so on. But to seize this opportunity to redeploy our analytic, activist, and psychic energies toward the process of change, we must relinquish the attachment to guarantee and embrace the indeterminacy—and possibility—that communist class processes may offer more advantageous conditions for the pursuit of our various radical aspirations. Those with the impression that they can relax their vigilance in the expectation that some guaranteed radical attributes of a particular class structure will necessarily be forthcoming will squander the opportunity to parlay communist class processes into the "good" communisms they ostensibly seek.

Neoliberal precarity and the resignification of the promise

Our relationship to guarantees is overdetermined by a range of contextual factors, including (of course) class processes. Despite the persistence of capitalism as the hegemonic class process in more affluent "advanced" capitalist societies, there is immensely consequential diversity in the capitalisms of each overdetermined context. Much recent scholarship has focused on the emergence of an increasingly "precarious" neoliberal era, which has evolved in contrast to the relatively more stable and equitable welfare state era. To investigate the possible implications of these different contexts as they inform our relationship to guarantees as an expression of our social hopes, we focus on the interplay of cultural and economic processes in both the welfare state and the neoliberal era. In particular, we consider the emergence of certain cultural attributes prevalent in the neoliberal era that might promote process–oriented conceptions of collective economic futures premised on the rejection of guarantees. Two attributes of the neoliberal milieu will be highlighted: the resignification of the notion of the promise and the attachment of hope to collectivist processes.

The concept of "precarity" is currently influential in the examination of contemporary neoliberal capitalism, particularly among those who emphasize a cultural perspective on precariousness (Berardi 2011, Berlant 2011, Butler 2011, Horning 2012, Lorey 2010). Resnick and Wolff's rethinking of Marxism is hospitable to this concern with precarity. Their "aleatory" Marxism emphasizes that attention to instability and its implications pervades Marx's thought. Even outside of systemic crises of capitalism, profound upswings, downswings, and many dislocations are a "normal" characteristic of capitalism as it continuously remakes (and is remade by) its conditions of existence (Resnick and Wolff 2006, 252). Indeed, overdeterminist Marxists regard moments of relative stability as the (fleeting) exception rather than the norm, since even conjunctures of seeming stability are animated by the dynamics that undermine that stability. These ubiquitous instabilities include unemployment, income insecurity, and many other troubling economic, political, cultural, and natural pressures (including environmental destruction) on workers and their communities. The economic dimensions of precarity are overdetermined by (and overdetermine) the cultural processes by which we make meaning of this precarity, including the meanings that might propel us toward (or deter us from pursuing) class transformation in response to precariousness.

Since Marxists influenced by Resnick and Wolff's engagement with overdetermination see precarity as ubiquitous, why is it that the concept of precarity is only recently attaining such prominence? Conceivably contemporary intellectual and activist preoccupation with precarity reflects the previous prominence of its antithesis. Neoliberal precarity is widely contrasted with an earlier era associated with relative stability and more widely shared affluence: the "golden age" of the welfare state. For a historically specific period in certain geographical locations and among certain workers and citizens, the harsher face of capitalism was softened (however imperfectly, unevenly, and briefly) in an environment of diminished economic crises and somewhat more equitable distribution of economic resources. The welfare state was contingent upon any number of contextual specificities (such as the ascendency of Fordist production processes, the Cold War geopolitical environment, the conspicuous role of the Great Depression in the cultural and political framing of government responsibility for delivering certain standards of economic wellbeing, etc.). But where it became the hegemonic framework in which capitalism flourished in the post-war period, the welfare state was associated with a degree of stability and comfort (for some) that was a sharp contrast to the preceding two world wars and Great Depression.

One prominent dimension of the discursive environment celebrating the possibility of a "good" capitalism was the influence of Keynesianism in reinterpreting economic possibility. While there are many interpretations of Keynes's economic thought, the Keynesianism that dominated public debate in the post-war era focused on the pursuit of economic stability and broadly shared affluence via a set of government policies (counter-cyclical aggregate demand stabilization).[4] Central to this Keynesian approach to creating a more stable and generous capitalism was an explicit and widely institutionalized[5] governmental promise to pursue the counter-cyclical and redistributive economic policies that would achieve full employment. A variety of conditions enhanced the credibility of this full employment promise, including the remarkable success of Keynesian economic theory in discrediting the free market orthodoxies that previously dominated economic theory and policy-making circles, the general prestige and credibility of modernist conceptions of technocratic management and progress that conferred legitimacy on the proposition that the economy could be "fine-tuned," the political reassurances that buttressed public faith in government commitment to such promises, and the unique Fordist competitive and technological conditions among prominent capitalist firms that encouraged them to acquiesce (for a time) to full employment as a desirable public policy commitment.

By promising to ameliorate some of capitalism's most reviled characteristics, the welfare state undermined the attractiveness of economic alternatives (however understood). Thus welfare state promises were a *de facto* bargain, in the sense that exploitation was tolerated (and even eclipsed as a theoretical lens with which to understand the economy) in return for the promise of a capitalism that would deliver stable employment, rising real wages, and increased consumption (Resnick and Wolff 2010). In the unique confluence of many distinctive post-war factors, the welfare state did deliver (however unevenly and briefly) on some of its promises. Unemployment was comparatively low, real wages rose, and economic crises were more infrequent and moderate. Thus in both society at large and within more oppositional social movements, promises concerning economic outcomes gained legitimacy as a credible response to (and means of channeling) hopes for a better future.

In this context, the radical energies of unions and other oppositional actors became tethered to welfare state promises. Rather than mounting more systemic challenges, these actors tended to focus on extending and contesting the promised benefits of the welfare state era. Thus the design of welfare state policies or the relative well-being of various types of workers became a central preoccupation of struggles over the division of the benefits of the welfare state. As some groups benefited more than others (while some lost ground entirely) divisions among radical movements were reinforced. Sexism, racism, and other oppressions differentially shaped who might be privileged by various government stabilization and redistributive policies or who might access the more secure and remunerative jobs that became available in the welfare state era.

In this economic and cultural milieu, promises became the means through which hopes were articulated. (Even those who opposed capitalism in its welfare state manifestation also tended to frame their opposition in terms of promises offered by some alternative arrangement.) But as long as radicals are engaged in negotiating the terms on which the benefits of welfare state promises might be divided, they become invested in the promise *per se*. Demands for new or more extensive promises imply that promises are both possible and credible. The devotion of radical energies to securing promises reinforces the proposition that promises are the currency with which the legitimacy of capitalism (or its alternatives) might be secured.

In the neoliberal era, capitalist firms, governments, and international institutions have increasingly abdicated their previous commitments that attenuated the vicissitudes and privations of capitalism. The promises of the welfare state—such as full employment—have been rescinded (where they were made explicit) or remain only as vestigial but discredited artifacts that are incongruent with the neoliberal era. The resonance of the concept of precarity today possibly reflects the degree to which the instabilities of capitalism are more acutely felt by those who became accustomed to enjoying (or aspired to enjoy[6]) some modicum of protection afforded to those beneficiaries of welfare state promises. While for many precariousness was never meaningfully abated, those who enjoyed some enhanced security in the previous era have had to grapple with an economic, political, and cultural landscape that violates the promise of relative stability and entitlement that for decades was important to the legitimation of capitalism. New discourses of precarity reflect the ramifications of this loss. The mourning (and melancholy) over the lost promise of the security and prosperity conferred by the welfare state is palpable:

> Precarization means living with the unforeseeable, with contingency. In the secularized modernity of the West, however, being exposed to contingency is generally regarded as a nightmare, as a loss of all security, all orientation, all order. This monster of the bottomless pit can clearly no longer be really tamed even in the post-Fordist industrial nations of the 'West'.
>
> (Lorey 2015, 2–3)

An outpouring of literature examines the attempts to secure alleviation from insecurity as the "central preoccupation" of the neoliberal subject (Butler 2015, viii). These Foucauldian examinations of the cultures of governmentality explore the countless ways in which neoliberal subjects are compelled to govern themselves in pursuit of an illusory stability even as they are precarized via this submission to neoliberal dictates. But while the cultures of neoliberalism include the desperate veneration of security and the fixation on its illusive pursuit, they also create conditions that problematize aspirations that have become invested in illusory guarantees. The lament for the violation of a promised security is incomprehensible to those who were never in a position to become accustomed to the welfare state's uneven largesse, but even its former beneficiaries are increasingly estranged from the optimistic attachment to the welfare state bargain. As high wages, secure jobs, and government supports have become more rare and unreliable, the ebullient rhetorical environment reflecting welfare state promises of progress and abundance seems distant and, in retrospect, even implausible. The conditions of contemporary capitalism may make the conception of security as a possible social goal increasingly dissonant.

Not only do the cultures of neoliberal capitalism reflect the consequences of the repudiation of the welfare state bargain, they also may impugn promises as such in political, economic, and cultural imaginaries. In a context in which welfare state promises are widely discredited, promises may now even be regarded as an obstacle to possibility. Berlant describes her interest in precarity as "a rallying cry for a thriving new world of interdependency and care that's not just private, but it is also an idiom for describing a loss of faith in a fantasy world to which generations have become accustomed" (Puar et al. 2012, 166). Perhaps relinquishing attachment to this lost fantasy world encourages left cultures to repudiate their investment in certainties in favor of the pursuit of potentialities. The embrace of possibility without promise might overcome the pathological melancholic fixation on (and repetition of) past losses and instead turn toward thriving amidst uncertainty. As Brown discusses in a more recent work, "[a] radical democratic critique and utopian imaginary that has no certainty about its prospects or even about the means and vehicles of its realization, that does not know what its imagined personae will be capable of—this would seem to be the left political sensibility that could give our mourning a productive post-revolutionary form" (2005, 114).

The negation (and abnegation) of the promise of security offers new possibilities in terms of political imaginaries focused on collective processes. As precariousness is experienced and interpreted as an existential state that characterizes every human (and non-human) life (Butler 2004), this recognition of our shared precariousness may invite different kinds of optimistic attachments. Suspicious of promises of security, and the manipulative motivations of such promises, our hopes might reside in collectivist response to precarity rather than in the illusion that insecurity can be overcome (Dean 2012). If we realize the futility of the quest to govern ourselves individually in a manner that might exempt us from precarity, we might attach our political hopes to our collective engagement in the processes through which we seek to manage the precarity of existence.

Many political theories and movements illustrate this rejection of the promise of security, and promises as such, as they focus their hopes on the collective encounter with imaginaries devoid of formulaic prescriptions or preconceived outcomes. "Occupy Wall Street," for example, famously refused to announce explicit demands and programs of action and instead focused on organizing collective processes through which to act upon the desire to effect change in favor of the 99%. A rejection of the discourse of promising and sensitivity to the collective engagement with contingency propel a diverse debate among many radical thinkers and activists (Noys 2011). Amidst their many contesting points of view, the essentialisms and teleologies of previous radical praxis are themselves a fetter to be overcome:

[I]t is no longer a matter of foretelling the collapse or depicting the possibilities of joy. Whether it comes sooner or later, the point is to prepare for it. It's not a question of providing a schema for what an insurrection should be, but of taking the possibility of an uprising for what it never should have ceased being: a vital impulse of youth as much as popular wisdom. If one knows how to move, the absence of a schema is not an obstacle but an opportunity. For the insurgents, it is the sole space that can guarantee the essential: keeping the initiative.

(The Invisible Committee 2009, 8–9)

Conclusion: celebrating precarity, reviling promises

Radicals hope for and struggle to achieve a society that is (in whatever ways) "better" than the status quo. But only in a determinist political culture would such imaginaries be conceivable in promissory terms. Resnick and Wolff have consistently cautioned against quests for certainty, as when they compare the search for "last instance" determinisms as a "search for god" (2006, 6). Indeed all attempts to fortify our political aspirations via recourse to promises is a cruel optimism, in that it deprives our radical movements of the capacities to respond to precarity by colluding with the fantasy that precarity might be controlled. Opportunities are squandered if the mature reconciliation with precarity is foreclosed and we stagnate in melancholic attachment to illusory promises.

Relinquishing the attachments to guarantees to shield ourselves from the encounter with precarity may well animate a vigorous and creative response to precarity. Whether or not this response to precarity includes the struggle to end exploitation is not knowable *a priori*. But this context may be conducive to the rethinking of Marxism that Resnick and Wolff have pursued throughout their lifework. Theirs is an epistemological outlook premised on changefulness and instability, alert always to the ways in which contradiction ceaselessly reconfigures the totality of our economic, political, cultural, and natural context in ways that may offer opportunities to advance radical agendas. Rather than repressing this radical indeterminacy, their Marxism confronts precarity without the (dubious) comforts of promises. Not only are such promises unintelligible, they are fraught with peril. As Stephen Cullenberg might say, such promises form part of "socialism's burden" that should be lifted (1992, 65).

Alongside this engagement with overdeterminist praxis, Resnick and Wolff advocate for the elimination of exploitation. This advocacy is not based in any promise, any assertion of truth, or any other appeal to essentialized or teleological compulsion. By renouncing the purported legitimacy conferred by either essentialist or necessitarian claims, theirs is an intellectual and political project that is self-consciously persuasive. They are persuaded that exploitation has horrific economic, political, cultural, and natural entailments and that a situation in which the communist class process is hegemonic would be preferable. They marshal a compelling case to argue that many radical agendas might be supported in a social totality overdetermined by the ascendency of collective production, appropriation, and distribution of surplus value. But his debate cannot be foreclosed by any conclusive promises. Perhaps the evident precarity of life in the neoliberal era makes this unpretentious call for debate compelling in itself. We must muddle through without certainties, finding confidence in the process of muddling through as we navigate a horizon in which our collective confrontation with instability is a more genuine engagement with uncertainty than the submission to still more promises.

Acknowledgments

Many thanks to Ted Burczak, Eva-Lynn Jagoe, and Sean O'Brien for their stimulating comments on an earlier draft of this paper.

Notes

1 An overdeterminist entry point carries no assertion of causal or analytic hierarchy. It reflects the necessity of beginning an analysis somewhere, without implying that this point of embarkation conveys an essentialist primacy in the subsequent analysis. The choice of entry point reflects that the analyst is persuaded (for whatever reasons) that a certain place is a compelling place to begin, without implying that these compelling qualities constitute a determinist claim.

2 Many theorists have productively engaged with both Brown's essay and the political significance of the mourning/melancholy distinction. For example, see Özselçuk (2006) on the various interpretations of Eric Santner, Slavoj Zizek, and others, as well as Dean (2015).

3 The act of promising also prompts scrutiny of the promiser in other ways. As Schlesinger (2008) reflects in the context of his clinical work, the very act of promising as a speech act suggests that a patient is conflicted about the promise and seeks additional reinforcement to overcome a wish to undermine the promise.

4 Several adoptions of Keynes's economic thought differ from the "bastard Keynesianism" discussed below, particularly with respect to the role of uncertainty in economic theory. However, the Keynesianism discussed here had an immense influence on the public policy discourse of the welfare state era, and this Keynesianism continues to frame the arguments of defenders of remaining welfare state attributes.

5 Various national commitments to full employment, as well as the dilutions in these commitments made to appease capitalists who objected to full employment, are detailed in Apple (1980).

6 Even those who were not directly supported by public policies characteristic of the welfare state may have hoped to mount a successful struggle to have their constituencies included in ameliorative welfare state policies. Thus, even those who were excluded from welfare state promises but who aspired for inclusion in the welfare state bargain may be deeply impacted by the renunciation of welfare state promises.

References

Apple, N. 1980. "The Rise and Fall of Full Employment Capitalism." *Studies in Political Economy* (4): 5–39.

Benjamin, W. 1999. "Left-Wing Melancholy." In *Walter Benjamin, Selected Writings: 1931–1934*, volume 2, part 2, M. Jennings, H. Eiland, and G. Smith, eds., 423–7. Cambridge, MA: Harvard University Press.

Berardi, F. 2011. "Cognitarian Subjectivation." *E-flux* 20 www.e-flux.com/journal/20/67633/cognitarian-subjectivation/ (accessed January 1, 2017).

Berlant, L. 2011a. *Austerity, Precarity, Awkwardness*. Durham: Duke University Press.

────── 2011b. *Cruel Optimism*. Durham: Duke University Press.

Brown, W. 1999. "Resisting Left Melancholy." *Boundary 2* 26 (3):19–27.

────── 2005. *Edgework: Critical Essays on Knowledge and Politics*. Princeton, NJ: Princeton University Press.

Butler, J. 2004. *Precarious Life: The Powers of Mourning and Violence*. London: Verso.

────── 2011. "Bodies in Alliance and the Politics of the Street." European Institute for Progressive Cultural Policies, www.eipcp.net/transversal/1011/butler/en? (accessed January 1, 2017).

────── 2015. "Forward." In *State of Insecurity: Government of the Precarious*, I. Lorey. Brooklyn, NY: Verso.

Cullenberg, S. 1992. "Socialism's Burden: Towards a 'Thin' Definition of Socialism." *Rethinking Marxism* 5 (2): 64–83.

Dean, J. 2012. *The Communist Horizon*. New York: Verso.

Hall, S. 1983. "For a Marxism without Guarantees." *Australian Left Review* 1 (84): 38–43.

Horning, R. 2012. "Precarity and 'Affective Resistance'." *The New Inquiry*. http://thenewinquiry.com/blogs/marginal-utility/precarity-and-affective-resistance/ (accessed February 14, 2016).

Lorey, I. 2010. "Becoming Common: Precarization as Political Constituting." *E-flux* 17 www.e-flux.com/journal/17/67385/becoming-common-precarization-as-political-constituting/

────── 2015. *State of Insecurity: Government of the Precarious*. Brooklyn: Verso.

Noys, B., ed. 2011. *Communization and Its Discontents*. Brooklyn: Autonomedia.

Ozselcuk, C. 2006. "Mourning, Melancholy, and the Politics of Class Transformation." *Rethinking Marxism* 18 (2): 225–40.

Puar, J., L. Berlant, J. Butler, B. Cvejić, I. Lorey, and A. Vujanović. 2012. "Precarity Talk: A Virtual Roundtable." *TDR: The Drama Review* 56: 162–77.

Resnick, S. and R. Wolff. 1987. *Knowledge and Class: A Marxian Critique of Political Economy*. Chicago, IL: University of Chicago Press.

────── 2006. *New Departures in Marxian Theory*. New York: Routledge.

────── 2010. "The Economic Crisis: A Marxian Interpretation." *Rethinking Marxism* 22 (2): 170–86.

Schlesinger, H. 2008. *Promises, Oaths, and Vows: On the Psychology of Promising*. New York: Analytic Press.

The Invisible Committee. 2009. *The Coming Insurrection*. Cambridge, MA: MIT Press.

Part IX

Knowledge and class in everyday life

26 The work of sex

Harriet Fraad

Introduction

The anti-essentialist class theory of Stephen Resnick and Richard Wolff can be called New Marxism or Overdetermined Marxism. This versatile Marxism allows Marxism to travel into the intimate terrain of the home from the living room to the bedroom, two places that mechanical Marxism never enters.[1] In this chapter, I use New Marxism to travel into three kinds of intimate relationships. Two take place inside the bedrooms of two different kinds of committed heterosexual couples. The other unfolds in the bedroom of a female heterosexual sex-worker, a "Sugar Baby." These different personal and sexual relationships represent three of many variations and class arrangements of emotional labor and sex work. I discuss only heterosexual relationships because they are more directly shaped by particular gender ideologies that form part of the context for this discussion.

A New Marxist analysis of sex work

Before getting into the particulars of the three kinds of intimate relationships, I will briefly present a class analysis of sex work based on Wolff and Resnick's New Marxist Class Theory. That theory defines class as a process, a relationship to the work being performed. The key questions one asks to understand that relationship are:

1   Who labors to produce a surplus, i.e., more than s/he consumes?
2   Who appropriates the fruits of that surplus labor?
3   Who reaps the benefits of the surplus labor performed?

These precise, versatile questions allow us to look at work relationships, whether those relationships occur in a factory or a household, a brothel, or anywhere else that surplus is produced. Surplus can be the extra produced whether that is extra money; use values like cooked food, or services like cleaning; emotional care; or sexual care and satisfaction.

Sexual labor is the expenditure of time, effort, and energy utilizing brain, muscle, and emotion to fulfill someone else's sexual needs. I define emotional labor in a parallel fashion, as the expenditure of time, effort, and energy utilizing the brain and emotion to fulfill emotional needs (Fraad 2009). Sex work can be isolated from emotional labor or performed together with emotional labor. They are often performed together because sexual labor usually demands the emotional labor of at least feigning excitement and desire for the sex partner. In order to understand this application of New Marxism, let us look at some of the different class relationships in which sexual and emotional work are performed.

Sexual labor and emotional labor can be performed within the slave class process. The slave class process entails ownership of the life and labor of another human being. Within the slave class process, the slave's sexuality, ability to marry, leisure, clothing, food, and housing—all of the physical conditions of her/his existence—are controlled by the master, who also appropriates the slave's surplus labor. Although fully 98% of sex slaves are girls and women, many thousands of boys and men are sexual slaves (Lillie 2014). Slave owners are overwhelmingly men. Young women or young girls or boys may travel to a job advertised as legitimate work and unexpectedly find themselves enslaved (Daughters Rising 2016). A sexual slave is a dehumanized, exploited commodity who performs sexual services for a person or an organization employing the class process of slavery. Her/his sexual surplus is appropriated by her/his owners. The emotional labor of feigning pleasure and welcome is often part of the sexual slave's job. A slave's owners maintain her/his survival over which s/he has no control. Sexual labor can be commodified when the slave's sexual services are sold for money. Sexual and emotional slavery are not commodified when sex slaves are used sexually outside of the market place, as they are in various places including the United States, where girls are enslaved and used for the sexual and emotional pleasure of their owners alone.[2]

Sex work and emotional labor can be performed in a way that is similar to feudal labor. Like a feudal serf, the feudal wife or prostitute is tied to her husband or her pimp by laws of "fidelity and love," or as the medieval serf and Lord promised, love and "fealty," which allow him to exploit her sexual and emotional surplus labor. The feudal sex worker is intimidated into serving a pimp or voluntarily devotes him/herself to a feudal husband or a pimp as an act of "love." Like the feudal serf, the sex worker and emotional worker in the feudal arrangement cannot easily change employers. The feudal lord (as pimp or exploiting husband) is supposed to protect the serf. However, that feudal lord or husband has the power to protect or to victimize. In the U.S., all 50 states only criminalized spousal rape in 2005. Before that a wife's sexual labor was legally the sexual property of her husband for him to use at will (McMahon-Howard, Clay-Warner, and Renzulli 2009). A wife's domestic and emotional labor was likewise an entitlement of her husband. Men invited their parents and children of former marriages to live with the couple and be cared for by his wife's physical and emotional labor. It was his right. The feudal class process is a dehumanizing, exploitative, class process.

A sex worker can work in a capitalist enterprise like a brothel in which s/he is hired to perform sexual and emotional services that create surplus for capitalist employers.[3] S/he is paid a salary, his/her necessary labor, which is only a portion of the money the brothel receives for his or her sexual and emotional labor. The capitalist employer appropriates and distributes the surplus produced by the sex worker. All three class processes—slave, feudal and capitalist—are exploitative forms of theft and disempowerment in which workers have no control over the surplus they produce. All three class processes operate in sex work that involves both sexual services and the emotional labor of feigned desire and pleasure on the part of the sex worker.

There is sex work without exploitation where sex workers decide what services to produce and how to produce them. Sex workers themselves allocate and distribute the fruits of their sexual and emotional labor. A sex worker can work for him- or herself in an independent class process where s/he produces, appropriates, and distributes the fruits of her/his own labor. Or a sex worker can be part of a cooperative partnership that produces, appropriates, and distributes the fruits of its labor communally. A cooperative partnership could produce sexual and emotional services as a commodity, as in a communist brothel, or in a non-commodity form, as in a communal marriage. In a communal marriage, both partners communally and equally share all aspects of their lives, including their sex lives.

A dramatic example of the communal class process is a successful sex worker's coop in Calcutta, the 20,000-member USHA Cooperative, which has its own bank to empower its members economically and politically (Restakis 2010). The communal class process here is not exploitative in a Marxian sense; surplus labor is not appropriated and distributed by others. The benefits of the sexual and emotional labors that USHA members produce are appropriated and distributed by the USHA members who perform that labor. Although the sex worker's sexual and emotional services that she provides might not be not equally desired, fulfilling, or enjoyed by her, the proceeds of that sexual labor are appropriated and distributed communally.

Applying New Marxism to two modern kinds of sex work

I will apply New Marxian class analysis to two modern forms of sex work in the U.S. One exemplifies the independent class process and the other, the communal class process. Both reflect America's changing attitudes toward sexuality. One form of sex work I discuss is the phenomenon of sugar daddies and sugar babies. The other is changing sexual dynamics in two modern love relationships. Let's begin with the form of sex work called "sugar arrangements, sugar, or sugar baby dating," which illustrates the independent class process. I will use a variation of David Montrose's precise definition of sugar arrangements (Montrose 2010, 9).

In sugar arrangements, women (sugar babies) garner financial and or material benefits from sugar daddies in exchange for providing emotional, often sexual, and other services on which they both agree. It's a pay to play arrangement negotiated between young women and wealthy, usually older men. Sugar arrangements are not only about sex. In fact, 40% of all high end sex-worker transactions do not involve sex (Ventakesh 2010). The terms are negotiated early in the relationship. After the initial negotiation, money is rarely mentioned. A credit card is given, tuition or rental bills are paid, etc., with no reminders of the cash nexus that binds the sugar partners. Sugar involves an exclusive relationship on the part of the sugar baby. That relationship usually includes intensive emotional labor. Sugar babies are overwhelmingly female.

Although similar arrangements have existed seemingly forever, they are now prevalent, advertised, and part of an active sub-culture at colleges and graduate schools. While sugar arrangements can and do exist outside of an educational context, I am focusing on the women who enter sugar arrangements to escape education debt. At least 44% of sugar babies are paying for school. One popular website is called "Sugar Baby University" (https://www.seekigarrangement.com/sugar-baby-university). It features an attractive young woman wearing scholarly eyeglasses. Her prominent video on the site, entitled "Say Goodbye to College Debt," attests to her success in escaping educational indebtedness via a sugar daddy arrangement. U.S. college debt now outstrips credit card debt or mortgage debt (Touryalai 2014). It now takes, on average 21 years to pay off college debt (Bidwell 2016). Sugar steps in as an ever more prevalent form of sex work.

Women who work in the sugar arrangements industry are performing their labor in the independent class process. They negotiate the terms of their own employment jointly with their sugar daddies and are paid well for their labor. They produce, appropriate, and distribute their own surplus themselves, and thus they are not exploited in a Marxian sense. They operate within U.S. capitalism where higher education is sold at a high price. They flourish in the economic conditions and values imposed by corporate capitalism within which young people suffer an unemployment rate of about 16%, twice the rate of older adults (Steinberg 2013). Sugar babies provide one of the many personal services, like personal trainers, massage therapists, life coaches, personal chefs, wedding planners, party organizers, dog walkers, and personal shoppers that proliferate to serve those at or near the top of our 1%/99% society.

Changed economic conditions promote the lure of sugar arrangements, but so too do evolving gender dynamics. A changed gender landscape leaves many men feeling insecure about their position in relationships. Many are unable to negotiate the emotionally communal relationships increasingly demanded by educated, professional women. Sugar arrangements protect sugar daddies from negotiating the new gender terrain. Daddies achieve the illusion of emotional and, sometimes, sexual and intellectual intimacy with attractive young women. Their money accomplishes what in sex work is referred to as a GFE, a girl friend experience. A sugar daddy's money replaces his partner's demands for reciprocal and communal emotional, sexual, and/or intellectual labor. Sugar daddies also buy out of any demands for marriage or future security. Both parties refrain from the frequent financial negotiations that may mar the sugar daddy's fantasy of a purely romantic connection.[4]

Sugar arrangements are comfortable for such men. They can appear at business-related or other social gatherings with smart, attractive, socially appropriate young women, who are generally able to understand their business dealings, converse intelligently with their colleagues, and also impress with their youth and looks. Daddies can have dates without concern for their adequacy as partners. They have paid in advance for appreciative partners. Men now face a different gender terrain in which to navigate personal relationships. The economic dependence that forced women to remain in destructive relationships has changed. In sugar arrangements the rules are clear and determined in advance. Daddies can maintain financial dominance,[5] which may be a great relief to them. They are comfortable in that terrain.

Gender ideology is another condition of existence for the sugar industry. Women are designated sex objects by virtue of their gender. In adolescence, girls suddenly become the focus of boys' and men's intense sexual attention. Their sexuality makes them interesting on a new and often bizarre level (Olivier 1989). Their allure as youthful sex objects is commodified in the sugar industry. In an ironic twist, the South is the area of greatest participation in the sugar baby industry (Ross 2015). The South is the primary home of Christian purity cults in which virginal girls pledge to their fathers that they will remain virgins until marriage. Part of the South's continuing infatuation with the Confederacy is their retention of patriarchal norms for white female purity (Wyse 2012). These purity norms put huge pressure on young women's sexuality. When Southern women enter university life, they encounter entirely different and opposing sexual norms and practices (Clark Felty 2007). They rebel, abandoning purity cults and Victorian morality. They have been trained to regard their sexuality as a precious resource, and they can and do disproportionally use that resource to escape educational debt. They have been steeped in patriarchal values, trained to disregard their own sexual needs and to serve men. Those skills are useful to sugar babies.

In another twist, the gender transformations that allow sugar arrangements to flourish without much moral or legal condemnation were fought for in the 1960s, when sexual liberation was advocated as part of the hippie and peace movements (Allyn 2001). Ironically, those movements with their slogan, "Make love, not war" declared freedom from capitalist money values and constraints.[6] Sugar is not as stigmatized as it would have been previously. In a final twist, the very sex object status that may mark women as inferior can be commodified and bartered for freedom from the college debt that haunts their male peers. Gender ideology has sufficiently changed so that sugar arrangements are tolerated as one part of university culture.

Sugar babies have advantages beyond freedom from debt. They can pursue careers without fearing that emotional intimacy with men will result in their losing focus on professional priorities. They may fear the kind of compromises that marriage and family still entail for women.[7] Sugar babies can pursue their ambitions with neither emotional nor financial debts. The terms of sugar arrangements are clear. The violence and inappropriate rage that many women experience from romantic partners or spouses are seldom present in purely voluntary sugar relationships with clear boundaries and sporadic voluntary meetings.

Both parties in sugar arrangements thrive, while what many consider to be traditional sexual and emotional pairings dissolve under the weight of collapsing traditional families. Yet, at the same time, both parties in sugar arrangements are deprived of the thrill and personal fulfillment of being freely chosen as lovers and partners.[8] Neither babies nor daddies benefit from the intense interactive experience and learning one can have from a truly honest emotionally intimate and communal love relationship.

Resnick's and Wolff's New Marxian class theory can also be used to explore some of the tensions and contradictions in the attempt to establish a communal class process in intimate relationships. I will look at two different kinds of intimate partnership relationships. One is a relationship between a married, higher-income professional couple and the other is a long-term relationship between an unmarried couple of mixed incomes and education levels. I discuss these two kinds of representative couples because marriages and partnerships today face starkly different futures depending on a couple's jobs, incomes, and education levels.

The bifurcation in marriage possibilities is a result of U.S. capitalist desertion of American workers through outsourcing and computerizing jobs. For generations, marriage prospects were similar for the wealthiest, middle-, and lower-income Americans. Marriage is now a luxury good mainly available to wealthy and solidly middle-class Americans (Carbone and Cahn 2014; Linn 2013). Successful marriage depends on many things available to people with money, such as job stability[9] and higher salaries that afford help with household maintenance and childcare. Family wages are no longer paid to working class men who thus cannot afford women to work for them full time in households. Marriages are now usually supported by two working professional salaries or at least one highly paid partner's earnings. Better professional credentials enable the economic security on which marriage can rest. More money buys a wide range of services to the ease burdens of home maintenance and childcare. Couples with money can outsource meal preparation, cleaning, laundry, mending, daycare, etc. They can afford vacation time to spend together. Only the wealthiest can maintain a stay-at-home-wife who becomes a feudal household manager. Professional women usually manage the labor of others in their homes, while they pursue careers. In her best-selling book, *Lean In*, Sheryl Sandberg describes how her husband and she alternated taking time off to be there for their children (2013). She does not mention the relevant fact that "[she] employs a staff to help keep house, raise her children and throw her women's leadership dinners" (Grant 2013).

If we explore the intimate life of a couple, we will see how the conditions of their working lives help to facilitate or hinder struggles for sexual and emotional connection. We can employ the sharp lens of New Marxian theory to see class dimensions that operate in intimate relationships, dimensions that were previously invisible. Of course, as in all else, class is not alone in determining intimate relationships. Each member of a couple may have psychological problems. In order to relate intimately on an emotional level, both members may need to negotiate their differing needs. However, neither partner may even realize his/her needs, no less be able to negotiate them with each other. With funds, each member of the couple can seek and find quality help. Quality personal psychotherapy or couple's counseling is a luxury.[10] Couples struggle to find their way to intellectual, emotional, and sexual intimacy on changed terrain. They need the help that only more prosperous couples can afford.

Many couples want financial security and adequate funds before they marry. They look for jobs with benefits they can depend on. Secure jobs have become steadily less available to the vast majority of Americans. Changes since 1970 have robbed U.S. men in particular of their stable well-paid jobs in manufacturing, high power sales, and construction. America has switched to a service economy in which the fastest growth areas are in food service and lower-paid medical assistance fields (Lacey and Wright 2010). These are traditionally female fields. Unlike women who have entered mostly male fields en masse, men are reluctant to enter pink collar jobs (Reeves and Sawhill 2015).

Blue collar men are hurt in other ways as well. Better jobs are increasingly professionalized, requiring higher education, and men's greater resistance to higher education has contributed to their lower incomes. Although men predominate in science, engineering, mathematics, and technology, women are the majority in college overall. While all couples suffer from the same range of emotional problems, they have not all been similarly affected by the vast changes and dislocation of male jobs in our current corporate capitalism.

Let us look first at a mixed blue-collar and professional couple, John and Jane, and then a professional couple, Michelle and Michael. In the mixed couple, John is a carpenter, as was his father. Jane has just entered her career as a pharmacist for the huge corporate drug store chain, Walgreens.[11] John and Jane are both 30 years old. They have a three-year old child. They are both from blue-collar families. They were high school sweethearts; however, they never married. Jane worked to put herself through six years of education to achieve a pharmacist degree. Jane's parents and John's mother care for their child when John and Jane are both busy. John did not want to return to school and did not pursue post high school education. Jane is exhausted but proud that she finished school. John's life has been less tiring. Jane will not marry John. Both find that John's future is economically precarious and insufficient for a marriage.

Jane is one of the 41% of U.S. women who bear children outside of a marriage (Cohen 2015a, 307). As a pharmacist, Jane will earn a median salary of just about $116,000 a year (Goldin and Katz 2016; Rosin 2012, 136–43). John earns about $40,000 (Payscale 2014). Jane and John are part of an ever-increasing number of cohabiting couples who do not marry. There is a high correlation of cohabitation with lower educational attainment (Cohen 2015a, 282). Jane and John usually enjoy each other's company; however, their intellectual and cultural tastes are diverging. Jane is increasingly contemptuous of the ways that John uses his discretionary time, from his choices in television viewing to the choice of hanging out with his buddies fishing, playing video games, getting stoned, or going to the bar instead of pursuing higher education.

John and Jane have had a satisfying communal and egalitarian sexual and emotional relationship. Nonetheless, the lack of shared ambition, different work environments and friends, and the inability to plan a stable future enters their lives on every level, including sex. The distance between the different worlds that John and Jane inhabit erodes even their lively and mutual sexual pleasure.

Like so many American men whose partners out-earn them, John is feeling unmanned.[12] He is beginning to demand more emotional labor from Jane to compensate him for his inability to be a traditional manly provider. In addition to raising his emotional demands, John is raising his sexual demands on Jane as an additional way to assert his manhood. He is behaving like a husband in a feudal marriage who has automatic access to his wife's sexual and emotional labor because he provides the income that sustains her in their feudal household. However, John's lesser salary and Jane's economic superiority help to create Jane's expectation of communality, including shared financial status, emotional support, and mutual sexual satisfaction. Jane is angry and exhausted. She wants a communal household of equals. The combination of John's inadequate earnings, lack of ambition, and increased emotional and sexual demands make John intolerable. His demands are feudal and inappropriate to their initial understanding of communality. John is educationally, financially, and now emotionally and sexually not a communal partner. Even though they are not legally married, Jane is following a trend in which 90% of the divorces of college-educated women are initiated by the women (Cohen 2015b). Jane is beginning the process of leaving the relationship.

The better-educated and married couple we are studying is Michelle and Michael. They are both well-paid professionals. Michelle is an optometrist and Michael is an engineer (Martin and Nudelman 2014; Sethi 2011). They follow the fastest growing trend among married couples: they have no children (Fraad and Fraad-Wolff 2014; Cohen 2015a, 318). After long days at work, Michelle and Michael discuss their daily activities and shared concerns over dinners out or take-out food brought in. They are free to focus on each other without concern for cooking, serving, cleaning, child care, etc. Both of them enjoy their careers. They can jointly process the professional and personal challenges they each face. They are financial, intellectual, and emotional equals in their communal relationship. They take occasional weekends to spend time relaxing and enjoying each other's company. Every year, they take at least two weeks off in which they travel to an exciting destination to explore and enjoy the place, their connection, and their personal space. Vacations allow time to process the irritations and frustrations that arise between them. With time off, there is possibility for conversations that are too difficult to have without ample opportunity to process the issues raised. They have on-going support from their respective psychotherapists for their own personal problems or difficult issues in their marriage. They cultivate their sexual connection on their weekends off and also on their vacations, which they reserve for each other.[13] They have time and space to experiment sexually, communicate, and relax. Michael goes to a costly gym where he can work out and relieve tension. Michelle takes early morning yoga classes several days a week to calm herself for the work ahead and for her life with Michael.

Michelle and Michael illustrate the fact that communal marriage has become a luxury good available to couples with money and who typically are educated with well-remunerated, stable employment. The array of services and opportunities that educated wealthy professionals can afford allows them time and money with which to address life's problems.

If we look at this phenomenon through the lenses of New Marxian class theory, we see an ironic picture. Communal class processes in sexual and emotional labor are enabled by the income bestowed upon participants in corporate capitalism. In our John and Jane example, Jane is able to earn a six-figure salary as a professional, skilled worker with stable employment. Jane's surplus labor on the job also contributes to the corporate profits of Walgreens, a huge drug store chain. John contributes less than half of

Jane's salary to the household budget. He is an independent worker with an unstable, less remunerative job. John tries to bolster his failing male confidence through asserting what were feudal privileges, which allowed automatic access to a dependent woman's emotional and sexual labor. The conditions of existence for John's feudal demands no longer exist. John is rejected as an inadequate communal partner. New Marxist class theory provides the analytic tools with which to see another dimension of John and Jane's emotional and sexual relationship.

New Marxian class theory also allows us to look at Michelle and Michael's emotional and sexual relationship differently. Michelle and Michael share income status, sexual labor, and emotional labor as general equals (no couple is equal in every dimension). When their lives together are difficult, their respective psychotherapists and couple's counselor help them to establish a satisfactory and equal emotional and sexual labor balance. They have time and space to enjoy their emotional and sexual relationship and to process the difficulties they face. They can outsource their domestic labor to others through restaurants, house cleaning services, dry cleaners, etc. Ironically, their higher incomes garnered in profitable capitalist enterprises—their surplus labors at work, which contribute to both their employers' profits—enable the communal class process to operate in their emotional and sexual lives together.

Both couples exemplify a majority trend in American mating called "assortative mating" (Greenwood, Guner, Kocharkov, and Santos 2014). Americans now depart from what has been their traditional pattern. They now marry people who share similar earning capacity. Changed U.S. economic and gender conditions and class relationships in personal life no doubt shape that shift.

Conclusion

I focus on the class dimension of relationships because class is the most repressed discourse in America. That focus in no way denies the crucial impact of such ideological processes as gender, morality, sexuality, and religion. These processes interact with, shape, and are shaped by class processes. They mutually interact to shape political and legal processes. Gender and religious ideologies, political processes, legal transformations, and myriad other processes interact with class processes and each other to change the terrain of married and unmarried cohabiting couple relationships, sex work, and the prevalence of sugar arrangements. The acceptance of cohabitation without marriage and sugar arrangements in turn influences and is influenced by class processes, gender and religious processes, economic processes, etc. The class transformation of marriage is shaped by and shapes gender ideologies, religion, morality, and laws defining both marriage and all forms of sex outside of marriage.

Marxist class analysis of sex work enters a contentious moral terrain. Moralists seem to decry paid sex work for two basic reasons. One is a protest against the commodification of sex as a violation of the exclusive employment of sex within marriage (O'Brien and Hayes 2013). Another is that in sex work, a human being is being used for sex alone, and it is immoral to use another human being for only one aspect of his/her being (Mappes 2008, Klepper 2008, and Soble 2008). In arguments against prostitution, a traditional feudal wife is often presented as a moral matrimonial ideal. This ignores the fact that a feudal wife often trades her sexuality with her husband for his use in exchange for a place to live and work. Women's sexuality has been the property of men for a long time; the husband's use of his wife's sexuality regardless of her wishes was present in the U.S. as late as 2005, when marital rape was finally declared illegal in all 50 states (McMahon-Howard, Clay-Warner, and Renzulli 2009).

Moral outrage at women who sell access to their sexuality appears to be more an indignation about women's freedom to control their own sexuality than a rejection of commodification, per se. Arguments that it is immoral to use one aspect of another human being ignore the basic fact that capitalism is based on using only one aspect of a human being, his/her labor, for capitalist profit. The sale of labor power ignores all other aspects of a worker's humanity. New Marxist class theory introduces a very different sexual morality. In the analysis presented here, exploitation itself is immoral. Sexuality is neither inherently moral nor immoral, and neither is the sale of sexual access. Sexual practice within the slave, capitalist, and feudal class processes *is* immoral, however, because exploitation cheats people of the right to control the process and to appropriate and distribute the product of their work. Exploitation is theft. That theft is immoral. Sexual sale within either the independent or communal class process is not economically exploitative and therefore not immoral. In this brief discussion, New Marxian class analysis allows us to use class to differentiate exploitative sex work from independent and cooperatively organized sex work, which are respected and respectful forms of labor.

Human life is infinitely complex. By separating the different processes that mutually shape our complex lives we can see each influence and trace its complex interaction with the others. New class theory provides a new view of each thread in the complex fabric of our lives and how those threads combine to weave the tapestry of human reality in ever-changing patterns. New Class Theory with its precise analysis of different processes permits us to decide where and how we can see our reality in order to transform it. We owe a huge debt of gratitude to Stephen Resnick, Richard Wolff, and all of the people who have taken the sharp analytic tools they gave us to reweave the tapestry of what we see as human reality. This volume is a testimony to the breadth and profundity of the new class theory and the new perspective on reality that we are building together.

Notes

1 Two other scholars who have applied New Marxism to sex work are van der Veen (2002) and Mulder (2015).

2 Several stories in recent memory that received wide media attention involved American girls or young women kidnapped and kept as personal sex slaves. They were not sold but kept for excusive personal use. They were terrorized into portraying enjoyment of their slave master (*New York Times* 2003).

3 Although Las Vegas brothels usually sell the surplus of female sex workers, males also work as prostitutes in these capitalist enterprises (Associated Press 2012, Netter 2010).

4 In my practice as a mental health counselor, I have noticed that many wealthy men confuse themselves with their money. They imagine that they are giving themselves emotionally when they support their intimates financially.

5 Wednesday Martin's book, *Primates of Park Avenue* (2015) is a "cute" illustration of the problems that may occur when educated women are completely financially dependent on their husbands. Martin, an anthropologist, describes women of the 1% who are highly educated and often accomplished. They leave high power jobs to be full-time wives and mothers. Their husbands may give them yearly bonuses for their wifely performance in getting the children into appropriate, elite schools, in making the "right" social connections, and even for their performance in bed.

6 Both the hippie and antiwar movements of the 1960s decried capitalistic materialism and advocated peace. In an ultimate expression of those values, John Lennon and Yoko Ono took advantage of the enormous media coverage of their marriage in 1969 to schedule two peace events, which consisted of "Bed Ins," where for two weeks they remained nude in bed to personify the slogan "Make love, not war." This observation is based on a wise comment by Michael Pelius.

7 In their important article on gender identity and income within households, Bertrand, Kamenica, and Pan (2015) meticulously document married women curtailing their employment opportunities after they exceed their husband's earnings. They also meticulously document that the 29% of married women who earn more than their husbands perform more domestic labor than their husbands to redress their husbands diminished sense of manhood. In addition, their study indicates that superior female earnings result in less marital stability. Rebecca Traister (2016a, 2016b) convincingly disputes the common wisdom that single status means poverty and privation for women. Traister persuasively argues that addressing family leave policies and wage inequities would prevent poverty more powerfully than does marriage.

8 I am indebted to Shane Knight for this insight.

9 Even skilled jobs that require higher education are far more precarious than they used to be. However, degrees in higher education afford the job mobility that permits educated workers to more easily replace jobs they lose.

10 Most insurance plans will pay a larger portion of costs only to members of their own panels. Psychotherapists and counselors are paid so little for belonging to insurance panels, that most experienced quality therapists will not join insurance panels. Some plans accept out-of-plan-providers. However, out-of-plan-providers are paid a fraction of what their services cost. Quality psychotherapy is another luxury good. Marriage counseling is very rarely covered at all.

11 Pharmacists are in a profession in which males and females are equally represented. One reason for the gender equality among pharmacists is that the field has changed. Huge drugstore chains are pharmacists' primary employers. They have set hours and shifts permitting women with children to work

the predictable hours that are needed for childcare arrangements. When pharmacists were independent capitalists, they worked long hours in their own pharmacies. They also had to lift the heavy sacks of ingredients for making pills. All of that is now mechanized. The combination of regulated hours and the elimination of physical labor have permitted women to enter and catch up with men in the field (Rosin 2012).

12 Twenty-nine percent of wives out earn their husbands (U.S. Bureau of Labor Statistics 2014). There is ample evidence that the number of cohabiting heterosexual women who out earn their mates would probably be even higher. However, that statistic is unavailable.

13 The US is alone among all of the OECD nations in requiring no paid vacation time for US workers (Ray, Sanes, and Schmitt 2013, Picchi 2015). Americans who earned less than $25,000 per year were the least likely to take vacation days, with almost half of that income bracket taking no days off in 2014 while the other end of the spectrum, workers earning more than $150,000 reported taking at least some vacation. Perhaps it is no coincidence that the US has the highest divorce rate of all the OECD nations and less wealthy American couples have the highest divorce rate in the United States. Time off together may improve a couple's chances of staying connected.

References

Allyn, D. 2001. *Make Love, Not War: An Unfettered History of the Sexual Revolution.* New York: Routledge.

Associated Press. 2012. "Men Back on Menu at a Brothel in Nevada." *The Arizona Republic.* August 6 <http://archive.azcentral.com/offbeat/articles/20120806nevada-men-back-menu-brothel.html> (accessed Aug. 19, 2016).

Bertrand, M., E. Kamenica, and J. Pan. 2015. "Gender Identity and Relative Income within Households." *Quarterly Journal of Economics.* 130 (2): 571–614.

Bidwell, A. 2014. "Student Loan Expectations: Myth and Reality." *U.S. News and World Report.* October 7 <www.usnews.com/news/blogs/data-mine/2014/10/07/student-loan-expectations-myth-vs-reality> (accessed July 19, 2016).

Carbone, J. and N. Cahn. 2014. *Marriage Markets: How Inequality Is Remaking the American Family.* New York: Oxford University Press.

Cohen, P. 2015a. *The Family: Diversity, Inequality, and Social Change.* New York: Norton.

———. 2015b. "Family Inequality." July 15 <https://familyinequality.wordpress.com/2015/07/> (accessed July 12, 2016).

Daughters Rising. 2016. "Didn't Slavery End?" <http://daughtersrising.org/the-sex-trafficking-issue/> (accessed July 10, 2016).

Felty, D. C. 2007. "Christian Group Files Suit Against SSU." March 7. <http://savannahnow.com/coastal-empire/2007-03-07/christian-group-files-suit-against-ssu> (accessed June 15, 2016).

Fraad, H. 2009. "Toiling in the Field of Emotion." In *Class Struggle on the Home Front.* G. Casssano, ed., 137–54. New York: Palgrave

Fraad, H. and T. Fraad-Wolff. 2014. "Capitalist Profit and Intimate Life: A Cruel Couple." *Journal of Psychohistory* 41 (4): 258–67.

Goldin, C. and Katz, L. 2016. "A Most Egalitarian Profession: Pharmacy and the Evolution of a Family-Friendly Occupation." *Journal of Labor Economics* 34 (3): 705–46.

Grant, M. 2013. "Sheryl Sandberg's 'Lean In' Campaign Holds Little for Most Women." *Washington Post* February 25.

Greenwood, J., N. Guner, G. Kocharkov, and C. Santos. 2014. "Marry Your Like: Assortative Mating and Income Inequality." Cambridge, MA: National Bureau of Economic Research, working paper 19829, January.

Klepper, H. 2008. "Sexual Exploitation and the Value of Persons." In *The Philosophy of Sex: Contemporary Readings*, 5th edition, A. Soble and P. Nicholas, eds., 249–58. New York: Rowman & Littlefield.

Lacey, A. and B. Wright. 2010. "Occupational Employment Projections to 2018" *Monthly Labor Review*. December 22. Washington, DC: Bureau of Labor Statistics.

Lillie, M. 2014. "Invisible Men: Male Victims of Sex Trafficking." *Human Trafficking Search*. February 24 <http://humantraffickingsearch.net/wp/invisible-men-male-victims-of-sex-trafficking/> (accessed July 14, 2016).

Linn, A. 2013. "Marriage as a Luxury Good." Today.com. October 26 <www.today.com/money/marriage-luxury-good-class-divide-who-gets-married-divorced-8C11457474> (accessed July 14, 2016).

Mappes, T. 2008. "Sexual Morality and the Concept of Using Another Person." In *The Philosophy of Sex: Contemporary Readings*, 5th edition, A. Soble and P. Nicholas, eds., 229–48. New York: Rowman & Littlefield.

Martin, E. and M. Nudelman. 2014. "The 20 Highest Paying Jobs for Women." *Business Insider*. September 17 <www.businessinsider.com/highest-paying-jobs-for-women-2014-9> (accessed July 14, 2016).

Martin, W. 2015. *Primates of Park Avenue*. New York: Simon and Schuster.

McMahon-Howard, J., J. Clay-Warner, and L. Renzulli. 2009. "Criminalizing Spousal Rape: The Diffusion of Legal Reforms." *Sociological Perspectives* 52 (4): 505–31.

Montrose, D. 2010. *Sugar Daddy Diary*. San Francisco: Bush Street Press.

Mulder, C. 2015. *Transcending Capitalism through Cooperative Practices*. New York: Palgrave.

Netter, S. 2010. "Prostitution Not Just for Women: Nevada Brothel Cleared to Hire Men." ABC News. January 7 <http://abcnws.go.com/Business/shady-lady-ranch-cleared-legal-male-prostitutes/story?id=9493257> (accessed July 14, 2016).

New York Times. 2003. "Man Admits Keeping 5 Women in a Bunker as Sex Slaves." June 11 <www.nytimes.com/2003/06/11/nyregion/man-admits-keeping-5-women-in-bunker-as-sex-slaves.html> (accessed July 18, 2016).

O'Brien, E. and S. Hayes. 2013. *The Politics of Sex Trafficking: A Moral Geography*. New York: Palgrave.

Olivier, C. 1989. *Jocasta's Children*. Trans. G. Craig. New York: Routledge.

Payscale. 2014. <www.payscale.com/research/U.S./Job=House_Painter/Hourly_Rate> (accessed July 14, 2016).

Picci, A. 2015. "The United States of No Vacation." CBS Money Watch. January 6 <www.cbsnews.com/news/the-united-states-of-no-vacation/> (accessed July 14, 2016).

Ray, R., M. Sanes, and J. Schmitt. 2013. "No-Vacation Nation Revisited." Washington, DC: Center for Economic and Policy Research, May <cepr.net/documents/publications/no-vacation-update-2013> (accessed July 26, 2016).

Reeves, R. and I. Sawhill. 2015. "Men's Lib." *New York Times Sunday Review*. November 14: P1.

Restakis, J. 2010. "The Daughters of Kali." In *Humanizing the Economy: Co-operatives in the Age of Capital*, J. Restakis, 135–48. Gabriola Island, B.C.: New Society Publishers.

Rosin, H. 2012. *The End of Men*. New York: Riverhead Penguin Books.

Ross, T. 2015. "Where the Sugar Babies Are." *The Atlantic*. January 15.

Sandberg, S. 2013. *Lean In*. New York: Knopf.

Sethi, C. 2011. "Engineering Salary Survey." ASME.com. <www.asme.org/career-education/articles/early-career-engineers/engineering-salary-survey-your-value> (accessed July 19, 2016).

Soble, A. 2008. "Sexual Use." In *The Philosophy of Sex: Contemporary Readings*, 5th edition, A. Soble and P. Nicholas, eds., 259–88. New York: Rowman & Littlefield.

Steinberg, S. 2013. "America's 10 Million Unemployed Youth Spell Danger for Future Economic Growth." June 5. Washington, DC: Center for American Progress <www.americanprogress.org/issues/economy/report/2013/06/05/65373/americas-10-million-unemployed-youth-spell-danger-for-future-economic-growth/> (accessed July 19, 2016).

Touryalai, H. 2014. "1 Trillion student Loan Problem Keeps Getting Worse." *Forbes*. February 21 <www.forbes.com/sites/halahtouryalai/2014/02/21/1-trillion-student-loan-problem-keeps-getting-worse/> (accessed July 19, 2016).

Traister, R. 2016a. "The Single American Woman." *New York Magazine*. Feb. 22–Mar. 6.

———. 2016b. *All the Single Ladies*. New York: Simon and Schuster.

U.S. Bureau of Labor Statistics. 2014. "Wives Who Earn More than Their Husbands, 1987–2012." *Current Population Survey*. March 24 <www.dol.gov/dol/topic/workhours/vacation_leave.htm> (accessed July 19, 2016).

van der Veen, M. 2002. "Rethinking Prostitution: Analyzing an Informal Sector Industry." Ph.D. dissertation, Department of Economics, University of Massachusetts, Amherst.

Ventakesh, S. 2010. "Five Myths about Prostitution." *Washington Post*. September 12 <www.washingtonpost.com/wp-dyn/content/article/2010/09/10/AR2010091002670.html> (accessed July 19, 2016).

Wyse, D. 2012. "To Better Serve and Sustain the South: How Nineteenth Century Domestic Novelists Supported Southern Patriarchy Using the 'Cult of True Womanhood' and the Written Word." M.A. Thesis, Department of History, Buffalo State University.

27 Homelessness as violence

Bad people, bad policy, or overdetermined social processes?

Vincent Lyon-Callo

Introduction

In early April of 2014, a friend of mine reposted on Facebook an article from the *New York Times* (Kilgannon 2014) that had been getting quite a bit of attention—a story about an adjunct professor who happens to sleep in her car. Perhaps not surprisingly, this brought about lots of consternation among his fellow Ph.D. students who were rightly feeling angst about their own economic futures. To me, the fascinating aspect of this news story was not so much that this particular woman happened to be homeless (although, of course, that is awful). Rather, my fascination was that the story was even deemed newsworthy, when homelessness had become so taken-for-granted, and that the story didn't hint at what underlying mental health issues must be at the root of her homelessness.

I want to suggest that the *Times* publishing this story (and the large number of highly educated, liberal academics who were disturbed by it) illustrates an important aspect of the resiliency of homelessness. The reactions to this woman's difficulties demonstrate the power of two enticing and compelling fantasies. Might it be that this particular person being homeless was disturbing precisely because it disrupted the fantasy that so many people are trying so hard to hold onto—that of meritocracy mixed with a faith in investing in one's individualized human capital? Obviously, the logic goes, someone so highly educated does not deserve to be homeless. Of course, this also points out the other popular fantasy (a fantasy that makes it ok to routinely move right by homeless and poor people living around us each day)—that most homeless people are somewhat deserving of their circumstances. This is a powerful and popular imaging, one that, truth be told, I still find myself falling into at moments. After decades of critiquing this fantasy, there are times when I meet a person who is homeless and catch myself thinking, "I don't get it. What's wrong with her that made her homeless?"—as though within each homeless person lies some essential flaw(s) just waiting to be revealed as the cause of their situation. These dual fantasies are important precisely because they have driven social policy, social service practices, and much of the advocacy around homelessness for the last three decades. While neoliberal social and economic restructurings continue to produce increasing inequities throughout the United States, homelessness remains a routine feature of life across the nation despite, and partly perhaps because of, such fantasies and the types of practices and policies they encourage and support.

For over two decades I have been conducting ethnographic research, giving talks, taking part in policy making efforts, participating in community based homelessness and poverty reduction organizing, and struggling within various activist interventions around homelessness. When I started working in homeless shelters back in the 1980s, I understood my work to be part of a broad policy effort. At that time, homelessness was an issue that was given lots of popular attention and news coverage as a sort of national problem that needed to be resolved. Today, widespread homelessness is as American as apple pie and debt. Homelessness has become normalized. Now a routine part of the social landscape of the country, homelessness is understood as warranting little personal, political, or media attention as homeless people have become a problem to be managed.

During the late 1980s, I worked as a housepainter during the day and as an evening counselor at a homeless shelter in southwestern Connecticut. Both jobs were learning experiences. There was something satisfying about seeing a home transformed through your and your co-worker's labor and sitting down for lunch with the rare homeowner who treated us as fellow human beings. On the other hand, I have had few experiences as soul draining as spending multiple twelve-hour days sanding layers of lead paint off an old Victorian home, repainting, and then being told that the white isn't white enough for the home owners association, followed by a night in the shelter two miles down the road working with a few dozen people who have been suffering and struggling in myriad ways through their lives in that community.

Working at the shelter quickly dispelled me of any conscious belief in the fantasy mentioned above of homelessness being simply the result of people being social deviants. Sure, some of the people there harmed themselves and others. One experience still stands out nearly three decades later. While playing the nightly game of finding the small bottle of vodka one sixty-year-old man would try to sneak into the shelter, "Tommy"[1] reacted badly when I found it. Pulling a switchblade out of his pocket with what remained of his fingers (he had lost most fingers and toes due to frostbite after passing out drunk on a winter night years earlier), he shouted, "OK, asshole, where do you want it? The heart or the throat?" Spending the next fifteen minutes with a rusty knife pressed against my throat while trying to convince this gentleman that I preferred not to be stabbed at all was an interesting experience—but, not completely out of the ordinary. Abuse and violence were frequent events in the lives of the people I met in the shelters. The violence done to themselves and other poor people was traumatic at times. But there were also moments of joy, charity, community, passion, and incredible intelligence. Taking that one bottle of vodka from Tommy did not stop him from drinking every other day, and he could be a real jerk at times. But, I got to know him as so much more than that. He's a man who acted as a protector and guide for several young people struggling with living on the streets. One young woman in particular was made safer by Tommy's looking out for her. He was also incredibly funny and kind at moments. In fact, after I argued that we should not kick him out of the shelter after the knife incident, we'd spend lots of quieter moments in the shelter playing cards and sharing stories. Like everyone I came to know, he was much more than what was on the surface during his worst moments.

After working in the shelter for a few years, the tension between wanting to help and seeing that our practices were doing little to actually alter the conditions causing homelessness began to wear on me. Helping people have a safe place to sleep and decent food to eat was gratifying. On the other hand, there was an incredible frustration on a personal level about spending so much of my time working with homeless people who themselves were not working collectively to change what I saw as the two primary causes of homelessness: lack of affordable housing and rising economic inequalities. Using a basic concept of class consciousness, I concluded that many of the homeless people I met were suffering from false consciousness, which disabled them from challenging the "real" problems that had given rise to their homelessness in the first place.

Needing time and space to think about how to better do this work, I entered graduate school at the University of Massachusetts, Amherst. As a committed economic determinist Marxist, I pursued a Master's degree in Labor Studies. Where better to focus my attention than on what I perceived to be the fundamental obstacle to emancipation: exploitation in the labor process. I followed that up with studies in anthropology, attracted by the rhetoric about holistic approaches. Shortly after beginning the anthropology program, I began working in another shelter that became the primary setting for much subsequent research (Lyon-Callo 2004).

In my second semester in graduate school, I took a class on the range of Marxian thinking with Rick Wolff. Keep in mind that this was the late 1980s when there was no Internet, there was no Marxism taught in schools except as pure evil tied to China and the USSR, and I was a middle-class kid from a conservative Connecticut community whose nascent understandings came from my own attempts at reading Marx and Lenin. Rick opened my eyes to an entire field of rich intellectual discussions and debates. Cultural Marxism, Gramsci, the Frankfurt School, and more were all new and exciting ways to develop my understanding of the world. It was an opening for thinking and acting in new ways. Through Rick, I was introduced to Steve Resnick and the Association for Economic and Social Analysis. Their work has been transformative in many ways, but in this paper I want to focus on two main aspects of the work: anti-essentialism and overdetermination. These interventions have guided much of my subsequent work as I've sought to reimagine how we understand and respond to homelessness.

Anti-essentialism and overdetermination

One of Resnick and Wolff's primary interventions is their critique of essentialism (Resnick and Wolff 1987, 8–10, 49–52). On a most basic level this was a critique of simplistic Marxist conceptions that ignored the dialectic in favor of a one directional economic determinism. It was not difficult to see the implications for Marxian analyses that found a determinant cause in complex situations. My experiences with Tommy and others I came to know while working at the shelter prepared me to be receptive to anti-essentialism. I had already come to understand that homelessness was not simply caused by deviance within homeless people and that people who invested in their human capital could still end up homeless. The idea that there was never one determinant factor producing a social situation was compelling to me.

However, the real challenge came in moving beyond this into an understanding that Resnick and Wolff neither simply replaced unidirectional determinism with a bidirectional view of the dialectic nor called for a multi-causal approach. The approach of trying to account for multiple causes of given outcome certainly appears to be an improvement, especially when factors such as race and sexuality that may have been previously neglected are added to the analysis. With homelessness, this might mean not just focusing on substance abuse or mental illness but also considering factors such as employment, wages, racism, a poor foster care system, or housing policy. However, adding more determinants into the equation maintains a cause-and-effect conceptualization. It is not simply a matter of finding the key determinant or adding more determinants. Rather, the challenge is in understanding how social situations like homelessness cannot be delinked from the overlapping interplay of material, historical, psychological, ideological, and other aspects of society that are woven together and not easily untangled into one or several determinants.

Likewise, it is certainly a step toward complexity to analyze how material and ideological conditions shape but do not determine each other. Which comes first, ideas or actions? Is it agency or structure? Are poverty and homelessness caused by structures of violence or individuals' behaviors? Is it the chicken or the egg? The critique of economic determinism helps to clarify how these questions themselves are all wrong. We all know intuitively that there is interdependence, but neither the chicken nor the egg would exist without a whole host of conditions that produce the setting conducive to their existence. Equally, asking whether homelessness is caused by homeless people or social structures is posing the question in a problematic fashion. It is of course both, but so much more, in a complex web of interconnected determinants. As Wolff and Resnick would suggest, the important question is not so much determining which it truly is as in understanding that how we think about the question influences how we act in response (which, of course, then challenges, reinforces, or shifts each of those interconnected determinants in a priori unknowable ways).

Drawing upon and refining the concept of overdetermination developed by Freud and later by Althusser, Resnick and Wolff move beyond unidirectional and multidirectional determinisms to a much more complex view of the world: one with multiple webs of interconnections acting dialectally with all the others in a constant, evolving, shifting process rather than a static state (Resnick, 2016). Class relations, social structures, human subjects, and everything else are understood to be part of processes that are overdetermining each other. The notion of deterministic cause and effect is challenged. Resnick and Wolff understand all aspects of life to be in a web of relations that impact all the rest.

I try to explain this approach to my students using a piece of yarn. You pull on one end, it impacts the other. Or, to make the example more complex, you can tie multiple pieces together at one end then pull on one of these pieces—again impacting the opposite end via simple cause and effect. But what if we took thousands of pieces of yarn, put them into a box, then tied, twisted, or mixed them with the others. These pieces represent various things that have shaped the possibilities of your existence such as interactions with your parents, educational policy in your community, the quality of the water you drank as an infant, events that may have happened to one of your siblings, environmental conditions, historical events, and so on. All of these are mixed together in this box and shift and shape the others. Adding more or shifting some will impact the others. Everything is causing and affecting everything; nothing acts alone. It's a web of interconnections among diverse elements, always in process. Neither ideas nor material conditions determine the other, but all have impacts in overdetermining everything. And when you try to find the one strand of yarn that holds everything else in place, you find this to be an impossible task as they are now interwoven. In fact, you will find that it is impossible to separate out one thread (though the rest of the web will be affected every time you pull on one strand). For every social intervention, therefore, there is a multiplicity of possible entry points.

Resnick and Wolff are most often criticized on this very point. If everything is determining everything else, there can be no empirical or rationalist mode of uncovering truth. Our thoughts, our material conditions, indeed our world is in a process of constituting. And, this process is different for different people in different moments and relations. As they explain in *New Departures in Marxian Theory* (2006) different people experience different worlds. There is no general truth to be uncovered.

This leads to a third popular fantasy around homelessness. Throughout my activist and academic work on homelessness one tendency that I have encountered repeatedly is the quest for uncovering and sharing the truth. From researchers to advocates, there is a desire for dispelling stereotypes and sharing truths. The truth will set us free is the notion. Perhaps, though, the search for one truth blinds us instead? I'll explore that dynamic later in this paper.

Of course, though, the notion of there not being a rationalist or empirical truth to be uncovered can lead to an accusation that this way of thinking is potentially politically debilitating. If there is no absolute truth, if there are no ultimate determinants, how do we act politically? Resnick and Wolff respond to that criticism by suggesting that this approach actually opens more avenues for acting upon the world. To think in particular ways or to act in particular ways changes all the other processes in multiple ways in an endless dialectical process that then changes thinking and acting and material relations and thinking and so on. Multiple spaces for political intervention are opened as everything we think and do has impacts on the world. Wolff and Resnick prioritize class as their entry point in the hope that a Marxian intervention will move people to think and act in ways that might promote different kinds of class processes and relations. Where we start, what we prioritize in thinking about things influences how we act and impacts how we intervene and then how we think and act and intervene again. To demonstrate this process, let me return to the project of rethinking homelessness.

Rethinking homelessness

What if there is no truth about homelessness to uncover and lay bare? If there is not a truth that can be uncovered through empirical or rationalist inquiries, how do we respond to homelessness? What I want to suggest is that where we start and what we prioritize in thinking and acting about these things all influence the processes producing more or less homelessness in multiple ways.

What if the three fantasies about homelessness mentioned above (homelessness is caused by deviant homeless people, meritorious people would not be homeless, and uncovering and educating policymakers and the public about the truth about homelessness is key to solving the problem) are just that? Fantasies, and perhaps fantasies that have helped normalize homelessness. But, by calling something a fantasy I am not implying that is it somehow less real. Indeed, fantasies are ways of imagining and making sense of the world that then have impacts upon how we think and act. There are multiple theories about homelessness that guide how we see, experience, and respond to homelessness and thus help to craft different outcomes. And, that is exactly the beauty of this approach. There are infinite possibilities for how to think and act and each has an impact on reshaping that complex web of overdetermined inter-connections. Some may move us toward reinforcing processes maintaining homelessness as a normal, routine aspect of life or others may move us in different directions. Let me demonstrate this through a discussion of popular thinking and policy responses to homelessness starting with two events in April 2016.

The day after discussing homeless youth in my introductory cultural anthropology course, perhaps the largest study of homeless youth was released by the US Department of Health and Human Services. Eight hundred and seventy-three homeless people aged 14 to 21 in 11 different cities were surveyed. The report detailed how more than 60 percent of these people had been assaulted, 41.1 percent reported their race as African American, more than half had spent some time in foster care, most described difficulties in accessing shelters or even services like bathrooms or laundries, and nearly 40 percent identified as lesbian, gay, bisexual, or transgender. More than half of those studied identified the reason for their homelessness as being told to leave by family (2016). Coinciding with this report, the Department of Health and Human Services announced a series of new public service announcements designed to raise awareness by giving a voice to the experiences of homeless youth as well as a call for research and social service interventions to address these concerns.

A few days later, I received an email request from a reporter in upstate New York wishing to interview me regarding a new program being advocated there. Building upon a relatively new "housing first" approach to homelessness that was increasingly popular, this community was proposing a policy of prioritizing military veterans for housing. The plan was to construct new affordable housing units but to prioritize veterans as the supply would not meet demand for many years. The reporter wanted to know my thoughts on this issue based upon my experiences and research on homelessness.

What is noteworthy about these two events, besides that homelessness was getting a bit of coverage in the print press, is how both represent significant shifts in thinking about and responding to homelessness from when I started working on homelessness. In the 1980s, the common perception was that homelessness resulted from deinstitutionalization from state mental hospitals, an economic recession, substance abuse, and perhaps post-traumatic stress for Vietnam War veterans. The answer was to shelter people until conditions improved while managing the worst pathologies within individuals. At that point it was unimaginable that three decades later homeless shelters in every community be commonsensical or that we would be exploring the multiple impacts of sexuality, race, family dynamics, employment, and impacts of abuse on young people or debating which group of people should have priority for new affordable housing units. That was as unthinkable at the time as imagining that there would be gay marriage, farmer's markets everywhere, legalized marijuana, and Rick Wolff on syndicated television talk shows. The point is that through thoughts and actions, change occurred. But none of that happened through a simple causation of an identifiable policy or advocacy effort. These processes of change occur through multiple factors interacting in an overdetermined fashion.

With homelessness, the first significant shift in policy happened with Bill Clinton's election. One of his first acts was to bring together leading experts to discuss what was needed to solve what was still being represented as a social crisis. What emerged from those meetings was a call for a "continuum of care" approach. The argument went that homelessness was caused by both a lack of affordable housing and problems within the individualized bodies of homeless people such as substance abuse or mental illness. Unfortunately, the funds for housing options did not emerge, so the continuum focuses on the individualized homeless person with a medicalized mode of analysis. Focused attention on the homeless person becomes understood as the logical or most realistic way of responding to homelessness. Social workers and counselors were tasked with figuring out what was wrong with homeless people and then helping them to access services or programs to fix those issues. The array of social, economic, and public policy practices that continued to disrupt communities and wreak havoc on many people and community's economic and emotional stability largely went unaddressed as a result. For example, the war on young black men (often referred to as a war on drugs) was expanded during this period, yet there was virtually no focused attention on the relationship of racism, criminal justice policies, and homelessness.

When the emergency shelters and the new continuum of care practices did not significantly reduce homelessness, rhetoric and practices in communities across the nation turned to punishing and criminalizing public homelessness. The thinking seemed to be that we tried to solve the problem and that didn't work so perhaps the best we can do is to keep certain areas clear of homeless people. That too did not do very much to diminish the overall number of homeless people (although it was useful for gentrification efforts).

By 2000, homeless shelters and homeless services were a routine part of life across the nation's landscape. No longer was homelessness represented as a social crisis. In fact, it is barely even newsworthy—except perhaps when a formerly middle-class or highly educated person becomes homeless. Recent years have brought two new shifts in policy. During the last years of the Bush administration, the Department of Health and Human Services announced a move to focus on so-called "chronic homelessness." Some suggested that a disproportionate amount of resources were being spent on just a few people who had been homeless for a long time. Most recently, the focus on chronic homelessness has moved in many cities into "housing first."

Housing first is pretty much just what the name implies. The plan is to provide housing for homeless people first. And, then, once housing is somewhat stabilized, to help them work on the various other issues causing problems in their lives. In some ways, this is a repackaging of the old story as it is not a question of whether homeless people are pathological, but rather what is the most efficient way of dealing with the perceived pathologies. On the other hand, it clearly helps individual people.

In 2006 the City and County of Kalamazoo, Michigan, responded to an organized and vocal movement in the community by establishing the Local Housing Assistance Fund—LHAF as a "one-time-funded" prototype to help the County better understand solutions to the homeless problem. Through various sources $1.5M was raised and was used to provide rent subsidies and create more affordable housing. Qualifying for the housing came with the condition that applicants needed to work closely with a religious or social service mentor on identifying and working on resolving the issues within their individualized selves that contributed to their homelessness. The County oversaw the program and provided housing for 117 families or individuals. For people I know well, often this was a tremendous assistance. Forty percent of recipients were able to "graduate" off this subsidy. The program also remodeled three apartment buildings to increase affordable housing in the community. Those were tangibly important interventions for several people.

What it did not do, however, was to disrupt the violence, inequality, and poverty of which homelessness is one manifestation. The focus remains on homeless people rather than social processes. If we hope to actually significantly decrease contemporary social suffering, I suggest that a serious engagement with the complexity of the dialectical processes that overdetermines the production of homelessness as a routine, largely taken for granted aspect of contemporary life while maintaining exploitation, oppression, and authoritarianism would produce different thinking and practices. Rather than continue to search for the essential or determinant causes of homelessness (whether they be veteran status, the chronically homeless, youth from foster care situations, or underpaid workers), an approach that promoted thinking about the interconnections and overdetermined processes at work between a broad range of aspects of contemporary life and how those might relate to homelessness could result in different sorts of activism, advocacy, and interventions in both thought and action.

For example, two racial groups are vastly over-represented among counted homeless people: African Americans and Native Americans. As mentioned earlier, the 2016 HHS report on homeless youth had African American youth significantly over-represented in the homeless population. Similarly, a report by the Institute for Children, Poverty and Homelessness (2012) showed that black families depended on homeless shelters at a rate that was seven times higher than white families. Yet, there is little discussion exploring possible connections between institutionalized, systemic racism and homelessness with even less attention focused on Native Americans. To be clear, my suggestion is not that race is the essential issue with homelessness or even a determinant issue. But, what if we took race as an entry point for thinking about the wide-ranging factors that produce the processes that result in homelessness at different levels for "whites" and "blacks" and "Native Americans" in the US today? Would that not open discursive space for imagining a wide range of possible interventions that are not currently being advocated or implemented?

Or, let me return to one of the fastest growing groups of people living on the streets or couch surfing across the nation: teens and young adults. What if we extended our analysis from just homeless teens and young adults to include housed and homeless? Reported rates of anxiety and depression continue to be understood as an increasing public health problem. What sorts of emotional, material, and ideological processes are factoring into their lives? It would of course be important to know that close to one-half of those young people living on the streets or in shelters identify abuse within their families and that over one-third identify as LGBT with many of these young people suffering physical, sexual, and emotional abuse within their families and schools. Why does being identified or self-identifying as LGBT seem to be connected to those who end up homeless? What can be done to alter those dynamics? I ask because we really don't know. That research has not been done. There are few if any activist or policy interventions focused on this issue. When a student of mine did some research on the understandings about and interventions aimed at such concerns in southwest Michigan a couple of years ago, what he found was a complete lack of programs accompanied by a desire to not know. If we don't look for the cause of youth homelessness but instead consider a whole web of interconnected aspects of lives, what sort of different ways of thinking and acting might become imaginable? It is just this point that I suggested to the reporter asking about prioritizing veterans for housing.

How does it make sense to prioritize veteran status as a preferred condition for accessing affordable housing units? What thoughts guide such practices? What types of alternative interventions might be possible through shifting the focus from identifying the most deserving toward a different entry point that might call into question broader conditions causing suffering on such large scales despite the wealth within the nation?

My first impulse when the reporter asked my thoughts on the policy was to problematize the notion that being a veteran itself should be the essential, determining category in deciding who was most deserving of housing. What is it about veterans that might make them more susceptible for becoming homeless? Is that even accurate? Is it all veterans or need we explore more fully what leads to someone becoming a veteran in today's volunteer army and how different people with different experiences (before, during, and after their military experience) might have different outcomes regarding being securely housed or not? Those questions would perhaps be worth exploring, but that remains within the mind frame of needing to determine who is deserving.

Imagine if the focus were shifted and instead of debating whether veterans are more deserving of housing than a woman leaving a violent partner or a seventeen year old who was kicked out of her home for being bisexual or a million other possible scenarios, the dominant thinking were shifted so that it became common sense that housing and a basic income was just a normal feature of life for all people? What sorts of activisms, policies, or practices would that make possible? Or, what if the idea of democracy at work as Wolff (2012) has been proposing became more widespread and that became an entry point for considering a range of responses to social situations of which homelessness is one manifestation. Similarly, in the work Resnick and Wolff did with Harriet Fraad (1994) they pointed out how the household is also a site of class processes and relations. Can we imagine if that became taken seriously and thoughts and practices on democratizing the household and/or the family became commonsensical? What if we began to understand homelessness as just one aspect of a larger web of discursive processes that is producing much social suffering despite the production of wealth and technology? The point is that different understandings make different entry points for activism and social policy possible and desirable, which would lead to different sorts of interventions that would have different impacts upon the world. Approaching the problem in that way could help move us beyond the no-win debate of how to divide up limited supplies of affordable housing among those suffering or how best to treat the symptoms of perceived pathology among people into considering what types of practices, policies, and ideas might make possible working toward a fantasy of economically and environmentally sustainable and supportive communities.

In looking at homelessness, it is of course imperative to think carefully about what remains problematic in most of the dominant responses both to homelessness and to growing inequality and economic insecurity. Believing that there is no alternative, ignoring the complexity of homelessness in favor of a simplistic embracing of housing first, or thinking one can best respond to systemic violence by reforming or punishing poor or homeless people is a powerful ideology. Whether elided and naturalized through charitable giving, enacted as a commonsensical approach to improving social conditions, or viewed as intractable or unchangeable, capitalism (based upon the violence of exploitation) and institutionalized racism remain dominant features of life. Likewise, we would want to explore what it is that people want and how those desires are manifested. Emotional and psychological processes must be considered along with the political and economic if we are to understand the violence of our currently dominant thoughts and practices as well as the possibilities for shifting these.

We need to engage in challenging that reality if we hope to make another world, one without homelessness, really thinkable and doable. To alter homelessness, we need to work at disrupting the fantasies that maintain homelessness. Drawing on Resnick and Wolff demonstrates that a fourth fantasy is the belief in determinist logic and that we can somehow uncover the truth. Perhaps embracing overdeterminism and thinking of how such an approach might make it possible to create spaces where non-punitive, non-neoliberal, cooperative policies, practices, and programs make sense would be a step toward making a world with less social suffering and without homelessness a reasonable goal. Shouldn't that be our aim?

Note

1 Name changed to somewhat protect identity.

References

Department of Health and Human Services Administration for Children and Families Family and Youth Service Bureau. 2016. "Data Collection Study Final Report." http://www.acf.hhs.gov/sites/default/files/fysb/data_collection_study_final_report_street_outreach_program.pdf (accessed April 18, 2016).

Fraad, H., S. Resnick, and R. Wolff. 1994. *Bringing it All Back Home: Class, Gender and Power in the Modern Household*. London: Pluto Press.

Institute for Children, Poverty and Homelessness. 2012. "Profiles of Risk No. 11: Race and Housing Instability." http://www.icphusa.org/index.asp?page=16&report=102&pg=83 (accessed August 11, 2015).

Kilgannon, C. 2014. "Without Tenure or a Home." *New York Times*, March 27.

Lyon-Callo, V. 2004. *Inequality, Poverty, and Neoliberal Governance: Activist Ethnography within the Homeless Sheltering Industry*. Toronto: University of Toronto Press.

Resnick, S. 2016. "Econ 305, Lecture 04, Richard Rorty and Overdetermination." goo.gl/62xGqW (accessed April 21, 2016).

Resnick, S., and R. Wolff. 1987. *Knowledge and Class: A Marxian Critique of Political Economy*. Chicago: University of Chicago Press.

———. 2006. *New Departures in Marxian Theory*. London: Routledge.

Wolff, R. 2012. *Democracy at Work: A Cure for Capitalism*. Chicago: Haymarket Books.

28 Family farms, class, and the future of food

Elizabeth Ramey

Introduction

Stephen Resnick and Richard Wolff's efforts to breach the doorstep of the household and bring the insights of their class analytical framework to bear on contemporary families have produced a unique Marxist-Feminist theoretical framework (Fraad, Resnick, and Wolff, 1994; Resnick and Wolff 2009). In this essay, I apply and extend Resnick and Wolff's class analytical framework to critically examine an iconic American institution, the family farm—its role in the twentieth century rise of industrial agriculture, and its potential future in alternative agricultural economies.

The family farm has been an idealized institutional form in the United States for over two centuries. As such, it has been harnessed in the service of widely disparate goals and agendas. As one food blogger puts it, "Everybody loves small family farms, from Republicans to Democrats and hipsters to ultra-religious folks. As a nation, we romanticize them—the last link to our pioneer past" (Ganzler 2014). The agrarian attachment to family farms has pervaded the left via various alternative food movements critical of the mainstream industrial agrifood system (Allen 2004; Walker 2012). This New Agrarianism combines nostalgia for an imagined ideal of the past with visions for the future. The local foods movement is one notable example.

The question of food—what we eat, where it comes from, and with what consequences—may well be unlike any other issue in demonstrating enormous power to tap people's motivation for change—systemic as well as personal. The local foods umbrella includes a plethora of activities and initiatives reflecting this appetite for change. With its broad appeal and motivational power, the political potential of the local foods movement is undeniable. It is, in fact, a *movement*—not just an alternative business model. It stands in explicit opposition to industrialized food—to global corporate giants that have hijacked and corrupted the more radical promise of other alternatives such as organic foods. The local foods movement provides an important site of concrete oppositional politics and practices at a time when systemic, global, ecological, and social threats can induce defeatism in even the most dedicated activist. It may also provide a gateway to political and economic practices that can begin to reverse capitalist domination over social relations and relations between humans and the non-human natural world. At a time when there appear to be so few opportunities for building non-capitalist futures, the local foods movement represents tremendous capacity to advance alternative visions of how to live and be in the world.

Its very significance, however, suggests the importance of engaging the movement respectfully, but critically. It may be the case, as I will explore here, that even while it generates new insights and even incursions into the capitalist domination of food systems, it may nevertheless accept too readily and uncritically certain aspects of the current food and agricultural system that can be and have been constraining and even exploitative—namely, family farms.

Family farms and local food

Local food is about more than just geographical proximity between food production and consumption. It is a complex and comprehensive alternative vision in which the local (unlike the global) is not only intrinsically valuable, but is also a means to an end of a variety of other goals. It is counter to what local foods pioneer Gary Nabhan refers to as the "transnational vending machine," or the industrial food system, as well as the means to address the many ills associated with that system. Nabhan chronicled his year-long quest to eat locally in his "manifesto of local food," *Coming Home to Eat: The Pleasures and Politics of Local Food* (2002). Nabhan views eating locally as an ethical act and advocates a return to and re-valorization of traditional, place-based, food practices. For him, as for many others in the movement, knowing where our food comes from is the key to change.

> What if each of us, day by day, fully fathomed where our food comes from, historically, ecologically, geographically, genetically? What would it be like if each of us recognized all the other lives connected to our own through the simple act of eating?
>
> (163)

Hence, one of the key imperatives of local food is to "Know Your Farmer." Knowledge is key to unlocking the cornucopia of benefits that flow from local food systems. Local foods advocates seek to change how and by whom food is marketed by decreasing the geographic and social distance between farmers and eaters. Local communities are strengthened by these increased opportunities for face-to-face interactions. Consumers get the power to vote properly with their food dollars because they know the story behind their food. Farmers are subjected to the scrutiny of personal interaction and accountability and therefore can capture the benefits of their efforts to deliver fresh, safe, healthy, environmentally sustainable, and humane products. A local foods economy aims to deliver a variety of benefits to move us toward a safer, healthier, more sustainable and just food system. Unlike the immoral economy of industrial agriculture, the production and consumption activities associated with the local foods economy are therefore virtuous and ethical acts. As noted local foods advocate Brian Halweil argues,

> so many of these activities and arrangements seem intrinsically valuable: chefs using fresher, tastier, and less processed foods; farmers linking up to offer busy consumers a diversity of products in one location; empty downtown parking lots sprouting farmers' markets on the weekends.
>
> (2002, 13)

In this way, "profits" and "people" align, and those profits go to "good" people—the local farmers delivering the local food.

One key, yet unexamined, assumption underlying local foods is that family farms are the ideal institution to produce and deliver this local food. The imperative to "know your farmer" resonates only if we implicitly assume that "your farmer" is someone worth knowing. *That* you know your farmer somehow stands in for *what* you know about him. Within the local foods movement, family farmers enjoy the elevated ethical status that comes with agrarian ideology. The local foods movement therefore incorporates the romantic, sentimental attachment to family farms while also assuming that these institutions are somehow outside of, alternative to, and untainted by the capitalist, industrial agriculture system and therefore a suitable model for alternative food economies.

As with other unexamined ideological attachments, the contradictions and complications of that model are also overlooked. As I argue, some aspects of family farms may be barriers to the establishment of more just food economies; I focus here on class. I first examine how the production, appropriation, and distribution of surplus were organized in those idealized models for the future, the family farms of the past. In doing so, I hope to illuminate aspects of family farms today or to at least caution against the uncritical acceptance of the family farm as the most and perhaps only desirable model of agricultural production. The discussion is grounded in the detailed class analysis of Midwestern family farms at the turn of the twentieth century in Ramey (2014). While a similar analysis of present-day local farms and local foods has yet to be made, I offer some initial thoughts along these lines. In thinking about a class-based critique of local foods, my goal is not to dismiss the movement entirely out of hand but to push toward a definition of "alternative" and "local" that is more robust, more radical, and more just.

Specifically, alternative food movements such as local foods should include concern for class exploitation and explicitly strive to encourage non-exploitative forms of agricultural production. Otherwise, they stand to reproduce one of the damaging aspects of the system they see themselves as replacing with more "ethical" food economies. Some local foods activists and consumers seek to include farm workers' wages and working conditions in their definition of ethical eating, but a discussion of exploitation—whether capitalist or some other form—is largely or wholly absent (Greenhouse 2015). Even if we do not accept that the presence of exploitation is itself intrinsically unethical, and hence worthy of attention from local foods advocates, it connects with other negative impacts that are of direct concern to those in the movement such as the erosion of community, self-determination, and social connection.

To begin, let us go to the early twentieth century Midwestern United States, to the diversified, small, general-purpose family farms that dominated the agricultural economy. Standing on the precipice of the industrial agriculture revolution, these "pre-industrial" entities most resemble the idealized family farm that serves as the fodder for the "agrarian dreams" of the future (Guthman 2004). In the discussion below, I highlight two key aspects of these family farms of the past, which should lead us to question their use as a model for the future: First, family farms were places of intense exploitation of farm families—men, women, and children. Second, family farms participated in the rise of the industrial agricultural system. They are not somehow outside of it, but rather integral to it.

Family farm feudalism

In many ways, the historical context then parallels that of today: In the first decades of the twentieth century, much like today, food was a hot topic. The food system appeared to be standing at a crossroads. Then, as now, a perceived crisis in the food and agricultural system provoked increased attention to family farms. Flagging productivity growth in agriculture had been pushing up food prices for over a decade and threatened to derail capitalist industrial growth. Rural backwardness was identified as the culprit. Then, as now, the desirability of the family farm as an institution was not in question. The question was how to restore, protect, and preserve it as a means of promoting rural progress. This goal remains at the forefront of the local foods movement as well.

Disparate concerns for the problems of rural life coalesced into what became known as "the farm woman problem." The burdens of the farm wife's job, it seemed, were creating a shortage of farm women and thereby threatening the survival of the family farm. Decades before the mass extinction of farms grabbed national attention after World War II, farmers' daughters were leading the charge to the city. Robert and Martha Bruère summed up the situation in their 1912 article in *Harper's Bazaar*: "Shall the nation go hungry because the farmer's wives don't like their jobs? For, after all, a man will not live on the farm without a wife."

In fact, the "farm woman problem" was actually a "feudal woman problem," exacerbated by the harsh conditions of farming and rural life at the time. Farm life was hard for everyone involved. Men, women, and children worked long hours doing strenuous work for minimal and uncertain compensation, in relative isolation, with little time for many diversions including education, and few alternative economic opportunities. While farmers labored in the farm fields in the context of an ancient class process, appropriating and distributing their own surplus, farm women worked in the context of a gender-based feudal class process. Their surplus labor, in the form of services like childcare, cooking, and gardening; products like canned produce, cooked meals, and sewn shirts; and cash from the sale of farm products like butter, eggs, and milk was appropriated by their farmer/husbands. As feudal serfs, farm women were tied to their exploiters by "marital oaths, ideology, tradition, religion, and power" (Fraad et al. 1994, 7). Hence a typical family farm included a feudal class structure, in which farm wives worked in the farm household and environs, such as the barnyard, garden, orchards, henhouse, and dairy.

Not only the farmer's wife, but also his children constituted a reserve labor force that could be called upon as needed. Children's labor was also typically part of the feudal class process as children were integrated as additional serfs in both farm and household production. Child labor on family farms was ubiquitous during the early twentieth century. Even though all 48 states had child labor restrictions and compulsory education laws in place by 1920, there were numerous exceptions and loopholes for family farms.[1] Chores were assigned to children as young as three or four, and older girls and boys took on gendered assignments as serf-apprentice wives and farmers to their mothers and fathers. Older boys took on work in the farm fields, with livestock and operating farm machinery, and girls specialized in the tasks their mothers performed as farm wife serf-apprentices in the household, barnyard, and garden. Even though by 1920, the "right to childhood" was widely recognized, most farm families could ill afford the luxury of "emotionally priceless" but "economically useless" children (Riney-Kehrberg 2005).

Pre-industrial, early-twentieth century family farms, then, included primarily non-capitalist class structures, but these were generally exploitative. Farm women and children performed a variety of labor processes within the context of an exploitative feudal class structure in the family farm's two sites of production: the farm household and the farm enterprise. In addition to the feudal class structure, the family farm included an ancient class structure in which the farmer himself labored in the farm enterprise. Family farms often also included a capitalist class structure in which hired hands were employed for a wage, usually on a seasonal or temporary basis, as needed in the farm enterprise. Then, as today, however, family labor accounted for the vast majority of labor hours required in farm production (Hoppe 2014).[2] Different kinds of class processes, therefore, combined differently in the family farm's two sites of production. While the farm household was mostly feudal, the farm enterprise was ancient, feudal, and sometimes capitalist. Whenever different kinds of class processes combine in a single site, a class structural hybrid is formed (Levin 2004). A typical family farm, therefore, was a hybrid of hybrids.

The feudal exploitation of women and children in the farm household and farm enterprise helped facilitate and subsidize the ancient self-exploitation of farm men in the farm enterprise. If the farmer also had hired workers to help him, this feudal exploitation also helped facilitate and subsidize the capitalist exploitation of those workers by the farmer, also in the farm enterprise. This occurred primarily in two ways. First feudal workers produced services, products, and proceeds to meet the needs of farm family members (and hired hands when they were present), thereby reducing the ancient farmer's (and hired hands') necessary labor to virtually nothing. This practice was known as "making do." Second, feudal workers supplemented the hired hands' and ancient farmer's surplus in the production of commercial farm commodities through the practice of "helping out" in fieldwork and other activities. The work of farm women, with the aid of their children, provided substantially for the reproduction of the farm family and, in so doing, provided an important source of subsidy to the family farm's ancient class structure, enabling it to survive and prosper, even as the burden of work was shifted onto the shoulders of feudal serfs—farm wives and their children. It was the work of feudal serfs that purchased the "self-sufficiency" of farm families, feudal dependence that purchased the ancient farmer's "independence," and insulated the family farm from the uncertainties of the farm enterprise income.

The transfer of surplus to the ancient from the feudal class structures in family farms is analogous to the transfer of goods and services to children in the form of childcare in contemporary feudal households (Resnick and Wolff 2009). Just as the husband transfers his wife's appropriated surplus to children to facilitate their survival and growth, the farm husband transferred his wife's appropriated surplus to the ancient farm enterprise in order to facilitate its survival and growth. The farm wife and children's feudal exploitation therefore helped reproduce the ancient farmer's own self-exploitation. These transfers helped push the ancient farmer's necessary labor toward zero, allowing him to devote most of his time to producing ancient surplus to secure the conditions of existence for the ancient farm enterprise.

Such transfers were enabled by the primacy of the ancient class process, which was viewed as the heart or essence of the family farm and therefore that for which all family members toiled and sacrificed, even at the expense of the family farm's feudal class structures in the household and enterprise. One condition of existence of this primacy of the ancient, and of the exploitative family farm hybrid, was agrarian ideology. Agrarian ideology celebrated the "independence" and moral virtue of family farmers and thereby helped mask their dependence on the work of farm women and children, as well as their position as feudal exploiters. For the ancient farmer/feudal lord, agrarianism helped define him culturally, politically, and economically as an independent producer, citizen, and head of family. For the feudal farm wife, it meant she was less likely to recognize or rebel against her exploited class position in the farm household, viewing it instead with a sense of service and fulfillment. For farm children, who often worked long hours at the expense of their formal education, it meant their labor was viewed as virtuous and educational, an affirmation of industry, thrift, and independence, rather than an abusive violation of childhood.

In elevating the masculine realm of the ancient farm enterprise over the feminine realm of the feudal farm household, agrarianism was also a gendered ideology, reflecting, assigning, and reinforcing a gendered hierarchy (Fink 1992). Farm women's work in the farm household and in reproducing the farm labor force was therefore constructed as less important and less like work. It was viewed instead as part of the natural order, as simply what women did. Farm women's work in the farm enterprise was similarly devalued. Even though farm women did much of the work of farming—caring for chickens, gardening, and milking, for example— farm women were never considered farmers themselves. Their work in the family farm enterprise was considered "helping out." Agrarian ideology hence helped reflect and reinforce men's privileged access to farming as an occupation, as well as their agency and authority (and the subordination of their wives and children) within the farm family.

The family farm's complex combination of different kinds of class structures—ancient, feudal, and sometimes capitalist—in its two linked sites of production—farm household and farm enterprise—help explain its continued persistence in the face of perpetual economic crisis across the twentieth century. This class structural complexity increased vulnerability to crisis while increasing the flexibility and means to respond to those crises. As we have seen, feudal class structures in the family farm could be used to supplement and expand ancient surplus so that its conditions of existence could be secured. The survival of the ancient, however, came at the cost of crisis in the family farm's feudal class structure. The farm woman problem was one manifestation of that crisis as overworked and exhausted farm women and children fled the burden of their feudal exploitation. The use of family labor was one way that family farms remained viable, yet its use was stretched to its limit. There was limited opportunity to increase production and absolute surplus by working family laborers for longer hours and hired farm workers were scarce and expensive. The feudal class structure supported the growth of the ancient but also presented a barrier to its further expansion. As the farm woman problem made clear, internal feudal to ancient subsidies needed to be supplemented in some way.

Family farms and industrial agriculture

The answer came in the form of farmers' rapid adoption of new labor-saving farm technologies and the rise of industrial agriculture, particularly in Midwestern grain crop farms. Farmers who successfully improved productivity relative to their neighbors could capture what Marx referred to as super profits from laggard ancient farmers, thereby increasing the surplus available to secure their own conditions of existence while displacing crisis onto others. Technological change became the new preferred strategy for weathering crises or expanding during prosperous times. Farmers began adopting new mechanical technologies in the form of tractors in the 1920s, biological technologies in the form of hybrid seeds in the 1930s, and chemical technologies in the form of pesticides and synthetic fertilizers in the 1940s. Once again, by "making do" and "helping out," the unpaid labor of farm family members helped generate the necessary savings or cash to allow the ancient farmer to make these purchases. From 1933 on, state subsidies supplemented these intra-farm transfers and aided in accelerating the processes of technological change. The result was nothing short of a revolutionary transformation in farming as well as in the broader food and agricultural system. The veritable flood of cheap foodstuffs, not to mention newly "freed" farmers and rural laborers that resulted helped finance the "Golden Age" of U.S. industrial economic development as well as its geopolitical position as a global superpower in the decades following World War II.

Industrial agriculture, itself a response to the contradictions associated with the intense exploitation and long, strenuous hours of work for women, children, and men on family farms, generated its own contradictions. In engaging in the hunt for super profits, farmers jumped on a "technology treadmill," running faster and faster only to end up in the same place or even fall behind as new technologies continually cheapened farm commodities but not costs of production (Cochrane 1993). The strategy that farmers employed to survive crisis itself threw them constantly into crisis. Technological change exacerbated inequalities among farmers, as the first movers leveraged their super-profits into ever larger, wealthier, and more productive farms and gobbled up the land and assets of their failing neighbors. The farmers that remain today, after nearly a century of this technology-induced crisis, are the most productive in the 10,000-year history of agriculture.

Industrialization involved the transfer of farm production processes away from farmers and into agribusiness corporations, thereby lightening considerably the strenuousness of farm work but reducing the value captured by farmers in the food supply chain. Inputs previously produced on farms, such as traction power, seeds, and fertility, were increasingly produced by capitalist agribusiness corporations and then sold back to farmers. Agribusiness firms, many of which became global behemoths, therefore both relied upon and reproduced the technology treadmill in ancient farming. As one observer notes "The agribusiness giants do not farm the land. They farm the farmers" (Pyle 2005, 196).

All but the largest and wealthiest of farmers have stayed in the game by altering strategies of "making do" and "helping out" but continuing to rely on the labor of family members to subsidize the farm enterprise. Mechanization tended to reduce the need for both hired and family workers to help out in crop production, but hired workers were the first to go. The reduced physical strain of field work meant that farm women could help out more regularly by driving machinery, keeping farm books, or running to town for machinery parts. "Making do" changed form, as well. During the 1950s, agricultural publications began noting the new phenomenon of farm women taking jobs in town to meet the increased cash expenses associated with the new industrial farming techniques. Hence, off-farm work increasingly replaced or supplemented household production as a source of feudal subsidies to farm family members and the farm enterprise. Today, both farm men and women work off-farm to subsidize the family farm, and most farms rely on this income to supplement farm receipts (Hoppe 2014).

Industrialization was accompanied by the expansion of capitalist class processes outside the farm gate and the retreat of capitalist class processes within. The family farm's feudal and ancient class structures changed as the strategies of "making do" and "helping out" evolved. Farm men and women participated increasingly in off-farm work in capitalist enterprises, and capitalist enterprises captured more and more of farm production processes, yet industrial agriculture relied upon and reproduced the growth of non-capitalist (feudal and ancient) class processes and the retreat of capitalist class processes within significant sectors of family farms that remained. For example, this retreat was particularly evident for Midwestern grain crop farmers for whom labor-saving technical change dramatically reduced the need for hired workers or for workers of any kind. Aided by their complex hybrid class structures, these industrial family farms have participated in and shaped the industrialization of agriculture (and vice versa), persisting as non-capitalist entities not in spite of, but because of that industrialization.

Family farms and the locavore: eat sustainably, exploit locally?

Today, the family farm stands at another crossroads. The shift to local agriculture, like the shift to industrial agriculture during the early decades of the last century, has been one response to crisis in the family farm's class structures. This time, crisis is associated with the contradictions of industrial agriculture. For its advocates, local food offers farmers a respite from the technology treadmill, a market niche sheltered from the ruthless price squeeze driven by corporate-dominated global commodities markets. For consumers, local food promises to remedy the human, environmental, and community ills associated with industrial agriculture's ill-gotten gains of abundant and cheap food.

There is no doubt that the industrial agricultural system is implicated in many of the world's most pressing problems ranging from poverty, hunger, and political unrest to environmental degradation, species loss, and climate change. An alternative system is necessary. It is true that local foods seem to deliver important benefits in many contexts (Martinez et al. 2010). Like the industrialization of agriculture, we would expect the localization of agriculture to be accompanied by contradictions. There are many reasons to temper our enthusiasm for local food, as numerous other authors have pointed out (see for example Allen 2004; Born and Purcell 2006; DuPuis and Goodman 2005; Gray 2013; Guthman 2004, 2008; and Hinrichs 2003). Here, I add to that critique a focus on class analytics and its ramifications. What lessons can we learn from our class analysis of family farms of the past?

First, we need to consider that the class implications of a transition to local foods are likely complex, or at least not automatically desirable. As we have seen, the transition to a capitalist industrial agriculture system has not necessarily been accompanied by a transition to capitalist farming. Nor is it clear that non-capitalist class structures in farming are more desirable or less exploitative than capitalist ones. Food system localization is not concerned directly with farm production itself, but with the circulation, or marketing, of farm commodities. A change in how and to whom agricultural products are marketed will not necessarily be accompanied by a shift to non-exploitative class structures in farm production. Indeed, evidence suggests the opposite.

Unlike industrial agriculture, which favored a shift toward non-capitalist class structures in crop production, a shift toward local markets seems to be favoring the expansion of capitalist class processes in family farm hybrids. This is because those farmers most likely to be able to take advantage of the opportunities offered by direct marketing channels such as CSAs and farmer's markets are those producing agricultural products that for the most part cannot be heavily processed, like corn or soybeans can, into the plethora of products the industrial food system spits out. As a result, these farmers already occupy the margins of the industrial food system, much like their products occupy the margins of supermarkets. These are the products that consumers can already readily identify as food without the help of expensive advertising campaigns and product placements: fruits, vegetables, and livestock products.[3] Local food delivers on a promise: farmers retain more of the value-added in local food because there are fewer opportunities for agribusiness to capture value-creating activities from these farmers in the so-called "short food supply chain."

One of the goals of local foods—boosting the income of local family farms—is therefore likely to be achieved. Agrarian mythology not withstanding, farmers are not philanthropists; they are businessmen. Where does that "value-added" come from on these family farms? In other words, how is the surplus production and appropriation organized? Compared to the massive mechanized monoculture grain farms producing raw material for the sprawling complex of processing and marketing activities that form the industrial food chain, these producers of the so-called "specialty crops" still use labor-intensive production processes and therefore are more likely to rely on hired labor to supplement their own and that of their family members. Hence, family farms participating in local foods economies, unlike industrialized crop farms, are likely to include a capitalist class process along with the feudal and ancient in the family farm hybrid. While the presence of wage workers is not a sufficient condition for the presence of capitalist class processes, it seems likely that these workers are in fact capitalist workers, exploited by their family farmer-employers.[4]

That exploitation has enabled the shift toward local foods, much like the exploitation of farm women and children enabled the shift toward industrial food in an earlier time. In her study of Hudson Valley family farms supplying local foods, Margaret Gray documents the "systematic conditions of treatment, which include meager wages, long hours of difficult manual work, lack of overtime pay, run-down housing, lack of respect, and paternalistic management practices" that characterize the working conditions of the mostly Latino immigrant farm workers on these farms (2013, 5). Not only is farm work among the lowest paid and most strenuous jobs in the United States, it is also among the most dangerous (Bureau of Labor Statistics 2015). The working conditions of farm workers harvesting field crops such as fruits and vegetables are similar to those of farm women and children at the turn of the twentieth century. Indeed, jobs such as these that are low-wage, require little education, lack worker protections, and are seasonal or part time are referred to as feminized occupations. Regardless of their gender, the workers who occupy these positions are "feminized" due to their marginalized, disempowered, and vulnerable status, which both enables and is enabled by their working conditions (Standing 1999). Like the unpaid labor of farm women and children helped subsidize the cheap and abundant food of the industrial food system, now the low-paid labor of farm workers subsidizes local food. Even though local foods proponents advocate for paying the "full cost" of our food, consumers and family farmers are still getting something for free: the surplus labor of their farm workers.

Just as for farm women, various conditions of existence enable and are enabled by this exploitative relationship. Like farm family workers, hired farm workers lack the federally mandated legal protections enjoyed by other workers, including overtime, restrictions on child labor, collective bargaining rights, the right to a day of rest, and in some cases, a minimum wage.[5] Like for farm women in an earlier time, farm workers' isolation—both geographic and social—provides a condition of existence for their exploitation. Most hired crop farmworkers are foreign born, and according to official numbers, about half are undocumented.[6] Language barriers and immigration status, as well as the remote location of farm labor camps, seasonal nature of work, and lack of access to transportation all contribute to farm workers' isolation and vulnerability. As Gray argues, it is a paradox of local food that while its advocates tout the importance of trust and community-building, the family farms supplying local produce rely upon and reproduce the isolation, fear, and lack of community for their farmworkers (2013, 64). These participate in producing the conditions of their exploitation on family farms. Unlike the situation of farm women at the turn of the twentieth century, there is no shortage of people fleeing economic conditions and lack of employment opportunities in their home countries. These conditions contribute to farmworkers' dependence on their farmer-exploiters at the same time that they lack avenues to improve their wages and working conditions. As one of the farmworkers in Gray's study expressed, "Even if the cage is golden, we are still locked up" (ibid.).

In addition to their lack of legal protections, isolation, and overall marginalization, agrarianism is one of the conditions of existence for farmworker exploitation, just as it was for farm women's and children's serfdom. A central component of the agrarian vision is a celebration of individualism, independence, and self-reliance. Our agrarian attachment to farmers therefore renders invisible the exploitative class structures financing the family farm. We maintain the illusion of agency, democracy, and independence for the ancient farmer only if we do not see the farm workforce on which he depends. Agrarianism allows us to conflate the family farm with ancient farm production and view the ancient farmer as the "real" farmer. Farm ownership and management are viewed as somehow distinct from other forms of profit-seeking business enterprises. As Gray argues, the "lack of big profits allows [farmers] an imagined distance from capitalism" (2013, 74). Because we essentialize the ancient class process in family farms, obscuring the capitalist and feudal class processes that coexist with the ancient, we see the family farm as somehow outside of capitalism, allowing local foods proponents to celebrate it as an alternative form of production.[7]

Agrarianism is both a gendered and racialized ideology. Jefferson's vision of agrarian democracy was for white, propertied men only. The existence and expansion of family farms in the United States has been predicated on the dispossession of non-white people from their land. Today, that process continues as dispossessed Mexican farmers become hired farmworkers in the United States. Racialized (and gendered) agrarianism thus assigns the role of farmer to white men and naturalizes his

privileged position of "independence." His non-white, immigrant workforce can then be cast in the role of dependent for whom the farmer is
providing an "opportunity."

Conclusion

Our association of local food with "virtuous consumption" reinforces the
class-blindness embedded in our notion of family farms. Simply purchasing food at a farmer's market or participating in a CSA is enough for us
to feel like we are doing a good deed. Class exploitation is masked by
the conflation of our local family farm with environmental sustainability, community-building, fairness, and social justice. Yet, if our definition of social justice is to include the absence of class exploitation in food
production, developing alternative marketing channels—the local foods
solution—is an imperfect one at best.

While failing to address class exploitation, and even encouraging it,
the local foods solution also participates in foreclosing communal, non-
exploitative alternatives in favor of individual action. Much like industrial
eaters, locavores are individualists: the individual acts of shopping and
eating are valorized over other forms of cooperative labor and social action. Changing one's personal shopping and eating habits is enough to
belong to the "social" movement. We are told that we can eat our way—
individually—to a better world. Complementing this individualism in
consumption is a reverence for the individual in production as well. The
conflation of the ancient class process with a family farm, and the resulting mythology of virtue and independence, remains embedded in local
foods discourses.

A class-based understanding of family farms reveals just how much
they have relied upon and reproduced exploitative class structures—then
and now—as well as gender and race-based oppression. The agrarianism
embedded in our public discourse about food and agriculture across the
ideological spectrum participates in rendering that exploitation invisible.
Because family farms have suffered decline as a result of the industrialization of agriculture, they are often viewed as alternatives to that system.
The analysis above shows that this is not the case. Not only did industrial
agriculture with its associated negative impacts on the health of our food,
our environment, and our communities depend upon the continued existence of family farms and vice versa, but the family farm is something
quite different from the mythical ideal.

Truly knowing our farmer requires revealing the man behind the cur-
tain of agrarianism, expanding our definition of social justice to take
exploitation into account.[8] Alternative food systems are not just about
producing food more sustainably, or increasing the proportion of healthier whole foods in our diets—although these are important goals. A truly
alternative food system also rejects exploitation, subordination, and

inequity in all of its forms and supports and fosters a truly democratic food economy.

While a class analysis reveals the family farm to be an imperfect institutional model for alternative food production, it also reveals that it has been a persistent yet dynamic—not contingent and passive—partially or wholly non-capitalist class structural form. As such, it may nevertheless be used in the service of fostering alternative food production models by helping us to develop an alternative discourse of capitalism, socialism, and what Gibson-Graham refer to as a "politics of economic possibility" (2006b). Gibson-Graham argue for a vision of capitalism that is "uncentered, dispersed, plural, and partial in relation to the economy and society as a whole" (2006a, 259). Likewise, Resnick and Wolff's view of society as a complex and contradictory configuration of economic, political, cultural, and natural processes, including capitalist and non-capitalist class processes, implies ceaseless, open-ended development and change. The centrality of change "necessarily implies that nothing about any social formation is still or stable" and that "the reproduction of the conditions of existence of any particular class relation is always an open question" (Resnick and Wolff 1979, 8). In this way, space is opened to imagine, expect, and identify the presence of non-capitalist entities, including non-exploitative ones, in society today and to ask new questions about their role in social change. No longer is capitalism an all-encompassing monolith that must be changed all at once or not at all. With non-capitalist spaces opened up, the possibilities for effective political and economic interventions are thereby multiplied. With such a perspective, non-capitalist forms of agricultural production—including family farms—become viable and visible on their own terms, rather than solely in relation to capitalism. Imagining capitalism and the family farm in this way moves us down the path toward imagining and creating not only non-capitalist, but also non-exploitative entities and a more just alternative agriculture economy.

Notes

1 This "agricultural exceptionalism" survives today. Agricultural workers are exempt from the minimum wage, overtime, and youth employment standards established by the Fair Labor Standards Act of 1938. While non-family workers in agriculture have succeeded in winning some of these protections, there is still no minimum wage, no overtime, and no age restrictions for youth employed on their parents' farms. See "Handy Reference Guide to the Fair Labor Standards Act" at www.dol.gov/whd/regs/compliance/hrg.htm#8.

2 Note that USDA figures on farm labor hours count only the production of commercial farm products such as field crops and usually exclude the labor of farm women and children in producing farm products for family use, family income, or for household production.

3 According to the 2007 Census of Agriculture, farms producing fruits, vegetables, and livestock products accounted for 84 percent of direct marketing farms and 87 percent of income from direct sales (Martinez et al. 2010, 21).

4 Hired farm workers account for one-third of all farmworkers in the United States. Self-employed operators and their family members account for the other two-thirds of those working on farms. (USDA Economic Research Service 2015).

5 For a discussion of gendered and racial impacts of New Deal labor legislation, see Mutari et al. (2002).

6 In 2009, 29% of hired crop farmworkers were born in the United States or Puerto Rico, and 68% were born in Mexico. Since 2001, the share of foreign-born hired crop farmworkers who are not authorized to work in the U.S. has been around 50% (USDA Economic Research Service 2015).

7 We also conflate industrial agriculture with capitalism, thus ignoring the ways in which non-capitalist class structures constitute and support the system.

8 In 2012, only 14 percent of principle operators of farms in the United States were women. See "2012 Census Highlights" at www.agcensus.usda.gov/Publications/2012/Online_Resources/Highlights/Farm_Demographics/.

References

Allen, P. 2004. *Together at the Table: Sustainability and Sustenance in the American Agrifood System*. University Park: Penn State University Press.

Born, B., and M. Purcell. 2006. "Avoiding the Local Trap." *Journal of Planning Education and Research* 26: 195–207.

Bureau of Labor Statistics. 2015. "National Census of Fatal Occupational Injuries in 2014." http://www.bls.gov/news.release/cfoi.nr0.htm (accessed October 1, 2016).

Cochrane, W. 1993. *Development of American Agriculture: A Historical Analysis*. Minneapolis: University of Minnesota Press.

DuPuis, M., and D. Goodman. 2005. "Should We Go 'Home' To Eat? Toward a Reflexive Politics of Localism." *Journal of Rural Studies* 21: 359–71.

Fink, D. 1992. *Agrarian Women: Wives and Mothers in Rural Nebraska, 1880–1940*. Chapel Hill: The University of North Carolina Press.

Fraad, H., S. Resnick, and R. Wolff. 1994. *Bringing It All Back Home*. London: Pluto Press.

Ganzler, M. 2014. "What Small Farms Actually Need Will Surprise Even Locavores." *The Huffington Post*. October 1. http://www.huffingtonpost.com/maisie-greenawalt/what-small-farms-actually_b_5907610.html (accessed October 1, 2016).

Gibson-Graham, J. K. 2006a. *The End of Capitalism (As We Knew It): A Feminist Critique of Political Economy*. Minneapolis: University of Minnesota Press.

———. 2006b. *A Postcapitalist Politics*. Minneapolis: University of Minnesota Press.

Gray, M. 2013. *Labor and the Locavore: The Making of a Comprehensive Food Ethic*. Berkeley: University of California Press.

Greenhouse, S. 2015. "Farm Labor Groups Make Progress on Wages and Working Conditions." *New York Times*. July 3. http://www.nytimes.com/2015/07/04/business/economy/farm-labor-groups-make-progress-on-wages-and-working-conditions.html (accessed October 1, 2016).

Guthman, J. 2004. *Agrarian Dreams*. Berkeley: University of California Press.

———. 2008. "'If They Only Knew': Color Blindness and Universalism in California Alternative Food Institutions." *The Professional Geographer* 60 (3): 387–97.

Halweil, B. 2002. *Home Grown: The Case for Local Food in a Global Market.* Washington, DC: Worldwatch Institute.

Hinrichs, C. 2003. "The Practice and Politics of Food System Localization." *Journal of Rural Studies* 19 (1): 33–45.

Hoppe, R. 2014. *Structure and Finances of U.S. Farms: Family Farm Report, 2014 Edition.* Washington, DC: USDA Economic Research Service.

Levin, K. 2004, "Enterprise Hybrids and Alternative Growth Dynamics." Ph.D. dissertation, Department of Economics, University of Massachusetts, Amherst.

Martinez, S., et al. 2010. *Local Food Systems: Concepts, Impacts, and Issues.* Washington, DC: USDA Economic Research Service.

Mutari, E., M. Power, and D. Figart. 2002. "Neither Mothers nor Breadwinners: African American Women's Exclusion from U.S. Minimum Wage Policies, 1912–38." *Feminist Economics* 8(2): 37–61.

Nabhan, G. 2002. *Coming Home to Eat: The Pleasures and Politics of Local Food.* New York and London: W. W. Norton & Company.

Pyle, G. 2005. *Raising Less Corn More Hell.* New York: Perseus Books Group.

Ramey, E. 2014. *Class, Gender, and the American Family Farm in the 20th Century.* London and New York: Routledge.

Resnick, S., and R. Wolff. 1979. "The Theory of Transitional Conjunctures and the Transition from Feudalism to Capitalism in Western Europe." *Review of Radical Political Economics* 11 (30): 3–22.

———. 2009. "The Class Analysis of Households Extended: Children, Fathers, and Family Budgets." In *Class Struggle on the Home Front: Work, Conflict, and Exploitation in the Household,* G. Cassano, ed., 86–115. London and New York: Palgrave Macmillan.

Riney-Kehrberg, P. 2005. *Childhood on the Farm: Work, Play, and Coming of Age in the Midwest.* Lawrence: University Press of Kansas.

Standing, G. 1999. "Global Feminization Through Flexible Labor: A Theme Revisited." *World Development* 27 (3): 583–602.

USDA Economic Research Service. 2015. "Farm Labor Briefing Room." http://www.ers.usda.gov/topics/farm-economy/farm-labor/background.aspx#Numbers (accessed November 18, 2015).

Walker, M. 2012. "Contemporary Agrarianism: A Reality Check." *Agricultural History* 86 (1): 1–25.

29 A long shadow and undiscovered country

Notes on the class analysis of education

Masato Aoki

Introduction

Amid the resurgent emphasis on students' non-cognitive skills as predictors of educational and labor market outcomes (Heckman and Rubinstein 2001; Heckman 2011), "grit" has emerged as a focal point of education research and policy discussion (Tough 2009, 2012, 2014, 2016; Duckworth and Gross 2014; Duckworth 2016). According to the "grit hypothesis," students' lack of self-control, resilience, tenacity, and perseverance can put them at risk, and the task of teachers and schools is to help students develop their grit. Further, as long as this ultimately crucial factor goes unaddressed, structural reforms in U.S. public education—market choice, testing, accountability—are unlikely to improve academic performance. Even at the college level, at-risk students are vulnerable to grit deficits. To help such students, Tough and others urge faculty members and student support staff to strategically deploy extra classes, confidence-affirming text-messaging, and other resources to "get inside the mind" of college students and help them develop a "new sense of identity," so that "germs of self-doubt" do not "metastasize" into crises (Tough 2014).[1]

From a Marxian perspective, grit advocates like Tough are a revealing symbol and mirror. As a symbol, Tough represents the continued hegemony of an economistic view of education, a view entrenched since the early 1980s, when *A Nation at Risk* (U.S. Department of Education 1983) declared that the U.S. public education system was failing to produce a world-class labor force at a time of intensifying global competition. Tough's rationale for actively developing the non-cognitive capabilities of at-risk students is unabashedly economistic:

> Beyond the economic opportunities for the students themselves, there is the broader cost of letting so many promising students drop out, of losing so much valuable human capital…And it is hard to imagine that the nation can regain its global competitiveness, or improve its level of economic mobility, without reversing them.
>
> (2014)

As a mirror, Tough reminds us of the prescience of Samuel Bowles and Herbert Gintis's classic *Schooling in Capitalist America*, which included the argument that the structural relation of the formal education system to the capitalist class structure made the reproduction of certain non-cognitive attributes critical to the maintenance of the economic system. Moreover, Tough's "human capital" rationale has a Marxian analogue: a core concern with capitalist productive labor. Indeed, productive labor has long served as an essence in the Marxian discourse on education, and in the last four decades Marxists and postmodernists alternatively embraced, rejected, and returned to capitalist labor as an analytical focus.

The long shadow cast by *Schooling* is its contradictory effects on the long-term trajectory of the Marxian analysis of education: namely, the essentialist oscillation around education's reproduction of capitalist productive labor and, ultimately, the restrictive narrowing of the broad theoretical and political project of understanding class-education relationships. In contrast, overdeterminist class theory, the alternative approach to Marxian analysis led and inspired by Stephen Resnick and Richard Wolff, sheds light on the vast analytical domain—the undiscovered country—existing outside the capitalist labor silo. By applying specific class categories and an expansive, anti-essentialist logic, overdeterminist class theory analyzes the mutual constitution between the cultural process of education and the class process. This approach treats the innumerable education-class interactions as the contradictory results and causes of the countless and distinctive configurations of political, cultural, natural, and economic processes. The expansiveness of the overdeterminist class theory of education results also from a conceptual specificity that is structured by categories and distinctions such as class versus non-class process, productive versus unproductive labor, fundamental versus subsumed class process, and capitalist versus non-capitalist class process/structure.

The long shadow of *Schooling in Capitalist America*

Bowles and Gintis's own focus on non-cognitive traits begins with a critique of "IQism," the view that the distribution of educational merit—measured in grades, degrees, etc.—reflects the distribution of intelligence. They argue that grades reward punctuality, obedience, and self-control more than test-measured intelligence (Bowles and Gintis 1976, 102–24). The overall argument of *Schooling* reframes non-cognitive traits—and their correlation to parental income—within a Marxian theory of the capitalist economy's need for a reliable workforce conforming to a capitalist division of labor (Bowles and Gintis 1976, 26–36).

Bowles and Gintis argue that securing a compliant labor force requires a segmented education system that confounds true meritocratic functioning while maintaining the appearance of a functioning meritocracy (Bowles and Gintis 1976, 81–84). The educational system thereby provides crucial supports—political and cultural as well as economic—to capitalist production and exploitation. The fundamental mechanism is a set of structural correspondences among (1) the political relations of the school and the workplace, (2) the reward structures in education and the labor market, and (3) the capitalist economic division of labor and the educational division of labor-reproduction (Bowles and Gintis 1976, 125–48).

The focus on the reproduction of productive labor results in part from the rhetorical tack of *Schooling*. Bowles and Gintis present their analysis as a Marxian response to a liberal puzzle: Why can't the educational system make good on its "promise" to perform all three of its great functions in the U.S. capitalist democracy? First, education should *develop* the skills and creativity of the youth. Second, it should *integrate* youth and immigrants into the economic, political, and cultural mainstream. Third, as the "Great Equalizer," education should perform its *egalitarian* function by equalizing opportunity (Bowles and Gintis 1976, 21–2).

Whereas liberals regard the three functions as mutually compatible, Bowles and Gintis argue that the educational system's structural relationship to the capitalist class structure determines the dominance of the integrative over the developmental and egalitarian functions. That is, the integrative function determines which forms of knowledge are developed and which segments of the population receive which kinds of development. Therefore, mass public education develops the skills and trainability of industrial workers and sorts other students into paths of a hierarchical higher education system, so capitalists can meet their "knowledge work" needs in finance, law, information technology, and so on. Parents with the means can augment their own child's public education through sizable private donations (Kozol 2005, 46–9) or enroll their children in private schools, thereby providing privileged access to the most elite and prospect-enhancing undergraduate and graduate institutions. Income and wealth thus impact individual educational and economic outcomes. But *Schooling*'s primary contribution is the larger social-economic context of this influence, namely, the myriad ways in which the educational system is structured to correspond to the complex needs of the capitalist division of labor. Though schools develop the skills and motivations of the entire labor force, the most important to capitalism is the reproduction of productive labor-power (Bowles and Gintis 1976, 53–84).

While the developmental function—divided, allocated, and contoured by the integrative function—is critical to laborers' *ability* to perform productive labor, the reproduction of their *willingness* to perform labor under capitalist conditions is where Bowles and Gintis make their most well-known contribution to the Marxian analysis of education. According to the "correspondence principle," the hierarchical structure of order-giving and order-taking in capitalist firms is replicated in schools, where children learn, through a system of grading and sorting, the rules that dictate rewarded behaviors. In other words, schools are structured to inculcate in youth and immigrants a certain understanding of the capitalist rules of the game, so they can repopulate a labor force that must perform productive labor within the structure of capitalist political relations (Bowles and Gintis 1976, 125–31). The school is where students learn punctuality, how to take direction, self-discipline, and that they do not possess ownership rights to the school's instruments (computers, books, lab and sports equipment) or the students' own outputs (exams, papers, projects).

On the other hand, wage laborers do have the right and the freedom to sell their labor-power. According to Bowles and Gintis, a primary objective of education is to reinforce workers' willingness to participate in capitalism as sellers of labor-power and performers of productive labor, and an important mechanism is the legitimization of education's role in a meritocratic system, in which (1) schools provide all children with a fair opportunity to apply their intelligence, creativity, and work ethic (including grit) to achieve as much educational merit as they will and (2) the capitalist labor market objectively and efficiently rewards educational merit with an appropriate place in the economy (Bowles and Gintis 1976, 92–100).

The hegemony of the meritocratic ideology is crucial in U.S. capitalism because a broad faith in meritocracy is a fundamental and overarching motivator for students to internalize the hierarchical rules and the extrinsic reward system of the school and capitalist economy. In addition, the ideology of meritocracy legitimizes the distribution of income and wealth, supports faith in the equality of opportunity for mobility, and encourages competitive participation in education so that education can perform its specialization and sorting functions (Bowles and Gintis 1976, 125–48). Indeed, the educational system's success in legitimizing meritocratic outcomes is reflected in the seeming eclipse of class struggle by economic sport; that is, competitiveness in school and the economy overshadows the class-oriented awareness of and political action against exploitation, the struggle over shares of extracted surplus value, and the concern over the class structure's impact on economic well-being, stability, and growth.

In *Marxism and Educational Theory* (2008), Mike Cole characterizes the critical role of *Schooling in Capitalist America* in the British scholarship on education. By the time of *Schooling*'s publication in 1976, the New Sociologists of Education (NSE)[2] had established a research agenda that focused on the political aspects of meaning construction. However, the NSE lacked a political-economy framework that could inform their analysis. Bowles and Gintis provided this framework. Indeed, *Schooling*, especially its correspondence principle, was deeply influential in the Open University curriculum on education and was added—along with Louis Althusser (1971), Michael Young (1971), Paulo Freire (1970), and Paul Willis (1977)—to the canon comprising what Glenn Rikowski termed the "Classical Age of Marxist Education Theory: 1970–82" (cited in Cole 2008, 33, 144).

The intervention of Bowles and Gintis's analysis had major contradictory effects for the Marxian analysis of education. First, its underlying structuralism added repulsive force to the NSE's anti-structuralist shift. The NSE represented a "radical departure from traditional sociological concerns with functionalist explanations (how schools and other institutions 'function' to maintain cohesion in societies)" (Cole 2008, 32). Postmodernists, too, rejected *Schooling*'s reproduction orientation for its "mechanistic and overly determined" cause-effect relationship:

> reproduction accounts of schooling have continually patterned themselves after structuralist-functionalist versions of Marxism which stress that history is made "behind the backs" of the members of society. The idea that people do make history, including its constraints, has been neglected.
>
> (Aronowitz and Giroux 1985, 70)

> Consequently, there has been an overemphasis on how structural determinants promote economic and cultural inequality, and an underemphasis on how human agency accommodates, mediates, and resists the logic of capital and its dominating social practices.
>
> (ibid, 90)

Similarly, Madan Sarup argued that "structuralists tend to stress domination and constraint, the power of the dominant ideology; the emphasis is always on the integrative, functionalist, adaptive, *deterministic* features" (1983, 147). More recently, Rikowski's critical summary of postmodernist objections to Marxian class analysis includes that the base-superstructure model's "determinism leaves no theoretical space for class struggle and engenders fatalism" (Cole 2008, 34).

The suffocation of struggle, as the critics saw it, engendered a twofold reaction to reproduction theory. First, following Paul Willis (1977), Stanley Aronowitz and Henry Giroux supported combining Marxist reproduction theory with "resistance theory," which analyzes acts of resistance within schools by educators and students against the dominant reproductive dynamics. Resistance theory "emphasizes the importance of human agency and experience as the theoretical cornerstones for analyzing the complex relationship between schools and the dominant society" (Aronowitz and Giroux 1985, 71).[3]

The second reaction to *Schooling*'s structuralism resulted in the blurring of Marxian theory's class focus. Postmodernist theorists of education argued for a radical openness toward multiple interpretations of education's social position and cultural role, and they based this move on various objections to Marxian approaches. In "Marxism, Class Analysis, and Postmodernism," Dave Hill, Mike Sanders, and Ted Hankin catalog the postmodernist criticisms as follows:

> 'class is dead'; 'we live in a classless society'; 'class identity and affiliation are archaic formulae'; 'relations of production have been

superseded in political, educational and social importance by relations of consumption'; 'we live in a postmodern and post-Fordist society and economy'; 'there is no class struggle'; and the notion that
'political and educational practices and theories of class struggle are
totalitarian, oppressive of other social groups, and doomed to failure'.
(2002, 159)

For postmodernist critics, Marxian class analysis had become unnecessary and domineering, like an odor-masking perfume: unnecessary because finance capital and merchant capital had replaced industrial capital
as the principal offender in contemporary capitalism and domineering
because it takes up too much discursive and analytical space relative to
other, non-class analyses.

Hill et al. mount a defense of Marxian analysis, but their definition
of what needs defending further diffused the scope of class analysis.
They argue that "a Marxist analysis and understanding of social class
is crucially significant for an understanding of contemporary capitalism." Specifically, Marxist analysis is necessary for explaining injustice
in its diverse dimensions: income inequality and poverty, health issues
(especially teenage pregnancy and accidental death), unemployment, and
savings and wealth disparities. The authors present data on these dimensions to demonstrate that Britain is not a "classless" society (Hill et al.
2002, 160–61).

To those who never stopped finding Marxian class analysis useful in
economic and social analysis, the claimed necessity to argue "class still
matters" is startling. Nonetheless, the argument by Hill et al. is instructive with regard to the shifts occurring within the Marxian analysis of
education. Referring to the postmodernist theorists of education as the
"neo-Marxists," Cole was one of the early critics of reproduction theory
who later found that "by the late 1990s the neo-Marxist pendulum had
swung too far in the cultural direction and too far away from the structuralist" (Hill et al. 2002). The instructive point: the postmodernist reaction to
reproduction theory led to a retreat from political economy in general and
class in particular, and subsequent defenses of Marxism have vitiated the
concept of class used by education theorists, arguing that Marxian theory
is necessary to explain (1) the class-related advantages enjoyed by those
in the small tail of the distributions of property, power, "cultural back-
grounds and aspirations," and connections and (2) the resulting inequities
measured in terms of income, wealth, health, and employment.[4]

The proliferation of Marxism's explanatory tasks and the diffuse definition of class have led some to call for narrowing the focus of analysis.
In particular, Cole recommends that "we dissolve Marxist sociology of
education altogether and develop an understanding of the schooling/cap-
italist economy relation around the material concept of labor power—to
return to Marx in order to develop a Marxist educational theory of the

twenty-first century" (Cole 2008, 35). In addition, Rikowski enlists himself in Michael Hardt and Antonio Negri's (1994, 4) army of "dinosaurs" who remain steadfast in their commitment to Marxian analysis and priorities (Hill et al. 2002, 17). Why does Rikowski find Marxian theoretical categories still necessary?

> Marxist theory affords potentialities for articulating a multitude of forms of oppression in relation to people of color, women, gays and lesbians, and other social groups de-valued by capitalist society. Furthermore, Marxism expresses, theoretic-politically and empirically, the dynamics of social class as the form of oppression within capitalist society that is constituted by its own development. Marxist theory also allows me to perspectivize gender, 'race' and other forms of oppression through the lens of social class. Finally, it articulates the fragility of capitalist oppression.
>
> (Rikowski 2002, 16)

Rikowski thus advocates a rededication to the "materialist" analysis of capital and, specifically, "the role that labor power (human capital) plays in society, the generation of value and profit, the social production of labor power and the role that education plays in this productive form" (2002, 22).[5] The reaffirmation of class analysis is "the first and most important critical moment":

> explaining the social existence of phenomena by exploring the social forms they attain in capitalist society and their relations within a developing totality. In the case of capitalism, this totality is nothing less than the social universe of capital whose substance is value. The fact that education and training play a role in the creation of value, through the laborer's labor power, fixes these as processes constitutive of this social universe.
>
> (Rikowski 2002, 23)

In effect, Cole and Rikowski propose using labor-power as the conceptual standard-bearer and beacon for a Marxian theoretical project that has lost its way.

Rikowski also argues that contemporary economic and political conditions warrant the focus on labor-power. In particular, the implementation of the neoliberal agenda—marketization, privatization, and the penetration of capital into schools and colleges—has resulted in the "heavy managerialism, bureaucratization and regulation of education" (2002, 19). The prime underlying motive: "the drive to reduce education and training to labor power production 'on the cheap'" (ibid). Cole agrees, adding that globalization intensifies the pressure on capitalists to secure "labor power with more human capital than their competitors." This intensified pressure "is apparent in the global drive to privatize schooling, both in order to increase profits from the schooling process itself...and in the attempt to massively increase capitalist control over the form and content of schooling" (Cole 2008, 35). For Rikowski and Cole, the centrality of labor-power makes education as a site and educators and students as agents critical to fundamental social transformation.

In sum, since the 1970s, Bowles and Gintis's classic study incited an anti-structuralist reaction and a postmodernist critique that resulted in the diffusion of class analysis. The resulting drift from class inspired a call to regroup behind the concept of productive labor-power. The gravitation toward labor-power is understandable for theoretical, political, and cultural reasons. However, while labor-power is a distinctive concept in Marxian theory—indeed perhaps because of this status—education's reproductive role has overwhelmed the Marxian imagination of education's significance in constituting a social formation's class structure. An important consequence is the narrowing of the field of battle and the limiting of the potential contestants. For example, in the work of Aronowitz and Giroux, Cole, and Rikowski, the key political agents are teachers as labor-power reproducers and students as embryonic bearers of labor-power. We thus see *Schooling's* long shadow—the profound influence it has exerted on the trajectory of theoretical development, namely, confining the Marxian analysis of education to the analytical silo of the reproduction of capitalist labor-power.

Undiscovered country: the expansive domain of the overdeterminist class analysis of education

That the Marxian analysis of education has been tethered to the reproduction of capitalist productive labor-power is visible from the perspective of overdeterminist class theory, which combines two fundamental theoretical commitments. First, overdeterminist class theory is committed to the entry point concern over the qualitative and quantitative dimensions of surplus labor production, appropriation, and distribution, the class struggles over these objects, and the interaction between class and non-class objects and struggles. Second, the logic of overdetermination and contradiction fundamentally commits the analysis to a methodological openness toward all cultural, political, natural, and economic concerns. Therefore, overdeterminist class theory would regard the entry point concerns of the New Sociology of Education and postmodernists—political aspects of meaning construction, the multiplicity of meanings, agency, and resistance—as existing in overdetermination with its own class-focused entry point. It is in the particular manner that overdeterminist class theory navigates the expansive methodological openness and the specific analytical focus on class processes and structures that we can define the vast domain of analysis of class-education interactions. The conceptual specificity is structured by categories and distinctions such as class versus non-class process, productive versus unproductive labor, fundamental versus subsumed class process, and capitalist versus non-capitalist class process/structure.

In analyzing education-class interactions, overdeterminist class theory begins by identifying the exploitative and non-exploitative ways in which class occurs and proceeds to investigate the nature of the mutual constitution between the class processes and the myriad non-class processes, including education—defined here as the cultural process of systematically producing and disseminating meanings. Following Marx's analysis in *Capital,* volume 1, the endless list of non-class processes begins with the conceptual building blocks of exploitative class relations: production, sale, purchase, and consumption of use-values; reproduction of labor-power as a commodity; consumption of labor-power; direct laborers' production of commodities; and realization of surplus-value. For overdeterminist class theory, Marxian class analysis investigates the mutual constitution between these (and progressively more) non-class processes and the production and appropriation of surplus value, which overdeterminist class theory terms the capitalist fundamental class process. The theoretical agenda quickly expands when we break down concepts such as the reproduction of labor-power. Marx begins this analysis with the consumption bundle that laborers need to replenish their working strength and health, which includes procreation and repopulating the labor force. Marx also notes the role of education ensuring that the labor force possesses—generation after generation—the requisite skills and attitudes (Marx 1977, 276 and 719–21).[6]

Certainly, the fascination with education's role in reproducing exploited laborers emerges directly from Marx's conceptual presentation of surplus value. But this fascination should not limit imagination. In the undiscovered country of the overdeterminist class theory of education, capitalist productive labor-power represents but one form of labor, so while the analysis of class-education relationships may begin with the reproduction of capitalist productive labor, it must not get mired there. The analysis of education-class interactions is as far ranging as the infinite ways in which the capitalist class structure exists in overdetermination with labor, production, consumption, technological change, finance, merchanting, state activities, education reforms, feudal and other non-capitalist class structures, and so on. The remainder of the chapter describes the vast analytical terrain by illustrating how overdeterminist class theory can be applied to class-education interactions.

To repeat, overdeterminist class theory would begin by identifying the various modes in which surplus labor is produced, appropriated, distributed, and struggled over. Solo practitioners of various services—law, accounting, psychoanalysis, health care, plumbing, and consulting, to name a few—may engage in the *ancient* class process, in which the performer of surplus labor is also the receiver of its fruits. Farming cooperatives and printing collectives may embody the *communal* class process, in which the surplus labor performers, as a group, are also the appropriators and distributors. Prison labor, prostitution rings, and forced labor of captured stowaways are examples of *slave* labor. Some traditional households[7] and pimp-prostitute relationships may conform to *feudal* class relations, in which the surplus appropriator controls the feudal production in exchange for lending productive resources to and/or protecting the surplus-producer. Moreover, corresponding to the matrix of class structures is an immense array of education processes occurring in multiple sites. Marxian theory would investigate the complex ways in which education reinforces and undermines the various class structures and the contradictory interaction among them. For example, for some the American Dream is to become "my own boss," which may mean either becoming the boss of everyone else or breaking from capitalist employment altogether and becoming an ancient producer-appropriator. Considering the latter case, what notions are systematically produced and disseminated that both motivate capitalist employees to work and save enough so someday they could shift from the capitalist to the ancient class structure, while countering the formation of an explicitly anti-capitalist class consciousness?

Acknowledging that various forms of class process and class structure constitute a social formation, suppose we choose to focus on the capitalist class structure. A Marxian analysis of the capitalist class structure might investigate how education overdetermines the expansion of capital in its various modes: that is, money-lending and merchanting, in addition to the industrial. *Money-lending capitalists* convert a quantity of money capital M into an increased quantity M' (= M + ΔM), where interest comprises ΔM, and they might encourage, through the recruitment of graduates, development of college curricula focusing on Financial Mathematics and Financial Economics. Similarly, merchant capitalists gain ΔM by buying commodities from industrial capitalists at a discounted price, then selling them at a higher, full-labor-value price. *Merchant capitalists* might therefore promote Retail Management as a college curriculum. In short, the class analysis of education should be mindful that the *"industrial capitalist"* mode of valorization, which Marx primarily theorizes in *Capital*, volume 1, is not the only mode. Indeed, capitalist economies increasingly are comprised of "unproductive" modes of valorization—money lending and merchanting—and the class analysis of education must be inquisitive about the education processes in a "post-Fordist" economy seemingly overrun by "financialization" and "Walmartization."

So far, the vastness of the class analysis of education results from the multiple forms of surplus labor production (feudal, slave, ancient, communal, and capitalist) and the various modes of valorization (industrial, money lending, merchant). When we focus on what Marx called the industrial capitalist mode of valorization, we can see the centrality of productive labor. Through the lens of overdeterminist class theory, we can also see that the class analysis of education must be expansive enough to match the complexity of non-class processes that overdetermine the capitalist class process and structure. This is true even when considering the relatively compact activity of capitalist production, which Marx theorizes as the general circuit of industrial capital.

In contrast to money-lending, merchant, and landowning capital, industrial capital seeks valorization through the production and appropriation of surplus value and the exploitation of labor. The path from M to M' must go through the capitalist production process, represented as P in Marx's progression, M–C–P–C'–M'. Figure 29.1 highlights production and the class process; it also contextualizes these two economic processes.

As Figure 29.1 indicates, labor-power (LP) figures centrally in the circuit. During the productive phase (thick arrow), the industrial capitalist's "productive consumption" of labor-power yields a triple result: (1) the labor process results in produced commodities for market sale, (2) the valorization process results in the transference (from means of production, mp, to constant capital, C) and production (by living labor to V + S) of value, so the total commodity value is W = C + V + S, and (3) the capitalist fundamental class process results in the laborers' production and the capitalists' appropriation of the surplus-value, S, embodied in the produced commodities.

Of course, various education processes overdetermine the productive laborers' ability and willingness to participate in the capitalist class process. For example, the direct laborers' production of commodities requires the application of technical knowledge of how to use equipment and materials. This application combines the cultural process of calling forth knowledge of productive skills and the natural processes of transforming materials via mechanical, electrical, chemical, and other processes. In addition, education may support workers' willingness to perform capitalist labor by reinforcing the notion that working is about earning a living and achieving the "American Dream" and not an elemental part of an exploitative and unstable economic system. Certain education processes influence workers' ability to follow their supervisors' directions and instructions—a central concern of Bowles and Gintis's correspondence principle. And education may enhance capitalist laborers' resilience or "grit" in the face of speed-up, intensified monitoring, or overwhelming indebtedness. The principal point here is that, as important as surplus producer is as a class position, it is not the only class position existing in overdetermination with education processes.

The general circuit frames additional class positions and different forms of labor, all variously overdetermined by education. In a corporation, for example, the board of directors occupies two class positions: fundamental class appropriators of surplus value and subsumed class distributors of surplus-value shares. In the capitalist subsumed class process, the board distributes surplus shares to various providers of conditions of surplus-value production and appropriation. The surplus distributors and receivers—all enablers of exploitation—occupy subsumed class positions. Therefore, in addition to the fundamental class struggle over the rate of exploitation, the general circuit also contextualizes capitalist subsumed class struggle, in which surplus distributors and receivers battle over surplus-value distributions and the conditions provided in exchange.

Equation 1, which summarizes the total revenue and expenditure of a capitalist enterprise, provides a framework for analyzing

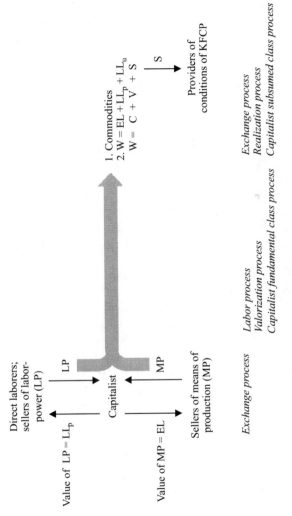

Figure 29.1 Class and nonclass aspects of capitalist commodity production.

fundamental and subsumed class struggles and their connection to education processes[8]:

$$S + SCR + NCR = \sum SC + \sum X + \sum Y \qquad (1)$$

In addition to surplus value (S), the total enterprise revenue includes subsumed class revenues (SCR) paid by other industrial capitalists and non-class revenues (NCR) such as interest paid by employees or non-capitalist institutions. The three expenditure categories on the right side correspond to the type of revenue they secure. $\sum SC$ represents the sum of subsumed class distributions to secure conditions of surplus-value revenue. $\sum X$ consists of expenditures to secure SCR, and $\sum Y$ to secure NCR.[9] We can use equation 1 to analyze various class-education relationships. Seven illustrative examples follow.

First, $\sum Y$ could include expenditures for education processes. For example, webpages may be used to educate employers on the contract terms of a company-provided loan or to instruct customers on how to seek extended warranty support. In these cases, the firm receives NCR in the form of interest payments or a warranty fee. Some of the employees and warranty customers may be productive laborers, for either the firm in question or other firms, but the education process accompanying the webpage would not directly affect surplus production. Therefore, the interest or fee payment would be included in NCR, and the firm's expenditure on webpage development would be part of $\sum Y$.

The next five examples involve the subsumed class process and struggle. To highlight education processes, we will focus on certain subsumed class expenditures: budgets paid to the advertising department (SC_a), dividends paid to the firm's owners or shareholders (SC_o), budgets paid to managers responsible for productive workers' training (SC_t), budgets paid to the research and development division (SC_r), discounts to merchant capitalists (SC_m), and taxes paid to state legislators (SC_s), who provide various conditions including a public education system. Assuming these are the only subsumed class expenditures for our illustrative industrial enterprise, Equation 1 can be expanded as follows:

$$S + SCR + NCR = [SC_a + SC_o + SC_t + SC_r + SC_m + SC_s] + \sum X + \sum Y \qquad (2)$$

In the second example of class-education interaction, a firm may expand its advertising budget to improve commodity sales and surplus realization. The head of advertising may engage in subsumed class struggle with the surplus distributors to secure a larger budget. The advertising chief may also clash with other subsumed class recipients, who are lobbying for their own greater surplus shares. If the advertising, which includes education processes, is aimed at consumers, the additional expenditure would appear in the subsumed class distribution for advertising, SC_a.

In a third example, suppose an equipment-manufacturing capitalist increases its advertising budget to promote sales to other industrial firms, which use the equipment in their own production process. The equipment-purchasing firms would contribute to the selling firm's S and SCR: surplus value because equipment is sold as a capitalist commodity, and a subsumed class revenue because the equipment is used as means of production in capitalist production by another firm. In this case, the equipment manufacturer's promotional effort would include education processes aimed at equipment-buying managers of industrial firms and expenditures would appear in two categories: (a) a subsumed class distribution for sales promotion (SC_a), which is aimed at increasing surplus value, and (b) a non-class expenditure, included in ΣX, to increase subsumed class revenue paid by the equipment-buying firms.

Fourth, suppose a capitalist firm seeks to improve its rate of exploitation by purchasing training services from a consulting firm, which would try to raise worker productivity.[10] The purchasing firm would make a subsumed class payment (SC_t) to the consulting firm, for which the payment would count as both surplus value and subsumed class revenue. As before, the training managers may engage in subsumed class struggle with surplus distributors and with other subsumed class recipients.

Fifth, suppose consulting firm A sells a commodity called "supervisor training" to manufacturing firm B. The trainers instruct supervisors in the use of new worker monitoring equipment. Suppose further that the trainers themselves need instruction in the technology. Firm B's subsumed class expenditure to acquire the supervisor training would appear in both S and SCR of firm A: surplus value because the training is sold as a capitalist commodity, and SCR because the training improves the effectiveness of firm B's supervisory labor. Finally, firm A's expenditure on instruction for its trainers would appear in its ΣX.

Sixth, suppose a few global merchant capitalists become so dominant that they pressure industrial capitalists to cut costs and offer greater discounts, so manufacturing firms must pay a larger SC_m. In other words, merchant capitalist firms such as Walmart prevail in a subsumed class struggle and secure larger surplus shares from industrial capitalists. The increased SC_m represents an additional strain on surplus value: firms must either generate additional surplus value or increase revenue from other sources, or reduce some subset of the remaining subsumed class payments, ΣX, and/or ΣY. Recognizing the vulnerability, major shareholders threaten to sell their shares unless the firm finds some way of addressing the crisis caused by Walmart.

Suppose further that the board of directors of one of the affected manufacturing firms becomes concerned that a significant stock selloff would dampen share prices and therefore threaten both the ability to raise future capital and the directors' continued board membership. The board therefore pressures both the R&D managers to find a productivity-enhancing technology and the training managers to improve worker productivity. The R&D managers and training managers engage in subsumed class struggle over increased surplus shares (SC_r versus SC_t) so they can augment their research and training activities, and both subsumed class receivers pressure the board to lobby for lower state taxes (SC_s) to protest the undertrained workers the public schools are graduating and the underprepared STEM (science, technology, engineering, math) students they are sending to college. Some board members, being also on boards of hedge funds that invest in charter school start-ups and school system management companies, lobby state legislators to expand the eligibility of vouchers to include private, for-profit schools. Expanding the market base of for-profit schools would, in turn, improve the surplus-value potential at schools that operate as capitalist firms.

In a final example, overdeterminist class theory might interpret the educational privatization movement in terms of a struggle between competing class structures, capitalist and feudal. In their theoretical justification of the privatization position, Chubb and Moe (1990) argue that the bureaucratic control exerted by state departments of education, school boards, and unions thwarts improvement in public education. School boards, they continue, enforce union-negotiated work rules, provide access to the means of production (furniture, books, lab equipment, athletic facilities, computers, etc.), and honor the tenure system, which provides teachers with labor protections. According to Chubb and Moe, the imposition of market choice and market-led responses would bring about educational improvement, because choice would allow parent-consumers to signal desired outcomes and lead product development by innovative and profit-seeking education enterprises, all following the neoclassical economic script of consumer sovereignty:[11]

> Schools that fail to satisfy a sufficiently large clientele will go out of business...Of the schools that survive, those that do a better job of satisfying customers will be more likely to prosper and proliferate.
>
> (Chubb and Moe 1990, 33)

For Chubb and Moe, the stagnation resulting from bureaucratic control is analogous to the social and technological stagnation attributed to feudal class societies in medieval Europe and Tokugawa Japan.

From a Marxian perspective, we could interpret the market-choice movement as a protracted attack on the feudal class system of public education by a proliferating array of private for-profit charter schools, for-profit management companies that operate public school systems, and voucher schools, many backed by major foundations and hedge funds.[12] How might we outline a class analysis of U.S. public education as a feudal class structure? Teachers (or "instructors," if we include coaches, music directors, librarians, guidance counselors, etc.) are the feudal producers of surplus labor, which is embodied in instructional services. The school board is the feudal class appropriator and the seller of the feudal output, "public education," to the local government. The local government purchases the output with a budget financed mostly by local property taxes and supplemented by state and federal outlays. The feudal school board appropriators grant the teachers the use of educational facilities and equipment, analogous to the access to land parcels granted by feudal lords. The school board engages in the feudal subsumed class process of distributing shares of the surplus to secure conditions of the instructors' surplus production. One such distribution finances the cost of negotiating with the teachers' union, which provides the condition of labor peace in exchange for a tenure system and a wage-benefit premium. The teachers pay the union a non-class expenditure, membership dues, in exchange for the union's securing of the tenure system and the wage-benefit premium.[13] The tenure system grants labor protections to the teachers; the wage-benefit premium supplements the feudal wage paid by the school board, where the wage is a monetized substitute for in-kind feudal payments made to reproduce the laborers' ability and willingness to perform feudal instructional labor.

Conclusion

The overdeterminist class theory of education seeks to illuminate cultural and political constituents of exploitation as much as economic ones, where the economic conditions are infinitely more extensive than capitalist productive labor. This approach would frame questions that take us far beyond the grit deficits of poor students or the reproduction of only one— albeit special—form of labor. For example, the allure of "being my own boss" might mean occupying a position of power within a corporate hierarchy, but it might also mean producing and appropriating as an ancient or as a member of a collective of producer-appropriators. What configuration of education-class processes might transform the vision and vocabulary of worker-citizens so that they could distinguish between surplus producer and appropriator, capitalist and non-capitalist, and exploitative and non-exploitative? And if the ability to frame such distinctions were to grow, what education processes might make worker-citizens grittier so they can transcend the passivity of "It is what it is" and move toward the dissonance of "We could do better"? And what class and non-class processes condition the forms and purposes of formal education and the endless array of education processes constituting activities such as curriculum development in the liberal arts tradition, advertising, religious ministry, musical training, textbook publishing, union organizing, psychotherapy, and Supreme Court deliberation and ruling?

The overdeterminist class-analytic approach to Marxian theory makes two fundamental theoretical commitments. First, it keeps a vigilant eye on class processes—ancient, communal, capitalist, feudal, and slave— and watches how they shape and undermine non-class processes such as education. Its anti-essentialism commits the analysis to honor the distinctiveness of every non-class process and its contradictory constitution of and by class processes. Second, the logic of overdetermination commits this approach to making sure that, while class-analytic questions are always on the table, other analytical approaches—including those concerned about persistence and resistance, power and meaning, structures and agency—are always at the table, asking questions that reflect their own entry-point concerns and logics.

Notes

1 This strategic focus on non-cognitive skills has incited reactions from the cognitive knowledge corner (Hirsch 2013; Meyer 2013; Willingham 2013) and clinicians who object to basing a pedagogical approach on therapeutic techniques (Osgood 2012).
2 See Wexler (1987) for a critical review of the New Sociology of Education.
3 For an analysis of the anti-structuralist critique—which implicated Althusser—and the essentialism-bound response it spawned, see Aoki (1994).
4 See Resnick and Wolff (1987), especially Chapter 3, for a discussion of the different concepts of class prevalent in the Marxian tradition.
5 We should note that "labor power" and "human capital" are specific concepts in radically opposed economic theories, so treating them as synonymous runs the risk of blurring important theoretical and political purposes.
6 In passing, we should note education's role in shaping productive laborers' (and others') desire for goods and their susceptibility to preference manipulation through advertising, which is an education process distinct from formal education. Education processes play a contradictory role here, as elsewhere: through advertising, capitalist firms want to encourage workers' consumption, because demand supports realization and exploitation; but to minimize wage costs, capitalists want to limit the use-values included in the necessary consumption bundle, because the value of that bundle overdetermines the value of labor-power and the wage. See Wolff and Resnick (2012, 170, 178, and 250).
7 See Fraad et al. (2006) for an analysis of feudal class relations in households. Other contributors to the *Rethinking Marxism* project have added significantly to our understanding of the analytics of noncapitalist class processes and structures. For example, see Kayatekin (2001, 2009) on feudal class structure, Feiner (1988) on slave class structure, and Amariglio (2010) on communal class structure.
8 See Resnick and Wolff (1987, Chapter 4, and 2012, Chapter 4) for a systematic analysis of the class/nonclass revenues, expenditures, and struggles.
9 A non-capitalist enterprise may make payments constituting non-capitalist subsumed class revenue if it acquires conditions of non-capitalist surplus labor production. For example, if a shipping firm replaces an engine in a ship that enslaves stowaways (Urbina 2015a, b) the payment to the engine manufacturer would constitute a slave subsumed class distribution by the shipping company and a slave subsumed class revenue (included in SCR) for the engine manufacturer. Again, the analysis of education processes must match the complexity of the class analysis.
10 See Aoki (1994, Chapter 3) for an analysis of the various ways capitalist firms may secure educational conditions of the capitalist fundamental class process.
11 See Aoki and Feiner (1996) for a critical analysis of Chubb and Moe's neoclassical, consumer sovereignty argument.

12 See Ravitch (2014, Chapter 3) on the involvement of major foundations and hedge funds.
13 See Annunziato (1990) for a class analysis of trade unions and "commodity unionism."

References

Althusser, L. 1971. *Lenin and Philosophy and Other Essays*. Trans. B. Brewster. New York: Monthly Review Press.

Amariglio, J. 2010. "Subjectivity, Class, and Marx's 'Forms of the Commune'." *Rethinking Marxism* 22 (3): 329–44.

Annunziato, F. 1990. "Commodity Unionism." *Rethinking Marxism* 3 (2): 8–33.

Aoki, M. 1994. "Education and the Economics of Class: A Critical Alternative to Political Economy Approaches." Ph.D. dissertation. Department of Economics, University of Massachusetts, Amherst.

Aoki, M., and S. Feiner. 1996. "The Economics of Market Choice and At-Risk Students." In *Assessing Educational Practices*, W. Becker and W. Baumol, eds., 75–98. Cambridge: MIT Press.

Aronowitz, S., and H. Giroux. 1985. *Education under Siege: The Conservative, Liberal, and Radical Debate over Schooling*. South Hadley: Bergin & Garvey.

Bowles, S., and H. Gintis. 1976 (2011). *Schooling in Capitalist America*. New York: Basic Books.

Chubb, J., and T. Moe. 1990. *Politics, Markets, and America's Schools*. Washington, D.C.: Brookings Institution.

Cole, M. 2008. *Marxism and Educational Theory: Origins and Issues*. New York: Routledge.

Duckworth, A. 2016. *Grit: The Power of Passion and Perseverance*. New York: Scribner.

Duckworth, A., and J. J. Gross. 2014. "Self-Control and Grit: Related but Separable Determinants of Success." *Current Directions in Psychological Science* 23 (5): 319–325.

Feiner, S. 1988. "Slavery, Classes, and Accumulation in the Antebellum South." *Rethinking Marxism* 1 (2): 116–41.

Fraad, H., S. Resnick, and R. Wolff. 2006. "For Every Knight in Shining Armor, There's a Castle Waiting to be Cleaned: A Marxist-Feminist Analysis of the Household." In *New Departures in Marxian Theory*, S. Resnick and R. Wolff, eds., 159–95. London: Routledge.

Freire, P. 1970. *Pedagogy of the Oppressed*. New York: Continuum.

Hardt, M., and A. Negri. 1994. *Theory Out of Bounds*. Minneapolis: University of Minnesota Press.

Heckman, J. 2011. "The Economics of Inequality: The Value of Early Childhood Education." *American Educator* 35 (1): 31.

Heckman, J., and Y. Rubinstein. 2001. "The Importance of Noncognitive Skills: Lessons from the GED Testing Program." *American Economic Review* 91 (2): 145–149.

Hill, D., M. Sanders, and T. Hankin. 2002. "Marxism, Class Analysis and Postmodernism." In *Marxism Against Postmodernism in Educational Theory*, D. Hill, P. McLaren, M. Cole, and G. Rikowski, eds., 159–94. Lanham, MD: Lexington.

Hirsch, E. D. 2013. Review of Howard Forman, "How Children Succeed: Grit, Curiosity, and the Hidden Power of Character." *Education Next* 13 (1) http://educationnext.org/primer-on-success/, (accessed December 4, 2016).

Kayatekin, S. 2001. "Sharecropping and Feudal Class Processes in the post-Bellum Mississippi Delta." In *Re-Presenting Class: Essays in Postmodern Marxism*, J.-K. Gibson-Graham, S. Resnick, and R. Wolff, eds., 227–46. Durham: Duke University Press.

———. 2009. "Ambivalence of Class Subjectivity: The Sharecroppers of the Post-Bellum Southern USA." *Cambridge Journal of Economics* 33 (6): 1187–1203.

Kozol, J. 2005. *The Shame of the Nation: The Restoration of Apartheid Schooling in America.* New York: Crown.

Marx, K. 1977. *Capital.* Vol. 1. Trans. B. Fowkes. New York: Vintage.

Meyer, P. 2013. "Paul Tough's Grit Hypothesis Doesn't Help Poor Kids." *Education Next.* Dec. 9. http://educationnext.org/paul-tough%E2%80%99s-grit-hypothesis-doesn%E2%80%99t-help-poor-kids/, (accessed December 4, 2016).

Osgood, K. 2012. "Paul Tough Is Way Off-Base. And Stop Saying 'Grit'." *The Chalk Face.* http://atthechalkface.com/2012/09/30/paul-tough-is-way-off-base-and-stop-saying-grit/, (accessed December 4, 2016).

Ravitch, D. 2014. *Reign of Error: The Hoax of the Privatization Movement and the Danger to America's Public Schools.* New York: Random House.

Resnick, S., and R. Wolff. 1987. *Knowledge and Class: A Marxian Critique of Political Economy.* Chicago: University of Chicago Press.

Rikowski, G. 2002. "Prelude: Marxist Educational Theory after Postmodernism." In *Marxism Against Postmodernism in Educational Theory*, D. Hill, P. McLaren, M. Cole, and G. Rikowski, eds., 15–32. Lanham, MD: Lexington.

Sarup, M. 1983. *Marxism/Structuralism/Education: Theoretical Developments in the Sociology of Education.* New York: Falmer Press.

Tough, P. 2009. *Whatever It Takes: Geoffrey Canada's Quest to Change Harlem and America.* New York: Mariner.

———. 2012. *How Children Succeed: Grit, Curiosity, and the Hidden Power of Character.* New York: Random House.

———. 2014. "Who Gets to Graduate?" *The New York Times Magazine*, May 15.

———. 2016. *Helping Children Succeed.* New York: Houghton Mifflin Harcourt.

Urbina, I. 2015a. "'Sea Slaves': The Human Misery that Feeds Pets and Livestock." *New York Times*, July 7.

———. 2015b. "Stowaways and Crimes aboard a Scofflaw Ship." *New York Times*, July 17.

U.S. Department of Education, National Commission on Excellence in Education. 1983. *A Nation at Risk: The Imperative for Educational Reform.* Washington, D.C.: U.S. Government Printing Office.

Wexler, P. 1987. *Social Analysis of Education: After the New Sociology.* London: Routledge & Kegan Paul.

Willingham, D. 2013. "How Children Succeed." Blog. October 29 http://www.danielwillingham.com/daniel-willingham-science-and-education-blog/how-children-succeed, (accessed December 4, 2016).

Willis, P. 1977. *Learning to Labour: How Working Class Kids Get Working Class Jobs.* Farnborough (UK): Saxon House.

Wolff, R., and S. Resnick. 2012. *Contending Economic Theories: Neoclassical, Keynesian, and Marxian.* Cambridge: MIT Press.

Young, M. 1971. *Knowledge and Control: New Directions for the Sociology of Education.* London: Collier-Macmillan.

30 Ecological challenges

A Marxist response

Andriana Vlachou

Introduction

The significance of nature for society has long attracted the interest of economists and social thinkers. Natural resource depletion and pollution have been considered major ecological challenges. In our day, sustainable development is defined in neoclassical environmental economics as development that meets the needs of the present generation without compromising the ability of future generations to meet their own needs, along the lines of the Brundtland report (World Commission on Environment and Development [WCED] 1987, 43). It is realized that pollution and resource depletion threaten sustainability, and so neoclassical economists search for ways to solve these problems. Ecological problems are interpreted as cases of market failures or as the consequence of the complete absence of markets in certain natural resources and conditions. Consequently, most neoclassical economists propose the intervention of the state to establish policies, such as a tax or pollution permits system that will help the perfection of markets or create ones in cases they do not exist, in order to achieve a dynamically efficient use of natural resources and the environment. As neoclassical economics is the dominant economic discourse, actual environmental policies have been indeed suitably justified along these lines.

Neoclassical economists, however, admit that dynamic efficiency is not sufficient to achieve sustainable development. Following utilitarianism and a Rawlsian ethical framework, most of them define sustainability as the state in which consumption is non-declining through time (see, for instance, Hartwick 1977, 1978). Furthermore, they suggest that the concept of sustainability focuses on maintaining production opportunities for future generations and not on bequeathing some fixed quantity of natural capital to future generations. Productive capacity can be maintained, according to neoclassical economists, as long as reduction in natural capital can be balanced by human-made capital so that output and consumption remain non-declining over time. This argument, however, presupposes that there is a significant degree of substitutability between human-made and natural capital. The policies that neoclassical economists propose to satisfy sustainability basically amount to achieving dynamic efficiency and to compensating future generations for natural resource depletion and pollution by bequeathing them human-made capital.

Their proposals, however, have been challenged on several grounds (Daly and Townsend 1996; Daly and Farley 2004; Foster 2000). Substitution possibilities between natural and human-made capital have been questioned. Issues of irreversible consequences of human activities on life support systems have been raised. The utilitarian focus of the neoclassical approach has been challenged in terms of its assumptions about human values and preferences and its implications for assessing cost and benefits of environmental goods and services. The assumption of rational, optimizing behavior on the part of individuals, for example when they discount the future, is also disputed. The approach of neoclassical economics to issues of intra- and inter-generational justice has been presented as problematic for sustainability.

In this paper, a distinct dialectical, value-theoretic and class-based approach is developed to respond to ecological challenges, especially to the ecological sustainability question, from a Marxist standpoint. In particular, a distinct perspective is offered from the overdeterminist epistemological position informed by the work of Stephen Resnick and Richard Wolff, above all their book *Knowledge and Class* (1987). In this framework, drawing from my published work, ecological problems in capitalism and adjustments are theorized as inseparably articulated with the process of extracting surplus value.

The structure of this paper is as follows. In the next section, a Marxist theory of knowledge is presented that enables us to approach nature, society and their interaction from an overdeterminist epistemological standpoint. In the third section, a value theoretic and class-based approach is employed to explain ecological degradation in capitalism and the contradictory nature of its greening. In particular, the non-environmentally friendly technological development and the consumerist culture in capitalism, often implicated for ecological problems, are critically inspected. It is explained that the development of science and technology cannot guarantee ecological sustainability in capitalism, since the knowledge produced about nature is not only fragmented and incomplete but also class-biased. In addition, the consumerist culture, analyzed as a "complex product of the capitalist societies," will tend, through its multiple constitution, to jeopardize the greening of capitalism while questioning moral ecological calls on individuals. In the epilogue, some concluding remarks and suggestions for a radical transformation of a capitalist society towards an ecologically defendable socialist society are offered.

Knowledge, nature and society

Marxist theory, as I understand it, produces its own knowledge of the relationship between nature and society by deploying its specific historical materialist standpoint centered on the concepts of overdetermination, contradiction, and class.[1] Overdeterminism perceives reality as an integrated whole of natural and social processes that cannot be reduced to a mere effect of any of its constituent aspects. Human societies meet nature from the inside and through social labor, the latter being itself an overdetermined process constituted by physical and social aspects, transform nature into its historically produced forms.

Human nature itself is constituted by the influences of many natural and social processes in interaction, and in this sense it is produced by means of human nature, in the words of Richard Lichtman (Marx and Engels 1969; Lichtman 1990; Resnick and Wolff 1987; Vlachou 1994, 2005b). The biologists Levins and Lewontin (1985) question the reduction of human individual and social life to some underlying ideal uniformity, called "human nature" that could be revealed in and served by human development. The physiological needs of human beings, as well as their vulnerabilities and ways of coping with the environment, are very similar to those of other mammals, they argue. For example, we share with other mammals the need for food. However, what people eat has been determined by their social position, which itself depends on the whole social organization (Marx 1973). "Hundred-dollar-a-plate dinners sustain the body politic, not the body physical. What begins historically as the act of mere nutrition ends as a totally symbolic one" (Levins and Lewontin 1985, 262). In short, human nature as we know it in historical time has been shaped by the interaction of natural and social processes.

Knowledge(s) about nature cannot be construed as mere representations of nature in thought, as statements about "what is really out there"; they are always mediated by conceptual frameworks (Resnick and Wolff 1987). Different discourses produce different knowledges, different "truths" about nature. Human nature, for instance, is "experienced" and "known" in different ways by medicine, ecology, psychoanalysis, philosophy or art discourses. Knowledges about extra-human nature are the product of the thinking process and as such are not a mirror image of the real (Resnick and Wolff 1987; Vlachou 1994).

Exposed to Kant-Laplace's nebular hypotheses[2] and to Darwin's theory of evolution,[3] Marx and Engels believed that these theories showed that "nature has a history" and that the natural sciences were themselves evolving from a static conception of nature towards a recognition of its historicity (Edley 1990; Levins and Lewontin 1985; Foster 2000). Transformation of nature is a continuous process. As nature itself is continually changing, thought-concretes of natural processes, species and systems produced by the discourses of natural sciences should be received with caution. They have proven to be incomplete and transitory. As Levins points out, all theories ultimately prove to be inadequate and nature appears stranger than *we* can know (Levins 1990, 115).

Knowledges about nature are then discourse-specific. Such knowledge is produced within diverse and evolving theoretical frameworks (Resnick and Wolff 1987). Observations, facts, empirical results and conclusions arise within a theoretical framework, not prior to theory and not in its absence (Feyerabend 1975, 168). Einstein similarly observed in a letter to Werner Heisenberg (quoted in Broad and Wade 1982) that on principle it is quite wrong to try founding a theory on observable magnitudes alone. In reality the very opposite happens, argues Einstein. Theory decides what we can observe, argues Einstein. Moreover, as Kuhn indicates, "truth" and "proof" are terms with only intra-theoretic application (1979, 256–66).

The development of ecology as a science exemplifies, I believe, the epistemological positions presented above. Trepl (1994) argues that since its emergence ecology has been marked by two fundamental approaches, the holistic and the individualistic concepts, while Levins and Lewontin (1994) challenge Trepl's topography by adding another approach, the dialectical view with which they are associated. These different approaches of ecology conduct different analyses, produce different knowledges of communities and ecosystems, and arrive at different strategy recommendations. In particular, these different ecological theories exert different influences on social theories and policies towards sustainability (Vlachou 2005b).

Levins and Lewontin, informed by Marxism, argue for a dialectical approach that, in my understanding of dialectics, has certain commonalities with Resnick and Wolff's overdeterminist epistemological position.[4] Their ecological view is centered on the idea of the instability and constant motion of systems in the past, present and future and on the notion that the organism is both the subject and the object of evolution. Equilibrium and harmony cannot be assumed to be the normal state of things. Change is an open-ended process. However, the time scales of change differ among species and systems; when they are very slow, a stationary state appears to have emerged. Moreover, organisms do not simply adapt to their environment but they also change it (Levins and Lewontin 1985, 272–88). "Environment" cannot be conceived as a given set of physical conditions but rather needs to be conceived in a dialectical sense as an interpenetration of organisms and environment. In the struggle for survival every living species chooses, transforms and defines its environment: species *construct* their environments. Moreover, such an approach does not require that

> communities and ecosystems are highly integrated 'wholes'; they could also be loosely integrated wholes. Communities and ecosystems as 'wholes' are not bound together by mutual need but by history; the integrating principle which gives the 'whole' its dynamics is the array of opposing processes that link its parts and transform them.
>
> (Levins and Lewontin 1994, 36)

According to the dialectical approach, "ecology does aim to display concrete reality but also to understand it, that is, to display the relation of the particular to the general without doing violence to either." Moreover, "in a dialectical approach, phenomena at the individual, population, community, ecosystem, and biogeographic levels are all equally real, equally 'fundamental,' and mutually conditioning" (Levins and Lewontin 1994, 36–37). Moreover, dialectical ecologists, according to Levins and Lewontin, do not commit themselves on philosophical grounds to the relative roles of the various possible philosophical interactions, such as competition and predation. "And not only because it is an empirical question; competition itself is abstracted from the complex and contradictory relations between the same pair of organisms" (*ibid.*, 38).

With respect to programmatic imperatives, Levins and Lewontin argue that

> the attempt to find such imperatives in nature (outside the contentions of actions, beyond politics) has led to many claims of political ecology which resonate with our moods, but which either dissolve into meaninglessness upon inspection or are simply wrong.
>
> (1994, 39)

These include claims and calls regarding non-substitutability, the fragile resilience of life mechanisms, the rights of other species and habitats, the embeddedness of society in nature and so on.

In many warnings and calls to embed society in nature and to respect the "rights" of other species and habitats, one can actually observe a latent, if not open, naturalistic determinism (Vlachou 1994). Such arguments tend to reverberate with older natural law philosophies that gave rise to beliefs in a "natural order" of the world to which human activity should adjust and in "natural rights" (determined by nature, thus being universal) to be respected. The response of Levins and Lewontin to such arguments is direct and bold:

> The imperative to live as part of nature is empty in one sense: of course, we live as parts of nature, albeit a socialized nature. There is no choice available. The claim that removal of a species could bring the whole edifice crashing down upon us is also not true: there is a redundancy in natural communities, species substitutions are common from one forest to the next and many ecosystems are remarkably resilient in the face of even gross perturbations.
>
> (1994, 39)

With reference to "natural rights," unless one wants to appeal to some form of idealism,[5] rights are social, no matter how socially important it might be to respect other species and natural systems. Thus Levins and Lewontin correctly argue that

> [W]e might be enjoined to respect the rights of habitats. But "rights" are social creations. A group has rights when it asserts them. We may apply notions of rights to natural objects, but that is a choice we make as a protection against uses we consider harmful.
>
> (1994, 39–40)

In the same way, as has been noted before, quite a few people might be willing to respect the right of the AIDS virus to be consistent with an "intrinsic rights" line of argumentation (Grundmann 1991).

For Levins and Lewontin, the search for ecological principles to guide our relations with the rest of nature, the escape from human-based politics into a natural, ecological politics, is futile.

> We have to work out how to live, rather than find answers in natural laws, and since "we" are divided by conflicting interests, that working out is to be reached neither by meditative contemplation of a tropical reef nor by computer-assisted calculation alone, but in political struggle.
>
> (1994, 40)

These epistemological insights set the ground for investigating the political-economic organization of contemporary societies in terms of social divisions and conflicts over the appropriation of nature, resulting in ecological degradation in capitalism experienced and perceived by various subjectivities that, in turn, gives rise to processes and agencies that strive to contain or eliminate ecological problems.

Capitalism and ecological sustainability

Marxist theory, deploying a materialist standpoint, takes society – in particular, the class process – as the point of departure and return for its analysis, not the individual. The class process, the extraction and appropriation of unpaid surplus labor, is the driving force for capitalist production, and its detrimental interchange with nature (Vlachou 2002, 2004). In particular, environmental problems are rooted in the historical patterns of capitalist development that has resulted in increased energy use and related pollution, deforestation, changing land use, changing climate conditions and so forth (see also Burkett 1999; O'Connor 1998; Vlachou 2002, 2004).

Capitalist firms need natural resources and conditions to be available in requisite quantities and qualities, and, if priced, at prices that make profit possible (Vlachou 2002, 2005a, 2005b). Nature also sustains human life and, for that matter, provides elements that are parts of firms' variable capital. Consequently, capitalism cannot be negligent of its natural conditions of existence for long. This argument, however, does not mean that capitalism will necessarily secure its natural conditions of existence, as will be elaborated later.

Following Marx (1991), the value of a commodity is determined by the *regulating conditions* of production, which are the *normal* conditions for industry and the *least favorable* natural conditions for primary sectors, both inclusive of natural aspects. When increased pollution or the depletion of better natural resource bases becomes part of the regulating conditions for a particular sector, it will register as an increase in the value (and price of production) of the commodity, *ceteris paribus*. On the other hand, differences in environmental quality, given the regulating conditions, result in either reduced or surplus profits, which might be appropriated as *differential rents* by the owners of better lands on the basis of their power to exclude producing capitalists from using the lands (Vlachou 2002, 2004).

Changes in prices and differential rents due to increased pollution and scarcity impact, in turn, profits, wages and other class payments. Environmental degradation may also have direct adverse social effects such as discomfort and pain to human and other living species, not necessarily captured by economic categories.

Various conflicts, tensions and changes can be instigated between offenders and various victims of natural degradation (capitalists, landlords, workers, local residents and so forth) because of these negative impacts of environmental degradation and scarcity on profitability, income and life conditions. I have argued elsewhere (Vlachou, 2004, 2005a) that these multiple struggles give rise to environmental regulation and change in contemporary capitalism.

In particular, policies for the appropriation of nature are shaped by *the struggles waged by the workers-citizens*. Striving to protect their physical conditions of life and their standards of living, workers-citizens may turn to the state to set environmental and health safety regulations.

Moreover, the *inter-capitalist struggle or competition* among capitals plays an important role in the shaping of environmental regulation. On the one hand, the capitalist firms adversely affected by pollution tend to confront polluting capitalists and make them control their emissions. They may also turn to the state and demand pollution regulatory institutions and mechanisms. On the other hand, polluting capitalists tend to resist pollution control measures on the ground of cost increases and deteriorating competitive position. However, several capitalist firms are beginning to view environmental issues as an opportunity for entry, change and growth. Properly designed environmental regulation can trigger innovation, which may in part or in full offset the costs of complying and can even lead to absolute competitive advantages in global markets (for a further discussion, see Vlachou 2004, 2005a, 2005b).

The *state* is thus called upon to mediate access to nature. In particular, the state becomes engaged in identifying the "appropriate" level of environmental protection and in establishing different types of regulation, such as emission standards, taxes, permit systems, subsidies and so on. The state actually becomes the site of different struggles over access to nature and has to answer many conflicting demands made upon it. Consequently, state policies tend sometimes to accommodate and other times to restrict the access to nature to certain class and non-class agents (Vlachou 2005a, 2005b).

Pulled and pushed by all these influences and forces, capitalism changes by altering (or creating new) meanings and values, restructuring production and designing anew commodities, i.e., it is becoming more ecologically responsive. Science and technology, in particular, influenced by market forces and state regulation, have started developing new environmentally friendly commodities and promoting conservation, pollution reduction and substitution of man-made capital or renewable resources for exhaustible resources.

An evaluation of specific environmental policies and adjustments from a class standpoint provided in Vlachou (2005a, 2014) and Vlachou and Konstantinidis (2010) revealed that those put in practice in recent decades have been under the strong influence of capitalists. Capitalist firms have attained free initial allocation of permits, extensive exemptions from environmental taxes, revenue recycling and subsidies. In contrast, the poor and the unprivileged not only suffer greater harm from environmental degradation than the wealthy and the privileged, but also incur the regressive impacts of environmental regulation. This implies that current environmental regulation and change take place at the expense of working people. The workers-citizens movements have indeed experienced instances and possibilities for interventions to protect their natural conditions of life, but these did not result in an effective overall influence on their part. This class bias captures in turn the present vulnerable position of labor and other social movements that stand fragmented and disorganized and thus politically ineffectual. The shaping and the application of the EU emissions trading system to mitigate climate change exemplifies these arguments (Vlachou 2005a, 2014).

Can capitalism be ecologically sustainable? The answer to this question depends crucially on the notion of sustainability. The notion of ecological sustainability I would like to apply to capitalism is a "narrow" concept that acknowledges that natural conditions are important for the existence of capital as a social relation. This means that the workings of capitalism will tend to secure these important natural conditions for the capitalist process of surplus labor extraction. On this ground, I consider capitalism to be ecologically sustainable if it can secure the natural conditions and processes necessary for its existence. But an ecologically sustainable capitalism is still capitalism. The arrival of ecological sustainability in capitalism is not expected to reverse the class nature of the system and its many negative effects on working people. In this sense, I try not to conflate an ecologically sustainable capitalism with socialism or any other desirable type of society envisioned by critics of capitalism (Vlachou, 2004, 2005b).

I next turn to showing that the transformation of capitalism to a more environmentally defensible (though still capitalist) alternative is a contradictory process whose outcome is fundamentally uncertain. I first focus on scientific and technological change, which can help in the green restructuring of capitalist firms. I will then return to discuss ecologically favorable changes in values and preferences of individuals against present-day consumerism in the process of greening capitalism.

Scientific research and development

Innovating – "the business of business" according to Hart (1997) – is emerging as a major strategy to respond to ecological problems. Science and technology is implied in the discussions of substitutability, irreversibility, carrying capacity, thresholds and natural limits. For example, absolute scarcity is argued by appealing to the second law of thermodynamics (Daly and Townsend 1996). However, the development of science and technology, invoked to define, analyze and solve ecological problems, can only be uneven, contradictory and class-biased as it is inseparably interwoven with capitalist motives and institutions.[6] Let us further investigate the reasons this is the course of science and technology.

Scientific research and technical development, to my understanding, are relatively autonomous but complex social activities. Knowledge is produced, as mentioned above, within diverse and evolving theoretical frameworks. History matters for scientific and technical change. In particular, research and development is a "path-dependent" social practice in the sense that past developments in science and technology exercise significant influences on current ones. Scientists deploy intellectual resources developed and shaped not only by competing scientific traditions throughout the centuries but also by the contested needs and resources of the wider society. Knowledge is always influenced by social divisions and conflicts in each historical epoch (Freeman 1994; MacKenzie and Wajcman 1999).

Economic considerations directly influence scientific and technical activity. In particular, in contemporary capitalism, firms introduce new technologies with the motive to maximize their profits. By innovating, they increase productivity and reduce costs, thus increasing relative surplus-value. Significantly, the first capitalist firms to innovate are able to reduce their individual unit costs and capture excess profits. At the same time, firms weigh savings in current operating costs against losses on the value of existing machinery and the plant and, thus, they may delay innovation.

However, high cost producers will be driven out of business if they do not soon innovate. Technological change has always been an important element of capitalist competition, as Marx (1991) argued. Interestingly, in complying with environmental regulation, internationally competitive firms, based on innovation, might be able to advance their positions on a global scale at the expense of less competitive firms.

Research and development has become an important economic activity in itself. Firms specialize (or partly invest) in research and development activities with the motive of securing a profit rate as high as that of any other alternative investment. In the cases of long-range research or research with highly uncertain results, as is the case of global warming for example, the costs are often socialized. These kinds of research are funded by government or international public funds, and they are typically undertaken by national institutes, universities, UN organizations and in some cases heavily subsided private companies. When such publicly supported research comes close to producing a commercial product, the final development stages are assumed by private companies in order to realize an exclusive property (see also Levins and Lewontin 1985, 201; Vlachou 2005b).

The work of natural and social scientists is now more than ever conditioned by the entrepreneurial organization of research. It is influenced by the economic goal of the firm, the resources available to the firm, its reward structure, the patterns of professional recognition the research market fosters and so forth. Moreover, the division of labor within science tends to resemble the division of labor in other economic activities.

> The creative parts of scientific work are more and more restricted to a small fraction of the working scientists, the rest are increasingly proletarianized, losing control not only over their choice of problem and approach, but even over their day-to-day, and sometimes, their hourly, activity.
>
> (Levins and Lewontin 1985, 202)

Moreover, important scientific assessment research involving physical knowledge is financed by business in order to comply with regulatory requirements. The fact that most countries also run research programs relating to more general problems identified by ministries' scientific advisory committees appears to create a countervailing force to balance the strong influence of biotechnology interests on such research. However, Butler and Reichhardt (1999) noted that green groups are concerned about the relatively large numbers of government scientific advisers with links to the biotechnology industry in countries such as Britain.

At present, we also experience the commodification of university science, which results from the financial needs of universities (Vlachou 2005b). These needs are fulfilled by research grants from corporations, (less and less) from government agencies and by tuition fees charged to students to be employed mostly by the business sector. Scientists in the universities are being pressured in this context to turn their research in more commercial directions (Butler and Reichhardt 1999). Scientists, obviously, need to publish in time for tenure review, a job hunt or a raise and in journals that confer prestige, which turns out to be practically impossible without funded research projects. Scientists may thus become pragmatists and limit their research agenda to the domain of what is acceptable to the current capitalist social order (Levins and Lewontin 1985, 207).

Given a global capitalist system, the kind, the level and the economic valuation of research and development will depend on the particular market developed for it. In short, the *nature*, the *direction* and the *pace* of technological change are shaped by, among other social factors, the economic aspects (motives and structures) of capitalist firms and markets. These arguments point to the fragmented and incomplete knowledge about nature, which is invoked by many critical advocates of sustainable development, and to its class-biased course in capitalism, about which non-Marxist critics are rather silent.

In particular, in the world of business, the concept of sustainability largely means not the need for preserving nature for future generations in some abstract, all-embracing sense (WCED 1987, for example), but the promotion of profitable ideas of radical change through new technology. Robert Shapiro, the former chairman and CEO of Monsanto Company, for example, maintains that by using information technology and biotechnology, one can increase productivity without abusing nature (Magretta 1997). Significantly, for Shapiro, "far from being a soft issue grounded in emotion or ethics, sustainable development involves cold, rational business logic" (*ibid.*, 81). However, in the process of dealing with certain environmental risks, scientific and technical change following business logic may even create new ones. The case of Monsanto and other genetically modified crops companies reveals the many problems arising from the hasty and unsafe path of development the industry followed in biotechnology that led it to a significant setback (Vlachou 2004). As it is inseparably interwoven with capitalist motives and institutions, the pro-ecological development of science and technology can only be uneven, contradictory, and class-biased.

Human nature, consumerism and ecological ethics

Sustainability can also be secured by changes in the realm of culture, by changes in the values and preferences of individuals towards an ecologically defendable way of life and consumption. Such behavioral change is often based on "a narrative of individual guilt and redemption" (Lohmann 2006, 193) and presupposes methodological individualism – shared both by neoclassical and ecological economics (see, for instance, Daly and Farley 2004).

From a Marxist standpoint, a change in human nature is a possibility in all societies since human nature is neither exogenously given nor reduced to some unchanged natural constants. That is, human nature is socially shaped and therefore ever changing. The rational and productive abilities of individuals, their needs, tastes, preferences and moral values and rules are developed within social contexts. Ecological ethics could then be developed through cultural processes such as education. However, the current social context of capitalist societies tends to cultivate certain personal attributes such as consumerist behavior that are conducive to capitalist class processes, but these may undermine the greening of capitalism.

Based on utilitarianism, neoclassical theory grounds consumerism in the insatiable needs of human beings. This common psychic property (insatiability) of human nature seems to be treated as inherent in human beings by neoclassical economics since needs and preferences are not the subject of its analysis, although they are fundamental for its value/price theory. From our perspective, however, the consumerist culture in modern societies is the "product of social organization" (Wolff 2012).

The consumerist individual is shaped by the economic, political, physical and psychological processes that constitute social life and condition individual life. In the economic sphere, production and circulation play an important role in the shaping of needs and their satisfaction. "Production," Marx observed, "not only supplies a material for the need, but also supplies need for the material" (1973, 92). As production became increasingly dependent on internal combustion engines, for example, the need for fossil fuels assumed enormous dimensions. Moreover, capital accumulation leads to extended reproduction – an increasing scale of production. Increasing volumes of produced commodities require expanding markets for profitable production. There is a constant effort on the part of capitalists to discover new use values and to create new needs in order to realize the surplus value produced. Marx included in these efforts

> the exploration of all of nature in order to discover new, useful qualities in things; new (artificial) preparation of natural objects, by which they are given new use values. The exploration of earth in all directions, to discover new things of use as well as useful qualities of the old; such as new qualities of them as raw materials, etc.; the development, hence, of the natural sciences to their highest point; likewise the discovery, creation and satisfaction of new needs arising from society itself.
>
> (1973, 409)

Moreover, he observed that "to each capitalist, the total mass of all workers, with the exception of his own workers, appear not as workers, but as consumers, possessors of exchange values (wages), money, which they exchange for his commodity" (*ibid.*, 419). "He therefore searches for means to spur them on to consumption, to give his wares new charms, to inspire them with new needs by constant chatter, etc." (*ibid.*, 287). Thus, although advertising absorbs a significant portion of surplus value away from accumulation, it ensures the realization of capital in circulation and consequently the continuance of accumulation.

Labor productivity increases with the expansion of capital as production is also technically revolutionized through accumulation. Increased productivity allows for real wage increases and the satisfaction of new needs required for the continuation of profitable expansion. The growth of workers' needs may simply follow the consumption standards already set by capitalists. Such a process of workers' emulation of the ways of life of the dominant class leads us to the political and psychological aspects of consumerism that are important constitutive aspects of contemporary capitalist societies.

The needs of workers in capitalism are determined not only by the physical aspects of existence but also and in crucial ways by the selling of their labor-power and the use values they can obtain by wages earned. They part with the use value of their capacity to labor in exchange for a wage, and consequently their laboring activity confronts them as an alien power under the control of capitalists. Similarly, they have no control over the commodity being produced, which confronts them again as an alien thing. Labor, which is an enabling activity and an expression of human life, appears alien to workers and coerced from them, as a *burden, sacrifice* (Lebowitz 1977–78).[7]

Dispossessed from any means of life except their labor power and deprived of the use value of their labor power, the only way for the workers to sustain themselves is to work for a wage in order to obtain direct possession of commodities (possessed by others) and to appropriate their use value by consuming them. However, while laboring activity is conceived by the worker as an alien power over him, the sphere of consumption appears to him as "the realm of freedom." Worker's inability to exercise creativity, initiative and participation in decision-making in the labor process and social life is presumably compensated through free choices over consumption goods.

However, workers' choices are limited by the income they derive on the basis of their class position. Even if wages were to rise as a result of accumulation, this increase is contained within the reproduction of the exploitative relation between capitalists and workers. As the capitalist world of wealth expands, it faces the worker as an alien world dominating him and increases his/her poverty and personal misery. Moreover, as social standards of consumption are rising, workers' efforts to catch up increase their bonding to capitalist production (Lebowitz 1977–78). Consumerism then, as a cultural process celebrating consumers' freedoms, helps the ideological and political "cementing" of social relations and disposing of individuals into social positions in capitalism.

All the above points to the conclusion that the ecological aspects of commodities' use values may not assume importance in consumption choices rapidly enough, as long as consumerist culture continues to prevail. Consequently, *ceteris paribus*, consumerism will tend to seriously limit the greening of capitalism.

Epilogue

This paper has presented a distinct Marxist response to the current ecological challenges. The negative effects of ecological problems, the enduring conflicts over them and state regulations give rise to environmental adjustments of capitalism. Such a greened capitalism, however, will still be characterized by economic, social and environmental injustices and inequalities. Consequently, ecological transformation that benefits the many and especially the unprivileged cannot be achieved without ending the class divisions of contemporary capitalist societies. Moreover, the possibility of an ecological crisis is not eliminated by the ongoing and prospective environmental adjustments of capitalism. This is because the complex interaction of the ecological, economic and social aspects of capitalist societies gives rise to old and new contradictions, including ecological ones, rendering the ecological adjustments and potentials of capitalism uncertain.

Eco-socialists work hard to build their distinct visions for an ecologically defendable socialist society. Commitment to this cause is an ethical and aesthetic judgment emerging out of our constitution as "products" of the exploitative societies in which we were born and live and rebel against, albeit in different and conflicting ways. For many socialists, the predominance of collective non-exploitative production relations is a worthy goal in itself as it connotes egalitarian economic well-being, cultural freedom, democracy, social justice and ecological sustainability.

Ecological sustainability will be collectively managed in future communist societies within the then-available interacting scientific, technological and social contexts, not according to absolute demands and principles dictated to human beings by nature or its positivistically conceptualized intermediary, science. An important different constitutive element of communal (compared to capitalist) ecological sustainability will be the predominance of collective rather than capitalist surplus appropriation.

It is reasonable for one to believe that a communist society will generally develop stronger incentives to engage its members into a more careful and just management of society's interchange with nature than capitalism does. This is because the impacts of important decisions regarding the interaction between nature and surplus production will be equally experienced by surplus producers and appropriators, as in the main they will be the same people. For instance, deteriorating natural conditions will harm human health, decrease labor productivity and surplus produced and, *ceteris paribus*, could jeopardize the reproduction of collective appropriation and/or restrict options for a good life as then-defined. These arguments suggest that ecological sustainability will be valued by collective producers who would tend to appreciate nature, not only as a source of economic resources enabling growth, but also for its nurturing, inspiring, scientific, aesthetic and moral values to human society.

The incomplete and fragmented knowledge reached by a communist society about extra-human and human nature will ground the *precautionary principle* in society's interchange with nature, including issues of non-substitutability, irreversibility, and relative scarcity. In particular, the precautionary principle would first require that when the physical/ecological impacts of a social action are uncertain, the potential long-term harmful effects should be carefully studied in advance; furthermore, it may also involve socially arrived-at restrictions to such an action, informed by the available knowledge, in order to avoid socially undesirable risks for present and future generations (Vlachou 2005b).

In short, collective surplus appropriation and ecological sustainability could be mutually supportive. However, achieving a collective organization of surplus does not *necessarily* guarantee ecological sustainability. This is because of the tensions that may arise between collective surplus production and ecological sustainability in certain instances (for example, the use of non-environmentally friendly technology that increases labor productivity). Therefore, collective producers have to desire and struggle for ecological sustainability in order to make it happen.

Notes

1 For the notion of overdetermination, see Althusser (1970), Resnick and Wolff (1987), and Vlachou (1994).
2 Kant and Laplace rejected Newton's view that the planets move around the sun in processes ruled by the laws of motion and gravity and associated with a repetitive or cyclical movement in a system that itself remained unchanged and unchanging. Kant and Laplace developed instead a theory representing the present solar system as the latest stage in a long and ongoing evolution (Edley 1990).
3 According to Levins and Lewontin:

> Darwin's revolutionary insight was that the differences among individuals within a species are converted into the differences among species in space and time...The force [for that conversion] postulated by Darwin was natural selection, which resulted from the struggle for survival ... that follows from overproduction in a world of finite resources...As time passes, the population will become more and more enriched with the variant that has a greater reproductive rate, and the species will change progressively...The reason some variants leave more offspring is that they are better able to appropriate resources in short supply...This superior efficiency is a manifestation of their greater degree of engineering perfection of solving the problem set by the environment. The mechanism then accounts not only for change, but for adaptation as well.
>
> (Levins and Lewontin 1985, 31–33)

4 Levins and Lewontin dedicate *Dialectical Biology* (1985) to Frederick Engels, "who got it wrong a lot of the time but who got it right where it counted" (*ibid.*, v).
5 For instance, early natural law philosophy appealed to the idea that God created the universe, including human beings, together with the laws that regulate.
6 For a critical though non-Marxist survey of the economics of technical change, see Freeman (1994).
7 According to Adam Smith and present-day neoclassical theorists, workers derive negative utility from work.

References

Althusser, L. 1970. *For Marx*. Trans. B. Brewster. New York: Random House.
Broad, W., and N. Wade. 1982. *Betrayers of the Truth*. New York: Simon and Schuster.
Burkett, P. 1999. *Marx and Nature: A Red and Green Perspective*. New York: St. Martin's Press.
Butler, D., and T. Reichhardt. 1999. "Long-term Effect of GM Crops Serves up Food for Thought." *Nature* 398: 651–656.
Daly, H., and J. Farley. 2004. *Ecological Economics: Principles and Applications*. London: Island Press.
Daly, H., and J. Townsend. 1996. *Valuing the Earth*. Cambridge: MIT Press.
Edley, R. 1990. "Dialectical Materialism." In *Marxian Economics*, J. Eatwell, M. Milgate, and P. Newman, eds., 115–120. London: W.W. Norton & Company.
Feyerabend, P. 1975. *Against Method*. London: New Left Books.
Foster, J. B. 2000. *Marx's Ecology: Materialism and Nature*. New York: Monthly Review Press.
Freeman, C. 1994. "The Economics of Technical Change," *Cambridge Journal of Economics* 18: 463–514.
Grundmann, R. 1991. "The Ecological Challenge to Marxism." *New Left Review* 187: 103–120.
Hart, S. 1997. "Beyond Greening: Strategies for a Sustainable World." *Harvard Business Review* 95: 66–76.
Hartwick, J. M. 1977. "Intergenerational Equity and the Investing of Rents from Exhaustible Resources." *American Economic Review* 67 (5): 972–974.
Hartwick, J. M. 1978. "Substitution among Exhaustible Resources and Intergenerational Equity." *The Review of Economic Studies* 45: 347–354.
Kuhn, T. 1979. "Reflections on My Critics." In *Criticism and the Growth of Knowledge*, I. Lakatos, and A. Musgrave, eds., 231–278. Cambridge: Cambridge University Press.
Lebowitz, M. A. 1977–78. "Capital and the Production of Needs." *Science and Society* 41: 430–447.
Levins, R. 1990. "Towards the Renewal of Science." *Rethinking Marxism* 3 (3–4): 101–25.
Levins, R., and R. Lewontin. 1985. *The Dialectical Biologist*. Cambridge: Harvard University Press.
———. 1994. "Holism and Reductionism in Ecology." *Capitalism, Nature, Socialism* 5 (4): 33–40.
Lichtman, R. 1990. "The Production of Human Nature by Means of Human Nature." *Capitalism, Nature, Socialism* 1 (4): 13–51.

Lohmann, L. 2006. "Carbon Trading: A Critical Conversation on Climate Change, Privatisation and Power." *Development Dialogue 48* www.thecornerhouse.org. uk/pdf/document/carbonDDlow.pdf, (accessed November 10, 2009).

MacKenzie, D., and J. Wajcman, eds. 1999. *The Social Shaping of Technology.* Philadelphia: Open University Press.

Magretta, J. 1997. "Growth Through Global Sustainability: An Interview with Mosanto's CEO, Robert B. Shapiro." *Harvard Business Review* 75 (1): 79–88.

Marx, K. 1973. *Grundrisse.* New York: Vintage Books.

———. 1991. *Capital: A Critique of Political Economy.* Vols. 1–3. New York: Penguin Books.

Marx, K, and F. Engels. 1969. "Theses on Feuerbach." In *Selected Works* I: 13–15. Moscow: Progress Publishers.

O'Connor, J. 1998. *Natural Causes.* New York: Guilford Press.

Resnick, S., and R. Wolff. 1987. *Knowledge and Class: A Marxist Critique of Political Economy.* Chicago: University of Chicago Press.

Trepl, L. 1994. "Holism and Reductionism in Ecology: Technical, Political and Ideological Implications." *Capitalism, Nature, Socialism* 5 (4): 13–31.

Vlachou, A. 1994. "Reflections on the Ecological Critiques and Reconstructions of Marxism." *Rethinking Marxism* 7 (3): 112–128.

———. 2002. "Nature and Value Theory." *Science & Society* 66 (2): 169–201.

———. 2004. "Capitalism and Ecological Sustainability: The Shaping of Environmental Policies." *Review of International Political Economy* 11 (5): 926–952.

———. 2005a. "Environmental Regulation: A Value-Theoretic and Class-Based Approach." *Cambridge Journal of Economics* 29 (4): 577–599.

———. 2005b. "Debating Sustainable Development." *Rethinking Marxism* 17 (4): 627–638.

———. 2014. "The European Union's Emissions Trading System." *Cambridge Journal of Economics* 38 (1): 127–152.

Vlachou, A., and C. Konstantinidis. 2010. "Climate Change: The Political Economy of Kyoto Flexible Mechanisms." *Review of Radical Political Economics* 42 (1): 32–49.

Wolff, R. 2012. *Democracy at Work: A Cure for Capitalism.* Chicago: Haymarket Books.

World Commission on Environment and Development (WCWD). 1987. *Our Common Future.* Oxford: Oxford University Press.

Index